How to Use This Book

This book provides a well-grounded background on ActiveX control creation using Microsoft Visual Basic 5.0. The motivated reader can cover the material in 21 days, progressing from beginning fundamentals to more advanced topics by the end of the three-week period. The book is intended for use with Visual Basic 5.0 to develop the controls. Visual Basic 5.0 is also used to illustrate control integration. Some samples also are based on a Web browser that supports ActiveX controls such as Microsoft's Internet Explorer. If you have these tools available, you can attempt the examples as you cover the material. However, the material was written so that it will also be clear and easy to learn if you use it without a computer.

Ideally, you can cover this book at the rate of a chapter a day. Each day covers a specific topic. Every day builds on the days that precede it, so the best approach to the material is a sequential one. Each week provides a new plateau of experience. The weekly material is covered at the beginning of each seven-day period and briefly reviewed again at the end of each week to put it all in context.

Through the course of 21 lessons, you will build a specific ActiveX control, making it increasingly powerful and usable as the days progress. The book is accompanied by a CD-ROM that contains all the code used in each lesson. On the CD-ROM you will find a directory for each day. In that directory, you'll find the completed, fully functioning example for that day's material. You will also find in that directory a folder called Your Start that contains the code as it should exist at the start of the day. You can then build up the control using the material for that day's lesson, and continue to build up the control as you progress through the book. Or, if you prefer, you can look at and use the code already completed as it should look at the end of each lesson, just in case you don't want to write the code yourself.

Teach Yourself ActiveX™ Control Programming with Visual Basic® 5 in 21 Days

Teach Yourself

ACTIVEX™ CONTROL PROGRAMMING WITH VISUAL BASIC® 5

in 21 Days

Keith Brophy
Timothy Koets

201 West 103rd Street
Indianapolis, Indiana 46290

From Keith to Ginny, Emma, and Ben.
From Tim to Grandma Barwacz and Uncle Jim.

Copyright © 1997 by Sams.net Publishing

FIRST EDITION

International Standard Book Number: 1-57521-245-5

Library of Congress Catalog Card Number: 96-71217

2000   99   98   97   4   3   2   1

Interpretation of the printing code: the rightmost double-digit number is the year of the book's printing; the rightmost single-digit, the number of the book's printing. For example, a printing code of 97-1 shows that the first printing of the book occurred in 1997.

Composed in AGaramond and MCPdigital by Macmillan Computer Publishing

Printed in the United States of America

Trademarks

Publisher and President   Richard K. Swadley
Publishing Manager   Greg Wiegand
Director of Editorial Services   Cindy Morrow
Managing Editor   Kitty Wilson Jarrett
Director of Marketing   Kelli S. Spencer
Assistant Marketing Managers   Wendy Gilbride, Rachel Wolfe

Acquisitions Editor
Christopher Denny

Development Editor
Anthony Amico

Software Development Specialist
Brad Myers

Production Editor
Kitty Wilson Jarrett

Copy Editors
Sarah Burkhart
Kimberly K. Hannel

Indexer
Sat-Kartar Khalsa

Technical Reviewer
BCI & Associates

Editorial Coordinator
Katie Wise

Technical Edit Coordinator
Lynette Quinn

Editorial Assistants
Carol Ackerman
Andi Richter
Rhonda Tinch-Mize

Cover Designer
Tim Amrhein

Book Designer
Gary Adair

Copy Writer
David Reichwein

Production Team Supervisors
Brad Chinn
Charlotte Clapp

Production
Jennifer Dierdorff
Michael Dietsch
Michael Henry
Shawn Ring

Overview

Contents

Foreword

This is a very exciting time to write software if you are a Visual Basic programmer! Microsoft has been touting the strategic importance of Visual Basic for several years now, and underscored this with improved capabilities of Visual Basic 4.0. The continuing software demand and the Internet and intranet push have raised the stakes even higher. Then along comes Visual Basic 5.0 with ActiveX control creation capability and native code generation. Visual Basic programming evolution takes a hyperspace leap ahead. ActiveX control creation is the backbone for a new generation of programming. Proclaiming "The future is here!" sounds way too much like a corny marketing slogan. But when it comes to ActiveX control creation and the corresponding importance of Visual Basic in your development arsenal, Microsoft has made it happen.

The fulfillment of the strategic vision is no longer something endlessly expounded on in suspect presentations by youthful Microsoft program managers at conferences. It is here today. You can now easily accomplish very important software architecture tasks with Visual Basic that were impossible six months ago. Best of all, you can take this hyperspace leap with little jolt. Sure, there are some new techniques to master and new concepts to understand to harness all this new capability. But it is built so well into the existing Visual Basic model that the hyperspace leap in capability is gained by a relative finger lift of exertion. We'll show you how.

Keith and Tim
April 1997

 NOTE

This book is based on a final release candidate version of Visual Basic 5.0. If any discrepancies between the material covered here and the official product release come to light, they will be fully documented and available online. Refer to the Web site `http://www.DoubleBlaze.com` for information on the latest updates, if any.

Acknowledgments

Thanks to Sams.net for the opportunity to meet another software technology milestone head on. We are grateful for the Sams.net team behind us, including Chris Denny, acquisitions editor; Tony Amico, key development editor; Kitty Jarrett, ever-patient production editor; BCI & Associates, technical editor; and the rest of the great Sams.net team. Thanks also to Kevin Schultz for checking out our early control work and offering helpful suggestions along the way. As usual, we must extend a big thanks to our friends and families who make it all possible, as reflected in our individual notes below. We consider ourselves fortunate to be software technology enthusiasts at a time when the most exciting evolution of software in history is taking place.

Tim adds: Every time I proceed to write another book, I can't thank my family enough for their support and encouragement. It's an awesome undertaking that I could never accomplish without my wonderful wife, Michelle, and my loving and supportive family. As I finish this book, I'd especially like to recognize my Grandmother, Ms. Mary Barwacz, and my uncle James Barwacz for their love, care, and concern in helping me climb the ladder of success to this point in my life. I have been so fortunate to receive their love and support all my life. I'd especially like to thank my Uncle Jim for helping to foster my interest in the wonderful world of electronics, computers, physics, chemistry, and astronomy. We've covered a lot of ground, he and I!

Keith adds: Persistence and inspiration give birth to books. Sometimes it seems that only the moonbeam in the window is keeping you going, and then along comes the next day's sunshine to provide renewed energy. Thanks to the sunshine of my life: Ginny, Emma, and Ben.

About the Authors

Keith Brophy

Keith Brophy is currently a software release coordinator for X-Rite, Incorporated, a leading worldwide provider of Color and Appearance quality control software and instrumentation in Grandville, Michigan. He manages a group of the world's best software test engineers as well as carries out Visual Basic– and intranet-related development. Keith previously served as a lead software developer for IBM's System Integration Division in Washington, DC. His experience includes a variety of Internet, operating system, distributed system, performance, and graphical user interface research and development projects. He has taught open system programming, Visual Basic, and Internet classes in various venues, including Northern Virginia Community College and Grand Rapids Community College.

Keith, along with Tim Koets, coauthored *Visual Basic 4 Performance Tuning and Optimization* (Sams, 1995) and *Teach Yourself VBScript in 21 Days* (Sams.net, 1996). He has also served as a contributing author and technical editor on various other Sams publications. He has a B.S. in computer science from the University of Michigan in Ann Arbor and an M.S. in information systems from Strayer College in Washington, DC. Mr. Brophy is the founder of DoubleBlaze Software Consortium (`www.DoubleBlaze.com`), an ActiveX Internet research and development company involved in endeavors such as research for this book.

Keith's outside interests include activities with his children and running trail ultramarathons. Ultramarathons are races of 50 to 100 miles over challenging trails. Since this pursuit is commonly viewed by nonparticipants (most of the world) as rather bizarre, one of Keith's goals is to someday explain the Zen and virtues of such endeavors on his Web site at `www.DoubleBlaze.com`. Keith recently extended his forays into snowshoe racing as well. He states that these undertakings complement Visual Basic development well, as many of his best programming insights have occurred out on the trail.

Timothy Koets

Timothy Koets is a software engineer at X-Rite, Incorporated, a leading worldwide provider of Color and Appearance quality control software and instrumentation in Grandville, Michigan. Prior to this, Mr. Koets was a computer systems engineer in the Systems Engineering and Integration division of Martin Marietta in the Washington, DC, area. In addition to developing Visual Basic applications, Tim has experience in many other areas, including Visual C++, computer networking, client/server application design, parallel processing, and performance analysis. He, too, has previous experience building systems that were Internet-aware in the days before the Web. Tim is an adjunct faculty member at the

Grand Rapids Community College, where he teaches Internet and Advanced Visual Basic classes, and has prior teaching experience at other institutions ranging from computer programming and engineering laboratory classes to Lotus Notes training courses.

Tim, along with Keith, coauthored *Visual Basic 4 Performance Tuning and Optimization* (Sams, 1995) and *Teach Yourself VBScript in 21 Days* (Sams.net, 1996). He has also served as a contributing author on various other Sams publications. He has a B.S. in electrical engineering and an M.S. in electrical engineering from Michigan Technological University in Houghton, Michigan. Mr. Koets is the founder of Cockateil Software, an Internet research and development company that is an affiliate of DoubleBlaze Software Consortium (`www.DoubleBlaze.com`).

Tim is an avid reader and spends lots of his free time collecting and reading books. He's also quite busy putting together Web sites these days. Although this has been an incredibly busy year, it's his first year as a married man and he's loving it! He's really looking forward to this summer when Lake Michigan once again beckons him and his wife to its friendly shores for peaceful, relaxing walks and talks along the beach. You see, so-called computer geeks actually do have a life!

Tell Us What You Think!

As a reader, you are the most important critic and commentator of our books. We value your opinion and want to know what we're doing right, what we could do better, what areas you'd like to see us publish in, and any other words of wisdom you're willing to pass our way. You can help us make strong books that meet your needs and give you the computer guidance you require.

Do you have access to CompuServe or the World Wide Web? Then check out our CompuServe forum by typing GO SAMS at any prompt. If you prefer the World Wide Web, check out our site at http://www.mcp.com.

NOTE

> If you have a technical question about this book, call the technical support line at 317-581-3833.

As the publishing manager of the group that created this book, I welcome your comments. You can fax, e-mail, or write me directly to let me know what you did or didn't like about this book—as well as what we can do to make our books stronger. Here's the information:

Fax: 317-581-4669

E-mail: programming_mgr@sams.mcp.com

Mail: Greg Wiegand
            Sams.net Publishing
            201 W. 103rd Street
            Indianapolis, IN 46290

You are also welcome to provide feedback directly to the authors. Due to the large volume of comments, authors may not be able to respond to individual requests, but will review all comments. The authors can be contacted through e-mail links on their Web site at http://www.DoubleBlaze.com.

Introduction

ActiveX control creation is an exciting new Visual Basic capability that greatly expands the range of software a Visual Basic programmer can produce. ActiveX controls serve as the building blocks for other programs and Web pages. Until now, these controls could only be created in C++. All that has changed with Visual Basic 5.0. You not only can create controls, you can do it with remarkably little effort.

Anyone who has purchased many software packages is familiar with the something-for-nothing promises. It always sounds easy until you start to do it. But with Visual Basic ActiveX controls, it really seems to be true. If you are familiar with the old model of control programming, you will particularly appreciate the ease of the current approach. A multitude of low-level details are transparently carried out for you by Visual Basic. You can concentrate on the important part of control development—getting your control to carry out the task you intend it for. You no longer have to worry about the arcane of how the control is packaged and whether the standard interfaces are in place.

This book shows you how to create a control with Visual Basic. If you want to create low-level Windows guru–level programs you may find that once you have digested this material, you will want to gain further knowledge from other sources. However, this book will show you everything you need to provide useful, functional controls. Some experts in the consulting field have claimed that even Visual Basic control developers need to be immersed in the low–level details; they have produced some pretty intimidating documentation and samples to reinforce those claims. They are, in many respects, missing the mark. The beauty of Visual Basic 5.0 control creation is that you *can* easily create controls. You don't need an advanced doctorate of Windows suffering to be successful at Windows control creation. It's at your fingertips.

Our goal in this book is to teach you and prove to you just how easy it is. We purposely steer far clear of the guts of Windows programming to make the learning easy and clear for you. Most of the controls that you'll create won't need to deal with these guts. If you do need to get into it, this book will still give you the starting foundation you need before tackling them. If you just need to write controls that get your job done, you may well find everything you need right here. This book teaches you how to incrementally expand the capabilities of a question control from day to day. By Day 3, you will have a control that is useful and production caliber. By Day 21, you will have created a remarkably sophisticated and refined control. Please take the time to look at the control and consider its capabilities. This type of control is representative of the type of development that can be easily accomplished with Visual Basic 5.0. You might use the same approach to contain your company's business rules or extend the capabilities of your applications in other ways. If you have the ideas, the packaging in the control format is certainly well within your grasp.

We're excited at the opportunity to show you what you can accomplish with this technology. Perhaps you may recall from your childhood the exhilarating feeling of taking off on a bike for the first time without training wheels. Microsoft has taken off the training wheels with Visual Basic 5.0. We will show you that as long as you know what you're doing, riding without the training wheels is a piece of cake. You can cover far more ground than you ever could have before. We'll run along beside you and catch you if you should wobble these first few weeks. After that, you'll no longer need us. You'll be pedaling faster than we could keep up!

Who Should Read This Book

This book is for you if you find yourself in one of the following categories:

- ☐ You are a Visual Basic programmer who wants to create your own ActiveX controls for use in your own applications or Web pages.
- ☐ You are a Visual Basic programmer who wants to create ActiveX controls for use in applications by others.
- ☐ You are not a Visual Basic programmer, but wish to explore ActiveX control creation and want to use the easiest tool available to make those components.
- ☐ You are a programming manager or information systems analyst and need to understand how much effort is really required for ActiveX control development on projects you plan or manage.
- ☐ You are a student who wants to learn about state-of-the-art component-based Windows technology.

What This Book Contains

This book is intended to be completed in 21 days—one chapter per day—although the pace is really up to you. We have designed the book as a teacher would teach a course. We start with the basics and continue to introduce more of the aspects of control creation as the chapters progress. By the end of the third day, you will be creating your first ActiveX control. As you work through the chapters, you will continue to incrementally add more and more powerful features to this control. In the second and third weeks, you will be exploring the more advanced features of ActiveX control creation. In addition to instruction, we will furnish an abundant amount of examples, as well as exercises for you to try. You can learn a great deal by reading, but only when you try building ActiveX controls of your own can you become truly experienced.

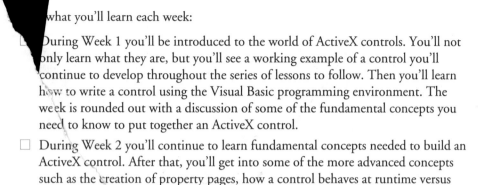

what you'll learn each week:

☐ During Week 1 you'll be introduced to the world of ActiveX controls. You'll not only learn what they are, but you'll see a working example of a control you'll continue to develop throughout the series of lessons to follow. Then you'll learn how to write a control using the Visual Basic programming environment. The week is rounded out with a discussion of some of the fundamental concepts you need to know to put together an ActiveX control.

☐ During Week 2 you'll continue to learn fundamental concepts needed to build an ActiveX control. After that, you'll get into some of the more advanced concepts such as the creation of property pages, how a control behaves at runtime versus design time, and how to debug your controls if they contain errors.

☐ During Week 3, you'll learn about some of the features you can add to fine-tune your controls and make them as useful and powerful as possible. You'll learn about data-bound controls, controls for the Internet, and self-painting controls. This week also covers control testing, preparing controls for the real world, and control licensing, distribution, and security. At the completion of this week's material, you will have the well-rounded background needed to tackle all aspects of ActiveX control development.

With this book, you will become comfortable enough with Visual Basic to design and implement your own powerful ActiveX controls. Working through all the examples in each lesson, you'll be confident in your abilities to use Visual Basic effectively to write professional controls—all in three weeks or less!

What You Need Before You Start

Because this is a book about creating ActiveX controls with Visual Basic, we assume that you are already familiar with the fundamentals of Visual Basic. This book is based on Visual Basic 5.0, the first commercial version of Visual Basic that supports ActiveX control creation. If you are not experienced with Visual Basic 5.0, you will find that this book provides plenty of help to get you up to speed as control creation concepts are introduced. Many readers may have experience with the freely distributed Visual Basic Custom Control Edition of Visual Basic, which was available for Internet download prior to the release of Visual Basic 5.0. Much of the material in this book also applies to controls that can be created with this edition. However, some features covered are specific only to the more powerful Visual Basic 5.0 itself, and you will need Visual Basic 5.0 to load and modify the examples. Some controls are also illustrated in a World Wide Web browser that supports ActiveX controls, such as Microsoft's Internet Explorer 3.0. So if you want to run the examples, make sure to have Visual Basic 5.0 handy. If you are content to learn by reading, you will find the book is well structured for that as well. You are ready to learn how to create your own ActiveX controls. Now that the formalities are out of the way, it's time to start the fun.

Conventions Used in This Book

Over the years we have found that a *Teach Yourself* book should be friendly and easy to read. Much of the text will be formatted as you see here. We have also found that some important details should stand out and be separated from the normal text. So we have established some conventions:

- [ ] Code/reserved words: Terms, functions, variables, keywords, listings, and so on, that are taken from or are part of code are set in a `monospaced type`.

- [ ] Placeholders: Placeholders are words that stand for what you will actually type. They are formatted in `monospaced italic`.

- [ ] Arguments: In lines of code, required parameters are shown in **`bold monospaced italic`**. Optional arguments are `monospaced italic`.

- [ ] Commands: When we are identifying commands from menus, we separate the different levels by using a vertical bar (|). For example, File|Open indicates that you select the File menu and select the Open command.

- [ ] Code continuation: When a line of code exceeds what we can show on a line in the book, we use a continuation character (➡). When you see this character, it means that the code continues on the next line. If you are typing, you should just ignore the character and continue typing. Do not use the Enter key to separate the code.

- [ ] Line numbering: We have numbered the lines in code listings for ease of reference. The line numbers are not part of the code.

The following are some of the special visual elements used in the book:

WARNING

These boxes point out areas where care must be taken to prevent catastrophe. They should be avoided until you become more experienced.

NOTE

These provide essential background material or different ways of viewing the information to help you understand the concepts behind the implementations.

This icon provides a definition for an important term that you will encounter as you progress through the book. The term shows up in *italics*.

 TIP

> These boxes tell you about techniques that are beneficial and that you might pursue.

ANALYSIS This icon tells you that we're describing an example in detail. You might think of it as a kind of detour to a scenic overlook on your journey to learning this new technology.

SAMPLE This icon indicates that a sample is available to help you enforce your learning. You should try to follow the instructions and perform the process until you feel comfortable with the procedure.

Though we have many code snippets embedded in the pages to illustrate the use of important concepts, we also have longer, more involved examples. In some cases we might build on a previous example.

Week

1

1
2
3
4
5
6
7

At a Glance

This book was written with one major goal in mind—to empower you with the knowledge and experience you need to create ActiveX controls that do just what you want them to. This week will get you started on a journey that will enable you not only to create ActiveX controls, but to create powerful, friendly, and reliable controls that your customers will love to use. You'll learn many of the fundamental concepts you need to know to create ActiveX controls with Microsoft Visual Basic 5.0. This exciting new release of Visual Basic gives you the ability to quickly and easily put together ActiveX controls. It is perhaps one of the only programming tools on the market today that lets you create controls so easily and quickly.

Where You Are Going

The week begins by showing you just what an ActiveX control is and what it can do. This is extremely important because you want to make sure ActiveX controls are right for you before you start learning how to create them. You'll see a simple example of a working ActiveX control, followed by a detailed guide through the new Visual Basic 5.0 programming environment. Then you'll start a series of lessons that teach you how to use and create properties, methods, and events for your ActiveX controls.

Day 1

Introducing ActiveX Controls

ion of this first day is to understand the journey that lies ahead. Before
the details of ActiveX controls, there are some basic questions to
r instance, what is an ActiveX control? Why would you want
d how do you go about creating one? You will find those answers

Is an ActiveX Control?

's start out with the most basic question. What exactly is an ActiveX control?
An ActiveX control is a component that can be integrated by other applications.
For example, assume that you are a Web page creator. You need to provide a Web
page that includes interactive questions. You must present a series of questions
to the user and have your page display feedback in response to the user's answers.

You could write your own code to accomplish this. Or, if a commercially available ActiveX control already existed for this purpose, you could simply purchase that control and insert it into your page where you wanted the questions to appear. You'd still have to initialize each instance of the control to tell it what question to show, what answer to look for, and so on. However, setting these initial values (called *properties*) is a far simpler and quicker process than writing all the code for the control.

How do you know the control will work if you purchase it? You can take assurance from the fact that it is an ActiveX control. The component must be generated according to industry-recognized ActiveX conventions to be called ActiveX. If the component is created according to these conventions, it can be easily incorporated into applications by a variety of development tools that support ActiveX.

You can see an example of the question control incorporated into a Web page in Figure 1.1. We will discuss this control in progressively more detail throughout the rest of this book. For right now, we'll focus on just a couple simple but major control integration fundamentals.

Figure 1.1.

The ActiveX question control incorporated into a Web page.

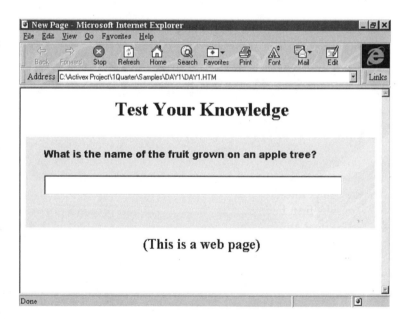

First of all, it's important to recognize how the control itself is packaged. A control is stored in a file with the file extension .OCX. This file is generated in a special manner defined by the ActiveX conventions. It contains the binary instructions that are loaded into memory and carried out to make the control function when applications reference it. This packaged component is referred to as an ActiveX control.

NOTE

> **SAMPLE** The sample page shown in Figure 1.1 can be found in file
> Day1.htm on the CD-ROM under the Samples\Day1
> subdirectory. You need Microsoft's Internet Explorer browser, available
> free of charge from http://www.microsoft.com, to view this page.
> Alternatively, if you do not have access to the browser, you can view the
> equivalent Visual Basic application, which is stored in Day1.exe under
> the Samples\Day1 subdirectory.

The developer who integrates the control into his application will be able to use the control through the interfaces it provides, but will have no insight into the source code behind it. For example, assume you have written the question control to sell. Then assume that a hypothetical Web page developer, Nola Nosering, purchases it. Nola can take full advantage of your control and its interfaces to make snazzy questions appear on her Web pages with built-in answer analysis. She doesn't have to worry about writing the answer-processing logic. You've already done it for her in your control. However, if she doesn't like the way your question control works, she can't change it. She does not have access to the source code that you as the control developer used to originally create it. She only has the OCX file she integrates, which contains no source code.

The ease with which Nola can integrate the question control into her Web page also illustrates the second important concept of controls. They can be integrated into any language. In our hypothetical example, you created the control in Visual Basic. Nola then used HTML to integrate it into her Web page without any knowledge of Visual Basic. Similarly, the question control could have been integrated into J++ applications, Visual Basic applications, C++ applications, and any other environment that supports ActiveX.

The Web page shown in Figure 1.1 uses a question control that was created with Visual Basic. The page itself was created with the Windows Notepad text editor and specified in the HTML format recognized by the Internet Explorer browser. When the page is loaded into the Internet Explorer browser, the browser correctly loads the control along with the page.

The control could just as easily be integrated into another environment. Figure 1.2 shows the same question control integrated into a Visual Basic application. In this case, the application was generated using the Visual Basic environment. The question control, once appropriately installed on the system, appears as another choice on the Visual Basic toolbox. The question control was integrated into the application at design time just as any other standard control would be with Visual Basic. (The specific steps for generating the question control and then incorporating it into an application are covered in more detail on Day 2, "Creating a Simple Control.")

Figure 1.2.

The ActiveX question control incorporated into a Visual Basic application.

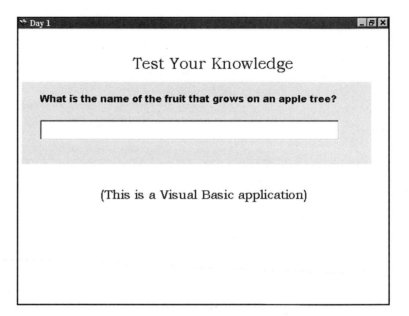

NOTE

SAMPLE The sample application shown in Figure 1.2 can be found in file Day1.exe under the Samples\Day1 subdirectory. Before you run the sample applications in this book, you must install and register the required OCXs on your system. You can run the program setup.exe in the Samples\OCX_Prep directory to carry out this step.

The question control will behave the same, regardless of which environment hosts it. The purpose of the control is to display a question and then respond to the user's answer. The code of the control is unchanged, and therefore the logic works exactly the same, whether the user is interacting with the Web page shown in Figure 1.1 or responding to the question in the Visual Basic application of Figure 1.2.

NEW TERM The application that incorporates a control is often referred to as the host or hosting application. You'll find this term throughout the remainder of the book.

Consider the actions of the question control. It displays a question based on an initial setting received from the host application. The host application also supplies an initial setting for an expected answer. When the user of the application types in a response and presses the Enter key, the question control compares the user's answer to the expected answer. The control displays feedback based on whether the user's response hits paydirt.

The two sample host applications shown so far provide identical feedback because they are based on the same control and have the same initial settings. Figure 1.3 shows another view of the Web page first shown in Figure 1.1. Now the Web page is displaying feedback in response to a user's incorrect answer to a question.

Figure 1.3.

The Web page question control with feedback on an incorrect response.

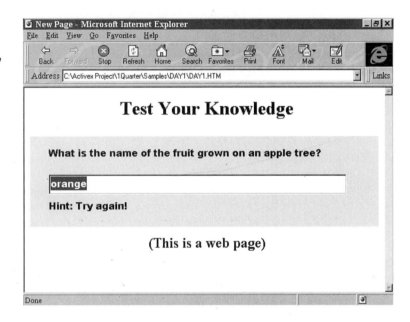

Test Your Knowledge

What is the name of the fruit grown on an apple tree?

orange

Hint: Try again!

(This is a web page)

NOTE

SAMPLE The sample page shown in Figure 1.3 can be found in file Day1.htm on the CD-ROM under the Samples\Day1 subdirectory. You need Microsoft's Internet Explorer browser, available free of charge from http://www.microsoft.com, to view this page. Alternatively, if you do not have access to the browser, you can view the equivalent Visual Basic application, which is stored in Day1.exe under the Samples\Day1 subdirectory.

Similarly, Figure 1.4 shows an additional view of the Visual Basic application first demonstrated in Figure 1.2. In this view, the Visual Basic application shows feedback in response to a user's correct answer to a question.

Figure 1.4.
The Visual Basic application question control with feedback on a correct response.

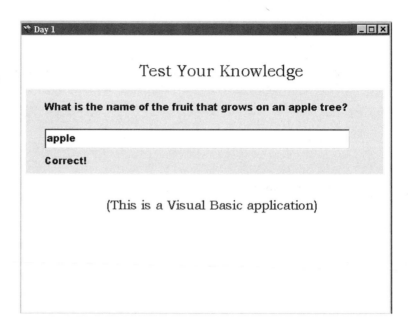

 NOTE

| SAMPLE | The sample application shown in Figure 1.4 can be found in file Day1_feedback.exe under the Samples\Day1 subdirectory. |

Both the Web page application and the Visual Basic application consist of no real programming. The question control does all the work of these applications. The control shows the question onscreen, looks for an Enter key keystroke from the user to signal a response, and provides feedback when a response is detected. Both applications just merge in the question control component with the rest of the application user interface in order to take advantage of the function the control provides. This approach is sometimes referred to as *gluing in* controls. Languages such as Visual Basic that facilitate this integration approach through high support for integrating controls are sometimes referred to as *glue tools*.

NEW TERM *Glue code* is the developer-written statements that are used to integrate the functions a control provides into an application.

Occasionally, simply gluing a control into an application and providing initial control settings accomplishes what an application developer needs his application to do. More often, however, the application developer must build further code around the control so that the application can interact with it. Suppose that an application were produced to deliver a test to students, collect their responses, and then grade the tests against a predefined grading scale.

1

This would require code in the application that interacts with the question control as the application runs.

You provide the means for an application to interact with your control by specifying certain interfaces when you create the control. You can define interfaces called *properties* to let a host application pass information to your control. You can define interfaces called *methods* to let a host application launch a block of code within your control that accomplishes a given action. You can even define actions called *events* that the host can supply as subroutines in their application. Then you can launch the application's event subroutine from your control code at some desired time, based on the current state, property settings, or methods called in your control. You will gain a much more detailed knowledge of properties, methods, and events in the days to come. They are the only means by which an application communicates and cooperates with the controls it hosts.

In the general sense, a control is a building block that can be integrated into other programs. The typical Visual Basic developer is already familiar with many controls created by Microsoft. The Visual Basic toolbox contains a whole collection of prefabricated controls that the Visual Basic developer can host in his applications, including the label control, the image control, the textbox control, and many more. A wide variety of commercial controls are available for purchase for similar purposes. There are many businesses devoted to producing controls, and many Web sites and catalogs devoted to hawking them in exchange for a quick grab into your billfold. If you purchase a control that lets you avoid many hours of development time, this arrangement may be to your mutual benefit.

Now with Visual Basic 5.0, you can make your own contributions to this wide world of controls. You might be among the majority of Visual Basic programmers who simply wish to create controls that serve as the building blocks for their own internal projects and applications. Or you might be among the enterprising group of programmers creating controls to market commercially to Nola Nosering and her contemporaries as general-purpose application-building blocks. Whatever the case, ActiveX controls are likely to be an important part of your development life.

Types of Controls

The horizons of the control world are broad. Many types of controls can be created. Virtually any code idea that can be embodied in an application can be packaged in an ActiveX control. Whether it makes sense to package a given set of code into a control is another matter, and is addressed throughout the remainder of this book. But for right now, recognize that the sky is the limit when it comes to types of controls that you can implement.

You can make fat controls (controls that take up a lot of disk and memory space). You can make skinny controls (controls that take up little disk space or memory). You can make invisible controls that perform their work without being seen by the user. You can make pretty visible controls with fancy, graceful graphics. You can make ugly visible controls if you wish, with loud, garish graphics. A control is really like a small mini-application built to serve a special purpose for the applications that incorporate it. Since you're a reader of this book, it's likely that you've developed many applications and realize that you can give an application any look, feel, style, and behavior you want. The same is true with controls.

Several construction frameworks are available under Visual Basic for creating controls. The framework used influences the control's behavior and appearance. One framework is the user-drawn control. A user-drawn control is a control that the control developer creates from scratch. No other supporting controls are incorporated as part of it. The user-drawn control paints itself on the host application's form and manages its actions based on code you write from the ground up. For example, you might create a whale control that shows a whale that swims back and forth across the screen and periodically blows water out its spout. If you embed all the code to manage this interaction and continual repainting within your control, rather than piggy-backing off an existing control, you have created a user-drawn control.

NEW TERM The word *user* in the term *user-drawn control* refers to the control code itself as the user of the application's form. This term is used to indicate that the control draws itself on the space it occupies. Do not confuse this user with the individual who is the end user of the application. The end user of the application is certainly not involved in drawing the control!

The meaning might be clearer if you think of this as a *component self-drawn control* instead. However, user-drawn control is a term referenced in the Microsoft documentation. Because Microsoft employees outnumber our author team by a considerable margin, we have used their term here for consistency.

Another control construction framework available is to simply enhance an existing control. Suppose you want to create a custom label control that displays a caption in black text normally, but in orange text if there is a full moon. (Admittedly, there might not be a large market for such a control, but perhaps Nola Nosering has some reason to need it for her Web pages.) You could create this from scratch as a user-drawn control, but it would be far easier to simply leverage the standard label control that is already available with Visual Basic. You can base your control on the standard label control as the starting point of your design and then enhance it. The standard label control already offers you a full range of functions, including the capability to paint itself. You simply have to modify the aspects of the standard label control's behavior that you wish to change, such as providing implicit control of the caption color. Then you save this modified version as your own custom label control.

The remaining control construction framework is particularly useful because it serves as the foundation for the majority of complex controls you are likely to write. This framework is

that of the aggregate control. An aggregate control is a control that defines a new control by using existing controls as building blocks. A control serves as a host to other controls when it is implemented as an aggregate control, just as an application normally does. Visual Basic even provides a `UserControl` object that lets you easily merge other controls with the foundation of your new control. The question control you saw in today's examples is one control that uses this technique. It was implemented by incorporating standard label controls and a textbox control into the question control's `UserControl` object.

 An *aggregate* control is a control that defines a new control by using existing controls as building blocks and serves as a host to those controls.

Which framework is right for you—user-drawn control, enhanced control, or aggregate control? That will depend very much on the goals you want to accomplish with your specific control. As you gain more knowledge from this book in the days ahead, you will build up the background to make that call. Whatever the need, Visual Basic offers a starting foundation that is appropriate to the type of control you wish to provide.

Why Would You Use an ActiveX Control?

Why do you care about ActiveX controls? The answer differs depending on your background. Some developers want the ability to write code once and easily share it among multiple applications. Others might need to share code without sharing source listings. Easy distribution of functional components over the Internet via Web pages might be the primary motivation of some. Developers might be attracted by the building block approach that is possible with controls.

You might be interested in ActiveX controls for some or all of these reasons. They all add up to the same advantage. ActiveX controls allow you to create applications that are more maintainable, more conveniently distributed, and easier to create in the first place. The bottom line is better applications. Now let's consider each of these motivations in more detail.

The Easy Building Block Approach

The use of controls allows you to construct applications with a building block approach. You simply add the pieces you need to your host application to instantly expand the function the application is capable of. Think back to Figure 1.1, the Visual Basic application that incorporated the question control. A Web page developer such as our friend Nola Nosering wouldn't have to write any lines of code to create an application such as this. She can create an application that carries out meaningful work with no programming effort. All the underlying logic needed to deliver a one-question test to the user is present in the control.

What if Nola wanted to expand this application to be more sophisticated? Say, for example, she wanted a Web page that asked three questions instead of one? Once again, the creation is a breeze thanks to the building-block approach of custom controls. The same control can be included repeatedly into an application, and each instance can have its own property settings. The developer does not have to do anything special to help the controls keep track of which instance they are. This is inherent in the control architecture. Figure 1.5 shows an example of such a Web page. Two instances of the question control have been incorporated into the page.

Figure 1.5.

A Web page that includes two question controls.

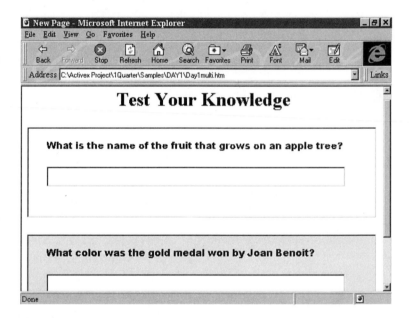

Test Your Knowledge

What is the name of the fruit that grows on an apple tree?

What color was the gold medal won by Joan Benoit?

NOTE

SAMPLE The sample page shown in Figure 1.5 can be found in the file Day1Multi.htm on the CD-ROM under the Samples\Day1 subdirectory. You need Microsoft's Internet Explorer browser, available free of charge from http://www.microsoft.com, to view this page. Alternatively, if you do not have access to the browser, you can view the equivalent Visual Basic application, which is stored in Day1Multi.exe under the Samples\Day1 subdirectory.

Figure 1.6 shows the same approach with a Visual Basic application rather than a Web page. The capability to host multiple occurrences of a control in a pain-free fashion exists in any host environment, including J++, C++, and others, as well as the Visual Basic and Web page hosts shown here.

Figure 1.6.

A Visual Basic host application page that includes two question controls.

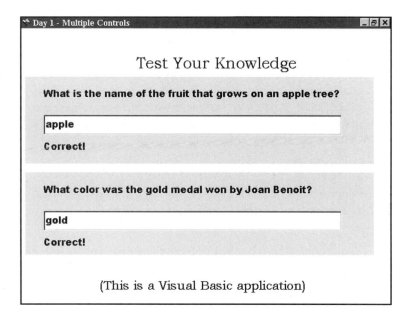

Day 1 - Multiple Controls

Test Your Knowledge

What is the name of the fruit that grows on an apple tree?

apple

Correct!

What color was the gold medal won by Joan Benoit?

gold

Correct!

(This is a Visual Basic application)

NOTE

SAMPLE The sample application shown in Figure 1.6 can be found in the file Day1Multi.exe under the Samples\Day1 subdirectory.

This ease of control integration provides a very strong motivation to base almost all development efforts on controls. A developer can increase the sophistication and functionality of his host application dramatically by simply adding controls. Some glue coding may be required if the application needs to interact with the controls. Glue code is required for the majority of controls integrated into host applications. However, even in these instances, the overall amount of coding needed will be far less than if no control were used and all the logic had to be programmed from scratch. Controls are an easy time-saving trick a developer can pull from his hat time and again on almost any project.

Reusability Payoffs

The reusability advantage of packaged components such as ActiveX controls is one of the strongest reasons to create controls. A control can be incorporated into many types of applications, as you have already seen in the previous examples. If you are making a control to sell commercially, your customer set is not limited to just Visual Basic programmers, or just Access programmers, or just C++ programmers. The entire development world is your potential marketplace.

If you are simply making controls for use on your own projects or at your own company, this same principle still applies. Once you make a control, you can use it over and over across all types of projects. In fact, my experience has shown that typically the best uses for a component are not the application that first drives you to design it. Once you get a component completed and perfected, you'll typically find other new application needs down the road where the control fits in perfectly and saves you time in an unforeseen manner. Controls allow you to make a coding investment once that pays off many times over down the road.

Ease of Distribution

Suppose you create an application for use at your company that tracks time worked across various projects. You distribute it to 100 employees. Then…oops!…management generates new requirements for some key trend analysis calculations.

Your first step is to regenerate the entire application so that you can get the corrected version in everyone's hands. In addition, assume that you originally inserted the same logic into another managerial tracking application as well. You regenerate that application, too, rebuilding the entire executable even though just a couple lines have changed. Now you have two updated applications to redistribute. You have to figure out which users get just one or the other, and which users get both.

There's still more reason for fear. You suspect that management will give you some new requirements for this frequently changing function next week and some more new requirements the week after that. It looks like frequent updates to both applications will be a part of your life for some time to come.

The simpler alternative would be to originally break off the trend analysis function into a separate control. This control could be utilized by both applications. Then, when the frequent updates come, you only need to change one body of code—the control source code. Instead of having to redistribute one application to some users, a different application to another pool of users, and both applications to still another group of users, all you need to do is simply redistribute the control's OCX file to everyone. The applications themselves can remain unchanged.

This distribution method becomes even more powerful with some of the emerging Internet-related control distribution technologies. When a Web page incorporates a control, it can list a home location for a master copy of the control. This location could be local or across an intranet or across the Internet. As soon as the browser loads a control, it compares the local control version with the latest version available in the master location. If the local control is out-of-date or does not exist on the user's system, the browser initiates download of the newer version of the control from the master location. The browser even installs the control on the user's PC and updates the Windows 95 System Registry (where systemwide control information resides) accordingly. It's a reasonable guess that in the future you might find similar support built into other applications as well as in the browser.

There are many advantages to this type of distribution model. Updating applications becomes much easier. Updates for a control can be provided directly over the Internet. It is far quicker to download just a control than to download an entire application since the control is just a fraction of the size.

Control updates offer some security advantages as well. Assume that you have a high-priced commercial product and a bug is discovered in it. You might be reluctant to provide the entire product for download if you don't have a good scheme to keep it from being stolen. However, you can provide a control update with a much higher level of comfort. It won't do a theft-minded user much good to download your latest virtual reality spreadsheet graphics engine control if he does not already own the application that uses it.

NOTE

> On the flip side, controls can introduce some security disadvantages from the user's perspective. When a Web page with controls is encountered, the code in those controls will be running on the user's system. Since a control can be written to do virtually anything, malicious behavior could result. The current industry solution to this dilemma is control certification, sometimes called code signing. Control certification does not eliminate this problem but does provide trackable ownership of controls that lessens the risk. This topic is addressed in more detail on Day 21, "Licensing, Distribution, and Security."

Reliability and Maintainability

Controls also offer reliability and testing advantages. A basic principle of software engineering is that the less code you touch, the less chance you'll break things. There is a chance that you will break unexpected areas if you make a change in the middle of a 10,000-line application. Such errors could consist of anything from altering use of a global variable to accidentally doing an unintended global search and replace across the entire program. There are a million other such unexpected strange and unnatural occurrences that can break code.

But suppose you had previously packaged the area that needed to be changed in a control generated from 100 lines of source code. Would you feel safer taking your chances of introducing a bug anywhere in 100 lines of code, or 10,000 lines? The answer is obvious (unless you have too much time on your hands). The testing time required for a control change is significantly less than for an entire application change.

In theory, you should retest the entire application after a change in any part, including a control. After all, a change in the way a control works could introduce an application bug. In practice, however, testing is usually a matter of risk assessment. The risk that a side-effect is introduced in the same body of code as the location of a change is very high. The risk that a side effect is introduced in a body of code that uses a component, but was not changed itself, is significantly lower. If just a control has changed, the odds that the developer understood the task and the entire body of code in the control are high. After all, he just had 100 lines to review. However, if the change was in the application, the developer would have to sift through 10,000 lines to determine which lines pertained to him. Knowledge of more total lines of software would be required for him to tackle this task. You should test the control-related function of the application in either case. However, the required test time, and the risk of bugs, is significantly lower if you change just a component instead of the monolithic application itself.

Commercial Packaging

If you were running a consulting business and had to make a business decision about how to provide a custom building block solution to other developers, you probably would already be leaning toward a control-based solution for the reasons mentioned earlier. There are a few other points to keep in mind that make commercial distribution of controls very easy and attractive. Control distribution allows you, of course, to distribute your product without source code, which is very important from a business perspective. You don't want to give your competitors the intellectual property embodied in your source code if it is worth much to you. Likewise, there are now code-signing techniques that provide means for a control to be certified from an independent auditing agency. Then a digital signature is embedded into the control so that it is always identified as a legitimate control produced by that company. If the control is tampered with and the contents of the file change, the digital signature breaks and the rogue control can't be passed off as your company's. The driving force for a company is to make money, and perhaps that's the biggest reason for a company to get into the commercial control market. The most universal market for any piece of software right now is for controls. That's where the action is!

How Do You Create an ActiveX Control?

By now you should have a general feel for what an ActiveX control is and why you would want to use one. The next thing you are likely wondering about is how to go about creating one. That question was most probably even your prime motivation for purchasing this book (unless you are one of the small handful of hard-core computer book fans who simply like the Brophy and Koets writing style)! You've come to the right place to find the answer. Throughout the rest of this book we will expose you to more and more of the techniques for

1

creating ActiveX controls. We'll start with a simple approach and work our way up to more advanced issues.

First things first, though. It's important to understand the high-level picture before diving right into the nuts and bolts. That high-level picture starts with an understanding of the ability to create ActiveX controls with Visual Basic.

The Evolution of Controls

You can be a perfectly effective control programmer without having any awareness of the history of ActiveX controls. However, there is some benefit in looking back at the heritage of this control family. It underscores how far controls have come and how important they are in the development world today.

Let's take a look back at where controls got their start. My father has told me many a time that it wasn't so easy being a child of the Depression era. We take for granted what we have now. And so it is with controls. Believe it or not, there was once a time when you couldn't see symbolic representations of the controls in your application-development environment and drag and drop them onto your form. As a matter of fact, there once wasn't even a form to drop them onto!

The great-great granddaddy of controls, back before forms existed and before Windows was even a gleam in Bill Gates's eye, was a traditional library. A library is just a collection of routines or functions bundled together in a file for easy calling by an application's source code. Many programming languages provide libraries of useful functions and allow the developer to create additional libraries of their own functions.

The great advantage of libraries was readily apparent. You could write code once and it could be easily integrated into other programs. When Windows was created, support was included for a similar entity called the dynamic link library (DLL). A traditional library was bound into each and every program that used it. If you had five programs that used a financial library and had all five up in a separate window, the identical five copies of the library would be loaded into memory as part of the five program executables. Loading the same thing repeatedly into memory was correctly perceived to be an expensive use of memory that could be avoided. The way to avoid this overuse of memory was with DLLs. A DLL could be loaded dynamically into memory only when it was needed rather than as soon as an application was called. Better yet, a DLL could be shared. After it was loaded into memory the first time for the first program, each subsequent program that required that library would simply reference the DLL already loaded, rather than loading another identical copy.

DLLs quite naturally became the backbone of Windows programming. This trend was accelerated, too, in large part because Windows itself was almost one big DLL. Operating system actions were carried out by making calls to Windows DLLs. Other programmers followed this model and soon began bundling functions in DLLs as a commonplace method to provide reusable shared component code.

This worked well enough in the early days. Then along came a language that some say revolutionized Windows computing—Visual Basic. Others adamantly dispute this, but most of those who do are probably still suffering the dazed effects of too many years spent coding in C and chasing down pointer problems! Quite seriously, the advent of Visual Basic was a very significant one in the computing world. Windows programming had been a difficult, challenging task that could only be tackled by experienced C gurus until the introduction of Visual Basic. Once Visual Basic was on the scene, the quicker learning curve made Windows programming possible for the masses. Corporate information systems groups, hard pressed for time, could now tackle Windows projects much more effectively. Individual solutions developers and consultants interested in putting quick solutions in their customers' hands now had a means to do it. The body of Windows programs grew, and interest and appetite for Windows grew along with it.

Visual Basic did provide the means to make use of DLLs. However, one of the strengths of Visual Basic was the new visual programming model it offered. Dropping a component onto a Visual Basic form to integrate it was far easier than writing the specific code to achieve the same result and fit in far better with the visual model. A way for others to provide these components for use in Visual Basic was needed. The VBX component model was the answer. VBXs appeared in the Visual Basic toolbox in the early '90s and worked according to the visual model. Furthermore, they went a step further than DLLs in providing a new type of interface to the Visual Basic applications that incorporated them. The way the Visual Basic application communicated to the VBX was through properties, methods, and events.

Sound familiar? Sure enough, the traces of VBX genetic heritage are just as strong on ActiveX controls as the family resemblance you would see if you happened to compare my childhood photos with my Grandpa Samuel's. Still, things were different in Grandpa's day, and so they were in the era of VBXs as well.

VBX controls started to cause developers some pain and suffering. A VBX control would work great in a Visual Basic application. Then it would only be a matter of time until someone wanted to merge it into a C program (or C++, which was just emerging as a Windows programming language at that time). Unfortunately, these languages didn't support VBXs. The answer, of course, was to fix those languages so they could support VBXs. Eventually they did, but more pain was ahead. About that time another version of Visual Basic came out, which supported a version of VBXs with even improved capabilities. Many VBX control creators started creating their controls to that standard. You guessed it—the other languages now supported the old, largely dead, VBX standard, but not the new one.

An odd paradox about VBX creation became apparent as well. VBX controls were a creature of Visual Basic. However, due to some internal requirements and limitations of the Visual

Basic language, VBXs could only be created with C (and later C++). The very pool of developers that was incorporating the most VBX controls had no means to create these controls in their own language!

Despite these speed bumps, the use of VBXs thrived. An enormous VBX control creation industry sprung up virtually overnight, with dozens and eventually hundreds of vendors offering different VBX controls for various specialized purposes. The time-saving advantages of a development model based on incorporating visual components were clear, even though shortcomings existed with the VBX approach. The next stage in the evolution began to address some of the shortcomings.

While the VBXs were flourishing, a different Windows technology, OLE, was also making headway in the mid '90s. OLE, or object linking and embedding, was actually a broad collection of specifications relating to areas including communication between objects and file storage structure. Early versions of OLE used as the backbone of communications between applications were slow, but then the technology began to mature and improve. As the technology matured, the anticipated arrival of the 32-bit Windows 95 operating system to replace the 16-bit Windows operating system drew nearer. New releases of 32-bit development products such as Access and Visual Basic also approached.

A new generation of controls was announced in the midst of this cluster of evolving technology: OLE controls. OLE controls, packaged in OCX files, served the same purpose as the VBX controls before them. However, OLE controls had several important differences. OLE controls could be created in 32-bit versions, unlike their predecessor VBXs, which were only a 16-bit technology. The 32-bit versions could take better advantage of the 32-bit Windows 95 and Windows NT operating systems. OLE controls were also, as the name implied, based on the powerful and now relatively mature OLE technology. This technology in turn provided a clear standard path for development environments to support the integration of these controls. Therefore an OCX could be hosted in a variety of environments, including Visual Basic, C++, and Access.

OLE controls made their mark. The control component industry continued to thrive as this standard was supported. The rapid growth of the Internet led to yet one more evolution, however. Microsoft responded to the Internet-driven direction of the industry by coming up with a new technology direction called ActiveX, in 1996. ActiveX was intended to be a natural outgrowth of current Windows technologies rather than a replacement of them. ActiveX encompasses many areas and one very important one is controls. An ActiveX control definition was released. This definition was actually a subset of the old OLE control definition. For this reason, existing OLE controls in the form of OCX files automatically met the definition of ActiveX control requirements. A new control could do even less than the old OLE controls to make the grade as an ActiveX control.

Microsoft carried out very heavy promotion of the ActiveX technology, and the number of development environments that supported ActiveX controls continued to grow. One environment was especially significant. That was the browser frontier, which opened the door to the Internet. Microsoft's Internet Explorer browser for Windows 95 was the first browser to support ActiveX. The browser could display ActiveX controls that had been included as part of Web pages. This allowed Web page developers to begin to integrate commercially available controls into their pages and share them across the Internet. Microsoft also began working in earnest with the rest of the industry on a control distribution scheme that addressed the nuances of sharing controls on servers across the Internet. At the same time, Microsoft pushed the ActiveX frontier further, demonstrating versions of its browser with ActiveX support on the Macintosh and UNIX platforms. ActiveX add-ons for the Netscape browser appeared, with more talk about future ActiveX support in that and other browsers. Microsoft even introduced Active Server Pages that could incorporate controls for enhanced back-end support of Web servers. The reach of controls, in the blink of an eye as far as most technologies go, had been extended to millions more users and hundreds of thousands more developers by extending to the Internet.

Visual Basic programmers found themselves still facing their old quandary, however. Controls were more important to all aspects of the development world than ever before. Alas, there was still no way for even a bright, hard-working Visual Basic developer to create a control with Visual Basic. It was technically impossible with the then-currently available version of Visual Basic.

This last obstacle was removed with the release of Visual Basic 5.0. A full-fledged version of Visual Basic capable of creating custom controls had at last arrived!

Visual Basic as a Control Development Language

Visual Basic 5.0 is the first full-fledged version of Visual Basic to offer ActiveX control creation capabilities. Not coincidentally, Visual Basic 5.0 is also the first version of Visual Basic to offer the ability to generate executables in native code format. Native code is code that can be executed directly by the operating system without requiring the assistance of another layer of code. Some programs are not in native code format, but instead require the assistance of another layer of software known as an interpreter to carry out their instructions. Programs produced by earlier versions of Visual Basic could not be generated in native code format, but required the presence of Visual Basic runtime interpreter software as well.

 NOTE

The official release of Visual Basic 5.0 was actually not the first version of Visual Basic available to create custom controls. Microsoft made the Visual Basic Control Creation Edition available free of charge on the

Internet several months before the release of Visual Basic 5.0. The Visual Basic Control Creation Edition was a technology preview of some of the capabilities available in Visual Basic 5.0.

The free availability of this preview product from Microsoft was very interesting in its own right. It demonstrates how firmly Microsoft stands behind the control creation model and how intent Microsoft is on spreading the gospel of control creation.

Visual Basic 5.0 provides the technology to create sophisticated controls in Visual Basic for the first time. This opens up the control creation world to a gigantic group of programmers who would not have considered writing a custom control before. A good way to assess the significance is to consider what happened earlier with Windows development. Earlier in today's discussion on control evolution I described how Windows applications were once the domain of experienced C gurus only. That (aside from assembly code) was the only language available for producing Windows programs in the early days. Then came Visual Basic, and the ability to create Windows applications was suddenly available to the common programmer who couldn't afford to spend weeks on end struggling with a gigantic learning curve, but just wanted to get down to business. The number and scope of Windows applications flourished with the boost from Visual Basic.

A very similar situation exists with control creation. Until a short time ago, the only way you could create controls was with a language such as C++. This was fine for the many C++ programmers out there. But the hundreds of thousands of hard-core Visual Basic programmers and the millions of occasional Visual Basic or Visual Basic for Applications users were left out in the cold, with no way to create their own controls. Visual Basic 5.0 changed all that. Now the very developers who use the most controls have been given the ability to create those controls with the same language they are accustomed to. It is a reasonable assumption that the world will now see a marked increase in the number of controls developed for use in Windows and Internet programming.

So how do you go about creating controls with Visual Basic? A knowledge of the Visual Basic 5.0 control creation features is necessary to generate the controls and will be provided in the days ahead. However, the process of laying out the control and writing the control code underneath is in many respects the same as the process used to lay out a regular Visual Basic form. The Visual Basic 5.0 IDE allows you to add a special control class to your Visual Basic project, just as you add other components such as forms, modules, and regular classes.

NOTE   IDE stands for Integrated Development Environment. This is the work
environment that comes with Visual Basic and allows you to carry out
development tasks such as editing, project management, and debugging. The Visual Basic 5.0 IDE is also a part of the Microsoft Developer Studio suite. This means that to a large extent the Visual Basic
IDE has the look and feel of other Microsoft development tools.

If you have developed Visual Basic applications before, you take for granted the capability
to view a form that is part of your project, add controls to it, and associate code with it. This
model still applies with control development. You can look at the visual representation of the
UserControl object associated with your control class. It looks very much like a standard
form, as you can see in Figure 1.7. You can add controls and associate working with
UserControl, just as with a standard form.

Figure 1.7.

The UserControl
*object from a new
control project.*

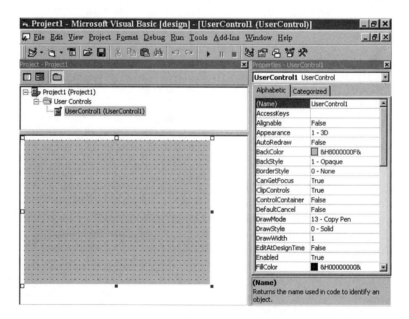

The UserControl object in Figure 1.7 is the standard starting point you will see when you
select the option to create a new control in Visual Basic 5.0. The steps for creating a new
control will be described in detail on Day 2. However, if you're really anxious to see this now
and just can't wait, follow these steps: Start Visual Basic 5.0. The New Project window will
appear with various project options visible. Select ActiveX Control. Then an ActiveX control

design window will appear right before your eyes, with the UserControl object ready for further design. I know that if you have just carried this out at your computer, it is now very tempting to dive in and begin madly designing! However, I recommend that you lean back and read a bit further. Soon you will reach the Day 2 sample that takes you the rest of the way through creating a control.

You take advantage of predefined properties, methods, and events of the UserControl and other controls you incorporate as you build up your own control. You can see a property window in Figure 1.7 to the right of the UserControl area. This window displays the properties of UserControl. They look very much like the properties of a form. You set the name of UserControl by supplying the Name property. You can change the background color of UserControl (and hence your ActiveX control itself) by changing the BackColor property. If you double-click on the UserControl object, a code window appears, just as it would for a form. Figure 1.8 shows the UserControl code window with the UserControl_Initialize event subroutine. This is where you associate the code with events just as you would for a form.

Figure 1.8.

The UserControl *code window showing the* UserControl_ Initialize *subroutine.*

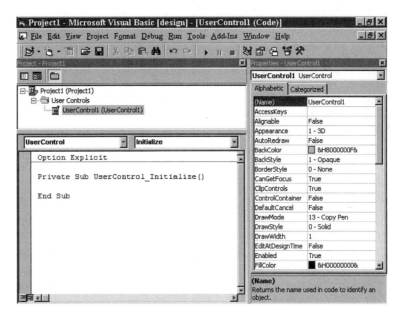

The point of showing you UserControl is to demonstrate that if you're already a Visual Basic programmer, the process of creating controls will be largely familiar to you. Granted, you'll encounter some new twists and turns as well. But you can think of Visual Basic control creation as getting behind the wheel of a deluxe sedan after you've been driving an economy model car. It might take you a while to get used to the power locks and cruise control, but you'll drive in largely the same manner. The leap is comfortable, and with the right tips, easily made. By contrast, if you'd just gone from your car to the wheel of a fighter jet, you might risk not only crashing the plane but also accidentally hitting the eject button at 30,000 feet (and more than one C++ control developer has stumbled across the eject button).

Visual Basic 5.0 comes with wizards that can make the control creation process even easier. Wizards are covered in more detail on Day 3, "The Programming Environment." You can think of a wizard as a friendly backseat driver who offers suggestions on where to go at every turn. The ActiveX Control Interface Wizard can help you define your controls. Then the Property Page Wizard can help you build up property pages to assist other developers in using the controls you create. These tasks are not hard to accomplish on your own once you have learned about controls. The wizards just make these tasks even more approachable.

Control creation is no longer a daunting task. A technical feat that was formerly a specialization has been transformed to be within reach of everyone with knowledge of Visual Basic and a will to learn (that's you!). You don't even have to be a Windows guru to create controls with Visual Basic—as a matter of fact, in writing this book, we have assumed that you are not. You do, however, need to develop a wider perspective than you may have brought to the previous application programming you did. There are some interesting concepts involved in creating controls you will learn about in the days to come that you might not have faced before. The new ground includes considerations of how to test an independent control, design time versus runtime event coding, exposing properties of constituent controls, and other interesting technical considerations. This book will provide you with the new approach, style, and way of thinking needed for effective control programming. Then you will be ready to jump in among the ranks of ActiveX control developers.

Summary

Today you have gotten an introduction to ActiveX controls. The question control is demonstrated as a representative sample of ActiveX controls. This is a simple control that can be integrated into a host application to provide question and answer feedback. This concept is seen in the Web page and Visual Basic application samples that both incorporate the question control.

A host application must be able to communicate and interact with a control in order to incorporate it. Properties are used to assign and retrieve control settings. Methods are used to launch code within the control. Event subroutines are used to respond to event states of the control. At times additional code is needed to integrate a control into an application. This is commonly referred to as glue code.

Three specific control frameworks are available. One is the user-drawn framework, where your control code carries out drawing on the application. Another framework is one that builds on enhancing an existing control. The final approach is the aggregate control framework, where a control is built on other existing controls.

There are many motivations for using ActiveX controls. These include the convenience of the easy building block approach of controls, reusability payoffs, ease of distribution, reliability and maintainability, and ease of commercial packaging. Many of today's ActiveX control concepts were present in early programming language libraries. Then windows provided dynamic link library packaging. The VBX controls that could be integrated by earlier versions of Visual Basic became the next link in the control evolutionary chain. Windows OLE technology contributed to VBXs' descendants, the OLE controls. Once Microsoft revamped its entire approach around the Internet and announced the ActiveX strategy, ActiveX controls arrived. An ActiveX control is a subset of the OLE control standard.

The UserControl object is the foundation of control creation under Visual Basic. There is strong similarity between traditional application development based on forms, and ActiveX control development based on the UserControl construction. Wizards can automate the control creation even further. Once you learn a few tricks and techniques, Visual Basic 5.0 allows you to create awesome controls with relative ease.

Q&A

Q **Which environments can you integrate Visual Basic–generated ActiveX controls into?**

   a. **C++ Windows applications**

   b. **Visual Basic Windows applications**

   c. **J++ Windows applications**

   d. **Web pages targeted for the Internet Explorer browser**

   e. **All the above**

A The answer is e. All the development environments listed can host ActiveX controls created in Visual Basic.

Q **What is not an advantage of ActiveX controls?**

   a. **Ease of distribution/updates**

   b. **Fewer files to install**

   c. **Reusability**

A The answer is b. An ActiveX control is an additional file that must be installed with the application that incorporates it if it does not yet exist on the user's system.

Workshop

Review the largest Visual Basic program you've implemented. Assess the code and identify candidate pieces that could have been broken off and implemented as separate controls. Pieces of the user interface with specialized underlying code that serves a fairly independent function are good candidates.

Quiz

NOTE   See Appendix D, "Answers to Quiz Questions," for the answers to these questions.

Fill in the blanks in the following sentences:

1. The foundation for a new control in Visual Basic 5.0 is the _____ object.

2. The host application interacts with the controls it integrates through properties, _____, and _____.

3. The three control construction frameworks available under Visual Basic 5.0 include using the user-drawn control, enhancing an existing control, and using the aggregate control. If you want to incorporate other controls, you would use the _____ framework.

Day 2

Creating a Simple Control

You're at the point where you know what ActiveX controls are, you understand what a great boon they are to your development efforts, and you have Visual Basic 5 in front of you. Now you're ready to dive in and experience the thrill of control creation for yourself! The dive will be a comfortable one, thanks to the Visual Basic 5 IDE. Some of the features of this development environment greatly assist the control developer.

 NOTE

Just a reminder from Day 1, "Introducing ActiveX Controls"—IDE refers to Integrated Development Environment. This is the work environment that comes with Visual Basic and allows you to carry out development tasks such as editing, project management, and debugging. As you'll soon see, you need to know your way around the

IDE to create controls in Visual Basic 5. Navigating the IDE is a snap once you learn the tips and techniques presented here over the next few days.

Now you find yourself approaching the quandary that faces anyone who learns a new programming language or technique. You should understand the nuances of the development environment to create the software. At the same time, you really need to experience the feel of software creation to fully understand the nuances of the environment. The dilemma is where to start. Should you learn the IDE and its features that you have no context for yet? Or should you forge ahead and create a control even though you don't yet know all about the IDE?

This time, you don't have to choose. The choice has been made for you in the structure of today's material. I once sat at the driver's seat of a brand new automobile, listening to the salesperson prattle on about the power locks and antilock breaks and stain-proof carpet. Little that she said registered. All I wanted was to turn the key and take it for a spin. Sometimes you have to experience before you absorb. So fasten your seat belt and prepare to venture straight ahead to the hands-on steps for creating your first control. You'll find just enough IDE tips to cover the necessities of control creation in this first sample. The real emphasis today is to provide you with the immediate insights and satisfaction of control creation. You'll get a fuller look at all the nuances and capabilities of the environment on Day 3, "The Programming Environment."

What Is the Question Control?

There is one more item to take care of before we barrel out of the parking lot. Control development should always start with a clear roadmap, even on this first sample trip. Clear definition of what a control is expected to do is very important to subsequent development steps. The definition should spell out the services the control will provide to the host application. This, in turn, will influence how you structure the control itself and which properties, methods, and events you provide.

NOTE

You will be hearing a lot more about properties, methods, and events in the days ahead. For now, keep in mind that properties allow a host application to pass information to and receive information from your control. Methods allow a host application to launch a block of code within your control that accomplishes a given action. Events are generated by a control in response to some predefined condition so that the host application can respond to them through an event-handling subroutine.

The question control that you first saw on Day 1 will be the first control you create. You can see this control integrated into a Visual Basic test application in Figure 2.1.

Figure 2.1.

The ActiveX question control incorporated into a Visual Basic test application.

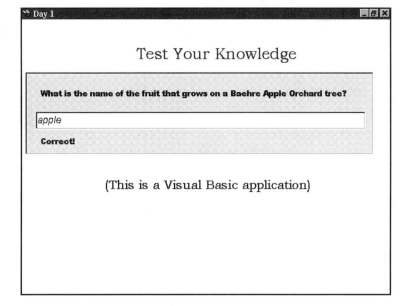

Consider what the question control should do. The purpose of the question control is to present questions to the user and to evaluate user responses. The control will do this from within the host application that incorporates it. The most convenient approach from the perspective of the host application development would be to have the control take care of all the question-related user interface aspects. In other words, the question control should directly display the question, collect the user response, and supply feedback on whether the answer was right or wrong, using its own control display area.

A couple major requirements are already clear. Recall from Day 1 that there are three types of control frameworks. A user-drawn control is built on no other controls, but includes the logic to draw itself. An enhanced control is built on an existing standard control by further modifying the characteristics of that standard control. An aggregate control is constructed by blending other controls into a new control. That new control uses the standard controls to help carry out its work. Your first requirement definition step is to assess the needs of your question control to determine the control creation framework you will use.

NOTE

> If you're an experienced Visual Basic programmer, you realize that the product comes with many standard controls you can use to build applications. These include the label control, textbox control, and shape control. These same controls can serve as building blocks for an aggregate control, just as they can for a normal application.

The question control will need a rather involved user interface. You could write intricate code to manage drawing out the question information you want letter by letter in a user-drawn control. Unfortunately, you'd have to worry about a lot of sticky coding details then, like how to position the drawing of the text and how to recognize and handle the user's key input in the answer area. There's really no reason to go through all that pain and suffering. After all, some highly paid Microsoft programmers have already addressed these issues in creating the standard controls, and you have full access to the function they contain. Use these existing standard controls as the foundation for your question control.

Next identify the specific standard controls you need to integrate. The question control needs to display question text that the user views but doesn't interact with. It also must provide an answer area that the user can type text into, and display a feedback area that the user views but does not interact with. If this sounds suspiciously similar to a need for a label control, a textbox control, and another label control, you're right! You should include a standard label where the question is displayed, a standard textbox where the user can respond, and another standard label that shows the answer feedback.

Now the user interface requirements can be clearly stated, at least in their rough draft form. You know that you want to proceed with an aggregate control framework and have an idea of which standard controls you need to integrate into it. Names can be defined for the standard controls at this point for ease of identification. Table 2.1 summarizes the standard control building blocks to use for the aggregate control.

Table 2.1. Aggregate control building blocks for the question control.

Name	Type	Purpose
lblQuestion	Label control	Displays question
txtAnswer	Textbox control	Receives answer
lblFeedback	Label control	Displays feedback

Next consider how the control will share information with the host applications that incorporate it. The control must provide interfaces for the application to communicate with it. For example, the designer of a host application will need a means to specify the question to be displayed in the control's question area. The expected answer will also need to be supplied so that the control can determine whether the user's answer is a match.

Have you ever grappled with a question and wished for a hint to help you out? Why not provide this capability in the control as well? In order to carry this out, a hint interface must be provided to specify the hint for the control to display. One control design rule of thumb already looms before you with this addition. You now have several different interfaces that you want to provide. This increases the complexity of control integration. Once you start to add interfaces, you'll often find that you need to add even more interfaces to facilitate the use of those that have been defined.

For example, some control integrators might want the control to display the correct answer whenever the question is missed. Others might want to see the hint displayed if the question is missed. There might even be some integrators who don't want to display any feedback at all in response to a missed question. You can solve this problem by adding one more interface. This interface should allow the integrator to specify whether he wants the control to display the hint, the answer, or nothing at all when the user misses a question.

You now have quite a lengthy list of interfaces for your control to provide. Don't let this list intimidate you, however. It's very easy to define this type of interface in your control. You simply declare a property for each piece of data you want to share with the host application. Planning the properties in the first part is often the hardest part of making them available in your control. Table 2.2 shows a list of the properties that have been discussed so far for the question control, along with the expected values and description for each property.

NOTE

> The properties that your control makes available for host applications to use are called *public*, or *exposed*, *properties*. They have been exposed to the outside world. You may also have many private properties defined in one way or another within your control. These are properties that can be used only by your control code itself, and not by outside applications. For instance, assume that your aggregate control incorporates a label control and you take no special steps to publish its properties beyond the bounds of your control. Then your control code could set the color of the label's text, but a host application would not have access to that internal property. These concepts are discussed more on Day 4, "Predefined Control Properties." For now, just remember that the only properties of your control that an application can see are those that you explicitly make public.

Table 2.2. Properties for the question control.

Name	Values	Purpose
DisplayOnIncorrectResponse	0 = nothing 1 = hint 2 = answer	Determines what is displayed after an incorrect response
ExpectedAnswer	Answer string	Compared to user's answer to see whether it is correct
Hint	Hint string	Hint to be displayed after incorrect answer
Question	Question string	Question to display in the control

After identifying the properties your control will need to support, the next step is to identify the required methods and events. I guarantee that this will be easy for our first simple question control. No methods or events are needed! A method is a way a host application can make a call to a control to cause some action. The only action your question control needs to carry out is to evaluate the user's answer to a question. The question control can be designed so that this evaluation takes place automatically whenever the user presses the Enter key. There is no need for the host application to call the control through a method when this approach is used. The same is true of events. A control can put an event mechanism in place to notify the host application about a designated state of the control. The simple question control, however, has no need for this level of complexity.

The host application has to carry out very little integration to incorporate the question control. The host application serves as a backdrop and container for the question control. The question control displays the question and checks the answer on its own, with no additional interaction with the host application it is integrated into. At this point, you've seen everything you need to know in the way of requirements for the question control. Now it's time to move from theory to reality. Fire up the IDE and prepare to create your first control.

Creating the Question Control Project

Now it is time to step through the actions you must carry out in Visual Basic 5 to create the question control. You will need Visual Basic 5 if you wish to follow along here. On the other hand, if you're reading this book on the sandy beach during a Caribbean island vacation and don't have Visual Basic 5 handy, that's okay too. The steps are outlined in enough detail for you to get the hands-on feel of what is required. (I suggest that you go easy on the cocktails during the next few chapters if you're one of our vacationing readers.)

2

NOTE

You will need Visual Basic 5 Professional or Enterprise Edition for the samples in this book. If you have the Visual Basic Custom Control Preview Edition that was available for free Internet download prior to the release of Visual Basic 5, you will also find that the samples are very relevant, although you will detect some differences in the IDE and other areas. The fact that Visual Basic 5 is only available as a 32-bit program implies that you must carry out these examples on Windows 95 or Windows NT, the 32-bit Windows operating systems.

The place to begin is at the start, or in this case, the Start button. Go to the Windows Start button and select Visual Basic 5 from the program choices. When Visual Basic 5 starts, you will see the New Project dialog come up. Figure 2.2 shows this dialog.

Figure 2.2.

The New Project dialog.

NOTE

The New Project dialog appears by default with Visual Basic 5. However, this behavior can be customized differently by the user. If you do not see the New Project dialog but instead see a default project when you go into Visual Basic, select File | New Project from the menu. This will display the New Project dialog.

If you don't want the New Project dialog to appear every time you start Visual Basic, you must set your options accordingly. Select Tools | Options from the menu. Then change the When Visual Basic Starts setting under the Environment tab.

The New Project dialog shows you the icons for a variety of project types, including standard applications, wizards, and ActiveX controls. You can probably guess which icon to pick to proceed (unless you're one of those Caribbean beach readers who has ingested a few cocktails). Double-click the ActiveX Control icon to start up a new ActiveX control project.

A new ActiveX control project will be loaded into Visual Basic. The IDE will show several different windows that pertain to this new control project. Figure 2.3 presents this view.

Figure 2.3.

The IDE with a new control project.

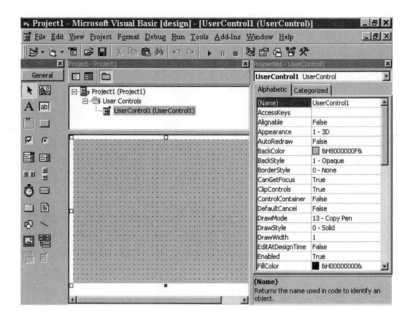

The full details of how a control project is managed in the IDE are examined on Day 3. Today's focus is on forging ahead for a test drive of your first control. However, there are a few quick points you must understand about the IDE even prior to our first test drive. You can see a toolbox area and three other windows in Figure 2.3. The toolbox area is at the far left. It contains the standard controls you can incorporate into your aggregate control. The upper-left window is the project window. This shows all the entities that make up your project. Your new default control project automatically starts out with one `UserControl` object named `UserControl1`, and that is reflected in the project window.

NOTE

You might not initially see all the windows described. Visual Basic remembers window arrangements from prior sessions and shows you the same arrangement when you start a new project. Your windows may differ if you established a different arrangement during a prior session. Or perhaps your cat walked across the keyboard and inadvertently closed a window. In any case, it is an easy matter to make a window appear if you don't see it. Select View|Toolbox from the Visual Basic menu to make the toolbox appear. You can make the project window visible by selecting View|Project Explorer from the menu. You can see the properties window by selecting View|Properties Window. If you don't see the UserControl window, highlight the UserControl entry that appears in the project window. Then right-click the mouse and select View Object.

Defining the UserControl Object

The UserControl object window is directly beneath the project window. This object serves as the foundation of your control. It is added to your project automatically when you choose a new ActiveX control project. You add other controls to this area to incorporate them into your control. To the right of the UserControl area is the properties window. This shows the properties of the currently selected object on the UserControl window. Initially, this window displays the properties for the UserControl object itself since you have not yet added other objects to it.

Laying Out the Interface

Now that you know some of the basics of the IDE, the creation of your control can commence. Begin by laying out the interface of the control. You already have the requirements needed to lay out the interface. Figure 2.1 illustrates a question control integrated into an application. Your question control should have the same general appearance as the one shown there. Table 2.1 lists the specific controls that should be incorporated into your UserControl object. The ability to use other controls as building blocks to construct your user interface makes this layout phase an easy task.

NOTE

When you incorporate other controls into your UserControl object, you are creating an *aggregate control*. The controls that you incorporate are called *constituent controls*. The end result of your control creation effort will be the creation of your own aggregate control, the question control. This question control will be built on the UserControl object, code you write, and other constituent controls you incorporate.

I promised you earlier that the initial steps for control creation would feel much like creating a regular Visual Basic application. You design a normal application by dragging controls onto a form, associating characteristics with the form or control objects through the properties window, and associating code with the objects through a code window. The same model applies to building aggregate controls. You start with the UserControl object and then drag the standard controls you wish to incorporate onto the UserControl form area.

You have a toolbox of standard controls to work with to accomplish this task. You can see this toolbox at the left of Figure 2.3. This is the same toolbox you use for regular form design. You're almost ready to start dragging constituent controls onto your aggregate control. There are just a couple more preparation steps to carry out on UserControl first.

UserControl **Properties**

One piece of preparation in particular is critical to make the subsequent control layout task a little easier. If you compare the question control user interface you want from Figure 2.1 with the space you have to lay it out in Figure 2.3, you can see that you don't have much room to work with. The UserControl object form area isn't big enough for the control you wish to create. This can be easily remedied with a bit of window closing and border dragging, though. Close the project window for now by clicking on the × at the upper-right corner. Then resize the property and UserControl object windows so that one appears above the other. Stretch your borders until you have reshaped the windows to approximate those of Figure 2.4.

Figure 2.4.

A rearranged window layout for the new control project.

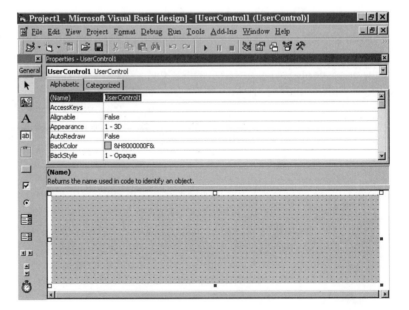

NOTE

It can be a bit intimidating when you first attempt to rearrange all the windows of a Visual Basic 5 project if you don't have much prior experience with stretching and docking. When you move the mouse to the edge of a window area, the mouse cursor changes to a double-arrow, indicating that you can stretch out borders. Once you see the double-arrow, just drag the mouse to stretch the borders in the desired direction.

You might notice when you move them that Visual Basic 5 windows seem to behave differently than those you're used to. They seem to stick themselves to certain areas as you drag them around and release them. This is because they are *dockable* windows by default. They dock themselves in a certain arrangement within the IDE for your convenience. (This really is intended as a convenience feature, even though it may seem just the opposite for first-time users as windows hop around unexpectedly!) You can switch between docked behavior and non-docked behavior of a window by simply double-clicking on its title bar. The best way to understand the difference is to experiment with both approaches.

Once you have rearranged the windows, turn your attention to the UserControl object itself. This object will define the visible boundaries of your control. Resize it using the same techniques you used for the windows. Stretch the UserControl object so that it becomes a long horizontal rectangle rather than a square, as shown in Figure 2.4.

You are beginning to implement the visual aspects of your control. You've defined its boundary. Now define its name and color. Click once anywhere on the UserControl area to ensure that it is the active control. The properties window displays the properties of the active control, which should now be your UserControl object. You can tell that the UserControl object is the current object displayed in the properties window by examining the Name property shown there. The UserControl object's default appears in the name properties area and is UserControl1. Click on UserControl1 and type over it with your own name. You should use the name ucQuestion if you want to be consistent with the samples to come. However, you could name your new control anything you want—Reba, Jane, Keith, Tim, or Rover if you wished.

NOTE

The name ucQuestion was used for clarity in referring to the UserControl object. The prefix uc is a standard naming convention that indicates that the named object is a user control. The second part of the name, Question, is used to communicate the purpose of the control as clearly as possible.

You will see other examples of this naming convention in the days ahead. For example, label controls are referenced with a leading lbl, textbox controls are referenced with a leading txt, and image controls are preceded by a leading img.

Control-related standards are discussed in more detail later in this book. For a review of naming conventions in general, you may wish to refer to an introductory programming book such as *Teach Yourself VBScript in 21 Days*, by Keith Brophy and Tim Koets.

You've defined the boundaries of your control and given it a name. The next customization step is to define the color of the UserControl object. Since the UserControl object is the backdrop for your entire control, the object's color will also be the default color of your control. Locate the BackColor property. You'll see a fairly cryptic number next to this property. This number represents the current color setting. Click on the drop-down area to the right of the current setting. You will see a tabbed palette set appear, with System and Palette choices available on the tabs. Choose the Palette tab so that you can view the selection of colors available in the current color palette. Figure 2.5 shows the Palette tab you will see. From there, click on the color of your choice. (Light green was used for the sample version on the book's CD-ROM if you are striving for consistency.) The UserControl background area will fill with the color you designate.

Figure 2.5.

Specifying a color for the UserControl *object through the color palette.*

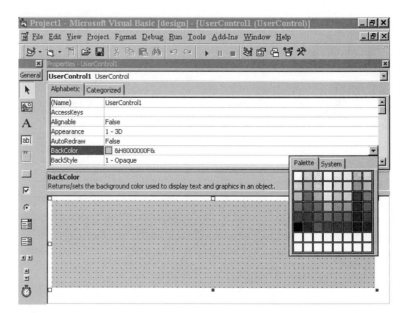

You have now modified properties of the UserControl object. Properties you have modified so far, like the BackColor property, are accessible only within your control code. These are properties you can interact with, but not ones that the integrator of the control will be able to read or change. The properties of the UserControl object are not automatically visible to the outside world unless you take explicit steps to expose them. You will see an example of this on Day 4.

Adding Constituent Controls

So far you have created a plain green rectangle. You could save your creation at this point in a control file. Then other developers could include your control in their applications if they wanted a plain green rectangle that did nothing as part of their programs. They couldn't do anything useful with this control in its current form, though.

So it's not time to rest on your laurels and celebrate the creation of your first control yet. There is some more work to be done to make this control useful. The toolbox can spring to action now that you have an adequately sized UserControl object. Click on the standard label control tool that is contained within the toolbox. This selects the label as the target control. The background of the label control tool changes to indicate that it is selected. The label control that you are about to add to your UserControl object will be used to display the question to the user. Position it at the very top of your UserControl area, as shown in Figure 2.6. Click at the left corner where you wish to place the label control, and then drag its boundaries to extend down to the desired lower-right corner of the label.

Figure 2.6.

A standard label control has been added to the UserControl *object to display the question text.*

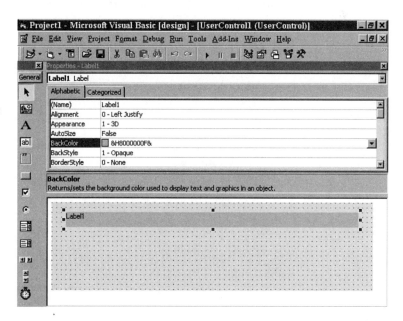

Congratulations! You have just integrated your first constituent control! Now that the label control is part of your UserControl object, your question control can take full advantage of it. There are a few properties of the label control that should be set to complete the integration. Make sure the label is still the active object. If it's active, it will be highlighted with dots on the corner and center of its boundaries. If it is not the active object, click once on it so it becomes active.

The properties for the active object, your new label control, are now visible in the properties window. The first item of business is to assign the control a more meaningful name that your program code can refer to. Replace the default name Label1 with the clearer name lblQuestion. Just click in the name property area and type in the new name to make this replacement.

Next replace the default caption of your constituent label control. The initial default caption automatically specified when you incorporated the control is the less-than-descriptive Label1. When your control is used by host applications, this label caption will be set by the host application through a property the host application initially sets. The end user will see that application-supplied caption and should never really see the default label caption. So in a sense it doesn't matter what the default label caption says. However, it is important to keep clear on constituent control usage as you design your control and as integrators integrate it in the design environment. For this reason, set the Caption property of the label control to This is where the question goes!. This will remind you that the purpose of the first label control is to display the question as you continue to design your control.

The BackStyle property of the label should be set to 0 - Transparent. This setting lets the green background of the UserControl object show through the area covered by the label. This gives your control a more pleasing overall aesthetic appearance. However, as you'll soon notice when you add other constituent controls, the disadvantage of a transparent background is in design mode. You cannot see where the outer boundaries of a transparent label fall if it has no text filling those areas. You will have to make sure to not lay any subsequent controls across the area already covered by your transparent label. Check the label's boundaries again to ensure that you have it sized the way you want before proceeding.

The integration of the label control is complete for now. Refer to Table 2.1, the table from the original control specification that lists required controls. The answer recipient textbox area is the next control on the list to integrate. If you had forgotten what was to come next, you can see from the table the benefit of planning the list of constituent controls in advance. When you start with a well-defined list, it is easy to march steadily through the list of needed constituent controls during control design.

Proceed on to integrate the textbox control, adding it much the way you did the label control. The textbox control tool appears in the toolbar as a text area containing the letters ab. Select this tool and then click and drag to define the boundaries of the textbox constituent control on the UserControl object. Since this textbox will receive the user's typed-in answer response, this control should appear immediately below the question label control and be of the same dimension.

The initial step to integrate the textbox control is the same as that for the label control. Start by supplying a more meaningful name for the textbox. Specify txtAnswer in the Name property area. The next property setting is different for the textbox than the label, however. The label's caption was set to an explanatory string to aid us at design time because that string will always be replaced by a question string from the host application before the program starts. The textbox, however, is intended to receive the user's answer. The initial contents of the textbox won't be replaced with the answer until the user starts typing there. The Text property was set to Text1 by default when you created the control. You want the end user to start out looking at a blank answer for the answer area rather than at a string that means nothing to him. You need to set the Text property to an empty state to ensure that it is initially empty. You can do this by highlighting the current text property value and pressing the Delete key to delete the old contents and replace them with an empty string.

The last constituent control to add to your aggregate control is the label that provides user feedback. Position this immediately beneath the answer textbox using the same positioning technique described earlier. Set the Name property of this control to lblFeedback. Make the BackStyle property transparent, as you did for the first label. The feedback string should initially appear as blank to the end user. The question control will not generate any feedback until the end user presses the Enter key when answering a question. The default caption of this label control is Label1. Replace this caption with an empty string to cause the feedback label to start in the blank state.

All the required constituent controls are now on your UserControl object form. There is one more property setting that should be made to all the controls to enhance the appearance of the aggregate control. A larger font should be used for the question, answer, and feedback areas. You can assign one font to all three constituent controls in one fell swoop. Highlight the top label control first to make it active. Then hold down the Ctrl key and click on the textbox control. It becomes active as well. Finally, hold down the Ctrl key and click on the bottom label control. Now all three controls are marked as active. Select the Font property in the properties window, and you will see the Font dialog, which is shown in Figure 2.7. Assign the font to be Arial Black with a regular font style and a font size of 12. This changes the font for all three constituent controls. You have completed the definition of the whole user interface portion of your control with this step.

Figure 2.7.

The Font dialog, for setting the font of all the constituent controls.

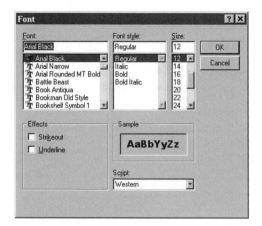

Defining Question Control Properties with the Wizard

You have defined the visible user interface of your control now. This is the representation of your control that will appear in a host application for the end user to see. There is still another level of interface to define below the user interface, however. That is the programmatic interface that your control provides to the host application. The host application needs a set of explicitly defined properties, events, and methods so that it can communicate with your control.

Properties were already discussed in today's material as you set up the UserControl object and then added constituent controls to it. All the properties referred to so far have been interfaces internal to the question control, and not exposed to the application. The question control properties themselves, however, must be exposed to the application. You saw the list of external properties needed for the question control back when the control requirements were defined. Those property requirements are summarized in Table 2.2.

The difference between the internal properties your control has access to and the external properties it exposes has been stressed several times here. If you fully understand this important distinction, you are well on your way to mastering ActiveX control creation. Remember that your control code can make use of the properties of constituent controls and objects it incorporates. The host application cannot see all of those when it integrates the control. It can only see the properties of your control that have been explicitly exposed.

A good analogy is that of notes around your house. You might have plenty of notes and lists you use to help you carry out your daily life. You may rely on grocery lists, gift lists, and a datebook. These are for your own information, and you don't share them with the outside

2

world. You also have a pretty steady stream of information that you do share. Bills come in through the mail, payments go out through the mail. Letters from your Aunt Dorothy arrive in the mail, and your response goes back out through the mail. The grocery list type of information is like the constituent label control properties—internal and not shared. The pieces of mail that travel through the postal service are similar to the exposed properties of your aggregate control. You explicitly decide what to share with the outside world. Your Aunt Dorothy won't be able to read your grocery list unless you decide to send it to her. Similarly, a host application can never read the caption of a constituent label in your question control unless you expose that label's Caption property.

By this point hopefully you're convinced that you must expose some properties for your question control. You just need to know how to go about doing it. You could directly insert the needed property declarations into your control code using some code statements. You'll see a detailed look at this approach on Day 4. Fortunately, there's an even easier way than that to insert the statements, which is today's focus. Visual Basic 5 comes with an ActiveX Control Interface Wizard that automates most of the property insertion process. You simply respond to a series of wizard questions, and the wizard generates the needed code for your control based on your answers. This automatically generated code becomes code that you can then inspect, modify, or make direct use of after the wizard session is complete.

Setting Up the Wizard

The ActiveX Control Interface Wizard, and the other Visual Basic wizards as well, are known as add-ins. They are not automatically available when you first use Visual Basic. You must carry out the step of adding the add-ins to have access to them. Select Add-Ins and then Add-In Manager from the Visual Basic menu to make your way to the Add-In Manager form. You can see this form in Figure 2.8.

Figure 2.8.

The Add-In Manager form for adding the ActiveX Control Interface Wizard.

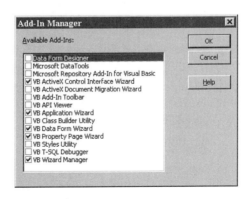

One of the available add-ins listed on the Add-In Manager form is the VB ActiveX Control Interface Wizard. Click on the corresponding checkbox to specify that you want it to be available under Visual Basic 5. Another available wizard choice is the VB Property Page Wizard. Select this one as well. It will be of use in days to come when you wish to have an enhanced property page for your control. (This topic is covered in more detail on Day 11, "Property Pages.") Click on the OK command button to close the Add-In Manager form. This is all you need to do to make the wizards available under Visual Basic 5.

Using the Wizard

Starting the ActiveX Control Interface Wizard is even easier than setting it up. Just choose Add-Ins from the Visual Basic menu. You will see that ActiveX Control Interface Wizard now appears as one of the available selections on the Add-Ins submenu. Click on this selection to start the wizard.

The first wizard dialog that appears is shown in Figure 2.9. This dialog is essentially just a greeting and introduction to the wizard session. Background information on the wizard is provided. The information on this dialog includes a reminder to lay out the user interface before proceeding through the wizard. Since you have already completed the user interface portion of your control, you are ready to proceed. You do not have to make any choices on this dialog. Select the wizard's Next command button to proceed to the next dialog.

Figure 2.9.

The initial ActiveX Control Interface Wizard dialog.

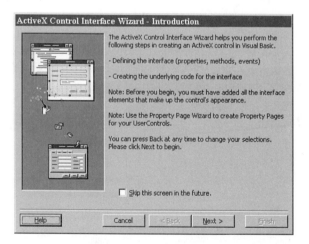

The next wizard dialog you see is the Select Interface Members dialog. This dialog is shown in Figure 2.10. You are presented with a list of available names and selected names for some of the routine control properties, events, and methods that are universal to most controls. For example, most controls support a BackColor property so that the host application can set the background color of a control. Most controls also support a `Click` event so that an application can receive notice that a given control it incorporates has been clicked on. The dialog provides an easy way to define which of those standard interfaces you wish to support.

Figure 2.10.

The wizard's Select Interface Members dialog.

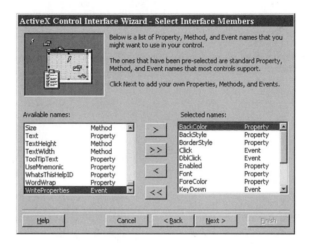

Typically you would use many of the standard properties the wizard has suggested for your control. Since this is your first control, however, this example uses only a limited number of the standard properties to keep the explanation simple in subsequent steps. Your first step is to remove all the selected controls except for the `BackStyle` property. Do this by using the less-than arrow command button to move individual properties over from the selected to the nonselected listbox. Then when you have only the `BackStyle` property displayed in the Select Names listbox you are ready to move on. Select the wizard's Next command button to accept these choices and proceed to the next dialog.

The next wizard dialog in the sequence is the Create Custom Interface Members dialog, as shown in Figure 2.11. This dialog prompts you to supply the names of any of your own nonstandard properties that you want the aggregate control to include. Back when you looked at the requirements for the question control, you saw a list of user-defined properties it needed. Refer to Table 2.2 to refamiliarize yourself with this list. Then select the New command button to add each of the properties from the table to the control.

When you select the New command button from the Create Custom Interface dialog, an Add Custom Member window appears over the dialog. Figure 2.12 shows this window. Add each of the four properties in Table 2.2 through this window: `DisplayOnIncorrectResponse`, `ExpectedAnswer`, `Hint`, and `Question`. Type the name of the property into the Name area of the Add Custom Member window. There is an option to specify whether you are creating a property, a method, or an event under the Name area. You will create a property in each case. Since this is the default setting, you do not have to change this option.

Figure 2.11.

*The wizard's Create
Custom Interface
Members dialog.*

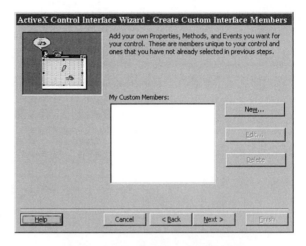

Figure 2.12.

*The Create Custom
Interface Members
dialog Add Custom
Member window.*

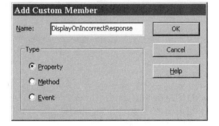

Once you have defined all the properties, select the Next command button from the Create Custom Interface dialog to proceed to the next dialog in the series. You reach the Set Mapping dialog, one of the more complex dialogs the wizard presents. This dialog allows you to associate exposed properties of your question control with specific properties from one of the underlying constituent controls or UserControl object. You can see the Set Mapping dialog in Figure 2.13, along with the question control properties it lists for you to consider mapping.

The Set Mapping dialog shows a list of everything that has been exposed, or defined to have a public name, so far. Consider each of these in turn to evaluate whether you should directly associate them with a specific property internal to the control. First in the list is the BackStyle property. This is a standard property that was suggested by the wizard on the Set Members dialog. You included it so that you can allow the host application to control the BackStyle property of the question control. This enables the application to determine whether your question control will appear as transparent when it is integrated. You know that the UserControl object within your control provides your control's visual backdrop. Therefore, if the host wants to control a BackStyle property of your question control, that property should really tie in to the UserControl object's BackStyle property. The Set Mapping dialog allows you to make exactly such an association.

Figure 2.13.

The wizard's Set Mapping dialog.

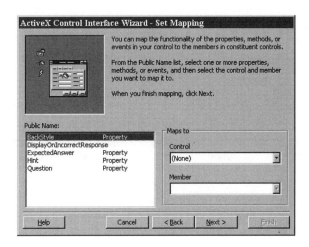

First make sure that BackStyle is highlighted in the Public Name listbox on the Set Mapping dialog. This indicates the question control property that you will map to a constituent control. Then select UserControl from the Control combo box to indicate that this is the corresponding constituent control. After you make this match, the wizard is smart enough to detect the presence of UserControl's BackStyle property and set the Member combobox to BackStyle based on this finding. This combobox indicates the specific constituent control property that you want to match to the question control BackStyle property.

In this case it worked out that both the question control property and the constituent control property had the same name (which is why the wizard could automatically match them for you). This is not always the case when mapping properties, however. You could map a question control property to a constituent control property with a completely different name. You will see an example of this in just a moment when you map the question control's Question property to the label constituent control's Caption property. This first association that you have made means that your question control's BackStyle property will correspond exactly to the underlying UserObject's BackStyle property. The code to make this happen will be automatically added to your UserControl object when you finish your session with the wizard.

Look at the list of public names again. The next item in the list is the question control's DisplayOnIncorrectResponse property. Recall from Table 2.2 that this property will contain a value indicating whether the hint, an answer, or nothing at all should be displayed after the user enters an incorrect response. This is a piece of information very specific to the needs of your question control. There is no preexisting property in any constituent control that serves the same purpose. Therefore, you can leave the Maps To Control information set to none for this property.

The next item in the list is ExpectedAnswer. This is a property that the question control will use to compare the user's answer to the expected answer. This property value will be displayed in the feedback label, but not continuously like the question text in the standard label caption. Instead, the expected answer will only be displayed after the user incorrectly answers a question and at the same time the DisplayOnIncorrectResponse property calls for answer display. Because of these special circumstances, this property cannot be mapped directly to the feedback label's caption. The ExpectedAnswer question control property, like the DisplayOnIncorrectResponse property, has no direct equivalent in a constituent control property. For this reason, leave the Maps To Control information set to none for this property as well.

The same situation holds true for the next question control property in the Public Names list. The Hint property like the ExpectedAnswer property is displayed in the feedback label caption, but only under special circumstances. It is not displayed unless the user incorrectly answers a question and at the same time the DisplayOnIncorrectResponse property calls for hint display. Once again, you leave the Maps To Control information set to none to indicate that this question control property has no equivalent constituent control property.

The final control property in the Public Names list, the Question property, can be correlated directly to a constituent control property. This property is simply used to present the question. The string that the host application supplies to the question control's question property should appear directly in the label. No special handling is required for this property. Highlight the question control in the Public Names list to make this association. Then select lblQuestion from the Maps To Control combobox to associate the question property with this control.

When you made the BackStyle property association earlier, the wizard automatically deduced that you wanted to map the question control BackStyle property to the constituent control BackStyle property. This was possible because the constituent control property had the same name as the question control property. In the case of your current mapping, however, the constituent label control has no Question property. You must specify a different property on the label control to display the question. The label's Caption property is the obvious candidate since its purpose is to display text. Select Caption from the Maps to Member combobox to complete this association.

Now all your property mappings are complete and you are finished with the Set Mapping dialog. Select the Next command button to proceed to the next dialog. You will arrive at the Set Attributes dialog shown in Figure 2.14. This dialog lets you describe the type and default value for each property. You can supply this attribute information for every property, with one exception. Attributes are automatically assigned for any control properties that are already mapped to a constituent control. The Question property mapped to the label caption property is one such example. The Question property will have the attributes of the standard label caption. No further attributes can be specified, so it does not appear in the Public Name list of this dialog as the other properties do.

Figure 2.14.

The wizard's Set Attributes dialog.

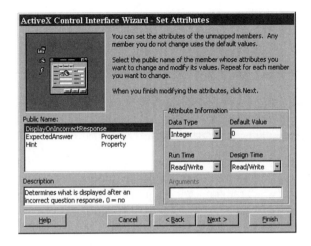

The other question control properties do need to have their attributes defined. Highlight the `DisplayOnIncorrectResponse` property in the Public Name listbox to begin. Then you can fill in the attributes that correspond to this property. First, fill in the Description field for the `DisplayOnIncorrectResponse` property. The Description text entry area appears right below the Public Name listbox, as shown in Figure 2.14. The description serves as a reminder to you, the developer, of what this property is intended for. In addition, the integrator of your control can view this description in the properties window of Visual Basic or other environments when he integrates your control into his host application. Your goal should be to provide a description that is clear, yet informative. For example, supply the following text for the `DisplayOnIncorrectResponse` description:

```
Determines what is displayed after an incorrect question response.
0 = no response, 1= hint, 2 = answer.
```

The next `DisplayOnIncorrectResponse` attribute to supply is the type of the property. Select the Integer type from the drop-down combobox labeled Data Type on the Set Attributes dialog. Set the corresponding Default Value field to 0. This sets the property's initial data to a value of 0. This value tells your control (once you write the corresponding control code) to provide no response to an incorrect question. This behavior is what an integrator of your control would most likely want by default since it is the most intuitive response.

NOTE

Generally, when you have multiple choices for a default setting and one of the choices is a none or no response state, that is a good candidate for the default. If integrators haven't taken explicit action to assign a property's value, they are likely to assume that no special handling will be carried out for actions relating to that property.

Next you have to supply values for the Run Time and Design Time fields. These attributes specify whether a property can only be read by a host application, can only be written, can be read and written, or is not available at all. There are two different situations where these settings are relevant. Run Time is when the host application runs normally for end user interaction. Design Time is the period when the host application is laid out by the integrator with a development tool such as Visual Basic. The considerations of whether a control property can be read or written may vary between these two situations, depending on the control. These considerations are examined in more detail on Day 10, "Coding for the Design Environment."

You could make the case that the question-related properties should be set to the read-only setting when the application runs. After all, the integrator of the host application would be expected to set up the question text he wants in the design environment in advance when he integrates the question control. If the property is read/write at design time, the integrator could supply the initial value. If it is subsequently restricted to read-only for runtime, then the host application can't inadvertently alter its value.

You could take this view, but it might make your control overly restrictive. Suppose the integrator wanted to write code that carried out a logic branch based on the time of day or the name of a student, and then dynamically supply the appropriate question text and settings as the program ran. If you had defined the properties as read-only at runtime, the host application code would not be able to modify the properties.

A better approach in this case is to provide more freedom so the control can be configured during design time or on-the-fly as the program runs. Such decisions on the read/write permissions of a control property may differ from control to control and property to property. The choice you make here is one that may influence the flexibility of your control. For this example, assume that all properties of your control can be freely read and written to regardless of whether the control is accessed during the design process or when the host program is actually running. Set both the Run Time and Design Time fields to Read/Write.

That completes the definition for `DisplayOnIncorrectResponse`. The next property to address is `ExpectedAnswer`. The required attribute assignments for `ExpectedAnswer` are not exactly the same as for `DisplayOnIncorrectResponse`. Highlight `ExpectedAnswer` in the Public Name listbox, and then supply the following description:

```
The correct answer to the question, used to match against user response,
and displayed after incorrect response when DisplayOnIncorrectResponse = 2
```

In this case, the data type should be set to `string` rather than `integer` since the `ExpectedAnswer` property is defined in terms of a text string. Supply `"Unknown"` for the default string value for this property. That way if no answer has been supplied to the control by the application developer and the answer is displayed, it will be clear that the correct answer is unknown to the control. Once again, leave the Run Time and Design Time fields set to Read/Write.

Finally, highlight the Hint field in the Public Name listbox, and then supply the following description:

```
The hint to assist the end user in answering the question.
This is displayed after an incorrect response when the
DisplayOnIncorrectResponse property is set  to 1.
```

The Hint property data type should also be a string since a hint is a string of text. In this case, however, the default value should be an empty string. If the control logic attempts to generate a hint for the user but none has been supplied by the application developer, you don't want the user to see anything since there is no meaningful information to help out. When you set Hint to the default empty string, the setting ensures that this will be the case. Make sure to delete all characters from the Default Value textbox to ensure that there is no default hint.

Take a moment to celebrate. You have now defined every property for your control. Click the Next command button to proceed to the wizard's final dialog. There you will see the window shown in Figure 2.15.

Figure 2.15.

The wizard's Finished! dialog.

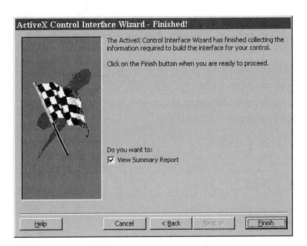

This dialog just confirms that you have finished the interface definition process. There is also a checkbox to view a summary report. When this is checked, a report will be generated and presented to you in a viewer. The summary report provides suggestions on further testing of the control interfaces. Similar material will be presented on Day 3, "The Programming Environment."

You have now generated all the definitions required to produce a working ActiveX control. It is important to periodically save your work during any type of software activity, and this is certainly true of Visual Basic control development. Create a directory to store this project in on your local drive. Select File | Save Project from the Visual Basic menu to save your control project. You will first be prompted to supply a location and name for the control file via a standard Windows file save common dialog. When you create a control, the control definition is stored in a class module. The wizard filled in code in the class module for you. You must now provide a name for the file that contains this control class module. Specify your directory of choice and a name of Day2Question.ctl for the control file. Next you will be prompted to supply a location and name for the project file itself. The project file can be thought of as the organizing file of your control project. A project file could reference multiple controls, although in the case of this example, it references only one. Specify your directory of choice and the name Day2QuestionControl.vbp for the project file. Your first control project is now safely tucked away on disk.

At this point you are already a bona fide control developer. You could now choose File| Make Question OCX from the Visual Basic menu and build an ActiveX control file that could be integrated into other applications. Don't give in to this temptation yet, however. There is some more important ground to be covered yet for this control. You could now assign properties to the current control from a host application and even see the question property display your control within the host application at runtime. However, there still is no logic in the control to evaluate an answer and provide a reaction to a correct or an incorrect response. You still need to test your control. There are still some refinements to your property definitions that can enhance your control, such as basing some property definitions on enumerated types that will show up for the integrator as property combobox value choices at design-time. The programming environment framework and the specific steps to address all these issues are provided on Day 3. Keep your seat belt fastened just a bit longer. By the end of Day 3 you will have a full-fledged, integrated ActiveX control.

Summary

Control development fundamentals are demonstrated today through a series of creation steps for a simple control. The targeted control is a question control that presents a question to the end user and evaluates the answer. The first step in creating a control is to plan your control and think through the requirements in advance. A list of the necessary control user interface objects and a list of the required control properties is essential.

Several windows in the Visual Basic IDE are used to create a control. The project window shows the components of your project. The properties window shows the properties of whatever your current active object is. The UserControl object window enables you to view and enhance the UserControl object. This object is the foundation of your control and is the foundation for any other controls you might subsequently add to it. You can work with it much as you would with a standard form, modifying properties and adding standard controls from the toolbox. The easiest and most common type of control to build is an aggregate control. An aggregate control is built on other constituent controls that you incorporate from the toolbox.

The ActiveX Control Interface Wizard speeds up control development. You simply respond to a series of wizard questions to describe the properties, and then the wizard does the work of generating the code. You can expose properties of the UserControl and constituent controls as properties of the question control itself. A wizard property mapping dialog lets you make associations between the question control and underlying control properties to make this happen. You can also define your own properties that have no underlying property association.

Once you have defined a control with the wizard, you have all the initial makings of a control before you. You could create the control file and integrate it into a host application at this point. You still need to add code, test your control, and shine up the way it exposes its properties to make it fully functional, however. This is the topic of Day 3.

Q&A

Q Can a host application have access to any of the properties of the constituent controls that are incorporated into your ActiveX control?

A Yes, if you take the proper steps to expose the properties. By default a host application cannot see any of the properties of the underlying controls that go into your overall aggregate control. However, you can take steps to make individual properties visible. Suppose you have three label controls that make up your aggregate control and you want the host application to be able to directly modify one of the label's captions. You define a property that will be used for this purpose as part of your control. Then you use the wizard to map this property to the specific label caption property that you want to associate.

Q Will the ActiveX Control Interface Wizard automatically generate your control requirements for you?

A No! First you need to plan your control requirements so you know what properties to define to the wizard. Then the wizard can generate the code for you in response to your requirements. The wizard automates control creation in a very intelligent matter, but it can't do your creative thinking and idea formulation for you.

Q Do you have to use the wizard to create an ActiveX control in Visual Basic?

A No. Anything the wizard does, you could do yourself by typing in code. You will see much more of the manual method for creating properties on Day 4, "Predefined Control Properties," and Day 5, "User-Defined Control Properties."

Workshop

Return your attention to the control you have started to create today. Examine each object that is a part of the control (the UserControl object and the textbox and label controls). Make the object the active object by clicking on it and then view the properties of that object in the properties window. Consider whether any of the other properties of the object should be made visible to the host application. Would it make sense for the host application to be able to modify the text color of the question label, for example? Make a list of the additional properties you could expose. You will see that there are many more properties you could expose for the question control if you wanted to give the host application greater control over the control's look and feel. The question of how many such properties to expose is usually a subjective matter with no definitive right or wrong answer. However, as a general rule, the more properties you can expose and the greater flexibility you give to integrator, the better. For example, if you force the background of your snazzy new tax calculation control to be pink, it might work fine for most users. If I try to integrate your control into my business application with a purple color scheme though, I would soon be wishing you had provided me with access to the background color of your control.

Quiz

NOTE   See Appendix D, "Answers to Quiz Questions," for the answers to these questions.

Fill in the blanks in the following sentences:

1. Before you plunge into creating a control with the wizard, you first need to understand the _____ of the control and lay out its _____ in the IDE.

2. You assign a background color for an aggregate control by setting the _____ of the _____ object.

3. The wizard lets you specify several pieces of information for a property. The _____ you supply will document for you as the control developer as well as the integrator of your control what the purpose of this property is. You provide a _____ value to determine the initial settings for the property.

Day 3

The Programming Environment

You are on your way to authorship of a full-fledged ActiveX control. On Day 2, "Creating a Simple Control," you began creating a simple question control. You used the toolbox, object layout area, and properties window to interactively design the user interface of your control, and you used the ActiveX Control Interface Wizard to define the public properties of your control. These design steps resulted in the generation of the Visual Basic files that define your project. You haven't directly used these files yet, but today you will see how to use the programming environment to inspect and enhance these files. In the process, you will add additional code to your question control to round out its question-handling abilities.

You will also learn how to use the programming environment to test your control today. Producing the code for a control is only half the development effort; the other half is testing the control to ensure that it works correctly. The programming environment has features that will assist you in this task.

You will learn about many other features of the programming environment as you put the finishing touches on your question control today. Once the control is done, you will see how to use the programming environment to generate the control's OCX file, which contains the binary representation of your control for other programs to integrate. By the time you are done with today's material, you will find that you not only have your very own custom-developed control in your hands, but that you have gained a solid understanding of the programming environment as well. This knowledge will come in handy in the days ahead as you tackle progressively more challenging control-creation scenarios. So start your engine and prepare to speed up the knowledge curve. I'm ready to navigate you through new areas of the Visual Basic IDE.

NOTE

> You may have noticed the use of several different terms that refer to the Visual Basic environment in which programs and controls are created. Such environments are often called *IDEs*, or Integrated Development Environments. Sometimes they are referred to as *development environments* for short. Another common usage is to refer to them as *programming environments*, the convention used for the title of this chapter. All these terms simply mean the Visual Basic windows, menus, dialogs, debug facilities, and the corresponding function they provide for you to put programs together. The programming environment, in other words, is what many developers simply think of as Visual Basic itself.
>
> If you want to be a technical stickler with your wording, you should say that you use the Visual Basic IDE programming environment to create programs in the Visual Basic language. If you're not such a purist, or if you're telling your grandmother what you do and she's not a programmer, it suffices to say that you use Visual Basic to create cool programs. Other Visual Basic developers will know that this implies use of the Visual Basic programming environment, because that's the only practical way to create Visual Basic programs today.

The Project Window

It's time to take a look at the control code the wizard has created for you so far. To do this, you first need to understand the project window. The project window is somewhat like the air traffic control tower at an airport, where planes are tracked and coordinated: It is the organizational nerve center of your project. From there you can see an inventory of the components in your project, add components to the project, delete components you no longer want from the project, and launch the object window or code window for those components you want to work with in the design environment.

Opening a Previously Saved Project

Today you'll work with the Day 3 sample project. Yesterday you saw the steps needed to create the initial portions of the question control. If you were really conscientious or had lots of time on your hands, you might even have carried out the creation steps that were presented and ended up with your own first attempt at a control. The focus today is on improving the control so that it's an impressive, ready-to-use question control by the end of the day.

Today you can start out with a clean slate. Begin with the Day 3 sample on the CD-ROM to ensure that you have a stable starting point and aren't hindered by any bugs or typos you may have introduced in your explorations on Day 2. This question control has been built with exactly the same steps as those outlined on Day 2, including the use of the wizard. The only difference is that the control and project names have been assigned to correspond to Day 3, and extra care has been taken to ensure that this version is bug free (not that there is any reason to suspect that your initial efforts were anything less than perfect!).

If you had a previous project up in Visual Basic, close it down. In fact, close Visual Basic all the way down. Exit the program and prepare to begin from the ground up. Start up Windows Explorer or any equivalent file-management system and turn your attention to the `Day03` directory of the samples. Under that directory is a subdirectory named `Your Start`. This subdirectory contains a project named `Day3QuestionControl.vbp`. Double-click on the project. Visual Basic starts up and proceeds to load the project. (You could have carried out the same feat by simply starting Visual Basic and then selecting File | Open Project from the menu.) Once the project is loaded into Visual Basic, you should see a project window for the question control project like the one shown in Figure 3.1.

Figure 3.1.

The project window with the Day3 *question control project loaded.*

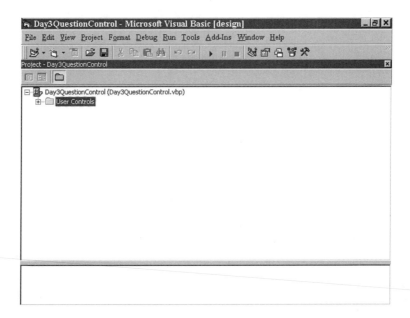

NOTE

> **SAMPLE** The sample to start with for today's exercise can be found in the file Day3QuestionControl.vbp on the CD-ROM under the Source\Day03\Your Start subdirectory. Because you will modify this project in the course of today's material, copy the entire subdirectory to your local drive before proceeding to work with it, if you did not already do so when previously installing the CD-ROM. The sample program for today is presented in somewhat of a before-and-after state. The version in the Your Start directory is intended to show the code as it would appear at the end of Day 2 (with names revised to correspond to Day 3). There is another version of this project one directory level higher in the Source\Day03 subdirectory. That version contains the completed project as it should appear by the end of the steps in today's material.

Viewing the Windows You Want

Now that the project is loaded, you can start to manipulate the project window—if you can find it, that is! If you have already opened this project in an earlier session, you might not even see the project window. Depending on your options and the state the project was in the last time you viewed it, your window display can differ from that shown in Figure 3.1. Visual Basic gives you all kinds of ways to look at windows. Just as an accountant can spread a dozen ledgers willy-nilly across her desk or just take out one at a time with great fastidiousness, Microsoft has provided you with the same type of professional license to indulge your organizational skills. You can change the window configuration at any time throughout your session. You learned on Day 2 that you can change your view by simply closing down a view window or by bringing up new views under the Visual Basic View menu. Modify your views in this manner until the project window appears before your eyes, if it is not already there.

You might be greeted by another puzzle if you have not yet used Visual Basic 5 very much. The windows are self-docking, as was briefly discussed yesterday. A docking window will glue itself on the Visual Basic border area. If you try to drag it away from the border and release it, it will spring back to the border again, clinging tightly to it. Parents can easily identify with the docked-window concept. A docked window functions much like a shy two-year-old child at a large family gathering: You can place the child in the middle of the room, but when you have barely even set him down, he will already be diving for your leg. Even if you stagger across the room, vigorously shaking your leg, the child remains, tenaciously clinging. If you bend over to pry him off, he might seize your arm instead of your leg, but he's still not letting loose for more than a moment.

This behavior can be annoying when it occurs in a window. Fortunately, you can also undock a window. This is much like distracting the same shy child with an amazing toy at the same family gathering. Now if you place him in the middle of the room, you can wander off and consume three plates of food and come back to find the child still happily playing right where you left him. So it is with undocked windows: They stay where you leave them. Figure 3.2 shows the window in its undocked form. You can toggle between the docked and undocked states by double-clicking the title bar of a window.

Figure 3.2.

An undocked project window.

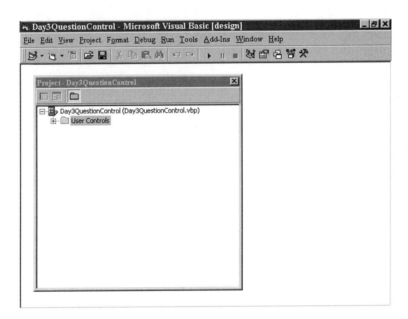

You can also alter the docking behavior ahead of time. Figure 3.3 shows the Docking tab of the Options dialog. You can display this dialog by selecting Tools | Options from the Visual Basic menu. This dialog allows you to control the default docking behavior of the various windows available within the programming environment.

If you don't like docking, you can turn it off altogether from the Options dialog. Note that your screen might look very different here based on the views you're displaying, your docking options, and even the resolution of your screen. The higher the screen resolution, the more Visual Basic windows you can comfortably display at a time. You should be able to display at least a similar window configuration with the tips given here and some experimenting. Take some time now to make sure you have a clear view of the project window.

Figure 3.3.

The Docking tab of
the Options dialog.

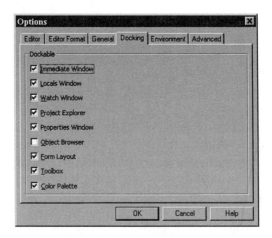

Why is there so much effort devoted here to the mechanics of viewing windows? Because you'll find that this has a big effect on your productivity in Visual Basic. This is true for any kind of development, but it's especially so when working on controls. Later today, you will see that control testing and development can involve multiple projects working in conjunction with one another.

A Visual Basic ActiveX control developer will likely find that he is spending a great deal of time hopping from one project to another and bouncing back and forth between windows within the same project. Experiment to find the most efficient work flow for yourself. It might be many windows littered across your screen with absolutely no docking. It might be a few neatly stacked, prim-and-proper windows aligned with the Visual Basic border. There is no one right answer for everyone. I can assure you, though, that you'll spend a lot of time bouncing around between those windows in your days ahead as an expert control developer!

Manipulating Objects from the Project Window

The project window should now be clearly visible in your Visual Basic session. Prepare to view the control object. Only one problem remains: If your project window looks like that in Figure 3.2, you can't view the control object yet! You have to be able to select an object before you can display the corresponding object view, property, or code window. But the window shown in Figure 3.2 provides no way to highlight the individual question control object itself.

If you look closely at the project window, you can see that it displays two entities in a hierarchical fashion. The control project itself, labeled Day3QuestionControl, is at the top. Underneath that is the User Controls folder. The User Controls folder groups together all the individual controls that are a part of the Day3QuestionControl project. Often, when you make a control you will just develop that single control individually. However, there may be times when you want to develop several related controls in tandem. You might even want to store them all in the same OCX file. A control project allows for multiple files to be present, and the folder metaphor provides a convenient way to view the controls. Your controls can make use of standard Visual Basic forms as well. If forms were present in your project, they would be grouped under a forms folder.

The specific `Day3QuestionControl` control file is grouped underneath the `User Controls` folder, in keeping with this folder model. Click on the plus sign (+) to the left of the `User Controls` folder to cause it to expand. The expanded view, shown in Figure 3.4, reveals the `Day3QuestionControl` control file associated with this folder.

Figure 3.4.

The `User Control` *folder expanded to show the underlying control objects.*

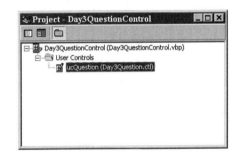

The folders really just provide an additional layer of abstraction you can use when viewing your project. Maybe you're one of those people who likes to keep things as simple as possible and avoid any unneeded abstraction. If so, you're in luck: You don't have to view your project using the folder metaphor. You can turn it off by clicking on the folder icon at the top of the project window. (It's the rightmost icon on the top row of the window.) You can see the state of the project window change between displaying the folders and not displaying the folders as you click on the icon. When the folders are not displayed, the underlying objects simply are associated with the project directly by the hierarchy lines to indicate their relationship. Your capabilities for interacting with the objects in the properties window are the same regardless of whether the folder-based display style is used.

NOTE

A common task to carry out in the programming environment is to add and delete files such as forms or control files. The project window can serve as the focal point for this activity. To add or delete a project or a supporting object, highlight the object to be affected. Then right-click to see the variety of choices available for manipulating the project, including options to add to the project or remove the current object.

The name displayed for the control file on the expanded view is ucQuestion(Day3Question.ctl). This is the standard name-display format you will see with each entity displayed in the project window. The leftmost portion of the name, ucQuestion in this case, is the name of the object represented by that entity. ucQuestion is the control object this entity represents. At the top of the hierarchy you can see an entry for Day3QuestionControl(Day3QuestionControl.vbp). In that case, Day3QuestionControl is the name of the project represented by that line. The rightmost portion of the name indicates the file in which an object is stored. The ucQuestion control object is stored in the file Day3Question.ctl. The Day3QuestionControl project is stored in the file Day3QuestionControl.vbp.

You probably have never seen the .ctl control file format for storing control information if you are new to control development. A .ctl file is very much like a form file. It contains text descriptions of the user interface and the declarations and routines the developer has defined for a control. Visual Basic reads and saves this text information as needed to support the developer's interaction and control definition in the design environment. Thanks to Visual Basic, you never have to edit the .ctl file itself. However, you should realize that this is where the source code will live for any control you define.

A .ctx file is used to store binary information that corresponds to a control, such as icon information. This model again parallels that of the traditional form, which uses an .frx file for this type of information. The .ctx file will not show up in the project window, however. It is implicitly handled behind the scenes for any control that has been created.

Now it's time to view the question control object. Click on the control object in the project window. The object you need to select is labeled ucQuestion(Day3Question.ctl). When you click on this control entry, it will be highlighted to indicate the current selection. Once you have the control highlighted, displaying the corresponding views becomes an easy matter, as you saw on Day 2. You can choose the corresponding object window view in several ways: You could click the middle icon at the top of the project window, which is the View Object icon; you could right-click and then select View|Object from the submenu that appears; or you could select View|Object from the main Visual Basic menu. No matter how you do it, the end result is the same. You will see the question control object view shown in Figure 3.5.

This is the view that allows you to modify the user interface. The UserControl object is displayed. This object is the foundation of your control, and you can place additional controls on it as well. You can also modify the properties of the UserControl object and any objects it contains. Just select the object for which you want to view properties. If you want to work with the UserControl object itself, click anywhere on its background to select it. Then press F4 or select View|Properties Window from the Visual Basic menu. You will then see the corresponding properties window.

Figure 3.5.

The question control object view, displayed from the project window.

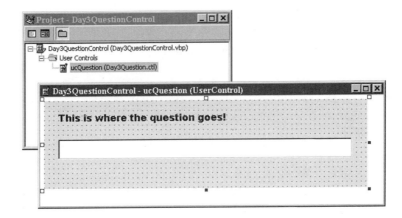

Another way to view the properties window for the UserControl object is to use the organizational nerve center of your project—the project window. Highlight the control object in the project window and then click on the View Object window icon, which is the middle icon at the top of the window. When you select it, you will see the properties window that corresponds to your control object. You can see this window in Figure 3.6.

Figure 3.6.

The question control properties view displayed from the project window.

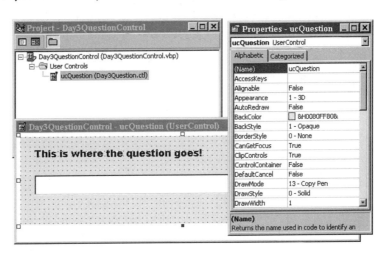

Some clarification on the different types of properties windows you can view may be helpful at this point. You can view properties windows for your constituent controls. You can view the properties window for your UserControl object. That is the same as viewing the properties window for your control because the UserControl object essentially defines the control. Whether you are viewing properties of your constituent control or of the aggregate control itself, you are looking at properties you can set within your control code. The properties window shows you properties at the disposal of the control developer. If you want to see the properties that a host application integrator will see when he incorporates your control, you must do the same. You would have to incorporate your control into a test form and view its properties from that container to see the same view of exposed properties that the integrator will see. You will see this step later today, in the section titled "Testing the Control in a Project Group." For now, realize that the properties you can get at through the project, the UserControl object, and the properties window when designing your control are those that you can use within control code.

The process for viewing code is very similar. You can double-click a control object on the UserControl form or double-click on the UserControl object itself to see the underlying code window. Alternatively, you can highlight the desired control in the project window and then select the Visual Basic View|Code menu option. The ever-present icon approach is available, too. Click on the leftmost icon at the top of the project window to show the code for the control that is currently highlighted. You can see the window that was displayed in response to this action in Figure 3.7.

Figure 3.7.

The question control code window view displayed from the project window.

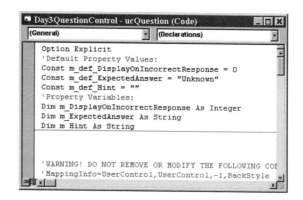

```
Day3QuestionControl - ucQuestion (Code)
(General)                              (Declarations)
Option Explicit
'Default Property Values:
Const m_def_DisplayOnIncorrectResponse = 0
Const m_def_ExpectedAnswer = "Unknown"
Const m_def_Hint = ""
'Property Variables:
Dim m_DisplayOnIncorrectResponse As Integer
Dim m_ExpectedAnswer As String
Dim m_Hint As String



'WARNING! DO NOT REMOVE OR MODIFY THE FOLLOWING CO
'MappingInfo=UserControl,UserControl,-1,BackStyle
```

NOTE

You might experience a slight panic if you are new to control development and Visual Basic 5.0. Suddenly your View Code and View Object buttons will be disabled. No matter how long you stare at them, they continue to stare unflinchingly back, remaining in their disabled state. This can happen if you do not have an object highlighted in the project window. If you have highlighted the User Controls folder, for example, both icons become disabled. Visual Basic realizes that it makes no sense to interact with these icons when there is not a specific object selected in the project window. When you click on the control object, you will see the icons become enabled.

3

The code window displays the code associated with the selected object in the traditional Visual Basic color-coded text format. You can add, delete, or modify code in the .ctl file here just as you would for any normal form or module file. Two drop-down comboboxes at the top of the code window allow you to select the current object and the corresponding procedure to view in the code window. You can use these comboboxes to navigate to any of the code in your control project, just as you would move between procedures in a conventional form.

The Code Window

Now you've seen quite a bit of the project setup for a control and have likely noticed how similar it is to regular application development. You know how to manipulate a control project in the programming environment. You can even get to the code window. As the saying goes, you know just enough to be dangerous now! The next step is to learn more about the code structure so you can make informed modifications to your control code.

You should start by considering the code that the wizard generated for you automatically on Day 2. You specified a series of properties to the wizard, and the wizard did all the work of generating the required code for your .ctl and .ctx files. So far, if you followed along on Day 2 as the user interface was created and the properties were defined, you have avoided typing any code for the control. All the code that's there is from the wizard. This code is shown in Listing 3.1.

NOTE Line numbers have been added to listings in this book for illustrative purposes. They are not a part of the Visual Basic source itself, but are used so we can easily tell you which line we're talking about.

Listing 3.1. Question control source code generated by the Interactive ActiveX Control Wizard on Day 2.

```
1: Option Explicit
2: 'Default Property Values:
3: Const m_def_DisplayOnIncorrectResponse = 0
4: Const m_def_ExpectedAnswer = "Unknown"
5: Const m_def_Hint = ""
6: 'Property Variables:
7: Dim m_DisplayOnIncorrectResponse As Integer
8: Dim m_ExpectedAnswer As String
9: Dim m_Hint As String
```

continues

Listing 3.1. continued

```
10:
11:
12: 'WARNING! DO NOT REMOVE OR MODIFY THE FOLLOWING COMMENTED LINES!
13: 'MappingInfo=UserControl,UserControl,-1,BackStyle
14: Public Property Get BackStyle() As Integer
15:     BackStyle = UserControl.BackStyle
16: End Property
17:
18: Public Property Let BackStyle(ByVal New_BackStyle As Integer)
19:     UserControl.BackStyle() = New_BackStyle
20:     PropertyChanged "BackStyle"
21: End Property
22:
23: 'WARNING! DO NOT REMOVE OR MODIFY THE FOLLOWING COMMENTED LINES!
24: 'MappingInfo=lblQuestion,lblQuestion,-1,Caption
25: Public Property Get Question() As String
26:     Question = lblQuestion.Caption
27: End Property
28:
29: Public Property Let Question(ByVal New_Question As String)
30:     lblQuestion.Caption() = New_Question
31:     PropertyChanged "Question"
32: End Property
33:
34: 'Initialize Properties for User Control
35: Private Sub UserControl_InitProperties()
36:     m_DisplayOnIncorrectResponse = m_def_DisplayOnIncorrectResponse
37:     m_ExpectedAnswer = m_def_ExpectedAnswer
38:     m_Hint = m_def_Hint
39: End Sub
40:
41: 'Load property values from storage
42: Private Sub UserControl_ReadProperties(PropBag As PropertyBag)
43:
44:     UserControl.BackStyle = PropBag.ReadProperty("BackStyle", 0)
45:     lblQuestion.Caption = _
46:         PropBag.ReadProperty("Question", "This is where the question goes!")
47:     m_DisplayOnIncorrectResponse = _
48:         PropBag.ReadProperty("DisplayOnIncorrectResponse", _
49:         m_def_DisplayOnIncorrectResponse)
50:     m_ExpectedAnswer = _
51:         PropBag.ReadProperty("ExpectedAnswer", m_def_ExpectedAnswer)
52:     m_Hint = PropBag.ReadProperty("Hint", m_def_Hint)
53: End Sub
54:
55: 'Write property values to storage
56: Private Sub UserControl_WriteProperties(PropBag As PropertyBag)
57:
58:     Call PropBag.WriteProperty("BackStyle", UserControl.BackStyle, 0)
59:     Call PropBag.WriteProperty("Question", _
60:         lblQuestion.Caption, "This is where the question goes!")
61:     Call PropBag.WriteProperty("DisplayOnIncorrectResponse", _
62:         m_DisplayOnIncorrectResponse, m_def_DisplayOnIncorrectResponse)
63:     Call PropBag.WriteProperty("ExpectedAnswer", _
```

3

```
64:          m_ExpectedAnswer, m_def_ExpectedAnswer)
65:      Call PropBag.WriteProperty("Hint", m_Hint, m_def_Hint)
66: End Sub
67:
68: Public Property Get DisplayOnIncorrectResponse() As Integer
69:      DisplayOnIncorrectResponse = m_DisplayOnIncorrectResponse
70: End Property
71:
72: Public Property Let DisplayOnIncorrectResponse _
73:      (ByVal New_DisplayOnIncorrectResponse As Integer)
74:
75:      m_DisplayOnIncorrectResponse = New_DisplayOnIncorrectResponse
76:      PropertyChanged "DisplayOnIncorrectResponse"
77: End Property
78:
79: Public Property Get ExpectedAnswer() As String
80:      ExpectedAnswer = m_ExpectedAnswer
81: End Property
82:
83: Public Property Let ExpectedAnswer(ByVal New_ExpectedAnswer As String)
84:      m_ExpectedAnswer = New_ExpectedAnswer
85:      PropertyChanged "ExpectedAnswer"
86: End Property
87:
88: Public Property Get Hint() As String
89:      Hint = m_Hint
90: End Property
91:
92: Public Property Let Hint(ByVal New_Hint As String)
93:      m_Hint = New_Hint
94:      PropertyChanged "Hint"
95: End Property
```

ANALYSIS   What does all this code mean? What does it do? You will gain full insight into this code over the next couple days. Remember what you defined when you used the wizard—properties. All the lines of code in your control so far relate to definitions for the properties you first defined through the wizard. The warning messages you see such as that on line 23 are also inserted by the wizard. They designate lines that the wizard needs in order to redisplay information if you should start it up again later in this session for the same control.

Property Definitions

The same basic code approach is used with each property. Focus your attention for a moment on one specific property and the pattern of code around it to better understand this general approach. Recall the DisplayOnIncorrectResponse property from Day 2. This property setting determines what happens when an end user types in the wrong answer to a question. If DisplayOnIncorrectResponse is set to 0, nothing happens after the incorrect answer. If the property is set to 1, the hint is displayed for the end user. If the property is set to 2, the answer is displayed. Listing 3.2 shows the pieces of the control code that pertain just to this property.

In the actual control file, these code statements would be interspersed with statements relating to the other properties. They are shown together here for your reading convenience.

Listing 3.2. Question control source code generated by the Interactive ActiveX Control Wizard relating to one property.

```
 1:  'Default Property Values:
 2:  Const m_def_DisplayOnIncorrectResponse = 0
 3:
 4:  'Property Variables:
 5:  Dim m_DisplayOnIncorrectResponse As Integer
 6:
 7:
 8: 'Initialize Properties for User Control
 9: Private Sub UserControl_InitProperties()
10:     m_DisplayOnIncorrectResponse = m_def_DisplayOnIncorrectResponse
11:     '…similar statements for other properties also in this routine
12: End Sub
13:
14: 'Load property values from storage
15: Private Sub UserControl_ReadProperties(PropBag As PropertyBag)
16:
17:     m_DisplayOnIncorrectResponse = _
18:         PropBag.ReadProperty("DisplayOnIncorrectResponse", _
19:             m_def_DisplayOnIncorrectResponse)
20:         '…similar statements for other properties also in this routine
21:
22: End Sub
23:
24: 'Write property values to storage
25: Private Sub UserControl_WriteProperties(PropBag As PropertyBag)
26:
27:     Call PropBag.WriteProperty("DisplayOnIncorrectResponse", _
28:         m_DisplayOnIncorrectResponse, m_def_DisplayOnIncorrectResponse)
29:     '…similar statements for other properties also in this routine
30:
31: End Sub
32:
33: Public Property Get DisplayOnIncorrectResponse() As Integer
34:     DisplayOnIncorrectResponse = m_DisplayOnIncorrectResponse
35: End Property
36:
37: Public Property Let DisplayOnIncorrectResponse _
38:     (ByVal New_DisplayOnIncorrectResponse As Integer)
39:
40:     m_DisplayOnIncorrectResponse = New_DisplayOnIncorrectResponse
41:     PropertyChanged "DisplayOnIncorrectResponse"
42: End Property
```

ANALYSIS Carefully examine the code in Listing 3.2 to see the many statements that relate to just one property. The first two groups of statements on lines 1 through 5 are simply internal control declarations that correspond to the property. The first declaration at line 2 specifies a default constant value for the control. The second declaration at line 5 sets aside a variable within the control to store the current value assigned from the host application for the property.

The `UserControl_InitProperties` event routine on line 9 is shown in abridged form. Normally it includes statements initializing all the properties. Here, for illustration purposes, it is shown with just the statement that initializes the `DisplayOnIncorrectResponse` property. This event is called as the control is initialized. Notice that the default value set up through the constant declaration is used to supply an initial value for the property when this event is called.

Next, you see a `UserControl_ReadProperties` and a `UserControl_WriteProperties` routine at line 15 and line 25, respectively. The first routine reads in the property settings from the host application at design time to retrieve startup values, and the second hands off any changed property settings back to the host application so that the host application can retain their values between design sessions. (These routines typically have statements for all properties, but only the `DisplayOnIncorrectResponse` property is shown here.)

Finally, you see the property routines themselves that define the property's interface. The `Get DisplayOnIncorrectResponse` routine of line 33 is called when the host application attempts to retrieve the value of the property. This routine does the work of supplying back a value. The `Let DisplayOnIncorrectResponse` routine of line 37 is called when the host application assigns a new value to the property. This routine does the work of storing the value within the control for later reference. The `Get` and `Let` routines are property specific; each property has a separate such routine for each property.

This quick look at the code behind a property might have raised several questions for you. For example, you might still be fuzzy on how properties are assigned, or you might wonder what the strange entity called `PropBag` is that's referenced in some of the routines. Full details about these issues will be supplied soon—on Day 4, "Predefined Control Properties," and Day 5, "User-Defined Control Properties." There are more fundamental points to concentrate on for the moment to gain insight into the entire control-generation process.

NOTE

> Have you seen enough to make you curious about how other controls might be structured? Or does control creation code seem so new that your head is still spinning a bit? In either case, you can gain further knowledge when you encounter the quiz at the end of today's material. One of the best ways to understand control code like that which you have just seen is to take a look at lots of different controls and the code behind them. Just as pilots in training need so many hours of flying to

> soar on their own, you may require a certain number of hours studying and reflecting on samples.
>
> The answer to today's quiz question serves as a very clear example of how a simple control is constructed. It has even less code than the question control described so far, so it's an easy example to understand. Make sure to check it out!

First of all, notice from Listing 3.1 that the wizard generated a considerable amount of code relating to property assignment. Second, notice from Listing 3.2 that this same code generation occurred for each and every property you specified to the wizard. Third, note the code that relates to maintaining the state of the property within the control itself while the control is loaded. Code is also present to ensure that the state of a property setting is preserved by the host application. The end result is a control that is nearly ready to use, with properties that are fully implemented. You haven't typed in a single line of code yet, and you already have a control capable of managing its property state. The next step is to add the logic for the control to evaluate responses. By now you know enough about the programming environment to make this code insertion fairly easily.

Adding Routines to Make the Question Control Work

The control should respond whenever the end user supplies an answer. There are two situations that can occur in the control's user input area that can indicate that the end user has finished supplying an answer in the answer field. The first is that the end user might conclude his answer by pressing the Enter key. The question control code can check for this by watching for any occurrences of an Enter key keystroke, and spring into action when Enter has been pressed. The second situation is that the end user might type in an answer and then press Tab or click the mouse to advance to the next field on the host form (changing from one field to another is called *changing focus*). Therefore, the question control code can likewise watch for the situation where the current answer input area loses focus. When it detects that it has lost focus, the control code can evaluate the answer just as it does after the Enter key is pressed.

These two cases are both associated with the answer input area. This input area consists of a constituent control textbox that you named txtAnswer when you laid out the user interface. Now you must supply code for events associated with this constituent control. Constituent control event routines are called automatically when the corresponding event they are defined to respond to takes place. The events you care about are when a keystroke occurs in the textbox and when the textbox loses focus.

3

The affected events will be the textbox's KeyPress event and Lost_Focus event. You can insert this code into the control directly in the code window. There are two ways you can go about inserting the code. You could define a new constituent control event subroutine area by selecting the appropriate object (txtAnswer) and event (KeyPress or Lost_Focus). These selections will result in the display of the event routine declaration in the code window, and you can supply the corresponding code within this routine. Alternatively, you can simply type the entire event routine, declaration, and code into the code window between two existing routines. Either way results in definition of the new constituent control event subroutine. Listing 3.3 shows the two subroutines to add to the question control definition.

Listing 3.3. Additional code to make the question control respond to a user-supplied answer.

```
 1: ' Process answer in response to Enter key
 2: Private Sub txtAnswer_KeyPress(KeyAscii As Integer)
 3:
 4:      ' Check if Enter key was pressed
 5:      If KeyAscii = vbKeyReturn Then
 6:
 7:          Call ProcessAnswer
 8:
 9:      End If
10:
11: End Sub
12:
13:
14: ' Check the answer if the user moves to next field
15: Private Sub txtAnswer_LostFocus()
16:
17:      Call ProcessAnswer
18:
19: End Sub
```

ANALYSIS   The txtAnswer_KeyPress routine of line 2 checks each keystroke to see if it is for the Enter key. If so, another routine is called to process the answer. The txtAnswer_LostFocus routine of line 15 calls another routine to process the answer whenever the event occurs. This means that whenever the end user starts to interact with the question control and then shifts to another area of the host application, his answer will be evaluated.

The next step is to enter the code that handles the evaluation of the answer. This code will be contained in the subroutine ProcessAnswer. The previous routines you supplied were event routines associated with a control. This routine is simply a user-defined subroutine. As you can see, constructing control code consists of building calls and routines just as you would for any other type of application. You can type the ProcessAnswer subroutine directly into the code window to add it to your control (see Listing 3.4).

Listing 3.4. Additional question control code to handle evaluation of the user-supplied answer.

```
1: ' See if answer is correct
2: Private Sub ProcessAnswer()
3:
4:     ' Only check the answer if it has not yet been evaluated.
5:     '   This control processes the answer in response to either the
6:     '   Enter key being pressed or when focus moves from the current field.
7:     '   Since the Enter key also removes focus, we have to make sure that
8:     '   the answer is not checked twice in a row.
9:     If m_bAnswerHasChanged Then
10:         If UCase(txtAnswer.Text) = UCase(m_ExpectedAnswer) Then
11:             lblFeedback.Caption = "Correct!"
12:         ElseIf m_DisplayOnIncorrectResponse = 2 Then ' Answer display
13:             lblFeedback.Caption = "Expected Answer: " & m_ExpectedAnswer
14:         ElseIf m_DisplayOnIncorrectResponse = 1 Then ' Hint display
15:             lblFeedback.Caption = "Hint: " & m_Hint
16:             ' Highlight the answer areas so user can retry after seeing hint
17:             txtAnswer.SelStart = 0
18:             txtAnswer.SelLength = Len(txtAnswer.Text)
19:         End If
20:
21:         ' Set the flag so we won't check again until answer has been altered
22:         m_bAnswerHasChanged = False
23:
24: End Sub
```

ANALYSIS The ProcessAnswer routine starts by checking a global flag on line 9 to see if the answer has changed and currently requires checking. This is because you structured the answer evaluation to respond to either an Enter key or a shift of focus to the next field. However, these actions could potentially occur as a pair. If the end user presses Enter, has his answer evaluated, and then moves to another field, there would be no need to evaluate the answer twice.

If the answer has changed, the end user answer is compared to the expected answer. Notice that a UCase function is used on line 10 so that the comparison takes place on two uppercase strings. This frees the integrator and end user from the burden of having to worry about case. Appropriate feedback is displayed by the code on line 11 if the answer is correct. If it is incorrect, feedback is also displayed if the integrator set the control properties to display an answer or a hint after an incorrect response.

The only piece of code you have yet to enter is the code that keeps track of when an answer has changed. That code appears in Listing 3.5. The variable declaration statement can be typed directly into the code window near the top of the module. The txtAnswer_Change subroutine is the event routine that is called automatically whenever text in the txtAnswer textbox changes. You can specify txtAnswer as the object and Change as the procedure in the comboboxes at the top of the code window to see the declaration for this event. Then fill in the code within the declaration. Alternatively, you could type the entire event subroutine, including the declaration, directly into the code window before or after other existing subroutines.

Listing 3.5. Additional code to make the question control aware that the user-supplied answer has changed.

```
 1: ' Keep track of when answer has changed so we know when to check it
 2: Dim m_bAnswerHasChanged As Boolean
 3:
 4:
 5: ' Records the fact that the answer has changed
 6: Private Sub txtAnswer_Change()
 7:
 8:     ' Keep track of when answer has changed so we know when to check it
 9:     m_bAnswerHasChanged = True
10:
11: End Sub
```

 The m_bAnswerHasChanged variable declared on line 2 serves as the indicator of when a new answer has been supplied for the control. The m_ prefix is a convention used to indicate that this is a module-level variable that can be referenced by any routine.

This variable will be updated whenever the end user types anything in the txtAnswer textbox. Any type of keystroke will call that textbox's Change event, which in turn sets the changed flag to true on line 9. The ProcessAnswer routine resets the changed flag to false after every time it processes a new answer.

Now you have entered all the code required to get your control up and running. It's time to turn your attention to verifying that it works correctly. The programming environment provides you with a convenient way to tackle the test task.

Testing the Control in a Project Group

The obvious way to test a control is to create a separate application that incorporates it. However, this will require that you work with two applications—your control project and the test application. If you've done much development at all, you are aware that the odds of perfectly defining a control the first time through are slim. There are likely to be bugs that need to be worked out in any software development activity, control creation included. The difference is that you can't test a control by itself. You need to incorporate a control into a host application to make it do much of anything useful. You also need to incorporate a control into a host application to do any useful testing and debugging.

Fortunately, Visual Basic provides a feature called a program group that facilitates this type of testing. A program group allows you to add a test form project alongside your existing control project and treat these as a group. You add the control as part of your test form. Then you can run the form, inspect the control behavior, and immediately stop and modify the control if you need to. You don't have to load one project and then another, or switch between two versions of Visual Basic. You can do all your work from the same project group session. On Day 13, "Debugging Controls," you'll even see how you can have breakpoints in the control code itself as well as in the form as you run your project group tests.

Adding a Form to the Control Project

Your mission is to integrate your control into a form so you can test it. The vehicle to do this will be the project group. Your first step then is to create a project group itself. First, locate your project group window and move it where you can easily observe it. (If you've lost it, you can use View | Project Explorer from the Visual Basic menu to get it back.) Then select File | Add Project from the Visual Basic menu. In response, the Add Project dialog will appear.

With all this talk about project groups, you might have expected to have a menu choice called Create a project group. Don't be deterred; you're on the right track. You're not really creating a brand new project group here. You are really taking a lonely control project and adding a friendly companion project to it. Merely by virtue of introducing these projects to one another, a strong bond will be formed and, with no more special action on your part, they will unite and turn into a unified project group!

The Add Project dialog offers choices for many different types of projects. Select the Standard EXE icon. A new form project is then added alongside your control project, and your project window now displays your new project group. You can see the new form in Figure 3.8.

Inspect your project window. You should have two projects reflected in the window now— your control project and your new form project. If you have your project window set to display folders, you will see that the control project is still grouped under the User Controls folder, and the new form project is grouped under a new Forms folder.

The new form project is named Project1 by default. Change this to a more meaningful name. Click on Project1 in the project window to make sure it is currently selected. Then select Project | Project1 Properties from the Visual Basic menu. The Project1 properties window will be displayed in response. This window is shown in Figure 3.9.

There is only one field you really need to change right now. Replace the default project name Project1 with the name Day3Tester. Then click on the OK command button. The name change will be reflected in your project window immediately. In addition, the default filename for your test form project file will correspond to your new name now. Next click anywhere on your new form to select it. Then select View | Properties from the Visual Basic menu. Replace the default form name in the properties sheet with the new name frmDay3Tester. Return once again to the project window. At this point your test form project and the form itself should show up with meaningful names. You can see such a project window in Figure 3.10.

Figure 3.8.

A new form project added to the question control project.

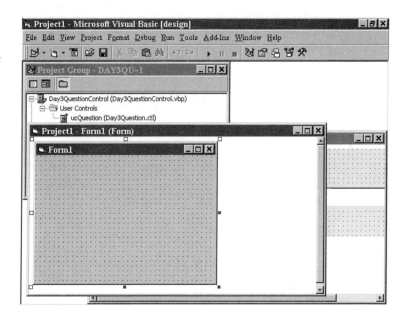

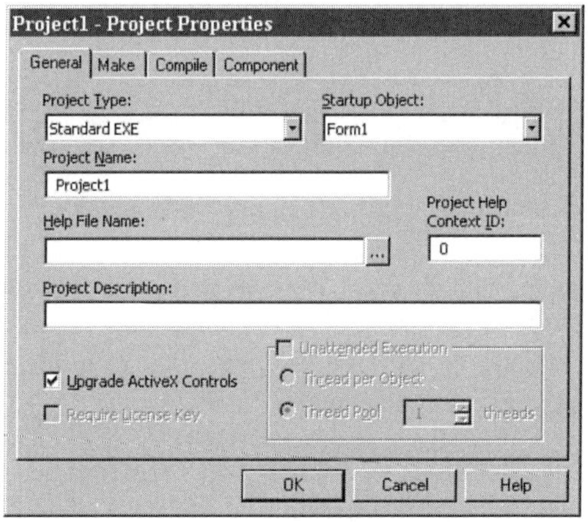

Figure 3.9.

The Project Properties window.

Figure 3.10.

The project group window, containing control and form projects.

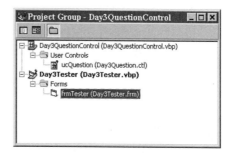

There are a couple points to make sure you are clear on before proceeding. When you created a project group by adding a test form, you really added three new files to your working space. One is the file that will contain the definition of frmDay3Tester (when you save your project, you should save it with the name Day3Tester.frm). Another is the file that contains your new form project, Day3Tester (when you save your project, you should save this file with the name Day3Tester.vbp). The third file is the file that will contain the definition of your new group itself. If you click on the Visual Basic File menu choice, you will see that you now have a Save Project Group choice. The group file (which you should save with the name Day3Question.vbg) can be directly loaded in future sessions to bring up your entire group into Visual Basic.

If you are the contemplative type, you might have another question flitting through your mind: "Why didn't we just add a form to the existing control project to check it out?" The answer to this question comes when you consider the purpose of the project file. Keep in mind that everything in the control project will become part of the eventual control OCX file. All the forms and control objects that make up the control project will be generated together into the OCX. You don't want your test form to end up shipping as part of your control! A far cleaner implementation is to test it through the project group.

Now the project group is ready for use. Your control is defined. You have a blank form just aching for some user interface definition. It is time to proceed to the integration of your first control.

Integrating the Question Control into a Form

This is the fun stage of control programming. You can see the fruits of your labor emerge right before your eyes as you add your control onto your test form. Start by selecting the test form in the project window and selecting Display Object so the form object is in front of you. Now select View | Toolbox from the Visual Basic menu. Look at the toolbox until you locate the icon for your question control.

3

NOTE

Wondering how to locate the icon for your control among the many in the toolbox? Simply move the mouse over each control tool in the toolbox. A tooltip (a small box of text with the name of the corresponding control) will pop up for each tool you point to. Point to all the tools until you locate your question control. If you're following along with the book's sample, you will find it to be the control named ucQuestion. If you specified some other name during its creation or kept the default name QuestionControl1, the tooltip will show that information accordingly.

You can also visually locate the control in the toolbox by looking for its icon. If you did not specify an icon for the UserControl object's ToolboxBitmap property when you designed it, you will see the Visual Basic default icon of a grid with an overlapping pencil. You should return to the UserControl object property view and assign a more meaningful icon for this property. The recommended step for this sample is to set ToolboxBitmap to indicate the Question.bmp file (available in the Source\Day03 subdirectory on the CD-ROM).

It's possible that your question control might simply show up as a nonresponsive, nonselectable gray outline in the toolbox at this point. If this is the case, any attempts to click on the icon result in the warning message This control's designer is open. To use the control you must first close its designer (design window). If you are confronted with this situation, don't despair. It is easily remedied but does require a bit of knowledge about how control integration works.

From the perspective of Visual Basic, you still have the control in design mode if you get this message. Visual Basic does not allow a control to be integrated into a host application (such as your test form) when the control implementation itself is still in the process of changing. If your control is not enabled in the toolbox, it means that you still have the UserControl object user interface window open somewhere in your project. Sift through your windows, find your UserControl object window, and close it. Then your question control icon will appear in the toolbox in an enabled, ready-to-roll state that warms the heart of any control integrator.

TIP

> If your UserControl object design window appears to be open but you can't find it among the clutter of other windows, just select Window | Tile Vertically from the Visual Basic menu. All your windows will be laid out side-by-side in the Visual Basic environment. You don't have to do any more window jockeying to locate the UserControl object window. If it's open, it will be tiled right in front of you, and you can click the close box to close it.

Now you can return your attention to integration of the control onto your form. Select your question control from the toolbox by clicking on it. Then click on your form background and drag the boundaries of the control to the desired proportions just as you would for any control. You now have the first question control on your test form.

Resize the form so that it will have room to accommodate two question controls and a title label, as shown in Figure 3.11. Place the title label at the top of your form. Then add another question control underneath the first.

Figure 3.11.

The test form for the question control in the design environment.

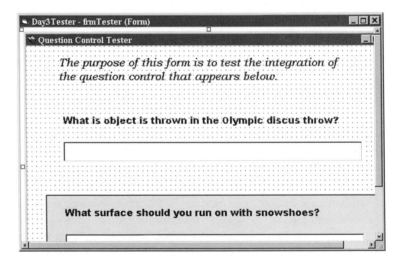

Now set the properties of your test form and the controls you have incorporated onto it. Property settings for the label control are summarized in Table 3.1.

3

Table 3.1. Property settings for the test form's label control.

Property Name	Value
BackStyle	0 - transparent
Caption	The purpose of this form is to test the integration of the question control that appears below.
Font	Bookman OldStyle, 14, Italic

You set the settings for your question control just like you would for any other control on a form. Select the property and display the properties window. You will see the same familiar properties you created with the wizard when you designed the control. The difference is that now you are setting the properties as the control integrator of the host application, rather than defining them as the control developer. You wear three hats when you create a control—first that of designer when you create the control. Next comes the integrator hat you're currently wearing as you build the test application for the control. Soon you will run the test application and pull on the end user hat. For now, pull your integrator hat on snugly and modify the question control properties. This is the same process that any integrators of your control will go through. Property settings to assign for the question control you placed on the top of the test form are summarized in Table 3.2.

Table 3.2. Property settings for the test form's first question control.

Property Name	Value
DisplayOnIncorrectResponse	2 - answer
ExpectedAnswer	Discus
Question	What object is thrown in the Olympic discus throw?

Now only one control remains to be addressed. You still need to assign property settings for the question control you placed at the bottom of the test form. This control will demonstrate use of the hint display feature, so you have an additional property value to supply. The property settings to assign to this control are summarized in Table 3.3.

Table 3.3. Property settings for the test form's second question control.

Property Name	Value
DisplayOnIncorrectResponse	1 - hint
ExpectedAnswer	Snow
Hint	It is cold and white.
Question	What surface should you run on with snowshoes?

Finally, all the test application steps are complete. Due to the nature of the question control, you don't need to write any code in the host application to test it. You just need to integrate the controls and set their properties accordingly, and you're ready to go.

Running the Test Program with Your Control

It's time to put on the third of the three hats you wear when you develop controls. You've already set aside the control designer hat for the host application integrator hat. Now take off that hat and strap on the end user beanie. You're about to see your control in action.

Use the Visual Basic Run | Start menu selection to launch your test form. This form was automatically assigned as the startup form when it was added to the project. The test application will be launched and you will see your test form displayed in the center of the screen. You can see the test form in Figure 3.12.

Figure 3.12.

Running the question control form.

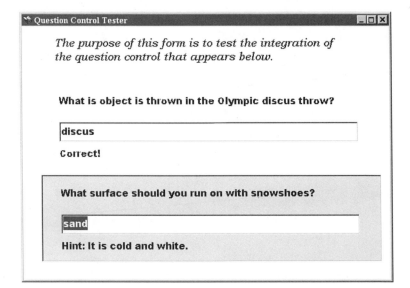

3

You can interact directly with the test form. Try out both correct and incorrect answers. The first control should display the correct answer when you miss a question. The second control should display a hint in response to a bad answer. If your test application uncovers problems, you can stop the application, modify the code, and start it again. You can even place break-points in the control code and in the form code and proceed to debug it. You'll see this technique in more detail on Day 13.

Revising the Control

Now that you've seen the question control in action, it's time to add some additional features. One aspect of control development that makes for quick, easy implementation is that you can add additional features and properties to a control incrementally. After you get the first version of the control up and running, you can go back and add more properties to it. Then you don't have to check out as much, or worry about as many new problems cropping up, in any one test run.

3

Adding Additional Properties to the Question Control Properties

Adding more properties to the question control is as easy as it was to originally implement them. Simply start up the ActiveX Control Interface Wizard again using the steps outlined on Day 2. Add the properties specified in Table 3.4.

Table 3.4. Additional properties for the revised question control.

Name	Values	Purpose
BorderStyle	0 = none 1 = fixed single	Determines the type of control border.
EnterCausesTab	Boolean true/false (read only at runtime)	When true, the Enter key causes a tab to the next control.

The BorderStyle property should be mapped to the UserControl object's BorderStyle property in the wizard. This is the same technique that was used to originally expose the BackStyle property of the control. This property allows the integrator to specify whether a border should appear around the control.

The EnterCausesTab property determines whether the input cursor should automatically shift from the current control to the next control on a form. You can see the need for this from the test form of Figure 3.12. After you enter an answer and press the Enter key, your feedback appears, but your cursor remains on the same textbox. If you had to respond to many consecutive questions, you might wish that the input cursor would automatically shift from one question control to another. Listing 3.6 shows some of the additional code added by the wizard when you defined this property.

Listing 3.6. Let `EnterCausesTab` property code.

```
1: Public Property Let EnterCausesTab(ByVal New_EnterCausesTab As Boolean)
2:     ' This property shouldn't be changed at runtime, only design time.
3:     '   If the host app does naughtily try to change this property
4:     '     at runtime, allow it, but give them an error msg to clue them in.
5:     If Ambient.UserMode Then Err.Raise 393
6:     m_EnterCausesTab = New_EnterCausesTab
7:     PropertyChanged "EnterCausesTab"
8: End Property
```

ANALYSIS   The code for the Let `EnterCausesTab` routine looks slightly different than what you have seen so far. This is because the `EnterCausesTab` property was specified to the wizard as read-only at runtime. The intention is to prevent the host application from changing this property through code statements as the program runs. The control code shown would raise a runtime error message for the user through the code on line 5 if an attempt were made to change this value as the program ran. This concept, and this specific example, is explained in more detail on Day 8, "Predefined Events." The key concept to recognize for now is that you can continue to substantially enhance a control on subsequent passes through the wizard.

You also need to add more code to the control to fully implement this feature. You need to add code at the end of the already existing `ProcessAnswer` routine to tab over to the next control when the `EnterCausesTab` property is set to `true`. You can modify the routine directly through the `UserControl` object's code window. The modified code is shown in Listing 3.7.

Listing 3.7. Additional code for `EnterCausesTab` property.

```
1: ' See if answer is correct
2: Private Sub ProcessAnswer()
3:
4:     ' Only check the answer if it has not yet been evaluated.
5:     '   This control processes the answer in response to either the
6:     '   Enter key being pressed or when focus moves from the current field.
7:     '   Since the Enter key also removes focus, we have to make sure that the
8:     '   answer is not checked twice in a row.
9:     If m_bAnswerHasChanged Then
```

```
10:          If UCase(txtAnswer.Text) = UCase(m_ExpectedAnswer) Then
11:              lblFeedback.Caption = "Correct!"
12:          ElseIf m_DisplayOnIncorrectResponse = 2 Then
13:              lblFeedback.Caption = "Expected Answer: " & m_ExpectedAnswer
14:          ElseIf m_DisplayOnIncorrectResponse = 1 Then
15:              lblFeedback.Caption = "Hint: " & m_Hint
16:              ' Highlight the answer areas so user can retry after seeing hint
17:              txtAnswer.SelStart = 0
18:              txtAnswer.SelLength = Len(txtAnswer.Text)
19:          End If
20:
21:          ' Set the flag so we won't check again until answer has been altered
22:          m_bAnswerHasChanged = False
23:
24:          ' Now send tabkey so focus goes to next question if that property
25:          '     option is set
26:          If EnterCausesTab Then
27:              SendKeys "{Tab}"
28:          End If
29:
30:      End If
31: End Sub
```

ANALYSIS The new code checks the EnterCausesTab property on line 26 to see if a tab is needed. If it is, the Visual Basic SendKeys routine is used to send the tab to the host application. The control communicates a keystroke to the application that contains it to cause that application to shift input focus to the next field. Note that this behavior will be host application dependent. A Visual Basic application that uses this control may respond to the Tab key, for example. On the other hand, a browser that displays a page with this control might not respond to the Tab key keystroke in the same manner.

Adding Enumerated Types to the Question Control Properties

There is one last change to make to enhance the control today. That is to add enumerated properties. The intent of this step is to emphasize the extent to which you can work with and modify code that was originally generated by the wizard. Enumerated properties are explained in greater detail on Day 4. For now, recognize that they let you define the type of a property at a more explicit level. This more explicit information from an enumerated type will also show up in the host application property view. When the integrator looks at properties for your control, it will see a drop-down combobox of property setting choices rather than just a blank entry area.

Add enumerated types that correspond to the BackStyle, BorderStyle, and IncorrectResponseDisplay properties values. You can see these additions in Listing 3.8. Since the BackStyle and BorderStyle properties are just exposed UserControl object properties, you can model your enumerated type after what you see in the properties windows for that object. Model the IncorrectResponseDisplay enumerated type after the values you originally identified as expected responses. Enter the code for these enumerated type declarations in the UserControl object code window near the top of the file.

Listing 3.8. Enumerated types added to the question control.

```
 1: 'Constants that correspond to settings for the exposed BackStyle property
 2: '  Even though this property is exposed, the corresponding constants
 3: '   of the underlying control are not exposed unless we declare them here.
 4: Public Enum BACKSTYLE_SETTINGS
 5:      Transparent
 6:      Opaque
 7: End Enum
 8:
 9: 'Constants that correspond to settings for the exposed BorderStyle property
10: '  Even though this property is exposed, the corresponding constants
11: '   of the underlying control are not exposed unless we declare them here.
12: Public Enum BORDERSTYLE_SETTINGS
13:      None
14:      FixedSingle
15: End Enum
16:
17:
18: 'Constants that correspond to settings for IncorrectResponseDisplay property
19: Public Enum RESPONSE_SETTINGS
20:      ucNone
21:      ucHint
22:      ucAnswer
23: End Enum
```

You need to make one more change to support the new enumerated types. You need to change the declaration type of any variables that correspond to the affected properties. The variables should now be declared to have the same enumerated type as the property they correspond to. Listing 3.9 shows the areas of code to change. Make these changes directly in the code window.

Listing 3.9. Property routines modified to use enumerated types.

```
 1: 'Property Variables:
 2: Dim m_DisplayOnIncorrectResponse As RESPONSE_SETTINGS
 3:
 4: 'Default Property Values:
 5: Const m_def_DisplayOnIncorrectResponse = ucHint
 6:
 7:
 8: Public Property Get DisplayOnIncorrectResponse() As RESPONSE_SETTINGS
 9:      DisplayOnIncorrectResponse = m_DisplayOnIncorrectResponse
```

```
10: End Property
11:
12: Public Property Let DisplayOnIncorrectResponse _
13:     (ByVal New_DisplayOnIncorrectResponse As RESPONSE_SETTINGS)
14:     m_DisplayOnIncorrectResponse = New_DisplayOnIncorrectResponse
15:     PropertyChanged "DisplayOnIncorrectResponse"
16: End Property
17:
18:
19: 'WARNING! DO NOT REMOVE OR MODIFY THE FOLLOWING COMMENTED LINES!
20: 'MappingInfo=UserControl,UserControl,-1,BorderStyle
21: Public Property Get BorderStyle() As BORDERSTYLE_SETTINGS
22:     BorderStyle = UserControl.BorderStyle
23: End Property
24:
25: Public Property Let BorderStyle(ByVal New_BorderStyle As_
26:     BORDERSTYLE_SETTINGS)
27:     UserControl.BorderStyle() = New_BorderStyle
28:     PropertyChanged "BorderStyle"
29: End Property
30:
31:
32:
33: 'WARNING! DO NOT REMOVE OR MODIFY THE FOLLOWING COMMENTED LINES!
34: 'MappingInfo=UserControl,UserControl,-1,BackStyle
35: Public Property Get BackStyle() As BACKSTYLE_SETTINGS
36:     BackStyle = UserControl.BackStyle
37: End Property
38:
39: Public Property Let BackStyle(ByVal New_BackStyle As BACKSTYLE_SETTINGS)
40:     UserControl.BackStyle() = New_BackStyle
41:     PropertyChanged "BackStyle"
42: End Property
```

ANALYSIS   The modified code works the same as before, but now relies on the more explicit enumerated type declarations. These enumerated types appear in bold in Listing 3.9. Observe how the variable declarations that rely on these types match up to the type declarations of Listing 3.8. The use of enumerated types is covered in detail in tomorrow's lesson. You have now enhanced the code that was originally generated by the wizard. As you can see, there is nothing sacred about wizard-generated code once it has been added to your project. You can modify and expand it just like any other type of code.

You can verify that your property settings took effect by viewing the properties window for the question control in your test application form. You can see the properties window in Figure 3.13. The DisplayOnIncorrectResponse property setting now shows the enumerated type value rather than just an integer. You should carry out an additional round of testing with the project group to ensure that your test form still works normally. As long as you don't uncover any new bugs introduced when you entered the sample steps, you can consider the design of your Day 3 question control nearly complete.

Figure 3.13.

*The question control
properties window,
displaying the new
properties.*

Turning the Control Project into an OCX File

One last step remains. You need to save your control in the standard OCX format so that other applications can incorporate the control without requiring the source code.

Saving the Control to an OCX File

Saving the OCX file is almost a bit anticlimactic after all the control design steps you have been through. Make sure your control project is active in the project window. Then select File | Make Day3QuestionControl.ocx from the Visual Basic menu. You will see the file generation dialog shown in Figure 3.14.

Figure 3.14.

*Saving the question
control to an OCX
file.*

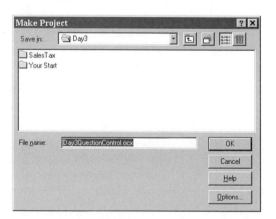

Before you save the OCX file, you should check out some related options. Select the Options button at the bottom of the window. You will then see the options dialog shown in Figure 3.15.

Figure 3.15.
Selecting options when saving to an OCX file.

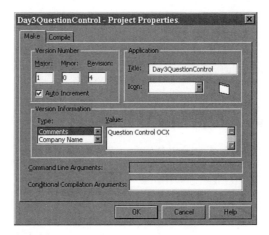

This dialog lets you set options related to control generation. Check the Auto Increment checkbox so that the version number of your OCX file will be automatically generated each time you generate the file. The Version Information area lets you supply a variety of information about control comments, company, copyright info, and other areas. Users can inspect this information through Windows Explorer and many other file managers by looking at the properties of the OCX file. Make sure that you are a responsible control developer and provide this information when you generate controls. It can come in very handy to integrators or frustrated users trying to figure out where a control came from. After you have specified make information, click on the Compile tab at the top of the dialog. You will see the Compile dialog shown in Figure 3.16.

Figure 3.16.
Compile options when saving to an OCX file.

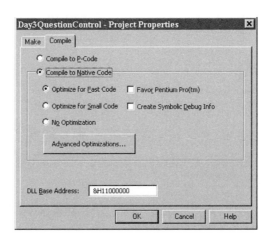

The compile dialog has many options related to how code is generated that are covered in days to come. The key setting here is whether your control will be generated in p-code, the interpreted language that requires support files, or native code, that machine code format of the PC. Unless you have reason to choose otherwise, you would likely choose native code here for the speed advantages it provides.

Once you've inspected this window, click OK to close it. You will be back at the OCX generation dialog. Click OK to generate the OCX to disk. You now have a real OCX file, ready to integrate into an application.

Integrating the OCX into a Host Application

Time for the last step of the day! You should now carry out a quick integration of the OCX into a brand new project to prove to yourself that it works. Create a new standard EXE project in Visual Basic. Then display the toolbox. You will see windows similar to those of Figure 3.17.

Figure 3.17.

A new project without the question control in the toolbox.

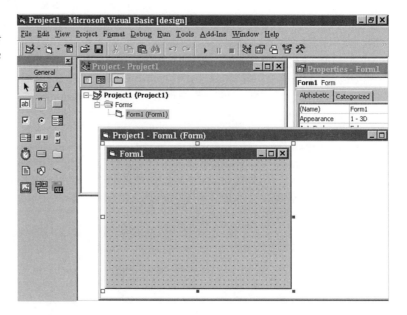

Look at the toolbox associated with this project. Notice that the question control does not appear. You have to tell this project that it should include the question control OCX as an available component. To do this, select Project|Components from the Visual Basic menu. You will see the dialog shown in Figure 3.18.

3

Figure 3.18.

Making the question control OCX available through the Components dialog.

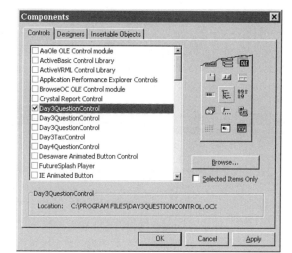

Now find the entry for Day3QuestionControl.ocx. Notice that a file location that corresponds to this control is listed at the bottom of the dialog. You might see more than one entry for the same OCX if you have generated multiple controls to different locations. Check the checkbox for the OCX you just generated. Then click on OK to make this change take effect for your project. When you look at your toolbox now, you will see that the question control is available in the toolbox and ready for use. You can see the revised toolbox in Figure 3.19.

Figure 3.19.

The new project with the question control in the toolbox.

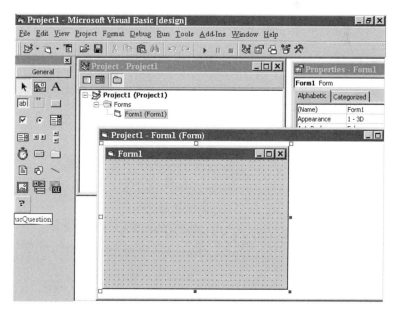

Now you can proceed to integrate the control onto your form from the toolbox. Modify properties and test it as before. The difference is that this time your project is truly based on an OCX. When you worked with the project group earlier, your control testing was initially based on the source code of the control project rather than on the OCX itself. The test form to verify the OCX is shown in Figure 3.20.

Figure 3.20.

The test form to independently verify the OCX.

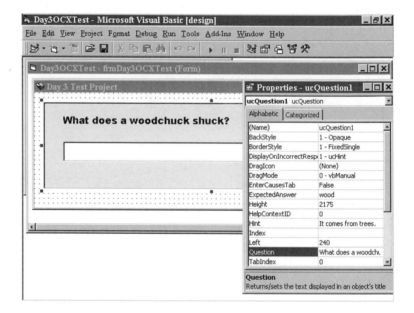

Control Creation Steps

Congratulations! You are now a full-fledged ActiveX control developer! The steps you have progressed through yesterday and today are summarized here:

1. Plan requirements.
2. Lay out the user interface.
3. Use the ActiveX Control Interface Wizard to define properties.
4. Use the project window to display wizard-created control code.
5. Use the code window to add your own code to the control.
6. Create a project group with a form to test the control.
7. Save the final control into an OCX file.

3

You might not always follow exactly this sequence, but the core elements will always be the same:

- ☐ Plan the control first.
- ☐ Define the layout.
- ☐ Add properties.
- ☐ Supplement with additional code.
- ☐ Test it.

If it works, create an OCX and prepare to share it with the world!

Summary

Today you joined the ranks of full-fledged ActiveX control developers. You started with the simple question control you defined with the wizard on Day 2. Then you used the programming environment to add code statements to the control definition, test the control, and integrate it into another host application. The programming environment served as the tool for these steps.

A clear-cut, no-holds-barred knowledge of the programming environment is crucial for any effective control development in Visual Basic, just as it was for this exercise. Today you learned about key concepts and details of the programming environment in context with the development of the sample to help you gain this critical knowledge and to see how it applies. By now you have seen how to manipulate the multiple view windows of Visual Basic. You have used the project window to manage your control project. You've recalled a previously saved control project back into Visual Basic and added more code to it. You've created a project group and added a test form to test your control. Last but not least, you have saved the resulting control into a binary OCX file so that it can be easily integrated into other applications.

Don't feel that you've arrived at the top of the mountain when it comes to control creation quite yet, however. There are still many more approaches, techniques, and tricks you will need to know for some of the more advanced controls you might want to tackle (at least 18 more days worth!). On the other hand, you've certainly scaled the first control creation hill. You are now able to create a basic control under Visual Basic, a feat that was completely impossible as recently as late 1996. It's now time to turn your attention to some more of the details behind control implementation.

Q&A

Q **Can you have both a form project and a control project be part of a project group?**

A Yes. One of the main uses of project groups that you've seen so far is to group a control project and a form project into the same combined project. A project group combines the form and control into one project entity for convenient handling during testing. You can use the form to test your control. If control changes or debugging are needed, you can monitor and edit your control right within the same project.

Q **What are two different ways to display the control code window that corresponds to your control?**

A Select the control module that appears in the project window. This module will be grouped under the main project. If you have the folder view active in the project window, it will be under the User Controls folder as well. Once you locate the module, click on it so that it is highlighted. Then, with the module still highlighted, click on the View Code icon at the top-left corner of the project window. The code window for your control module will be displayed.

Alternatively, select the control module from the project window by highlighting it with a mouse click, just as with the first approach. Then click on the View Object icon. This is the middle icon of the three icons at the top of the project window. You will see the UserControl object form area displayed in a UserControl window in response to this selection. Then double-click directly on the UserControl form area. The code window that corresponds to the UserControl object will be displayed.

NOTE

> There are many different ways to carry out an action on a highlighted item in the project window. Instead of clicking on the View Code icon to view the highlighted object's code, you could have selected the Visual Basic View menu choice and then selected the Code submenu choice. Or you could even have right-clicked in the Project window and then selected View Code from the resulting submenu. The same type of alternatives are available for the View Object icon. With so many selection choices, even the most finicky developers should be able to find something that suits their tastes!

3

Q Is the property code generated by the ActiveX Control Interface Wizard protected so that you cannot inadvertently alter it?

A No. You can view the code through the Visual Basic code window and directly edit it if desired. Often you will want to modify the code to add additional logic to the simple property assignment subroutines made by the wizard. You will see examples of supplying detailed property code on Day 5.

Workshop

Consider a hypothetical sales tax control you could create. This aggregate control would have one constituent textbox control where the end user would enter a pretax sales price. The sales tax control would also have a constituent label control that showed the amount of tax due, and another constituent label control below that which showed the grand price of the sale. The tax rate would be based on a TaxRate property of the sales tax control set by the host application integrator at design time.

The set of recommended control creation steps used to develop the question control was summarized earlier today and is repeated here:

1. Plan requirements.
2. Lay out the user interface.
3. Use the ActiveX Control Interface Wizard to define properties.
4. Use the project window to display wizard-created control code.
5. Use the code window to add your own code to the control.
6. Create a project group with a form to test the control.
7. Save the final control to an OCX file.

Consider each of the steps in turn in relation to the hypothetical sales tax control. Think about how long it would take you to carry out a given step. Also consider how easy it would or would not be for you to carry out that step with your current knowledge of the programming environment and control creation.

Quiz

NOTE See Appendix D, "Answers to Quiz Questions," for the answer to this question.

Show the object declaration you would need to use to declare a Java applet that you can access by the name jvaGifts in your script. If you've ever had a sneaky professor for a class, you probably saw this one coming. Now take the sales tax control from the hypothetical realm to reality. Implement the sales tax control described in the workshop. When you're done, create a project group for the control and use a test form to verify that the control works. Then inspect your code and compare it to the code in the sample solution.

Day 4

Predefined Control Properties

On Day 2, "Creating a Simple Control," and Day 3, "The Programming Environment," you got a good start putting together an ActiveX control. Now that you've learned a bit about the Visual Basic environment and you've used the various wizards in Visual Basic for easy creation of properties, events, and other control characteristics, it's time to look in more detail at what properties are really all about. Over the next two days, you will learn everything you need to know about ActiveX control properties. On Day 2 you saw how to create properties using the ActiveX Control Interface Wizard. The wizards can save you a lot of time and make it easy for you to create properties, but you need to understand the fundamentals in order to use properties as effectively as possible.

By now you should have a pretty good understanding of what a property is. This lesson expands on the basic concepts you've already learned. You should not only know what a property is, but you should also understand *why* properties are important in the design and creation of ActiveX controls. Today you'll be introduced to the first of two types of properties—the predefined control property. Predefined control properties are properties that are already a part of the control they belong to, whether that control is an aggregate or a constituent control. They come along automatically and are a part of the control. That's what you'll learn about today. Tomorrow you'll learn about the second type of property: the user-defined property. User-defined properties are ones you create from scratch. They are not already part of a control; you add them to the property list yourself along with all the properties your control already has.

Properties are just one of the many fundamental elements that make up a control. You need to understand them because you'll be using them extensively as you design ActiveX controls of your own. The nice thing about properties is that you can expose them to the host application or you can keep them hidden so that only you, the one creating the control, have access to them when you design the control. If this sounds a bit confusing right now, that's perfectly all right. By the end of this lesson, you should have a much clearer idea of properties and how they are used. Without further ado, let's talk more about what a property is and why you'd want to use one.

What Is a Property?

Waking up on a cold, brisk morning in the dead of winter, you struggle out to your frosty car, ready for another exciting day of work. What's the first step in getting to work? To get inside the car, of course. How do you do that? Well, you must first open the car door. At this point, the door is shut and locked. The door can be either locked or unlocked, open or closed. Suddenly, you realize just how brilliant you really are! You've just discovered two important properties of your car door. The first property indicates whether the door is open or closed. Let's call this property Position. Now the door is either open or not, so the Position property can be either Open or Closed. The second property of your car door is Locked, which can be either True or False.

So what characterizes a property? Well, a property can take on one or more different possible values, or settings. In the case of the car door position, it can be either opened or closed. Consider your washing machine. While washing your favorite bundle of clothes, the machine might be in the soak, spin, or rinse cycle, just to name a few. Let's call the property Cycle. The Cycle property can therefore take the settings Soak, Spin, or Rinse. The point is that a property must be set to some value, and that value can be changed.

The second characteristic of a property is that it always belongs to an object. Thus far we've considered a car door and a washing machine. Now let's think about ActiveX controls. Suppose that within your ActiveX control you have a label. That label is a constituent control inside your ActiveX control and, as you might expect, it too has several properties. One property is called Visible, which can be set to True or False. This determines whether the user can see the label inside the control. Another property of the label is Caption, which allows you to enter any string value, such as Jose's Cafeteria, into the label control for the world to see.

Properties, then, are a set of attributes that have the potential to modify the characteristics of a control in some way. Using properties, you can provide the outside world the ability to interact with the control and change its characteristics. Just as you can set the Locked property of your car door to True or False by clicking the lock on or off, you can set the Enabled property of a label control by setting that property to True or False. Properties, then, provide the programmer with an interface to the control that allows the programmer to change its characteristics.

NEW TERM A *property* is an interface to a control that allows the program to change its characteristics in some way.

Properties are an essential part of a control because they provide the host application the ability to get the control to do what it is intended to do in the program. Control properties come in several shapes and sizes. But before we discuss the different kinds of properties, you first need to know about the controls to which they belong.

A property is always associated with an object, and in our case we focus specifically on control objects, or controls. An ActiveX control can contain several controls. In this case, the ActiveX control acts like a container to contain the controls. The controls that are placed inside the ActiveX control are called *constituent controls*. The container that contains the constituent controls is called the UserControl object. To better understand this relationship, consider a simple ActiveX control that consists of a label. This is illustrated for you in Figure 4.1.

Figure 4.1.

A label within the UserControl *object is called a constituent control.*

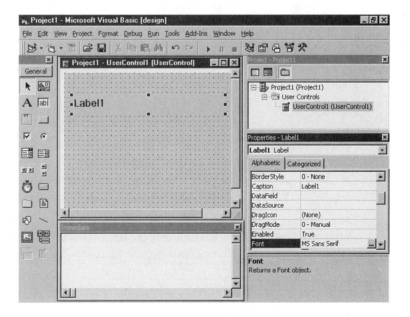

4

The label control resides inside the UserControl object. Taken together, both constitute the ActiveX control. As you know, the label control has properties of its own, as does the UserControl object, even though the label is inside the UserControl object. For example, consider the label control's Caption property. Likewise, the UserControl object has its own set of properties. For example, UserControl has a Visible property. Since the UserControl object is a container in which all the constituent controls reside, if you set the Visible property of the UserControl object to False, the container becomes invisible, making all the constituent controls inside the container invisible as well.

So you see that there are two levels of properties here. Both are available to you, the designer of the control, when you're writing the code for your ActiveX control. You get to choose which properties you want to expose to the host application, whether they be UserControl object properties or properties of a constituent control inside the UserControl object.

UserControl Object Properties at a Glance

So what exactly are the properties of the UserControl object? These are the properties of the object, not any of the constituent controls that may reside within it. Let's look at some of the properties of a UserControl object that are available when you're designing the ActiveX control. They are summarized in Table 4.1.

Table 4.1. Some of the important properties of the UserControl object.

Property Name	Purpose
ControlContainer	Returns or sets a boolean value determining whether a control can contain controls placed in it by the developer or the end user at the control's runtime.
Enabled	Returns/sets a value that determines whether an object can respond to user-generated events.
FillColor	Returns/sets the color used to fill in shapes, circles, and boxes.
InvisibleAtRuntime	Returns or sets a value determining whether a control should not have a visible window at runtime.
Public	Returns or sets a value determining whether a control can be shared with other applications.
ToolboxBitmap	Returns or sets a bitmap that will be used as the picture representation of the control in the toolbox.

This is just a small sampling of the total number of properties a UserControl object has. You may, in the course of the design of your control, use many of these properties. Many of these properties you would never want to expose to the user of your control. You would never, for example, want to expose the ToolBoxBitmap property to the user! The user should never be able to change the picture that appears in the toolbox when the control is included in the project. You might, however, want to expose a property such as Enabled to the user since you might want to allow him to disable the control when it's on his form in his project. So we can classify predefined properties into two categories—those you want to hide from the host application and use only in the internal code of the control, and properties you want to expose to the user. Let's take a look at the hidden properties first.

Hidden Properties

Properties are hidden (that is, private) by default, unless you decide to expose them. Therefore, you can use the properties directly in your code without fear of the user's being able to manipulate them. Since the UserControl object has properties of its own, and any constituent controls you may have in your project also have their own properties, there are two kinds of hidden properties you can have in your project. The first are hidden properties of the UserControl object. The second are the properties of the constituent controls you wish to keep hidden.

Exposed Properties

Similarly, you may want to expose several of the properties of either the UserControl object or any constituent controls to the user. You have to write a little bit of code to expose a property to the outside world, but it's not that difficult. You'll see how it's done in just a bit. As was the case with hidden properties, you can choose to expose the properties of the UserControl object, or you can expose the properties of the constituent controls within the UserControl object itself. You may, for instance, wish to expose the Caption property of the label inside your control. That way, the host application would be able to access that property and change the caption directly. Let's take a closer look at the process of using hidden predefined properties and exposing those predefined properties to the application that uses your control.

UserControl **Object Properties**

Let's take a look at the UserControl object first, before considering the constituent controls you can place within it. Open the question control project group for today's lesson. The project group, named Day3QuestionControl.vbg, can be found on the CD-ROM that comes with the book. Or, if you've installed the source code to your hard drive, locate the Day4 directory and open the file in that directory. When you open the project group, the question control should appear in the design environment, as shown in Figure 4.2.

Figure 4.2.

The question control and the UserControl *object's property sheet as they appear in the design environment of a host application.*

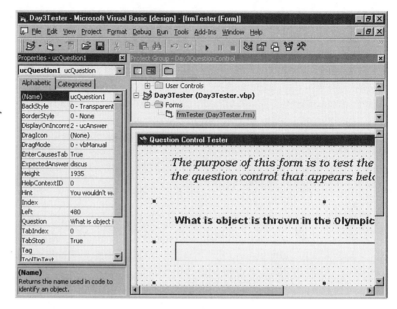

Hidden Properties

As a designer of the control, you will likely want to access many of the properties of the UserControl object, some of which are summarized in Table 4.1. Let's suppose, for example, that you need to define a bitmap for the question control so that the control appears with an appropriate icon in the Visual Basic toolbox. Open the test application within the project group and move the mouse pointer over the question control icon found in the toolbox. You should notice a generic icon. Visual Basic chooses this icon as a default if you haven't chosen a different one.

Your goal at this point is to place a better icon in the toolbar than the default one. To do so, you need to set the ToolBoxBitmap property. Bring up the question control project once more. Click on the UserControl object and bring up the property sheet for it. Find the ToolBoxBitmap property. You'll notice that this property is currently set to (None), as shown in Figure 4.3.

To set this property, simply double-click on ToolBoxBitmap in the property sheet. You should now see a dialog asking you for a bitmap file like the one shown in Figure 4.4. Go ahead and select the bitmap named Question.bmp, which is found in the same directory the project is in.

Figure 4.3.

The ToolBoxBitmap *property in the question control's design environment is not set at this point.*

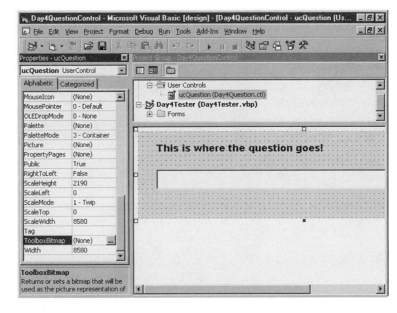

Figure 4.4.

Setting the ToolBoxBitmap *property in the question control's design environment.*

Now close down the question control project and switch back to the test application project. Notice this time that the bitmap you've selected for the question control now appears in the toolbox. This is shown in Figure 4.5.

Figure 4.5.

The question control now appears in the host design environment with the appropriate bitmap in the toolbox.

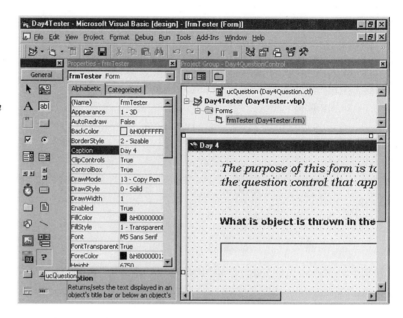

In the previous example, the `ToolBoxBitmap` property was set in the property sheet of the `UserControl` object. Many of the properties of the `UserControl` object can only be set using the property sheet and cannot be set in code. The reason for this is that the property cannot be changed once it is initially set using the property sheet in design mode. In other words, the property can never be set at runtime because it was never intended to be changed once the control is running. For example, it is impossible to set the `ToolBoxBitmap` property at runtime. This makes sense because Visual Basic won't and shouldn't have to change the picture in the toolbox that represents the control. Not only is it nonstandard, but it also makes no sense. So if you try to set the `ToolBoxBitmap` property in code, Visual Basic will generate an error because the property will not be recognized. You can, however, set many of the properties using code. The following subroutine, for example, can be used to force the background color of the control to light red whenever the control is displayed on a form, whether at design time or at runtime:

```
Private Sub UserControl_Initialize()
    BackColor = QBColor(12)
End Sub
```

Therefore, using hidden properties within an ActiveX control is really quite simple. You can either work with them directly on the property sheet at design time, or access them via code using the syntax `UserControl.PropertyName`. Since the `UserControl` object is the default object if none is specified, you can often omit the term `UserControl` from the syntax, simply using `PropertyName` directly. You can only do this, however, when there are no naming conflicts between predefined properties and the name given to the exposed property. You'll learn more about this in a bit.

Exposed Properties

Hidden properties are quite easy to work with because they can be used as-is. If you want to expose properties to the host application, however, you must either add a bit of extra code to do the trick or use the wizard.

It is often useful for a host application to disable a control. When a control is disabled, it does not respond to events such as mouse clicks or keystrokes. Often, when a program wants to keep the user from using a control, the program will set the `Enabled` property of the control to `False`. In this simple example, you will learn how to expose the `Enabled` property of the `UserControl` object so that the host application can disable the ActiveX control.

Typically, the name of the property you wish to expose is the same name you want to use for the public interface. The property name, however, doesn't necessarily have to be. For example, if you wanted to provide a public property on the ActiveX control that sets the `Enabled` property of the `UserControl` object to `True` or `False`, you might want to call that public property `On` rather than `Enabled`. In most cases, however, it is desirable to keep the name the same.

The host application will not know what's in the ActiveX control other than the properties you provide. To the host, the `On` property simply determines whether the control is active. The host isn't aware of what goes on within the control itself. The only knowledge the host application has is of the property itself and the values the host can assign to that property.

First, let's expose the `UserControl` object property named `Enabled`, sticking with the same property name as the `UserControl` object does—`Enabled`. Before you begin, bring up the host application in design mode, select the question control, and bring up the property sheet. As you can see from the host application design environment, shown in Figure 4.6, the `Enabled` property does not appear in the property sheet.

Figure 4.6.

The question control hasn't exposed the Enabled *property yet, as can be seen from the property sheet.*

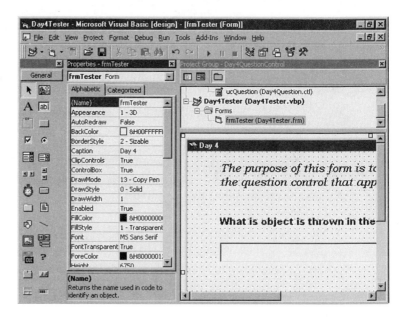

You can expose the Enabled property to the host application by creating a set of *property procedures.* A property procedure tells Visual Basic to expose the property using the name of the property as specified in the procedure. When you create a property procedure, a set of procedures is always generated—one procedure for when the property is read, the other for when the property is written. The syntax for the property procedure that is used to retrieve the value of a property is

```
Public Property Get PropertyName() As Variant
    ' property procedure code goes here
End Property
```

where *PropertyName* is the name of the property you wish to expose. In our case, we wish to call the property Enabled, so that's what you'd type where you see the expression *PropertyName*. To expose the property, you must make the procedure Public, which is indicated by the first keyword. The second keyword, Property, is the keyword that indicates that the procedure is indeed a property procedure. Both you and Visual Basic can then recognize a property procedure in your code listings by the presence of this keyword. The third keyword, Get, indicates that this procedure will be called whenever the host application wishes to read the property. As such, the property procedure takes no input parameters but returns an output parameter. The default data type for this return value is Variant since Visual Basic does not know what kind of data is in your property when you first create the property procedures. Typically, you should change the data type from Variant to the data type of the property you're dealing with. We'll talk more about this later, but for now, since Enabled is a boolean property, you would want to change Variant to Boolean.

The second property procedure is used when the host application wants to change the value of the property. The syntax for the second of the property procedure set is

```
Public Property Let PropertyName(ByVal vNewValue As Variant)
    ' property procedure code goes here
End Property
```

The syntax is similar, except the keyword Let is used rather than Get. Let indicates that this is the property procedure used to save a new value. Both procedures must have the same *PropertyName* parameter because both are used to represent the same property. Also notice that the procedure requires an argument and returns no arguments. This makes sense when you consider how you use the procedure. In the host application, imagine an ActiveX control called ucQuestion1. To set the Enabled property of the ucQuestion1 control, you would enter the statement

```
ucQuestion1.Enabled = False
```

Notice that you pass one parameter—the value of the property. No return arguments are expected. This corresponds perfectly to the Let property procedure. As before, you will likely want to change the data type from the default of Variant to the data type that best represents your property.

The Property Get procedure requires no arguments and returns a single argument: the value of the property. This makes sense when you once again consider the code statement that the host application would need to execute to read a property. The statement

```
bEnabled = ucQuestion1.Enabled
```

would read the Enabled property of the question control and assign it to a boolean variable. To accomplish this, the Property Get procedure must return a value, and obviously, no arguments can be passed in. The convention for calling a property procedure is unlike a conventional procedure. In the case of property procedures, you refer to the object and its property using the

```
object.property
```

convention as you've been used to doing with any Visual Basic object whose properties you use. Visual Basic takes care of handling the property and passing it along to the appropriate property procedures you've created in code.

It's time to get back to the task at hand. Your goal here is to expose the Enabled property of the UserControl object to the outside world through the ActiveX control property sheet. To do this, you need to create a set of property procedures as just described. In order to create the property procedures, select the UserControl object within the Visual Basic design environment. Then click on Tools | Add Procedure, which prompts you with the dialog shown in Figure 4.7.

Figure 4.7.

*The Visual Basic 5.0
dialog used to create a
property procedure.*

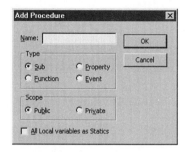

Enter the name of the property in the Name textbox, and then specify Property in the Type radio button group. The scope must always be public when you're creating a property you wish to expose. If you chose Private rather than Public, you could use the property in your ActiveX control project, but it would still be private, so you wouldn't really be accomplishing very much. After you enter these parameters, simply click the OK button and you will find the following two procedures in your `UserControl` object's code window:

```
Public Property Get Enabled() As Variant
End Property

Public Property Let Enabled(ByVal vNewValue As Variant)
End Property
```

At this point, you have two empty property procedures, both properly named `Enabled`. Close the question control project and bring up the test project within the project group in design mode. You should see a new property appear on the property sheet, aptly termed `Enabled`. If you click on the `Enabled` property, however, you'll be able to set `Enabled` to anything you want—not just `True` and `False`. This isn't exactly what you had in mind. What went wrong? Why, you forgot to change the data type in both property procedures from `Variant` to `Boolean`! Close down the test application project and reopen the question control project. Go ahead and change the property procedures so they look like the following:

```
Public Property Get Enabled() As Boolean
End Property

Public Property Let Enabled(ByVal vNewValue As Boolean)
End Property
```

Close the question control project and bring up the test application again. This time, you should get the kind of behavior shown in Figure 4.8.

You've now created the interface procedures that bring the property into existence in the host application. But if you try to use the property, you will find that it has no effect. Why not? Because you haven't linked the hidden property of the `UserControl` object to the exposed property of the ActiveX control. To do this, simply add the following lines of code to both procedures:

```
Public Property Get Enabled() As Boolean
    Enabled = UserControl.Enabled
End Property

Public Property Let Enabled(ByVal vNewValue As Boolean)
    UserControl.Enabled = vNewValue
    PropertyChanged "Enabled"
End Property
```

Figure 4.8.

The question control in the host application's design environment. Now that the data types have been set to Boolean, *the* Enabled *property can only be set to* True *or* False.

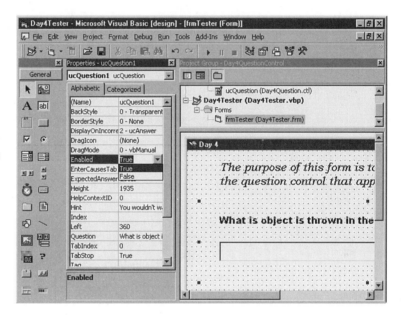

Let's consider what both procedures do. The first procedure, as you recall, is used when the user wants to retrieve the value of the property. This procedure returns the boolean value that the property is equal to. Inside the procedure you find the statement

```
Enabled = UserControl.Enabled
```

This statement uses the name of the procedure, Enabled, as if it were a variable, and sets it equal to the UserControl object's Enabled property. Just as when creating normal Windows applications with Visual Basic, if you treat the name of a function like a variable, that value gets returned as the argument of the function. The same approach works here with property procedures. This one line of code links the private Enabled property of the UserControl object to the public interface of the ActiveX control. Both the exposed and hidden properties are named Enabled. This is why you must enter the expression as

```
Enabled = UserControl.Enabled
```

rather than

```
Enabled = Enabled
```

which would obviously be illegal. Whenever you give the exposed property the same name as the hidden property, you must be careful when making assignments in code. In this case, you must be explicit so that Visual Basic can tell what it has to work with. If you ever hesitate, always be as explicit as possible when working with properties in code.

The second procedure is used when the host application changes the property to some other value. The statement

```
UserControl.Enabled = vNewValue
```

sets the Enabled property of the UserControl object to the new value being passed in. The next statement

```
PropertyChanged "Enabled"
```

notifies Visual Basic that a property has changed. This makes sure the property is saved later. You'll learn about property saving and retrieving tomorrow, so don't worry about this at the moment.

Now let's consider what to do differently if you want to use a different name for the exposed property than for the hidden property. To do that, change the name of the property procedures. For example, if your property procedures look like this:

```
Public Property Get Alive() As Boolean
    Alive = UserControl.Enabled
End Property

Public Property Let Alive(ByVal vNewValue As Boolean)
    Alive = vNewValue
    PropertyChanged "Alive"
End Property
```

then the host application design environment will look like that shown in Figure 4.9.

Now, when the host application wants to enable or disable the question control, this statement:

```
ucQuestion1.Alive = False
```

must be entered rather than this one:

```
ucQuestion1.Enabled = False
```

Figure 4.9.

The question control in the host application's design environment. The property name has been changed to `Alive` *rather than* `Enabled`.

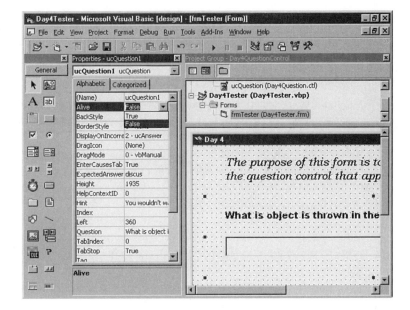

Keep in mind that you cannot simply use just any property name. There are many reserved words that you can't use, such as `On`, for example. Visual Basic will notify you immediately if you are using a reserved word that is illegal to use. Also, you can't use the same name as another property that exists in the interface.

That's all there is to exposing properties. You simply have to create the property procedures and then write the code to do the link. As you might expect, you can get pretty fancy when writing the linking code. You may wish, for example, to do some sort of validation when the user attempts to set a property. Furthermore, you may want to do some additional processing of some sort when presenting the result to the user. Tomorrow you will see much more of this type of interaction when you learn how to create your own user-defined properties, where you have more latitude in the design.

Before we move on to constituent controls, it might be helpful first to mention that you should become familiar with the hidden properties of the `UserControl` object. Some of the more important ones are summarized in Table 4.1. As you progress through the book, you will see more and more uses for these properties and should have a good understanding of how they all fit together by the time you finish.

Constituent Control Properties

Now that you've seen how to manipulate the `UserControl` object properties, it's time to look at the constituent controls within the `UserControl` object. You'll see that working with constituent controls is really quite simple and isn't much different from working with the `UserControl` object properties.

Hidden Properties

As was the case when looking at `UserControl` objects, accessing the properties of a constituent control and keeping them hidden from the user is the default condition and therefore requires no extra work on your part. Let's consider our question control. As you know from Day 2, the question control contains two labels, `lblQuestion` and `lblFeedback`, and a textbox, `txtAnswer`. All three controls reside within the `UserControl` object and are therefore referred to as *constituent controls*. The first label is used to display the question. One of the properties of this first label is the `Alignment` property. `Alignment` can be set to `0` for left justification, `1` for center justification, or `2` for right justification. Go ahead and select the `lblQuestion` label and bring up its property sheet. To set the alignment of the label, click on the `Alignment` property of the property sheet for the label and change it to whatever value you want. Figure 4.10 shows you what the process should look like.

Figure 4.10.

Changing a constituent control property using the property sheet in the design environment.

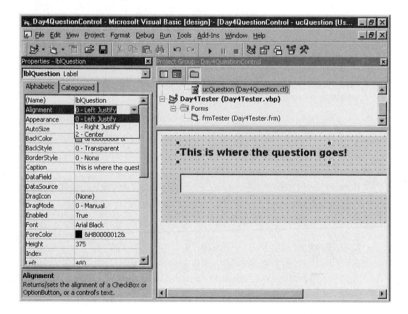

Rather than setting the property here at design time, you can also set it in code. Bring up the Initialize event of the UserControl object and enter the following code:

```
lblQuestion.Alignment = vbCenter
```

```
The Initialize procedure should now look likePrivate Sub_
    UserControl_Initialize()
    lblQuestion.Alignment = vbCenter
End Sub
```

First of all, you must specify the specific control within the UserControl object—in this case, the label control named lblQuestion. Then you simply set the Alignment property of the control to 1 in this case, which centers the text within the label.

Exposed Properties

As will often be the case, you'll want to expose various properties of the constituent controls within your application. The process of exposing such properties is essentially the same as with the UserControl object, with the additional reference to the control within the UserControl object when making the link between the public interface and the hidden property. Let's consider how we might expose the ForeColor and Font properties of the text control, txtAnswer. Both of these properties are special in that they use a data type other than the standard ones (that is, Integer, Long, Single, Double, and Boolean).

Let's begin with the ForeColor property of the text control. When the user chooses a foreground color, it's best to open up the color picker dialog so that the user can select from a predefined set of colors. This requires the use of a special data type called OLE_COLOR. To expose this property, you need to create two property procedures in the UserControl object. Go ahead and type in the following Property procedures:

```
Public Property Get AnswerColor() As OLE_COLOR
    ForeColor = txtAnswer.ForeColor
End Property

Public Property Let AnswerColor(ByVal vNewColor As OLE_COLOR)
    txtAnswer.ForeColor = vNewColor
    PropertyChanged "AnswerColor"
End Property
```

This is one of those cases where it's wise to rename the exposed property. If you left it as ForeColor, the host application programmer might mistake the property for the foreground color of the entire control rather than just the txtAnswer control. To avoid this problem, simply call the property something else, such as AnswerColor.

Go ahead and switch to the test application project. Click on the question control and bring up the property sheet. Go ahead and click the ellipsis next to the AnswerColor property. If you specify OLE_COLOR for the data type, the color dialog box appears when the user clicks on the property, as shown in Figure 4.11.

4

Figure 4.11.

The color selection dialog box that comes up as a result of adding the `AnswerColor` *property to the question control.*

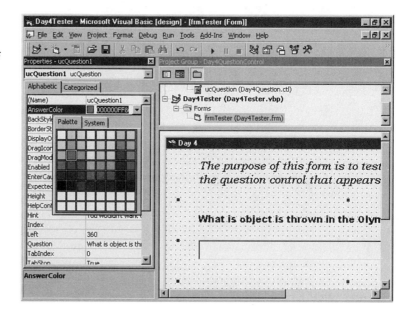

If you use the `OLE_COLOR` data type, the host application will always display this color window whenever the property is changed by the programmer.

Now to the procedures themselves. Let's first consider the `Property Get` procedure. The `Property Get` procedure includes the following code statement:

```
ForeColor = txtAnswer.ForeColor
```

which sets the return value, of type `OLE_COLOR`, to the `Foreground` property of the `txtAnswer` constituent control of the `UserControl` object. The `Property Let` procedure contains the following code statement:

```
txtAnswer.ForeColor = vNewColor
```

Here, the order is reversed in the statement and the new color, passed through the system using the color dialog, is assigned to `ForeColor` of the `txtAnswer` control, which resides in the `UserControl` object.

Now consider a second property you can expose to the host application—the `Font` property of the text control into which the user enters the answer. To expose this property, it is once again wise to rename the property so that the host application programmer has a clear understanding of what the property will do. You'll call this property `AnswerFont`. Go ahead and enter the following property procedures into the `UserControl` object code window:

```
Public Property Get AnswerFont() As Font
    Set AnswerFont = txtAnswer.Font
End Property
```

```
Public Property Set AnswerFont(ByVal vNewFont As Font)
    Set txtAnswer.Font = vNewFont
    PropertyChanged "AnswerFont"
End Property
```

These procedures use yet another type of return object called the Font object. This particular data type is actually an object, which means that you must treat it differently from all the properties you've seen so far. One of the differences is that you must use Property Set rather than Property Let because Property Set must be used when passing objects as properties.

In both cases, you must use the Set command to assign one object to an object variable either being passed to the procedure or returned. In the case of the Property Get procedure, the font object is being returned. The statement

```
Set AnswerFont = txtAnswer.Font
```

places the txtAnswer Font object, accessible through the Font property, into the AnswerFont font object that is passed into the procedure. Using the Set command, the font is returned through the property procedure to the caller. Likewise, when the property is assigned by the host application, the statement

```
Set txtAnswer.Font = vNewFont
```

is used. This statement sets the txtAnswer control's Font property to the object passed, which is named vNewFont. The variable vNewFont is defined as an object using the Font object designator. Once you've entered the property procedures, switch back to the test application project. Figure 4.12 shows what you should see when you click on the AnswerFont property in the property sheet.

Figure 4.12.

The font selection dialog box that comes up as a result of adding the AnswerFont *property to the question control.*

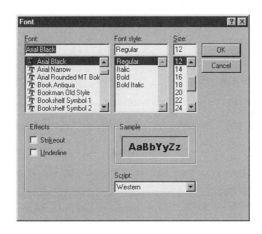

The selected font then appears on the property sheet of the question control, as shown in Figure 4.13.

Figure 4.13.

The AnswerFont
*property, as it appears
in the property sheet of
the question control.*

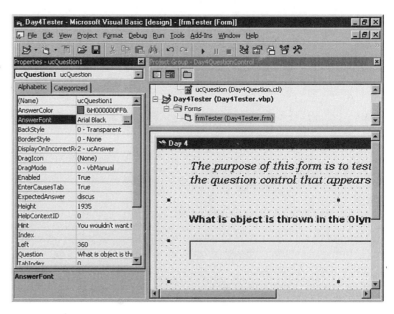

Standard Control Data Types

In addition to these special types of properties, there are standard types, all of which are briefly summarized in Table 4.2.

Table 4.2. A summary of the standard control property types.

Property Type	Description
OLE_COLOR	This property type is for properties that return colors. As you have seen, the properties window uses the color picker dialog, which allows the user to select a color rather than specify a numeric value.
OLE_TRISTATE	This property type is used to represent exposed properties for three-state checkbox controls. The three values used are 0 - Unchecked, 1 - Checked, and 2 - Gray.
OLE_OPTEXCLUSIVE	This property type is a special type used for option buttons. When you have multiple option buttons grouped together, this property makes sure that only one button has its Value property set to True at a time.
Font	You have also seen this object used to bring up a font picker dialog and store the font using the Visual Basic Font object.

These are just some of the variety of property types you can use in Visual Basic. While we can't delve into the specifics of each of these data types, you have been presented with the general concepts of how to expose predefined properties or use hidden properties. Those concepts will always be true, regardless of the type of property you're working with.

Properties and the Extender Object

But wait, there's more! So far today, you've seen how to expose predefined properties to the host application of an ActiveX control. But take a look at the property sheet of the control at this point, which is shown in Figure 4.14.

Figure 4.14.

The property sheet of the question control.

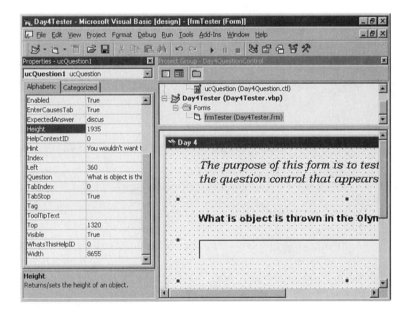

If you look closely, you'll see on the property sheet several properties that you haven't created or exposed through the property procedure method you've seen in this chapter—properties such as Name, Visible, Left, and Top, to name a few. These properties are actually provided by the container into which the host application programmer places the ActiveX control, yet they appear in the ActiveX control property list as a seamless extension of the properties that are a part of your control. For example, if the host has a form that contains an ActiveX control, these properties actually come from the form that the control resides in. A UserControl object can access these runtime properties, however, through what is called the Extender object.

The purpose of the Extender object is to provide you, the developer of the ActiveX control, access to properties the user has access to within the container during the control's runtime.

The Extender object saves you a great deal of work because you have access to all those properties at design time. You have no way of knowing if the properties exist or what settings they have at design time because the control doesn't get placed into a container until runtime. It's important to keep in mind that many of the properties of the Extender object may or may not exist, depending on the container. Table 4.3 shows some of the more important properties of the Extender object.

Table 4.3. A summary of important Extender object properties.

Property	Description
Name	Returns the name the user has assigned to the control in the host environment.
Visible	Indicates whether the user has made the control visible or invisible in the container in which the control has been placed.
Parent	Returns a reference to the container object into which the control was placed. This enables you to have access to other parts of the container inside your control's code.
Cancel	Determines whether the control serves as the cancel button for the container. If the control serves as a cancel button, when the user presses the Esc key, the control's Click event will be triggered.
Default	Determines whether the control serves as the default button for the container. If the control serves as a default button, when the user presses the Enter key, the control's Click event will be triggered.

Now consider a simple example. Suppose you've created an ActiveX toolbar control that you want to appear at the top of the container into which it is placed. In order to do this, you must set the Top and Left properties of the control to 0, regardless of where the user places the control on the form. You could place the following simple statements in a control method, for instance, to snap the control to the top of the container:

```
Extender.Top = 0
Extender.Left = 0
```

It is conceivable that you may create properties and assign names to them that already exist in the Extender object. What will happen if you do? The Extender object will win every time. In other words, the user will see the Extender property and never actually set the property you've exposed in the UserControl object. For instance, if you expose the Visible property of a label within the question control and use Visible as the property name, the Extender object's Visible property will appear instead and be used instead. This important fact underscores the importance of using clear and unique property names whenever possible to avoid such confusion.

Let's consider another simple example of using the Extender object. Suppose we want to center the control within the container as the result of a particular control method. To do this, we need to place the following statements in the method procedure:

```
Extender.Left = (Parent.Width - Extender.Width) / 2
Extender.Top = (Parent.Height - Extender.Height) / 2
```

The net effect will be to set the Extender object's Left property to half the difference between the width of the form, represented through the Parent object's Width property, and the width of the control, represented through the Extender object's Width property. Remember that the UserControl object's Width property is the width of the control in design mode, whereas Extender's Width property gives you the actual width of the control in the host environment. The same logic is used for the Extender object's Top property. The result is a perfectly centered control, as shown in Figure 4.15.

Figure 4.15.

A centered control using the Extender *object.*

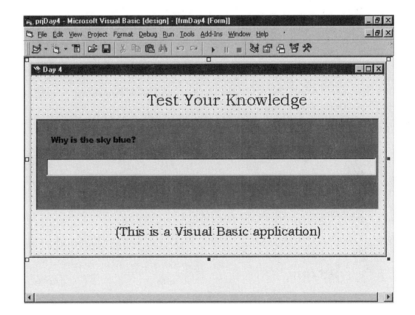

Another important point to remember is that the Extender object is not available in the Initialize event because at that point it is too early to ascertain what is inside the container. Even in the InitProperties event, many of the properties are still not available, so you must exercise caution and be sure to test your application thoroughly. Both of the examples you've just seen do not work if placed in the InitProperties event. They must instead be placed in a control method, which we'll cover on Day 5, "User-Defined Control Properties," or in an event, which will be covered in Day 6, "Predefined Control Methods," and Day 7, "User-Defined Control Methods."

One final point you should be aware of is that some of the Extender properties may not always be available, depending on the container you place them in. Visual Basic calls the properties that always exist *standard properties* and those that do not *container-specific properties*. For instance, if your control exists in a container other than a Visual Basic form, you may or may not have access to the Parent property, for instance. The moral of the story? Be careful to use properties you know will always exist at runtime. The best way to avoid errors is to write your code to gracefully handle trying to access the properties that don't exist. In other words, you must make sure your code can properly handle errors. Error handling is discussed on Day 15, "Preparing Your Control for the Real World," and on Day 16, "Testing Your Control."

Properties and the Ambient Object

Another important object that works with ActiveX controls is the Ambient object. The Ambient object also provides to the UserControl object properties that are a part of the container in which the control exists. The primary difference between the Ambient object and the Extender object is that the Ambient object gives you hints about how you can best display your controls in the host container. Furthermore, the properties of the Ambient object always exist, regardless of the container the control is placed in.

How is the Ambient object used? Suppose the user has placed your ActiveX control into a form. To make sure your control blends in with the form, you may want to set the background color of your ActiveX control to the background color of the form itself. How would you go about obtaining the form's background color? Through the Ambient object, of course.

In the InitProperties event of your UserControl object, you can simply place the code

```
BackColor = Ambient.BackColor
```

which will set the background color of the ActiveX control to the background color of the form onto which it was placed. Other important properties of the Ambient object are summarized in Table 4.4.

Table 4.4. A summary of important Ambient object properties.

Property	Description
UserMode	Determines whether the control is being used at design time or at runtime. UserMode is True when the control is being used at runtime and False when in design mode. This is one of the most important properties of the Ambient object because it allows the program to do different things based on where the control is being run. The differences between runtime and design time will be discussed in more detail on Day 10, "Coding for the Design Environment."

4

Property	Description
LocaleID	Used to determine the locale where the control is being used. Useful for international and translation purposes.
DisplayName	Used to get the display name of the control while being run for the purposes of correctly identifying the control when errors arise.
ForeColor, BackColor, Font, TextAlign	These properties can be used to set the ActiveX control to match the host form where necessary. All four properties are designed to synchronize the ActiveX control with its container to make them appear fully integrated.
DisplayAsDefault	Indicates whether the control is the default button for the container. If so, an extra heavy border is typically drawn around the control.

Connected with the Ambient object properties themselves is the AmbientChanged event. This event can be used in code to determine when an Ambient object property has changed, allowing the ActiveX control to respond accordingly. By the way, events are fully discussed on Day 8, "Predefined Events," and Day 9, "User-Defined Events," so don't worry about this at the moment. When you learn about events, you'll see how the properties can be used accordingly.

Now let's consider an example using the Ambient object. One of the Ambient event properties is the Font property. Suppose you want to synchronize all the fonts in the labels and text control within the UserControl object to match that of the container into which the control is placed. To do that, you can simply add the following statements to the InitProperties event:

```
' Using the Ambient object to synchronize all the fonts
lblQuestion.Font = Ambient.Font
txtAnswer.Font = Ambient.Font
lblFeedback.Font = Ambient.Font
```

This segment of code will make sure the fonts of the relevant constituent controls within UserControl synchronize with the container's font—in this case the form into which the ActiveX control was placed.

Summary

Today you have learned a great deal about UserControl object properties. The chapter begins by discussing the properties that you, the designer of the control, have access to. These properties are hidden unless you want to expose them to the host container into which they are placed. Doing so is a simple matter of adding property procedures for the properties you wish to expose. When doing so, however, you must make sure the property name you assign is clearly identifiable to the user and does not collide and clash with other properties on the property page of the ActiveX control. You can also use the properties of constituent controls, and you can choose to expose them. Here it is even more important to make each property name clear and distinct. You would not want, for example, to use the property name Caption if you were going to expose two label controls. The user would not be sure which caption you would be changing. Likewise, you would not want to call your property Name because it would conflict with the Extender object and would never be reachable by the end user.

The Ambient and Extender objects are a very important part of using ActiveX controls. Their use is explored later on in the book, when you learn about integration issues of bringing a control into the environment in which it will be used. For now, these important concepts will serve as the diving board that will allow you to jump more deeply into the concepts you need to explore to create ActiveX controls.

Properties are an essential part of ActiveX control design and usage. Today you've taken a look at predefined properties. In tomorrow's lesson, you will learn how to create brand-new properties of your own. You'll also learn more about how to save and load properties to your control both in the host application's design environment and its runtime environment. So hang on! There are plenty of exciting topics ahead.

Q&A

Q Can I expose any predefined property I want to?

A Even though a property can be exposed, it is often a read-only property. In other words, if you try to change it in a Property Set procedure, you'll get an error from Visual Basic saying you can't set the property.

Q Why does Visual Basic distinguish between the Ambient object and the Extender object?

A The two objects are separate because they behave a bit differently from one another. The property set of the Extender object changes based on the type of container your control is placed in. The Ambient object, on the other hand, maintains all its properties regardless of the container. Even though they're used the same way, the properties you have access to depend on what object you're talking about.

Q Why do I have to worry about setting all these properties manually when the wizard can do it for me?

A True, the wizard can do a lot of things for you, but if you don't have a fundamental understanding of how properties are created and used in the design environment, you're likely to get stuck when trying to do something the wizard can't help you with. Remember, it's a wizard, not a genie. If you don't understand what's really going on, you won't be as confident when designing your control, and you may be limited if you're dependent on it.

Q **It seems that a lot can go wrong behind the scenes when I'm trying to read and set properties. What happens if an error occurs?**

A It's very important to be able to handle errors if they occur. That's why the lesson on error handling will be so important. For now, concentrate on how the properties should work in an ideal world. Once you understand that, you'll be ready to recover from errors if and when properties don't work in reality. On Day 15 you'll learn all about error handling and recovery.

Workshop

Determining what properties to expose can be challenging and requires some advance planning. Go through the list of predefined properties in a UserControl object as well as the constituent controls of the question control. Considering these objects, along with the Extender and Ambient objects, make a list of those properties you cannot expose and those you can. Of the properties you can expose, which ones would you be most likely to expose? Think about possible applications for each property.

Quiz

NOTE

See Appendix D, "Answers to Quiz Questions," for the answers to these questions.

1. Suppose that you want to expose the Visible property of the lblQuestion control. Can you use the property name Visible for the control? Why or why not?

2. Write out the property procedures for the ForeColor property of UserControl.

3. Write the property procedures to expose the caption of the label lblFeedback. Make sure there are no property name conflicts.

Day 5

User-Defined Control Properties

In yesterday's lesson you learned about predefined control properties and how to use them in code and expose them to the public. All the properties you learned about were predefined; that is, they already existed. All you needed to do was either use them directly or expose them to the public. In some cases, you could use the same name as the property you were exposing. In other cases, you had to rename the property to avoid a naming conflict with another property or to make the meaning of the property more clear to the user. Today you will learn how to actually create brand new, unique properties of your own. You'll also learn how to save and restore property settings within the containers in which you place your controls. So turn on your computer, grab a cup of coffee, get comfortable, and prepare to round out your knowledge of ActiveX properties.

What Are User-Defined Properties?

First of all, you need to understand the difference between predefined and user-defined properties. User-defined properties are those properties that already exist in the UserControl object or one of its constituent controls. That means that when a predefined property is changed, the control responds by modifying the characteristics of the control in some way. You don't have access to the code that changes the characteristics, nor do you need to. For example, if you expose a property that sets the background color of a label, you don't care about the code inside Visual Basic that actually changes the color. When you set the property, the color changes, and that's all you care about.

When you bring a user-defined property into existence, however, the rules change. Now you are creating a brand new property that is not predefined. The code for a property like this doesn't exist. For instance, suppose you wish to create a property that determines whether you want to give the user a certain amount of time to answer a question. For a property like this, there is no constituent control you can pass the work off to—you have to implement the code yourself. This is a simple example of perhaps thousands of possibilities, but it illustrates that a user-defined property must often be handled differently than when you can simply call a predefined property of the UserControl object or use an exposed property of a constituent control.

Of course, there are times when you can create a user-defined property that can call various properties of existing objects or constituent controls. In that case, you're simply using a user-defined property to call predefined properties of existing controls. That's a simpler case, but that's not always possible. Sometimes you have to do all the work in code yourself. You'll learn about both cases.

When you create properties, you can write code to do many things. In some cases, you may set properties of constituent controls or the UserControl object itself. That might cause various activities to take place, as was just discussed. In other cases, it might be a simple matter of changing a module-level variable. Then, when an event occurs later on or a method is called, some activity will take place based on how that variable was set when the property was changed.

In today's lesson, the first thing you'll learn is how to create properties that set the properties of several controls at a time. Then you'll learn about properties that set module-level variables used later on to change the characteristics of the control. Then we'll take a look at how to restrict the user to a specific set of possible values for a property. This is similar to when we looked at the font and color picker dialogs that were used in the AnswerFont and AnswerColor properties of the question control in yesterday's lesson. Today, however, you'll learn how to create your own customized set of possible choices for a property.

Properties That Set Constituent Control Properties

Creating user-defined controls is virtually identical to exposing predefined properties of the UserControl object. One way, of course, is to use the Control Wizard. The alternative, manual, approach is to simply select Tools|Add Procedure when you're in the design environment of Visual Basic, type in the name of your user-defined property, and select Property from the type selections available. The only difference is that in this case, the name of the property you choose is totally user defined and doesn't have to be tied down to a specific predefined property of an existing control.

Consider the following example based on the question control of yesterday's lesson. We wish to provide the end user with the ability to choose a question to display to the user. The easiest way to do this is to create a property, let's call it Question, that sets the caption of the question label to whatever the user types in the label.

The first step is to create the property procedures with the property name Question. This results in the creation of the following pair of property procedures:

```
Public Property Get Question() As Variant
End Property

Public Property Let Question(ByVal vNewValue  As Variant)
End Property
```

The first step is to change the input and output data types of the property to String because the caption will always be a string. Then we need to consider what we want the property to do when set. Since we want to change and retrieve the caption of the question label, the simplest way to code this is as follows:

```
Public Property Get Question() As String
    Question = lblQuestion.Caption
End Property

Public Property Let Question(ByVal New_Question As String)
    lblQuestion.Caption() = New_Question
    PropertyChanged "Question"
End Property
```

Here, you can see that the caption of the control lblQuestion is used to set the Question property. Notice the addition of this statement:

```
PropertyChanged "Question"
```

This statement notifies the container of your custom control, the host application, that a property's value has changed. Then the container can synchronize its properties window with the new values of your control's properties. We'll talk much more about the PropertyChanged statement later on in today's lesson.

5

The net result is that when the user enters text into the Caption property at design time in the host application environment, the label caption will indeed change to the new property value. Figure 5.1 shows the question control with the Question property set to the string indicated on the control.

Figure 5.1.

Setting the user-defined Question *property of the question control.*

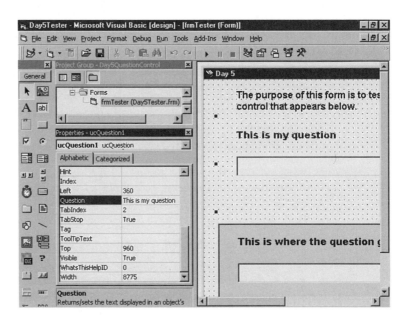

When you put the finishing touches on your controls, you might want to consider adding some validation code to the property procedures where properties are set. This prevents the user from doing anything weird that might cause an error in your control code. Consider, for example, the user who decides to enter 1,000 characters into the string for the Question property. Obviously, a string that long would never display properly on the screen—there's not enough room! To make sure this doesn't happen, you could write validation code such as the following:

```
Public Property Let Question(ByVal New_Question As String)
    If Len(New_Question) >= 30 Then
        MsgBox "The Question must be no more than 30 characters in length!", _
               vbExclamation, "Error"
    Else
        lblQuestion.Caption() = New_Question
        PropertyChanged "Question"
    End If
End Property
```

This would ensure that the length of the Question property string is correct and that the question will look correct as presented within the control.

Properties That Set Module-Level Variables

The property you've just seen sets a constituent control property and has some extra code in it to make sure an appropriate value is entered. You've also seen properties that set module variables that are acted on in control events or methods. It's also possible to have control properties that simply set a variable that is used later on. For example, consider the question control again. We've already provided the user with a Question property. We also need to give the program the capability to recognize whether the user's answer is correct. We can do this with a new property. The goal is for the control to simply compare the user's answer with the correct answer. Let's call the property that allows the program to store the correct answer ExpectedAnswer. The property procedures required to set up this property are as follows:

```
Public Property Get ExpectedAnswer() As String
    ExpectedAnswer = m_ExpectedAnswer
End Property

Public Property Let ExpectedAnswer(ByVal New_ExpectedAnswer As String)
    m_ExpectedAnswer = New_ExpectedAnswer
    PropertyChanged "ExpectedAnswer"
End Property
```

Once again, the data type of the property is set to the string, as you'd expect. You'll also notice that the PropertyChanged function is called once more. Notice, however, that in this case, the module-level variable m_ExpectedAnswer is set. No constituent controls or anything else, for that matter, takes place. The variable that is set is declared in the declarations section as

```
Dim m_ExpectedAnswer As String
```

So what effect does changing this property have? None, at least until the user types his answer to the question within the control at runtime. When that happens, the ProcessAnswer subroutine, shown in Listing 5.1, is called. The ProcessAnswer subroutine is called when the user presses the Enter key when typing in an answer. This subroutine checks whether the answer the user has typed in is equal to the value stored in m_ExpectedAnswer.

Listing 5.1. The ProcessAnswer subroutine.

```
1: Private Sub ProcessAnswer()
2:
3:     ' Only check the answer if it has not yet been evaluated.
4:     '    This control processes the answer in response to either the
5:     '    Enter key being pressed or when focus moves from the current field.
6:     '    Since the Enter key also removes focus, we have to make sure that the
7:     '    answer is not checked twice in a row.
8:     If m_bAnswerHasChanged Then
9:         If UCase(txtAnswer.Text) = UCase(m_ExpectedAnswer) Then
10:            lblFeedback.Caption = "Correct!"
```

continues

Listing 5.1. continued

```
11:          ElseIf m_DisplayOnIncorrectResponse = ucAnswer Then
12:              lblFeedback.Caption = "Expected Answer: " & m_ExpectedAnswer
13:          ElseIf m_DisplayOnIncorrectResponse = ucHint Then
14:              lblFeedback.Caption = "Hint: " & m_Hint
15:              ' Highlight the answer areas so user can retry after seeing hint
16:              txtAnswer.SelStart = 0
17:              txtAnswer.SelLength = Len(txtAnswer.Text)
18:          End If
19:
20:          ' Set the flag so we won't check again until answer has been altered
21:          m_bAnswerHasChanged = False
22:
23:          ' Now send tabkey so focus goes to next question if that
24:          ' property option is set
25:          If EnterCausesTab Then
26:              Call SendTab
27:          End If
28:
29:      End If
30:
31: End Sub
```

On Day 3, "The Programming Environment," you learned about how this procedure works to process the answer the user has entered. The point in showing it today is to confirm that the variable m_ExpectedAnswer is needed in the procedure and is set through the property that changes it.

Creating Properties with Customized Settings

Most of the properties you've worked with so far have been created using standard Visual Basic data types. You also saw a special data type called OLE_COLOR used for assigning a color value to a property. Now suppose you want to provide the user a property that lets him choose from a list of possible settings that you define. For example, you might want to create a speed property and provide three settings—fast, medium, and slow—for the user to choose from. How would you do this?

To learn how, let's look at another property in the question control. When the user enters an incorrect answer, what do we want the control to do? Why not let the programmer decide by setting a property? That's what the property named IncorrectResponseDisplay will do. The property gives the programmer three choices—to do nothing, to display a hint, or to display the correct answer. A bad thing to do would be to give the user some confusing, cryptic integer to set. An even worse thing to do would be to leave it up to the user to type in some string such as Hint or Nothing, relying on him to get the spelling right. The best solution is to allow him to set only one of the three conditions, displaying each in plain English so he can easily understand what he's doing. To make this happen, you need to create an *enumerated type* for the property. An enumerated type is simply a list of the values you want to provide the user as they should appear on the property sheet. Enumerated types must always be placed in the declarations section of the UserControl module. Consider the following enumerated type:

```
Public Enum RESPONSE_DISPLAY
    ucNone
    ucHint
    ucAnswer
End Enum
```

A property that uses this enumerated type allows the user to select one of three choices— ucNone, ucHint, or ucAnswer. Only one of these three values can then be selected. Notice the structure of the user-defined type. The first keyword is Public. The enumerated type must be public so that the property values can be shared. Otherwise, Visual Basic will show an error when you try to compile the control or use it in a project group. The next keyword, Enum, tells Visual Basic that it's dealing with an enumerated type. The third keyword is the name of the user-defined type that gets used in the property procedures.

Note that the designer has listed three types. Because this is an *enumerated* type, the first value is always assigned the integer value 0, the second 1, the third 2, and so on. These numbers also appear in the property sheet, as shown in Figure 5.2.

Figure 5.2.

The property sheet of an ActiveX control whose property settings were created using an enumerated type.

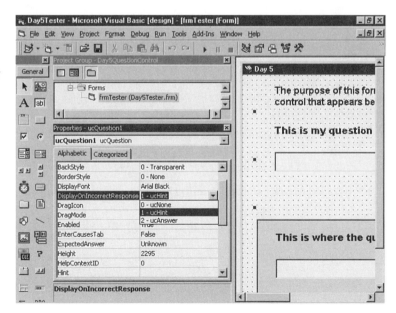

Take a look at the property sheet and zero in on the IncorrectResponseDisplay property. Click on the property and you'll notice the possible values you can set this property to. As you can see, the numbers are to the left and the text strings used in the enumerated type are displayed. Visual Basic places a hyphen between the numbers and the text strings and automatically sets up the property values in the property sheet for you. All you have to do is create the enumerated type itself.

Why the choice of ucNone, ucHint, and ucAnswer rather than None, Hint, and Answer? The prefix uc, which stands for UserControl, is recommended so that the programmer who uses your control can easily distinguish the property settings of your control from the settings of others. If the property settings you've chosen are common settings, such as Enabled, for instance, the user might get confused about what he's really setting. When the programmer sees the following statement, he knows the property setting is specific to the control he's using:

```
ucQuestion1.IncorrectResponseDisplay = ucHint
```

After you've created the enumerated type, all you have to do is link it up with the property procedures themselves. The property procedures are defined as follows:

```
Public Property Get IncorrectResponseDisplay() As RESPONSE_DISPLAY
    IncorrectResponseDisplay = m_IncorrectResponseDisplay
End Property

Public Property Let IncorrectResponseDisplay(ByVal
            New_IncorrectResponseDisplay As RESPONSE_DISPLAY)
    m_IncorrectResponseDisplay = New_IncorrectResponseDisplay
    PropertyChanged "IncorrectResponseDisplay"
End Property
```

As you can see, the data type used is the enumerated type RESPONSE_DISPLAY as defined in the declarations section of the UserControl module. The value m_IncorrectResponseDisplay is used to hold the value for when it is needed later. That variable is declared as

```
Dim m_IncorrectResponseDisplay As RESPONSE_DISPLAY
```

which is necessary in order to make the data types correspond. If you take a look back at Listing 5.1, you'll notice that this variable is used when the ProcessAnswer subroutine is called, just like the ExpectedAnswer property uses a different variable in the same subroutine.

As for the number of possible settings you want to use, you can, for all practical purposes, use as many as you want (well, up to 65,535 of them!). Even though they are stored internally inside the enumerated type as integers, both your code and the host application that uses the control can use the setting strings that you've defined in setting the appropriate property.

So, as you've seen, there isn't much difference between constructing a user-defined property and a predefined property. Although the two types of properties are different, they are created and work essentially the same way. Predefined properties are typically much simpler because you simply link the exposed property to the internal property of the UserControl object or the constituent control. User-defined properties are often more complex, however, because they may bring in several constituent controls, contain validation code, or perform more complex tasks with more advanced Visual Basic code.

User-defined properties are almost always public in nature (that is, they're exposed to the host application code). They don't necessarily have to be, however. You can create hidden user-defined properties simply by specifying Private when declaring the property procedures. You might want to do this when you wish to create a property that sets a series of other properties. That way, you can avoid doing all the work yourself each time you want to make a change. By keeping the property private, you can use it but not expose it to the public.

Saving Control Properties

During the course of these two lessons on properties, you've learned how to create or use just about every possible property in an ActiveX control. There's one major missing piece, however, that you have yet to consider. You can create and use properties, but you need a way to save them to the container into which the control is placed. If, for example, the host application sets the Question property of the question control to some string, the user would expect to see the same string the next time he loads the project into Visual Basic and brings up the form with your control on it. Furthermore, he would expect to see that question displayed on the form if an executable file were to be created.

Whether a programmer is using your control to write an application, or a user is using the control at runtime, instances of an ActiveX control are constantly brought into and out of memory. The ActiveX control defines property interfaces but doesn't actually store the initial property settings for the control in the host application. In fact, the control itself never stores anything. The control simply tells the container to store the property settings, which it does by placing those settings in the file used to represent the host application container.

Where Are Property Settings Saved?

The first question you may have is "Where do the property settings get saved, anyway?" After all, the control is usually placed inside a container such as a form. Where does it put all its property settings? You've probably figured out by now that the property settings actually are stored in the container that the control is placed into. Specifically, the property settings are written into the file that is used to represent the container. In the case of a form, for instance, the settings are simply stored in the same file used to store the form definition, that is, the .frm file. Table 5.1 shows a summary of the extensions used for various container files.

Table 5.1. File extensions used for various containers.

Container	Container File(s)
Visual Basic form	.frm, .frx
Visual Basic UserDocument objects	.dob, .dox
Visual Basic UserControl objects	.ctl, .ctx
Visual Basic property pages	.pag, .pgx
Web page (HTML document)	Within <OBJECT> tag of .html file

The extensions that end with an x are often called *binary files.* They are binary because they contain binary data—values of properties that can be represented using simple data types such as strings and integers. For instance, the picture of a form or an icon may be stored in a binary file. The term *binary file* is used because these files cannot easily be read by the user in a text file.

Now let's take a look at the form we've been using to test our question control in this chapter. The code is shown in Listing 5.2.

Listing 5.2. The raw code of the Day 5 test form for the question control.

```
 1: VERSION 5.00
 2: Begin VB.Form frmTester
 3:    BackColor       =   &H00FFFFFF&
 4:    Caption         =   "Day 5"
 5:    ClientHeight    =   6345
 6:    ClientLeft      =   165
 7:    ClientTop       =   465
 8:    ClientWidth     =   9480
 9:    Icon            =   "Day5Tester.frx":0000
10:    LinkTopic       =   "Form1"
11:    ScaleHeight     =   6345
12:    ScaleWidth      =   9480
13:    StartUpPosition =   3   'Windows Default
14:    Begin VB.Label Label1
15:       BackColor    =   &H00FFFFFF&
16:       BackStyle    =   0   'Transparent
17:       Caption      =   "The purpose of this form is to test the_
18:                         integration of the question control that_
19:                         appears below."
20:       BeginProperty Font
21:          Name      =   "Bookman Old Style"
22:          Size      =   14.25
23:          Charset   =   0
24:          Weight    =   300
25:          Underline =   0     'False
```

```
26:            Italic          =   -1   'True
27:            Strikethrough   =    0   'False
28:        EndProperty
29:        Height          =   855
30:        Left            =   840
31:        TabIndex        =   0
32:        Top             =   240
33:        Width           =   7455
34:    End
35:    Begin Day5QuestionControl.ucQuestion ucQuestion1
36:        Height          =   1935
37:        Left            =   360
38:        TabIndex        =   0
39:        Top             =   1320
40:        Width           =   8655
41:        _ExtentX        =   15266
42:        _ExtentY        =   3413
43:        Question        =   "What object is thrown in the
44:                    ➥Olympic discus throw?"
45:        DisplayOnIncorrectResponse=   2
46:        ExpectedAnswer  =   "discus"
47:        Hint            =   "You wouldn't want to get hit in
48:                    ➥the head with it!"
49:        EnterCausesTab  =   -1   'True
50:        AnswerColor     =   255
51:        BeginProperty AnswerFont {0BE35203-8F91-11CE-9DE3-00AA004BB851}
52:            Name        =   "Arial Black"
53:            Size        =   12
54:            Charset     =   0
55:            Weight      =   400
56:            Underline   =   0   'False
57:            Italic      =   0   'False
58:            Strikethrough =  0   'False
59:        EndProperty
60:    End
61:    Begin Day5QuestionControl.ucQuestion ucQuestion2
62:        Height          =   2175
63:        Left            =   360
64:        TabIndex        =   2
65:        Top             =   3600
66:        Width           =   8775
67:        _ExtentX        =   15478
68:        _ExtentY        =   3836
69:        BackStyle       =   1
70:        BorderStyle     =   1
71:        Question        =   "What surface should you run on with snowshoes?"
72:        ExpectedAnswer  =   "Snow"
73:        Hint            =   "It is cold and white."
74:        BeginProperty AnswerFont {0BE35203-8F91-11CE-9DE3-00AA004BB851}
75:            Name        =   "Arial Black"
76:            Size        =   12
77:            Charset     =   0
78:            Weight      =   400
79:            Underline   =   0   'False
80:            Italic      =   0   'False
```

continues

Listing 5.2. continued

```
81:             Strikethrough   =   0   'False
82:          EndProperty
83:     End
84: End
85: Attribute VB_Name = "frmTester"
86: Attribute VB_GlobalNameSpace = False
87: Attribute VB_Creatable = False
88: Attribute VB_PredeclaredId = True
89: Attribute VB_Exposed = False
90: Option Explicit
91:
92:
93: Private Sub Form_Load()
94:
95: ' Center the form
96: Me.Move (Screen.Width - Me.Width) / 2, _
97:         (Screen.Height - Me.Height) / 2
98:
99: End Sub
```

ANALYSIS If you look closely at the source code, you'll notice the section that specifies the first ActiveX control (starting at line 35):

```
Begin Day5QuestionControl.ucQuestion ucQuestion1
       Height          =   1935
       Left            =   360
       TabIndex        =   0
       Top             =   1320
       Width           =   8655
       _ExtentX        =   15266
       _ExtentY        =   3413
       Question        =   "What object is thrown in the
                  ➡Olympic discus throw?"
       DisplayOnIncorrectResponse=   2
       ExpectedAnswer  =   "discus"
       Hint            =   "You wouldn't want to get hit in
                  ➡the head with it!"
       EnterCausesTab  =   -1  'True
       AnswerColor     =   255
       BeginProperty AnswerFont {0BE35203-8F91-11CE-9DE3-00AA004BB851}
          Name         =   "Arial Black"
          Size         =   12
          Charset      =   0
          Weight       =   400
          Underline    =   0   'False
          Italic       =   0   'False
          Strikethrough =  0   'False
       EndProperty
    End
```

As you can see, the Question property does indeed appear in the list. There are, of course, many other properties inherent to the question control in addition to those shown. Why don't they appear? Because only those property settings that differ from their defaults are saved. You'll see the reasoning behind this in a bit.

NOTE

> You need to understand the difference between a property and a property setting. *Properties* are the interfaces that the host application using the ActiveX control can use to change the characteristics of the control. *Property settings* are the specific values that are assigned to those properties. The property settings, not the actual properties themselves, are what get stored inside a container.

How Are Property Settings Saved?

Now that you know where the property settings themselves get saved, the question is how to save them there. There is one very important time that you must save the property settings of the control to the container it resides in—whenever the container is removed from memory. When the container is removed, the control goes along with it. Before it is removed from memory, the property settings must be saved so that when it enters memory later on, the settings will be retained.

Suppose, for instance, that the programmer is writing a host application that contains your control. He changes a bunch of property settings of your control. Then the user decides to close the form that houses the control and switch to another form. When the form your control resides in is closed, the control on that form is destroyed. At this point you need to save your properties to the form. Since the form file is in memory, the changes are temporarily written there. Then, if the user later decides to exit Visual Basic, bring up a new project, or save the existing project, the form will be pulled out of memory and written to permanent storage on disk. That way, when the form is reloaded and displayed onscreen, the property settings can be read back out of the container file and set properly on the property sheet.

Now to the specifics. Property settings are actually saved through what is called, oddly enough, a *property bag*. The `PropertyBag` object is a simple object designed to retrieve property settings from or save property settings to a container. To store a property setting in the property bag, you use the `WriteProperty` method of the `PropertyBag` object. The `WriteProperty` method uses the following syntax:

`Object.WriteProperty propertyname, propertyvalue, defaultvalue`

where `Object` is a `PropertyBag` object, `propertyname` is the name of the property, usually placed in quotes, `propertyvalue` is the value you wish to store in the property, and `defaultvalue` is the default value you want to store in the property.

NOTE   The `PropertyBag` object can only be used within your ActiveX design code. Anybody who uses your control in his own programs is not able to access `PropertyBag`.

You might be wondering why a default value should be supplied here when we're already passing in a value for the property. The answer to this question is efficiency. If Visual Basic sees that the property you wish to set in the control is the same as the default value, it simply won't write the value. That's why the form code you saw earlier contained so few properties. All the ones not present, such as `IncorrectResponseDisplay`, were not displayed because the default values are the current property values. Only when the property changes to something different is the property stored.

This is done in order to keep the container files as small as possible. If the form always had to store the value of every single property of a control, it could become quite large. If you don't specify a default, the property will always be written. In the case of a sophisticated control such as an option button or a picture control, saving every single property could make the container file rather large indeed. This approach, therefore, keeps Visual Basic forms lean and efficient.

To store, for example, the `Question` property of the question control, you could enter this statement:

```
Call PropBag.WriteProperty("Question", lblQuestion.Caption, m_def_Question)
```

where `m_def_Question` is a constant that stores the default question string just in case the caption of the label has not been set.

So how do you get access to `PropertyBag`, and where do you actually save the properties? The `UserControl` object has a special event called `WriteProperties`. `WriteProperties` is called every time Visual Basic is ready to save the properties of a control. This could happen when the control is destroyed, or perhaps when the container is saved. Consider the `WriteProperties` event in our question control, shown in Listing 5.3.

Listing 5.3. The `WriteProperties` event of the question control.

```
 1: Private Sub UserControl_WriteProperties(PropBag As PropertyBag)
 2:
 3:     Call PropBag.WriteProperty("BackStyle", _
 4:                             UserControl.BackStyle, _
 5:                             0)
 6:
 7:     Call PropBag.WriteProperty("BorderStyle", _
 8:                             UserControl.BorderStyle,
 9:                             0)
10:
```

```
11:     Call PropBag.WriteProperty("Question", _
12:                                 lblQuestion.Caption, _
13:                                 m_def_Question)
14:
15:     Call PropBag.WriteProperty("DisplayOnIncorrectResponse", _
16:                                 m_DisplayOnIncorrectResponse, _
17:                                 m_def_DisplayOnIncorrectResponse)
18:
19:     Call PropBag.WriteProperty("ExpectedAnswer", _
20:                                 m_ExpectedAnswer, _
21:                                 m_def_ExpectedAnswer)
22:
23:     Call PropBag.WriteProperty("Hint", _
24:                                 m_Hint, _
25:                                 m_def_Hint)
26:
27:     Call PropBag.WriteProperty("EnterCausesTab", _
28:                                 m_EnterCausesTab, _
29:                                 m_def_EnterCausesTab)
30:
31:     Call PropBag.WriteProperty("AnswerColor", _
32:                                 txtAnswer.ForeColor, _
33:                                 vbWindowText)
34:
35:     Call PropBag.WriteProperty("AnswerFont", _
36:                                 txtAnswer.Font, _
37:                                 UserControl.Font)
38:
39:     Call PropBag.WriteProperty("Enabled", _
40:                                 Enabled, _
41:                                 True)
42:
43: End Sub
```

ANALYSIS As you can see, the PropertyBag object is passed in from the container to the UserControl object. Here is where all the WriteProperty statements are executed, one for each exposed property, whether user defined or predefined. Notice that each property has a default value, stored either in a module-level variable or supplied as a literal in the WriteProperty statement. This sequence of statements writes the values into the container file, which is eventually stored to disk.

So what makes the WriteProperties event occur? The most obvious is when the user goes to save the form. This forces the WriteProperties event to occur for every UserControl object contained within the container. But there's another important statement connected with the WriteProperties event, and you've actually seen it already. It's the PropertyChanged statement.

You'll notice that in every Property Let procedure, where property settings are stored, the PropertyChanged statement is called and passed the name of the property. This informs Visual Basic that the specific property passed in as the argument to this statement has changed, requiring the execution of the WriteProperties event when the control is destroyed. Keep in mind that WriteProperties is always called when a form is manually saved by the user, so this especially applies to controls that are destroyed by forms that are closed without being saved yet. In other words, the values are temporarily stored in memory until the time when they are saved.

Retrieving Property Settings with the Property Bag

So much for how property values are stored. Now let's see how they are retrieved. A UserObject control also contains a ReadProperties event. This event can be used to get the properties back out of the PropertyBag object associated with the container using the ReadProperties method of the PropertyBag object. In this way, you can read the properties and store them back into the UserControl properties. The syntax of the PropertyBag object's ReadProperties method is

```
Object.ReadProperty propertyname, defaultvalue
```

where *Object* once again is the PropertyBag object passed to the event, *propertyname* is a string naming the property, and *defaultvalue* is the value to be stored in the property if the property wasn't originally placed in the PropertyBag object. In other words, the ReadProperty method returns the saved property value, if there is one, and the default value if there is not. If you assign the return value of this method to the property of the UserControl object, the Property Let procedure will execute, giving you the opportunity of validating and otherwise properly assigning the property to the hidden or constituent control properties it is associated with.

Consider, for example, the ReadProperties event taken from the question control. This event is shown in Listing 5.4.

Listing 5.4. The ReadProperties event of the Day 5 question control.

```
 1: Private Sub UserControl_ReadProperties(PropBag As PropertyBag)
 2:
 3:     UserControl.Enabled = PropBag.ReadProperty("Enabled", True)
 4:
 5:     UserControl.BackStyle = PropBag.ReadProperty("BackStyle", 0)
 6:
 7:     UserControl.BorderStyle = PropBag.ReadProperty("BorderStyle", 0)
 8:
 9:     Question = PropBag.ReadProperty("Question", _m_def_Question)
10:
11:     txtAnswer.ForeColor = PropBag.ReadProperty("AnswerColor", _
12:                             vbWindowText)
```

```
13:
14:      m_DisplayOnIncorrectResponse = PropBag.ReadProperty(
15:                             "DisplayOnIncorrectResponse", _
16:                             m_def_DisplayOnIncorrectResponse)
17:
18:      m_ExpectedAnswer = PropBag.ReadProperty("ExpectedAnswer", _
19:                             m_def_ExpectedAnswer)
20:
21:      m_Hint = PropBag.ReadProperty("Hint", m_def_Hint)
22:
23:      m_EnterCausesTab = PropBag.ReadProperty("EnterCausesTab", _
24:                             m_def_EnterCausesTab)
25:
26: End Sub
```

ANALYSIS Focus on the following code statement:

```
Question = PropBag.ReadProperty("Question", _m_def_Question)
```

Here, the `PropertyBag` object is queried for the `Question` property as denoted within quotes. If the property wasn't previously saved, the value in the module-level variable `m_def_Question` is returned instead. Regardless of the value returned, it is assigned to the `Question` property. This, in turn, fires off the following procedure:

```
Public Property Let Question(ByVal New_Question As String)
    lblQuestion.Caption() = New_Question
    PropertyChanged "Question"
End Property
```

which sets the label `lblQuestion` caption to the new property value that was retrieved from the `PropertyBag` object and alerts Visual Basic that a property value was changed. Keep in mind that you could also skip the routing path through the exposed property by simply using the following statement rather than working through the property procedure:

```
lblQuestion.Caption = PropBag.ReadProperty("Question", m_def_Question)
```

In general, however, it's a good idea to route your property settings through the property procedures in order to ensure proper validation and correct synchronization of the container with the aggregate control.

NOTE The `ReadProperties` event is always called *after* the `Initialize` event. This means that you cannot access properties during the `Initialize` event. `ReadProperties` is called *after* `Initialize`, and only when loading in the instance of an object whose properties have already been saved.

5

Assigning Default Properties

As you learned on Day 2, "Creating a Simple Control," when a control is first brought into existence on a container, the InitProperties event is called. It is typically called only once because from that point forward, whenever the form is reloaded or displayed, the control will already exist and only the ReadProperties event will be called. The nice thing about this is that you can set the default values for the properties in the InitProperties event. The InitProperties event for today's question control is shown in Listing 5.5.

Listing 5.5. The InitProperties event of the Day 5 question control.

```
1: Private Sub UserControl_InitProperties()
2:     lblQuestion.Caption = m_def_Question
3:     m_DisplayOnIncorrectResponse = m_def_DisplayOnIncorrectResponse
4:     m_ExpectedAnswer = m_def_ExpectedAnswer
5:     m_Hint = m_def_Hint
6:     m_EnterCausesTab = m_def_EnterCausesTab
7:
8: End Sub
```

As you can see from the code in this event procedure, all the variables used to store the associated property settings are given default values. Notice, however, that the properties are not assigned directly. Why not assign the properties directly, as in Listing 5.6?

Listing 5.6. An incorrect implementation of the InitProperties event.

```
1: Private Sub UserControl_InitProperties()
2:     Question = m_def_Question
3:     DisplayOnIncorrectResponse = m_def_DisplayOnIncorrectResponse
4:     ExpectedAnswer = m_def_ExpectedAnswer
5:     Hint = m_def_Hint
6:     EnterCausesTab = m_def_EnterCausesTab
7:
8: End Sub
```

It's better not to set the properties directly because doing so will cause the Property Set or Property Let procedures to execute. These procedures will, in turn, execute the PropertyChanged statements for each property assigned, provided that the statement exists inside each property procedure called for that property. In such a case, Visual Basic will be told that the program has changed the properties, when in fact it hasn't. All that has happened is that the default properties have been assigned to a brand new instance of the control placed into a container.

You might argue that this isn't a big deal anyway, and you get the added benefit of correct property validation. Yes, but if you, the designer, are responsible for assigning the default properties yourself, you can quite easily make sure that the default properties are valid. They will never change, so if they are invalid, you'd have to change them. Validation code wouldn't be needed for default property settings anyhow. So to avoid making the program think it has to save properties when it may in fact not have to, it's best to avoid calling the property procedures yourself.

Having said that, default property settings are very important because each property must have an initial value when a control is first placed inside a container. When you place code in the InitProperties procedure, make sure to set all the properties you've created or exposed to some default value. If not, your control could start off in a state you'll never expect to occur, which could cause major problems if the program begins to interact with a control where false assumptions are made.

Suppose, for example, that you fail to set a particular property that stores an integer value. Later, you query the property to see what the value is. Your code might not take into account that the property hasn't been assigned yet, and might then take an unexpected turn and behave in a way you hadn't intended. So you must make sure every property is assigned a value right up front in order for your control to be happy.

Mapping Properties to Multiple Controls

Before closing out today's lesson, let's take a look at some other important issues to consider when creating properties. The first of these issues is the case where you want a user-defined property procedure to change the same property of a set of constituent controls within the UserControl object. Let's suppose, for example, that you want to create a property that changes the font of every aggregate label and text control within UserControl. You decide to give this property the name DisplayFont. When the user changes the DisplayFont property, you want the Font property of every aggregate control within the UserControl object to change. One way you to do this is shown in Listing 5.7.

Listing 5.7. Mapping a user-defined property to multiple constituent controls.

```
1: Public Property Get DisplayFont() As Font
2:     Set Font = UserControl.Font
3: End Property
4:
5: Public Property Set DisplayFont(ByVal NewFont As Font)
6:
```

continues

Listing 5.7. continued

```
 7:     Dim objCtl As Object
 8:
 9:     UserControl.Font = NewFont
10:
11:     For Each objCtl In Controls
12:         objCtl.Font = NewFont
13:     Next
14:
15:     PropertyChanged "DisplayFont"
16:
17: End Property
```

ANALYSIS Let's take a look at these two procedures in detail. The Property Get procedure is simple enough. It returns the UserControl object's Font property. The easiest way to implement a universal font in the control is to set the UserControl object's Font property and use that property to store the property value for all the controls. Since all the controls will have the same font, if we make the font of each constituent control the same as the UserControl object's, then all we have to do is return the Font property of UserControl here.

Now on to the Property Set procedure. Notice, first of all, that we must use a Property Set, not a Property Let, because we're dealing with an object, not a Visual Basic data type. Next, notice that the first thing we must do is create a generic variable of type Object. This generic object variable is then used in a For-Next loop to scan down the control through each object it encounters, setting the font of that object to the desired font passed into the procedure by the user. Notice that the loop cycles through each objCtl in controls, meaning basically that it temporarily assigns every constituent control it finds inside the UserControl object to objCtl inside the loop. Then the Font property of the objCtl variable holding each constituent control in turn is set to the NewFont variable, which is passed in by the user.

The net result is that each control inside the UserControl object gets its font changed to the new font passed in via the NewFont variable. This technique can be used to effect a global change with every constituent control in the UserControl object. Suppose, however, that you only wanted to change the label controls and not the textbox controls. One simple modification of the code could be implemented, as shown in Listing 5.8.

Listing 5.8. Mapping a user-defined property to multiple constituent controls based on the control type.

```
1: Public Property Set DisplayFont(ByVal NewFont As Font)
2:
3:     Dim objCtl As Object
4:
5:     UserControl.Font = NewFont
```

```
 6:
 7:     For Each objCtl In Controls
 8:         If (TypeOf objCtl Is Label) Then
 9:             objCtl.Font = NewFont
10:         End If
11:     Next
12:
13:     PropertyChanged "DisplayFont"
14:
15: End Property
```

ANALYSIS By using the TypeOf function, we can apply the change selectively to the type of controls we want. For more information on the TypeOf statement and the various controls you can compare it with, refer to the Visual Basic online help documentation. It's quite complete, and it will give you as many details about this approach as you want.

Creating Read-Only Properties

At some point during your control creation endeavors, you'll likely want to create one or more properties that can only be read, whether at runtime or at design time. To illustrate how and why you would want to do this, let's consider our question control for the day.

When the host application that uses your question control is executed, the user might get the answer wrong many times before he gets it right. It might be useful to store the incorrect answers as they're being entered into a property for easy retrieval by the program. The program may, for instance, show the user all the incorrect responses at some point for whatever purpose the host application programmer intends. How would this be done?

First of all, you'd probably want to store the list of incorrect responses in an array. The array must be set up as a private array, however, because Visual Basic allows only one element of the array to be exposed to the user at a time. Therefore, the property would have to return one string out of the array of incorrect answer strings. This array of strings would have to increase as the user continues to enter incorrect responses. A second important aspect of this property is that the program should never be able to set the property directly because it should only be changeable as a result of the user's incorrect responses. Therefore, the property should be a read-only property. At no time, whether in design mode or at runtime, should the programmer or any program, for that matter, be able to modify the property setting.

In order to make this happen, you actually need three properties. These properties are identical to those that are implemented in a standard listbox, except that the property names are different. The first property is used to display one of the incorrect answers in the array of all the incorrect answers. Let's call this property IncorrectAnswer. It should be a read-only property. You also need a property that can tell you the total number of incorrect answers the user has entered thus far. Let's call that property IncorrectAnswerCount. That property, too, should be read-only. Finally, you need to have a way of setting the index of the incorrect response you want to retrieve. That property, called IncorrectAnswerIndex, should be a read/write property since the user must set the index and then retrieve the property value. None of these properties would need to be saved, since they all would apply only at runtime.

First, let's take a look at the private variables you'd have to declare in the declarations section of the UserControl code module. The declarations are

```
' Keep track of the incorrect reponses
Private m_IncorrectAnswerCount As Integer
Private m_IncorrectAnswers() As String
Private m_IncorrectAnswerIndex As Integer
```

These declarations store the module-level variables used to interface with the properties themselves. Now let's take a look at the first property, the IncorrectAnswerCount property. The property procedure for that property is shown in Listing 5.9.

Listing 5.9. The property procedure for the IncorrectAnswerCount property.

```
1: Public Property Get IncorrectAnswerCount() As Integer
2:     IncorrectAnswerCount = m_IncorrectAnswerCount
3: End Property
```

As you can see, there is no Property Let procedure here. The user can only query this property, not set it directly. To make a property read-only, all you have to do is get rid of the Property Let procedure. The property won't even appear in the property sheet of the host application when it's being designed within Visual Basic.

Let's move on to the IncorrectAnswerIndex property procedures, which are shown in Listing 5.10.

Listing 5.10. Property procedures for the IncorrectAnswerIndex property.

```
1: Public Property Get IncorrectAnswerIndex() As Integer
2:     If Ambient.UserMode = True Then
3:         IncorrectAnswerIndex = m_IncorrectAnswerIndex
4:     End If
5: End Property
6:
7: Public Property Let IncorrectAnswerIndex(ByVal iNewIndex As Integer)
8:     If iNewIndex >= 0 Then
9:         m_IncorrectAnswerIndex = iNewIndex
10:     Else
11:         MsgBox "Index must be greater or equal to zero!", vbExclamation, _
12:             "IncorrectAnswerIndex Error"
13:     End If
14: End Property
```

The Property Get procedure is designed so that the property setting can be changed only at runtime. If the programmer tries to change the property setting in the host application's design environment, the property sheet will change the setting back to zero as soon as the Enter key is pressed. Only when the program that uses your control actually runs can the property setting be changed, and then only in code. The return value is simply the value of the private variable.

The Property Let procedure puts up a message box if the caller passes in an invalid setting, namely one less than zero. Otherwise, the private variable is set.

Now on to the third and final property, the IncorrectAnswer property. The property procedure for this property is shown in Listing 5.11.

Listing 5.11. The property procedure for the IncorrectAnswer property.

```
1: Public Property Get IncorrectAnswer() As String
2:      IncorrectAnswer = m_IncorrectAnswers(m_IncorrectAnswerIndex)
3: End Property
```

This property procedure simply returns the element of the incorrect answers array that the IncorrectAnswerIndex property is set to. Therefore, in order for the caller to see a particular incorrect answer within the array, the caller must specify the index of that string. The caller can get the total number of items using the IncorrectAnswerCount property, and then must simply use that property in retrieving all the values. As you can see, this property too is a read-only property.

So how do the incorrect answers get stored in the internal array? In the ProcessAnswer subroutine, which takes place when the user presses the Enter key. The revised version of the ProcessAnswer procedure is shown in Listing 5.12.

Listing 5.12. The revised ProcessAnswer procedure.

```
1: ' See if answer is correct
2: Private Sub ProcessAnswer()
3:
4:      ' Only check the answer if it has not yet been evaluated.
5:      '   This control processes the answer in response to either the
6:      '   Enter key being pressed or when focus moves from the current field.
7:      '   Since the Enter key also removes focus, we have to make sure that
8:      '   the answer is not checked twice in a row.
9:      If m_bAnswerHasChanged Then
10:         If UCase(txtAnswer.Text) = UCase(m_ExpectedAnswer) Then
11:             lblFeedback.Caption = "Correct!"
12:         Else
```

continues

Listing 5.12. continued

```
13:                 ' Store the incorrect reponse in the array
14:                 m_IncorrectAnswerCount = m_IncorrectAnswerCount + 1
15:                 ReDim Preserve m_IncorrectAnswers(m_IncorrectAnswerCount)
16:                 m_IncorrectAnswers(m_IncorrectAnswerCount) = txtAnswer.Text
17:
18:                 If m_DisplayOnIncorrectResponse = ucAnswer Then
19:                     lblFeedback.Caption = "Expected Answer: " & m_ExpectedAnswer
20:                 ElseIf m_DisplayOnIncorrectResponse = ucHint Then
21:                     lblFeedback.Caption = "Hint: " & m_Hint
22:                     ' Highlight answer areas so user can retry after seeing hint
23:                     txtAnswer.SelStart = 0
24:                     txtAnswer.SelLength = Len(txtAnswer.Text)
25:                 End If
26:             End If
27:
28:             ' Set the flag so we won't check again until answer has been altered
29:             m_bAnswerHasChanged = False
30:
31:             ' Now send tabkey so focus goes to next question if that property
32:             ' option is set
33:             If EnterCausesTab Then
34:                 Call SendTab
35:             End If
36:
37:         End If
38:
39: End Sub
```

The three statements starting at line 14 are called whenever an incorrect answer is entered in the textbox:

```
m_IncorrectCount = m_IncorrectCount + 1
ReDim Preserve m_IncorrectAnswers(m_IncorrectCount)
m_IncorrectAnswers(m_IncorrectCount) = txtAnswer.Text
```

The count is updated, the array is redimensioned with the Preserve keyword (which keeps the array intact while expanding its dimension), and the newly added item of the array is set with the latest value.

How might this complement of properties be used? Consider Listing 5.13, which is designed to print each incorrect response to the debug window. This code resides in a command button in a host application that uses the question control.

Listing 5.13. Obtaining the incorrect responses.

```
1: Dim IncorrectAnswers As String
2:     Dim i As Integer
3:     Dim iTotal As Integer
```

```
  4:
  5:    iTotal = ucQuestion1.IncorrectAnswerCount
  6:
  7:    For i = 0 To iTotal
  8:        ucQuestion1.IncorrectAnswerIndex = i
  9:        Debug.Print ucQuestion1.IncorrectAnswer
 10:    Next
```

The first thing this code excerpt does is obtain the total number of incorrect answers. Then it sets up a loop to cycle through each one. Inside the loop, the index is updated so that the program points to the appropriate answer. Then that answer is output to the debug window. Here, all three properties—IncorrectAnswerCount, IncorrectAnswerIndex, and IncorrectAnswer—are all used to obtain the values. This example illustrates not only how to set up properties that allow you to index an array, but it also shows you how to create properties that can only be read at runtime and can only be changed at runtime. None of the properties are saved because they are not intended to be saved at design time.

Summary

This completes today's lesson! During the course of this and yesterday's lesson, you've learned a great deal about predefined and user-defined properties. Today's lesson has given you the background necessary to create and use user-defined properties. You have learned how to create a user-defined property by creating property procedures. You have also learned a bit about naming procedures and how to name a user-defined property without colliding with other properties that have the same name. You have learned how user-defined property procedures can set one or more constituent control properties, or they can set module-level variables that make a control behave differently when a method or an event takes place down the road.

You have also learned how to create customized settings for properties. This enables you to force the user to choose property settings that you create, rather than simply using the built-in data types of Visual Basic. Using enumerated types, you saw that it's really pretty easy to come up with property settings of your own.

Finally, you have learned the ins and outs of saving and retrieving property settings when a control is created or destroyed. This typically occurs when a control is placed on a form and the form is then saved or closed in the design environment when a programmer uses your control. It also occurs at runtime when the control is created when the user's program runs, and then destroyed when the program is closed or temporarily minimized.

It's very important that you understand these two lessons on properties since properties are a fundamental part of creating an ActiveX control. Take a moment to look back over these past two lessons, and make sure you have a good comprehension of what a property is and how to create one and make one work for you. Tomorrow we will begin another two-part lesson on control methods, followed by another two-part series on control events. By the end of these series of lessons, you should be well on your way to mastering the fundamentals of control creation. Good for you!

Q&A

Q **If I don't create or expose any properties for my control, what will appear on the user's property sheet when he uses my control?**

A The only properties the user will see are the `Extender` properties provided by the container—properties such as `Left`, `Top`, and `Visible` if the control is placed on a Visual Basic form. If those properties are adequate, you don't need to worry about creating any new ones. This is, however, pretty rare, since almost every control has its own custom set of properties the programmer can work with.

Q **Where are property settings saved?**

A They are saved in the container into which the control is placed during design time. So if, for example, the programmer places your control inside a form, all the property settings of your control will be saved inside the file used to hold the form.

Q **What happens if I forget to put a `WriteProperties` statement inside a `Property Let` procedure?**

A Suppose a programmer is creating an application and puts your control on one of his forms. Then the programmer saves his work and closes Visual Basic. If you had neglected to place a `WriteProperties` statement in your `Property Let` procedures, it's likely that when the programmer closes down the project, all the properties he set while in design mode will be lost. You want to avoid this at all costs because the user will consider your control unreliable if it does. What's worse is that he'll be right!

Q **How many times does the `InitProperties` event take place, and when does it occur?**

A `InitProperties` only occurs one time—when a programmer who is running Visual Basic in design mode clicks on the toolbox, selects the control, and drags it onto the container. Here the control is being created for the first time within that container, and `InitProperties` must be called. It makes sense, therefore, that you have to set the default properties in this event and nowhere else. After this event is called, the user can change property settings as he wishes, and you certainly don't want to erase the user's changes with the original defaults.

Q Why can't I just use the ActiveX Control Interface Wizard for all this stuff?

A The Interface Wizard is really useful, especially when you have a lot of properties you want to add at once. You can save a lot of time and extra work by using it. You still need to understand the underlying code that the wizard produces, however, in order to understand how your control works. If you treat the wizard like a genie, you may not be very happy if you've got to do all the hard work to help him grant your wish!

Workshop

Suppose you'd like to write a control that provides the user with a calendar that he can place on a form. The calendar control consists of a grid with buttons to switch between the months and years. The user can also click on the individual dates within a particular month. Make a list of all the properties you would want to provide to the user. Determine which properties would be predefined and which would be user defined. Do you have more predefined properties or more user-defined properties? Make sure you don't include properties in your list that already come through the `Extender` object.

Quiz

 NOTE

See Appendix D, "Answers to Quiz Questions," for the answers to these questions.

5

1. Write the code necessary to save and retrieve the `DisplayFont` property from the container into which the control is placed. Make sure you not only show the code, but also the procedures in which the code resides.

2. Now write the code required to set the default font of the `DisplayFont` to the font of the container the control is being placed into. Once again, make sure to indicate the procedure where the code is written.

3. Why was the property given the name `DisplayFont` rather than `Font`?

Day **6**

Predefined Control Methods

In these next two lessons, you'll be learning about the next fundamental concept of ActiveX control design: methods. Today's lesson teaches you just what a method is and why you might want to use one in a program. Then you'll learn about methods that have already been defined and are ready to use in your control. The lesson teaches you not only how to use methods that are not exposed to the host using the control, but also how to expose those methods so that the host application has access to them as well. In tomorrow's lesson, you'll learn how to create your own user-defined methods.

What Is a Method?

Let's start at the beginning: Just what is a method, anyway? Simply put, a method is a procedure that belongs to an object such as a control. This procedure accomplishes a specific task that typically relates to the control to which the method belongs. Methods can either be hidden or exposed. If a method is hidden—only available within an ActiveX control—the host application cannot call it directly. If, however, that method is exposed, the host—along with any code within the control—*can* call the method. In today's lesson, you'll learn how to handle hidden methods as well as to expose methods to the host.

To better understand methods, think back to the car analogy you read about on Day 4, "Predefined Control Properties." Remember that methods typically accomplish certain tasks within the control to which they belong. For instance, you could give the name Drive to a sample method for a car. You could name another method Stop. To invoke the Stop method in a car, you simply have to step on the brake. This is equivalent to calling a method of a control in code. When you hit the brakes in your car, you don't necessarily care how the car stops as long as it stops. Likewise, when you're calling control methods, you don't necessarily need to care how the methods happen. You simply call them and expect results.

In today's lesson, you'll consider the methods available in three different objects that come together in making an ActiveX control work. The first, the UserControl object, is the one in which the control is built. Then, if constituent controls exist in the UserControl object, those controls also have methods available that you might choose to expose. Finally, the Extender object provides methods from the container on which the control is placed. These methods act on the control itself. First, let's discuss the UserControl object and constituent control methods themselves.

UserControl **Object Methods**

There are many methods available for your use in the UserControl object. Table 6.1 summarizes them.

Table 6.1. A brief summary of UserControl **object methods.**

Method	Description
AsyncRead	Begins to have the UserControl object read in data from a file or a URL in an asynchronous manner.
CancelAsyncRead	Cancels the asynchronous reading operation.
CanPropertyChange	Asks the container whether a property bound to a data source can have its value changed. The CanPropertyChange method is most useful if the property specified in PropertyName is bound to a data source.
Circle	Draws a circle on a UserControl object.
Line	Draws a line within a UserControl object.

Method	Description
Point	Returns the color of a particular point within a UserControl object.
PSet	Sets a specific point within a UserControl object.
Cls	Clears the container of any graphics drawn using the Circle, Line, and PSet methods.
Print	Allows text to be printed on the UserControl object.
OLEDrag	Causes the UserControl to initiate an OLE drag/drop operation.
PaintPicture	Draws the contents of a graphics file (.bmp, .wmf, .emf, .ico, or .dib) within a UserControl object.
PopupMenu	Displays a pop-up menu on a UserControl object at the current mouse location or at specified coordinates.
Scale	Defines the coordinate system for a UserControl object.
ScaleX, ScaleY	Converts the X and Y coordinates from one scale unit to another.
TextHeight	Returns the height of the text specified as it appears on the UserControl object.
TextWidth	Returns the width of the text specified as it appears on the UserControl object.
Refresh	Forces a complete repaint of the UserControl.

As you can see, there are a number of methods for you to use. Many of these objects you will probably never use, but some you might wish to use from time to time. This chapter doesn't go into detail on all these methods, but you'll see an example of some of the more commonly used methods of the UserControl object in today's lesson.

All these UserControl methods are hidden to the host application unless you expose them. That is, you can use them in the code you write to put together your control, but you can't call the methods outside your control code. To do that, you need to expose the methods, which you'll learn how to do later. Before talking about exposing the methods, however, you'll first learn how to use them in the design environment of your control.

Hidden Methods

The best way to learn how and why you might want to use UserControl methods is to look at a simple example. Suppose you want to display the question number every time the user sees a new question. How would you do this? Suppose you create a property called QuestionCount. This property, when set, would then call the appropriate UserControl object methods to display the question number on the form. Listing 6.1 shows the property procedures for the QuestionCount property.

Listing 6.1. Using UserControl methods.

```
 1: Public Property Get QuestionCount() As Integer
 2:     QuestionCount = m_QuestionCount
 3: End Property
 4:
 5: Public Property Let QuestionCount(ByVal vNewCount As Integer)
 6:     If vNewCount > 0 And vNewCount < 10 Then
 7:         m_QuestionCount = vNewCount
 8:         ShowQuestionCount
 9:         PropertyChanged "QuestionCount"
10:     Else
11:         MsgBox "You can only enter up to 10 questions.", vbExclamation, _
12:                 "Invalid Property Value"
13:     End If
14: End Property
```

Notice first that you had to create a new module variable called m_QuestionCount. This variable keeps track of the question count. Notice also that in the Property Let procedure, the QuestionCount property can take on an integer value between 1 and 10. This restriction allows you to avoid a lot of additional code that might divert you from your primary purpose in today's lesson. When the new property value is stored in the module-level variable, the subroutine ShowQuestionCount is called. Listing 6.2 shows the procedure.

Listing 6.2. The ShowQuestionCount subroutine.

```
 1: Private Sub ShowQuestionCount()
 2:     UserControl.Cls
 3:     UserControl.CurrentX = 520
 4:     UserControl.CurrentY = 260
 5:     UserControl.FontSize = 12
 6:     UserControl.Print Str(m_QuestionCount)
 7:     UserControl.DrawWidth = 2
 8:     UserControl.Circle (660, 420), 250, RGB(0, 0, 0)
 9: End Sub
```

This is the primary piece of code that draws the question number, along with a bordering circle, on the UserControl object itself. This results in a control that looks like the one in Figure 6.1.

Figure 6.1.

The new question control using UserControl *methods.*

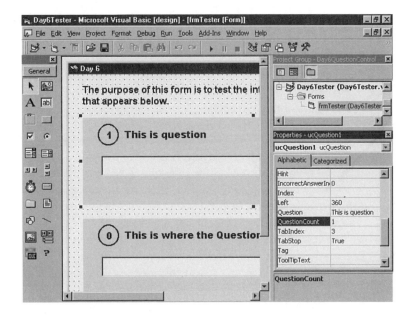

The question label had to be moved over a bit to accommodate the circle and question number. The reason the number of questions is restricted to 10 is that you'd need more room, which means you'd have to add a lot of code to take this into account. The purpose here isn't to get into a lot of details on graphics. Simply focus on what the methods are doing for you. The following three methods are used in the example: Cls, which clears UserControl of graphics produced using graphics methods; Print, which prints the text onto UserControl; and Circle, which draws the circle on the UserControl object. These three methods function together to produce the intended result.

Make sure the UserControl object's AutoRedraw property is set to True so that the graphics are redrawn as needed. Also check that the coordinates are fixed in place. A better implementation would allow the control to shift the coordinates when the control is resized, as well as allow a count greater than 10, making the circle as large as necessary.

Exposed Methods

The methods you've been using are not accessible to the host application. All the host can do is set the QuestionCount property and watch the number and circle appear. But suppose you want to give the host the capability to draw graphics on the UserControl object itself. By exposing all the UserControl object methods you've used to this point, the host application can do the drawing itself, rather than having it done in the predetermined fashion supplied in code.

6

To expose the UserControl object methods, you create public procedures for each of the methods you want to expose. Some methods are very simple, requiring no arguments. Take the Refresh method, for example. If you look up the Refresh method in the Visual Basic online help, you'll find that no arguments are required. Exposing the Refresh method, then, is a simple matter of writing the following procedure:

```
Public Sub Refresh()
    UserControl.Refresh
End Sub
```

This procedure, as you can see, is very simple. It requires no arguments, and the only line of code you need is the code to link the exposed Refresh method to the UserControl object's Refresh method. Suppose, however, that you wanted to expose the UserControl object's Circle method. If you were to look up the Circle method in the help file, you would find a number of arguments. Some are even optional! How in the world are you going to expose a complex method such as this? You don't have to. When you wish to expose methods of the UserControl object or any constituent controls within the UserControl object, the best way to do so is to use the ActiveX Control Interface Wizard that comes as an add-in to Visual Basic. You had the chance to use the wizard back on Day 2, "Creating a Simple Control," but you'll get the chance to use it again—this time specifically for methods.

NOTE

The ActiveX Control Interface Wizard is an add-in that comes with Visual Basic 5.0. If, when you click on Add-Ins on the Visual Basic menu, the ActiveX Control Interface Wizard does not appear as a selection, choose Add-In Manager, which will bring up the dialog shown in Figure 6.2.

Check the appropriate selection, and you'll be able to use the Control Interface Wizard in your Visual Basic applications. You must use the Visual Basic Add-In Manager in order to use this wizard.

Figure 6.2.

Using the Add-In Manager to make sure the ActiveX Control Interface Wizard is included.

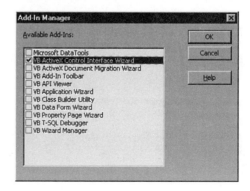

The first step is to click Add-Ins | ActiveX Control Interface Wizard. As you saw on Day 2, this might bring up an introductory screen, as shown in Figure 6.3.

Figure 6.3.

The introductory screen of the ActiveX Control Interface Wizard.

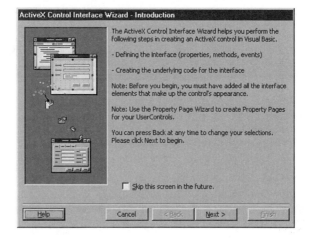

If this screen appears, click Next to proceed. Either way, you should then advance to the screen shown in Figure 6.4.

Figure 6.4.

The method selection screen of the ActiveX Control Interface Wizard.

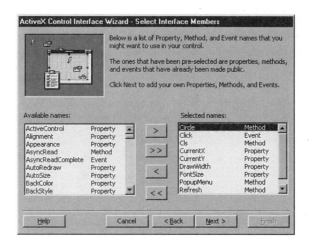

This first screen is where you select all the methods you want to expose to the host application. In this case, you wish to expose the Circle and Cls methods. Incidentally, you also need to expose the CurrentX, CurrentY, DrawWidth, and FontSize properties. The dialog can accomplish all this. Note that the properties and methods you need appear to the right-hand side.

What about the Print method? You'll notice that it doesn't appear in the list. The wizard doesn't want to automatically handle the Print method for you. That's why you're dealing with the wizard, not a genie! You'll deal with the Print method later. Okay. So far, so good. Click on Next to advance. The dialog shown in Figure 6.5 now appears.

Figure 6.5.

The user-defined method screen for the ActiveX Control Interface Wizard.

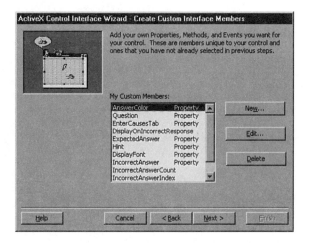

This dialog is used for user-defined methods. You'll also notice the user-defined properties you added on Day 5, "User-Defined Control Properties," and on earlier days already appear. We'll discuss user-defined methods in tomorrow's lesson, so let's move on. Click Next to advance. Now the dialog in Figure 6.6 appears.

Figure 6.6.

Mapping the methods to the appropriate controls using the ActiveX Control Interface Wizard.

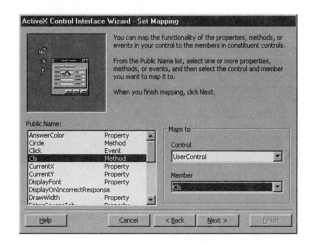

This dialog is important because here you must map the methods you wish to expose to the appropriate control. Mapping is the process by which you connect the exposed method to the control you want to expose. For instance, if you were exposing the Refresh method, you could map Refresh to the text control, the UserControl object, or any other constituent control that supported Refresh. You need to tell Visual Basic that you want to expose the UserControl object's Refresh method, not any of the other controls. That's what this dialog is for.

All you need to do is select each of the new methods you want to expose, select UserControl in the Maps to listbox, and then select the method you want to expose in the Member listbox. You can do the same for the properties, mapping them all to the UserControl object and selecting the property you wish to expose in the Member listbox. When you've properly mapped all the methods, click on the Next button to advance. The dialog shown in Figure 6.7 appears.

Figure 6.7.

Handling unmapped methods using the ActiveX Control Interface Wizard.

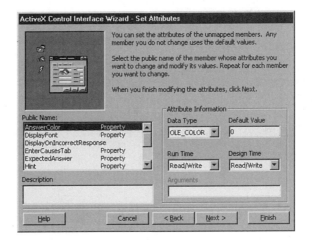

The dialog shown in Figure 6.7 is for unmapped methods. You don't need to worry about this dialog at the moment because you've already mapped every method and property you wish to expose. Let's wrap this up by clicking on the Finish button. You'll see a couple more dialogs confirming your choices. You can close these. The net result is that Visual Basic will build all your methods and property procedures for you. They should all appear as shown in Listing 6.3.

Listing 6.3. Property procedures needed to expose various `UserControl` properties.

```
 1: 'WARNING! DO NOT REMOVE OR MODIFY THE FOLLOWING COMMENTED LINES!
 2: 'MappingInfo=UserControl,UserControl,-1,Cls
 3: Public Sub Cls()
 4:     UserControl.Cls
 5: End Sub
 6:
 7: 'The Underscore following "Circle" is necessary because it
 8: 'is a Reserved Word in VBA.
 9: 'WARNING! DO NOT REMOVE OR MODIFY THE FOLLOWING COMMENTED LINES!
10: 'MappingInfo=UserControl,UserControl,-1,Circle
11: Public Sub Circle_(X As Single, Y As Single, Radius As Single, _
12: Color As Long, StartPos As Single, EndPos As Single, Aspect As Single)
13:     UserControl.Circle (X, Y), Radius, Color, StartPos, EndPos, Aspect
14: End Sub
15:
16: 'WARNING! DO NOT REMOVE OR MODIFY THE FOLLOWING COMMENTED LINES!
17: 'MappingInfo=UserControl,UserControl,-1,CurrentX
18: Public Property Get CurrentX() As Single
19:     CurrentX = UserControl.CurrentX
20: End Property
21:
22: Public Property Let CurrentX(ByVal New_CurrentX As Single)
23:     UserControl.CurrentX() = New_CurrentX
24:     PropertyChanged "CurrentX"
25: End Property
26:
27: 'WARNING! DO NOT REMOVE OR MODIFY THE FOLLOWING COMMENTED LINES!
28: 'MappingInfo=UserControl,UserControl,-1,CurrentY
29: Public Property Get CurrentY() As Single
30:     CurrentY = UserControl.CurrentY
31: End Property
32:
33: Public Property Let CurrentY(ByVal New_CurrentY As Single)
34:     UserControl.CurrentY() = New_CurrentY
35:     PropertyChanged "CurrentY"
36: End Property
37:
38: 'WARNING! DO NOT REMOVE OR MODIFY THE FOLLOWING COMMENTED LINES!
39: 'MappingInfo=UserControl,UserControl,-1,FontSize
40: Public Property Get FontSize() As Single
41:     FontSize = UserControl.FontSize
42: End Property
43:
44: Public Property Let FontSize(ByVal New_FontSize As Single)
45:     UserControl.FontSize() = New_FontSize
46:     PropertyChanged "FontSize"
47: End Property
48:
49: 'WARNING! DO NOT REMOVE OR MODIFY THE FOLLOWING COMMENTED LINES!
50: 'MappingInfo=UserControl,UserControl,-1,DrawWidth
51: Public Property Get DrawWidth() As Integer
52:     DrawWidth = UserControl.DrawWidth
```

```
53: End Property
54:
55: Public Property Let DrawWidth(ByVal New_DrawWidth As Integer)
56:     UserControl.DrawWidth() = New_DrawWidth
57:     PropertyChanged "DrawWidth"
58: End Property
```

The Cls and Circle methods form the first two procedures in the listing. The remaining procedures are property procedures that expose CurrentX, CurrentY, FontSize, and DrawWidth. The ActiveX Control Interface Wizard exposed both of these procedures. You should always use the wizard to make sure all the arguments required for the UserControl object methods are properly exposed using all the correct data types. The wizard even maps the methods to the correct object for you—in this case, the UserControl object. Doing this yourself would not only invite errors, but it would also be a lot of work. The wizard does all the work for you, and you can be sure it's correct.

The only code you must add manually is the Print method. The code for the Print method appears in Listing 6.4.

Listing 6.4. The Print method must be added manually because the wizard does not support it.

```
1: ' This method was added manually and only handles strings
2: Public Sub Print_(svText As String)
3:     UserControl.Print svText
4: End Sub
```

Notice a couple things about the Print method. First, to avoid using a reserved word, the wizard placed an underscore after the name Print in the procedure. This lets you use the method name Print while at the same time letting Visual Basic know you're not trying to take over its built-in syntax. If you look up the Print method in the help file, you'll notice that it requires an open-ended number of parameters depending on how it's used. Unfortunately, there's no easy way for Visual Basic to provide a single list of arguments for the method when such a wide variety of possible arguments could be used. This may be one of the reasons the ActiveX Control Interface Wizard does not give you the ability to expose this Print method using the wizard. You can add a wide variety of output parameters to this method that cannot be supported with the same level of flexibility. In this example, the method was exposed manually by creating a public function procedure that requires one variant as an input parameter. This is certainly more restrictive than the default method. But placing a restriction on the method is the only way possible if the wizard doesn't support the property directly. The Print method is one such example.

6

When you restrict the parameters for an exposed method, you are deviating from the conventional way that method is called. You should, as a rule, avoid this practice. If a user sees a Print method in your control, he should expect your Print method to behave just like any other Print method used in a Visual Basic program. If yours is different, a user might perceive it as a bug; or he might simply get confused when he tries to use it by looking at the help file. The best way to avoid this problem is to give the exposed method a different name so there is no confusion. You could, in the example you've just looked at, change the exposed method name from Print to PrintString, for example, which would clue users in to the fact that the method can only be used to print strings, and therefore will accept only string arguments.

The ActiveX Control Interface Wizard also takes care of the ReadProperties and WriteProperties events, as well as the InitProperties event. The net result of all this work that Visual Basic performed is that all the properties should be exposed in the property sheet in the host environment, as shown in Figure 6.8.

Figure 6.8.

All the properties that have just been added now appear in the property sheet.

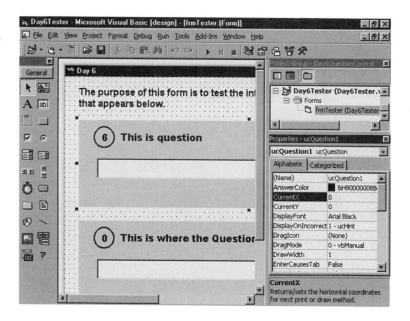

All the methods that have been exposed should be available as well. If the host application programmer wants to draw the graphics himself, he can simply add to the program the code shown in Listing 6.5.

Listing 6.5. Because the methods are now exposed, the host application can call them itself.

```
1: ucQuestion1.Cls
2: ucQuestion1.CurrentX = 520
3: ucQuestion1.CurrentY = 260
4: ucQuestion1.FontSize = 12
5: ucQuestion1.Print "1"
6: ucQuestion1.DrawWidth = 2
7: ucQuestion1.Circle (660, 420), 250, RGB(0, 0, 0)
```

Using the ActiveX Control Interface Wizard, then, is the best way to expose any methods, whether of the UserControl object or any other in the ActiveX control.

Constituent Control Methods

Just as you've been working with the methods of the UserControl object, you also have access to the methods of your constituent controls. You'll have different methods available, depending on the controls themselves. As when working with the UserControl object, you can choose to expose these methods to the host application, or you can keep them hidden and use them within the ActiveX code itself. Exposing constituent control methods, as you will see, has the benefit of giving the host more flexibility in using your control. The downside to exposing the methods is that you give the host a better chance to mess something up in your control or cause something to happen that you didn't quite predict.

Hidden Methods

By default, constituent controls within an ActiveX control are hidden. That is, the code you use within your control has access to any of the methods of its constituent controls. For example, the statement lstMembers.Clear clears out the contents of a listbox called lstMembers within an ActiveX control. You can use this statement anywhere within the code inside your ActiveX control. But the host application has no way of calling this method unless you expose it.

Exposed Methods

Exposing constituent control methods is essentially the same as exposing methods for the UserControl object. The primary difference, of course, is that the code inside the procedure used to map the method to the constituent control is different than when mapped to the UserControl object. Consider, for example, the code in Listing 6.6.

6

Listing 6.6. Exposing a constituent control method.

```
1: Public Sub Clear()
2:     lstMembers.Clear
3: End Sub
```

In this case, a public subroutine called Clear that clears the contents of the listbox lstMembers is created. When you expose methods of constituent controls, you might find that you use the same name twice. In this case, for instance, you might have another control on the form, such as a combobox, in which you also might want to expose the Clear method. If you decide to expose that method using the name Clear, you'll have a name conflict. Therefore, you must often be more specific when naming a method, just as you had to be when naming a constituent control property on Day 4.

Extender Object Methods

In addition to UserControl and constituent control methods, there are a host of additional methods the container into which your control is placed can provide you. These methods are available within your control through the use of the Extender object. Extender object methods are always available to the user. That is, they're always exposed. But you can call the methods yourself in the code you write within the UserControl object itself. Table 6.2 shows a summary of the methods you have access to if you place your ActiveX control within a Visual Basic form.

Table 6.2. A brief summary of Extender object methods.

Method	Description
Drag	Begins, ends, or cancels a drag operation of the ActiveX control.
Move	Moves the position of the control.
SetFocus	Sets the focus within the container to the ActiveX control.
ShowWhatsThis	Displays a selected topic in a help file using the "What's This" pop-up provided by Help.
ZOrder	Places the control at the front or back of the z-order within its graphical level.

Each of these methods is available to the host application. But you can also call them from within the container itself if you wish. Suppose, for instance, that you want to set the focus within the container to the ActiveX control during the course of a procedure. To do this you can simply enter this statement, which will assign focus to your control:

```
Extender.SetFocus
```

This will, in turn, assign focus to the first constituent control in the tab order if you're using constituent controls within your ActiveX control.

You can also use the `ZOrder` method within your code to make sure nothing can be placed on top of your control in the layer within which your control resides in the container. To do this, you can simply call this statement, which will set the control to the top of its z-order in the layer in which it is defined:

```
Extender.ZOrder 0
```

If for some reason you need to move your control within the container, you can invoke the `Move` method. For instance, suppose you want to move your control to the upper-left corner of the container for some reason. To do this, you simply add the statement

```
Extender.Move 0,0
```

and the control will move, as ordered, to the upper-left corner as you've instructed it. Keep in mind, however, that you can't use the `Move` method, or any other `Extender` method for that matter, in the `Initialize` or `InitProperties` events of the `UserControl` object.

With the host application, the program would refer to the method using the control name it has assigned. For example, to move the control to the upper left of a form in Visual Basic, this statement would be executed somewhere in the code within the form:

```
ucQuestion1.Move 0,0
```

So regardless of whether the method is executed inside the control code or within the code of the host application that uses the control, the same method actually is called. It simply depends on who wants to do the calling—the host application or the control code. Since `Extender` object methods are actually a part of the container the control resides in, there are no such things as "hidden" `Extender` object methods. These methods are always available to anyone who wants to use them because technically they're not a part of the control. They belong to the container in which the control resides.

Summary

This chapter takes a comprehensive look at predefined control methods. It begins by discussing briefly what a method is and why methods are used. Then it describes three different categories of methods: methods for the `UserControl` object, methods for constituent controls, and methods for the `Extender` object. In each case, you have learned how to use the methods of these various objects. The methods of a `UserControl` object and its constituent controls are hidden from the host application unless you expose them yourself. You have learned how to use the methods in their hidden state within the ActiveX control code. You have also learned how to expose those methods to the public using the ActiveX Control Interface Wizard, along with a small pinch of elbow grease where necessary. You use or expose constituent control methods the same way as a `UserControl` object, so you examined constituent control methods briefly. Then you looked at the `Extender` object. `Extender` object methods are provided by the container that hosts the control. As such, they are exposed and can simply be used in your ActiveX control code if you wish. You have learned how to do this and why you might want to call `Extender` object methods from time to time. In tomorrow's lesson, you'll learn how to create methods of your own.

Q&A

Q How many methods of an ActiveX control should I expose to the public?

A You should expose the methods of an ActiveX control judiciously. If you expose too many, you might give users too much power, enabling them to cause your control to behave erratically. Your best option is to give them only the methods, properties, and events they need to get the job done—but not at the cost of the stability of the control.

Q Why doesn't the ActiveX Control Interface Wizard let you expose any method you want it to? Some of them aren't on the list.

A The Interface Wizard only exposes those methods that have a clearly defined set of arguments. If you want to expose a method that takes a complex set of arguments the wizard can't handle, you might need to expose the method yourself. Keep in mind, however, that this makes your method unconventional and you should avoid this whenever possible. You might want to consider assigning the method a different name to make it more clear to the user.

Q The ActiveX Control Interface Wizard looks pretty powerful. Why can't I just use that and not worry about all these silly details?

A Well, you certainly can use the wizard, but you need to know the underlying concepts in order to use the code that the wizard generates. Don't look to the wizard as the magic tool that will solve all your problems. Use the wizard as a carpenter uses a hammer—the hammer can help you pound a nail, but you still need to know what's happening.

Workshop

Examine the controls available to you in your Visual Basic toolbox. Take a look at the methods each of these controls provides you, and think about why you might want to use them as hidden methods and why you might want to expose them to the public. Are there any methods you would never want to expose to the public? Why or why not?

Quiz

NOTE

See Appendix D, "Answers to Quiz Questions," for the answers to these questions.

1. Suppose you want to expose the Size method of the UserControl object to the public. Look up the Size method in the help file. How many arguments does it require?

2. Without using the wizard, write the procedure you would need to expose the Size method to the public.

3. Now use the wizard to produce the same method and compare the solution to your own. Are they the same?

4. It's a very good idea to expose the Refresh method of your UserControl object. Show the code required to do so, either manually or using the wizard.

Day **7**

User-Defined Control Methods

Now that you've seen the power of using and exposing predefined methods in your ActiveX controls, you're about to see the real beauty of using methods. Yesterday you started off with methods by learning how to work with hidden methods of the UserControl object and constituent controls within UserControl. You then learned how to expose some of those methods to the host. In today's lesson, you'll learn how to create methods of your own.

Yesterday all you had to do to expose the method of UserControl or a constituent control was to provide a public procedure that was named with the same name as the method you wanted to expose. Then you simply provided code within the procedure to connect the public procedure to the method itself. When you create your own methods, however, the rules change a bit. Now it's totally up to you to write the code that does the work your method is intended to do. So you not only need to know how to create a user-defined method, but you should also know what kinds of things you can do with a user-defined method to begin with.

Today's lesson, therefore, not only shows you how to create methods, but gives you several practical examples of how you might go about using a method and why you'd want to create one in the first place. Each example builds on the previous, and by the end of this lesson you should have a very good grasp on user-defined methods. So hop on board, and let's begin.

What Are User-Defined Methods?

Before getting into the specifics, let's review the purpose of user-defined methods. Basically, whenever you want the host application that uses your control to make something happen within your control, you can supply a method for the host to call. A method is created to execute a series of instructions that change the characteristics of the control or otherwise make something happen within it. The predefined methods you looked at yesterday, for instance, were used to create graphics. The `Circle` method drew a circle within the control. `Print` enabled the host to print text on the control. Any given method is used to cause something to happen in the control or within Windows itself.

Creating User-Defined Methods

Creating a user-defined method is even easier than exposing predefined methods. All you have to do is create a public subroutine or function, depending on whether your method returns arguments. Since most methods do not return arguments, the subroutine is likely to be the most commonly used type of procedure for your methods. To create user-defined methods, you can either enter the code manually or you can use the ActiveX Control Interface Wizard that you learned about in yesterday's lesson. For the purposes of learning just how a user-defined method is put together, we won't use the wizard in today's lesson. The wizard is a vital component when exposing predefined methods, but when you create the method yourself, there's little the wizard can do other than create the procedure. That's a fairly simple task, so it's safe to say we can get by without the wizard in this lesson.

To show you how to create and use user-defined methods, you'll see three examples as we further develop our question control. If you have a previous project up in Visual Basic, close it down. As a matter of fact, close Visual Basic all the way down. Exit the program and prepare to begin from ground up. Start up Windows Explorer or any equivalent file management system and turn your attention to the `Day07` directory of the samples. Under that directory is a subdirectory named `Your Start`. This directory contains a project named `Day7QuestionControl.vbp`. Double-click on that project. Visual Basic starts up and proceeds to load this project. (You could have carried out the same feat by simply starting Visual Basic and then selecting File|Open Project from the menu.) Once the project is loaded into Visual Basic, you should see a project window for the question control project like that shown in Figure 7.1.

NOTE

SAMPLE The sample to start with for today's exercise can be found in file Day7QuestionControl.vbp on the CD-ROM under the Source\Day07\Your Start subdirectory. Since you will modify this project in the course of today's material, copy the entire subdirectory to your local drive before proceeding to work with it if you did not already do so when installing the CD. The sample program for today is presented in somewhat of a before-and-after state. The version in the Your Start directory is intended to show the code as it would appear at the end of Day 6, "Predefined Control Methods" (with names revised to correspond to today, Day 7). There is another version of this project one directory level higher in the Source\Day07 subdirectory. This contains the completed version as it should appear by the end of the steps in today's material.

Figure 7.1.

The project window with the Day 7 question control project loaded.

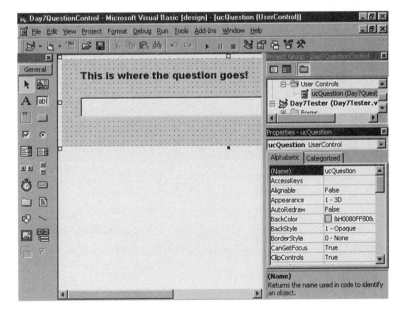

Now let's take a look at four examples of implementing user-defined control methods.

Example 1: The `Clear` Method

The first example will be to implement a method we'll call `Clear`. The purpose of the `Clear` method will be to erase the `IncorrectAnswers` array and zero out the number of incorrect responses in the `IncorrectResponseCount` property. This one method, therefore, will erase an array internal to the control as well as set a property.

 NOTE

> The `IncorrectAnswers` and `IncorrectReponseCount` properties were both discussed on Day 5, "User-Defined Control Properties." Refer to Day 5 for a detailed discussion of the `IncorrectAnswers` array and the properties used to manipulate that array.

Often, when creating a method procedure, the method may change properties, private variables, and other controls within the `UserControl` object. Creating the procedure for the `Clear` method is very simple. When your project has loaded into Visual Basic, bring up the code view of the `UserControl` object. Then simply click Tools | Add Procedure and create a public function named `Clear`. You will then see the empty procedure appear on the code sheet:

```
Public Sub Clear()
End Sub
```

Since you want to zero out the `IncorrectReponseCount` property using this method, we can simply set `IncorrectResponseCount` within the `Clear` procedure. To do this, click inside the `Clear` procedure and enter the following statement as the first line of code:

```
m_IncorrectAnswerCount = 0
```

The next step is to zero out the array that holds the incorrect responses. You can do this simply by redimensioning the array without using the `Preserve` keyword. The size of the array is set using the variable `m_IncorrectAnswerCount`, which has just been set to `0`. This statement empties out the array completely. Go ahead and enter this statement in the procedure:

```
ReDim Preserve m_IncorrectAnswers(m_IncorrectAnswerCount)
```

Finally, you want to notify Visual Basic that you've changed the `IncorrectAnswerCount` property. To do that, simply enter this statement below the other two:

```
PropertyChanged "IncorrectAnswerCount"
```

This updates the control's property in the host environment. The end result is shown in Listing 7.1.

Listing 7.1. The `Clear` method procedure.

```
1: Public Sub Clear()
2:     m_IncorrectAnswerCount = 0
3:     ReDim Preserve m_IncorrectAnswers(m_IncorrectAnswerCount)
4:     PropertyChanged "IncorrectAnswerCount"
5: End Sub
```

To see this method in action, close the control project and open the sample application project that's in the project group used to build the control. The form is shown in design mode in Figure 7.2.

Figure 7.2.

The test form in design mode.

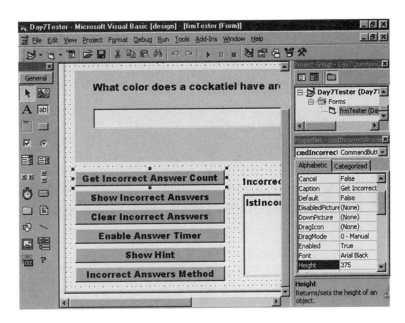

Right now, none of the buttons have any code behind them. Throughout the course of this lesson, you'll be adding the code necessary to both the control project and the test application project to build the final result. For this first example, let's zero in on the buttons labeled Get Incorrect Answer Count and Clear Incorrect Answers. When the user clicks the first button, you want the label to indicate how many incorrect answers the user has entered. To do this, enter this statement in the `Click` event of the command button:

```
lblIncorrectAnswerCount = "Incorrect Answer Count = " & _
              ucQuestion1.IncorrectAnswerCount
```

The code for the first button, which is designed to show the user the number of incorrect answers, is shown in Listing 7.2.

7

Listing 7.2. The `Click` event of the Get Incorrect Answer Count button.

```
1: Private Sub cmdIncorrectAnswerCount_Click()
2:     lblIncorrectAnswerCount = "Incorrect Answer Count = " & _
3:     ucQuestion1.IncorrectAnswerCount
4: End Sub
```

ANALYSIS This procedure simply creates a string and places it into the label just to the right of the button. The string reports the incorrect answer count using the IncorrectAnswerCount property of the question control, in this case named ucQuestion1.

The second command button, labeled Clear Incorrect Answers, invokes the Clear method, as shown in Listing 7.3. Enter the code from Listing 7.3 into the command button's Click event procedure.

Listing 7.3. The `Click` event of the Clear Incorrect Answers button.

```
1: Private Sub cmdClearIncorrectAnswers_Click()
2:     ucQuestion1.Clear
3:     Call cmdShowIncorrectAnswers_Click
4: End Sub
```

ANALYSIS The first statement in this procedure invokes the Clear method, which clears out the m_IncorrectAnswers array and sets the IncorrectAnswerCount property to 0. The second statement invokes the Click event of the middle command button labeled Show Incorrect Answers. This button's Click event uses the code we created back on Day 4, "Predefined Control Properties," only this time it places the incorrect answers in the listbox located just to the right of the button.

Bring up the Click event for the cmdShowIncorrectAnswers command button and enter the code for this command button, as shown in Listing 7.4.

Listing 7.4. The `Click` event of the Show Incorrect Answers button.

```
1: Private Sub cmdShowIncorrectAnswers_Click()
2:
3:     Dim IncorrectAnswers As String
4:     Dim i As Integer
5:     Dim iTotal As Integer
6:
7:     iTotal = ucQuestion1.IncorrectAnswerCount
8:
9:     lstIncorrectAnswers.Clear
```

7

```
10:
11:     For i = 1 To iTotal
12:         ucQuestion1.IncorrectAnswerIndex = i
13:         lstIncorrectAnswers.AddItem ucQuestion1.IncorrectAnswer
14:     Next
15:
16:     Call cmdIncorrectAnswerCount_Click
17: End Sub
```

ANALYSIS So what does the code you've entered do? The first statement in this procedure, after the variable declarations, sets the number of incorrect answers in a procedure-level variable. The second procedure calls the `Clear` method, which clears out the listbox used to show the incorrect responses. Then the procedure loops through the number of incorrect answers and writes them to the listbox. The procedure also updates the current count by calling the `cmdIncorrectAnswerCount_Click` event whose code you entered earlier, shown in Listing 7.2. The net effect is that all the incorrect answers are shown in the listbox.

So what happens when you run the application? Go ahead and click the Visual Basic Run button or press F5. Figure 7.3 shows the form in its initial configuration, asking the question of the user. This is what you should see when you run the program.

Figure 7.3.

The test form at runtime with a simple question the user has incorrectly answered.

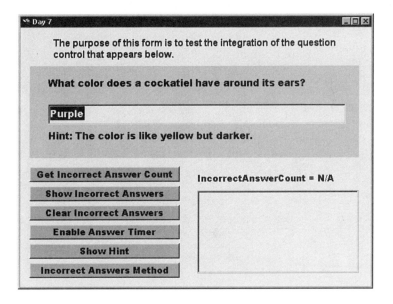

This figure shows an example where the user has entered an answer to the question, but has gotten it wrong. Now suppose the user enters two more incorrect answers, say Green and Blue, and clicks on the Show Incorrect Answers button. The result is shown in Figure 7.4.

Day 7
The purpose of this form is to test the integration of the question control that appears below.
What color does a cockatiel have around its ears?
Blue
Hint: The color is like yellow but darker.
Get Incorrect Answer Count
Show Incorrect Answers
Clear Incorrect Answers
Enable Answer Timer
Show Hint
Incorrect Answers Method
Incorrect Answer Count = 3
Purple
Green
Blue

Figure 7.4.
The test form with two incorrect answers that are displayed by clicking on the Show Incorrect Answers command button.

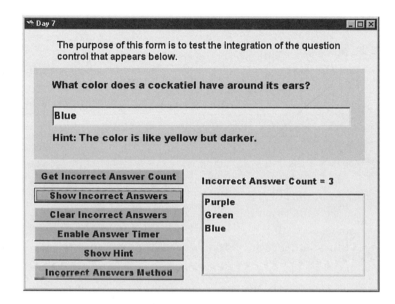

At this point, the two incorrect answers are displayed and the incorrect answer count is properly set to `2`. Now watch what happens when the user clicks on the Clear Incorrect Answers button. The listbox becomes empty and the incorrect answer label is set back to `0`. The result is shown in Figure 7.5.

Day 7
The purpose of this form is to test the integration of the question control that appears below.
What color does a cockatiel have around its ears?
Blue
Hint: The color is like yellow but darker.
Get Incorrect Answer Count
Show Incorrect Answers
Clear Incorrect Answers
Enable Answer Timer
Show Hint
Incorrect Answers Method
Incorrect Answer Count = 0

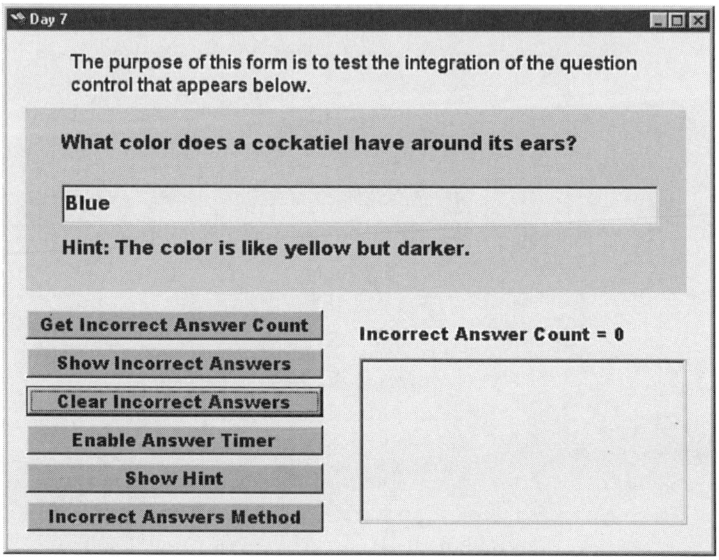

Figure 7.5.
The test form after the Clear Incorrect Answers button is clicked.

The Clear method does its job in clearing out the array of answers and resetting the IncorrectAnswerCount property back to 0. Now if the user goes back to enter more answers and they are incorrect, the count starts back from 0 and increments upward. The case where the user has entered another incorrect answer is shown in Figure 7.6.

Figure 7.6.

The test form after the user has entered another incorrect answer but has cleared the array.

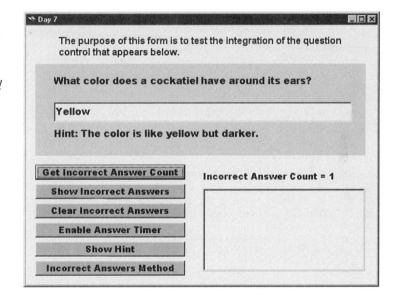

How might a method like this be useful to the programmer of the host application? Suppose the application is asking two people the same question and wants to clear out the incorrect answers before asking the question again. Or, perhaps the user has reached the maximum number of tries and the host application wants to clear out the buffer holding the incorrect answers. For these reasons, among others, methods like this are useful to the potential programmer of the host application.

Example 2: The ForceAnswer Method

This next method is designed to give the host application programmer a way to display the answer to the user if he wants to. One potential use for this type of method is if the host application has a timer designed to give the user a certain amount of time to respond. If the user fails to answer the question in the allocated time, the answer simply appears in the answer textbox.

The implementation of this method is very simple. Open the question control project once more and create a public subroutine called ForceAnswer. Then enter the code into the ForceAnswer procedure as shown in Listing 7.5.

7

Listing 7.5. The ForceAnswer method.

```
1: Public Sub ForceAnswer()
2:     txtAnswer.Text = "Answer = " & m_ExpectedAnswer
3: End Sub
```

That's all there is to it! The method you've created consists of a simple statement that fills the answer textbox with the module-level variable that holds the answer. Now let's write the code in the host application to make use of this method. Look back for a moment at Figure 7.2, where you see the host application at design time. Notice the timer in the upper-right corner of the form as well as the button in the lower-left corner labeled Enable Answer Timer. Let's write the code for these two controls. Close down the control project and bring up the test application project. In the Click event of the Enable Answer Timer button, enter the code shown in Listing 7.6.

Listing 7.6. The Enable Answer Timer button Click event.

```
1: Private Sub cmdForceAnswer_Click()
2:     If tmrForceAnswer.Enabled = True Then
3:         tmrForceAnswer.Enabled = False
4:         cmdForceAnswer.Caption = "Enable Answer Timer"
5:     Else
6:         tmrForceAnswer.Enabled = True
7:         cmdForceAnswer.Caption = "Disable Answer Timer"
8:     End If
9: End Sub
```

This simple procedure enables the timer if the user clicks on the button when the timer is turned off. If the timer is off when the user clicks the button, the button click turns the timer on. In this way, and by updating the caption appropriately, the button serves a dual purpose of both turning the timer on and turning it off. Make sure the timer's Interval property is set to 10,000 ms, or 10 seconds. Now you need to write the code to trigger the method when the timer expires. To do this, double-click on the timer control and enter the code shown in Listing 7.7 into the Timer event.

Listing 7.7. The Timer event of the host application timer.

```
1: Private Sub tmrForceAnswer_Timer()
2:     ucQuestion1.ForceAnswer
3: End Sub
```

As you can see, the Timer event simply invokes the ForceAnswer method of the question control. Go ahead and run the application, click Enable Answer Timer, and wait 10 seconds without typing in the answer. You should notice, after 10 seconds, that the answer appears in the answer textbox, as shown in Figure 7.7.

Figure 7.7.

Using a timer to limit the user's response time to a question. Here the time has expired and the correct answer is displayed.

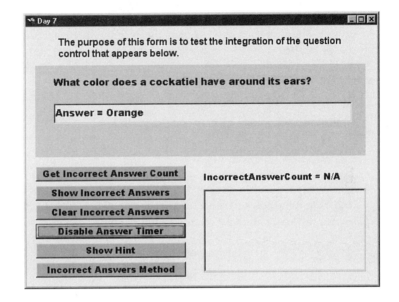

Voilà! Your method works like a charm. Now you could enhance the question control even further, for instance, by keeping some sort of score. That might be ideal, for example, if the question control were being used on the Internet to grade a user in some sort of test. The possibilities are numerous, but this simple example does show how you can use a timer in coordination with a control method to provide useful capabilities within the host application.

Example 3: The ShowHint Method

The next example in today's lesson shows how you can use a control method to display a hint to the user. The method will be called ShowHint. Put Visual Basic back in design mode and switch back over to the control project. Add a new, public procedure called ShowHint, and enter the code shown in Listing 7.8 into the procedure.

Listing 7.8. The ShowHint method.

```
1: Public Sub ShowHint()
2:     lblFeedback.Caption = "Hint: " & m_Hint
3: End Sub
```

7

Again, you can see just how simple the method code is here. When the host calls the method, the hint is displayed in the lblFeedback constituent control within the UserControl object. If, at some point in the host application, the programmer wishes to display the hint, he simply has to call this method. Close the control project and switch over to the test application project. The second-to-last button on the form should be labeled Show Hint. Enter the code shown in Listing 7.9 for the Click event of this command button.

Listing 7.9. The test application's cmdShowHint Click event.

```
1: Private Sub cmdShowHint_Click()
2:     ucQuestion1.ShowHint
3: End Sub
```

This simple little subroutine invokes the ShowHint method and lets the control do all the rest. Run the application and see what happens when you click on the Show Hint button. The result you see in Figure 7.8 should match the result on your screen.

Figure 7.8.

The hint is displayed at runtime as a result of the user clicking the Show Hint button.

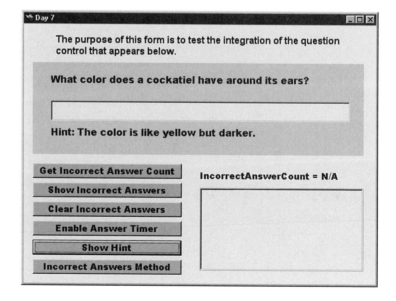

The possible applications for such a method are also diverse. You could, for instance, set a timer that, when expired, displays the hint automatically for the user. The application would be very similar to the second example, which limited the user to a fixed amount of time before which he can answer the question. This task is included as an exercise at the end of the chapter.

7

Example 4: The `ShowIncorrectAnswers` Method

The fourth and final example of today's lesson shows you how you can present a user interface through a method. To illustrate how this might work, you will create the `ShowIncorrectAnswers` method. This method is designed to bring up a form that shows the user all the incorrect answers in a listbox on that form. This method is unlike all the others you've seen so far because this one actually brings up a user interface rather than returning a value or changing properties of the control.

Before the method is actually created, you need to first create the form that the method will invoke. To do this, make sure you have the question control project loaded into Visual Basic. Then click Project | Add Form, which may bring up an Add Form dialog, upon which you should choose Form to bring up a simple, default form. The form should then appear, as shown in Figure 7.9.

Figure 7.9.

Bringing up a blank form for use in a control method.

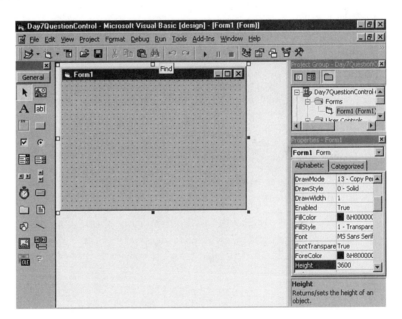

The form should be given a name, in this case `frmIncorrectAnswers`. Then the caption is assigned to the form as Incorrect Answers. To make the form behave like a dialog, the `BorderStyle` property is set to `Fixed Dialog` and the `StartUpPosition` property is set to `Center Owner`. The next step is to place an OK button on the form, name it `cmdOK`, and make it the default command button. You should also add a listbox control named `lstAnswers`. When all is said and done, the form should look like the one shown in Figure 7.10.

7

Figure 7.10.

The form and controls needed to implement the ShowIncorrectAnswers method.

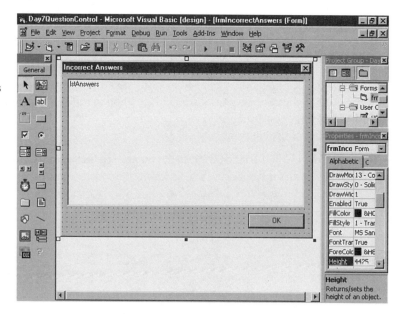

With all these elements in place, you're now ready to start writing some code. The first thing you need to do is to make sure the form unloads when the user clicks the OK button. To do this, simply add the following statement to the cmdOK_Click event:

```
Unload Me
```

You'll write the code to put the answers in the listbox in a moment. For now, though, you'll get the basic framework put into place to get the method working.

The next step is to create the method procedure and add the necessary code to get it working properly. Bring up the UserControl object within the question control project. Then add a method procedure titled ShowIncorrectAnswers and place the code shown in Listing 7.10 within that procedure.

Listing 7.10. The ShowIncorrectAnswers method is now exposed to the host application.

```
1: Public Sub cmdShowIncorrectAnswers()
2:
3:     Dim i As Integer
4:
5:     Load frmIncorrectAnswers
6:
7:     For i = 1 To m_IncorrectAnswerCount
8:         frmIncorrectAnswers!lstAnswers.AddItem m_IncorrectAnswers(i)
```

```
 9:     Next
10:
11:     frmIncorrectAnswers.Show vbModal
12: End Sub
```

ANALYSIS If you look closely, you'll notice that the code here is similar to the code you saw in today's first example, where the incorrect answers were displayed manually in the test application. To compare the two alternatives, refer to Listing 7.4. The difference is, of course, that the method takes all that code and puts it inside the ActiveX control so that the host doesn't have to supply the listbox and all the supporting code. What a benefit! Let's take a look at the code in detail.

The first thing this procedure does is to load the form you've just created. When a form is loaded, it is not yet displayed on the screen. The show command that appears at the end of the subroutine takes care of that for you. Once the form is loaded using this command:

```
Load frmIncorrectAnswers
```

a loop begins that loops from the first incorrect answer through to the total number of incorrect answers entered. This, of course, is available through the m_IncorrectAnswers variable. Then, one by one, each incorrect answer is added to the form's listbox control using the statement

```
frmIncorrectAnswers!lstAnswers.AddItem m_IncorrectAnswers(i)
```

Notice the syntax used in this statement. Visual Basic uses the ! symbol to indicate a reference to an object within an object—in this case, a listbox control object within a form object. Then the AddItem method is invoked and the appropriate string is passed to the listbox using the m_IncorrectAnswers array. After this, the Show statement is used to actually display the form to the host. Notice the use of the constant vbModal in the Show method. This constant is used to make sure the user must dismiss this dialog before the application does anything else. The program halts within this form, not executing any other code or doing any other activities until the user dismisses it. To see the method in action, close the UserControl object and the frmIncorrectAnswer form and switch over to the test application in the project group.

Earlier in today's lesson, you saw how the test application used the IncorrectAnswer and IncorrectAnswerCount properties along with a listbox to display the incorrect answers manually. Now you have a great method that does the work for you and even brings up a separate form. Figure 7.11 shows the test application form. At the bottom of the form, you will see the button labeled Incorrect Answers Method.

The Click event for this command button is shown in Listing 7.11.

7

Figure 7.11.

The Incorrect Answers Method button on the test application form, demonstrating the use of the ShowIncorrectAnswers method.

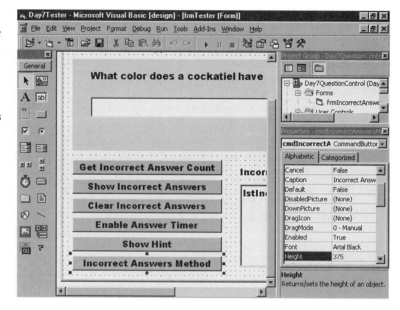

Listing 7.11. The ShowIncorrectAnswers method comes alive in the test application.

```
1: Private Sub cmdIncorrectAnswersMethod_Click()
2:     ucQuestion1.ShowIncorrectAnswers
3: End Sub
```

Run the program, enter some incorrect answers, and click on the Incorrect Answers Method button. The Click event does little more than call the ShowIncorrectAnswers method that belongs to the ucQuestion1 question control. The result you see in Figure 7.12 should match what you see on your screen.

You might be wondering why the code to display the incorrect answers was handled in the UserControl method procedure rather than the Load event of the form used to display the results. It turns out that when you load the form frmIncorrectAnswers, it has no knowledge of who called it. Therefore, the frmIncorrectAnswers form cannot refer to the UserControl object and access all the properties it needs to display the results. Therefore, in this case, you need to treat the form as a dumb container that really can't do anything other than close itself. All the intelligence lies back in the method procedure, which not only loads up the form, but feeds it all the information it needs and then waits for the user to close it down.

Suppose, for instance, you had tried to build all the intelligence into the supporting form. You might try to enter the code using a scheme like that shown in Listing 7.12.

7

Figure 7.12.

The Incorrect Answers Method button in action, bringing up a dialog that will ultimately show the incorrect answers the user has entered.

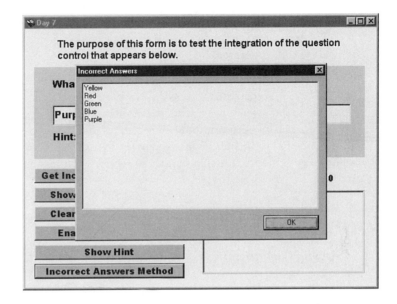

Listing 7.12. A form that your `UserControl` object calls can't refer to the `UserControl` object that called it.

```
1: Private Sub Form_Load()
2:     Dim i As Integer
3:
4:     For i = 1 To UserControl.m_IncorrectAnswerCount
5:         lstAnswers.AddItem UserControl.m_IncorrectAnswers(i)
6:     Next
7:
8: End Sub
```

The `UserControl` method procedure would then simply contain one statement:

`frmIncorrectAnswers.Show vbModal`

If you were to try to run this application, however, you would soon be stopped dead in your tracks with a runtime error. Why? Because a statement such as the following is illegal within the form

`For i = 1 To UserControl.m_IncorrectAnswerCount`

The form doesn't know what `UserControl` is. If you had entered the following:

`For i = 1 To ucQuestion1.m_IncorrectAnswerCount`

your program would still not run because the form doesn't know what `ucQuestion1` is either. There are no question controls on the support form, and you can't simply refer to the

7

UserControl that called the form. The form has no way of knowing who called it. Therefore, you can't expect the form to be capable of querying its caller for data. The caller has to pass the data to the support form!

Therefore, remember that if your UserControl object calls up a supporting form, that form will not have the capability to access the UserControl object that called it. The UserControl object has to spoon feed any information the form needs to the form directly. This limits the potential uses of supporting forms such as these, as you can only do so much useful work when all the code has to lie outside the container. Typically, however, forms such as these are designed with that intention in mind, and therefore are an appropriate application of this model.

Summary

With today's and yesterday's lessons, you should now have a firm understanding of ActiveX control methods. In yesterday's lesson you learned about predefined control methods, and today you learned about user-defined control methods. User-defined control methods are very simple to create—you declare them by declaring a public procedure and placing it within that procedure code to accomplish the purpose of the method. Four simple examples were presented in this lesson that illustrate the use of methods. The examples are used to modify the properties of constituent controls, set variables within the control, and update properties with new settings. The last example even shows you how to bring up a supporting form that presents a useful interface to the user when the host application calls up a method.

While the examples are fairly simple, they show you some of the capabilities that methods provide. Methods are the workhorses of controls. They are unique in that they can be directly called from the host to do useful work. Properties are used to set a control to various states. Events, as you will see in tomorrow's lesson, are used when the control has to notify the host that something has taken place. But methods are the primary mechanism the host has to cause a control to accomplish a specific task. Since methods do not appear on a property sheet as properties do, it is very important that you clearly document each method you provide to the user in your control's documentation and help file. In tomorrow's lesson, you'll learn about the last of the "big three" elements of an ActiveX control: events.

Q&A

Q What's the main difference between a property and a method?

A A *property* is an attribute of a control you can set to a specific setting. A *method*, on the other hand, is a procedure you call that performs some set of operations based on the purpose of the method. Properties must be set equal to some value.

Methods work like procedure calls, where arguments may or may not be required, and the method may return a value, depending on how it is constructed.

Q   How can I tell what methods a control provides me with?

A   The best way to determine what methods are a part of a control is to use the Object Browser. Figure 7.13 shows the object browser in action, displaying all the properties, methods, and events of the ucQuestion object used in the Day7QuestionControl project.

Figure 7.13.

The Object Browser in action, showing the properties, methods, and events of the ucQuestion *question control.*

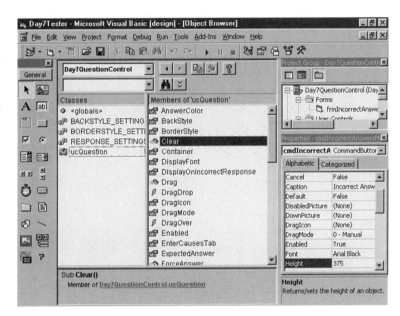

Events appear with the small, green, speeding block, as shown in Figure 7.13. Properties appear as a small card with a finger pointing on it. Events appear as a lightning bolt within the browser.

It's very important that you properly document every method you expose to the user. Provide a help file and/or written documentation so that those who use your control know exactly what it does and how it works. Poor documentation will lead to many wasted hours of frustration for the user of your control—make sure to document *properly!*

Q   I have a hard time knowing whether I should use a property or a method. How do I decide?

A   Sometimes it's a bit unclear whether to use a property or a method. Some properties cause actions to occur in a control as they are set. As a general rule, however, you should use properties only when you want the user to set an attribute of a control. A property shouldn't be used to cause the control to do something. For example, in the Common Dialog control of Visual Basic 3.0, you had to set the Action property to bring up a dialog. This would be better implemented as a method, because programmers don't usually expect major activity to take place by simply setting a property. Visual Basic 4.0 and higher uses methods such as ShowPrinter, ShowFont, and ShowColor, all of which take the place of the rather cryptic Action property. Learn this lesson as Microsoft has—use properties to change settings; use methods to accomplish tasks.

Workshop

Try to think of additional methods you could provide to the user for the question control. Do some of the methods you think of require the control to notify the host application when they're complete? In tomorrow's lesson you'll learn how you can handle such situations when you learn about events.

Quiz

NOTE   See Appendix D, "Answers to Quiz Questions," for the answers to these questions.

1. Enhance the test application you've learned about in today's lesson with another timer named tmrHint. Write the code necessary to display the hint to the user after 30 seconds.

2. Suppose that you're writing a control with a timer built in to the control. Show the code required to create a method that requires an interval, sets the interval to the timer, and enables the timer. Call the method Countdown. Have the method return True or False—True if the timing interval is valid, False otherwise.

3. Write a method that grabs the contents of a textbox named txtInformation in a control and copies it to the Clipboard. Call the method CopyAnswer.

In Review

This first week you got a basic understanding of what an ActiveX control is and how to create controls using Microsoft Visual Basic 5.0. You have seen a simple example of an ActiveX control and how easy it is to put together a simple control. Although you might not be an ActiveX control–building guru yet, you have reached the point where you can put together a simple control with a set of properties and methods the user of your control can take advantage of.

Where You Have Been

At the start of the week, you learned just what an ActiveX control is, a little bit about the history of ActiveX controls, and the underlying technology that makes them possible. After that, you saw a simple example that shows you just what a control is capable of providing its users. The third lesson started from scratch, showing you the Visual Basic programming environment and all the things you need to know to find your way around and work within that environment when building ActiveX controls. The rest of the week began to focus on the building blocks of ActiveX controls—properties and methods. As the lessons continue, you'll be able to build progressively more powerful controls.

Day 8

Predefined Events

By now you've learned how to make a control that a host application can communicate with. You provide properties the host application sets to manipulate the control's characteristics. The host application can also use these property settings to retrieve information about the control. You define control methods to allow the host to trigger an action within the control. What more could a host application ask for with the power of properties and methods at its disposal? The answer is *events*, and that is the topic of today's lesson.

What Are Events?

Events are conditions that occur in an integrated object of a host application to which the host application can react. Your control is one of the objects that can provide events for a host application to react to. Your own control can even respond to the events of the objects it is built on, just as a host application can respond to events of its integrated objects.

Picture a car on a racetrack, circling it repeatedly. When one lap remains, a flag is waved to alert the driver that he has reached a new stage. The action of raising the flag signals a new condition to the driver of the car. The philosophy is much the same when a control or another object raises an event. An integrated object raises a virtual flag to signal some new condition to its host. The host programmer can decide when building the program whether code should be supplied to deal with that condition. An event could be a user mouse click within a control, a keystroke, the entry of a certain number of characters in a textbox, or any other condition the control creator wishes to specify.

Some events are predefined in existing controls and Visual Basic objects. You can create others when you create your control. The focus of today's lesson is on understanding predefined events. These are events that are already available for your use with the standard Visual Basic controls and objects. Tomorrow's lesson, Day 9, "User-Defined Events," takes a look at events that you define yourself when creating a control.

How to Respond to Events

The host application developer can supply code to respond to each event condition he cares about. An event response routine must be declared in the host application code if a response is desired. This routine must have a name that consists of the name of the host application object, an underscore, and then the specific event name defined by the object that generates the event. The name of the subroutine that responds to a mouse click on the frmTest form would be frmTest_Click, for example. This event response routine is often called an *event handler* because it handles the event. The event handler defined in the host application will be called automatically through the magic of Windows and the host application framework whenever the event is raised.

A control might raise many different events and the host application might supply corresponding code for none, some, or all of them at its discretion. What if a control raises an event and no special code has been supplied in the host application to deal with it? Then there is simply no host application response to the event.

NEW TERM When a control *raises* an event, the calling code of the control has a chance to be notified. Calling code is only notified if it has a specific defined subroutine that is named with the object name, an underscore, and the event name. If this routine exists, it will be automatically called as a result of the control raising the event. If it does not exist, no action is taken for the event. Therefore, the act of raising an event really means providing notification. Code at higher layers may or may not respond to this notification, depending on the logic at that level.

The question of whether a host application should respond to an event is very event and application specific. Consider yourself in the role of the host application as you drive your car down the road. If someone waves a flag from the side of the road that says "You just crossed the state line," you might not want to carry out any special action at all. On the other hand, if someone waves a flag that says "Volcano three miles ahead just erupted," it might be prudent to mentally enact some event-handling behavior and carry out a quick U-turn. A host application won't often have molten lava streaming from it, but there will very likely be some events it cannot afford to ignore to carry out its purpose successfully.

The Difference Between Internal and Exposed Events

Any object can potentially generate events. This includes standard controls you incorporate into your control design as well as the controls you create. For this reason there are two levels of events to consider in control development, just as there are two levels of properties and methods. The two types of events are internal events and exposed events.

The control you design can generate events for a host application. These are called *exposed events*. At the same time, the control you design can incorporate constituent controls, which generate events your control must respond to. These are called *internal events*.

The label control, the textbox control, and virtually any other constituent control you might incorporate into your control design come with events you can respond to. Likewise, predefined objects such as `Extender` and `UserControl` raise events your control code can react to.

Your control code can react to these internal events through its own event-handling routines. These events and corresponding event-handling routines help your control carry out its own work. They are not visible to the host application that might include your control. Suppose you define a control that shows several constituent shape controls and changes the color of each shape a user clicks on. Within your own control code you would respond to the internal `Click` event of each constituent shape control. When a host application is defined and integrates your control, the host application code cannot make use of internal events within your control. For example, there would be no way the host application could respond to a click on a specific shape within your control.

By contrast, exposed events are those to which your host application has access. Several events are automatically exposed when you create a control. You can also explicitly expose additional events in your control code. You just have to make the appropriate event declaration. You will see later in this lesson how you can map events of constituent controls to exposed events for the main control. This allows you to give the host application the capability to use events raised by constituent controls if you deem it necessary. For example, you could allow a host application the capability to respond to a click on a shape in the aforementioned shape control.

> **NOTE**
>
> What if exposing the predefined events of a constituent control doesn't meet the full needs of your control for raising an event to a host application? Then you can define a brand new event of your own and expose it. This is the topic of Day 9.

Now that you know the difference between exposed and internal events, you can see why they are necessary. Visual Basic and the controls you incorporate come with a full set of predefined events ready for your use when you create a control. You must understand exposed events to provide a full interface from your control to the applications that incorporate it. You must be aware of internal events because they serve as building blocks in the control code you create. Events help you build more sophisticated controls and provide more sophisticated interfaces to the application that integrates your controls.

Extender **Object Events**

When you create a new control, several events are automatically available to any application that integrates it. These predefined events all come from the Extender object that is behind your control. The application developer who incorporates your control doesn't care what the object is behind your control's events. He just cares that he can access these events through your control. However, it is a good idea for you, as the control developer, to understand exactly what the Extender object is, as well as the events that it provides.

The Purpose of the Extender **and** Ambient **Objects**

Two important objects that you can use are a part of every control. They are the Ambient object and the Extender object. These objects are automatically available to your control code. Both of them provide information pertaining to how your control fits into the host environment.

The Ambient object is set by the host container. It provides recommended settings to your control. For example, this object suggests a background color that matches the host application's background color. Your control doesn't have to use this setting. However, if the control does set its own color based on this recommended color, it might blend in more closely with the host application. The Ambient object does not have any events associated with it. It has a close cousin, the Extender object, that does.

The Extender object provides information to the control about the current settings of the control that directly relate to the host container. Properties about the left and top location of the control in relation to the host application, whether the control is currently visible, and whether the control serves as the default button for the host application are all available through the Extender object. The Extender object also provides some key events for your control in addition to the various properties and methods it defines.

The Predefined Events

The Extender object provides four events for your control. These events are summarized in Table 8.1. They are available under the Visual Basic container framework, but might not be supported under other environments. The Microsoft Internet Explorer browser, for example, does not support these events.

Table 8.1. Predefined exposed events for a control.

Event Name	Description
DragDrop	Raised when another control on the form is dropped on this control
DragOver	Raised when another control on the form is dropped on this control
GotFocus	Raised when this control gets the focus
LostFocus	Raised when this control loses the focus

These are *not* events that you can interact with in the code that defines your control. Instead, they are events that the host application can respond to when it includes your control. The host application can provide an event-handling routine for each of these events if you desire. When the host application runs, the Extender object will raise these events on behalf of your control when the corresponding conditions occur. It requires no action from you, the control developer, to provide these important control events to users of your control.

The first two events shown in Table 8.1 are the DragDrop and DragOver events. These are events that are triggered when some other object is dragged over or dropped onto your control's area on a host application by the mouse. No code is needed in your control to make these events available. They are ready for use by the host application as soon as you create a control.

Listing 8.1 shows the handler routines for the two drag-related Extender events in a host application. If you want to test DragDrop yourself, add these handler routines to the Day 8 test application. You can type them directly in the code window for the test form. Select the ucQuestion1 control object from the leftmost drop-down listbox at the top left of the code window. Then click on the drop-down combobox at the top right of the code window, and you will see a list of all predefined events for the ucQuestion1 control, including the drag

events. Click on the name of the drag event, such as DragOver, and the subroutine declaration
will be inserted directly into the code for you. You just have to supply the code statement that
goes within the declaration. You could also simply type the entire declaration into the code
window without using the drop-down listboxes if that is your preference.

NOTE

> **SAMPLE** Follow along with the examples in this chapter by modify-
> ing the Day8QuestionControl.vbg group project file under
> the Samples\Day08\Your Start\ directory. This project contains the
> code that is intended to be your starting point for the modifications
> described in the rest of this chapter. Copy it to your hard drive so you
> can make subsequent modifications. The material is presented in before
> and after formats. If you want to see the final application with all of
> today's changes already implemented, you can view the
> Day8QuestionControl.vbg group project file in the Samples\Day08
> directory.

Listing 8.1. Host application event-handling routines for drag operations.

```
1: Private Sub ucQuestion1_DragDrop(Source As Control, X As Single, Y As Single)
2:     Msgbox "DragDrop occurred!"
3: End Sub
4: Private Sub ucQuestion1_DragOver(Source As Control, X As Single, _
5:         Y As Single, State As Integer)
6:     Msgbox "DragOver occurred!"
7: End Sub
```

ANALYSIS Listing 8.1 shows the event routines for the drag events. The event-handling routine
names are ucQuestion1_DragDrop on line 1 and ucQuestion1_DragOver on line 4. The
name assigned to your control when it was incorporated into the host application was
ucQuestion1. The event names were automatically defined based on this. The event name
definition consists of merging the object name (defined by the host application developer)
with the event name (predefined by the Extender object). An underscore separates the two
components of the name.

If the host application contains a routine with this expected name, that routine is automatically called when the corresponding event occurs in your control. The Extender object also
passes the relevant parameters at the time of the call. The number of parameters might differ
for different events. The DragDrop event routine has three parameters, and the DragOver event
has four parameters.

The DragDrop and DragOver events are used here just to illustrate the events Extender makes available. Once you have defined the event routines in Listing 8.1, you can observe the results. First, though, you have to drag a different control over the ucQuestion1 control so that the drag events get triggered. There is a ucKeithTimHelp control in the upper-right corner of the test form that can serve this purpose. This control already has internal coding to make it draggable. Click on the ucKeithTimHelp control and drag it over to the top of the ucQuestion1 control. You will see the result that is displayed in Figure 8.1.

Figure 8.1.

The result of the
DragOver *event*
routine in the test
application.

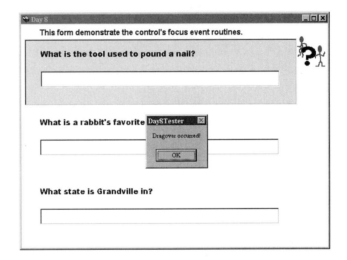

NOTE

The ucKeithTimHelp control has logic that was added to make it draggable. The intricacies of drag support are not the main goal of this lesson, so you don't need to understand what is going on within the control to follow the example. However, you might find it interesting because it is based on a series of events. The ucKeithTimHelp control checks whether it detects a MouseDown event without a corresponding MouseUp event. If so, the control initiates a UserControl.Extender.Drag vbBegin to trigger the drag operation. This allows it to be dragged by the user.

You might encounter some intricacies if you try to build sophisticated drag operations into your application around these events. For example, consider what happens if you implement the host application code shown in Listing 8.1 and then attempt to drag and drop another control onto the ucQuestion1 control. The DragOver event will occur first and cause the host application to display a message box. When the user clicks OK to acknowledge that message box, then by Windows convention the drag operation is canceled, so the subsequent DragDrop event will not be raised for the host application. Therefore, you would never see the two message boxes in sequence. If you remove the message box statement from the DragOver event-handling routine, then that message box does not occur to interrupt the sequence. In that case, the DragDrop event will occur immediately after the DragOver event and a message will be displayed.

NOTE

Don't worry if you don't understand all the nuances of DragDrop. The intention here is not to make you a drag expert, but to expose you to how control events work. For more information on the DragOver and DragDrop events, refer to the Visual Basic help file system. Supply DragOver or DragDrop as the target of the Help Index tab search field.

You can see a practical example of how to use the DragDrop event in the quiz at the end of this chapter. A multiple-choice exam is built around the question control by using the Extender object's DragDrop event in the host application. The source code for this application is provided in the quiz answer.

The next two events listed in Table 8.1 are the GotFocus and LostFocus events. These events pertain to the standard Windows concept of focus control. When a Windows entity such as a control has focus, it has the attention of Windows. It is the object that will receive the subsequent keystrokes the user enters until he changes focus to a different control with another mouse click or keystroke. If you have a window that displays five textboxes, for example, the one that has focus is the one that will display the characters you type at the keyboard.

Often focus is indicated by highlighting the control in some way. Standard textboxes indicate that they have focus by displaying an input cursor as long as focus remains on them. The GotFocus and LostFocus events can come in handy for implementing similar type behavior in an application that integrates custom controls. You can use these events to put special processing or display actions in place that should take effect while your control has focus.

Listing 8.2 shows the format that the focus-related event-handling routines should take in the test host application that integrates your control. Add this code to the test form via the code window.

Listing 8.2. Host application event-handling routines for focus operations.

```
1: Sub ucQuestion1_GotFocus()
2:     MsgBox "Got Focus!"
3: End Sub
4:
5: Sub ucQuestion1_LostFocus()
6:     MsgBox "Lost Focus!"
7: End Sub
```

ANALYSIS Listing 8.2 shows the event routines for the focus events. The event-handling routine names are ucQuestion1_GotFocus and ucQuestion1_LostFocus. These names are based on a combination of the name given to the control when it is integrated into an application and the predefined event name, just as the names for the drag operations are.

There is a significant difference between these events and the drag events. These event-handling routines have no parameters. No further special information needs to be conveyed when focus changes, so no parameters are required.

Once these event routines have been defined, you can observe the results by clicking on ucQuestion1 and then clicking off ucQuestion1. The corresponding message boxes are displayed as focus moves on and off the question control.

An Example of Using an Extender Event

Now it is time to look at a practical host application example of how to use a control's Extender events. Suppose you were creating an application based on our faithful question control. This control in its current form only indicates that it has Windows focus by displaying an input cursor in the answer textbox. This is an implicit capability of the constituent textbox control on which the question control is built. No special code is required to make this happen. However, there is a minor shortcoming with this style of indicating focus. It can be rather difficult to see. If you build an application that presents several questions to the user with the question control, the user might not be able to easily determine the current question by glancing at the application.

Consider Figure 8.2, for example. The user has skipped the first question and tabbed to the second question. When he starts typing, his response will appear in the second question control area. However, this is not easily visible. Suppose the user takes a break at this point. Perhaps the phone rings and he sits back from the computer and takes care of the call. Then when he returns his attention to the test, he might have forgotten where he was and expect that when he starts typing, his response will show up for question 1. How can you give the end user a more visible reminder of the current question?

Figure 8.2.

A question application with only an input cursor to indicate question focus.

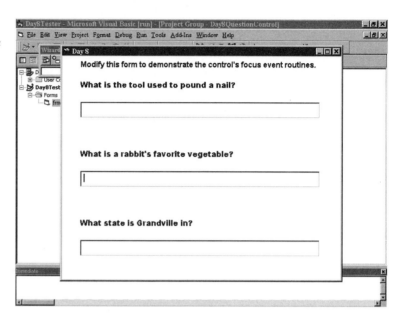

Why not take advantage of the control's Extender events? Then you can provide a highly visible focus indication right from the host application itself. Listing 8.3 shows the code required to add the more visible focus indicators.

Listing 8.3. Host application code to highlight the current question.

```
 1: Private Sub ucQuestion1_GotFocus()
 2:    ' Show the focus indicators so this control stands out to the user
 3:    ucQuestion1.BorderStyle = FixedSingle
 4:    ucQuestion1.BackStyle = Opaque
 5: End Sub
 6: Private Sub ucQuestion1_LostFocus()
 7:    ' Remove the focus indicators since this control no longer has focus
 8:    ucQuestion1.BorderStyle = None
 9:    ucQuestion1.BackStyle = Transparent
10: End Sub
11: Private Sub ucQuestion2_GotFocus()
12:    ' Show the focus indicators so this control stands out to the user
13:    ucQuestion2.BorderStyle = FixedSingle
14:    ucQuestion2.BackStyle = Opaque
15: End Sub
16: Private Sub ucQuestion2_LostFocus()
17:    ' Remove the focus indicators since this control no longer has focus
18:    ucQuestion2.BorderStyle = None
19:    ucQuestion2.BackStyle = Transparent
20: End Sub
```

```
21: Private Sub ucQuestion3_GotFocus()
22:      ' Show the focus indicators so this control stands out to the user
23:      ucQuestion3.BorderStyle = FixedSingle
24:      ucQuestion3.BackStyle = Opaque
25: End Sub
26: Private Sub ucQuestion3_LostFocus()
27:      ' Remove the focus indicators since this control no longer has focus
28:      ucQuestion3.BorderStyle = None
29:      ucQuestion3.BackStyle = Transparent
30: End Sub
```

ANALYSIS Listing 8.3 shows the code needed to more visibly indicate the current question to the user. This code is added directly to the host application through the code window. Event routines are defined for the GotFocus and LostFocus events for each of the three question controls on the host application. In this application the control properties BorderStyle and BackStyle are set up to normally have no border and have a transparent background.

The GotFocus event routine for each control turns on the control's border and makes the background opaque when the control receives focus. When the user shifts focus to that control, he will see it suddenly displayed with a background color and border, in contrast to the other question controls. The LostFocus event routine sets the control back to normal appearance by changing back the BorderStyle and BackStyle settings.

Figure 8.3 shows the host application with focus on the second question after this new code is in place. Compare the application shown in Figure 8.2 to that of Figure 8.3. Even the least observant of users will now probably be able to determine which question he is responding to!

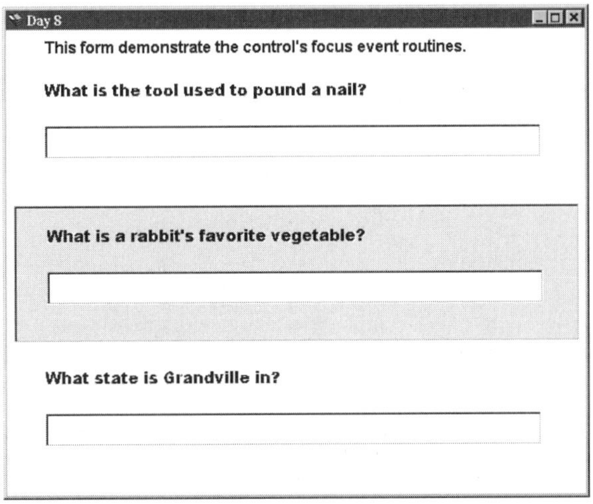

Figure 8.3.

A question application with a highlighted background and border to indicate question focus.

This example shows you how you interact with a control's events from a host application. You will not find this code in the Day 8 sample solution, however. That's because it can be refined even further. The indicate-focus capability is such a nice feature for the question control that you might want to include it in every application that integrates the control. In that case it would make more sense to add the indicate-focus code to the control itself rather than implement it in the host application over and over. To do this you need to know how to use the UserControl object's events within the controls you create.

UserControl **Events**

The four events summarized in Table 8.2 are the only events automatically available as part of your control after you create a new one. However, you can handle many more events in the code that is internal to the control. If you have integrated a lot of controls into host applications, you might have had other events you expected to see on this list. For example, you might have expected to see a Click event. Most controls let the host application respond to a Click event, but the click event is not automatically available as part of a new control. For instance, there is not a Click event that is part of the automatically exposed Extender object. There is an internal Click event for the control. This event is made available through the UserControl object that serves as the basis of your control.

NOTE

> An external or exposed event is an event your control raises. Exposed events can be handled by event-handling routines that are a part of the host application that integrates a control. Internal events, on the other hand, are events your control responds to. An internal event might be raised by a Visual Basic object or a constituent control that has been included as part of your aggregate control. Regardless of where it comes from, an internal event can be addressed through an event-handling routine that you can add to your control. Exposed events are the building blocks for a host application. Internal events are the building blocks for the control itself.

The UserControl object provides many other helpful predefined internal events. You don't have to carry out any special activity to have these events at your disposal when you create a control. They are predefined for you as part of the UserControl object that is the basis for every control. Table 8.2 shows the complete list of events the UserControl object raises.

Table 8.2. Predefined internal events for UserControl.

Event Name	Description
AccessKeyPress	Raised when the user presses control access key
AmbientChanged	Raised when ambient properties change
Click	Raised when click occurs on control
DblClick	Raised when double-click occurs on control
DragDrop	Raised when object is dropped on control
DragOver	Raised when object is dragged over control
EnterFocus	Raised when control or constituent gets focus
ExitFocus	Raised when focus leaves control
GotFocus	Raised when UserControl area gets focus
Hide	Raised when control is made not visible
Initialize	Raised when application first creates control instance
InitProperties	Raised when a new control instance is created
KeyDown	Raised when key is pressed down
KeyPress	Raised when key is pressed
KeyUp	Raised when key goes up
LostFocus	Raised when UserControl area loses focus
MouseDown	Raised when mouse button goes down
MouseMove	Raised when mouse is moved
MouseUp	Raised when mouse button goes up
OLECompleteDrag	Raised when OLE drag is complete
OLEDragDrop	Raised when OLE DragDrop occurs
OLEDragOver	Raised when OLE DragOver occurs
OLEGiveFeedback	Raised after OLE DragOver event
OLESetData	Raised for GetData method with unloaded data
OLEStartDrag	Raised at the start of OLE drag
Paint	Raised when object is exposed and needs repainting
ReadProperties	Raised when loading old instance with saved state
Resize	Raised when control is resized
Terminate	Raised when all control references are cleared
WriteProperties	Raised to save state of object instance

8

There is quite a variety of events available. Most likely you will only deal with a small subset of these when you create a control based on the specific needs of the control you are crafting. Many of these events, such as OLESetData, are quite specialized and are infrequently used. Other events, such as EnterFocus, are more commonly handled. You can find full documentation on all these events in the Visual Basic help file by looking up the topic UserControl on the index tab. From there, click on Events to see detailed definitions for the entire list of supported events summarized in Table 8.2.

You declare an event-handling routine for the internal events in your control just as you do for exposed events in a host application. The event-handling routine name must consist of the name of the object raising the event, followed by an underscore, followed by the name of the event. The declaration includes the list of relevant parameters. You can determine the parameters by referring to the help file. You can also use the drop-down selection boxes at the top of the code window to specify the object (such as UserControl) and event (such as EnterFocus) for which you want to define an event handler. This will insert the code declaration right into your code window, with appropriate parameter declarations already defined for you.

A UserControl Event Example

Now it's time to return your attention to the focus-indication problem you considered earlier in this lesson. You saw how you can modify the GotFocus and LostFocus events of the control in the host application to provide a handy indicator of which control is active. It is even better for your control integrators if you provide this support directly in your control by responding to a UserControl internal event. Then the integrators who use your control don't have to worry about providing the exposed event code to build this capability. The capability will already be built right into your control for anyone who uses it, with no further code required.

Before you begin to implement this capability in your control, first remove the GotFocus and LostFocus event routines from your test application. Go to the code window for the test form, highlight these event routines, and press the Delete key to delete them from the host application code. Then bring up your control through the project window. Display its UserControl area and double-click on it to view the code area for the control. Type in the event-handling routines shown in Listing 8.4.

Listing 8.4. Code to highlight the current question using internal UserControl events of the control.

```
1: Private Sub UserControl_EnterFocus()
2:
3:     ' Show the focus indicators so this control stands out to the user
4:     Me.BorderStyle = FixedSingle
```

```
 5:    Me.BackStyle = Opaque
 6: End Sub
 7: Private Sub UserControl_ExitFocus()
 8:
 9:    ' Remove the focus indicators since this control no longer has focus
10:    Me.BorderStyle = None
11:    Me.BackStyle = Transparent
12: End Sub
```

ANALYSIS Listing 8.4 shows the code needed to visibly indicate the current question to the user. This action all takes place within the control, using the UserControl EnterFocus and ExitFocus event-handling routines on line 1 and line 7, respectively. The EnterFocus event is raised whenever focus moves to the UserControl or any constituent control contained within UserControl. Therefore, using this event guarantees that the code will be carried out no matter how the user shifts focus to your control. When the EnterFocus event-handling routine is called, it simply sets the BorderStyle and BackStyle properties of UserControl. This is the same technique used in the example in Listing 8.3, which carried out this capability at the host application level. Likewise, the ExitFocus event-handling routine will change the BorderStyle and BackStyle properties of UserControl back to their normal settings.

Your test form will look and behave the same way it did in Figure 8.3 after you make this modification. The key difference is that now this behavior is being driven within the control. The test application no longer has to respond to exposed events of the control to show the user which question is active.

NOTE

SAMPLE The final test application with this change in place is available in the Day8QuestionControl.vbg group project file in the Samples\Day08 directory.

There is just one more change to make to fully round out the focus indicator in your control. Some integrators might love your new feature. Other integrators might hate it if they do not want the distraction of a very visible border and background shifting from question to question. It is good control design etiquette never to force a feature on your users. A better approach for the focus highlighting would be to add a corresponding property—FocusIndicator. If the integrator of the control sets this to True, you can carry out the highlighting. If the integrator sets it to False, you carry out no special highlighting of the current control.

Use the wizard to add the FocusIndicator property to the question control. Then insert an if-then condition in the control's EnterFocus and ExitFocus events. The modifications to your control code that relate to this property are shown in Listing 8.5.

Listing 8.5. Focusing handling based on a `FocusIndicator` property setting.

```
 1: Dim m_FocusIndicator As Boolean
 2: Public Property Get FocusIndicator() As Boolean
 3:     FocusIndicator = m_FocusIndicator
 4: End Property
 5: Public Property Let FocusIndicator(ByVal New_FocusIndicator As Boolean)
 6:     m_FocusIndicator = New_FocusIndicator
 7:     PropertyChanged "FocusIndicator"
 8: End Property
 9: Private Sub UserControl_EnterFocus()
10:
11:     If Me.FocusIndicator = True Then
12:         ' Show the focus indicators so this control stands out to the user
13:         Me.BorderStyle = FixedSingle
14:         Me.BackStyle = Opaque
15:     End If
16: End Sub
17: Private Sub UserControl_ExitFocus()
18:
19:     If Me.FocusIndicator = True Then
20:         ' Remove the focus indicators since this control no longer has focus
21:         Me.BorderStyle = None
22:         Me.BackStyle = Transparent
23:     End If
24:
25: End Sub
```

ANALYSIS This code has the effect of ensuring that the focus indicator changes are only carried out when the application integrator has set `FocusIndicator` to `True`. Note that property entries also were made to the `InitProperties`, `ReadProperties`, and `WriteProperties` event routines to carry out storage and retrieval of the property setting. Those changes are not shown here because they are of the standard format used for every property. The final test application with this change in place is available in the `Day8QuestionControl.vbg` group project file in the `Samples\Day08` directory.

Finally, set this property to `True` for each question control on your test form. You now have implemented a flexible, full-functioned level of focus indication that can make all the users of your control happy!

Guaranteed Events

The `EnterFocus` and `ExitFocus` events used in the preceding sample are internal events that occur only under specific circumstances. In other words, they do not necessarily occur every time the application that includes your control is carried out. They occur only in response to user actions as the user interacts with the application and your control. Many `UserControl`

8

events are in this category of circumstantial events. There is another group of events that will occur every time an application with your control is used, regardless of the user's interaction patterns. Consider these to be guaranteed events. Like death and taxes, there is no avoiding them. And it often is not wise to ignore them either!

You saw a list of all the internal events of `UserControl` in Table 8.2. Only a subset of these events falls under the category of guaranteed events. Those events are listed in Table 8.3, and they are listed in the sequential order in which they are likely to occur.

Table 8.3. Guaranteed events for the `UserControl`.

Event Name	Description
`Initialize`	Raised when application first creates control instance
`InitProperties`	Raised when new control instance is created
`ReadProperties`	Raised when loading old instance with saved state
`Resize`	Raised when control is resized
`Paint`	Raised when object is exposed and needs repainting
`WriteProperties`	Raised to save state of object instance
`Terminate`	Raised when all control references are cleared

Most of these events apply both when you are designing your control and when your control is running within an application. However, some of the events, in particular `WriteProperties`, apply only to design time when a control is integrated into an application. These events will be considered in more detail on Day 10, "Coding for the Design Environment."

The `Initialize`, `Resize`, `Paint`, and `Terminate` events have not been used yet for the question control. They are of more relevance for advanced controls that carry out activities such as painting their own interface rather than relying on constituent controls. The `Resize` event can take on a special importance in control design. This is because you, as control designer, do not normally have a say in how big your control will be when it is integrated into an application. The integrator can make it large or small, regardless of your default size. If you wanted to adjust the size of constituent objects within your control accordingly, you would rely on the `Resize` event for this purpose.

You had some brief exposure to many of the other events during earlier lessons as you saw code created by the ActiveX Control Interface Wizard. The wizard generates statements automatically to carry out the assignment of initial values to your control properties in the `InitProperties` event. You used the wizard to generate code to retrieve and save property settings in the `ReadProperties` and `WriteProperties` events.

The InitProperties, ReadProperties, and WriteProperties events are typically defined for any nontrivial control. They are the means by which a control retrieves its property value settings when it starts up. Listing 8.6 shows these event-handling routines, which you have already put in place for the question control in the course of the previous days' lessons.

Listing 8.6. The InitProperties, ReadProperties, and WriteProperties event-handling routines.

```
 1: 'Initialize Properties for User Control
 2: Private Sub UserControl_InitProperties()
 3:     lblQuestion.Caption = m_def_Question
 4:     m_DisplayOnIncorrectResponse = m_def_DisplayOnIncorrectResponse
 5:     m_ExpectedAnswer = m_def_ExpectedAnswer
 6:     m_Hint = m_def_Hint
 7:     m_EnterCausesTab = m_def_EnterCausesTab
 8:
 9:     Set DisplayFont = Ambient.Font
10:
11: End Sub
12: 'Load property values from storage
13: Private Sub UserControl_ReadProperties(PropBag As PropertyBag)
14:     UserControl.Enabled = PropBag.ReadProperty("Enabled", True)
15:     UserControl.BackStyle = PropBag.ReadProperty("BackStyle", 0)
16:     UserControl.BorderStyle = PropBag.ReadProperty("BorderStyle", 0)
17:     Question = PropBag.ReadProperty("Question", m_def_Question)
18:     AnswerColor = PropBag.ReadProperty("AnswerColor", vbWindowText)
19:     DisplayOnIncorrectResponse = PropBag.ReadProperty _
20:         ("DisplayOnIncorrectResponse", m_def_DisplayOnIncorrectResponse)
21:     ExpectedAnswer = PropBag.ReadProperty("ExpectedAnswer", _
22:         m_def_ExpectedAnswer)
23:     Hint = PropBag.ReadProperty("Hint", m_def_Hint)
24:     m_EnterCausesTab = PropBag.ReadProperty("EnterCausesTab", _
25:         m_def_EnterCausesTab)
26:     Set DisplayFont = PropBag.ReadProperty("DisplayFont", Ambient.Font)
27:
28: End Sub
29: 'Write property values to storage
30: Private Sub UserControl_WriteProperties(PropBag As PropertyBag)
31:     Call PropBag.WriteProperty("BackStyle", UserControl.BackStyle, 0)
32:     Call PropBag.WriteProperty("BorderStyle", UserControl.BorderStyle, 0)
33:     Call PropBag.WriteProperty("Question", lblQuestion.Caption, _
34:         m_def_Question)
35:     Call PropBag.WriteProperty("DisplayOnIncorrectResponse", _
36:         m_DisplayOnIncorrectResponse, m_def_DisplayOnIncorrectResponse)
37:     Call PropBag.WriteProperty("ExpectedAnswer", m_ExpectedAnswer, _
38:         m_def_ExpectedAnswer)
39:     Call PropBag.WriteProperty("Hint", m_Hint, m_def_Hint)
40:     Call PropBag.WriteProperty("EnterCausesTab", m_EnterCausesTab, _
41:         m_def_EnterCausesTab)
42:     Call PropBag.WriteProperty("AnswerColor", txtAnswer.ForeColor, _
43:         vbWindowText)
```

```
44:    Call PropBag.WriteProperty("AnswerFont", txtAnswer.Font, _
45:    UserControl.Font)
46:    Call PropBag.WriteProperty("Enabled", Enabled, True)
47:    Call PropBag.WriteProperty("DisplayFont", DisplayFont, Ambient.Font)
48:
49: End Sub
```

ANALYSIS The InitProperties event of line 2 is called whenever a control is created. For example, when you add a new control to a test form, this event is launched. ReadProperties, as shown on line 13, will occur whenever the control is loaded. Therefore, each time you start the application, ReadProperties will occur. WriteProperties, as shown on line 30, occurs at the end of a design session or when a design container such as Visual Basic detects that a change has been made to properties. Its purpose is to preserve the property settings for the next session.

The ReadProperties and WriteProperties event-handling routines communicate property information to the container through a special parameter called a *property bag*. This contains information about all properties for the control. To a large extent you can consider it a black box you don't need much insight into. You just carry out ReadProperty and WriteProperty methods against the property bag to read and save your settings. This technique is described in Day 5, "User-Defined Control Properties," and will be considered in more detail on Day 10.

Some special considerations apply to the ReadProperties event. The ReadProperties event typically makes assignments to the properties of the control based on the setting values it retrieves. What if an invalid value had been stored? The ReadProperties event-handling routine should take this into account with additional error checking if invalid property settings could be fatal. Listing 8.7 shows one such check that could replace the original UserControl.BackStyle assignment.

Listing 8.7. Checking a retrieved property value.

```
1: svTemp = PropBag.ReadProperty("BackStyle", 0)
2: if (svTemp = 0) or (svTemp = 1)then
3:    ' Assign the saved property value
4:    UserControl.BackStyle = svTemp
5: else
6:    ' The saved property value is wacky, provide safer default value
7:    UserControl.BackStyle = 0
8: end if
```

ANALYSIS These lines of code could be inserted in the ReadProperties event-handling routine to carry out the assignment of the BackStyle property. If for some reason the BackStyle property is incorrectly retrieved, the control will still be initialized in a normal state. The control code should not raise an error at this point because the host container might not be set up to handle the error. Instead, a safe setting is assigned to the property and the application can continue on its way.

The security that such additional checks provide versus the likelihood that such errors will occur is a tradeoff the control developer must make. However, if you are designing controls for wide distribution, it is much better to err on the side of unneeded caution than to subject your control integrators to potential problems!

Exposing Constituent Events

So far you've seen two of the three sides of predefined events. You've tackled handling exposed events from a host application and handling internal events within the control code. But how do you expose predefined events from the control code to the host application? Suppose, for example, that you want to let the host application detect a click on the question text. The question text is displayed within the question control by a constituent label control. If you can expose that label control's Click event, you have achieved this goal.

The easiest way to carry this out is to once again rely on the ActiveX Control Interface Wizard. You must define a new event of the question control itself in order to expose the underlying label's Click event. The step should be familiar because you've already carried out much of the same action for adding exposed properties and methods in previous lessons. Proceed to the wizard dialog that has the caption Create Custom Interface Members. Select the New button to specify the name for your new event. Name it QuestionClick.

Then proceed to the next dialog, which has the caption Set Mapping. You can see this dialog in Figure 8.4.

Figure 8.4.

Exposing a constituent control event with the wizard.

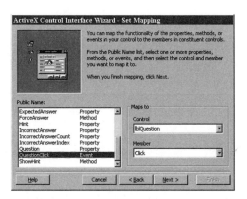

Select the QuestionClick event under the Public Name listbox so that you can map its characteristics. Then under the Caption drop-down listbox select lblQuestion. Select the Click event under the corresponding Member box and proceed through the rest of the wizard dialogs. Now you have exposed the Click event of the label control. Any host application that integrates your control can directly respond to this Click event. If you examine your control code, you will see several new lines of code pertaining to this new event. Listing 8.8 shows the additional lines. Some of the syntax keywords might look new to you. Because this approach is almost equivalent to defining your own events, the syntax is explained in more detail in Day 9.

Listing 8.8. The control code added by the wizard to expose a constituent control's Click event.

```
1: 'Event Declarations:
2: Event QuestionClick() 'MappingInfo=lblQuestion,lblQuestion,-1,Click
3: Private Sub lblQuestion_Click()
4:     RaiseEvent QuestionClick
5: End Sub
```

 The Event statement has been added to declare the QuestionClick event as a public event of the control. Then an internal event handler for a click on the constituent label raises the corresponding event with the RaiseEvent statement. This raises the specified event to containers that have provided corresponding event handlers.

Now return your attention to the test form. Add some code to take advantage of this newly exposed event. Define an event handler in the host application for the first question control. The easiest way to do this is to double-click directly on the control to bring up the code window for that control object. Then select the QuestionClick event from the rightmost drop-down listbox at the top of the code window. The QuestionClick event-handling routine will be inserted into the code window for you. You just have to fill in the body.

You can use this event to let users request a hint anytime they are answering a question. Supply the code shown in Listing 8.9.

Listing 8.9. Using the exposed constituent control event to let the user request hints at anytime.

```
1: Private Sub ucQuestion1_QuestionClick()
2:     ucQuestion1.ShowHint
3: End Sub
```

 This code is called in response to a click on the question label contained within the question control. In response, a call is made to the question control's ShowHint method to display the hint.

How to Find the Events an Object Supports

You've now been exposed to every fundamental concept of predefined properties, methods, and events. In the course of this activity, you have seen that Visual Basic control creation and integration requires you to frequently examine the properties, methods, and events of controls and other objects. The ability to quickly figure out the capabilities of a control can be a tremendous asset to you in your development. Let's consider several different approaches for rounding up this information. For the record, the following are the resources for uncovering object descriptions:

☐ The wizard—One of the easiest places to look for property, method, and event information (which I'll refer to from here forward as *object descriptions*) is in the ActiveX Control Interface Wizard itself. Just fire it up and proceed through the dialogs. It will display the underlying object descriptions for your control as well as constituent controls under the Maps To dialog.

☐ The Object Browser—If you want a really detailed look at object descriptions, you can use the Object Browser. Select View|Object Browser from the Visual Basic menu to start up this tool. It allows you to easily inspect object descriptions for any object you specify.

☐ The code window—If it's event-handling routine descriptions you want, particularly parameter information, you can always rely on the good old code window. Just display the object and event you are interested in, and the routine declaration will be added to your code window.

☐ Help files—Perhaps the best resource of all is the Visual Basic help file. Start up help, go to the Index tab, and then specify the name of the control object you're interested in. You will get hyperlinked help with a master list and description of each property, method, and event.

☐ Friends—And what about the often-used "ask the programmer down the hall" approach? Unless he happens to have a jar of candy on his desk, don't even bother to make the trip. Tried and true experience learned the hard way by legions of programmers before you has demonstrated that you are nearly always better off relying on your own detective work than your hallmate's conjecture. Besides, the information is right at your fingertips, and you are already well on your way to becoming a control creation expert!

8

Summary

In today's lesson you have discovered how to rely on the trigger points other objects send your way to help you write better programs. And you have seen how you can generate those trigger points, or events, yourself in the controls you create. This lesson's focus is on predefined events that are ready for your use without any special declarations. You have seen a fairly formal definition of events. You have also seen examples of how to respond to a control's events from a host application. You must supply an appropriately named event-handling routine in the host to have that code carried out when a given event occurs. The event-handling routine's name should consist of the object name, an underscore, and the event name.

This chapter presents the difference between internal and external events. Internal events are used within your control code to carry out its work. External events are exposed so that they can be recognized and handled externally to your control. Extender object events are automatically exposed. This chapter also considers drag- and focus-related events of this object in detail and describes a sample application that provides a focus indicator on the current question with the focus events.

Today's lesson also discusses UserControl events. UserControl events are available for use internally within your controls. A wide range of events is supported by the UserControl object. You have seen an example that handles the focus-indication display task entirely within the control, so that host application code is no longer required. We have discussed events that always occur in every application, and we have taken a look at the specific sequence of many key events and gotten an overview of the events that are related to the getting and setting of property information. We have considered an example of exposing the events of a constituent label and discussed the key reference approaches for looking up object description information. There is only one area of events that you have not yet explored: the opportunity to define your own events from scratch. This is one of the most powerful capabilities you have in your control, and it is the topic of Day 9.

Q&A

Q Are the events of the constituent controls in your aggregate control automatically exposed to the host application?

A No. The events of constituent controls can be used internally within your control but cannot normally be accessed by the host application. If you want the host application to be capable of using these events, you must explicitly expose them with an appropriate declaration statement.

Q What type of declaration is needed in your control code to expose the events of the Extender object?

A None. The Extender object events are automatically exposed as part of any controls you create.

Q What are the four events that are exposed for every control?

A The DragOver event, the DragDrop event, the GotFocus event, and the LostFocus event. These are all supported by the Extender object, which is a part of every control.

Q How can you find out which events are supported by a standard control?

A There are several ways to inspect the events for a control. You can inspect the help file that contains control information, using the help Index tab as your starting point and specifying the control name as the search. You can use the Object Browser to list events. You can see which event names are listed in the Procedure Name drop-down box at the top of the event code window for a given control. You can also use the ActiveX Interface Control Wizard mapping dialog to see which control events are available.

Workshop

Use the Object Browser to inspect the events supported by a standard label control. The question control you have constructed during the past several days' lessons uses a label control as a constituent control to display question text. You could expose any of the events for the constituent label control by adding the appropriate exposed event declarations through the ActiveX Control Interface Wizard. Consider each event of the label control in turn. Decide whether it would be useful to the host application integrator of the question control to have that event available as an exposed event of the question text label.

Quiz

NOTE

See Appendix D, "Answers to Quiz Questions," for the answer to this question.

Assume that you are the developer of a host application built on the question control. You want to present one question in the question control. Directly underneath that you want to

offer four potential answers, each displayed in a separate label. Show the code for the question control's DragDrop event that could make this type of multiple choice test possible.

Hints: You will need a way to assign the multiple choice answer to the question control so that the question control can evaluate it. You could expose the text property of the textbox control or find some other means to send the text to the control.

Day **9**

User-Defined Events

Yesterday you saw how to use the events that other objects provide for you. You can respond to events from constituent controls. You can take steps to raise those events from your control to the host application that integrates your control. You've had enough of a taste to see the power of the event model. And if you've thought about the power of events, you're likely hungry for more. There is one more capability that will vastly expand the support you can provide in your controls. That is the topic of today: user-defined events.

NOTE

NEW TERM The term *raise* was first introduced yesterday in discussing predefined events. The same concept applies to user-defined events as well. When a control *raises* a user-defined event, it calls the `RaiseEvent` statement, which notifies calling code of the event. Calling code is only notified if it has a specific defined subroutine that is named with the object name, an underscore, and the event name. If this routine exists, it will be automatically called as a result of the control raising the event. If it does not exist, no action is taken for the event. Therefore, the act of raising an event really means providing notification. Code at higher layers may or may not respond to this notification, depending on the logic at that level.

User-defined events allow you to define and raise your own events. With this capability, your control can signal the host applications that integrate it about any conditions that you want your control to react to. Recall the analogy from Day 8, "Predefined Events," of a car repeatedly circling a racetrack. When one lap remains, a standard flag is waved to alert the driver that this stage has been reached. This event notification happens at every race with exactly the same flag. Visual Basic predefined events are very similar. There are events that occur in your constituent controls and objects that are simply there for your use.

Now suppose you own the racetrack and you realize that a car on your racetrack overheats if the outside temperature hovers over 90 degrees and the drivers don't back off their speed. You could go to your tool shed and craft another flag. Since you are designing this flag, you can make it have any characteristics you want. Perhaps you make it lime green with a big ice cream cone drawing in the middle. At the next race, you wave this flag as soon as the temperature reaches 90. The race car drivers can choose to ignore it, respond by slowing down the pace, or perhaps respond by quitting the race entirely and grabbing an ice cream cone. The user-defined events you can create in your control are very similar to this hand-crafted flag analogy. You can make your own events if the predefined events don't suffice. They can have any characteristics you desire, such as your own name and parameter list. Once you raise an event from your control, it is up to the host applications to choose how to respond. Some may ignore it. Others may respond in various ways. You have done your job by providing the event, and the host applications take it from there.

When your control raises a user-defined event, essentially the control raises a flag up a flagpole that the host application can respond to if it chooses. The process of raising this flag, as you shall soon see, consists of using the `RaiseEvent` keyword with the name of the event that has occurred. You start by declaring and thereby attaching a name to an event in your control code. You identify through a meaningful name and comments what conditions cause the event to occur, so its purpose is clear. The control code is then coded to detect those conditions. When those conditions are detected, the control triggers a notice that that event has occurred. This process is called *raising* an event. The host application's event-handling routine will be called only if that event-handling routine has been defined by the application that integrates your control.

9

NOTE

If you are a deep thinker who has just started to consider events for the first time, a strange revelation may occur to you. Events are not really necessary! After all, a host application can check properties of a control. A control can set its own property settings. Therefore, if a control needs to trigger some response in the host application, it could just set the property setting accordingly. The host application just has to monitor the property setting, and when it detects a change, it can spring into action and carry out the appropriate event-handling code that is needed.

The problem is that this works at a conceptual level but not at a practical level. If a host application relied on property changes to goad it into action, it would have to continuously carry out checks of those property values, so it would notice any changes. This would require loops or timers in the host application code. If a host application had to check for several different events, it wouldn't take long to come up with a pretty messy-looking application!

A much cleaner solution is to allow the application to supply event-handling routines that are automatically triggered when an event occurs. This is a standard programming model used in many other languages and environments as well. Code design and maintenance is far easier, and system overhead far less. Visual Basic provides an elegant solution so that host applications do not have to resort to a more cumbersome manual approach.

User-Defined Event Constructs

It's time to take a closer look at the elements of the language that are used to declare user events. The first of these elements is used to define an event within your control. You have to have the event defined with an associated name before you can trigger it in your control code. The Event statement is used to declare an event, followed by the desired name for the event. You would use this statement, for example, to declare an event named MaxGuessesExceeded:

```
Event MaxGuessesExceeded()
```

This statement appears in the declarations area of your module. Once you have defined the event, it can be referenced anywhere within that module. You can then use the RaiseEvent statement from within any block of code in the module to cause the named event to occur.

The RaiseEvent statement just references the event that is to be raised by its name, as in this sample:

```
RaiseEvent MaxGuessesExceeded()
```

This causes the event to occur. Any code that integrates your control can potentially respond to this event. A host application must have a defined event-handling routine to respond. You saw on Day 8 how to define an event-handling routine in the host application. That routine is then automatically called when a predefined event of the same name occurs. Exactly the same approach is used by the host application to handle the user-defined events you supply. From the perspective of the host application that integrates your control, there is no difference between predefined events that Visual Basic and its controls raise and the user-defined events you have coded your control to raise. Every event becomes, in effect, a predefined event to the host application. As long as the host application has created a routine that consists of the name of your control, followed by an underscore, followed by the name of the relevant event, that routine will be called whenever the event is raised.

What about your old friend, the ActiveX Control Interface Wizard? You've seen how the wizard comes to the rescue. It lets you easily define properties and methods, and even expose predefined events through constituent control mappings. As you likely expect by now, the wizard can also assist you with user-defined events. However, the process for declaring an event is easy enough, as you saw from the Event statement, that you can easily declare your events without the wizard as well.

You'll see both approaches in the examples that follow. Steps are provided for creating several different types of events. These include events that are raised based on the setting of other properties and events that pass additional information as arguments. Most programmers are used to writing code that responds to events, but many programmers seldom encounter the need to raise events. This all changes when you are creating controls for other applications to integrate. The event mechanism is a very powerful form of interface between your control and the host because it is so easy for the host application to use. Fortunately, event mechanisms are also very easy for you, as the control developer, to implement, as you are about to see.

A Simple Event Triggered by a Property Setting

The time has come to implement your first user-defined event. Once again, you can build on the question control of the previous lessons. The event to be added is the MaxGuessesExceeded event. This is a fairly simple event that is used to indicate when a user has taken more than a set maximum number of attempts to correctly answer a question. Once this maximum number of guesses is exceeded, the MaxGuessesExceeded event will be raised.

NOTE

> **SAMPLE** Follow along with the examples in this chapter by modifying the Day9QuestionControl.vbg group project file under the Samples\Day09\Your Start\ directory on the book's CD-ROM. This project contains the code that is intended to be your starting point for the modifications that are described today. Copy the directory to your hard drive so you can make subsequent modifications. The material is presented in a "before" and "after" format. If you want to see today's changes already implemented, you can view the Day9QuestionControl.vbg group project that is available one directory level up in the Samples\Day09 directory.

In order to offer this as a meaningful capability to the host application, you must also provide a way for the host application to specify what the maximum number of attempts should be. You could arbitrarily pick the maximum number yourself when you write the control. But you might soon find that the maximum number you decided on doesn't fit the needs of all the applications that integrate your control. One application might be happy with a limit of 10 guesses per question. The next one might demand a limit of 20 guesses. You want your control to be as attractive and flexible as possible to the applications that integrate it to encourage its use. Therefore, it is a good idea to define a MaxGuesses property that the host application can set when it integrates your control. You will find this need often arises when you define events. Many events require corresponding properties to provide the widest range of control to an integrating application.

NOTE

> Some events require properties that go with them and others do not. How can you tell the difference? It depends on the purpose and needs of the event. Consider the standard Visual Basic controls and the events that they support. The label control generates a Click event when it is clicked on. You have no corresponding properties you can use in your host application to determine the characteristics of this event. It always occurs and you can choose to respond to it or ignore it if you wish. On the other hand, look at the timer control. The Timer event is raised by the timer control whenever the timer expires. But the timer will only expire when its Enabled property is set to True and the number of milliseconds specified in its Interval property has gone by. There is a strong relationship between properties and events in this case. The property–event relationship reflects the purpose of the event and control. You will make this subjective decision as the designer of controls and supplier of user-defined events.

The first step, then, is to define the MaxGuesses property in your sample application. Do this using the approach outlined on Day 5, "User-Defined Control Properties." Select Add-Ins and ActiveX Control Interface Wizard from the Visual Basic menu. Then proceed through the wizard pages and select the New command button on the Create dialog. Specify the name MaxGuesses. Proceed to the Set Attributes dialog and specify a type of integer and a default value of 0.

Once you have the supporting property defined, you are ready to define the event itself. Once again you can fire up the wizard by selecting Add-Ins and ActiveX Control Interface Wizard from the Visual Basic menu. You could have defined both the event and the property you just specified during the same wizard session. The definition sequence is broken into two steps here just for simplicity. Once again, proceed to the Create dialog of the wizard and select the New command button. This time specify the name of the event MaxGuessesExceeded. Also make sure that the Event radio button is checked, as shown in Figure 9.1.

Figure 9.1.

Specifying a user-defined event name through the ActiveX Control Interface Wizard.

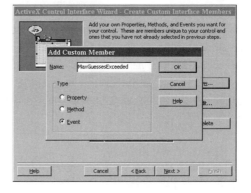

Select the OK button to complete the definition. Proceed to the next page of the wizard that is relevant to your user-defined control—the Set Attributes page. An event has no type to specify, unlike a property. However, you do need to supply a description for this event in the Description text area. Enter a description such as This event is raised if the user exceeds the maximum number of question guesses specified in the MaxGuesses property. You can see the wizard with this text entry in Figure 9.2.

There is also an Arguments field that you can supply for events on this wizard page. You will learn what that field is for in later examples. For now, just proceed through the remaining wizard pages with no other changes, and complete your wizard session so the event definition is added to your file.

Keep in mind the purpose of the event description you provided through the wizard. This description will serve as documentation of the event for the integrators of your control. When an application integrator uses your control, he will need some means to understand this event. You might provide a written manual or other documentation. However, you can count on the fact that many integrators will rely on the Visual Basic Object Browser to learn about your control. This tool, which you have seen several times during the previous days, is a very effective source of information when integrating controls. Try it yourself right now. Select View|Object Browser from the Visual Basic menu. Enter MaxGuesses in the search text area to the left of the binoculars icon. Click on the binoculars to carry out the search. This will search for this string among all the objects in your project. You will see a result similar to that shown in Figure 9.3.

Figure 9.2.

Specifying the user-defined event description through the ActiveX Control Interface Wizard.

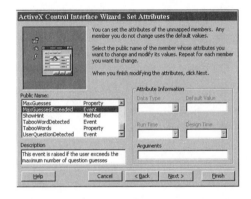

Figure 9.3.

The Object Browser with the event description for the MaxGuessesExceeded *control.*

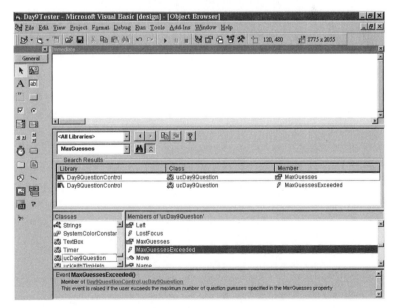

One of the match areas in the bottom listbox of the Object Browser display will be the
MaxGuessesExceeded event. Click on that event to make it the item that is displayed in the
description area. Then notice what is at the bottom of the Object Browser, just as in Figure
9.3. There is the complete description you supplied to the wizard. You can see why this
information often serves as a primary source of documentation to users of your control. It's
easily available, so integrators will rely on it. Therefore, even though a description is not
required by the wizard, you should never breeze by it.

NOTE

> This example uses the wizard to add an event. I mentioned that you
> could directly type in the equivalent event definition and bypass the
> wizard. There is even another alternative available. You can select
> Tools | Add Procedure from the Visual Basic main menu. Type in the
> name of the event and click the Event radio button. The event will be
> inserted into your code. Then you can select Tools | Procedure At-
> tributes and define the description that goes with the event. This is a
> quicker alternative to the wizard approach.

Now your event is defined and ready to be raised at the appropriate moment. If you examine
the source code behind the question control, you will see that the wizard has added a
statement like that in Listing 9.1.

Listing 9.1. The user-defined event declaration added by the wizard.

```
1: 'Event Declarations:
2: Event MaxGuessesExceeded()
```

The wizard did not add the code that actually raises the event for you. The wizard is
convenient, but doesn't have the intelligence to replace you, the control developer. The
wizard has no idea when and where you intend to trigger the event within your control code.
You must decide the appropriate place within your control logic to use the RaiseEvent
statements that will trigger this event.

In the case of the MaxGuessesExceeded event, this decision is straightforward. Recall the
methods you added on Day 7, "User-Defined Control Methods." One of those methods
relates to keeping track of the user's incorrect question responses for subsequent display. A
property called IncorrectAnswerCount was added at that time to support this incorrect answer
logging, along with the code to increment it. The module-level variable that corresponds to
the IncorrectAnswerCount property is incremented in the ProcessAnswer routine every time
an incorrect answer occurs. You can see this code in Listing 9.2.

Listing 9.2. `ProcessAnswer` routine code prior to adding the event-raising code.

```
 1: ' See if answer is correct
 2: Private Sub ProcessAnswer()
 3:
 4:     ' Only check the answer if it has not yet been evaluated.
 5:     If m_bAnswerHasChanged Then
 6:         If UCase(txtAnswer.Text) = UCase(m_ExpectedAnswer) Then
 7:             lblFeedback.Caption = "Correct!"
 8:         Else
 9:             ' Store the incorrect response in the array
10:             m_IncorrectAnswerCount = m_IncorrectAnswerCount + 1
11:             ReDim Preserve m_IncorrectAnswers(m_IncorrectAnswerCount)
12:             m_IncorrectAnswers(m_IncorrectAnswerCount) = txtAnswer.Text
13:
14:             If m_DisplayOnIncorrectResponse = ucAnswer Then
15:                 lblFeedback.Caption = "Expected Answer: " & m_ExpectedAnswer
16:             ElseIf m_DisplayOnIncorrectResponse = ucHint Then
17:                 lblFeedback.Caption = "Hint: " & m_Hint
18:                 ' Highlight answer area so user can retry after seeing hint
19:                 txtAnswer.SelStart = 0
20:                 txtAnswer.SelLength = Len(txtAnswer.Text)
21:             End If
22:         End If
23:
24:         ' Set flag so we won't check again until answer has been altered
25:         m_bAnswerHasChanged = False
26:
27:         ' Send tabkey so focus goes to next question if option is set
28:         If EnterCausesTab Then
29:             Call SendTab
30:         End If
31:
32:     End If
33:
34: End Sub
```

ANALYSIS   Listing 9.2 shows the code that checks whether an answer is correct. The module-level variable m_IncorrectAnswerCount is incremented for each incorrect answer, but no further checking on the number of incorrect answers takes place in the original code.

The code you need to add will compare the current number of incorrect answers to the maximum number allowed. The code you need to insert is shown in Listing 9.3.

Listing 9.3. The code that raises the event.

```
1:             ' See if a max number of guesses is in effect
2:             If Me.MaxGuesses > 0 Then
3:                 ' Check to see if maximum allowed guesses has been exceeded
```

continues

Listing 9.3. continued

```
4:                    If m_IncorrectAnswerCount > Me.MaxGuesses Then
5:                        RaiseEvent MaxGuessesExceeded
6:                    End If
7:                End If
```

ANALYSIS The first step to carry out is to make sure the integrator has requested that you limit the user to some maximum number of guesses. You should also provide the integrator the choice of not having any maximum cap. This is easily accomplished by using a convention for the MaxGuesses property. Recall that when you defined this in the wizard, you specified a default of 0. The code can then be structured on the assumption that when a value of 0 is defined for the maximum, the integrator has not specified any preference for a maximum limit. In that case, no further maximum limit checking is carried out.

If the maximum is specified, however, you need to carry out a check to see if the current number of guesses exceeds this maximum. The current number of incorrect answers is available through the m_IncorrectAnswerCount variable, as you have seen. The maximum number of guesses allowed is available through the MaxGuesses property you just defined with the wizard. All you have to do is compare the two values. If the answer count does exceed the maximum, the RaiseEvent statement is used to raise the event. Any host application event-handling routine for this event of the control will be called as a result.

This event-raising code should be inserted into the ProcessAnswer subroutine immediately after the area of code that increments the incorrect answer count. This is the aspect of event implementation that the wizard cannot automate for you. Just modify the ProcessAnswer routine directly in the code window and insert the new event-handling code in the appropriate area. Listing 9.4 shows the entire ProcessAnswer routine with the event modification included.

Listing 9.4. The ProcessAnswer routine with additional event-raising code.

```
1: ' See if answer is correct
2: Private Sub ProcessAnswer()
3:
4:      ' Only check the answer if it has not yet been evaluated.
5:      If m_bAnswerHasChanged Then
6:          If UCase(txtAnswer.Text) = UCase(m_ExpectedAnswer) Then
7:              lblFeedback.Caption = "Correct!"
8:          Else
9:              ' Store the incorrect response in the array
10:             m_IncorrectAnswerCount = m_IncorrectAnswerCount + 1
11:             ReDim Preserve m_IncorrectAnswers(m_IncorrectAnswerCount)
12:             m_IncorrectAnswers(m_IncorrectAnswerCount) = txtAnswer.Text
13:
```

```
14:                     ' See if a max number of guesses is in effect
15:                     If Me.MaxGuesses > 0 Then
16:                         ' Check to see if maximum allowed guesses has been exceeded
17:                         If m_IncorrectAnswerCount > Me.MaxGuesses Then
18:                             RaiseEvent MaxGuessesExceeded
19:                         End If
20:                     End If
21:
22:
23:                     If m_DisplayOnIncorrectResponse = ucAnswer Then
24:                         lblFeedback.Caption = "Expected Answer: " & m_ExpectedAnswer
25:                     ElseIf m_DisplayOnIncorrectResponse = ucHint Then
26:                         lblFeedback.Caption = "Hint: " & m_Hint
27:                         ' Highlight answer areas so user can retry after seeing hint
28:                         txtAnswer.SelStart = 0
29:                         txtAnswer.SelLength = Len(txtAnswer.Text)
30:                     End If
31:                 End If
32:
33:                 ' Set the flag so we won't check again until answer has been altered
34:                 m_bAnswerHasChanged = False
35:
36:                 ' Send tabkey so focus goes to next question if option is set
37:                 If EnterCausesTab Then
38:                     Call SendTab
39:                 End If
40:
41:         End If
42:
43: End Sub
```

ANALYSIS You can see in Listing 9.4 that the block of MaxGuesses event code was inserted immediately after the code that updates the incorrect answer information. The MaxGuesses event check code could alternatively have been added anywhere further on down in the procedure and would work just the same. However, from a practical standpoint, it is a good idea to include the new block right after the related area of code that updates the incorrect answer count. This makes the flow of the code easier to follow as you modify and maintain it in the future.

Only one step remains. You need to test your new event from a host application to make sure it is correctly supported. You must now simulate the role of the application developer who integrates your control to test this new event. For this purpose, you can use the familiar test project Day9Tester.vbp that is part of the question control project group. Since the test project is part of the same group as your control project, this test project is already loaded and ready for use.

The form named frmTest in the test project uses several question controls. Go to the form and select the first question control. Bring up the property sheet for the integrated control by selecting View | Properties Window from the Visual Basic menu. You will now see an entry for the MaxGuesses property listed in the properties view. It is set to the default value, 0. Replace this value with 3 to specify that only three tries at a question are allowed.

Now close the properties window and bring up the code window for the test form by double-clicking on the form area. Go to the object drop-down listbox at the top of the code window and select the first question control, ucQuestion1, as the current object. Now go to the procedure drop-down listbox directly to its right. This drop-down listbox shows all the events available for the current control. Your new user-defined event, MaxGuessesExceeded, appears as an entry on the list. Click this event to select it. This event becomes the current selection in the drop-down listbox and the corresponding routine declaration is added to your code window, as you can see in Figure 9.4.

Figure 9.4.

The event MaxGuessesExceeded *added to the test form from the procedure drop-down listbox.*

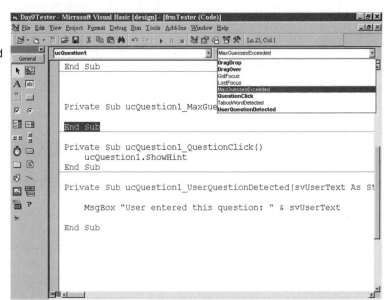

You can type your test code directly into the code window within this event-handling declaration. What will most applications do when the maximum number of guesses is exceeded? Should they hide the question control to force the user on to the next question? put up a message box to chide the user? refer the user to additional study material? Every application may handle the situation differently.

You might wonder why we didn't just write the control to carry out these activities directly. Why not have the control put up a warning message box when the maximum number of guesses is exceeded, and not even bother with an event? Again, the answer is that the needs of every application that integrates your control may be different. When you define an event within a control, you are really taking the position that you will let application integrators decide how to handle a given situation rather than fully respond to it in your control.

NOTE

> What if you know your control will be used by only one application? In that case, your need to provide a flexible interface suitable for all applications does diminish. However, even in the single application case, you'll find that providing a flexible approach pays off. The odds are very likely that as you integrate the control and modify the application, new needs will come up that you didn't originally envision. Then it is likely to be much quicker to change code at the application level based on a flexible control than to regenerate the control itself.

For this sample all you're really after is to prove that the event can be detected at the application level. So for your test simply display a message box when the event occurs. The code to enter for this response is shown in Listing 9.5.

Listing 9.5. Code to verify that the event-handling routine is called.

```
1: Private Sub ucQuestion1_MaxGuessesExceeded()
2:
3:     MsgBox "You have guessed too many times!", _
4:         vbOKOnly, "Warning"
5:
6:
7: End Sub
```

Next run the test application. Type in four different answers in the first question control. On the fourth try, you will receive a response like the one shown in Figure 9.5. Congratulations! Your first user-defined event has been handled!

Now try to enter four different answers in the second rather than the first question control. No warning message occurs. You only set the MaximumGuesses property for the first control and not the second. Each control raises events based on its own property settings, so only the first control is currently looking to see if the maximum number of guesses is exceeded. To have every control handle the maximum guesses situation, you would have to individually set properties for each one. Alternatively, you could use a control index. If you give each control that is integrated into the host application the same name and specify a separate index property value, the control is treated as a control array. Then you can make one property assignment and define one event-handling routine that will apply to all the integrated controls as a whole.

Figure 9.5.

The test application event-handling routine generating a response.

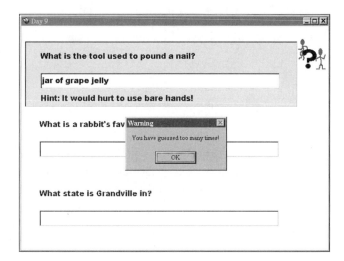

An Event with Arguments

You've seen how to raise a simple event to notify a host application of a given condition. In some cases, however, it may not satisfy your needs to simply notify the host application. You might want to make some additional information available as well. Suppose, for example, that you implement a TabooWordDetected event. The purpose of this event is to monitor the user's response and check to see if he has entered any forbidden words. (This sample is provided for illustrative purposes only, not to endorse any form of censorship built into your controls!)

If any forbidden words are detected, an event is raised that the host application can handle. It is then up to the host application integrator to decide how to deal with the situation. However, the host may want more information on which forbidden word was encountered in order to proceed. The application might display the taboo word, or provide a further error message based on the severity of the offense. In either case, the application needs to know specifically which taboo word was encountered.

Your control code that raised the event has to know what the specific word was that caused the offense, since it raised the event in the first place. What you need is just a way for your control code to share this information with the host application when the event is raised. Your first thought on how to share this information might be to provide a property that contains it. Both the control and the host application could use this property. This property approach would work. It is a bit of overkill, however. The only time the property would ever be used is in conjunction with this specific event.

Fortunately, the Visual Basic event-handling model gives you a much simpler way to share the event-related information. You can supply information right along with the event itself. This information is passed as a parameter from your control event to the host application event-handling routine.

Three levels of specification are required for an event parameter. Two of these areas are in the control itself. You must specify the parameter in the control event declaration statement. Then when you raise the event, you must pass the parameter information along with the event. The other area of specification is in the host application that integrates the control. The event-handling routine must include a matching parameter definition.

A control event declaration that includes a parameter appears like this:

```
Event TabooWordDetected(svTabooWord As String)
```

The corresponding statement to raise this event in the control then supplies the information for that parameter:

```
RaiseEvent TabooWordDetected("dagnabitall")
```

The host application event-handling routine that is called when the event is raised has a matching parameter to receive this information:

```
Private Sub ucQuestion1_TabooWordDetected(svTabooWord As String)
```

Based on these statements, the argument svTabooWord will contain the string dagnabitall when the host application ucQuestion1_TabooWordDetected routine is called.

You have already seen the key statements required to make this event work. Now turn to your sample program again and prepare to fully implement this event. The goal is to add an event that detects taboo words to your control. You certainly don't want to get in the sticky situation of imposing your views of what's taboo and what isn't on the integrators of your control. It's better to let them specify the list of taboo words your control should check for. You will need a property for this. Return to the ActiveX Control Interface Wizard and specify the property TabooWords on the Create Custom Interface Members page. Also specify a new event named TabooWordsDetected on this page. Make sure that the Property option is selected when you create TabooWords and that the event option is selected when you create TabooWordsDetected.

Then proceed to the Set Attributes Wizard dialog to set the attributes for your new property and event. First highlight the TabooWords property from the Public Name selection list. Specify an Attribute Information Data type of string, with no default value (to signal the empty string). Enter this information in the Description area: This property contains the list of all forbidden or taboo words that the user should not enter during the question response. The property value should consist of a string containing each forbidden word followed by a semicolon (;) after each word. The control does a check for the occurrence of any of these taboo words whenever a full answer is processed. If a taboo word is detected, the control raises the TabooWordDetected event, which the host application can catch.

Next highlight the TabooWordDetected event from the Public Name selection list. In the corresponding Arguments area specify the following:

svTabooWord As String

This entry tells the wizard that the new event will include a parameter named svTabooWord, which has a string data type. You also need to add a description for your new event. Supply this information in the Description area: This event is raised when a word on the taboo list, as specified in property TabooWords, is detected.

Proceed to the end of the wizard pages and close the wizard. Your new event and property definition will be saved to the project. Verify that these additions have taken place by inspecting the code and finding the new event statement and the new property statements in Listing 9.6:

Event TabooWordDetected(svTabooWord As String)

Listing 9.6. Property definitions added by the wizard.

```
1: Public Property Get TabooWords() As String
2:      TabooWords = m_TabooWords
3: End Property
4:
5: Public Property Let TabooWords(ByVal New_TabooWords As String)
6:      m_TabooWords = New_TabooWords
7:      PropertyChanged "TabooWords"
8: End Property
```

NOTE The wizard has also added property-related code to several other areas, including a module-level variable declaration and the ReadProperties and WriteProperties routines. Those are not shown here for the sake of simplicity. If you need more details on all areas affected by a new property, refer to Day 5.

The wizard has done its work. Now you have a property that the integrator can use to specify the taboo words. And you have an event that your control can raise when it detects that one of those words has been used. The next step is to modify the question control code to detect when taboo words have been used.

Various approaches can be used to implement this feature. One that keeps the implementation relatively simple is to supply a TabooWordCensor routine that is used only locally within the control. This routine checks the property list TabooWords for any sign of a taboo word and raises the TabooWordDetected event when needed. Code is also added to call the routine whenever the user enters a keystroke or changes focus away from the control.

First add the code for the TabooWordCensor routine. This code is shown in Listing 9.7. You can type the code directly in the code window, including the Sub and End Sub declaration.

NOTE

Make sure you are entering in the code window that corresponds to the question control, rather than the code window for the test form. You can verify that you are at the right code window by starting from the View | Project Explorer view on the Visual Basic menu.

Listing 9.7. Code to implement the TabooWordCensor routine.

```
 1: Private Sub TabooWordCensor()
 2:
 3:     ' Location index used in string match searches
 4:     Dim iPos As Integer
 5:     ' Used to rebuild a censored string for leftmost portion
 6:     Dim svLeft As String
 7:     ' Used to rebuild a censored string for rightmost portion
 8:     Dim svRight As String
 9:     ' Contains all the words on the taboo list
10:     Dim svRemainingTaboos As String
11:     ' The taboo word currently being processed
12:     Dim svTabooWord As String
13:     ' The string to evaluate
14:     Dim svCheckString As String
15:
16:
17:     ' Start with the entire taboo list.
18:     svRemainingTaboos = Me.TabooWords
19:
20:     ' Process the text in the answer textbox
21:     svCheckString = txtAnswer.Text
22:
23:     ' Extract each word on the taboo list and see if it
24:     ' occurs in the user string
25:
26:     Do While Len(svRemainingTaboos) > 0
27:
```

continues

Listing 9.7. continued

```
28:            ' Find the next word on the taboo list
29:            iPos = InStr(svRemainingTaboos, ";")
30:
31:            If iPos = 0 Then
32:                ' Take the last taboo word from the remaining
33:                ' string since no more separators
34:                svTabooWord = svRemainingTaboos
35:                '  Empty list of unprocessed taboo words to indicate no more
36:                svRemainingTaboos = ""
37:            Else
38:                ' Take the next taboo word based on the separator position
39:                svTabooWord = Left(svRemainingTaboos, iPos - 1)
40:                ' Remove this word from the list of unprocessed taboo words
41:                svRemainingTaboos = Right(svRemainingTaboos,
42:                    Len(svRemainingTaboos) - iPos)
43:            End If
44:
45:            ' See if the newly extracted taboo word occurs within the user string
46:            iPos = InStr(svCheckString, svTabooWord)
47:
48:            If iPos > 0 Then
49:                ' The prohibited word was found
50:
51:                RaiseEvent TabooWordDetected(svTabooWord)
52:
53:                ' Replace the prohibited word
54:                svLeft = Left(svCheckString, iPos - 1)
55:                svRight = Right(svCheckString, Len(svCheckString) -
56:                    (Len(svLeft) + Len(svTabooWord)))
57:                txtAnswer.Text = svLeft & String(Len(svTabooWord), "*") & svRight
58:
59:                ' Put the input cursor at the end of the selection
60:                txtAnswer.SelStart = Len(svCheckString)
61:
62:            End If
63:        Loop
64: End Sub
```

ANALYSIS The TabooWordCensor routine sequences through every word contained in the TabooWords property. It extracts each word and then does a comparison using the Visual Basic InStr function to see if the word is present in the answer supplied by the user. If the word is present, the TabooWordDetected event is raised. In addition, the taboo word is replaced by a series of asterisks, one for each character of the taboo word.

The message box and asterisk feedback are behaviors that you might not choose to provide at the control level. Often it is a good idea to leave the details of how to handle a condition to the host application and have a control simply raise the event for the host. Replacing text might not be what the host application integrator wants to have happen, and you could just leave all the user feedback up to the host. However, the logic is included here at the control level to illustrate that you do have the capability to merge your own processing in the control with subsequent raising of the event.

The control integrator has the option of using taboo word processing. Taboo word processing always takes place if a taboo word property string has been defined. If the integrator has not supplied this string, which is the default condition, then no taboo search occurs.

The next step is to call the TabooWordCensor routine whenever the user types a keystroke or the control loses focus. The routine should be called with each keystroke so that the user can get immediate feedback on any problem words. At first glance you might think that simply calling the routine whenever a keystroke changes is sufficient. But don't forget the complex nature of Windows! A user could copy and paste text into the question response area and then click the mouse on the next question, supplying an answer and moving on, all without ever using a keystroke. The call to TabooWordCensor when the control loses focus will address such situations.

You just need to add a single statement to call the routine:

```
Call TabooWordCensor
```

This statement needs to be added to both the txtAnswer_KeyPress event routine and the txtAnswer_LostFocus routine. These are both event routines for events that are addressed internally within the control code. You are, in turn, raising an exposed event in response to an internal event. You can modify these event routines from the control code window. Select the txtAnswer object from the drop-down list at the top-left of the code window, and then use the right drop-down list to specify the txtAnswer_Keypress and txtAnswer_LostFocus procedures in turn. Add the call statements to the top of each routine. The modified versions of these control routines, with the appropriate call statements added, are shown in Listing 9.8.

Listing 9.8. Code to implement the TabooWordCensor routine.

```
 1: Private Sub txtAnswer_KeyPress(KeyAscii As Integer)
 2:
 3:     ' Censure any taboo words that have been entered in the textbox so far
 4:     Call TabooWordCensor
 5:
 6:     ' Check if enter key was pressed
 7:     If KeyAscii = vbKeyReturn Then
 8:
 9:         KeyAscii = 0
10:         Call ProcessAnswer
11:     End If
12: End Sub
13:
```

continues

Listing 9.8. continued

```
14:
15: ' Check the answer if the user moves to next field
16: '    (in response to tab/enter keystroke or mouseclick on other control)
17: Private Sub txtAnswer_LostFocus()
18:
19:        ' Censure any taboo words that have been entered in the textbox so far
20:        Call TabooWordCensor
21:
22:        ' Evaluate the answer
23:        Call ProcessAnswer
24:
25: End Sub
```

Your control now has support for as much censorship as any integrator wishes to impose! Now you must step into the shoes of the application integrator and turn your attention to the test form to test this new capability. Select the test form `frmTester` from the Visual Basic View | Project Explorer menu. This test form includes several question controls. Select the first control and bring up the corresponding property view. Notice that the new `TabooWords` property now appears in the property view, as you can see in Figure 9.6.

Figure 9.6.

The property view for the question control with the new `TabooWords` *property.*

It is time to supply your list of forbidden words. Enter `disco;C++` in the `TabooWords` property area. The control will now raise the `TabooWordsDetected` event whenever the user types in either of these words. Add a host event-handling routine so you can see when this event occurs. To add this routine, first double-click on the first question control to bring up the corresponding code window. The `ucQuestion1` object will be selected in the leftmost drop-down list at the top of the code window, since that is the object you clicked on. Then select the `TabooWordDetected` event from the procedure drop-down list to the right. When you make this selection, an empty subroutine declaration for the corresponding event-handling routine is displayed. Even the `svTabooWord` parameter that you specified when you declared the event in your control is supplied for you in the declaration. Supply the code shown in Listing 9.9 in the event-handling routine.

Listing 9.9. The `TabooWordDetected` event-handling routine in the host application.

```
1: Private Sub ucQuestion1_TabooWordDetected(svTabooWord As String)
2:
3:     ' The prohibited word was found
4:     MsgBox "Please do not use the word " & svTabooWord & ".", _
5:         vbOKOnly & vbCritical, "Watch your language!"
6:
7: End Sub
```

ANALYSIS   This event-handling routine just displays a message box to the user when an offensive word is used. The taboo word that was detected is passed in to the routine through the `svTabooWord` parameter. This word is echoed back to the user in the message box statement.

The message box shown in Figure 9.7 is displayed when the event-handling routine is called. The host event handler could have taken more action, such as storing the response or disabling the question.

Figure 9.7.

The message box that is displayed by the host application when a taboo word is detected.

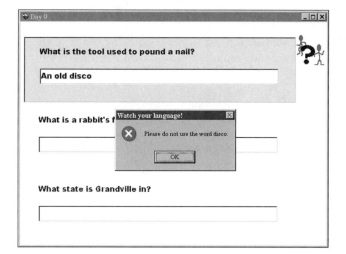

The control code itself also takes some corrective action after the event is called. After the user responds to the message box, processing flow returns to the control code right after the `RaiseEvent` (on line 51) statement in Listing 9.7. The control code replaces the taboo word with a sequence of asterisks. The user response is altered so that the offensive word is no longer visible, as you can see in Figure 9.8.

Figure 9.8.

The host application question control with the corrected text for the taboo word.

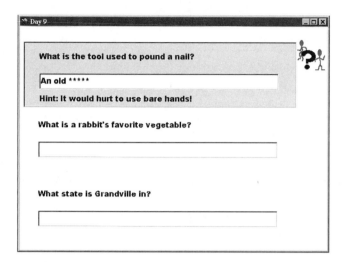

The control took the approach of notifying the host application through an event and altering behavior when a given condition occurred. It could also have simply notified the host application and left any changes up to the host. Better yet, the control could notify the host application, let the host supply a replacement for the taboo word if desired, or supply a replacement itself if the host did not. The revised code in the control's TabooWordCensor routine that accomplishes this is shown in Listing 9.10.

Listing 9.10. The control's TabooWordCensor **routine, modified to let the host application supply a taboo word replacement.**

```
 1: Private Sub TabooWordCensor()
 2:
 3:     ' Location index used in string match searches
 4:     Dim iPos As Integer
 5:     ' Used to rebuild a censored string for leftmost portion
 6:     Dim svLeft As String
 7:     ' Used to rebuild a censored string for rightmost portion
 8:     Dim svRight As String
 9:     ' Contains all the words on the taboo list
10:     Dim svRemainingTaboos As String
11:     ' The taboo word currently being processed
12:     Dim svTabooWord As String
13:     ' The string to evaluate
14:     Dim svCheckString As String
15:     ' The string to replace the taboo word
16:     Dim svReplacement As String
17:
18:     ' Start with the entire taboo list.
19:     svRemainingTaboos = Me.TabooWords
```

```
20:
21:        ' Process the text in the answer textbox
22:        svCheckString = txtAnswer.Text
23:
24:      ' Extract each word on the taboo list and see if it occurs in user string
25:
26:        Do While Len(svRemainingTaboos) > 0
27:
28:            ' Find the next word on the taboo list
29:            iPos = InStr(svRemainingTaboos, ";")
30:
31:            If iPos = 0 Then
32:                ' Take the last taboo word from the remaining string
33:                '      since no more separators
34:                svTabooWord = svRemainingTaboos
35:                ' Empty the list of unprocessed taboo words to indicate
36:                '      no more remain
37:                svRemainingTaboos = ""
38:            Else
39:                ' Take the next taboo word based on the separator position
40:                svTabooWord = Left(svRemainingTaboos, iPos - 1)
41:                ' Remove this word from the list of unprocessed taboo words
42:                svRemainingTaboos = Right(svRemainingTaboos, _
43:                    Len(svRemainingTaboos) - iPos)
44:            End If
45:
46:            ' See if the newly extracted taboo word occurs within the user string
47:            iPos = InStr(svCheckString, svTabooWord)
48:            If iPos > 0 Then
49:
50:                ' Extract strings needed to go around the prohibited word
51:                svLeft = Left(svCheckString, iPos - 1)
52:                svRight = Right(svCheckString, Len(svCheckString) - _
53:                    (Len(svLeft) + Len(svTabooWord)))
54:
55:                ' Tell the host application about the problem
56:                svReplacement = svTabooWord
57:                RaiseEvent TabooWordDetected(svReplacement)
58:
59:                ' Build the replacement string, using either the host supplied
60:                '    value or a string of "*"s if host did not supply replacement.
61:                If svReplacement = svTabooWord Then
62:                    ' Host did not supply a replacement string so fill with "*"s
63:                    svReplacement = String(Len(svTabooWord), "*")
64:                    ' Otherwise host supplied replacement in event handler
65:                End If
66:
67:                ' Replace the taboo word with the designated replacement
68:                txtAnswer.Text = svLeft & svReplacement & svRight
69:
70:                ' Put the input cursor at the end of the selection
71:                txtAnswer.SelStart = Len(txtAnswer.Text)
72:            End If
73:        Loop
74: End Sub
```

This routine now gives the host application the opportunity to supply replacement text for the taboo word. The host's opportunity occurs when the RaiseEvent statement of line 57 is processed. At that point, the code in the host's event-handling routine is carried out before the processing flow continues in the TabooWordCensor routine. The host's event-handling routine receives the parameter that is specified in the RaiseEvent statement. If the host's event-handling routine modifies that parameter, the changes are reflected back in the TabooWordCensor routine when processing flow returns to that routine. Therefore, a change from the host application is picked up as the new replacement value for the taboo word by the control.

You can provide your own replacement string in the host application event-handling routine now with this new version of the control. The revised version of the host application event-handling routine is shown in Listing 9.11.

Listing 9.11. The host application TabooWordDetected event handler, modified to provide a replacement value.

```
 1: Private Sub ucQuestion1_TabooWordDetected(svTabooWord As String)
 2:
 3:      ' The prohibited word was found
 4:      MsgBox "Please do not use the word " & svTabooWord & ".", _
 5:          vbOKOnly & vbCritical, "Watch your language!"
 6:
 7:      ' Specify a replacement for the control to display
 8:      svTabooWord = "<Censored>"
 9:
10: End Sub
```

This event-handling routine displays a message box to the user when an offensive word is used. It also replaces the taboo word with the phrase <Censored>. This replacement is carried out by assigning it to the event-handling parameter svTabooWord. SvTabooWord is the parameter passed to this routine by the control to indicate the taboo word that was found. That parameter, in turn, is read back by the control when this routine completes and processing flow returns to the control. Any changes you make to the parameter within this routine will be reflected back to the control since this is a ByRef parameter. If the parameter had been declared to be a type ByVal parameter, changes would not be reflected back to the control.

The message box that the host application would display in response to an offensive entry remains the same as that shown in Figure 9.7. However, the appearance of the corrected text will differ. The corrected text is now supplied by the host application, as you can see in Figure 9.9.

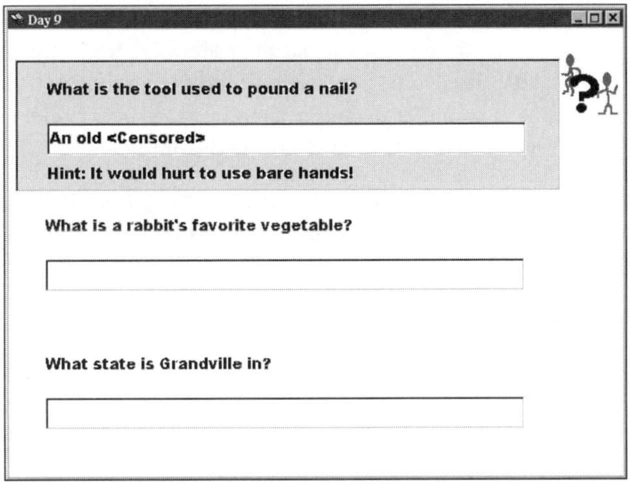

Figure 9.9.

*The question control
with corrected text
supplied by the host
application event
handler.*

Now you have a property that allows the integrator to restrict the user from using certain words in a question. By default, the control will replace these words with a series of asterisks when they are detected. However, you have also provided an event that an integrator can use to catch the occurrence of any word he doesn't like. Then he can use the event handler to replace it with whatever he chooses. You've provided a very flexible solution to the integrator, which is what events are really all about!

Summary

Today you have learned all about user-defined events. First you saw how to declare these events in your control using two key statements. The first statement was the Event keyword used to declare events. The second statement was the RaiseEvent keyword used to raise events within the code once an expected event condition is encountered. You have also learned how you can react to these events in a host application through an appropriately named event-handling routine, just as you can react to the predefined events.

You have seen how to use the ActiveX Control Interface Wizard to define events. The first event you added to the question control today is the MaxGuessesExceeded event. This event is raised when the number of user guesses for a question exceeds the number specified in the question control's MaxGuesses property. This example provides a good look at the basics of raising a user-defined event in a control and handling it in a host application.

You have also learned how to implement the TabooWordDetected event. This event is raised when a word on the TabooWords property list is detected within the user answer string. The host application can respond to the event in the manner of its choosing, and then the control will replace the offensive text with a series of asterisks. You have also seen how the control routine can be modified to replace the offensive text with some value supplied by the host event handler itself. The control code and the host event handler can exchange information through the parameter that is declared with an event declaration. The information can flow in both ways—from control to host and from host to control.

You may not have a need for your own censorship. But if you develop many controls, you will certainly have a need for your own events. If you have followed along with the examples in this chapter, you now have all the knowledge you need to produce sophisticated user events of your own.

Q&A

Q **What declaration statement would you use to declare an event named `QuestionMarkDetected` within your control?**

A Use the event statement `Event QuestionMarkDetected()` to declare the event.

Q **Do you need to include your control name as part of the name of an event that you declare within a control?**

A No, you can name the event anything you wish. However, when you reference the event from a host application, you must precede the control event name with the name you gave the control when you incorporated it into your application.

Q **Assume that you have declared the event `QuestionMarkDetected` in your control. What statement do you need to use in your control code to trigger that event in a host application with a corresponding event-handling routine?**

A Use the raise statement `RaiseEvent QuestionMarkDetected()` to raise the event.

Workshop

Consider what happens when you provide an event in a user-defined control. You are giving the host application the option to provide code to handle that event. On one hand, you want to provide as wide a range of events as possible to give the application integrator the most flexibility in using your control. On the other hand, designing additional events in your control takes time and can add to the complexity of the control code you maintain. It can also add to the complexity the integrator encounters in learning about your control's capabilities.

You must decide on a happy medium when designing your control so you support key events but not unneeded ones. Use the Object Browser to take a look at the events of the standard label control. How many of these events have you ever used in your application? Do all the events seem necessary to you? Are there any additional events you can think of that should be here but are not present?

Quiz

NOTE   See Appendix D, "Answers to Quiz Questions," for the answer to this question.

Add another event to the question control named `UserQuestionDetected` that is raised immediately when the user enters a question mark as part of his answer. You will have to supply an event declaration as well as modify the following `txtAnswer_KeyPress` routine:

```
' Process answer in response to enter key
Private Sub txtAnswer_KeyPress(KeyAscii As Integer)

    ' Censure any taboo words that have been entered in the textbox so far
    Call TabooWordCensor

    ' Check if enter key was pressed
    If KeyAscii = vbKeyReturn Then
        KeyAscii = 0
        Call ProcessAnswer
    End If
End Sub
```

Note that the ASCII code for the question mark character is 63.

Day 10

Coding for the Design Environment

So far you've learned how to use and create your own properties, methods, and events for ActiveX controls. You've learned quite a bit, and you now know most of the fundamental concepts needed to put a control together. But there's lots more to learn yet. One of the issues you've likely been thinking about throughout the lessons so far is the different ways your control behaves at design time versus runtime. In fact, writing a control is much more difficult than writing a simple application. A control has to behave properly both at runtime and at design time.

One of the reasons ActiveX controls behave and are designed so much differently than anything else in Visual Basic is that they have to be built to run properly for both the developer at design time and the user at runtime. That's also why Microsoft has added a number of new properties, events, and methods that at first might be a bit bewildering and strange to you. Even though you've been working with many of them so far, you may be a bit hazy on how they all work together, when they are called and when they're not, and why they are called in the order they are.

In today's lesson you'll learn about all the events that take place and the order in which they occur when you work with controls in various scenarios. You'll see the order of events as you first create a control on a form, dragging it from the toolbox over onto the form. Then you'll see what happens when it comes time to run your project within Visual Basic. You'll also learn what happens when you save the form, as well as when you compile a program that uses the control and run it as an executable. Throughout this lesson, I'm going to assume you're working with an ActiveX control being placed on a Visual Basic form within a standard Visual Basic application. It is possible to use ActiveX controls in many other platforms besides Visual Basic, but the overall sequence of events remains pretty much the same. On Day 21, "Licensing, Distribution, and Security," you'll learn about one possible exception—using controls on the Internet. But for now, the model you'll see should hold true for most platforms you're likely to use ActiveX controls within.

Placing the Control in the Container

Let's begin at the start. Imagine yourself sitting at your desk with a brand-new Visual Basic project open on your desktop. You see the question control icon in the Visual Basic toolbar, as shown in Figure 10.1.

Figure 10.1.

A brand-new Visual Basic application with the question control sitting in the toolbar to the left.

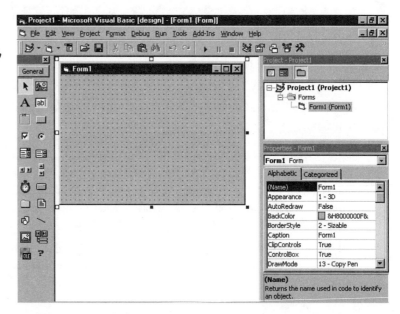

10

Now suppose you want to use the question control on the form. You double-click on the question control toolbox icon, and the control appears on the form. Being the astute programmer that you are, you know there are events going on behind the scenes. After all, you're in design mode and the control is properly displayed on the form. You even see a set of default properties the control knew enough to set for you. What makes all these things happen? Figure 10.2 shows a chronological list of all the events that take place to get you from the toolbox to a usable control on the form.

Figure 10.2.

The order of events when a control is first created.

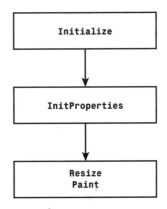

As you can see, only a few simple events are called. Let's look at each one in detail.

Initialize

One of the first things that happens before the control even appears on the form is that any constituent controls within your control are created in memory. Then the first event, Initialize, occurs. Keep in mind that any code that you put in the Initialize event is executed before the control is even placed on the form. This would be the place to put in code required before the control is to appear on the form. Most of the properties, methods, and events of the control cannot be accessed yet, so you should avoid setting properties, executing methods, or raising events here. In many cases, you don't even need to worry about the Initialize event. But it is there for cases where you want to add code to prepare the system or the control in some way before it appears on the form.

Let's look at a simple example of using the Initialize event. Suppose you want to keep track of the total amount of time from when the control first appears on a form. One way to do this is to create a new property that indicates the elapsed time since the control was initialized. The easiest way to do this is to create a variable that stores the time during the Initialize event. Then you simply create a property that can only be read at runtime, which indicates the elapsed time by comparing the current time with the startup time.

To try this yourself, open up the question control for Day 10. This control is on the CD-ROM that accompanies the book in the Samples/Day10 subdirectory. Open the question control project and bring up the code window for the question control. In the declarations section of the UserControl module, enter the statement

```
Private m_StartupTime As Single
```

This statement creates a private variable called m_StartupTime with the Single data format. This variable will store the number of seconds since midnight, indicating at what point the control was initialized. Now bring up the UserControl object's Initialize event and enter this statement into the event:

```
m_StartUpTime = Timer
```

When the control initializes, the Timer function is called. This function returns the number of seconds since midnight, which then gets stored in the m_StartupTime variable. Now you can create the property procedure. Since this property is a read-only property and is only available at runtime, you only need to add one property procedure. The procedure is shown in Listing 10.1.

Listing 10.1. The Property procedure for ElapsedTime.

```
1: Public Property Get ElapsedTime() As Integer
2:     ElapsedTime = CInt(Timer - m_StartupTime)
3: End Property
```

As you can see, this simple Property procedure calculates the current number of seconds since midnight and subtracts that value from the number of seconds at initialization time. The difference, which is a floating-point value, is converted into an integer and returned through the Property procedure. This approach is limited, of course, if the control is active for more than 24 hours. More sophisticated code would be required to handle that case. But anyone who was still answering questions after 24 hours needs a break anyway, so let's not worry about that here!

This is only one simple illustration of how you might use the Initialize event. Use Initialize whenever you need to store initial data, set up variables a certain way, or perform any other introductory tasks. Just remember that you won't be able to access the Extender object, the Ambient object, or any events, properties, or methods other than those already provided by the UserControl object. You'll use the Initialize event again in a moment.

10

InitProperties

After `Initialize` is called, the `InitProperties` event is called next. This event is the place where you should write code to set the default values for all the properties of the instance of the control being placed in the container. This event will be called only once—the time that the control is first placed into the container. It is the appropriate time for assigning default properties to the control. For instance, the code used for the question control is shown in Listing 10.2.

Listing 10.2. The question control's `InitProperties` procedure.

```
1: Private Sub UserControl_InitProperties()
2:
3:     lblQuestion.Caption = m_def_Question
4:     m_DisplayOnIncorrectResponse = m_def_DisplayOnIncorrectResponse
5:     m_ExpectedAnswer = m_def_ExpectedAnswer
6:     m_Hint = m_def_Hint
7:     m_EnterCausesTab = m_def_EnterCausesTab
8:
9: End Sub
```

Notice here that none of the properties are set directly using `Property` procedures. You should avoid doing so in this procedure. Why? Suppose you used all the `Property` procedures to set the properties. When each `Property` procedure is called, Visual Basic will typically execute the `PropertyChanged` statement, notifying Visual Basic that a property has been changed and that it needs to write out the new property value to the form.

The problem with this is that `PropertyChanged` is really intended to trap changes the programmer makes himself so that only those properties that were changed get stored to the form when it is saved. If you call the `Property` procedures, Visual Basic thinks that all the properties have been changed, when really all you're trying to do is set the initial values of the properties. Therefore, it's best to set the variables used to store the properties directly. Is this safe, you ask? After all, you don't get the benefit of all the error checking. No, but you're the designer, not someone who's using the control. You can make sure the properties are set correctly, so you shouldn't have to worry about errors here!

Resize **and** Paint

Now the control is ready to be displayed on the form. The `Resize` and `Paint` events are called when the control is first displayed. The `Paint` event is called as a result of Windows painting the control for the first time. The `Resize` event gets called because the control is sized for the first time. These two events give you the opportunity to write code to handle any resizing or repainting issues that you need to take care of.

One very beneficial use of the `Resize` event is to make sure the user can't change the size of your control. In many cases, you may be designing a control that you don't want the user to resize. In the case of our question control, this certainly holds true. Bring up the test application in design mode and resize the question control. You'll notice that you can change the size of the control any way you like, and if you make it smaller, the controls become clipped off the edge. Consider, for example, the form shown in Figure 10.3.

Figure 10.3.

Resizing a control can lead to undesirable effects if you don't plan for it in your code!

To avoid a problem like this, you have two options—you can either prevent the user from resizing the control or you can resize all the constituent controls and other elements within your control to match whatever size the programmer changes the control to. The first solution is easiest because the second solution means you'll have to write a lot of code. In a case like ours, it wouldn't be worth the effort. Realistically speaking, you don't need to give the user the ability to resize the control because it would likely be too small anyway.

One way to make sure the control size doesn't change is to enter these two lines of code in the `Resize` event:

```
Width = 8580
Height = 2190
```

Go ahead and add them to the question control. Then switch back over to the test application's form in design time. Try to resize the control, and you'll find that it always defaults to its original size. The code you've just entered may seem a bit crude. After all, if you change the size of the control during development, you now have these hard-coded numbers in your code that you'll have to change as well. A better solution is to use variables and store the original width and height of the control in the Initialize event. Bring up the question control in design mode and add the following two variable declarations in the declarations section of the question control module:

```
Private m_Orig_Width As Integer
Private m_Orig_Height As Integer
```

Then, in the Initialize event, enter the following two statements:

```
m_Orig_Width = Width
m_Orig_Height = Height
```

Finally, in the Resize event, enter these statements:

```
Width = m_Orig_Width
Height = m_Orig_Height
```

Go ahead and bring up the test form. Delete the existing question control and bring up a new one from the toolbox. Notice that the control appears in its proper size right from the start. If you try to change the size, it snaps back to its original size every time.

Since the Initialize event executes first, and the Height and Width properties are available in the Initialize event, you can assign them to the variables to store them for use later. Then, when the Resize event occurs, you can be sure Width and Height are always set to their original values. If the host program or the programmer decides to change the size of the control, their decision will be overridden by the code in the Resize event. You may find this handy technique useful when you create your own controls. You'll learn a lot more about the Paint and Resize events on Day 19, "Self-Painting and Invisible Controls."

That completes the list of events required to bring the control into existence. The programmer should now have a control on the form with a set of default units properly set in the property sheet.

Moving from Design Mode to Run Mode

Now that you've got the control inside the form, suppose you decide to change a few properties, add some code to the form, and then run the project to test it. When you run the project, you'll essentially be taking the project out of its design environment and be switching over to its runtime environment. You may or may not have your project options set to ask whether to save the form before you run the project. For now, let's assume you don't ask to save when you want to run. What will be the sequence of events? Figure 10.4 shows you a chronological list.

Figure 10.4.

The sequence of events in moving from design mode to run mode.

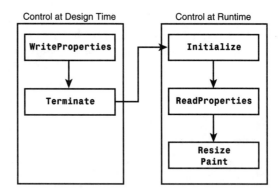

In order for Visual Basic to switch from design mode to run mode, Visual Basic has to close the form and run the application. When the form closes down, the instance of the control that appears on the form has to be destroyed. Let me take a minute to explain what a *control instance* is. Figure 10.5 shows you a graphical representation of the form and the control at design time and runtime.

Figure 10.5.

ActiveX control instances at design time and runtime. This illustration shows the form saved on disk.

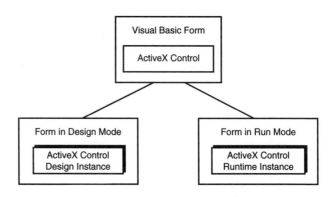

When you place a control on a form at design time, you actually create an instance of that control in memory for the control. This is illustrated in the box to the bottom-left of Figure 10.5. Later, when you decide to save the form, Visual Basic will store the control as it exists on the form. The saved, physical form is typically placed on disk. This is illustrated in the box at the top of the figure. Notice that any instances of the form are derived from the physical copy once it's been saved to memory. Any time an instance of a form exists, whether at design time or at runtime, an instance of the control exists as well. That will never change unless the control is physically deleted from the form.

What, then, is an instance? It's a copy of the control in memory that exists as long as the form exists in memory along with it. There are two types of instances—design-time instances and runtime instances. When a form is in design mode, a design-time instance of the control exists. When the project switches from design time to runtime (the user does this by running the program from within Visual Basic), the design-time instance of the control is destroyed and a new runtime instance of the control on the form is created.

Now when the design-time instance of the control is destroyed, that doesn't mean that the control itself is destroyed. A record of its existence remains on the physical form shown in the top of Figure 10.5. When the project moves into run mode, a new runtime instance is created. Also remember that only one instance of the control can exist at a time. When the program is in design mode, the design-time instance exists. When the program moves to run mode, the runtime instance is created and the design-time instance is destroyed. Both cannot exist in memory simultaneously.

WriteProperties

Refer to Figure 10.4, which shows you the sequence of events in moving from design mode to run mode. The first event that takes place is, as you might expect, `WriteProperties`. All the events on the left side in Figure 10.4 are events that take place in the design-time instance of the control. The events to the right take place in the runtime instance. The events execute from top to bottom, left to right.

Since the control is about to switch from design mode to run mode, the instance of the control in design mode needs to be destroyed. Then the instance of the control in run mode can be created. Before the design-mode instance is destroyed, the properties the programmer may have changed in design-mode first need to be saved. That is the purpose of `WriteProperties`, and that's why it takes place here.

The properties are written into the form that resides in memory. If the programmer decides to save the form before running the program, those property values will be stored permanently on disk as well as inside the form. If the user does not attempt to save the project before running the application, the copy of the container stored in temporary memory is used instead.

NOTE

Visual Basic will write the properties to the temporary copy of the form in memory. Only when the user decides to physically save the form will the property values be written to disk.

Terminate

The only step that remains is to destroy the instance of the control in design mode. Before that happens, the Terminate event is called. This is your last opportunity to write any additional code you need to implement before a control instance is destroyed. After the event executes, consider the instance of the control gone. A new instance of the control is now ready for creation during runtime.

Initialize

At this point, Visual Basic is ready to run the project. It is at this point that the form, and the question control within the form, switch from design mode to run mode. As you can see from Figure 10.4, the order of events shifts over to the right-hand side of the figure, showing the events that take place at runtime. The first event to be called is the Initialize event. The Initialize event is used in the same way as before, except that this time the control is being created in the runtime environment rather than in the design-time environment.

ReadProperties

Now that the control is initialized, it is created and exists in memory. The next step is to pull the properties out of the form and assign those properties to the control. That is why the ReadProperties event is called. It's up to you to write the code necessary to make sure the properties are correctly loaded from the form and placed into the instance of the control. Fortunately, when this event is called, the Extender and Ambient objects are available because the container has already been created. Here is the place where all the properties are read and assigned to the appropriate variables. Listing 10.3 shows the ReadProperties event of the question control.

Listing 10.3. The ReadProperties event of the question control.

```
1: Private Sub UserControl_ReadProperties(PropBag As PropertyBag)
2:
3:     UserControl.Enabled = PropBag.ReadProperty("Enabled", True)
4:     UserControl.BackStyle = PropBag.ReadProperty("BackStyle", 0)
5:     UserControl.BorderStyle = PropBag.ReadProperty("BorderStyle", 0)
6:     Question = PropBag.ReadProperty("Question", m_def_Question)
7:     AnswerColor = PropBag.ReadProperty("AnswerColor", vbWindowText)
8:     DisplayOnIncorrectResponse =
9:         PropBag.ReadProperty("DisplayOnIncorrectResponse",
10:            m_def_DisplayOnIncorrectResponse)
11:    ExpectedAnswer = PropBag.ReadProperty("ExpectedAnswer", _
12:                                  m_def_ExpectedAnswer)
13:    Hint = PropBag.ReadProperty("Hint", m_def_Hint)
14:    m_EnterCausesTab = PropBag.ReadProperty("EnterCausesTab", _
15:                                  m_def_EnterCausesTab)
16:
```

```
17:     UserControl.BackColor = PropBag.ReadProperty("BackColor", &H80FF80)
18:     txtAnswer.ForeColor = PropBag.ReadProperty("AnswerColor", &H80000008)
19:
20:     Set Picture = PropBag.ReadProperty("Picture", Nothing)
21:
22:     Set lblQuestion.Font = PropBag.ReadProperty("QuestionFont",
23:     ➥Ambient.Font)
24:     Set txtAnswer.Font = PropBag.ReadProperty("AnswerFont", Ambient.Font)
25:     Set lblFeedback.Font = PropBag.ReadProperty("HintFont", Ambient.Font)
26:
27:     lblQuestion.ForeColor = PropBag.ReadProperty("QuestionColor",
28:     ➥&H80000012)
29:
30: End Sub
```

In this event, all the constituent controls and the UserControl object itself are set based on the property values they have inside the container. While the user is in runtime, the properties of the control are changed in the control within the application. The executable file has no way of permanently storing the properties of an ActiveX control within the form, so when the application shuts down, any changes made to the properties of the ActiveX control are simply discarded.

Resize **and** Paint

Once again, the Resize and Paint events are called. The only difference is that this time, they take place in the runtime environment rather than the design environment. You'll learn more about these events on Day 19. For now, just remember that if there is any difference in the way your control is displayed at design time versus runtime, you must handle that here if it is not automatically handled for you. For example, if you set the InvisibleAtRuntime property of the UserControl object to True, the Resize and Paint events will never be executed. If not, however, any special kind of drawing operations you'll handle here.

That's all there is to bringing up a control in runtime. What happens when the user decides to exit the application? Since the application was started in Visual Basic, the runtime environment will be switched back over to the design-time environment. What happens in this case? Read on!

Moving from Run Mode Back to Design Mode

When the application switches back into design mode, the behavior is a bit different from that of going from design time to runtime. Figure 10.6 shows the sequence of events that take place.

Figure 10.6.

The order of events when closing a Visual Basic form when switching from runtime to design time.

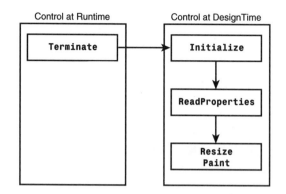

At first glance, the order of events simply looks reversed. But if you look closely, you'll see several key differences.

Terminate

The first event that takes place occurs in the runtime instance of the control. The control is destroyed, first calling the `Terminate` event. You might ask yourself why the `WriteProperties` event doesn't get fired off like it did when moving from design time to runtime. The reason is very simple. At design time, the user can change the property values and they are saved in memory or on disk at that point. At runtime, however, the user cannot permanently change the properties within the form. The code in the program can change the properties of the runtime instance, but they do not carry back over to the design-time instance. If any properties do change at runtime, they are simply discarded when the program exits. That's why when you change the `Caption` property of the question control at runtime, for instance, the caption doesn't stick when you switch back to design mode. The value you used in design mode reappears because it is stored inside the form as a property value.

Initialize

That's all there is to do with the runtime instance of the control. It is now gone. The next step is to create a new instance of the control in design mode. The first event that is always called when a new instance of a control is created is the `Initialize` event. There's really nothing new to say about this event that we haven't said already, so let's move on.

ReadProperties

As you might expect, the next step is for the design-time instance of the control to read back in the property values it had stored in the form before it went into runtime. Therefore, the control reads its properties as they are stored either in the memory copy of the container or from the disk they are stored on. Notice, however, that this time `InitProperties` is not called like it was when the control was created from scratch. The only time `InitProperties` is called is when the programmer places the control into a container from the toolbox or when a control is created the very first time in any particular environment. After that, the control exists in the container, regardless of whether it's at design time or runtime. When the programmer switches back and forth between the two, that same control is being used in either environment.

Resize **and** Paint

When the program returns from runtime to design time, the size of the control is set to whatever it was the last time the program was in design mode. That is, any changes made to the control at runtime, including resizing changes, are not saved. When the program switches back to the design environment, the `Left`, `Top`, `Width`, and `Height` properties are restored based on their settings within the container into which the control was saved.

So, as you can see from the order of events, there is one fundamental difference between the control at runtime and the control at design time. All the changes made to the control at runtime are not stored in the container within which the control resides. They are all discarded as soon as the runtime session is over.

Closing the Container

Now suppose you have an open form in the Visual Basic design environment. Your control is prominently displayed on the form. What if you want to close down the project to go take a nap? I do it all the time! See Figure 10.7 to see the order of events that take place.

In this case, Visual Basic has to destroy the current instance of the control—the instance in design mode. Visual Basic executes two events to help make that happen—`WriteProperties` and `Terminate`. `WriteProperties` is used to write the properties of the control into the form. At this point, the form resides in temporary memory. If the programmer decides to save the form when it's closed, this temporary form in memory will be transferred onto a disk for permanent storage. `WriteProperties` ensures that if the programmer decides to save the form, it will be saved with the latest property changes made to the control. If the programmer doesn't save, all the property changes will be lost.

NOTE   It's important for you to understand the distinction between an instance of a control and the control itself. When a control is placed on a form in design mode, an instance of that control exists in memory.

> The control is always a part of the container. When the program
> switches from design time to runtime, the design-time instance of the
> control is destroyed and the runtime instance of the control is created.
> Either way, the control exists on the form. The term *instance* simply
> refers to the fact that the control is currently being used by the
> program.

Figure 10.7.

*The order of events
when closing a Visual
Basic form by exiting
the Visual Basic
environment.*

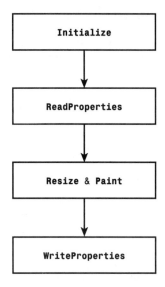

After the properties are written to the instance of the control in memory, and then to
permanent form on disk (if the user so chooses), the `Terminate` event is triggered. After that
event, the instance is destroyed, along with the form's instance. Then the entire project is
closed down and you're all set. Time to take that nap!

Reopening the Project

After your extended nap, you decide it's time to reopen the project and get busy once more.
As soon as you open the project and then open the form that holds your control, Visual Basic
needs to create a brand-new instance of your control in the design-time environment. The
events for this situation are shown in Figure 10.8.

10

Figure 10.8.

The sequence of events in reopening a project in Visual Basic that contains an ActiveX control.

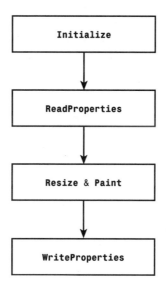

Let's explore each event in detail once more.

Initialize

The first event, as you might expect, is the `Initialize` event. This is always the first event a control receives when an instance of the control is brought into existence.

ReadProperties

The next event that is called is `ReadProperties`. Here is where the properties of the control that was saved to the form on disk are reloaded into the instance of the control in memory.

Resize **and** Paint

The control is then displayed and its `Resize` and `Paint` events are called. This ensures that any code you add to these events is carried out in aiding the proper display of the control in the design environment.

WriteProperties

You might be surprised to find `WriteProperties` in the list. Why would the `WriteProperties` event need to be called after the properties were just read in? When the properties are read off a disk, this additional event is necessary because the `ReadProperties` event takes the properties out of the disk file and then needs to write them to the instance in memory. To do this, Visual Basic needs to call the WriteProperties event. Thus, both events are called in this case. Normally, only one of the events is called at a time because the instances are always in memory. But in this case, since the properties are being brought from disk into memory, both events need to take place.

Compiling the Project

Now let's move on to some of the other interesting scenarios that may occur. Suppose you choose to compile into an executable file the project that uses your control. What happens then? Figure 10.9 gives you a diagram of the events in sequence.

Figure 10.9.

The sequence of events inside an ActiveX control when you're compiling the control into an OCX in Visual Basic.

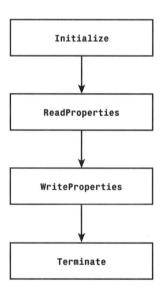

Visual Basic loads each form into memory and writes the contents into the executable file. What that means for your control is that the Initialize, ReadProperties, WriteProperties, and Terminate events will be called, all in that order. ReadProperties reads the properties from the disk, and WriteProperties places them in memory. Visual Basic then constructs the executable file and, in the process, removes the form from memory, destroying the instance of the control that was temporarily brought in. This triggers the Terminate event. If code in any of these events generates a compilation error, Visual Basic will be more than happy to notify you while the program attempts to compile. How nice can Visual Basic get?

10

Running a Compiled Program or Component

When a compiled executable is run outside the Visual Basic environment, the initial property values are read from within the executable file itself. Therefore, the usual events are called. Figure 10.10 shows the ordered sequence of events within the control.

Figure 10.10.

The sequence of events within an ActiveX control when the control is being run in its compiled version.

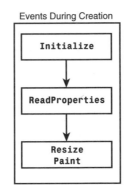

Events During Creation

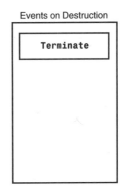

Events on Destruction

Initialize is called first, followed by the ReadProperties and Resize and Paint events. When the form within the application is unloaded from memory, the Terminate event is called. Again, notice that no properties are ever saved when a control is in the runtime environment. If the program changes any properties, they only apply to the runtime instance of the control. Once that instance is destroyed, as Figure 10.10 illustrates, any properties that were set are simply discarded. If, for some reason, you need to save properties of a control in the host application, you must write code yourself to store the properties in the Registry or in some other file. The control is incapable of doing so automatically for you at runtime.

Controls Placed on World Wide Web Pages

One other note about ActiveX controls. So far in our discussion you've been using controls in Visual Basic or in compiled programs. If an ActiveX control is placed in an HTML document, however, the rules change somewhat. You assign properties to an ActiveX control by specifying them between the <OBJECT> and </OBJECT> tags that specify the ActiveX control. Unlike properties set in the property sheet at design time within Visual Basic, these properties are not retrieved using ReadProperties, nor are they saved using WriteProperties.

When a Web page appears in a browser, any controls that come up on the page behave as if they were being created for the first time. In other words, the ReadProperties event is never called, but InitProperties is called every time. So what happens when an ActiveX control is loaded into a Web browser by way of an HTML document? Figure 10.11 illustrates the sequence of events.

Figure 10.11.
The sequence of events within an ActiveX control when you're running the control in a Web page on the Internet.

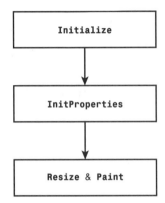

As you can see, the only events called are Initialize, InitProperties, and then Paint and Resize. The properties you set within the <OBJECT> and </OBJECT> tags that define the control are assigned once the control is running. When the page is unloaded from the browser, the Terminate event is called and any properties that were set or changed while the page was in the browser are discarded. You'll learn much more about ActiveX controls and how to design them for the Internet on Day 20, "Designing Controls for the Internet."

Runtime and Design-Time Coding Considerations

Now that you've seen the basic sequence of events in the various scenarios presented in today's lesson, here are a few more concepts you need to understand, along with some tips for writing your controls to work properly both at design time and at runtime.

Always Provide Adequate Error Handling!

One of the issues you, the developer of the control, need to watch out for is placing code in an event that causes an error. Errors can and do occur, but if they occur, you need to handle them as gracefully as possible. You should, of course, place error-handling code in every procedure of your control. Two event procedures in particular that you must watch out for, however, are the WriteProperties and ReadProperties events. As you know, WriteProperties only occurs when a design-time control instance is being destroyed. ReadProperties, on the other hand, occurs both at design time and at runtime. If the programmer assigns a property to the control whose setting is invalid, the procedure must be able to deal with the problem by putting up a message box or setting the property to some other value. If, however, the error is not handled with an error handler of some kind, the programming tool may not be able to gracefully recover from the error and the programmer may lose all the property settings he just made. How can you prevent this from happening? At the bare minimum, place an error handler in your procedure that looks something like the one shown in Listing 10.4.

Listing 10.4. Placing an error handler in the WriteProperties procedure.

```
 1: Private Sub UserControl_WriteProperties(PropBag As PropertyBag)
 2:
 3:     On Error Goto WriteProperties_Error
 4:
 5:     Call PropBag.WriteProperty("BackStyle", UserControl.BackStyle, 0)
 6:     Call PropBag.WriteProperty("BorderStyle", UserControl.BorderStyle, 0)
 7:     Call PropBag.WriteProperty("Question", _
 8:                             lblQuestion.Caption, m_def_Question)
 9:     Call PropBag.WriteProperty("DisplayOnIncorrectResponse",
10:             m_DisplayOnIncorrectResponse, m_def_DisplayOnIncorrectResponse)
11:     Call PropBag.WriteProperty("ExpectedAnswer",
12:             m_ExpectedAnswer, m_def_ExpectedAnswer)
13:     Call PropBag.WriteProperty("Hint", m_Hint, m_def_Hint)
14:     Call PropBag.WriteProperty("EnterCausesTab",
15:             m_EnterCausesTab, m_def_EnterCausesTab)
16:     Call PropBag.WriteProperty("AnswerColor",
17:                             txtAnswer.ForeColor, vbWindowText)
18:     Call PropBag.WriteProperty("AnswerFont", txtAnswer.Font, _
19:                             UserControl.Font)
20:     Call PropBag.WriteProperty("Enabled", Enabled, True)
21:     Call PropBag.WriteProperty("DisplayFont", DisplayFont, Ambient.Font)
22:
23:     Exit Sub
24:
25: WriteProperties_Error:
26:
27:     MsgBox "An error has occurred in writing your properties! Please make_
28:             sure each property is set properly.", vbExclamation, "Question_
29:             Control Property Save Error"
30:
31:     Resume Next
32:
33: End Sub
```

First of all, the statement

```
On Error Goto WriteProperties_Error
```

will make sure that if an unforeseen error occurs, the program will automatically jump down to the section of code labeled `WriteProperties_Error`. This, in turn, will execute the code

`WriteProperties_Error:`

```
MsgBox "An error has occurred in writing your properties! Please make_
       sure each property is set properly.", vbExclamation, "Question_
       Control Property Save Error"

Resume Next
```

which puts up a message box telling the developer there is a problem saving a particular property and then moves on with this statement:

```
Resume Next
```

Error handling is discussed in much greater detail on Days 13, "Debugging Controls," 14, "More Control Debugging Techniques," and 15, "Preparing Your Control for the Real World," when debugging and testing are taken up.

NOTE   Control error handling, debugging, and testing are covered in great detail on Days 13, 14, and 15.

Similarly, the `ReadProperties` event should include a similar error-handling approach. If an unhandled error takes place in the `ReadProperties` event, the program could cause the design-time programming environment to shut down or it could cause the program to terminate unexpectedly at runtime. So make sure your events can handle errors gracefully at all times.

Beware of Faulty Property Procedure Code

As you saw on Days 4, "Predefined Control Properties," and 5, "User-Defined Control Properties," there are several ways to implement `Property` procedure code. One way is to have a `Property Let` procedure set some internal variable that is used later on during a method or some other event in the control. Other properties, when set, change parameters, call functions, invoke methods, or raise events immediately when the property is being changed. If, for some reason, one or more of the pieces of code within the property procedure is unable to succeed, you may decide to avoid setting the property. For example, you may have a property in a control called `BaudRate` that sets the baud rate of the device attached to your serial port, say a modem. Your code might look like that shown in Listing 10.5.

Listing 10.5. A `Property` **procedure that may not successfully set the property.**

```
 1: Public Property Let BaudRate(ByVal New_Baud As BAUD_RATE)
 2:
 3:     Dim bSuccessful As Boolean
 4:
 5:     bSuccessful = ChangeBaudRate(New_Baud)
 6:
 7:     If bSuccessful Then
 8:         m_Baud = New_Baud
 9:         PropertyChanged "Baud"
10:     End If
11:
12: End Property
```

Alternatively, you could implement the `Property` procedure in such a way that it always succeeds, such as shown in Listing 10.6.

Listing 10.6. A `Property` **procedure that always successfully sets the property.**

```
 1: Public Property Let BaudRate(ByVal New_Baud As BAUD_RATE)
 2:
 3:     m_Baud = New_Baud
 4:     PropertyChanged "Baud"
 5:
 6: End Property
```

Using the approach in Listing 10.4, if the function `ChangeBaudRate` fails for some reason, the property will not get set. If the programmer of the host application that is using your control goes ahead and tries to change the property and the `ChangeBaudRate` function fails, the property setting he changed to won't remain in the property sheet. In fact, the property setting that was there before he tried to change will pop back up on the property sheet. In the case of Listing 10.5, the user will always be able to change the property with success. In both cases, since an enumerated type is used, you can be confident that no illegal values were entered into the property. What, then, is the best solution?

The first approach has the advantage of allowing the user to make an immediate change to the configuration of the control based on a property. The second approach requires that the baud rate be changed later, say when the user attempts to communicate with the device over the serial port. In most cases, the best approach is the latter. If the user tries to change a property at design time and the value isn't accepted, the programmer is very likely to think that the control has a bug in it when, in reality, the control simply may not be able to do what the property setting mandates. On the other hand, if you always allow the property to be changed by setting a simple variable, the user gets immediate, successful feedback. Later, when the user attempts to communicate with the device over the serial port, you can pop up a message box telling the user that the instrument can't communicate due to an incorrect baud rate setting. Then the programmer can make the changes necessary to get the application working properly.

You want to try to minimize the amount of unconventional behavior, especially within the design environment. If this property gives you trouble, perhaps you should use a method called ChangeBaudRate, which could return True or False depending on whether it was successful. You, the designer, must make the final call. But you want to make your control as predictable and reliable as possible at all times.

A Picture Is Worth a Thousand Words

You've heard this cliché before, but it still rings true, even in the world of control creation. When a developer sees your control in the toolbox, you want to make sure the bitmap used to represent your control is attractively presented and gives the developer some sort of visual cue as to what the control does. The question control, fittingly enough, gives the user a picture of a question mark. This should form in the mind of the person who sees the bitmap in the toolbox that the control represented there has something to do with a question. If the bitmap had been, say, a picture of a paper and pencil, the viewer would be much more uncertain of exactly what the control represents.

Make sure you keep your bitmap simple, but use attractive colors and effective graphics to get your point across. The bitmap should be 16 pixels wide and 15 pixels high, and never use an icon—icons will not scale well on monitors with different resolutions.

Keep in mind that it's not always easy to do this. If your control puts together a random series of words for your monthly status report and mails off the meaningless dribble to your boss, a picture of a piece of notebook paper probably won't convey the idea very well. If, however, you have a miniature picture of the status report, or even better, a picture of your boss, you're likely to give your viewers a much better idea of what the control does. And hey! Won't your boss be overjoyed at how much work everyone's doing? I thought so.

A Good Name Says a Lot

In addition to providing a practical and useful picture for the toolbox when your control is displayed there, you should provide a useful tooltip when the user moves the mouse over the control. What is a tooltip? Take a look at Figure 10.12.

10

Figure 10.12.

The question control displayed with the tooltip activated.

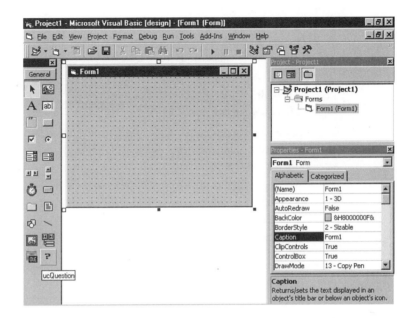

The small box that appears with the text ucQuestion is the tooltip text. The text that appears is taken from the name you assign to the UserControl object via the Name property. You should make sure you assign a name that gives the user an idea of what the control is. In the case of the question control, the name ucQuestion is used. The uc prefix is added to the name because the object in which the control resides is a UserControl object, ergo the prefix uc. You'll also notice that a new control is given the name ucQuestion, plus a number is tacked on at the end. Similarly, the image control has the name Image, and when you place an image control on a form, the control is given the name Image1. Make sure the name you assign to your UserControl object—that is, your ActiveX control—is easy to read and understand.

Summary

Many differences exist in the way a control behaves at runtime versus design time, particularly the order of events that are executed in each state. Here are the important concepts presented in today's lesson that you should remember:

☐ ActiveX controls are typically created and saved within containers. These containers, such as a Visual Basic form, are usually saved to disk. While loaded in memory, however, they are represented by instances within memory. Controls can exist in memory either in design-time instances or in runtime instances, but never both at the same time with the same control.

☐ When you create a control from scratch by dragging it from the toolbox onto an empty form, the `Initialize` event is called for the control. `Initialize` is used for code that must get called every time a control instance is created.

☐ The `InitProperties` event then takes place. This event sets the control properties to their default values. It is only called this one time, never to be called again for that particular control.

☐ The `ReadProperties` event takes place whenever a container is being loaded from disk or an instance of a control is being created in the runtime or design-time environments. It is very important that the `ReadProperties` event can handle errors gracefully.

☐ The `Resize` and `Paint` events are called whenever the control is first displayed on the screen, resized, or in need of repainting to the screen.

☐ The `Terminate` event is called whenever an instance of a control is destroyed.

You have learned the various sequences of events that occur during all kinds of different scenarios a control can pass through. These concepts are important to understand in the overall design of a control. You need to understand why an event executes, when it executes, and how to write code for the event. Later in the book, when you start learning about error handling, testing, debugging, and then more advanced concepts such as invisible controls, self-painting controls, and subclassed controls, just to name a few, the concepts you've learned in this chapter will be invaluable!

Q&A

Q Why can't I save and retrieve properties when I place my controls on a Web page?

A Web pages are unlike containers such as Visual Basic forms because they are completely temporary. Since a Web page can be distributed across the entire Internet, there is no easy way to store properties of ActiveX controls unless you could somehow write them to the user's computer and retrieve them later on. This capability could present security problems and garble up a system with a lot of information never to be used later, so that kind of idea is unlikely to be accepted.

Q I don't really understand the difference between the `Initialize` event and the `InitProperties` event?

A These two events are different because `Initialize` is executed every time a control instance is brought to life, whether it be in design mode or run mode, saved or not saved, in a Web page or in a Visual Basic form. `InitProperties`, on the other hand, is only executed the first time a control is brought to life within a form.

10

Q Do all the events of an ActiveX control execute in this order in other programming environments, such as Visual C++ or Delphi?

A In order for an ActiveX control to work, any programming environment in which you use the control must be able to support ActiveX controls. This might seem like an obvious statement, but if an environment supports ActiveX controls, all the events will take place as advertised. Web browsers that support ActiveX controls work a bit differently because there essentially is no programming environment—no container in a design environment—into which properties can be entered and saved. It is very possible, however, that such a tool may arise and give the programmer this capability. Basically, any programming tool that can save ActiveX control properties in the container and support the ActiveX control technology would make use of these events in a consistent manner.

Q Are there cases where some of these events will not execute?

A The only event that may never execute is the `WriteProperties` event. If Visual Basic is never notified via `PropertyChanged` (which is commonly placed within a property procedure) that a property has changed, it will need to call `WriteProperties` at the point where it may be needed. There is no danger in failing to call `WriteProperties` if none of the properties have changed since they were last saved.

Q I want to make sure my control handles errors correctly! Where do I go for more information?

A In Days 13, 14, and 15 you'll get much more information and experience with error handling, debugging, and testing.

Workshop

Take the question control from yesterday's lesson and place breakpoints in each of the events of the control. If no code exists in the event, insert a `Break` statement there in order to force a breakpoint. Go through the process of creating a new control, saving the form on which the control resides, running the project in which the control exists, and so forth. Do the events execute in the order you expected as revealed in this lesson? Any unexpected surprises?

Quiz

NOTE See Appendix D, "Answers to Quiz Questions," for the answers to these questions.

1. How many times is the InitProperties event called when you run a project previously saved to disk?

2. My ActiveX control needs to determine where it's located before it is loaded into the container. What event do I use to place that code?

3. Modify the following WriteProperties function so that it could gracefully recover from an error:

```
Private Sub UserControl_WriteProperties(PropBag As PropertyBag)
    Call PropBag.WriteProperty("Caption", m_Caption, m_def_Caption)
    Call PropBag.WriteProperty("Language", m_Language, m_def_Language)
    Call PropBag.WriteProperty("Answer", m_Answer, m_def_Answer)
End Sub
```

10

Day 11

Property Pages

Today you're going to learn about a very useful and powerful feature of ActiveX controls—property pages. Property pages give you the ability to create powerful properties that go beyond the simple ones you've seen so far, particularly on Days 3, "The Programming Environment," and 5, "User-Defined Control Properties." You need to know at the outset, however, that while property pages give you an incredible amount of power and flexibility, they are also more difficult to learn and can become incredibly complex.

The goal of this lesson is to make the challenging task of putting together a property page a simple one. I will step you through the creation of a very simple property page so you can see the framework and construction of property pages in general. Then, step by step, you'll see how to add functionality and complexity to your property page to make it even more useful to the programmer who uses your control. By the end of this lesson, you will be able to add your own property pages to your control interface and be able to make them quite functional and flexible. This lesson presents you with the basics. Tomorrow, you'll go a bit more in depth. Although I won't delve into all the advanced details of property pages, you should find enough information in these two lessons to get you moving in the right direction.

This lesson begins by introducing you to property pages and showing you how and why they can be important and useful to you. Then, from the ground up, you will learn how to build property pages. You'll start out simple and build from there. In tomorrow's lesson, I'll show you some more of the advanced issues you have to take into account as your property pages grow more dynamic and complex. As you journey through this exciting process, you'll be able to use the examples in this lesson to gain practice and confidence in building property pages so that you can create your own. So let's get started.

What Is a Property Page?

If you've never used a property page before, you're in for a real treat. Odds are that you have, at one point or another, used a property page, perhaps without even realizing it. So just what is a property page, anyway? A *property page*, at first glance, looks very much like a form. It basically consists of a set of controls that you use together to set one or more properties for a control. Yes, you can set more than one property on a page. But you can also use a series of controls that, when taken together, can set a single property.

Property pages, then, come in two basic varieties. First, you can create a property page to group several similar properties together. In the user's mind, all the properties fit together nicely and therefore work well together on a single property page. If you like, you can create several property pages, all of them grouping various properties together, and then combine those pages into a single interface. This gives the user a clean interface of property sheets to work with. As an example, let's consider a custom control that comes with Visual Basic 5.0.

If you haven't already done so, bring up Microsoft Visual Basic 5.0 and create a new project. If Visual Basic asks you for a project type, go ahead and select the standard EXE project. A blank form should then appear on your desktop. Choose Project|Components from the Visual Basic menu. This brings up a dialog box with a list of components. Scroll down the list until you find a control named Microsoft Access Calendar 7.0.

NOTE

This control may or may not appear on your components list, depending on whether you have Microsoft Access installed on your computer. If you can't find the control in the list, don't worry. Just keep reading the information here. This is just one of many examples of custom controls with property sheets. You can understand this example just as easily by reading along and looking at the figures.

If it's not already checked, click in the checkbox to the left of the component and click the OK button. You should then see the calendar control's icon appear in the toolbox within the project workspace. Click on the toolbox bitmap and drag it onto the new form. Make the calendar large enough so that it takes up most of the space on the form. Your workspace should now look similar to that in Figure 11.1.

Figure 11.1.

Using the Microsoft Access 7.0 calendar control within Visual Basic 5.0.

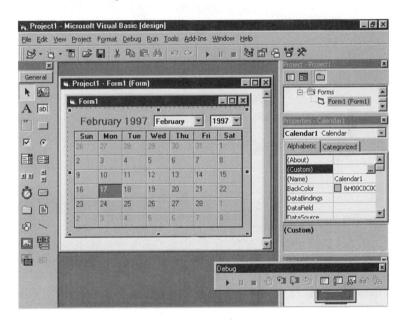

Now that you have the calendar control on the form, click on the properties sheet within your workspace. At the top of the property sheet list, you'll notice a special item on the list called Custom. It's special because it's one of the few items at the top enclosed in parentheses. It turns out that this particular item is not a property; instead, it brings up a series of property pages for the user of the control. To see the property pages, double-click the Custom item. This results in the dialog shown in Figure 11.2.

You'll notice that the caption of this dialog reads Property Pages. Great! You've brought up the right dialog. The first thing you'll notice is that this is very much unlike setting a typical property. Here you're actually presented with a user interface that allows you to set a bunch of various settings on the dialog. You'll also notice a series of tabs across the top of the dialog— in this case, three. What you're actually seeing here are three separate property pages all brought together within a single item back on the property sheet called Custom. In this case, you can actually change 10 properties in a single dialog! That's pretty powerful. And what's really great about this property page is that the user has them all grouped together in one place. That means the user can set all the properties right here instead of setting them one-by-one in the property sheet.

Figure 11.2.

A series of property pages for the calendar control. Here you see the General property page.

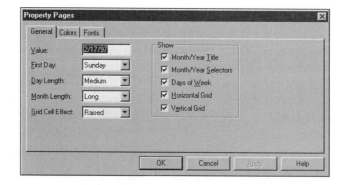

Notice, however, that the properties also happen to appear separately in the property sheet. If you look closely at the property sheet, you'll find the FirstDay, DayLength, MonthLength, and all the other properties listed in the property sheet individually. So the property page you're looking at isn't the only place the programmer using your control can set the properties. If he wants to, he can set them individually using the property sheet. What you, the control designer, have essentially done is to make the process of setting the properties more convenient for the programmer using your control.

Now click on the property page tab labeled Colors. The property page shown in Figure 11.3 should then appear.

Figure 11.3.

The Colors property page of the calendar control.

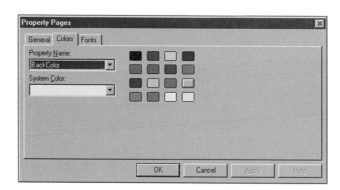

This property page is a bit different. Here you find a drop-down listbox, Property Name, that gives you the ability to choose from a wide variety of properties. What do all these properties have in common? They are all used to set colors for various constituent controls and other elements within the calendar control! You can, of course, set all these independently on the property sheet, but here is a convenient place to set them all. Below this listbox is another one, labeled System Color. This listbox gives the programmer using your control the ability to select from a series of Windows default colors. Or, if you prefer, you can select from the series of colors to the right of the two listboxes.

Now click on the Fonts tab to bring up the third property page. You should see a dialog similar to the one in Figure 11.4.

Figure 11.4.

The Fonts property page of the calendar control.

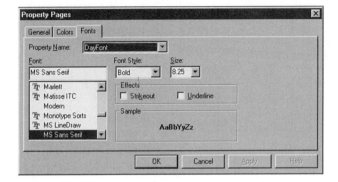

Once again, at the top, you see a listbox that is filled with all the properties within the calendar control that allow you to set a font for one of the elements of the calendar control. Notice all the functionality you get here. You can set the font type, size, style, and effects, and even see a sample of what the resultant font looks like when you're finished.

Now that you've seen three property pages, you may have a few questions. First of all, notice that the three property pages are all connected together in one dialog. Later in today's lesson, you'll learn how to tie multiple property pages together like this. This dialog is invoked using one item on the property sheet. You'll also learn how to do that. If you look closely at the property pages, you'll notice that they are all raised higher than the backdrop of the dialog. On the dialog itself are the OK, Cancel, Apply, and Help buttons. It turns out that all you, the designer, have to do is to create the property pages—that is, the part that's raised in the dialog. Visual Basic automatically takes care of the buttons, as well as the switching between the tabs if you have more than one property page in your set.

So right off the bat you can see that there's really quite a bit going on here. Not only do you have to design each property page, but you also have to connect them together and connect the entire set back to the property sheet of the control. You also have to write all the code to successfully set all the properties when the pages are displayed, as well as to store any properties that change while those pages are available to the user. Yes, you have your work cut out for you. This is a good time to be thankful you've got this book to guide you. Hey, maybe this wasn't such a bad idea after all.

So far, you've seen examples of property pages that essentially group together a series of properties that are similar in some way. The other reason you might create a property page is to set a single property with a series of controls designed to make it easier to set the property or to help you build the correct property setting. Consider the following example. Go back to the list of components in your project and select Microsoft Multimedia ActiveX Control. Place the control on your form, which should make the form appear similar to the one shown in Figure 11.5.

Figure 11.5.

A series of property pages for the Microsoft Multimedia ActiveX control. Here you see the General property page.

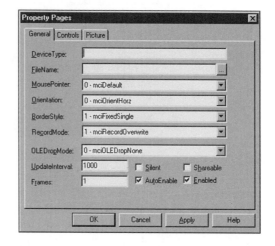

In this case, let's move directly to the third property page, labeled Picture. That dialog is shown in Figure 11.6.

Figure 11.6.

The Picture property page of the Microsoft Multimedia ActiveX control.

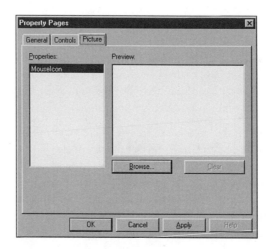

The goal in this property page is to set one property: the MouseIcon property, located in the listbox to the left. To help you make this decision, you are presented with three controls—a Browse button, allowing you to select a picture file; a Clear button that enables you to delete whatever picture you've chosen; and a picture control that shows you what result you've chosen. The user can use these three controls to make a selection, and he can even preview the picture before he clicks on the OK button. Very handy! In this case, the property page assists the user in making the right choice for a single property.

This is a simple example. You may find more elaborate examples where, for instance, the user has to make several choices before a single property value is assigned. The point here simply is that a property page is a powerful way to make setting a property (or a set of properties) more convenient, and that you can combine a group of properties on a single page so that they make more sense to the user. Now that you've had a sampling of what property pages are and what they can do, let's delve into the details of how to create your own property pages.

Creating a Property Page

Before you write any code for a property page, you need to know what properties you're going to represent on it. Table 11.1 shows a list of all of the user-defined properties you'll find in the question control up to this lesson.

Table 11.1. User-defined question control properties.

Property	Description
AnswerColor	The color of the answer the user enters into the control
BackStyle	The background style of the control
BorderStyle	The border style of the control
DisplayFont	The font used throughout the control for displaying text to the user
DispIncorrectResponse	Determines what the control will do when the user enters an incorrect response
EnterCausesTab	Determines whether the user's pressing the Enter key triggers the control to evaluate the answer the user has entered
ExpectedAnswer	The string that represents what the user is supposed to enter as an answer to the question
Hint	The hint displayed if the user doesn't answer the question correctly
Question	The question displayed for the user to answer

After looking over this list of properties, you should be able to group many of them into similar categories. One of the purposes you've seen for a property page is grouping similar properties together for the convenience of the user. The property pages you'll be designing shortly in today's lesson will accomplish that purpose. Before you can design the pages, though, you need to determine how many properties you want to put on a page and how you want to categorize multiple pages if you want to provide them. I'll take care of this task by doing the work for you (I'm such a nice guy). Take a look at Table 11.2 for the groupings.

Table 11.2. Property groupings for the question control.

Property	Description
General Properties	
BackStyle	The background style of the control
BorderStyle	The border style of the control
DisplayFont	The font used throughout the control for displaying text to the user
Question-Related Properties	
Question	The question displayed for the user to answer
Hint	The hint displayed if the user doesn't answer the question correctly
Response-Related Properties	
AnswerColor	The color of the answer the user enters into the control
EnterCausesTab	Determines whether the user's pressing the Enter key triggers the control to evaluate the answer the user has entered
ExpectedAnswer	The string that represents what the user is supposed to enter as an answer to the question
DispIncorrectResponse	Determines what the control will do when the user enters an incorrect response

There aren't a huge number of properties to deal with here, but this is a rough grouping of many of the properties into three camps—one to set general properties, one for properties involved in getting the user to answer a question, and the last group for deciding what to do with the answers. Over today's and tomorrow's lessons, you'll be creating three property pages that group the properties as they're shown in Table 11.2. Not only will you learn how to create the pages themselves, but you'll also get a feel for setting up different property types within the pages.

Let's get started. As always, if you have a project up in Visual Basic, save and exit Visual Basic. Start up the Windows Explorer or any equivalent file-management system and turn your attention to the Day11 directory of the samples. Under that directory is a subdirectory named Your Start. This directory contains a project named Day11QuestionControl.vbp. Double-click on that project. Visual Basic starts up and proceeds to load this project. (You could have carried out the same feat by simply starting Visual Basic and then selecting File | Open Project from the menu. The project would then load into Visual Basic.) Wait for the project to finish loading, and we're off.

NOTE

SAMPLE The sample to start with for today's exercise can be found in file Day11QuestionControl.vbp on the CD-ROM under the Source\Day11\Your Start subdirectory. Because you will modify this project in the course of today's material, copy the entire subdirectory to your local drive before proceeding to work with it if you did not already do so when previously installing the CD-ROM. The sample program for today is presented in somewhat of a before-and-after state. The version in the Your Start directory is intended to show the code as it would appear at the end of Day 10, "Coding for the Design Environment" (with names revised to correspond to Day 11). Another version of this project is located one directory level higher in the Source\Day11 subdirectory. This contains the completed version as it should appear by the end of the steps in today's material.

Constructing the Page

The first step in creating a property page is to construct the page. There are two ways you can create a property page, just as there are two ways to build a set of properties; you can use the Visual Basic Property Page Wizard, or you can do the work manually. Let's learn how to do the job manually first for this simple page. Later on, when you design more complex pages, we'll look at the wizard to make the job a bit easier. Let's begin with the easiest page: the Question page. To get started, choose Project | Add Property Page from the Visual Basic 5.0 menu. This should result in the dialog shown in Figure 11.7.

NOTE

If, for some reason, this dialog does not appear, it's likely you've chosen this menu item before. At that time, you may have selected the option Don't show this dialog in the future. If you did, you won't get to choose to use the wizard unless you select to elsewhere in the Visual Basic menu. You'll learn more about using the wizard later in this lesson.

Figure 11.7.

The Add PropertyPage selector dialog.

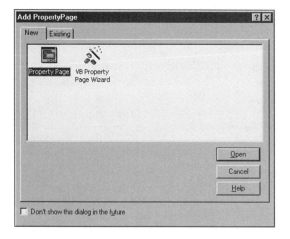

At this point, you can choose either to use the VB Property Page Wizard or bring up a blank property page and add the controls yourself. To learn how to create a property page yourself, go ahead and click the Open button. A blank property page like the one shown in Figure 11.8 appears.

Figure 11.8.

Starting with a blank property page.

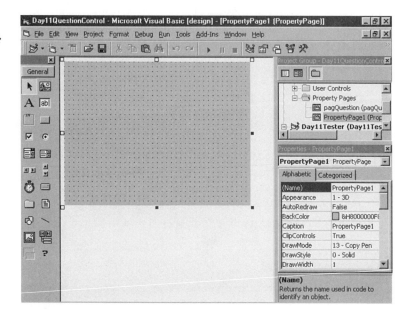

The first thing you should do is assign a name to the property page—name it pagQuestion. A property page is unlike a form because it doesn't have a window title bar. It does, however, have a tab, as you saw earlier in today's lesson. To assign that tab a caption, set the Caption property of the page to Question. So much for the default settings. Now, let's add the controls you need in order to allow the user to work with the properties you want to expose on the page.

You have just two properties, Question and Hint. Both are string values. Go ahead and place two text controls on the page alongside two labels. The first label/text control combination is for the Question property; the second is for Hint. Use the names lblQuestion and txtQuestion for the first set, and lblHint and txtHint for the second. Your form should look like the one shown in Figure 11.9.

Figure 11.9.

Adding the controls to the Question property page.

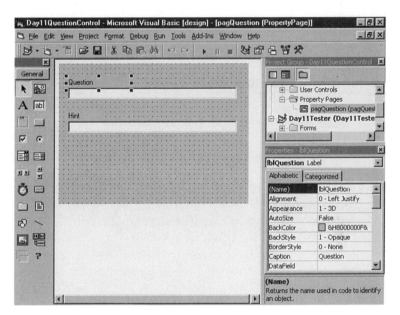

Don't worry about putting any buttons on the property page. Remember that Visual Basic automatically takes care of that for you. Also, don't worry about the size of the page. As you'll see later, Visual Basic can change the size of the property page as it sees fit. Just make sure there's enough room on the page to contain all your controls.

Coding the SelectionChanged Event

Go ahead and take a look at all the events of a property page. The first thing you might notice is that there is no Load event! And there's no Unload either. This might, at first, bewilder you. Don't worry; you'll see why this is later on. A property page, it turns out, is quite different from a form. One of the most significant differences is the set of events a property page contains; the way you interact with a property page can be quite a bit different from how you deal with a form. You'll see what I mean as you progress through the lesson.

The first thing you need to understand is the SelectionChanged event. This event occurs whenever a property page is first displayed. It's similar to a Load event, but is not quite the same due to the nature of property pages. The SelectionChanged event will also take place if the user selects more than one control and brings up a shared property page for multiple controls. (By the way, we'll talk about these more advanced issues more fully in tomorrow's lesson.)

To make your property page function, you have to write code in this event that puts the property values into the controls on the page. In this case, all you need to do is put the Question and Hint property settings into the two text controls on the page. For more complicated properties, however, the task isn't always so simple. Enter the code shown in Listing 11.1 into the SelectionChanged event of your new property page.

Listing 11.1. Adding code to the SelectionChanged event.

```
1: Private Sub PropertyPage_SelectionChanged()
2:     txtQuestion = SelectedControls(0).Question
3:     txtHint = SelectedControls(0).Hint
4: End Sub
```

The code in this event uses a special collection object for property pages called SelectedControls. This object is a collection of all the controls the user has selected within the container before bringing up the property page. The first control in the collection, SelectedControls(0) will be the only one in the collection if the user has clicked on one control and brings up the property page. That's the case we're going to consider in today's lesson. You'll learn about what happens when multiple controls are selected in tomorrow's lesson.

Setting the Changed Property

Refer for a moment to Figure 11.2. As previously mentioned, one of the characteristics of a property page is the presence of four buttons at the bottom of the dialog that contains the property page. One of the buttons is labeled Apply. The Apply button essentially takes the current values within the property page and applies them to the selected control or set of controls the property page belongs to. The Apply button should be grayed out until the user changes a property within a property page. At that point, the Apply button should be enabled, allowing the user to click on it if desired.

The Apply button always appears grayed out initially, but it's up to you to write the code necessary to enable the button when a property value changes. So how do you do this? Simply by setting the Changed property to True. When Visual Basic encounters the statement

```
Changed = True
```

the Apply button will become enabled, ready for the user to click on. The Changed property typically should only be set in the Change event of the various controls used to change the properties within the property page. In this example, there are two controls the user needs to manipulate to change the properties on the page: txtQuestion and txtHint. To make the Apply button work, you simply need to set the Changed property in the Change event of both of these controls. You must remember to set the Changed property in every Change event of every control on the page that the user uses to change a property. Otherwise, if you miss a control, the Apply button may not become enabled. That would confuse the user and make your boss very unhappy.

Listing 11.2 shows the code you need to take care of the Changed property in this property page.

Listing 11.2. Setting the Changed property in the Change events of the appropriate property page controls.

```
1: Private Sub txtHint_Change()
2:     Changed = True
3: End Sub
4:
5: Private Sub txtQuestion_Change()
6:     Changed = True
7: End Sub
```

Go ahead and enter the following into both Change events of the text controls on the property page:

```
Changed = True
```

Coding the ApplyChanges Event

Now that you've given the user the ability to click the Apply button, the next step is to add the code necessary to actually make the property changes to the control or controls the user has selected back in the host container. The user can, of course, also click the OK button at any time the property page is displayed. Apply and OK both change the properties, except that the property page remains on the screen when Apply is clicked. That way, the user can immediately see the effect of a property change and still make other changes on the dialog.

So when does the ApplyChanges event take place? When the user clicks the Apply button, the OK button, and when the user changes to another property page tab, if more than one exists. In all three cases, you need to be able to execute code that takes the values off the property page and applies them to the appropriate properties. The ApplyChanges event is, therefore, very important—just as important as the SelectionChanged event.

Because the user may have clicked on more than one control and then brought up the property page, you need to be careful in the ApplyChanges event. How do you go about assigning the properties? Do you assign the same property to all the controls that were selected, or do you just select the first one and change that control's properties only? There are no hard and fast rules because it all depends on the property you're dealing with. Let's see what would happen if you only changed the property values of the first control in the list of selected controls. This assumes, of course, that the user has selected more than one control. If the user hasn't, it's a moot point.

Listing 11.3 shows the code you need to enter into the SelectionChanged event if you only want the properties to apply to the first control in the set of controls the user has selected back in the host container.

Listing 11.3. Writing the code necessary in the ApplyChanges event to save the property settings to the first (or only) control selected.

```
1: Private Sub PropertyPage_ApplyChanges()
2:
3:     SelectedControls(0).Hint = txtHint
4:     SelectedControls(0).Question = txtQuestion
5:
6: End Sub
```

As this procedure shows, the contents of the text control txtHint are being stored in the Hint property of SelectedControls(0). SelectedControls(0) is the first element of a possible set of controls the user has selected. If the user has selected only one control, the array has only one element—element 0, or SelectedControls(0). In this case, you only want to change the properties of the first control selected. The code shown in Listing 11.3 accomplishes this. Because in today's lesson you're only learning about the case where the user selects one control, go ahead and enter the code shown in Listing 11.3 into the ApplyChanges event.

But suppose you want to change the properties for every question control the user has selected. To change the property for every question control in the entire collection, you would change the code in Listing 11.4 to that of Listing 11.5.

Listing 11.4. Writing the code necessary in the ApplyChanges event to save the property settings to all the question controls selected in the host container.

```
1: Private Sub PropertyPage_ApplyChanges()
2:
3:     Dim qc As ucQuestion
4:
```

```
 5:     For Each qc In SelectedControls
 6:           qc.Hint = txtHint
 7:           qc.Question = txtQuestion
 8:     Next
 9:
10: End Sub
```

This subroutine sets up a loop that begins with the first control in the collection and proceeds, one by one, to the last. For each control it encounters in the collection, it checks to see if that control is of the type ucQuestion, representing the question control object type. If the control is of that type, the subroutine takes and changes the Hint and Question properties and moves along to the next control in the collection. If it encounters a control other than a question control, say a label, it doesn't even attempt to set the properties. This, of course, is necessary because you don't want to go around setting controls where the properties don't even exist!

NOTE
In tomorrow's lesson, you'll learn how to handle situations when an error may occur in this event. It is conceivable that the user may enter a value that can't be successfully stored in a property. It's very important to handle errors gracefully. You'll learn how in tomorrow's lesson.

So the question is, do you want to set the first control in the collection or all of the controls? Basically, it's up to you. Let's say that in this case you want the Question property to apply to all the controls in the collection, but you only want the Hint to apply to the first control in the collection. How would you do this? You'd simply enter the code shown in Listing 11.5.

Listing 11.5. Writing the code necessary in the ApplyChanges event to save the property settings of the question controls selected in various ways.

```
 1: Private Sub PropertyPage_ApplyChanges()
 2:
 3:     SelectedControls(0).Hint = txtHint
 4:
 5:     Dim qc As ucQuestion
 6:
 7:     For Each qc In SelectedControls
 8:           qc.Question = txtQuestion
 9:     Next
10:
11: End Sub
```

This listing would only change the Hint property of the first control. All the question controls, however, would be assigned the Question property. Basically, the behavior of the properties and when they are saved are up to you. Allow us to give you a word of advice. First of all, the easier the property page is to understand, the better. If some of the properties are saved to all the controls, and others are saved to only the first, it will probably be very confusing to the user. You're better off making all the properties either apply only to the first control or to all the controls. We'll talk about the multiple-control case more in tomorrow's lesson. For now, let's see how you proceed to link up your property page with the ActiveX control.

Connecting a Property Page to an ActiveX Control

Before you move on to create the other two property pages, you're now going to learn how to connect the first property page to the ActiveX control. Go ahead and close the question control project and switch over to the test application project. Go to the property sheet. You'll notice that the property sheet looks just the same as it always has—no property page linkages yet. You're going to learn how to make the connection now.

To connect the property page to the control, you need to close down the test project and open the question control project. Then, when the project is inside the environment, open the property sheet by pressing the F4 key. This will result in the dialog shown in Figure 11.10.

Figure 11.10.

The Connect Property Pages dialog.

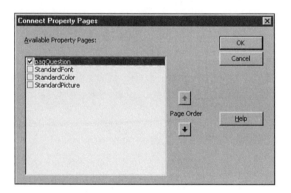

Notice in this dialog that the property page you've constructed appears at the top of the list. The other three property pages you see, StandardFont, StandardColor, and StandardPicture, are standard property pages that we'll discuss in the next section. Place a check in the box next to the name of the page you just constructed. Notice that you can order the number of pages, if more than one exists, with the arrow buttons to the right. When you add more pages later on, you'll see how to do this. When you're finished, click the OK button. Your property page has now been connected.

Now for the fun part. Close down the question control project and open the test application project. Bring up the test form and press F4 to bring up the property sheet. Click on a question control within the form and take a look at the property sheet. Your screen should look similar to the one shown in Figure 11.11.

Figure 11.11.

The test application at design time with the property page added.

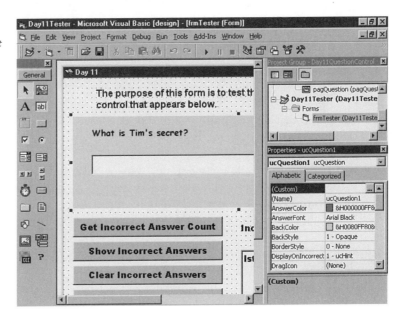

Notice the additional "property" shown toward the top of the property sheet, named Custom. This item is the link you need to get to the property page. The designer who uses your control will see this item. Because it's a standard representation for a series of property pages, the designer should know that if he clicks on Custom, the property pages defined for the control will appear. Have you been anxiously waiting to click on the item? Go ahead; give it your best shot. You should notice your property page in its finalized form, as shown in Figure 11.12.

Wonderful! You now have a property page. Notice that, just as discussed earlier in today's lesson, your page is enclosed in a tabbed dialog with only one tab—the Question tab. Notice also that your two properties, Hint and Question, both appear. Depending on what you set the properties to back in the property sheet, those values should appear in the textboxes on the property page. In the example shown in Figure 11.12, the Question property's text properly appears on the property page.

Figure 11.12.

The preliminary property page for the question control.

Notice also that all three buttons in the bottom of the dialog are enabled. Apply is enabled because when the textbox for the Question property was set in the SelectionChanged event, the Change event was triggered for the text control. This, in turn, enabled the Apply button. Go ahead and change the Question property in the dialog and click the Apply button. Thanks to the code you entered earlier, the property should change back on the control behind the property page, but the property page should remain intact. Figure 11.13 shows what should happen in this case when the Question property is changed and the Apply button is clicked.

Figure 11.13.

Using the Apply button of a property page.

Notice that the Apply button is disabled in Figure 11.13. The button is disabled after you click on it because once the changes are applied, there is no reason to click the Apply button again until a new set of changes is made. Change the Question property one more time in the property page. This re-enables the Apply button. This time, however, click on the OK button. Now you should see that the property page disappears and the Question property change takes effect. This completes the design of your first property page. But you have three to go. You'll be adding those property pages in tomorrow's lesson.

Using Standard Property Pages

Before you wrap up today's lesson, I want to tell you a bit about the standard property pages you saw earlier. These standard property pages give you a great deal of power without writing any code! The three standard property pages you can use are StandardColor, StandardPicture, and StandardFont. To see just how powerful these pages are, close the test application project and open the question control project. Open the UserControl object and bring up the property sheet. Then double-click on the Custom property and bring up the dialog that you saw in Figure 11.9. At this point, the property page pagQuestion is the only one checked. Go ahead and check the StandardColor property page and click the OK button. Now close the question control project and switch to the test application project. Click on the control and bring up the property sheet. Select the Custom item and notice the result. It should look like what's shown in Figure 11.14.

Figure 11.14.

Adding the
StandardColor
property page to the
question control.

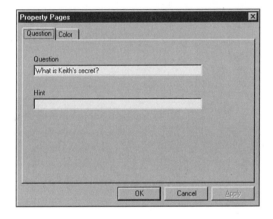

You now have two tabs—the first is labeled Question; the second is labeled Color. Click on the Color tab. You should then see the property page shown in Figure 11.15.

Figure 11.15.

The StandardColor
property page in the
test application.

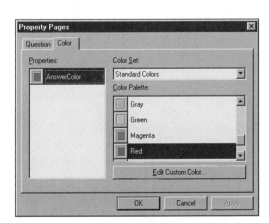

In what seems like magic, you should discover that your Color tab comes up with a property already present—the AnswerColor property! So how did that happen? The way you get properties to automatically find their way onto this property page is to define the property using the OLE_COLOR object type. Listing 11.6 shows the code you wrote back on Day 5 for the user-defined property AnswerColor.

Listing 11.6. The Property Get and Set procedures for the AnswerColor property.

```
1: Public Property Get AnswerColor() As OLE_COLOR
2:     AnswerColor = txtAnswer.ForeColor
3: End Property
4:
5: Public Property Set AnswerColor(ByVal vNewColor As OLE_COLOR)
6:     txtAnswer.ForeColor = vNewColor
7:     PropertyChanged "AnswerColor"
8: End Property
```

As you can see, you used the OLE_COLOR data type in the declarations of each property procedure you created. The first thing this data type does for you is to bring up the color dialog when the user selects the property directly on the property sheet. This was shown on Day 4, and if you look back to Figure 4.11, you'll see the Color Picker dialog appear. At the time, that's all I mentioned about the OLE_COLOR property, and that's probably all you thought it did. But now that you've learned about property pages, you see that it even places the property in the standard color property page. Refer to Figure 11.15. Notice the amount of flexibility you get with the StandardColor property page. If there were more than one property here that used the OLE_COLOR property, you could get that property to appear as well.

At this point, you may be asking, "What about the BackColor property?" Why doesn't it appear? The reason is that you haven't exposed the BackColor property to the host application. Use the ActiveX Control Interface Wizard to expose the BackColor property to the host. If you recall, you learned how to do this back on Day 4.

TIP

The Day 4 lesson taught you how to expose a predefined property using the ActiveX Control Interface Wizard. Refer to that day's lesson to review the steps you need to carry out.

The wizard will automatically take care of all the code required to pull this off. When it's finished, you'll have two new property procedures, as shown in Listing 11.7.

Listing 11.7. The `BackColor` property as exposed by the ActiveX Control Interface Wizard.

```
1: Public Property Get BackColor() As OLE_COLOR
2:     BackColor = UserControl.BackColor
3: End Property
4:
5: Public Property Let BackColor(ByVal New_BackColor As OLE_COLOR)
6:     UserControl.BackColor() = New_BackColor
7:     PropertyChanged "BackColor"
8: End Property
```

This newly exposed property will then appear in the property page. Switch to the test application project and bring up the property pages once more. Then switch to the Color property page. Your property page should now look like the one in Figure 11.16.

Figure 11.16.

The revised StandardColor *property page in the test application, now showing two color properties.*

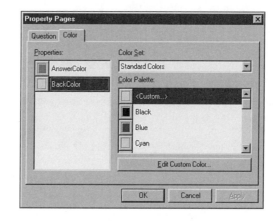

You can use the other two standard property sheets the same way. Go ahead and add the StandardFont property page to the control using the same steps as before. Once you do, you should notice a third property page in the test application (see Figure 11.17).

The DisplayFont property proudly appears on the property page. But suppose you want to let the user set the question font, the answer font, and the hint font all separately. How would you do that? Right now the control has one property for all the controls on the page. What you need to do is replace the single property with three separate properties, one for each font.

The first step in making this happen is to go in and delete the DisplayFont property procedures. Open the question control project and remove these two property procedures. You also need to go into the InitProperties, ReadProperties, and WriteProperties procedures and delete all references to the DisplayFont property. Then it's time to create three new properties—QuestionFont, AnswerFont, and HintFont. Use the ActiveX Control

Interface Wizard to create the three properties. You should map the font control of lblQuestion, txtAnswer, and lblFeedback to QuestionFont, AnswerFont, and HintFont, respectively. The wizard will place code in the InitProperties, ReadProperties, and WriteProperties subroutines, as well as generate the set of property procedures shown in Listing 11.8.

Figure 11.17.

The StandardFont *property page in the test application, now showing one font property.*

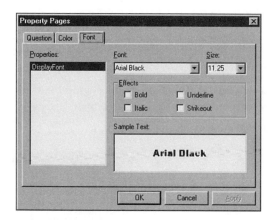

Listing 11.8. The QuestionFont, AnswerFont, and HintFont property procedures.

```
 1: Public Property Get AnswerFont() As Font
 2:     Set AnswerFont = txtAnswer.Font
 3: End Property
 4:
 5: Public Property Set AnswerFont(ByVal New_AnswerFont As Font)
 6:     Set txtAnswer.Font = New_AnswerFont
 7:     PropertyChanged "AnswerFont"
 8: End Property
 9:
10: Public Property Get HintFont() As Font
11:     Set HintFont = lblFeedback.Font
12: End Property
13:
14: Public Property Set HintFont(ByVal New_HintFont As Font)
15:     Set lblFeedback.Font = New_HintFont
16:     PropertyChanged "HintFont"
17: End Property
18:
19: Public Property Get QuestionFont() As Font
20:     Set QuestionFont = lblQuestion.Font
21: End Property
22:
23: Public Property Set QuestionFont(ByVal New_QuestionFont As Font)
24:     Set lblQuestion.Font = New_QuestionFont
25:     PropertyChanged "QuestionFont"
26: End Property
```

If you look carefully, you'll notice that the wizard failed to place the correct code in the `ReadProperties` and `WriteProperties` events. It placed these statements in the `ReadProperties` event:

```
Set Font = PropBag.ReadProperty("QuestionFont", Ambient.Font)
Set Font = PropBag.ReadProperty("AnswerFont", Ambient.Font)
Set Font = PropBag.ReadProperty("HintFont", Ambient.Font)
```

and the following statements in the `WriteProperties` event:

```
Call PropBag.WriteProperty("QuestionFont", Font, Ambient.Font)
Call PropBag.WriteProperty("AnswerFont", Font, Ambient.Font)
Call PropBag.WriteProperty("HintFont", Font, Ambient.Font)
```

Here, the mappings are not correct, although they are correct in the property procedures themselves. You need to make sure that the `ReadProperties` event contains the statements

```
Set lblQuestion.Font = PropBag.ReadProperty("QuestionFont", Ambient.Font)
    Set txtAnswer.Font = PropBag.ReadProperty("AnswerFont", Ambient.Font)
    Set lblFeedback.Font = PropBag.ReadProperty("HintFont", Ambient.Font)
```

and that the `WriteProperties` event contains the following statements:

```
Call PropBag.WriteProperty("QuestionFont", lblQuestion.Font, Ambient.Font)
Call PropBag.WriteProperty("AnswerFont", txtAnswer.Font, Ambient.Font)
Call PropBag.WriteProperty("HintFont", lblFeedback.Font, Ambient.Font)
```

This is a good time to once again remind you that the wizard isn't foolproof. Here you've caught it doing something wrong! Make sure you check your code after the wizard generates it rather than blindly accepting it. Remember that using the wizard should never take the place of thinking through the issue yourself and checking out the code to make sure it's correct.

Notice that each of the three new properties you've exposed uses the `Font` object as a return type. Now, when you bring up the property page in the test application, you should see all three properties appear in the `StandardFont` property page, as shown in Figure 11.18.

Figure 11.18.

The `StandardFont` *property page in the test application, now showing three properties for each constituent control.*

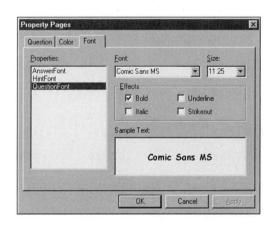

Notice that this property page allows you to set the font size, font type, and attributes such as bold and italics to the various font properties. It even shows you a sample of the font as it appears onscreen. Wow! You can't beat that!

The third and final standard property page is the StandardPicture property page. To have a property be automatically included in this property page, you have to create or expose a property using the Picture data type for the property to appear. Then, when you include the StandardPicture property page in your list, you'll be able to set and even preview the picture before assigning it to the property—another great piece of functionality! The process of exposing a picture property and linking it up to a property page is left as an exercise for you at the end of this lesson. It will give you good practice as a recap of what you've learned in this chapter.

Putting It All Together

Now that you've arrived at the end of this lesson, review the list of properties you've exposed on property pages in Table 11.3.

Table 11.3. Properties and property page assignments.

Property	Description
Properties in the QuestionProperty Page	
Question	The question displayed for the user to answer
Hint	The hint displayed if the user doesn't answer the question correctly
Properties in the ColorProperty Page	
AnswerColor	The color of the answer the user enters into the control
BackColor	The background color of the question control
QuestionColor	The color of the question text (you'll work with this in the Quiz at the end of the lesson)
Properties in the StandardFont Page	
AnswerFont	The font of the answer text control
HintFont	The font of the hint label
QuestionFont	The font of the question label

Property	Description
Properties in the **StandardPicture Page**	
Picture	The background picture of the control (you'll work with this in the Quiz at the end of the lesson)
Properties slated for a **GeneralProperty Page**	
BackStyle	The background style of the control
BorderStyle	The border style of the control
Properties slated for a **ResponseProperty Page**	
EnterCausesTab	Determines whether the user's pressing the Enter key triggers the control to evaluate the answer the user has entered
ExpectedAnswer	The string that represents what the user is supposed to enter as an answer to the question
DispIncorrectResponse	Determines what the control will do when the user enters an incorrect response

In tomorrow's lesson, you'll place these properties on the appropriate property pages and learn about more of the advanced features of property pages.

Summary

Today's lesson gives you an introductory look at what property pages are, how you use them, and how to create them for your controls. You started out with the basics, seeing several property pages of controls that already exist. Then, step by step, you put together property pages of your own, adding new properties as necessary so that the property pages make sense. You first had to create a new property page and add the controls necessary to let the users set properties. Then you needed to write code for two key events—SelectionChanged and ApplyChanges. Finally, you used the PropertyPages property of the UserControl object to tie the property page to the control. You added several property pages, including several standard property pages that give you built-in functionality with virtually no extra code. The end result is that you now have an even more powerful question control. You also understand that property pages add a great deal of flexibility and convenience for the user.

Q&A

Q **I understand what a property page is, but I'm still a bit confused on what happens when the user selects more than one control and then brings up the property pages.**

A Yes, this does get confusing. When the user clicks on one control and brings up its property page, the situation is very clear. But if the user clicks on two question controls and brings up the property page, you need to decide which properties will change on what controls. Hopefully, this will become more clear in tomorrow's lesson.

Q **All the property page code you showed me today had no error checking in it. What happens if errors occur in property pages?**

A It's very important to handle errors in property pages. Tomorrow, we'll show you how.

Q **How do I change the order in which the property page tabs appear?**

A In the Property Page builder dialog, you can use the up and down arrow buttons to rearrange the page order. You can position each page in the order you want it to appear in, and it will behave just as you want it to.

Q **How do I rearrange the OK, Cancel, and Apply buttons below the property pages? Is there any way to get at them?**

A No, you cannot change the position of the buttons. The property pages must conform to the Visual Basic framework for property pages. Unlike forms, they are a bit more restrictive in positioning and manipulation.

Workshop

Suppose you would like to create a brand-new ActiveX calendar control. What properties would your control include? How might you group those properties together using property pages? Write out a list of properties and assign them to a series of property pages.

Quiz

NOTE See Appendix D, "Answers to Quiz Questions," for the answers to these questions.

1. Expose the Picture property of the question control. This property allows the user to select a picture to be displayed on the UserControl surface. Use the data type necessary so that the property is included in the StandardPicture property page. Include the StandardPicture property page in your control and verify that the page appears with the correct property shown.

2. Add a new property to the control called QuestionColor and expose it through the Color property page.

Day 12

More Property Pages

In yesterday's lesson you learned a lot about property pages, how to create them, and some tips for designing them. Today's lesson brings you to even greater heights in property page design. In this lesson, you'll add more properties to the existing property pages and add a new property page to the set. You'll also learn more about how to handle situations when the user clicks on multiple controls and wants to bring up property pages for those multiple controls. Error handling is an important part of property page design. Today's lesson will give you some tips on how to handle errors gracefully. Throughout the lesson, you'll learn many useful tips and guidelines for building exceptional property pages.

A Brief Look at Where You've Been

Before you get started with today's lesson, let's take a brief moment to review what you implemented in yesterday's lesson (Day 11, "Property Pages"). Table 12.1 gives you a summary of all the property pages you created and the properties you can set on each page.

Table 12.1. Summary of the property pages from Day 11.

Property Page	Properties on Page	Page Type
Question	`Question`	Custom
	`Hint`	
Color	`AnswerColor`	Standard
	`BackColor`	
	`QuestionColor`	
Font	`AnswerFont`	Standard
	`QuestionFont`	
	`HintFont`	
Picture	`Picture`	Standard

By the end of today's lesson, you will have added a new property page as well as added some new properties to the existing property pages you created yesterday.

Property Pages and Multiple Control Selection

When you assembled the property pages in yesterday's lesson, you selected a single control, brought up the property pages, made changes to various properties, and saw the results on the control you selected. It's entirely possible, however, that the user might select more than one control and bring up property pages for the set of controls he's selected. How does that affect your property pages? Do the property changes apply to all the controls the user has selected, to none of them, or to only one of the controls?

To answer this question, you need to understand the two possibilities that exist when a user selects multiple controls. On the one hand, he might select a wide variety of controls, such as a text control, a label, a picture control, and your question control. Perhaps he wants to change the font in each of these controls. Another case is when the user selects several controls of the same type. For instance, he might select three question controls on a single form and attempt to universally apply a series of property changes to each control. We will now examine each of these cases.

Selecting Different Multiple Controls

What happens if the user selects different types of controls and attempts to bring up various property pages? Suppose, for instance, that the user selects a label, a text control, and the question control. What would happen in this case?

Load the Day 12 question control project found in the Day12/Your Start directory. Then bring up the test application project and open the test form. You'll notice it is entirely blank. Go ahead and place a question control on the form, along with a command button. Then select the question control only. Then choose View | Property Pages, which will display the property pages you created in yesterday's lesson, as shown in Figure 12.1.

You can also bring up the property pages by selecting (Custom) on the property sheet itself. Now that the pages are up, select the question control and the command button.

Figure 12.1.

Selecting the property pages for a single control.

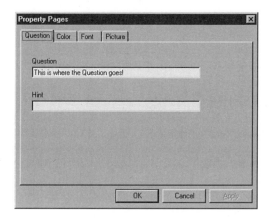

TIP

To select more than one control at a time, click on the first control. Then hold down the Shift key and click the second control. Both controls will be selected, and selector indicators will appear on the edges of both controls. Using the Shift key, you can select as many controls on a form as you want to.

Then click on View | Property Pages again. This time you should see the result shown in Figure 12.2.

Figure 12.2.

*No property pages
appear when the user
selects controls of
different types.*

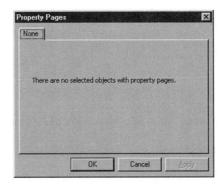

Notice that the property page does not appear. Instead, you get a dialog that says There are no selected objects with property pages. This message actually is a bit misleading. The question control does support property pages, but the command button does not. Therefore, the property pages don't appear. Why, you ask? Both controls have a Picture property, and that appears on one of the property pages; wouldn't it seem reasonable that at least one property page should appear with the Picture property on the page?

NOTE

You will also notice that the property page item does not appear in the property sheet. Actually, the property page item never appears in the property sheet when more than one control is selected, even if both controls use the same property pages. You can always get to the property pages using View | Property Pages, however, so that's the technique used in this lesson.

The reason that the property pages do not appear is simply because Visual Basic doesn't allow this sort of behavior to occur. In fact, the ActiveX technology itself prevents it. In order for the user to be able to bring up property pages with this assortment of controls selected, you would need to know which properties in the property pages would apply and which would not. That would be very difficult because you have no way of easily determining which controls the user has clicked on in the assortment of controls. Even if you could, the code to allow only certain properties common to all three controls would be cumbersome at best, and probably very confusing to the user. It turns out, therefore, that Visual Basic avoids the whole issue by not allowing it.

In order for a property page to appear when two different types of controls are selected, both controls must explicitly support the property page. If one does not, the property page doesn't appear. If you think about this a while, it really does make sense. The code you would need to write to enable some properties in a property page and disable others could potentially be very complicated. Not only that, but it has the potential to be unreliable and subject to error. That could make your control error prone and buggy. So, in a sense, having the property page not appear is a good thing because it keeps the interface simple and the rules clear.

Selecting Identical Multiple Controls

The more common case is when the user selects two identical controls within the form. Go ahead and delete the command button. Then place a second question control on the test form. You should notice that the (Custom) item does not appear on the property sheet to the right. This should not alarm you, however; you can bring up the property pages by choosing View | Property Pages. Go ahead and do that. The dialog shown in Figure 12.3 should then appear.

Figure 12.3.

Bringing up the property pages for two identical question controls.

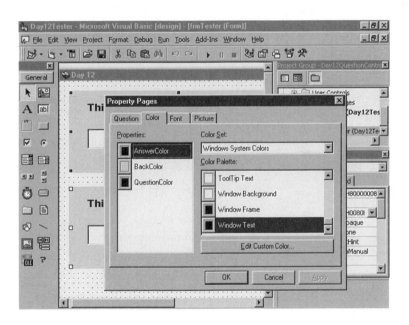

As you can see, the property pages appear as you would expect. Unfortunately, Visual Basic doesn't give you any special sort of queue that the property pages are in for all the controls you've selected. Now that the properties appear on the pages, the next logical questions you might ask are What happens if I change a property like the Question property? Does the question change for both controls, or just for the first? or maybe just for the second? What about the BackColor property? If you change that property, which of the two controls changes? the first, the last, or both?

In yesterday's lesson you learned that the answer to these questions is totally up to you, the designer. Let's briefly review the difference as it's implemented in code.

Applying Property Changes to a Single Control

You can make it so a property is changed in a property page where multiple controls are selected, and the change only applies to the control that was selected first. Visual Basic keeps track of the order in which the user selects the controls. Because Visual Basic knows which control was selected first, you have the option of only applying the property to the first control rather than all of them. To do this, you need to use the `SelectedControls` collection.

The `SelectedControls` collection was discussed briefly in yesterday's lesson. `SelectedControls` is basically an array of controls sorted in the order in which they were selected on the form. The first control the user selects, for example, is `SelectedControls(0)`. The second control selected is `SelectedControls(1)`, and so forth.

Listing 12.1 shows the code used in the `SelectionChanged` event you learned about on Day 11.

Listing 12.1. The `SelectionChanged` event for the Question property page.

```
1: Private Sub PropertyPage_SelectionChanged()
2:     txtQuestion = SelectedControls(0).Question
3:     txtHint = SelectedControls(0).Hint
4: End Sub
```

Here, you can see that `SelectedControls(0)` was used, and the `Question` property of that control is stored in the textbox on the property page. Likewise, in Listing 12.2 you see the code used in the `ApplyChanges` event.

Listing 12.2. The `ApplyChanges` event for the Question property page.

```
1: Private Sub PropertyPage_ApplyChanges()
2:
3:     SelectedControls(0).Hint = txtHint
4:
5:     Dim qc As ucQuestion
6:
7:     For Each qc In SelectedControls
8:         qc.Question = txtQuestion
9:     Next
10:
11: End Sub
```

12

In this listing, the statement

```
SelectedControls(0).Hint = txtHint
```

sets the Hint property for the first control in the collection of selected controls.

Applying Property Changes to Multiple Controls

The code in Listing 12.2 shows how to make changes to the Hint property apply across all the selected controls. This was presented to you in yesterday's lesson. Notice that a loop is constructed and a temporary control object variable is created to loop through all the selected controls in the collection. The same property change is applied to all the controls in the collection. To verify this behavior, go ahead and change the code in the ApplyChanges event so that it appears as shown in Listing 12.3.

Listing 12.3. The revised ApplyChanges event for the Question property page.

```
 1: Private Sub PropertyPage_ApplyChanges()
 2:
 3:     Dim qc As ucQuestion
 4:
 5:     For Each qc In SelectedControls
 6:         qc.Question = txtQuestion
 7:         qc.Hint = txtHint
 8:     Next
 9:
10: End Sub
```

Now go back to the test application, select both question controls, and bring up the property pages for the controls. Change the Question property to any value you like. Notice that after you close the property pages by clicking the OK button, the change applies to all the controls you've selected on the form. Figure 12.4 shows two controls on the test form, with the Question property changed for both controls.

It's very likely that the user will not want every Question and Hint to change across all the controls. Go ahead and modify the code so that only the first control in the collection changes. The code in the SelectionChanged event should look like Listing 12.4.

Figure 12.4.

Changing the Question *property now applies across all selected question controls.*

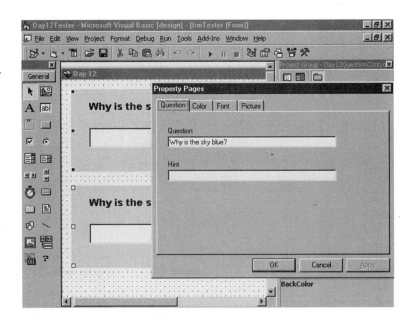

Listing 12.4. A new `ApplyChanges` event that changes only the first control in the collection.

```
1: Private Sub PropertyPage_ApplyChanges()
2:
3:     SelectedControls(0).Question = txtQuestion
4:     SelectedControls(0).Hint = txtHint
5:
6: End Sub
```

Now only the first control will accept the property changes you make in this property page.

Multiple Controls and the Standard Property Pages

What about the standard property pages? As you learned yesterday, the properties that appear in these pages are based on the data types of the properties that appear in those pages. For instance, all the data types of the properties that appear in the Font page are of type Font. Those that appear in the standard Color property page are of type OLE_COLOR. What happens, then, when you select more than one question control and change a font or a color within the property pages?

12

Go ahead and bring up the test application form. Select both question controls and choose View | Property Pages. Switch to the Font dialog and change QuestionFont to something other than the current setting. You should observe that all the question controls selected change fonts, as shown in Figure 12.5.

Figure 12.5.

Changing properties in standard property pages applies across all selected controls automatically.

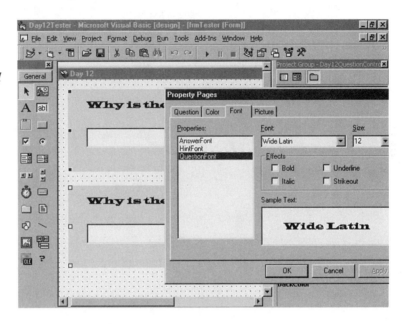

It turns out that Visual Basic automatically applies the changes to all the controls. There is no way to override or change this. So any changes you make to any color, font, or picture properties will be applied to all the controls included in the control collection. You should be aware of and understand that the user can make these universal changes to your control properties through these standard property pages.

Building a Property Page for a Special Property

In yesterday's lesson you learned that there are two types of property pages you can create. One type allows the user to set a series of properties logically grouped together on a single page. The other approach is to use a series of controls that, taken together, can set a single property. You can even create property pages that are a hybrid of these two approaches.

On Day 9, "User-Defined Events," you added the TabooWords property to the set of question control properties. As you learned at that time, you can set this property with a series of taboo words separated by a semicolon. While it's easy enough to type in all the words directly, the list could get rather long. It would be much more convenient to give the user an easier way to enter the taboo words than typing them all directly through the property sheet. That's where the beauty of a property page can really shine through! Now you'll construct a special page for the TabooWords property to practice implementing this technique.

First, switch over to the question control project. Yesterday you created a property page manually, so today go ahead and use the Property Page Wizard. Click Project | Add Property Page, which brings up the dialog shown in Figure 12.6.

Figure 12.6.

The opening dialog of the Property Page Wizard.

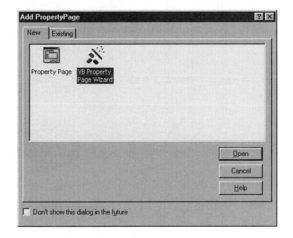

Select the VB Property Page Wizard icon and click the Open button.

NOTE

In order to use the Property Page Wizard, you must make sure it is included as an add-in within Visual Basic. If you don't see the Property Page Wizard appear when creating a new property page, click on Add-Ins and look for Property Page Wizard in the menu. If it doesn't appear, click on Add-In Manager and select the VB Property Page Wizard option within the dialog. This will ensure that the wizard comes up properly within Visual Basic.

You will probably see an introductory screen unless you've disabled the introduction screen before. If you see the Introduction dialog, click Next to proceed. You will then see a screen

12

that allows you to change an existing property page or add a new one. Go ahead and click on the Add button. You will then be prompted to enter a property page name. Enter pagTaboo for the property page name. Visual Basic creates the property page and then gives you the opportunity to order the page. Order your property pages so that they appear as shown in Figure 12.7.

Figure 12.7.
Ordering the property pages within the Property Page Wizard.

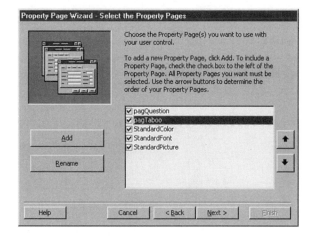

Now click the Next button again. You will see a dialog that shows all the property pages in tabs across the top of the dialog. Select the pagTaboo tab, which should be the second tab from the left. On the left side of the dialog, you'll see a series of properties you can add to the property page. You'll be adding most of these properties to the property pages at some point. For now, just move the TabooWords property over to the listbox to the right of the dialog. Your dialog should now look like the one shown in Figure 12.8.

Figure 12.8.
Setting the appropriate property for the Taboo property page.

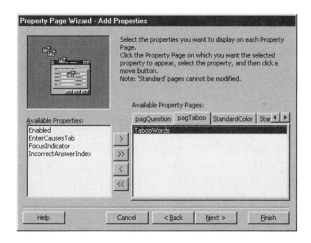

12

Click the Next button, which will present you with a Finished! dialog. You can go ahead and click the Finish button, which will show you a couple dialogs indicating that the process is finished and showing a summary of the actions taken. Close the summary dialog, and you'll notice the addition of the pagTaboo property page in the project window of the question control project.

Go ahead and open the pagTaboo page. You will see a simple property page with a text control and label at the top of the page. Change the caption of the property page from pagTaboo to Taboo so that the tab appears properly in the list of property pages. Then delete the existing controls on the page as well as the code that belongs with them. You're going to construct this page from scratch. Add the controls shown in Figure 12.9 to the dialog. These controls are described in Table 12.2.

Figure 12.9.

New controls for the Taboo property page.

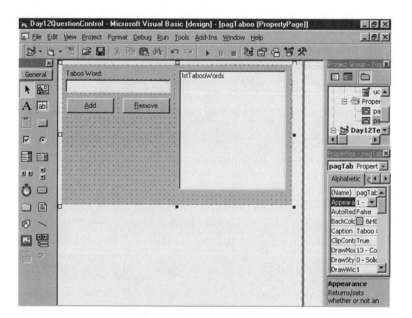

Table 12.2. Controls for the Taboo property page.

Control Name	Control Type
lblTabooWord	Label
txtTabooWord	Textbox
cmdRemove	Command button
cmdAdd	Command button
lstTabooWords	Listbox

These five controls will be used to add and remove taboo words from the listbox. The user will be able to enter a word in the textbox and have that word added to the listbox below. Then, when the user clicks the Apply or OK button, the words will be concatenated and separated with a semicolon in the property itself.

The first event to write code for is the SelectionChanged event. Enter the code shown in Listing 12.5.

Listing 12.5. The Taboo property page's SelectionChanged event.

```
1: Dim svTabooWords As String
2:
3:      Dim svItem As String
4:      Dim lStart As Long
5:      Dim iPos As Long
6:
7:      lPos = 0
8:      lStart = 1
9:
10:     lstTabooWords.Clear
11:
12:     cmdAdd.Enabled = False
13:
14:     svTabooWords = SelectedControls(0).TabooWords
15:
16:     Do
17:         ' Get the next semicolon
18:         lPos = InStr(lStart, svTabooWords, ";")
19:
20:         ' If no semicolons exist and the string has data in it,
21:         ' assume only one item and add that item into the listbox
22:         If lPos = 0 And svTabooWords = "" Then
23:             cmdRemove.Enabled = False
24:             Exit Sub
25:         End If
26:
27:         ' If no semicolons exist and the string has data in it,
28:         ' add the string and set the listbox to the first item
29:         If lPos = 0 And lStart = 1 And svTabooWords <> "" Then
30:             lstTabooWords.AddItem svTabooWords
31:         Else
32:             ' Semicolon found - parse and store
33:             If lPos <> 0 Then
34:                 svItem = Mid$(svTabooWords, lStart, lPos - lStart)
35:             Else
36:                 svItem = Mid$(svTabooWords, lStart)
37:             End If
38:             lstTabooWords.AddItem svItem
39:             cmdRemove.Enabled = True
40:             lStart = lPos + 1
```

continues

12

Listing 12.5. continued

```
41:          End If
42:
43:      Loop Until lPos = 0
44:
45:      If lstTabooWords.ListCount = 0 Then
46:          cmdRemove.Enabled = False
47:      Else
48:          cmdRemove.Enabled = True
49:      End If
50:
51:      lstTabooWords.ListIndex = 0
52:
53: End Sub
```

This procedure takes the TabooWords property value and parses out all the words between semicolons. The procedure must also take into account the case where only one word is specified and no semicolons exist, as well as if no words exist at all. Furthermore, the procedure needs to set the listbox to the topmost value, if one exists. You'll find that there are a lot of little issues that need to be taken care of, such as the Clear method at the top of the procedure. If you fail to include the Clear method, for example, and you bring up the property page through the (Custom) item on the property sheet, SelectionChanged is called twice, resulting in a duplication of the words in the listbox. To avoid situations like these, you need to test your control carefully to make sure this doesn't happen. You'll learn more about testing your control on Day 16, "Testing Your Control."

Now let's proceed on to the ApplyChanges event. The code for that event is shown in Listing 12.6.

Listing 12.6. The Taboo property page's ApplyChanges event.

```
 1: Private Sub PropertyPage_ApplyChanges()
 2:
 3:      Dim i As Integer
 4:      Dim svItem As String
 5:      Dim svTabooWords As String
 6:
 7:      ' If there are no words, make the property empty
 8:      If lstTabooWords.ListCount = 0 Then
 9:          SelectedControls(0).TabooWords = ""
10:
11:      ' If only one word exists, leave off the semi-colon
12:      ElseIf lstTabooWords.ListCount = 1 Then
13:          SelectedControls(0).TabooWords = lstTabooWords.List(0)
14:      Else
15:          For i = 0 To lstTabooWords.ListCount - 2
```

12

```
16:              svItem = lstTabooWords.List(i)
17:              svTabooWords = svTabooWords & svItem & ";"
18:           Next
19:           svTabooWords = svTabooWords & lstTabooWords.List(i)
20:           SelectedControls(0).TabooWords = svTabooWords
21:       End If
22:
23: End Sub
```

This procedure takes the words out of the listbox and concatenates them together, separating them with a semicolon. Extra code is needed to handle the last word so that it doesn't get a semicolon tacked on to the end of it. Alternatively, if only one word has been specified, a semicolon is not needed either. And if no words are specified in the listbox, the string is set to be empty.

The code for the Add and Remove buttons must be entered next. Enter the code shown in Listing 12.7 to get these two buttons working properly.

Listing 12.7. The Taboo property page's command button events.

```
 1: Private Sub cmdAdd_Click()
 2:     Changed = True
 3:     lstTabooWords.AddItem txtTabooWord.Text
 4:     cmdRemove.Enabled = True
 5:     lstTabooWords.ListIndex = lstTabooWords.ListCount - 1
 6: End Sub
 7:
 8: Private Sub cmdRemove_Click()
 9:     Changed = True
10:     lstTabooWords.RemoveItem lstTabooWords.ListIndex
11:     If lstTabooWords.ListCount = 0 Then
12:         cmdRemove.Enabled = False
13:     Else
14:         lstTabooWords.ListIndex = lstTabooWords.ListCount - 1
15:     End If
16: End Sub
```

These procedures make sure that when the user clicks Add or Remove, the appropriate action takes place. The listbox selection is changed and, if the user has removed the last item, the Remove button is grayed out. Conversely, if the user adds the first item, the Remove button is enabled. Finally, if more than one item exists in the listbox, Remove stays enabled until they all disappear. The only other helpful segment of code you can add is in the Change event of the txtTabooWord event. That code is shown in Listing 12.8.

Listing 12.8. The Taboo property's text control Change event.

```
1: Private Sub txtTabooWord_Change()
2:     If txtTabooWord.Text = "" Then
3:         cmdAdd.Enabled = False
4:     Else
5:         cmdAdd.Enabled = True
6:     End If
7: End Sub
```

This little snippet of code makes sure the Add button is grayed if there is no text in the textbox for adding a word. As soon as a word is entered into the textbox, the Add button becomes enabled. This way, there is no chance the user will click the Add button with no string defined, resulting in a possible error.

Now that you have all this code entered, you're ready to give the control a test run. Save the project and close the control project. Switch over to the test project and bring up the test form. Select the first question control and notice the TabooWords property. When you click on it, you'll see an ellipsis to the right. Clicking on that ellipsis brings up the property page for the TabooWord property. Similarly, clicking on the ellipsis for the Question or Hint property brings up the Question property page. So you can either click on Custom if you've selected one control or you can find the particular property and click the ellipsis. Finally, you can choose View | Property Pages in the case of multiple controls.

NOTE Any properties that connect to property pages will not appear in the property sheet when multiple controls are selected. The best way to access all the properties of a control when more than one are selected is to use View | Property Pages. Only those properties that do not use property pages can be selected in the property sheet when multiple controls are selected. All those properties that are used on property pages do not display, so you must access them using the View | Property Pages menu item.

Figure 12.10 shows the Taboo property page in action.

Go ahead and enter taboo words using the property page. Experiment with adding and deleting taboo words and seeing the result in the property sheet. Keep in mind that you can still edit the property directly if you want to.

The Taboo property page is an excellent example of how you can use a number of controls on a single property page to build a property setting. Rather than having to type all the words on a single line, the control user now has a much more convenient way of entering the properties. Keep in mind that you could enhance this page even further. You're limited only by your imagination.

Figure 12.10.

The Taboo property page in action.

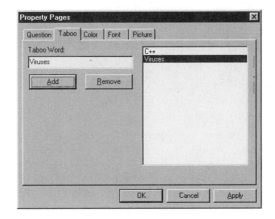

Building a Property Page with User-Defined Property Settings

In the process of building property pages, it is often necessary to build in properties with settings that are set to a user-defined type. The DisplayOnIncorrectResponse property, for example, can be set to three user-defined constants: ucNone(0), ucHint(1), or ucAnswer(2). The Property Page Wizard doesn't recognize properties that can be set using user-defined types; it only picks up on properties that use standard, built-in data types. If you bring up the Property Page Wizard and try to add the DisplayOnIncorrectResponse to the Question property page, for instance, you wind up with the dialog you saw in Figure 12.8. Notice the absence of this property. So how do you go about adding it? You have to do so manually. Let's step through the process of adding this property to the Question property page.

Switch back over to the Question property page and bring it up in design mode. Add a new label and a combobox, as shown in Figure 12.11.

Be sure to set the Style property of the combobox to 2 - Dropdown List and name the combobox cboDisplayOnIncorrectResponse. Because the property page does not recognize the property as a built-in data type, you basically have to add the code yourself to enable the user to see the same property settings as on the property sheet. To do this, go ahead and add the following lines of code to the SelectionChanged event:

```
cboDisplayOnIncorrectResponse.Clear
cboDisplayOnIncorrectResponse.AddItem "0 - ucNone"
```

```
cboDisplayOnIncorrectResponse.AddItem "1 - ucHint"
cboDisplayOnIncorrectResponse.AddItem "2 - ucAnswer"
cboDisplayOnIncorrectResponse.ListIndex =
      ➥SelectedControls(0).DisplayOnIncorrectResponse
```

Figure 12.11.

Adding the new label and textbox control for the DisplayOn IncorrectResponse *property.*

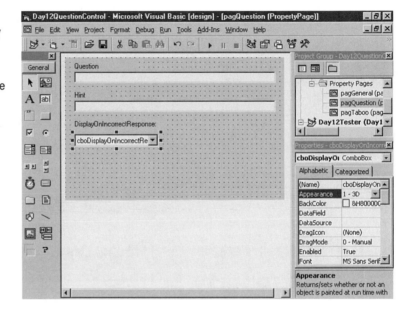

The first four lines of code place the correct property settings into the combobox. Then the last line of code sets the appropriate item based on the current property setting. The user then has the option of changing any of the items. All you have to do to store the property is add this line of code to the ApplyChanges event:

```
SelectedControls(0).DisplayOnIncorrectResponse =
      ➥cboDisplayOnIncorrectResponse.ListIndex
```

This simple line of code takes the current ListIndex of the combobox and assigns it to the DisplayIncorrectResponse property of the first control of a possible collection of selected controls. So, as you can see, you have to manually store the property settings into the control or controls used on the property page. Then you have to go back and set the property setting based on what selection the user has made with the controls you have provided.

One other side effect you'll notice is that an ellipsis does not appear to the right of a property with custom settings, even though it happens to be on a property page. You are presented with a drop-down list of choices, but the only way you can change the property on a property page is to specifically call up the property pages using the (Custom) property sheet item or by choosing View | Property Pages from the menu.

Sharing a Property Page Among Other Properties

So far in your experiences with property pages, every property you've set gets a distinct place on a property page or has its own property page assigned to it. But suppose you want to use the same property page layout for more than one property, or perhaps you would like one property to use a part of another property's layout on a property page.

Consider, for example, the TabooWords property. This property has its own Taboo property page that really does quite a lot. Suppose that you have another property that would require the same property page layout as the Taboo property does. Let's suppose you have a property called AlertWords that triggers an event whenever an alert word is typed in by the user. If the AlertWords property has the same characteristics as TabooWords, you can use the same property page. Let's begin by creating the AlertWords property and the code necessary to put it into effect.

First, you need to create the new variables for this property in the declarations section. Switch to the question control project and add the following declarations to the declarations section.

First, put this in the default property values section:

```
Const m_def_AlertWords = ""
```

Put this in the property values section:

```
Dim m_AlertWords as String
```

Then add this event in the event declarations section:

```
Event AlertWordDetected(svAlertWord As String)
```

Next, add the procedure shown in Listing 12.9.

Listing 12.9. The AlertWordCensor procedure.

```
 1: Private Sub AlertWordCensor()
 2:
 3:     ' Location index used in string match searches
 4:     Dim iPos As Integer
 5:     ' Used to rebuild an alert string for leftmost portion
 6:     Dim svLeft As String
 7:     ' Used to rebuild an alert string for rightmost portion
 8:     Dim svRight As String
 9:     ' Contains all the words on the alert list
10:     Dim svRemainingAlerts As String
11:     ' The alert word currently being processed
```

continues

Listing 12.9. continued

```
12:      Dim svAlertWord As String
13:      ' The string to evalute
14:      Dim svCheckString As String
15:      ' The string to replace the alert word
16:      Dim svReplacement As String
17:
18:      ' Start with the entire alert list.
19:      svRemainingAlerts = Me.AlertWords
20:
21:      ' Process the text in the answer textbox
22:      svCheckString = txtAnswer.Text
23:
24:      ' Extract each word on the alert list and see
25:      ' if it occurs in the user string
26:
27:      Do While Len(svRemainingAlerts) > 0
28:
29:          ' Find the next word on the alert list
30:          iPos = InStr(svRemainingAlerts, ";")
31:
32:          If iPos = 0 Then
33:              ' Take the last alert word from the remaining string
34:              ' since no more separators
35:              svAlertWord = svRemainingAlerts
36:              ' Empty the list of unprocessed alert words to
37:              ' indicate no more remain
38:              svRemainingAlerts = ""
39:          Else
40:              ' Take the next alert word based on the separator position
41:              svAlertWord = Left(svRemainingAlerts, iPos - 1)
42:              ' Remove this word from the list of unprocessed alert words
43:              svRemainingAlerts = Right(svRemainingAlerts, _
44:                  Len(svRemainingAlerts) - iPos)
45:          End If
46:
47:          ' See if the newly extracted taboo word occurs
48:          ' within the user string
49:          iPos = InStr(svCheckString, svAlertWord)
50:
51:          If iPos > 0 Then
52:              ' Tell the host application about the alert
53:              RaiseEvent AlertWordDetected(svAlertWord)
54:          End If
55:
56:      Loop
57:
58: End Sub
```

This procedure detects the presence of a word that should alert the host application. The presence of an alert word triggers the AlertWordDetected event on the host application.

Next, you need to add the two property procedures needed for the AlertWords property. These two procedures are shown in Listing 12.10.

12

Listing 12.10. The `AlertWords` property procedures.

```
1: Public Property Get AlertWords() As String
2:     AlertWords = m_AlertWords
3: End Property
4:
5: Public Property Let AlertWords(ByVal New_AlertWords As String)
6:     m_AlertWords = New_AlertWords
7:     PropertyChanged "AlertWords"
8: End Property
```

In order to save and retrieve property values, you must also add code to the ReadProperties and WriteProperties events. Add the following statement to the ReadProperties event:

```
m_AlertWords = PropBag.ReadProperty("AlertWords", m_def_AlertWords)
```

and the following statement to the WriteProperties event:

```
Call PropBag.WriteProperty("AlertWords", m_AlertWords, m_def_AlertWords)
```

Don't forget to also change the InitProperties event by adding the statement

```
m_AlertWords = m_def_AlertWords
```

To trap alert words, you must add the following code statements to the txtAnswer_KeyPress event:

```
' Notify program of any words that require an alert
Call AlertWordCensor
```

This statement checks for any alert words whenever the text control changes. You should place the same code statement in the LostFocus event of the txtAnswer control for the same reason. When you have all this code in place, switch over to the test project and bring up the Test application. In the Test application form, make sure the AlertWordDetected event looks like what's shown in Listing 12.11.

Listing 12.11. The `AlertWordDetected` event.

```
1: Private Sub ucQuestion1_AlertWordDetected(svAlertWord As String)
2:
3:     Static svWord As String
4:
5:     If svWord <> svAlertWord Then
6:         svWord = svAlertWord
7:         MsgBox "You cannot use this word in your answer!"
8:     End If
9:
10: End Sub
```

12

This event code will put up a message box the first time the alert word is encountered. Then the program warns the user that this particular word is not part of the answer. After that, the user is not notified again.

Go ahead and test the property by setting AlertWords to a word like Radishes. Run the test application and try typing the word Radishes into the question control. The result should look as shown in Figure 12.12.

Figure 12.12.

The AlertWords *event in action.*

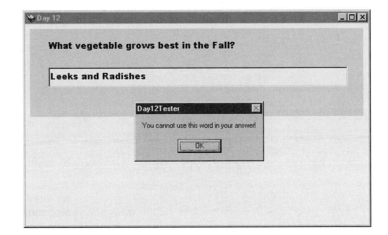

Now that the property is in place and the event works, let's return to our discussion of shared property pages. Because AlertWords is so much like TabooWords, it makes perfect sense to use the same property page. To do this, bring up the project window of the question control; then select View Code to open the code window. From the Tools menu, select Procedure Attributes, which will open the Procedure Attributes dialog. Click the Advanced button to expand the dialog. Then, in the Name box, select the AlertWords property. In the combobox labeled Use this Page in Property Browser, select the pagTaboo property page. Then click the OK button.

The result is that Visual Basic will place the AlertWords property within the TabooWords property page. Go ahead and open the test application and click on the AlertWords property in the property sheet. The ellipsis will appear. When you click, you'll notice that the Taboo property page appears and that all the TabooWord property settings show up. What you need to do now is write code to share the property page with the AlertWords property you've just created. To do that, you need to change the existing pagTaboo property page and write some more code.

First, go in and change the caption of the Taboo page from Taboo to Taboo && Alert Words. (The && places a regular ampersand character in the caption tab of the property page in the

Property Page dialog.) The new property page should look like the one shown in Figure 12.13.

Figure 12.13.

The New Taboo and Alert Words property page.

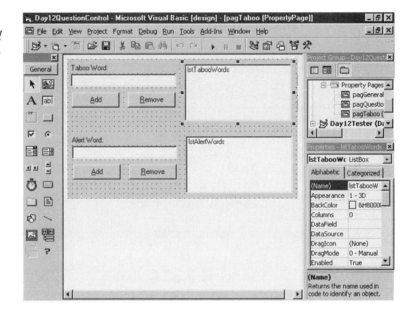

The controls should be labeled as shown in Table 12.3.

Table 12.3. Controls for the Taboo/Alert Words property page.

Control Name	Control Type
lblTabooWord	Label
txtTabooWord	Textbox
cmdTabooRemove	Command button
cmdTabooAdd	Command button
lstTabooWords	Listbox
lblAlertWord	Label
txtAlertWord	Textbox
cmdAlertRemove	Command button
cmdAlertAdd	Command button
lstAlertWords	Listbox

12

Now that you have all the new controls in place, it's time to modify the procedures. Make all the modifications shown in Listing 12.12.

Listing 12.12. Procedure modifications for the Taboo/Alert Words property page.

```
 1: Private Sub cmdTabooAdd_Click()
 2:     Changed = True
 3:     lstTabooWords.AddItem txtTabooWord.Text
 4:     cmdTabooRemove.Enabled = True
 5:     lstTabooWords.ListIndex = lstTabooWords.ListCount - 1
 6: End Sub
 7:
 8: Private Sub cmdTabooRemove_Click()
 9:     Changed = True
10:     lstTabooWords.RemoveItem lstTabooWords.ListIndex
11:     If lstTabooWords.ListCount = 0 Then
12:         cmdTabooRemove.Enabled = False
13:     Else
14:         lstTabooWords.ListIndex - lstTabooWords.ListCount - 1
15:     End If
16: End Sub
17:
18: Private Sub PropertyPage_ApplyChanges()
19:
20:     Dim i As Integer
21:     Dim svItem As String
22:     Dim svTabooWords As String
23:     Dim svAlertWords As String
24:
25:     ' Handle the Taboo words
26:     ' -------------------------------------------------
27:
28:     ' If there are no words, make the property empty
29:     If lstTabooWords.ListCount = 0 Then
30:         svTabooWords = ""
31:
32:     ' If only one word exists, leave off the semi-colon
33:     ElseIf lstTabooWords.ListCount = 1 Then
34:         svTabooWords = lstTabooWords.List(0)
35:     Else
36:         For i = 0 To lstTabooWords.ListCount - 2
37:             svItem = lstTabooWords.List(i)
38:             svTabooWords = svTabooWords & svItem & ";"
39:         Next
40:         svTabooWords = svTabooWords & lstTabooWords.List(i)
41:     End If
42:
43:     SelectedControls(0).TabooWords = svTabooWords
44:
45:     ' Handle the Alert words
46:     ' -------------------------------------------------
47:
```

12

```
48:      ' If there are no words, make the property empty
49:      If lstAlertWords.ListCount = 0 Then
50:          svAlertWords = ""
51:
52:      ' If only one word exists, leave off the semicolon
53:      ElseIf lstAlertWords.ListCount = 1 Then
54:          svAlertWords = lstAlertWords.List(0)
55:      Else
56:          For i = 0 To lstAlertWords.ListCount - 2
57:              svItem = lstAlertWords.List(i)
58:              svAlertWords = svAlertWords & svItem & ";"
59:          Next
60:          svAlertWords = svAlertWords & lstAlertWords.List(i)
61:      End If
62:
63:      SelectedControls(0).AlertWords = svAlertWords
64:
65: End Sub
66:
67: Private Sub PropertyPage_EditProperty(PropertyName As String)
68:
69:      If PropertyName = "AlertWords" Then
70:          cmdTabooAdd.Enabled = False
71:          cmdTabooRemove.Enabled = False
72:          lstTabooWords.Enabled = False
73:          txtTabooWord.Enabled = False
74:      ElseIf PropertyName = "TabooWords" Then
75:          cmdAlertAdd.Enabled = False
76:          cmdAlertRemove.Enabled = False
77:          lstAlertWords.Enabled = False
78:          txtAlertWord.Enabled = False
79:      End If
80:
81: End Sub
82:
83: Private Sub PropertyPage_SelectionChanged()
84:
85:      Dim svTabooWords As String
86:      Dim svAlertWords As String
87:      Dim svItem As String
88:      Dim lStart As Long
89:      Dim lPos As Long
90:
91:      ' Handle the taboo words
92:      ' --------------------------------------------------------------
93:
94:      lPos = 0
95:      lStart = 1
96:
97:      cmdTabooAdd.Enabled = False
98:
99:      lstTabooWords.Clear
100:
101:      svTabooWords = SelectedControls(0).TabooWords
102:
```

continues

Listing 12.12. continued

```
103:    Do
104:        ' Get the next semicolon
105:        lPos = InStr(lStart, svTabooWords, ";")
106:
107:        ' If no semicolons exist and the string has data in it,
108:        ' assume only one item and add that item into the listbox
109:        If lPos = 0 And svTabooWords = "" Then
110:            cmdTabooRemove.Enabled = False
111:            Exit Sub
112:        End If
113:
114:        ' If no semicolons exist and the string has data in it,
115:        ' add the string and set the listbox to the first item
116:        If lPos = 0 And lStart = 1 And svTabooWords <> "" Then
117:            lstTabooWords.AddItem svTabooWords
118:        Else
119:            ' Semicolon found - parse and store
120:            If lPos <> 0 Then
121:                svItem = Mid$(svTabooWords, lStart, lPos - lStart)
122:            Else
123:                svItem = Mid$(svTabooWords, lStart)
124:            End If
125:            lstTabooWords.AddItem svItem
126:            cmdTabooRemove.Enabled = True
127:            lStart = lPos + 1
128:        End If
129:
130:    Loop Until lPos = 0
131:
132:    If lstTabooWords.ListCount = 0 Then
133:        cmdTabooRemove.Enabled = False
134:    Else
135:        cmdTabooRemove.Enabled = True
136:    End If
137:
138:    lstTabooWords.ListIndex = 0
139:
140:    ' Handle the alert words
141:    ' --------------------------------------------------------------
142:
143:    lPos = 0
144:    lStart = 1
145:
146:    cmdAlertAdd.Enabled = False
147:
148:    lstAlertWords.Clear
149:
150:    svAlertWords = SelectedControls(0).AlertWords
151:
```

12

```
152:     Do
153:         ' Get the next semicolon
154:         lPos = InStr(lStart, svAlertWords, ";")
155:
156:         ' If no semicolons exist and the string has data in it,
157:         ' assume only one item and add that item into the listbox
158:         If lPos = 0 And svAlertWords = "" Then
159:             cmdAlertRemove.Enabled = False
160:             Exit Sub
161:         End If
162:
163:         ' If no semicolons exist and the string has data in it,
164:         ' add the string and set the listbox to the first item
165:         If lPos = 0 And lStart = 1 And svAlertWords <> "" Then
166:             lstAlertWords.AddItem svAlertWords
167:         Else
168:             ' Semicolon found - parse and store
169:             If lPos <> 0 Then
170:                 svItem = Mid$(svAlertWords, lStart, lPos - lStart)
171:             Else
172:                 svItem = Mid$(svAlertWords, lStart)
173:             End If
174:             lstAlertWords.AddItem svItem
175:             cmdAlertRemove.Enabled = True
176:             lStart = lPos + 1
177:         End If
178:
179:     Loop Until lPos = 0
180:
181:     If lstAlertWords.ListCount = 0 Then
182:         cmdAlertRemove.Enabled = False
183:     Else
184:         cmdAlertRemove.Enabled = True
185:     End If
186:
187:     lstAlertWords.ListIndex = 0
188:
189: End Sub
190:
191:
192: Private Sub txtTabooWord_Change()
193:     If txtTabooWord.Text = "" Then
194:         cmdTabooAdd.Enabled = False
195:     Else
196:         cmdTabooAdd.Enabled = True
197:     End If
198: End Sub
```

As you can see, the SelectionChanged and ApplyChanges events now handle both sets of controls. You also need to add new event code for all the Alert controls. These new events are listed in Listing 12.13.

Listing 12.13. New procedures for the Taboo/Alert Words property page.

```
 1: Private Sub cmdAlertAdd_Click()
 2:     Changed = True
 3:     lstAlertWords.AddItem txtAlertWord.Text
 4:     cmdAlertRemove.Enabled = True
 5:     lstAlertWords.ListIndex = lstAlertWords.ListCount - 1
 6: End Sub
 7:
 8: Private Sub cmdAlertRemove_Click()
 9:     Changed = True
10:     lstAlertWords.RemoveItem lstAlertWords.ListIndex
11:     If lstAlertWords.ListCount = 0 Then
12:         cmdAlertRemove.Enabled = False
13:     Else
14:         lstAlertWords.ListIndex = lstAlertWords.ListCount - 1
15:     End If
16: End Sub
17:
18: Private Sub txtAlertWord_Change()
19:     If txtAlertWord.Text = "" Then
20:         cmdAlertAdd.Enabled = False
21:     Else
22:         cmdAlertAdd.Enabled = True
23:     End If
24: End Sub
```

These three procedures handle the new Alert controls. If you bring up the test application at this point in design mode, you'll notice that the new AlertWords property appears in the property sheet. You'll also notice that when you click on either the ActiveWords property or the TabooWords property, the same dialog appears and allows you to change both properties.

When two properties share the same property page, however, it's often useful to disable the portion of the page that is unused. If, for instance, you've selected the AlertWords property, you should disable the TabooWords controls. How do you do this? Read on!

The EditProperty Event

The EditProperty event gives you the ability to determine which property has brought up the property page. The event is called after the Initialize and SelectionChanged events take place. The property that brings up the page is set through a parameter called PropertyName that is passed in. By intercepting the name of the property, you can disable various controls in the dialog, set focus to an appropriate control within the dialog, and enable or disable controls that apply or do not apply to the property being passed in. Listing 12.14 shows what you should enter for the question control project.

12

Listing 12.14. The `EditProperty` procedure for the Taboo/Alert Words property page.

```
 1: Private Sub PropertyPage_EditProperty(PropertyName As String)
 2:
 3:     If PropertyName = "AlertWords" Then
 4:         cmdTabooAdd.Enabled = False
 5:         cmdTabooRemove.Enabled = False
 6:         lstTabooWords.Enabled = False
 7:         txtTabooWord.Enabled = False
 8:     ElseIf PropertyName = "TabooWords" Then
 9:         cmdAlertAdd.Enabled = False
10:         cmdAlertRemove.Enabled = False
11:         lstAlertWords.Enabled = False
12:         txtAlertWord.Enabled = False
13:     End If
14:
15: End Sub
```

This procedure will enable or disable the appropriate set of controls depending on which property was selected. If the property page is brought up by selecting any other property or by selecting View | Property Pages, the `PropertyName` variable is set to neither property, so both are enabled. If, however, the user chooses one of the two properties and brings up a property page, only the relevant property will have enabled controls. The other one will not. This technique is very useful for cases like this, and lets you use fewer property pages, which conserves space and usually makes the control simpler to use.

Property Page Error Handling

Error handling is a very important part of property page design. One place that is especially critical when working with property pages is the `ApplyChanges` event. If you create a property page that cannot allow the user to enter invalid properties, you don't need to worry about error handling here. For instance, if your property page consists of a series of listboxes where the user must select from one of several valid choices, error handling is unnecessary because you're assured of getting correct entries.

If, on the other hand, the property page allows the user to enter values that the Property Let (or Set) procedures may reject without handling the error properly, it may be up to your property page to handle the errors itself. I might point out right away that it's always best to do your error handling in the Property procedures themselves. That way, you keep error handling at the lowest possible level, which is always desirable. If you need to do error

12

handling here, however, this is the most appropriate sequence of events to follow. When an error occurs, do the following:

1. Stop processing the `ApplyChanges` event.

2. Display an error message so the user can see what went wrong and knows how to fix it.

3. Set the focus back to the property that caused the error.

4. Set the `Changed` property of the `PropertyPage` to `True`. This re-enables the Apply button and prevents the property page from closing. Otherwise, the dialog will close and the property changes will be lost.

Listing 12.15 shows an example of error handling in the `ApplyChanges` event of the Question property page.

Listing 12.15. Error handling in the `ApplyChanges` event.

```
 1: Private Sub PropertyPage_ApplyChanges()
 2:
 3:     On Error Resume Next
 4:
 5:     SelectedControls(0).Question = txtQuestion.Text
 6:
 7:     If Err.Number <> 0 Then
 8:         MsgBox "Error: " & Err.Description & "(" & Err.Number & ") has
 9:             ➥occurred in setting the Question property. Please enter
10:             ➥the value correctly.", vbExclamation, "Question Property
11:             ➥Error"
12:         txtQuestion.SetFocus
13:         Changed = True
14:         Exit Sub
15:     End If
16:
17:     SelectedControls(0).Hint = txtHint
18:
19:     If Err.Number <> 0 Then
20:         MsgBox "Error: " & Err.Description & "(" & Err.Number & ") has
21:             ➥occurred in setting the Hint property. Please enter
22:             ➥the value correctly.", vbExclamation, "Hint Property Error"
23:         txtQuestion.SetFocus
24:         Changed = True
25:         Exit Sub
26:     End If
27:
28:     SelectedControls(0).DisplayOnIncorrectResponse = _
29:             cboDisplayOnIncorrectResponse.ListIndex
30:
31: End Sub
```

Notice that error handling is unnecessary in the case of the `DisplayOnIncorrectResponse` property because it is impossible for the user to select an invalid setting in that case.

Concluding Guidelines for Designing Property Pages

Here are some concluding guidelines and tips for making your property pages the best they can be. Many of these guidelines are recommended by Microsoft:

- [ ] Make sure you give focus to the first control in your property page. You can do this by setting the `TabIndex` property of the first control to `0`. Make sure the rest of the controls are set in order. Columns of controls should be ordered top to bottom, left to right.

- [ ] Give the user access keys for all the properties on a page.

- [ ] Group standard property pages at the end of a list of pages.

- [ ] Make sure all your property pages are the same size. You can use the `StandardSize` property of a property page at design time.

- [ ] Don't add too many property pages. Make sure you have a reasonable number of pages and group like properties together as much as possible.

- [ ] Don't attach other dialogs to property pages. Keep them simple. You can add common dialogs when necessary, but go no further.

- [ ] Avoid cross-tab dependencies, where setting the property on one page affects a property on another. Try to keep your pages as clean and distinct as possible.

- [ ] Most property pages start with a General tab at the beginning with a list of general properties. Although this is not a hard-and-fast rule, it is recommended for controls with properties that fit into that category.

12

Summary

Property pages are very powerful extensions of the property sheet. They enable you to group simple properties together on individual tabbed pages, and they also enable you to mass together several controls to craft a property setting for a specific property. Property pages can be used when a single control is selected or when multiple controls are selected. You need to write your property page code to handle multiple control selection. The biggest decision you have to make is which properties apply to all the controls selected and which ones apply to the first selected control. You, the developer, must make this decision on a property-by-property basis.

You've now been exposed to the techniques needed to create property pages, as well as some of the more advanced concepts such as error handling and shared property pages among multiple properties. You also have some tips and techniques that should help you when you're designing your own property pages.

By all means, use property pages. They add a great deal of power and capability to your controls. The best way to design effective and useful property pages is to practice. Go back through the exercises in this lesson and make sure you understand them. Also, the Quiz questions at the end of this lesson should help to reinforce the concepts you've learned over the last couple days.

Q&A

Q Why would I want to share a single property page with more than one property?

A The beauty of property pages is that you can group like properties together on a single page. The disadvantage is that if you select a single property and are brought to a property page, you can change any properties that appear on the page. Any time you don't want to distract the user with all the other properties, you can simply disable their interfaces. Also, if one property uses a subset of the controls needed in another property, you can use this technique to keep things simpler for the user, not to mention for yourself.

Q I'm having a hard time deciding how to group my properties together. How do I make this easier?

A This is a very important step, and one you need to work through carefully before you write any property pages. If you decide to change midstream, you might have to go through a lot of extra work. I suggest that you think as much about the various properties as you can before sitting down to create property pages. Try to find common functionality between the various properties; then experiment with different groupings of properties until they make the most sense to you. It might take a while, but the effort will be well worth the investment in time and energy.

Q Why can't I access property pages from the property sheet when I select multiple controls on a form?

A For some reason, this is not possible through the property sheet. I'm not quite sure why, but this is the way Visual Basic works in its current implementation. To avoid getting confused, always go to View | Property Page to make sure you see all the property pages you should see for the control.

12

Workshop

Take another look at the Taboo property page. Think of ways you can enhance this page to make it even more usable. Can you get the page to produce unwanted effects or errors? If so, write error-handling code to make the control more robust. Has this experience confirmed to you the importance of adequate error handling in a control?

Quiz

NOTE

See Appendix D, "Answers to Quiz Questions," for the answers to these questions.

1. Gain some more experience with property pages by adding the following properties to the Question page:

   MaxGuesses

   ExpectedAnswer

2. Create a General property page and add the following properties to it:

   Enabled

   FocusIndicator

   EnterCausesTab

12

Day 13

Debugging Controls

So far you have seen specific code statements to construct controls. You have, in effect, learned to hammer the nails and boards of the control together with these code fundamentals. However, any good carpenter will tell you that it takes more than just knowledge of how to nail boards to build a good house. The same is true of control construction. For the next two days, the focus changes to provide you with the broad background you need to make sure your controls work well. The earlier focus was on very specific code techniques to build your controls. Now it's time to consider a general approach for making sure your controls work smoothly after you have entered the code. This error-removal, troubleshooting, and refinement process is referred to as the *debug and test phase* of control development.

The process of debugging is closely intertwined with all phases of control development. You might debug, or isolate and remove errors, as soon as you start to enter your first line of code. You will likely continue to debug throughout your control-definition process. Then, once everything is done, most likely you will test your control in a more formal fashion and debug some more to fix the errors you find. Debugging is therefore addressed today because it is often a continuous part of the control development process. After you have debugging in context, you will learn about the broader topic of testing. Day 16, "Testing Your Control," provides guidelines for testing your controls in a systematic manner.

Some specific features of the Visual Basic programming environment will aid you in control debugging. Many relevant general software concepts that apply universally to any programming language will also aid your understanding of control development. A Visual Basic control is, in many respects, just another variation of a traditional Visual Basic program. It's not surprising, then, that much of the debugging knowledge that pertains to control development also pertains to applications in general. However, there are also some control-specific aspects to debugging. You will learn about both today.

Debugging is a broad topic in its own right, and one that is far too often overlooked. Your debugging skills will be one of the biggest determinants of how efficient your control development is, as well as of how robust your controls are. Debugging techniques vary from one type of development to another, but the same importance applies in virtually every development arena. Clearly every computer programming book should have at least one chapter devoted to debugging! But check out some of the other programming books you have available. Most likely you'll see that not much ink has been sacrificed to this topic.

Unfortunately, this is all too representative of the state of programming based on the experiences your authors have had working with a variety of developers. Many programmers use only a subset of the debugging capabilities available to them. Many others have just a minimal understanding of the most effective debugging concepts. Then control development throws in even a few more twists and considerations to the debugging model. Debugging knowledge directly correlates to programming skill. The goal of today's lesson is to ensure that you are in the skilled programmer category when it comes to control development. By the end of today you will have learned enough to be confident that you can efficiently and effectively debug the controls you develop.

The Concept of Debugging a Control

Consider what it means to debug a control. When you produce any software, you generally want it to work well, unfettered by bugs and problems. This goal is present in control development as well. Delivering bug-free code might even be more of a concern in control development than traditional development because a typical component is utilized by many different host applications. Therefore, if you unleash a bug into the world through your control, the users of any host application that incorporates your control might experience that problem. The audience of people affected by a bug can be quite large when a bug is present in a control.

In addition, the user of an application that integrates your control is typically powerless to stamp out the bug himself. Suppose your control does cause some problem when it is used within his application. If he just has your control file and not your source code, the user will have to depend on you to make a fix and redistribute the control. Control bugs can be very challenging to track and pin down.

In one sense, control code is straightforward to debug. The properties, methods, and events of a control provide a very well-defined set of interfaces between a control and the host application. Debugging is easier to carry out when you're chasing well-defined problems. In another sense, though, problems can be very subtle. Debugging now involves two pieces of software rather than one. You must often test both the host application and the control code to determine where a problem is being caused. Some problems may occur only when the control has a certain state of property settings that most host applications do not normally use. Problem re-creation can be difficult under these circumstances.

Once you suspect there is a problem in your control, you need to hone in on the area that causes a problem and rule out other areas from suspicion. Many Visual Basic features can help you with this task. The structure of your project may influence your ability to use features. You clearly need a host application to test your control (you must run a host application to cause your control to run because a control cannot run by itself). One structure you can use is to define a standard application project that just references the control OCX file you want to test (through the Project|Components menu option). However, if you simply run an application that references a control, you will not have access to the control code you want to debug. Without access to the control source code, you cannot apply the debugging tools to analyze the control. Instead, a project structure that allows you to simultaneously test a control at the source code level and the host application that drives it is needed for effective debugging. The Visual Basic project group is the answer.

You were introduced to the concept of the project group back on Day 2, "Creating a Simple Control." The samples you have worked through since then have been set up as project groups. These groups incorporate two projects: The standard application project contains a form that incorporates the question control, and the question control project itself defines the control.

13

You get a significant benefit when you group an application project with a control project in a project group. You can debug the control code at the same time you debug the sample application code. Because the application that includes the control is part of your project, it is an easy matter to start the application and cause your control code to run. And because the control code is part of your project, it is easy to sequence through that code as it runs and see how it responds to the sample application. You can use techniques that you will learn today— like breakpoints, watches, and the code window—to help put the code through its paces and pinpoint problems in the control as well as in the host application.

A Sample Project Group to Debug

Today you will use the project group structure once again. The biggest advantages of the project group structure is the ease of debugging it allows, and you will have a chance to observe this benefit firsthand. The project group you will use is the same question control sample you have used on past days. The project group consists of a test application that integrates the question control as well as the control project itself.

A nice little bug has been thrown into this control project to make things a little more interesting and relevant for you. Recall the example from Day 9, "User-Defined Events." In the course of that day's material, you added a MaxGuessesExceeded event. That event was raised by the question control whenever the user's guesses exceeded the number specified in the control's MaxGuesses property. The code worked very well when you saw it on Day 9. However, imagine that you were a little loose-fingered when you typed in the solution. One of the key checks of the logic behind raising the MaxGuessesExceeded event was the conditional check:

```
If m_IncorrectAnswerCount > Me.MaxGuesses Then
```

This check evaluates whether the incorrect answers exceed the guesses. What if this line had been entered as

```
If m_IncorrectAnswerCount > Me.IncorrectAnswerCount Then
```

The variable m_IncorrectAnswerCount is a module-level variable that tallies incorrect responses. Me.MaxGuesses refers to the MaxGuesses property of the user control itself. Me is Visual Basic shorthand notation for referring to the current object, which in this context is the UserControl object itself.

When you type the names of objects into the Visual Basic editor, the editor automatically offers a drop-down list of object properties you can choose from to complete your typing sequence. Suppose you scrolled down through this list, attempting to select MaxGuesses as the property you wanted to deal with. However, just as you were about to complete this selection, the phone rang, your spouse yelled at you to answer it, and the cat jumped on your lap and spilled your soda. In the midst of this commotion the cat's paw, unbeknownst to you, brushed the keyboard and caused the Width property to be selected rather than the intended MaxGuesses property. Therefore, you inadvertently introduce the use of the Me.IncorrectAnswerCount property when you intended your conditional to use Me.MaxGuesses. The resulting code is shown in Listing 13.1.

13

Listing 13.1. A bug in the conditional check for MaxGuessesExceeded.

```
 1: ' See if answer is correct
 2: Private Sub ProcessAnswer()
 3:     ' Only check the answer if it has not yet been evaluated.
 4:     If m_bAnswerHasChanged Then
 5:         If UCase(txtAnswer.Text) = UCase(m_ExpectedAnswer) Then
 6:             lblFeedback.Caption = "Correct!"
 7:         Else
 8:             ' Store the incorrect response in the array
 9:             m_IncorrectAnswerCount = m_IncorrectAnswerCount + 1
10:             ReDim Preserve m_IncorrectAnswers(m_IncorrectAnswerCount)
11:             m_IncorrectAnswers(m_IncorrectAnswerCount) = txtAnswer.Text
12:
13:             ' See if a max number of guesses is in effect
14:             If Me.MaxGuesses > 0 Then
15:                 ' Check to see if maximum allowed guesses has been exceeded
16:                         ' bug on this line for sample purposes!!
17:                 If m_IncorrectAnswerCount > Me.IncorrectAnswerCount Then
18:                     RaiseEvent MaxGuessesExceeded
19:                 End If
20:             End If
21:
22:             If m_DisplayOnIncorrectResponse = ucAnswer Then
23:                 lblFeedback.Caption = "Expected Answer: " & m_ExpectedAnswer
24:             ElseIf m_DisplayOnIncorrectResponse = ucHint Then
25:                 lblFeedback.Caption = "Hint: " & m_Hint
26:                 ' Highlight answer areas so user can retry after seeing hint
27:                 txtAnswer.SelStart = 0
28:                 txtAnswer.SelLength = Len(txtAnswer.Text)
29:             End If
30:         End If
31:
32:         ' Set the flag so we won't check again until answer has been altered
33:         m_bAnswerHasChanged = False
34:
35:         ' Now send tabkey so focus goes to next question if that
36:         ' property option is set
37:         If EnterCausesTab Then
38:             Call SendTab
39:         End If
40:     End If
41: End Sub
```

ANALYSIS This is an example of a logic bug. A bug has been introduced into the code in Listing 13.1. The conditional check on Me.IncorrectAnswerCount (line 17) should instead check Me.MaxGuesses to work correctly. The check is intended to detect when the maximum number of guesses specified by the user has been exceeded. Instead, with this bug left in the code, the condition will only be true when the number of user guesses exceeds the number of user guesses, which will never happen!

Is this an outlandish bug-introduction scenario? Perhaps so, but then every other scenario is equally outlandish. Bugs are unintended problems in your code. Because they are unintended, by definition you never plan to have them in your code! Bugs can be introduced through typos, through flaws in your thinking process, and through inattention, in a million different ways and flavors. In my years of programming, I have indeed had the misfortune to have had a bug introduced by the brush of a cat's paw on the keyboard. I've had many more bugs introduced by my own typos and flaws in thinking. No matter how they got in the code, the end result is always the same. Bugs can be tremendously hard to track down and exterminate.

You have a sample bug in the code that you will chase in the example ahead. You have a distinct advantage with this example that you will not normally have when debugging: You already know the solution to the bug that you are chasing. However, you may not know the most efficient way to track down the problem, which is the primary point of this lesson. How do you rid yourself of the bug? Should you use the insect repellent or the fly swatter, or simply open the window and let the bug fly away? Or, in more concrete Visual Basic terms, is it easiest to hunt down your `Me.IncorrectAnswerCount` bug by using code breakpoints, watches, the `debug` object, or a combination of these methods? The place to start is by learning a little more about each of these approaches.

The Easy Way Out of Debugging

First of all, before you start to chase the bug, verify that it is present. The test program was set up to limit the number of user guesses for the first question to three. Correspondingly, you will see a value of 3 in the control's `MaxGuesses` property. The host application catches the `MaxGuessesExceeded` event and provides a warning message to the user when he has exceeded this allotment of guesses. If the code were functioning correctly, after you entered three unique guesses, your fourth guess would cause this error message to be displayed. Check this out for yourself. Enter four different answers and notice that the message box never occurs.

NOTE

SAMPLE Follow along with the examples in this chapter by using and modifying the `Day13QuestionControl.vbg` group project file under the `Samples\Day13\Your Start\` directory on the book's CD-ROM. This project contains the code that is intended to be your starting point for today. Copy the directory to your hard drive so you can make subsequent modifications. The material is presented in a before-and-after format. If you want to see today's changes already implemented, you can view the corrected `Day13QuestionControl.vbg`

13

group project that is available one directory level up in the
`Samples\Day13` directory.

Now place yourself in the role of the developer who has just discovered this bug. Where do you start in the debugging process? The first step is one that is often overlooked because it is so obvious. Before you plunge into applying some of the Visual Basic debugging features, first lean back, take a breath, and think about what the code is doing. Briefly view the source code for the host application and control. Grab a piece of scrap paper and jot down some notes about the flow you expect the code to take.

Many bugs are far too subtle to discover by such a simple code inspection. On the other hand, several bugs might jump out immediately when you do this quick mental and visual inspection. If you can find your bugs with a quick first-pass application of this technique, you are best off. You've invested minimal time in debugging and already have a potential solution.

Consider how this approach would work for the `Me.IncorrectAnswers` bug. You know the program doesn't work. You should always start thinking through the highest, most obvious layer of the application, or the layer that the user interacts with, and then work your way down to progressively lower layers. Thus you are considering what the host application does before you worry about what the control does. The first thing you should do is inspect the properties of the control that is integrated into the host application. Make sure the `MaxGuesses` property is indeed set to 3. You don't want to spend time debugging code if you don't even have a code problem!

After you have verified that the property settings are okay, next consider why the message box is never displayed. When you review the code, you see that the `ucQuestion1_MaxGuessesExceeded` event of the host application should display the message box when it is called. This event-handling routine is shown in Listing 13.2. Display this routine in the code window and inspect it to see if you detect any problems.

Listing 13.2. The host application's event handler that should be called when the event is raised.

```
1: Private Sub ucQuestion1_MaxGuessesExceeded()
2:    MsgBox "You have guessed too many times!", _
3:        vbOKOnly, "Warning"
4:
5: End Sub
```

13

This event-handling routine displays a message indicating that too many guesses have been attempted. Because this message box has never been displayed, your first assumption is likely to be that the event handler has never been called.

Because no obvious code problems are apparent in this routine, and it appears that this event handler has never been called, next you can shift your quick visual code inspection to the control code itself. Select the question control project from the Project Explorer and view its code window. Now you want to move your inspection to the next lower level of code. This next suspect would be the code called in the control immediately before the event handler should be raised. Because you know the name of the event handler from your host application inspection, you can just do an Edit | Find from the main menu and specify that event name to locate the point where that event is raised in the control code. In the case of your question control, the event is only raised once in the control code. You saw that area of code in Listing 13.1. This is your next suspect.

Review the code here carefully. If the `RaiseEvent` seems to be in place correctly, you can assume that the problem is not there and must be in the circumstances that should cause it to get called. You can begin to shift your inspection upward. As you do, think about the logic of each line of code. If you have used good comments in your code, you will notice that at this point the mental debugging process is very easy. As you shift your gaze and thoughts upward, you are very likely to notice that the conditional comparison is incorrect. If so, you've nabbed your bug with hardly a fight, and would normally put a fix into place at this point.

I want to give you a couple warnings about this approach, however. One is that it often just does not work very well. If your code is somewhat complex, you may not be able to easily define the flow of the code, let alone the bug. Likewise, your analysis is based on a lot of assumptions that the code is working the way you expect. Some of your assumptions may be wrong and may lead you to the wrong places in your code.

For these reasons, you should use this approach but use it lightly. You need to have a general feel for the flow of the code before you debug with advanced debugging techniques anyway, so you are out nothing if you spend a small amount of time studying the code. However, the debugging techniques you will learn about are so powerful and easy to apply that you might as well put them to use right away unless the problem jumps out at you during the visual inspection. A good general rule is to spend 5 to 10 minutes on a visual inspection of the code as you begin your bug hunt. Get a feel for the code flow. You might even stumble across the bug. If you haven't found it after a few minutes, it's time to pull out the heavy artillery and continue the hunt.

13

Breakpoints

Your first round of bug hunting was based on speculation during your visual inspection. From here on in, it can be based on proof. It's time to insert a code breakpoint. You can use breakpoints to test and conclusively prove your hypotheses about exactly which code is being executed. A *code breakpoint* is an instruction to Visual Basic to temporarily halt the progression of the program when some source code line that you designate has been reached.

The first breakpoint to insert is one that lets you prove whether the event handler is ever reached. Return to the code for the event handler, shown in Listing 13.2. Bring up this source code in the code window. Now insert a breakpoint. You do this by placing the text cursor on a given source code line and then selecting Debug|Toggle Breakpoint from the Visual Basic menu. This will turn on a breakpoint for that line. Place a breakpoint on the line that reads

```
MsgBox "You have guessed too many times!", vbOKOnly, "Warning"
```

The line's color will change to a highlighted background to indicate that it has been selected as a breakpoint location. You can see the code window with this breakpoint inserted in Figure 13.1.

Figure 13.1.

Specifying a breakpoint in the event handler code window.

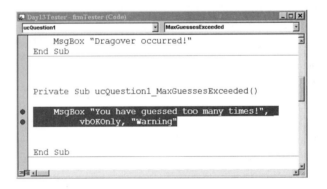

Now try your test case again. Start the Test application and enter four different answers to the question. If the breakpoint were reached, the code execution would be immediately suspended. The code window would be displayed to you with a breakpoint indicator on the line containing the breakpoint. This does not occur in response to your test case. You can conclude that the event-handler breakpoint has not been reached. That means that the event-handler code is never executed, as you suspected. This additional insight helps you narrow down the scope of the problem. The problem must lie in the fact that the control doesn't generate the event in the first place, rather than in some mistake in the event-handling routine itself.

13

NOTE

> The event-handling routine provides visual feedback when the event occurs by displaying a message box, as you can see in Listing 13.2. So it would seem that if the event had occurred, you would have seen the message box. You may wonder why you couldn't just conclude that the event didn't occur if the message box is absent, rather than resorting to a breakpoint to prove the same thing.
>
> In this particular case, that approach would have worked. But in the general sense, you want to avoid such assumptions. One of the fundamental rules of debugging is to never assume how a given line of code will act. There could have been some hidden problem that caused the program flow to reach the event handler, but the message box to be suppressed. But with your breakpoint you have eliminated this possibility. At this point you have conclusively proven that your breakpoint, and therefore the event-handling routine, is never reached.

Now it is time to wade deeper into the thicket to hunt down the bug. You have not been able to detect a problem at the application level, so next you must move down to the control layer. Fortunately, the project group structure of your test application and control makes it easy to test the control at the source code level, just as you tested the test application. Use the Project Explorer to bring up the code window for the question control. Locate the ProcessAnswer routine shown in Figure 13.1. Now place a breakpoint on the RaiseEvent statement in this routine. Place the text cursor on this source code line:

```
RaiseEvent MaxGuessesExceeded
```

Then select Debug | Toggle Breakpoint from the Visual Basic menu to add the breakpoint, just as you did for the first breakpoint you added.

Now you have two breakpoints set in this project: One is in the host application; the other is in the control. You can have as many breakpoints as you need in a project. Each breakpoint will be displayed in the code window as it is encountered.

The first test you ran proved that the host application's event-handling routine is never called because that breakpoint was never reached. This new breakpoint will allow you to test whether the event is raised within the control code. Because the event handler wasn't called, it is a good guess that the corresponding RaiseEvent statement in the control was not carried out either. However, once you start the methodical steps of debugging, you must abandon the temptation to draw final conclusions based on such guesses. Prove to yourself what is happening each step of the way. It might be true that the RaiseEvent statement is never called, but then again it might not be. Perhaps the wrong event name was coded in the RaiseEvent statement. In that case the RaiseEvent statement *would* be carried out, but the host application's event handler with the correct event name would never be called.

This second breakpoint will allow you to conclusively test whether the `RaiseEvent` statement is carried out. Carry out the second test now. If you still have the application running from a prior test, stop it at this point by selecting Run | End from the Visual Basic menu. You should start every test by running a new instance of the application. Then you can be confident you are testing the application in the same state every time, not testing the aftermath of changes from the earlier trial run. Now run the application again. All your breakpoints remain in effect from one test run to another. Enter four different responses as the answer for the first question.

Once again, no breakpoints are encountered in this test. You've definitively proved a bit more about the control code. The `RaiseEvent` statement is not carried out, as you suspected. And now you're starting to see a very important pattern of debugging. You often learn as much from what does *not* happen as by what does happen. It's time to plot your next debugging move. You saw that the high-layer host application code was never called. Then you proved that the statement in your control code that triggered the event was not called. You need to prove the code flow in the control to understand the problem. So now you must continue to backtrack through the control code until you locate some code that is called within it.

Examine the code in Listing 13.1 once again. It is a likely assumption that the `ProcessAnswer` routine is called because it should be called every time the Enter key is pressed. This is the next hypothesis to prove. If you want to make sure that the routine is called, it is best to place the breakpoint near the top of the procedure before any conditional branches are called that could affect code flow. Therefore, insert a breakpoint on this line:

```
If m_bAnswerHasChanged Then
```

NOTE

> You can use the regular Debug | Toggle Breakpoint menu option to insert the breakpoint, as you have for earlier breakpoints. You could also click the cursor on the line where you want to insert the breakpoint and press the F9 key. This has the same effect as toggling on a breakpoint through the menu selection.

13

Multiple Breakpoints

You could carry out your next test now, but you've already had a couple rounds of a one-shot-at-a-time breakpoint approach. You can see that it can take a considerable time investment to shift your attention a line at a time through your code with breakpoints. If you really want to make sure you have all your bases covered, you can take the scattergun approach. In this approach you use many breakpoints all at once. Add even more breakpoints in this round. Perhaps you have started to wonder if the code that is supposed to call the `ProcessAnswer` routine is even working correctly.

You can put your mind at ease by proving whether the code that precedes the ProcessAnswer call is reached. Select Edit|Find to initiate a search. Do a search of the entire module for all occurrences of the name ProcessAnswer in the control. You will find that it is called by both the txtAnswer_KeyPress event routine and the txtAnswer_LostFocus event routine. You can see these two control event routines in Listing 13.3.

Listing 13.3. The control routines that call ProcessAnswer.

```
 1: ' Process answer in response to enter key
 2: Private Sub txtAnswer_KeyPress(KeyAscii As Integer)
 3:     ' Declare a constant for the question mark since VB doesn't define one
 4:     Const vbKeyQuestion As Integer = 63  ' ASCII 63 is question mark
 5:     ' Censure any taboo words that have been entered in the textbox so far
 6:     Call TabooWordCensor
 7:
 8:     ' Check if enter key was pressed
 9:     If KeyAscii = vbKeyReturn Then
10:         KeyAscii = 0
11:         Call ProcessAnswer
12:     ElseIf KeyAscii = vbKeyQuestion Then
13:         ' Raise event to signify that user entered a question.
14:         '    Pass the entire text response entered by user with the event.
15:         RaiseEvent UserQuestionDetected(txtAnswer.Text)
16:     End If
17: End Sub
18: ' Check the answer if the user moves to next field
19: '    (in response to tab/enter keystroke or mouseclick on other control)
20: Private Sub txtAnswer_LostFocus()
21:     ' Censure any taboo words that have been entered in the textbox so far
22:     Call TabooWordCensor
23:
24:     ' Evaluate the answer
25:     Call ProcessAnswer
26:
27: End Sub
```

ANALYSIS   The ProcessAnswer routine is called in two cases. The first is in response to an Enter keystroke. The second is when focus changes from one control to the next.

The next task is to see which, if either, of the conditions that lead to the ProcessAnswer call occur when you run your test. You need to put two more breakpoints in your control code for this purpose. Place the first breakpoint on the ProcessAnswer call in the txtAnswer_Keypress event routine:

```
Call ProcessAnswer
```

13

Place the next breakpoint on the `ProcessAnswer` call in the `txtAnswer_LostFocus` event routine:

```
Call ProcessAnswer
```

Use F9 to toggle the breakpoint on in both of these cases. Now you will certainly have a good feel for where your code flow is going when you carry out the next test; the breakpoints will tell you quite clearly if the code flow moves in the direction of the `ProcessAnswer` routine. You took a scattergun approach for this round of testing, which provides a lot more information after the test. With this approach, you can draw a conclusion for each new breakpoint.

The scattergun approach can, however, make debugging a bit tougher. You now have more code breakpoint areas to keep track of and more statements your mind is thinking about. When you shift through your code using a single breakpoint at a time, it is often easier to stay completely focused on your mission. The scattergun versus single-shot breakpoint-insertion choice is a subjective one. You will probably find that in early stages of debugging a scattergun approach works best, and then as you hone in on the problem a single-shot, one-step-at-a-time approach will help lead you to the solution more quickly. Whichever approach you take, you should always be crystal clear on the reason for inserting every breakpoint. Each breakpoint should be intended to prove or disprove a hypothesis about your code flow.

You now have five breakpoints standing ready to serve you. Once you start to work with multiple breakpoints, it can become easy to forget where you have placed them all. It is a good idea to make a list on a piece of scrap paper as you go; then at a glance you can see a good summary of all the hypotheses your next test will prove or disprove. Table 13.1 shows such a summary for the five breakpoints you now have in place.

Table 13.1. Breakpoints currently in place.

Code Statement	Procedure	Where
MsgBox	ucQuestion1_MaxGuessesExceeded	Host app
RaiseEvent	ProcessAnswer	Control
If m_bAnswerHasChanged	ProcessAnswer	Control
Call ProcessAnswer	txtAnswer_KeyPress	Control
Call ProcessAnswer	txtAnswer_LostFocus	Control

13

You can see from this table that you currently have four breakpoints contained in your control code and one breakpoint in your host application. You can quickly see where every breakpoint occurs from this table. You should also be clear on the purpose of each breakpoint before running a test. It might be overkill to write out the purpose on your scrap paper because in many cases the purpose is intuitively obvious. But you should at least have a clear picture in your mind. Review the breakpoints in Table 13.1 and see if you can state what each is intended to prove. Table 13.2 provides a summary of the purpose of each breakpoint.

Table 13.2. The purpose of each breakpoint.

Breakpoint Location	Conclusion if Reached
ucQuestion1_MaxGuessesExceeded	Event handler in host app called
ProcessAnswer *RaiseEvent line*	Control raised event
ProcessAnswer *if line*	Answer change state evaluated prior to raising event
txtAnswer_KeyPress	ProcessAnswer call made in response to keystroke
txtAnswer_LostFocus	ProcessAnswer call made in response to losing focus

Now go ahead and run this new test. Restart the application. Your test goal is to supply four different answers to the first question, one at a time, and observe the behavior of the control. Start by entering TestOne as the response to the first question on the test form. The current breakpoint indicator appears after you type in the fourth response (see Figure 13.2). You finally have proof that at least some of your control code has been reached!

NOTE

You should stop the test application's previous run and then start the application anew before each test to make sure you are always running your tests under clean, comparable conditions. One quick way to start a new test is to select Run|Restart from the Visual Basic menu. This is equivalent to selecting Run|End and then Run|Start.

The test program has been suspended at this point. Visual Basic is waiting for instructions from you before it proceeds any further. Select Run|Continue from the menu to resume execution of the program and see if your next breakpoint is reached.

Figure 13.2.

The breakpoint indicator, displaying the control code statement that has been reached.

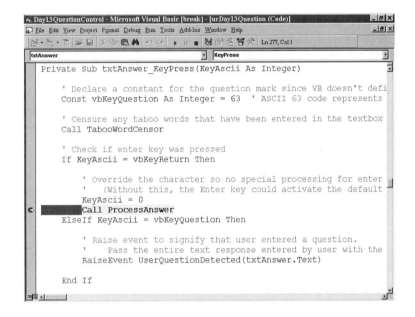

```
Day13QuestionControl - Microsoft Visual Basic [break] - [ucDay13Question (Code)]
File  Edit  View  Project  Format  Debug  Run  Tools  Add-Ins  Window  Help
                                                              Ln 277, Col 1
txtAnswer                                    KeyPress

    Private Sub txtAnswer_KeyPress(KeyAscii As Integer)

        ' Declare a constant for the question mark since VB doesn't defi
        Const vbKeyQuestion As Integer = 63    ' ASCII 63 code represents

        ' Censure any taboo words that have been entered in the textbox
        Call TabooWordCensor

        ' Check if enter key was pressed
        If KeyAscii = vbKeyReturn Then

            ' Override the character so no special processing for enter
            '   (Without this, the Enter key could activate the default
            KeyAscii = 0
            Call ProcessAnswer
        ElseIf KeyAscii = vbKeyQuestion Then

            ' Raise event to signify that user entered a question.
            '    Pass the entire text response entered by user with the
            RaiseEvent UserQuestionDetected(txtAnswer.Text)

        End If
```

NOTE

By now, you probably have caught on to the idea that Visual Basic gives you lots of choices on how to carry out any task. There are several ways to tell a program to continue running. One way is the Run | Continue menu selection. Another way is to click on the Continue button on the Visual Basic toolbar. The Continue toolbar button is easy to spot—it is shaped like a right arrowhead and will display the text Continue when you move the cursor over it. My favorite way to continue a program is, not surprisingly, the easiest. You can just press F5 to continue the program. After all, when you're in the middle of debugging you want to focus all your energy on finding the problem. Why waste any on mouse clicks?

13

Now you see the results of another breakpoint occurrence, as shown in Figure 13.3. The If statement in the ProcessAnswer routine has been reached. You know that this routine was called, and a condition is about to be evaluated. You're on to something here. Once again, press F5 to continue the program execution. Oops! No more breakpoints occurred. The program scampered merrily on its way, and is once again running and waiting for your input.

Figure 13.3.

The breakpoint indicator in the ProcessAnswer *routine.*

Because the condition you want to test is the behavior after you enter four incorrect answers, you are still in a good position to carry out this test. Supply a new incorrect answer of TestTwo and press the Enter key. Once again, you will arrive at the breakpoint in the txtAnswer_KeyPress routine, as shown in Figure 13.2. The control code is going through the same flow of statements for the second answer as it did for the first answer. The first time through you saw that the ProcessAnswer routine was correctly called, and you have a breakpoint at that level. Therefore, you really don't need the breakpoint here any longer. You are not gaining any additional insight by reaching it. Remove this breakpoint now so that it will not be reached on future cycles of this test. To remove the breakpoint, just make sure the cursor is on the same line as the highlighted breakpoint statement and then press F9. This toggles the breakpoint off so it is no longer in effect.

Now press F5 to cause the program to run again. Once again, you arrive at the breakpoint in the ProcessAnswer routine, as shown in Figure 13.3. From this breakpoint you can dig deeper into the code. However, right now you have just entered two incorrect answers. The behavior you really want to analyze occurs after four incorrect answers, so it is not time to dig deeper yet. Press F5 to continue the program again.

The test form window reappears when the program runs. This time type in TestThree and press Enter. The ProcessAnswer breakpoint is displayed in response. The txtAnswer_Keypress breakpoint no longer occurs because you removed it last time around. Press F5 to continue the program once more to type in the answer that should put the program over the MaxGuesses limit. Things are about to get more interesting!

13

Stepping Through Code

You have used breakpoints to follow the flow of your code through the entry of three answers. Now your program is running again and is ready for you to enter the critical fourth answer that is related to your program bug. Type in TestFour as the question response on the test form. The premise of your test is that the code should allow only three incorrect responses. Press Enter and you will once again see the familiar ProcessAnswer breakpoint of Figure 13.3. This time, however, is especially significant. You are now on your fourth incorrect response. If the control code was working as intended, it would raise the MaxGuessesExceeded event now. You need to probe deeper into the code at this point to understand why the event is not raised. Fortunately, you don't have to resort to adding more individual breakpoints. Visual Basic provides you with a step feature that lets you progress through the flow of the code a line at a time, observing results as you go along.

NOTE

You might be wondering why I didn't tell you about the step feature to begin with instead of asking you to enter all the breakpoints. First of all, it is important that you understand the breakpoint concept very well for control debugging, so it was good experience. But more importantly, this many-breakpoint approach is typical of much debugging. Often it is most efficient to start by scattering several breakpoints throughout the code. Then, once you have traveled to these breakpoints and start to have a feel for the code flow, you can more efficiently apply the step feature that is now our topic of discussion. You wouldn't want to hit just one breakpoint and then step through all your code a line at a time, or the stepping process would take far too long.

Select the Debug option from the Visual Basic menu. You will see the submenu displayed in Figure 13.4. There are many step-related choices you can make. Some of these features are described in more detail later today and on Day 14. Right now you can use one specific feature—Step Into—to probe further into this problem. The Step Into feature will cause your code to run for just one more line. Each time you select Step Into, one more line is carried out and then a breakpoint is automatically put into effect on that line. The code execution stops, and the current line indicator highlights the new current line. You can see the current line indicator that is displayed after the initial breakpoint in Figure 13.4; it is the arrow pointing to the If statement in the left side of the code window.

13

Figure 13.4.

Debug step options.

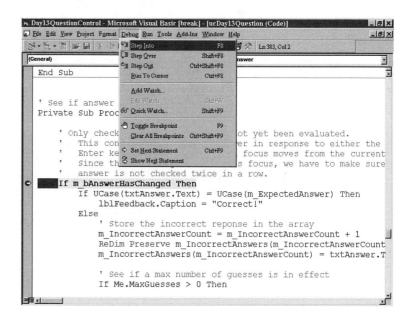

Try the Step Into feature for yourself. Choose Debug | Step Into from the menu. You could also use the F8 shortcut key to carry out the same action. After this selection is made, the current line indicator advances to the next code statement, as you can see in Figure 13.5. Study Listing 13.1, which shows the ProcessAnswer code, to see what information you can derive at this point.

> **NOTE**
>
> Step Into, rather than Step Over, is used to advance. The difference between the two occurs when you step across a procedure call. Consider what happens when your current line contains a call to a procedure and you carry out a step operation. The Step Into option will shift the next current line breakpoint to the code within that called procedure. Step Over, on the other hand, will shift the next current line breakpoint to the statement immediately below the call statement, without displaying the called procedure to you. When the current statement does not contain a procedure call, however, Step Into and Step Over will provide you with the same end result.

You can see from the new current line position that the preceding conditional statement If m_bAnswerHasChanged must have evaluated to true. You can deduce this from the fact that the code flow advanced to the If...then part of the conditional that is only reached when the condition is true. The next statement waiting to be carried out is the second conditional check. This conditional check is now indicated as the current line. Press F8 to carry out this statement now. The current line shifts to the `Else` statement, as you can see in Figure 13.6.

Figure 13.5.

The current line indicator after the first Step Into.

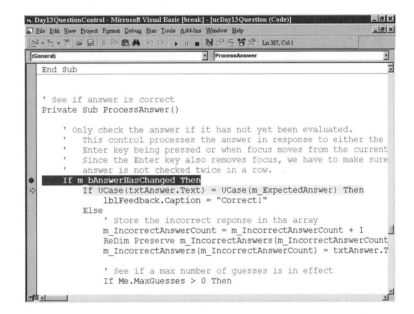

Figure 13.6.

The current line indicator after the second Step Into.

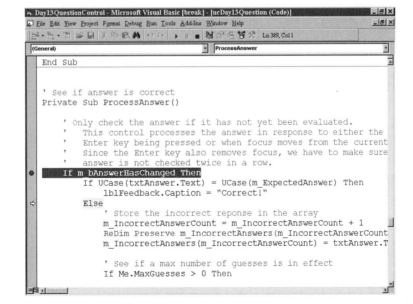

13

> **NOTE** When you step through code, Visual Basic will automatically skip over comments. Visual Basic will not allow you to place breakpoints on comment lines, either. A comment line is not a line that is processed by Visual Basic, but is simply there for your reading convenience.

Because the code shifted to the `Else` part of the `If` statement, you can assume that the second conditional evaluated to `false`. That means the user's latest answer was incorrect rather than correct. So far, everything is in order. This is what you would expect at this point. You entered the fourth incorrect answer, and your review of the code flow has verified that the control is processing it as an incorrect answer. Now you just need to continue the stepping to see why the number of incorrect guesses is not recognized correctly. Press F8 to proceed yet another step. The current line shifts down to the first line within the `Else` block of code.

Inspecting Variable Values

The program flow has now reached a critical juncture. The current statement increments the variable that keeps track of incorrect answers. You can easily verify the value of this variable: Just place the mouse cursor over the `m_IncorrectAnswerCount` variable name in that statement. A small display pops up immediately below the variable name. This display tells you `m_IncorrectAnswerCount = 3`. You can see this variable readout illustrated in Figure 13.7. The value 3 is what you'd expect at this point because the statement that increments the incorrect answer count is your current statement that has not yet been carried out.

Now press F8 again to step over one more statement. The statement that increments the `m_IncorrectAnswer` variable is carried out, and then the current line indicator shifts down by one more line. Move the mouse cursor back over the `m_IncorrectAnswerCount` variable of the preceding line. This time, when the display pops up it informs you that `m_IncorrectAnswerCount = 4`. The number of incorrect answers has been correctly incremented.

You have not tracked down the ultimate bug yet, but you have already learned a great deal from your debugging. Refer to Listing 13.1 to see what you can conclude at this point. There are two key observations you can make. The first is that you have verified that everything in the code flow is working fine up to the current code statement. The next observation is that the `RaiseEvent` statement looms just a few statements down. Earlier today you verified that that statement is not called as intended.

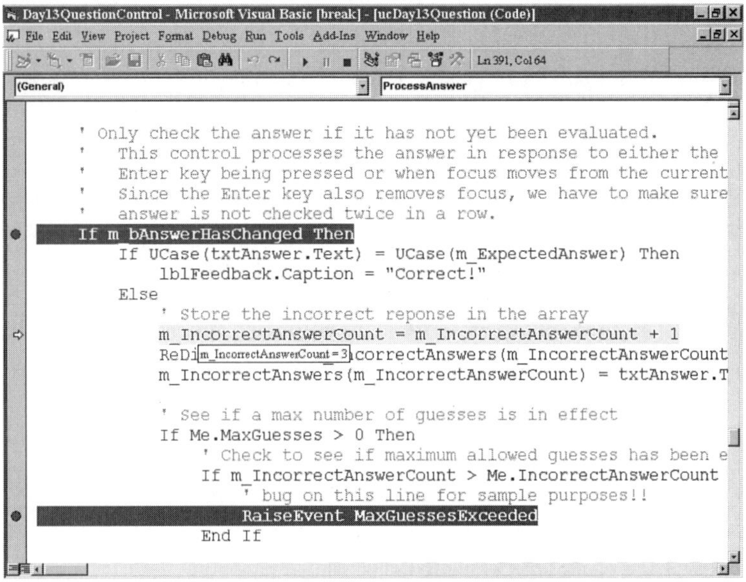

Figure 13.7.

The variable value is displayed when you place the cursor over the variable name after the program hits a breakpoint.

```
' Only check the answer if it has not yet been evaluated.
'   This control processes the answer in response to either the
'   Enter key being pressed or when focus moves from the current
'   Since the Enter key also removes focus, we have to make sure
'   answer is not checked twice in a row.
If m_bAnswerHasChanged Then
    If UCase(txtAnswer.Text) = UCase(m_ExpectedAnswer) Then
        lblFeedback.Caption = "Correct!"
    Else
        ' Store the incorrect reponse in the array
        m_IncorrectAnswerCount = m_IncorrectAnswerCount + 1
        ReDim m_IncorrectAnswerCount = 3 correctAnswers(m_IncorrectAnswerCount
        m_IncorrectAnswers(m_IncorrectAnswerCount) = txtAnswer.T

        ' See if a max number of guesses is in effect
        If Me.MaxGuesses > 0 Then
            ' Check to see if maximum allowed guesses has been e
            If m_IncorrectAnswerCount > Me.IncorrectAnswerCount
                ' bug on this line for sample purposes!!
                RaiseEvent MaxGuessesExceeded
        End If
```

These two observations are significant. You can now narrow down your bug hunt to a very specific block of suspect code. This block is bounded at the top by the place in the code flow up to which you know everything works, and is bounded on the bottom by a statement that you know is not carried out as expected. Somewhere between the top of this block of code and the bottom of the block of code, your code flow gets derailed. You can see this block of suspect code in Listing 13.4.

Listing 13.4. A suspect block of code.

```
 1:  ' Store the incorrect response in the array
 2:  m_IncorrectAnswerCount = m_IncorrectAnswerCount + 1
 3:  ReDim Preserve m_IncorrectAnswers(m_IncorrectAnswerCount)
 4:  m_IncorrectAnswers(m_IncorrectAnswerCount) = txtAnswer.Text
 5:
 6:  ' See if a max number of guesses is in effect
 7:  If Me.MaxGuesses > 0 Then
 8:      ' Check to see if maximum allowed guesses has been exceeded
 9:              ' bug on this line for sample purposes!!
10:      If m_IncorrectAnswerCount > Me.IncorrectAnswerCount Then
11:          RaiseEvent MaxGuessesExceeded
12:      End If
13:  End If
14:
```

13

You have proven that the m_IncorrectAnswerCount statement works correctly. You have proven that the RaiseEvent statement is not reached. Somewhere between lies your problem. There are only a few more statements that could be the cause of the problem. Your suspect list has narrowed!

Press F8 to advance to the next code statement. You have now proceeded past the ReDim statement and are at the m_IncorrectAnswers(m_IncorrectAnswerCount) statement. Press F8 again to continue to the following If Me.MaxGuesses conditional statement. This conditional centers on the MaxGuesses property that is so relevant to your problem. You specified the number of maximum guesses to allow in this property. Place the mouse cursor over the Me.MaxGuesses property name so that you can verify its current value. The pop-up display that results confirms that this value is 3. If you can recall way back to the start of today's lesson, remember when you first checked out the host application that integrated this control. One of the first steps you took was to verify the MaxGuesses property setting of the control in the properties window. This original property value was 3, just as the current value is. The current value of 3 is exactly what you'd expect at this point. So far, everything still seems to be on course. The number of suspects in your lineup is dwindling!

Press F8 to proceed past this conditional statement. Surprise! The next current line is perhaps not what you expected. The current line indicator appears, as shown in Figure 13.8. The Property Get routine Get MaxGuesses has become your new current line. The conditional statement you just carried out referenced the MaxGuesses property. Because you used a Step Into (F8) command, Visual Basic stepped you into the code that is processed to retrieve that property value. The debugging environment has provided a convenient reminder that the flow of code is about to sequence through the statements in Listing 13.5.

Listing 13.5. The property block of code that the Debug|Step Into operation has advanced to.

```
1: Public Property Get MaxGuesses() As Integer
2:     MaxGuesses = m_MaxGuesses
3: End Property
```

The statements in the Get MaxGuesses property routine will be carried out before program flow returns to the ProcessAnswer routine you were advancing through. The lineup of suspects is slightly larger than it appeared just a moment ago!

Now press F8 twice to step through the code in this property routine and advance to the End Property statement. You can use the mouse cursor to display the value of the MaxGuesses property. You will see it remains at 3, as you would expect. Now press F8 again to advance to the next statement. Visual Basic takes you back to the next statement in the ProcessAnswer routine, after the statement that references the MaxGuesses property.

Figure 13.8.

The current line becomes a statement in the Property Get *routine when a statement that references a control property is carried out.*

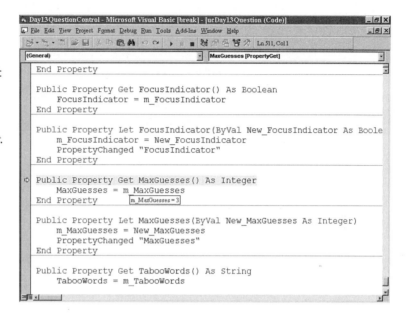

Consider once again your block of suspect code. You are at the very last statement prior to the RaiseEvent statement that never gets called. So far you have proven that everything is working as expected. The current statement is the last statement that could be causing the problem. Consequently, your suspicions about it should be very high! Use the mouse cursor to inspect all variables in that statement:

```
If m_IncorrectAnswerCount > Me.IncorrectAnswerCount Then
```

You will see from the pop-up value display that the module-level variable m_IncorrectAnswerCount contains the value 4. Then when you inspect Me.IncorrectAnswerCount, you observe that it contains a value of 4 as well. Your expectation was that your designation of three incorrect answers had been exceeded and would cause RaiseEvents to occur. At this point alarm bells should go off in your head. Your adrenaline should pump. Your heart should race. You are on to something! The suspicious values you see should make you carefully consider the logic of the entire statement. This inspection should lead you to the conclusion that Me.IncorrectAnswerCount is *not* the property that you want to compare with the module-level variable to decide whether to raise the event. Rather, the correct comparison should be

```
If m_IncorrectAnswerCount > Me.MaxGuesses Then
```

This insight is typical of most debugging. You spent a lot of time using the debug features to hone in on your problem. You have proven the soundness of statement after statement to advance toward the problem. Then, once you finally close in on the bug, you ultimately must rely on your judgment to recognize the cause of the problem.

13

Type the correction directly into the code window, replacing `Me.IncorrectAnswerCount` with `Me.MaxGuesses`. Now you can verify this fix. Because you don't want to have the test run interrupted by the series of breakpoints this time, clear all the breakpoints. You can use the Visual Basic option Debug|Clear All Breakpoints to remove every breakpoint you have inserted so far today. Then restart the program by choosing Run|Restart from the Visual Basic menu. Enter four different answers in response to the first question. Notice that you no longer encounter the breakpoints. When you enter the fourth incorrect answer, you see the message box shown in Figure 13.9.

This is the message box that is generated by the host application's event-handling routine, as you saw earlier today in Listing 13.2. Congratulations! You now have a fully functioning program again.

Figure 13.9.

The message box from the host application that indicates you have exceeded the maximum number of allowed guesses.

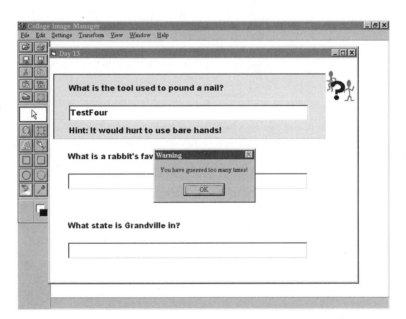

Special Control Debugging Considerations

You have seen a lot of debugging today. You have used a strategy of breakpoints, single stepping, and variable inspection. These techniques apply when debugging regular applications as well as controls. There are a few notable considerations for control debugging, however. First, you should always make sure to aggressively debug controls. Controls are, by the nature of their component packaging, usually intended for wide reuse and distribution.

A bug in a control may ripple through many applications and affect the lives of many users. A control may be integrated into host applications in ways you cannot anticipate. A fair number of programmers might generate normal applications without relying on extensive debugging techniques, but control developers cannot afford this luxury. The control developer should be intimately acquainted with debugging techniques such as breakpoints, steps, and variable inspection, and the emphasis on these techniques today is intended to ensure that you have this background.

In addition, you have seen some special techniques for control debugging. You should rely on the project group so that you can deal with your control source code and the source code of a test application within the same Visual Basic session. Then you can set breakpoints in the host application and the control code simultaneously. The primary way that controls and host applications communicate is through properties, methods, and events. If you have supplied user-defined properties, methods, or events in your control, you have introduced the potential for bugs. You can debug all these at the control level. A property setting in a host application might look straightforward, such as

```
VariableA = YourControl.CurrentCount
```

Remember that this assignment in the host application will cause the corresponding `Property Get` routine in your control to be carried out, however. A `Property Let` routine in your control is called in assignments where you set the value of the control property, such as

```
YourControl.CurrentCount = 0
```

Depending on the property, you might have many lines of code statements that are carried out to retrieve the property value for the host application. You can use breakpoints in your control to observe the behavior of these property routines and ensure that they do not introduce bugs.

The same approach applies when the host application makes calls to the methods of your control. Assume that the host application calls a method of your control in a statement such as this:

```
YourControl.ClearDatabase
```

When you debug a control, you must drive the start of your tests from a host application, but then plunge into the code at the corresponding control layers. This method is implemented as a normal procedure in your control code. You can insert breakpoints anywhere within that method to observe what is really going on at the control level.

Debugging the interface between control events and the host application code that handles them follows the same principles but is slightly more complicated. First, you need to detect if the event is occurring at the host application level. If it is, the control is doing its job, and

13

any event-related problems you see might well be in the host application. If the event never occurs in the host application, however, your suspicion must turn to the control. You will need to locate the `RaiseEvent` statement in the control that triggers the event. There may be multiple `RaiseEvent` statements that raise the same event from different areas of the control code. Once you find the location of the relevant `RaiseEvent` statements in the control code, you can start the breakpointing and debugging process to determine why the events do not occur.

You have seen only a subset of the rich set of features that Visual Basic offers to ease the process of testing and debugging your controls. You will encounter more tips on applying these to your controls tomorrow. The goal is to provide you with the background you need to be an expert debugger. Debugging is so important to the control development process that you need this knowledge to become an expert control developer.

Summary

Today you have learned how to debug the controls you develop. Debugging is important for any type of development. It takes on added importance for controls because they are likely to be widely integrated and distributed in ways that you may not anticipate. Visual Basic provides many features that can help you in the debugging process.

The first and most fundamental of these is the structure of the project itself. The project group allows you to work with source code for your control and an integrating host application within the same Visual Basic session. Today, a sample bug was introduced into the familiar question control so that you could observe the debugging techniques used to chase it down. This bug affected an event normally raised by the control, so communication between the control and host application was directly affected. You used breakpoints to hone in on the problem. You learned that you should work toward a control bug in a logical progression, ruling out possible causes in upper layers such as the host application right away. First a breakpoint was used to rule out the host application as a bug suspect.

Next, you used breakpoints to step through the control code. First a check was made to see if the event was correctly raised in the control. A breakpoint proved that it was not raised. Then you saw how to use multiple breakpoints across the control code to hone in on the problem. Once the breakpoints had narrowed down the possible area where the problem was caused, a process called *stepping* was used to isolate the problem. You also saw how to inspect the value of variables as you step through the code. Finally, through a combination of these techniques, you identified the problem and killed the bug.

Today's lesson concludes with some general guidelines on control debugging. A control communicates with an integrating host application through properties, methods, and events. Today's lesson provides a sound fundamental view of how to start the task of testing and debugging a control.

Q&A

Q Can you debug a control and a host application at the same time?

A Yes. The project group allows you to work with an application and a control project in the same session. You can view source code, breakpoint source code, and inspect it, whether it is the control or the host application.

Q Is it possible to have more than one breakpoint at a time?

A Yes. You can have as many breakpoints as desired, scattered anywhere in your source code.

Q What if you set up breakpoints, run your program, and then stop it? Do you need to reenter the breakpoints before the next run?

A No. The breakpoints will persist even if you stop your program and restart it, until you explicitly clear them. If you exit Visual Basic, however, the breakpoints will not be present when you start up the project the next time.

Q Suppose you're seeing goofy behavior with an application that uses your control. Should you assume that the control or the host application is causing the problem?

A Assume that the host application is the problem first, and then work your way downward in the software layers. Debug the host application, and if you don't find the problem, continue progressing down into the control itself after you have eliminated the host application as a possible culprit. If you start at the lower control layer first, you will likely have a harder time laying out your debugging steps in a manner that lets you effectively hone in on the problem.

Workshop

In today's lesson you saw how to single-step through code once you hit a breakpoint. You can also *start* a program with single stepping. Return to today's sample program. Make sure the program is not currently running. Now select Debug|Step Into from the Visual Basic menu. The program advances to the first line and stops. Keep pressing F8, the key for the step operation. You will see the current line advance a line at a time. Step through 20 or 30 steps and observe the code flow of the question control at startup. This is a good technique for understanding the starting behavior of any program.

13

Quiz

NOTE   See Appendix D, "Answers to Quiz Questions," for the answer to this question.

Two code statements are shown in the following code:

```
' Replace the taboo word with the designated replacement
txtAnswer.Text = svLeft & svReplacement & svRight

' Put the input cursor at the end of the selection

txtAnswer.SelStart = Len(txtAnswer.Text)
```

The first statement builds a string from partial strings. The second statement sets the selection cursor location. Assume that these statements are sequential in a block of code. You want to verify that the string has been correctly built. Where should you place a breakpoint?

13

Day 14

More Control Debugging Techniques

In yesterday's lesson you had a look at basic debugging techniques. You saw how you can stop execution of your control, step through it, and inspect variable values to isolate problems in your control source code. These techniques are the backbone of debugging. However, there are easier, slicker, more informative ways to carry out these tasks—especially when it comes to debugging control code. Advanced features of the Visual Basic debugging environment improve your ability to analyze program flow and data.

Features like watches, debugging objects, assertions, and call stacks are at your disposal. They provide you with insight into your code. These debugging features are available for any type of debugging, but they are particularly well suited to control debugging. Some of the terms might be new to you if you haven't been an intensive user of the debugging environment before. You can use a *watch* to monitor a property change, use an *assertion* to catch when an event is or is not raised, and inspect a *call stack* to see how code flow progresses from a host application to your control methods to your local subroutines. In today's lesson you will learn the meaning behind these terms and how to apply the concepts to your own control debugging.

Applying the Techniques to Your Code

In yesterday's lesson you saw how a succession of related debugging techniques was applied to the same body of code. You inspected a sample control with an intentionally introduced bug. We applied each new technique to this sample and progressed steadily from one to the next. You had a good look at the overall process of harnessing debugging techniques to isolate a problem. Today's lesson is a bit more staccato in nature. Although you probably understand the essence of debugging now, you need exposure to several more techniques that have specific relevance to control debugging. We will now introduce you to a range of these advanced capabilities without the backdrop and distraction of a broader sample. You can pick and choose from this smorgasbord of techniques when you need them and apply them to your own control debugging tasks in the same general fashion as you did in yesterday's lesson.

The Immediate Window

You can bring up the Immediate window by selecting View | Immediate window from the Visual Basic menu. This window can do many interesting things. When you reach a breakpoint, you can print out the value of an expression in this window. Suppose you have set a breakpoint on the `RaiseEvent` statement in the `ProcessAnswer` routine of question control. This routine has a module-level variable named `m_IncorrectAnswers`. You can type this command in the Immediate window to see the current value of this variable when the breakpoint is reached:

```
Print m_IncorrectAnswerCount
```

NOTE

> **SAMPLE** If you wish to experiment with the debugging techniques provided today, you can try them out on the question control. This source code can be found in the `Day14QuestionControl.vbg` group project file under the `Samples\Day14\Your Start` directory on the book's CD-ROM. This project contains the code that is intended to be your starting point for the modifications described in today's lesson. Copy the directory to your hard drive so you can make subsequent modifications. The material is presented in a before-and-after format. If you want to see today's changes already implemented, you can view the `Day14QuestionControl.vbg` group project, available one directory level up in the `Samples\Day14` directory.

14

The value of m_IncorrectAnswerCount will be displayed immediately below this line in the Immediate window, as you can see in Figure 14.1.

Figure 14.1.

The Immediate window.

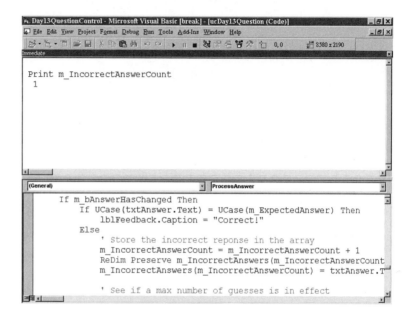

You can also use the convenient Print command shorthand provided in the Debug window by typing in a question mark instead of the word Print. For example, the following code has the same effect as the Print command:

```
? m_IncorrectAnswerCount
```

Of course you can inspect variables just by placing the cursor over them, even without the Immediate window. The advantage of the Immediate window is that it lets you do a whole lot more. You can type in procedure calls, control methods, built-in functions, or complex expressions as well. You can carry out any legal Visual Basic syntax, such as the following:

```
? m_IncorrectAnswerCount * 1000 & " Printed at " & Time
```

This would print the number of incorrect answers, multiplied by 1,000, along with the current time.

NOTE   Various keyboard shortcuts make working in the Immediate window easier. Enter is used to run whichever line of code the cursor is currently on. You can move the cursor to any line in the Debug window so you can easily repeat statements you have already carried out. Ctrl+Home will move the cursor to the top of the Immediate window, and Ctrl+End will move it to the bottom.

You can use the standard key combinations for copy and paste operations. Ctrl+C will copy to the Clipboard selected text in the Immediate window. Ctrl+V will paste Clipboard text into the Immediate window at the cursor.

What if you want to clear the entire contents of the Immediate window? You won't be the first programmer to get annoyed by the lack of a single command to do this! There is no one keystroke operation to clear the window. The safest way to do it is to use Ctrl+Home to go to the top of the window. Hold down Shift and Ctrl+End to highlight all the text in the window. Then press Ctrl+X to cut all the text out of the Immediate window and move it to the Clipboard. If you decide in the next step or two that you want the information back, it will still be on the Clipboard for easy retrieval.

The next sequence shows the Immediate window in use after a breakpoint is reached. The code has already incremented the variable m_IncorrectAnswerCount to 1. You can then inspect this variable, call a method of the control to clear the variable, and then inspect it again, before continuing the program. Listing 14.1 shows the series of commands.

Listing 14.1. Commands entered in the Immediate window.

```
1: ? m_IncorrectAnswerCount
2: me.Clear
3: ? m_IncorrectAnswerCount
```

You can see the results of this series of commands in Figure 14.2. The variable starts out as 1 and then is cleared to 0 after the method call. Any routine that can be called from code can be called from the Immediate window. This gives you the ability to interact with your control as it is being debugged. This is particularly useful when you need to activate control methods that reset the state of the control midway through a debugging session.

14

Figure 14.2.

The Immediate window calling a control method.

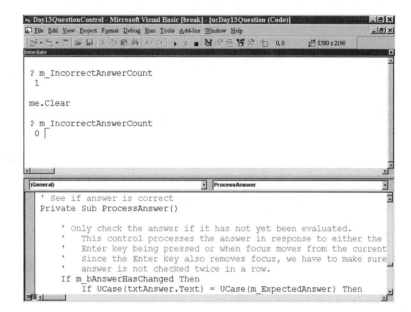

You can even use the Immediate window when your code is in normal design mode rather than at a runtime breakpoint. For example, you can use it to display current property settings of any instances of a control on your test form. Assume that you are working with form frmTester, which contains a question control named ucQuestion1. Ensure that the program is *not* currently running. Then highlight the test form in the Project Explorer view of your control group project to make it active. Close all other open project views. Now you can use the Immediate window to interact with this object and its underlying control code, even though no code is running. Then you can type the following into the Immediate window:

```
? frmTester.ucQuestion1.Question
```

The current property setting of this control property will be displayed in the Immediate window, as shown in Figure 14.3.

You can even use the Immediate window to call a method or property procedure in your control when the program is in design mode. Insert a breakpoint in the Get Question property procedure of your question control to test this. Make sure the test form is highlighted in the Project Explorer view—the only active view—just as before. Then type again in the Immediate window:

```
? frmTester.ucQuestion1.Question
```

14

Figure 14.3.

A control property displayed at design time from the Immediate window.

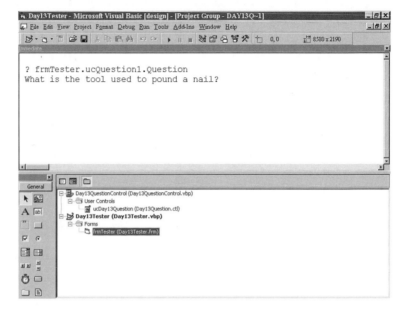

The property procedure for your control is called, and the breakpoint in your control is reached. You can see the result in Figure 14.4. Even though your test application wasn't running, you were able to use the Immediate window to cause the control code to be carried out.

Figure 14.4.

A control breakpoint reached in response to a design-time command in the Immediate window.

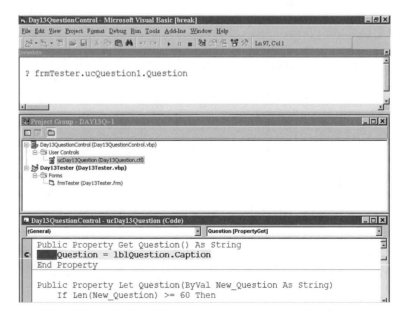

Much of the debugging you do will require that your test form be running because, after all, you want to analyze how your control responds to a running program. But there are some types of debugging activities that might best be carried out using the design-time Immediate window approach. If you need to test the effects of individual property procedures or methods in your control in an isolated fashion, you might find it easiest to debug this way. Then you can individually launch the areas of code you wish, without having to go through the overhead of launching your test application and driving it through the paces needed to cause the control property or method to be called.

There is yet another powerful aspect of the Immediate window. To understand this remaining aspect, you must also understand the Debug object, which is the next topic of discussion.

The Debug Object

Visual Basic provides a Debug object that can be used to aid in the debugging process. If you judge this object on the basis of quantity, you might not be impressed. It provides no events, no properties, and only two methods. If you judge it on the basis of quality, however, you might come to view it as one of the most helpful objects available to you. The Debug object provides a Print method and an Assert method. Both of these allow you to carry out more effective debugging of code flow.

These Debug object methods are particularly valuable for debugging controls. Control code, as you have seen, focuses on the interfaces you provide a host through properties, events, and methods. What if a complex host application doesn't work with your control? The first thing you will need to do is understand how the host application is exercising your control. Therefore, control code debugging often consists of monitoring a number of areas of code to understand when and where each interface is exercised by a host application.

The Debug.Print Method

The Print method provides a convenient way to monitor code. It also relies on the availability of the Immediate window you just learned about. You can insert a Print method statement anywhere in your code to print out a customized feedback message in the Immediate window. The feedback message typically indicates where in the code you have placed the statement. Then you can learn about the flow of your code by observing which Print method statements are reached.

For example, suppose you want to know when each and every property routine in your control is called. You can insert a Print method statement in every property Let and Get procedure. Listing 14.2 shows the Let Question property procedure of the question control with this addition.

14

Listing 14.2. The `Let Question` **property procedure with a** `Debug` **object** `Print` **method statement added.**

```
 1: Public Property Let Question(ByVal New_Question As String)
 2:     Debug.Print "Let Question property procedure called at " & Time
 3:     If Len(New_Question) >= 60 Then
 4:         MsgBox "Question must be no more than 30 characters in length!", _
 5:                 vbExclamation, "Error"
 6:     Else
 7:         lblQuestion.Caption() = New_Question
 8:         PropertyChanged "Question"
 9:     End If
10: End Property
```

ANALYSIS   The `Debug.Print` method statement has been added at the top of this routine. A print to the Immediate window will occur whenever the routine is called.

Now make the same type of addition to every property procedure, method procedure, and local procedure in the control. (Or if you want to save the time of making the numerous changes, you can open the `Day14\Day14QuestionControl.vpg` project, which already has these changes in place.) Then start the test application. As the test program is carried out, it makes use of the control. Correspondingly, the Immediate window will display a detailed printout of the control program flow from procedure to procedure. Figure 14.5 shows the resulting view of the Immediate window.

Figure 14.5.

`Debug.Print` *statements in every control procedure provide the flow of the control code in the Immediate window.*

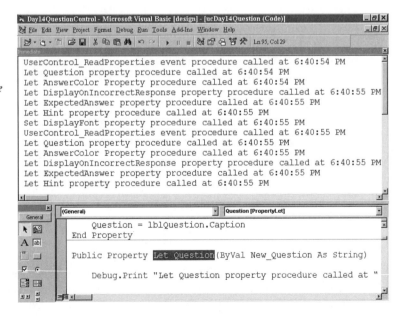

You can see that there's a wealth of information at your fingertips now! And you can insert even more of the Debug.Print statements into your control code anywhere you deem useful. You can even print out the value of properties and variables with this method. Any Visual Basic expression can be part of the print string. Suppose you want to check the current value of property MaxGuesses. You could use a statement like the following:

```
Debug.Print  "In routine ProcessAnswer, MaxGuesses = " & me.MaxGuesses
```

In response, you would see the value of me.MaxGuesses displayed as part of the information in the Immediate window.

This approach to providing information on the flow of your program without interrupting it is often called *tracing*. Tracing is very similar to breakpointing or stepping through a program. In either case you get insights into code flow and you can inspect data values along the way. The difference is that breakpointing or stepping through stops program execution at each step, and then you must explicitly send the code on its way again. Tracing is far less intrusive. It is therefore more convenient to use. Also, it allows you to collect a great deal more comprehensive information in far less time. You just sit back and let results accumulate in the Immediate window while you interact with the program. Then you can view the entire code flow and focus only on the parts that interest you.

You must understand how your control reacts in response to a host program to effectively debug it. Your control typically has many different properties, methods, raised events, and underlying procedures that you must monitor to fully understand all interactions. For this reason, tracing is often particularly well suited to control debugging. Typically, tracing is a first step to understanding code flow and allows you to narrow the scope of a problem area much more quickly than you could if you just used breakpoints. After you've isolated the problem to a general area, you would likely start using breakpoints or stepping through to examine the program line by line—perhaps carrying out more Immediate window statements as you sequence through the code.

The moral of the story is to use well-placed Debug.Print statements in your control code. At least one per procedure is a good guideline. They will pave the way for you to better understand your code as you test it, and they will make debugging easier and quicker. If you're encountering this guideline for the first time, you might have a major concern about this advice: Isn't it a lot of work to remove all these statements later on when you produce the final version of your control? The good news is you don't have to! The Visual Basic designers at Microsoft were kind enough to take this into account. On Day 15, "Preparing Your Control for the Real World," you'll see how to save your control as an OCX file. When you generate your final control file, the Debug.Print statements are automatically bypassed and do not become part of your control OCX file. You will still see the Debug.Print statements when you view your original source code, but you can rest assured that users of your control are completely unaffected by them. There are no extra bytes taking up space or time when the

14

program runs because you have used them. `Debug.Print` statements are purely a developer's convenience and are nonexistent from the user's perspective.

The `Debug.Assert` Method

You have learned about most sides of code flow analysis now. You can step through a program a line at a time, stop at specific lines if you designate them as breakpoints, or fly through the program, tracing out flow as you go. Only one major drawback remains: What if you want to stop at a given location if a problem is occurring, but otherwise continue on your way? Suppose you have a procedure that uses the `MaxGuesses` property. If the procedure is entered and `MaxGuesses` is `0`, you know you want to do more debugging. If it's not `0`, you have no need to debug the routine and should just continue.

Think about your choices. One alternative is to insert a breakpoint at the top of the procedure and inspect the value of the variable after the program suspends execution. But then your program will stop every time it reaches the procedure—even if everything is fine. You'll spend a lot of your debugging time carrying out the same check over and over. There are other alternatives. When I first became a Visual Basic programmer many years ago, I would handle such dilemmas by inserting a temporary block of code like this:

```
if me.MaxGuesses = 0 then Stop
```

`Stop` is a Visual Basic keyword that forces your program to suspend execution, just as if you had entered a breakpoint. This second alternative isn't too bad. After all, Visual Basic makes it easy to enter temporary code, and now this procedure will only stop when the problem condition is affected. The only drawback is that I have extra code in my control. It will take up bytes in my final OCX file unless I remember to remove it later on.

It turns out that Visual Basic provides a third alternative that neatly steps around the problems of the first two approaches. Your new friend the `Debug` object comes to the rescue with the second of its two methods: `Assert`. The `Debug.Assert` method lets you specify a statement that checks for a given condition. If the assertion condition you've provided is true, code flow continues normally with no break. If the condition is false, however, a breakpoint occurs. Like the `Debug.Print` method, `Debug.Assert` methods are automatically suppressed from the final controls you generate. Only the developer working in the design environment will ever see a program halt from a `Debug.Assert` statement. The statements will not affect end users of the control.

This method is easily applied to the problem of detecting when `MaxGuesses` has a value of `0`. The following statement causes a breakpoint to occur only when this is the case:

```
Debug.Assert Me.MaxGuesses > 0
```

This statement specifies that if `Me.MaxGuesses` is greater than `0`, everything remains as expected and the program should continue. Only if this is false will the program halt.

You can see a more detailed example of this in Listing 14.3.

Listing 14.3. The `txtAnswer_KeyPress` routine with an assertion statement.

```
 1: ' Process answer in response to enter key
 2: Private Sub txtAnswer_KeyPress(KeyAscii As Integer)
 3:
 4:     Debug.Print "txtAnswer_KeyPress event procedure called at " & Time
 5:     Debug.Assert Me.MaxGuesses > 0
 6:
 7:     ' Declare a constant for the question mark since VB doesn't define one
 8:     Const vbKeyQuestion As Integer = 63   'ASCII 63  is question mark
 9:
10:     ' Censure any taboo words that have been entered in the textbox so far
11:     Call TabooWordCensor
12:
13:     ' Check if enter key was pressed
14:     If KeyAscii = vbKeyReturn Then
15:         ' Override char so no special processing for enter key occurs
16:         KeyAscii = 0
17:         Call ProcessAnswer
18:     ElseIf KeyAscii = vbKeyQuestion Then
19:         ' Raise event to signify that user entered a question.
20:         '    Pass the entire text response entered by user with the event.
21:         RaiseEvent UserQuestionDetected(txtAnswer.Text)
22:     End If
23: End Sub
```

 ANALYSIS `Debug.Assert` has been added to this routine. Now a breakpoint will automatically occur whenever this routine is called and `MaxGuesses` is `0`. Otherwise the `Debug.Assert` statement will have no effect.

You can use the question control test program to witness firsthand the behavior of this statement. The test program in the `Day14QuestionControl` project group integrates three question controls. The first control was set with a `MaxGuesses` property of `4` when it was integrated. The remaining two controls were set to have a `MaxGuesses` property of `0`. Add the assertion statement from Listing 14.3 to the `txtAnswer_Keypress` routine of the control code.

 NOTE Don't dive ahead and look for a problem when `MaxGuesses` is `0`. The assertion statement is added here just to illustrate this technique. No code problem that occurs when `MaxGuesses` is set to `0`.

14

Now run the program. Click on the first question area and type a response. The test program functions normally, as shown in Figure 14.6. No assertion break occurs because the MaxGuesses property value for this first question is set to 4.

Figure 14.6.

The assertion breakpoint will only occur for the second and third question controls—not the first.

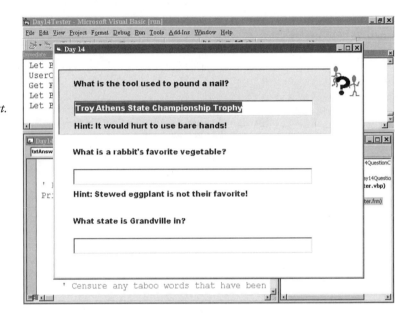

Next, move to the second question area. Start typing a response. Immediately the assertion breakpoint occurs. Program execution halts and the code window is displayed, as in Figure 14.7. The current statement where the code was suspended is the Debug.Assert statement. In this case the assertion is that the value of MaxGuesses is greater than 0. This assertion fails because the property setting of that property for this instance of the control is set to 0. Since the assertion failed, the assertion breakpoint occurred.

Assertions can be an invaluable debugging aid for the same reason that the Debug.Print method is. Assertions allow you to easily monitor the flow of your code without having to interact on a statement-by-statement step level. Breakpoints do not last from one Visual Basic session to another. Debug object statements do. This makes them particularly appropriate to control debugging. You will want to debug your control with a variety of different test host applications to ensure that it works correctly under a variety of circumstances. If you lean on the Debug object when you first put together your control code, you will find that it is easy to analyze the behavior of your control with each new host application you test.

14

Figure 14.7.

The code window containing the assertion breakpoint is displayed when the assertion fails for the second control.

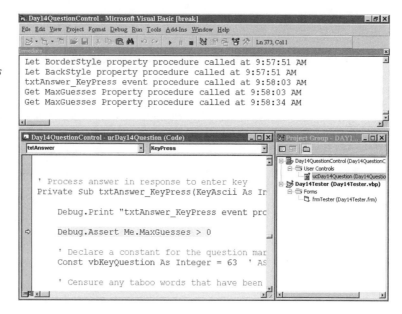

The Watches Window

So far you've seen a couple different approaches for inspecting the value of variables and properties used in your control code. On Day 13, "Debugging Controls," you saw how after a breakpoint was reached, you could just point the cursor to a variable and see a display of its value. Earlier in this lesson, you saw that you can get the same information by typing a `Print` statement in the Debug window. Guess what? There's still another way you can monitor the value of data. This technique is the most convenient of all—particularly for control debugging. It is called a *watch*.

You can associate a watch with any item of data. Then the current value of that data item will be displayed in a special Watch window as your program runs in the design environment. The value will change right before your eyes as the program proceeds. Whenever the program changes the data, the change is immediately reflected in your Watch window. There's no messy stopping at breakpoints, typing in the Immediate window, or even entering `Debug.Print` statements in advance. Just set up a watch and sit back and monitor your data as your program runs. Don't get too comfortable in the easy chair, though. The watch technique is just like any other debugging technique. It gives you a powerful information window into your program; but you still need to devote plenty of hard work to get to the bottom of any debugging problem. A watch is typically used in conjunction with all the other techniques you've already seen to analyze the code.

14

Adding a watch is easy. Suppose you've reached a breakpoint for a line of code like the following from the question control's ProcessAnswer routine:

```
ReDim Preserve m_IncorrectAnswers(m_IncorrectAnswerCount)
```

If the module-level variable m_IncorrectAnswerCount is one of the focuses of your debugging, you can add a watch on this variable. Carry out the steps to do this now. First, locate the code statement shown in the ProcessAnswer routine. Then set a breakpoint on that statement and run the test program. Enter an incorrect answer so that a breakpoint occurs. Click the cursor on the m_IncorrectAnswerCount variable name. Select Debug | Add Watch from the Visual Basic menu. This will cause a dialog like the one you see in Figure 14.8 to appear.

Figure 14.8.

The Add Watch dialog.

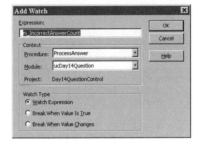

The Add Watch dialog already has the correct expression, procedure name, module, and project filled in, based on information it has extracted about the current variable. You also have an option that lets you specify the watch type. You can choose the option to monitor the basic expression only, or you can go even further and monitor the expression and have an automatic breakpoint triggered whenever the expression reaches a true state. Likewise, you can choose the option to suspend execution whenever the expression changes. Choose the first option to make this a regular watch, and then click the OK command button.

After you have defined this watch, the Watches window will appear in the Visual Basic design environment. You can see this window in Figure 14.9. This window lists the expression type and its current value. The expression type should be m_IncorrectAnswers for your current watch, and the value should be set to 1 if you've entered only one incorrect response in the test program so far.

NOTE

Normally the Watches window will appear automatically after you have added a watch. However, if you do not see it when you need it, just select View | Watches window from the Visual Basic menu to display it.

Figure 14.9.

The Watches window, which displays your current watches.

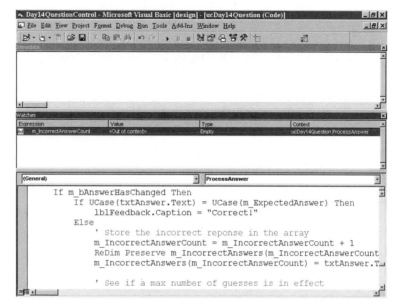

Continue execution of the program and enter more incorrect responses. Each time you enter an incorrect response, the breakpoint is reached again, and the watch reflects the current variable value. You can even interact directly with the Watches window by clicking on the data in the Value column and typing a new data value directly over it. Try changing the incorrect response value to 3. The program will proceed with this new data when you start to run it again. You can even click on the expression itself. Click on the variable name in the Watches window and replace it with the following:

```
m_IncorrectAnswers * 10
```

Now run the program again and cause the breakpoint to reoccur. You will see that the latest expression you entered in the Watches window remains the expression that is displayed.

This example focuses on using the Watches window within one procedure. It takes on far more relevance when you set up watches that function across the entire program. This is of particular use when debugging control property code. You can set up a watch directly on properties themselves. You can also set up a watch on the underlying module-level variables that correspond to properties. And you can specify that an automatic breakpoint should occur whenever the watch expressions change. An example of a Watches window where expressions have been set up to aid in debugging properties of the question control is shown in Figure 14.10.

14

Figure 14.10.

The Watches window with watches set up for properties and their underlying module variables.

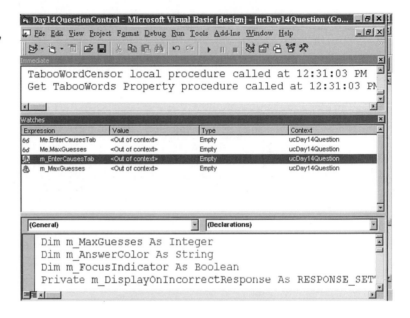

The first two entries you see in the Watches window are defined to watch the control properties themselves. The eyeglasses icon beside these entries indicates that these are monitoring watches that will not cause breakpoints. Below that, you can see two entries for the module-level variables that correspond to the first two properties. The open-hand icon next to these entries indicates that they are expression-change watches. Whenever these variables change, no matter where within the control code that occurs, an automatic breakpoint will result. You will see the current statement highlighted in the code window with execution of the program suspended. The concepts behind a watch are similar to those behind the breakpoints and variable display features you saw in yesterday's lesson. The difference is that watches let you easily put automatic monitoring and checking in place that can be carried out across your entire control. This capability can save you a great deal of time in debugging your control, particularly in tracking the changing states of your property values.

The Locals Window

The Locals window is a close cousin to the Watches window in terms of the benefits it provides. You have seen how easy watches are to use. There's a good chance that when you debug a procedure, you'll care about the values of any local variables defined in that procedure. Don't you wish you could automatically install watches on all the local variables any time you look at a routine? You can with the Locals window. Select View | Locals window from the Visual Basic menu to display this window.

The Locals window provides information very similar to the Watches window. You can see the current values of variables. These values are updated as you step through the code. However, when you use the Locals window, you cannot request automatic breakpoints when variables change or conditions are true. You would have to set up an individual watch on a local variable to carry that out. Still, the Locals window can be an incredible time saver during the debugging process.

There is one particular feature that makes this solution outstanding. That is the capability of the Locals window to display the state of the UserControl object itself. Now is a good time to make the question control reach a breakpoint so you can see the benefits of this feature. Go to the code window and locate the local routine TabooWordCensor in the control code. Then set a standard breakpoint on the code line as follows:

```
svCheckString = txtAnswer.Text
```

Run the program and enter a response into the first question control on the test application so this breakpoint will occur. You must type your response into the first question control to arrive at the breakpoint since the other two question control instances do not have the TabooWords property set to an active state. You will see the Locals window that is displayed in Figure 14.11.

Figure 14.11.

The Locals window after a breakpoint has been reached.

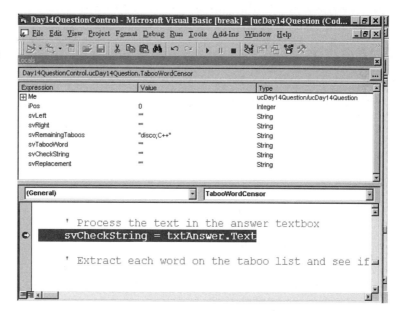

All the local variable values are displayed. Many of the variables are still in an uninitialized state since the current line is still near the beginning of the routine. Notice the very top entry in the Locals window. You'll see an object called Me, preceded by a plus sign. The plus sign indicates that this entry is an object that can be expanded. The Me object references the main object itself in the context of the current routine. Since you are viewing a control routine, Me refers to the control. Often when you are debugging control code, you need to refer to the control's property values themselves and module-level variables to analyze the state of the control. This is as easy as clicking on the Me entry, thanks to the Locals window.

Observe what happens when you click on the plus sign in front of the Me entry. The information in the Locals window expands. The expanded view shows you subentries for all the properties and module-level variables of the entire UserControl module. Some of the subentries can be expanded even further. Click on the plus sign in front of the subentry for the UserControl's module level m_IncorrectAnswer variable. This subentry expands as shown in Figure 14.12. Now you can see the individual array elements of this module-level variable.

Figure 14.12.

The Locals window after the Me *entry has been expanded twice.*

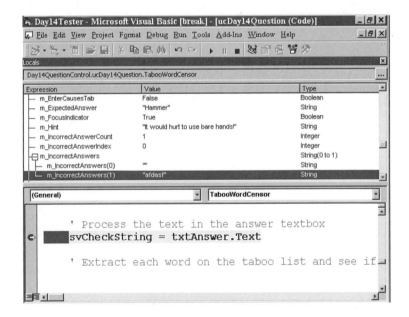

You can click on the Value column of the Locals window and type in new values for any UserControl module-level variable or property, just as you can within the Watches window. Effective debugging should start with at least a brief examination of the Locals window whenever a breakpoint is reached. It is the quickest technique around to verify the state of your control's property settings and adjust them if needed.

The Call Stack Window

There is one other view that can be very important when you debug a control. This is the Call Stack view. Like the other debugging-related views, this one is best illustrated by an example. Stop your test program from running and clear all breakpoints from your current project with the menu's Debug|Clear All command. Now bring up the code window for the test form. Locate the TabooWordDetected event routine for the ucQuestion1 object. This routine will be named ucQuestion1_TabooWordDetected. Place a breakpoint on the first line of this routine as follows:

```
MsgBox "Please do not use the word " & svTabooWord & ".", _
        vbOKOnly & vbCritical, "Watch your language!"
```

This breakpoint should be reached when the user types a forbidden word in response to a question. The TabooWords property of the ucQuestion1 control property should already be set to specify C++;disco as forbidden words. Now run the test program and enter disco as your response to the first question.

The code window pops up, indicating that this breakpoint has been reached. But this is normally only the beginning of the debugging effort. What if you wanted to understand how your control had raised this event? For example, which routine in your control called the RaiseEvent statement? This kind of backward tracing is possible with the help of the Call Stack window. Select Debug|Call Stack from the menu to display this view. The window pictured in Figure 14.13 will appear.

Figure 14.13.

The Call Stack window.

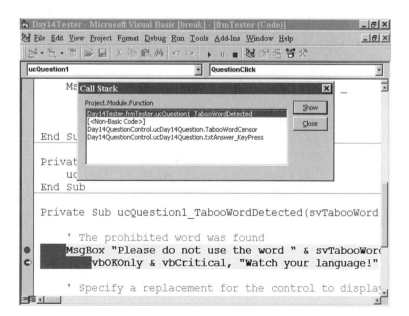

This window provides the sequence of calls that lead to the current statement. `Day14Tester.frmTester.ucQuestion1_TabooWordDetected` appears first in the list. This is the event routine itself. The call name is made up of the project name, form name, and routine name. This event-handling routine is in the host application. The next entry on the list says Non-Basic Code, which means there was an interface between components prior to the current statement. Following the Non-Basic Code entry is `Day14QuestionControl.ucDay14Question.TabooWordCensor`. This name is made up of the control project name, the control name itself, and the local procedure name within the control. This indicates that the local procedure `TabooWordCensor` was called in the control right before the host application event-handling routine was called. You can deduce from this that the control's `RaiseEvent` statement is in that routine. If you want to work back even further, you can view the next item on the list, `Day14QuestionControl.ucDay14Question.txtAnswer_KeyPress`. You can see that the keypress event-handling routine within the control is the routine that makes a call to `TabooWordCensor`.

Now, with relatively little debugging effort, you know a whole lot more about the flow of code between your control and the host application. You can also use the Call Stack window as a convenient way to navigate to any of the routines that appear in its list. Just double-click on the routine you wish to bring up in the code window. When you go to that routine, you will see an arrow in the left-hand margin of the code window that indicates the last statement-called in the routine. This allows you to trace the exact code flow. For example, when you go to the `TabooWordCensor` routine from the Call Stack window, you will see the arrow pointing to the `RaiseEvent` statement.

This navigational feature works for moving forward and backward. You can use the Call Stack window to move back to routines you already visited as well as to move forward to other routines in the call list. Every routine will have the last statement indicator. The Call Stack window gives you a high-level routine-level overview, a detailed statement-level trace, and the ability to jump back and forth between routines viewed in the code window. These features of the Call Stack window are handy for any type of debugging. By definition, control code debugging involves testing at least two interfacing modules, so the Call Stack window is a necessity for any control code debugger who wishes to work in the most efficient manner.

Other Debugging Options

We have discussed many techniques for debugging controls. There are a few other basic techniques to keep in mind. When you reach a breakpoint, you can type code modifications directly into the source code. Then when you resume program execution, these modifications will be in effect. In addition, you can tell Visual Basic to resume execution at an entirely different line than its current breakpoint. Just use the Debug | Set Next Statement option. You can also instruct execution to continue only until the code reaches the location of your

14

cursor in the source file through the Debug|Run To Cursor option. These are advantages few languages provide, and the advantages apply to Visual Basic control code as well as to traditional Visual Basic application code. In fact, this is one of the strengths of the entire Visual Basic control model. Control creation used to be an intimidating task with other languages. Now the features of Visual Basic allow you to approach control creation much the same as you would a regular application—in development and debugging.

Summary

Today's lesson covers various advanced debugging techniques that can be applied to controls. You can use the Immediate window when your program reaches a breakpoint state to gain further insight into its data, cause other code to run, or change data values. Essentially, you can insert any expression you wish into the program flow through this window before execution continues. The biggest advantage of the Immediate window for control debugging might be that you can use it at design time. With the proper setup, you can individually launch control property routines and methods even though no test form is running. This allows easy testing of isolated pieces of control code and is often handy in initial stages of control development.

The Debug object provides methods that are particularly useful for control debugging. You can insert Print method statements into your control code that aid in tracing the flow of your program, and Assert method statements that halt execution when your prespecified conditions occur. You will want to test your control code with many different test host applications, so insert Debug object statements once and test them with many different projects.

There are a wide range of other helpful features available for debugging. Watches provide automatic monitoring of expressions as a program runs and are particularly useful for debugging control property code. You can use the Locals window to easily inspect local variables in any routine when you reach a breakpoint. In addition, you can even view and modify UserControl-level property and module variable settings through the Locals window by expanding the UserControl Me object. You can use the Call Stack window to see the sequence of calls leading up to a breakpoint. It will show the flow of calls from a host application working all the way back to your control code, and it's a convenient way to locate the source of events within a control. There are many other helpful debugging features in Visual Basic. For the most part, control development is similar to regular application development under Visual Basic. Therefore, the rich Visual Basic debugging environment advantages apply to all forms of development, including controls.

14

Q&A

Q **If you are in design mode and have not yet started a program, can you provide statements in the Immediate window that cause code to execute?**

A Yes, with proper setup you can enter statements that cause property and method routines of your control to be executed. You can even set and reach breakpoints in these control routines.

Q **I want to use the Immediate window to debug my control in design mode so I can cause specific method or property routines to be carried out. What kind of setup is needed?**

A Make sure the No Test application is running. Then highlight the test form in the Project View window so it is the active project. Close all other project views. Now you can reference the control in the Immediate window. You must provide the test form name and the underlying integrated control name with the property or method reference in your Immediate window statements. Here's an example:

```
? frmTester.ucQuestion1.Question
```

Q **If I leave `Debug.Print` and `Debug.Assert` statements in my code, what is the effect on the host application that integrates my control when it runs outside of design mode?**

A Fortunately, there is no effect at all. The `Debug` statements are not generated as part of the control OCX file your control source code produces. Visual Basic takes care of this for you automatically. Therefore, you can leave `Debug` statements and not worry about the impact to the end user who experiences your control as part of a normal application outside the design environment.

Q **`Debug.Print` and `Debug.Assert` statements seem much more convenient to use than traditional breakpoints. Does a good programmer use these techniques exclusively?**

A No. Every programming task and debugging challenge is a bit different, but in most cases you will find that a blend of techniques is most appropriate. The `Debug` statements are nice for providing a high-level understanding of program flow. However, when you start to really hone in on a problem, you might find you want to do more detailed probing on a line-by-line basis. Then it might seem more natural to use traditional breakpoints or to step through the code one line at a time and evaluate expressions in the Immediate window. There is no definitive guideline on when to use which techniques. The best approach is to understand all techniques thoroughly and then use whichever approach seems most convenient for your particular debugging problem.

14

Q **What is the easiest way to view all of a control's current property settings after you hit a breakpoint in your control? What if you want to change the value of a property after hitting a breakpoint?**

A Display the Locals window and expand the Me object by clicking on the plus sign that precedes it. Then you will see a list of all properties and module-level variables you can directly modify within the window if you desire.

Q **You have reached a breakpoint in an event handler in the host application of a control project group. Is there any way to see where this event was raised in the control code?**

A Yes. View the Call Stack window. You will see the flow of routines that led up to the current statement. The first control routine listed prior to the host application event handler should contain the RaiseEvent statement. Double-click on that entry to bring that routine into the code window. An arrow in the left margin will indicate the last statement called within this routine.

Workshop

In this lesson you have seen how you can use Debug.Print statements to trace your program flow. Now turn your attention to the ProcessAnswer routine of the question control. Insert Debug.Print statements throughout this routine until you have enough to provide you with a clear guide to the overall flow of the code. Run the test application and observe the output of your statements in the Immediate window. How many statements do you feel are needed to fully convey the program flow? Would it be easier for you to insert individual breakpoints throughout the routine to gain insight into it, or do the Debug.Print statements work better? There is no definitive answer to these questions. The best technique depends largely on the code and the reason for debugging it.

Quiz

NOTE

See Appendix D, "Answers to Quiz Questions," for the answer to this question.

Suppose you are having problems with a control property. You want to limit the size of a Question property string to 50 characters, but the restriction doesn't seem to be in effect. The host application has been able to assign strings of 55 characters to the property. You just want to take the first step and try to re-create the problem and probe into the code. You've tried inserting a breakpoint at the top of the property procedure. However, your form uses 60 question controls, and most of those use short questions. When you load your form, you hit breakpoint after breakpoint for the short strings.

You remove the breakpoint and reassess your debugging needs. You really want to start debugging only when the property procedure processes a long string. Add a statement to the control's property procedure that will allow you to further probe what is occurring only when a string longer than 50 characters has been entered. The following is the code for the property procedure:

```
Public Property Let Question(ByVal New_Question As String)

    If Len(New_Question) >= 60 Then
        MsgBox "The Question must be no more than 30 characters in length!", _
              vbExclamation, "Error"
    Else
        lblQuestion.Caption() = New_Question
        PropertyChanged "Question"
    End If
End Property
```

ANALYSIS   This property procedure assigns the property string. This sample has been kept very simple for illustrative purposes. The sample problem is that the designer wants to allow only strings of 50 characters. If this were a real problem, the solution would be clear-cut. You would simply observe that the maximum number of characters is limited to 60 rather than 50 by the first conditional check in the property procedure and fix it easily. However, in most cases the solutions are not so simple, and you might need to insert a statement to help you isolate the problem further.

WEEK 2

In Review

The first week of this book took you through many of the fundamentals you need to get off the ground in writing ActiveX controls. The second week finished up looking at those fundamentals and moved forward to look at more advanced features and techniques. The techniques and strategies you learned about in the lessons this week should start you thinking not only about the features you can add to the controls themselves, but the entire process of designing a control from start to finish. Taken as a whole, the techniques covered in this second week bring you to the point where you can put together real, productive, ActiveX controls.

Where You Have Been

The week started with a look at predefined and user-defined events. Control events, along with properties and methods, form the core functionality of an ActiveX control. You need to know what these things are and how they work to move beyond the fundamentals. Then the book moved into more advanced features, such as writing controls to work properly both at design time and at runtime. Days 11 and 12 showed you how to create property pages for your controls, giving the developer a much easier way of setting properties that can be grouped together. The last two days focused on control debugging techniques so that you can clean up bugs quickly and effectively during the development process. During the third week, you'll learn more advanced techniques and round off all the control design concepts you need to understand to master ActiveX control development.

Week

3

At a Glance

Welcome to Week 3! At this point, you know quite a bit about ActiveX controls. You have learned what an ActiveX control is and how to create one using all the fundamental techniques and concepts. During this week you will learn about some of the more advanced techniques that you can add to your repertoire to make your controls even more effective and useful. By the end of this third week, you will know how to create invisible controls, aggregate controls, and controls for the Internet, plus you'll learn how to test your controls and prepare them for the real world.

Where You Are Going

The week begins with a look at how to prepare your control to behave properly on the systems on which the control will be used. Then you'll learn various techniques for testing your control so that the user will not only have powerful controls, but stable and reliable ones as well. Then you'll learn about some of the more advanced concepts, such as designing controls that can be bound to data sources. You'll also learn about invisible controls and controls that you must paint yourself. You'll learn about multiple, subclassed, and aggregate controls, and controls designed for a Web page. The week wraps up with a discussion on control security, distribution, and licensing. By the end of this week, you should be fully prepared to write the controls you've been wanting to write because now you'll know the techniques and be able to use them.

Day 15

Preparing Your Control for the Real World

You've scoured your control for bugs in the design environment. You've applied the state-of-the-art debugging techniques you've learned from this book to produce squeaky-clean code. You probably think you're ready to unleash your control to the real world. Unfortunately, I have to step in and pull back on the reins. The world can be a harsh, cruel place to controls that haven't paid their dues. You do know how to debug now. But there are still more techniques for preparing your control for the real world that we have not yet covered.

Now that you have the fundamental debugging skills under your belt, you are ready to tackle some of these other areas. Today's lesson focuses on the preparatory steps you need to carry out to get your control closer to final form. You must add sufficient error handling to ensure that your control is robust enough to last outside the design environment. You must package the control into its ultimate delivery form—the OCX control file. Along with packaging, you must consider issues of optimization and consistency of registration information. You will be ready to move on to more advanced topics after you have covered these preparation basics. Day 16, "Testing Your Control," expands on how to produce a simple setup for your control and carry out systematic testing of it after you have it in final form. Day 21, "Licensing, Distribution, and Security," expands on some more advanced distribution issues. First, however, you must understand the basics of preparing a control for the real world. That is the background you will gain today.

Error Handling

An *error handler* is special code that deals with errors that occur while your control is running. The premise of runtime error handlers is sometimes difficult to grasp for newcomers to programming. After all, an error handler is code that is intended to deal with errors that occur while the user is interacting with the program. The natural question might be, why not just write code that doesn't cause any errors in the first place? If you've been programming for a while, you intuitively know the answer to this. No matter how much debugging and testing you do, there is always a chance that some unforeseen error may occur as the software is used, based on some unique program or system state.

Unhandled Errors

Consider what happens to the host application that integrates your control if your control causes an error. Do you think the host application will gracefully handle it? A sample error condition can help you reach a conclusion. Go to the question control project and inspect the control's `ProcessAnswer` local procedure. The code appears as shown in Listing 15.1.

NOTE

> **SAMPLE** If you want to experiment with the debugging techniques provided today, you can try them out on the question control. This source code can be found in the `Day15QuestionControl.vbg` group project file under the `Samples\Day15\Your Start` directory on the book's CD-ROM. This project contains the code that is intended to be your starting point for the modifications that are described today. Copy the directory to your hard drive so you can make subsequent modifications. The material is presented in a before-and-after format. If you want to see today's changes already implemented, you can view the `Day15QuestionControl.vbg` group project that is available one directory level up in the `Samples\Day15` directory.

Listing 15.1. The `ProcessAnswer` **procedure, with a new percentage calculation.**

```
 1: ' See if answer is correct
 2: Private Sub ProcessAnswer()
 3:
 4:     Dim svPercent   ' Percent of responses used, based on calculation
 5:
 6:     ' Only check the answer if it has not yet been evaluated.
 7:     '   This control processes the answer in response to either the
 8:     '   Enter key being pressed or when focus moves from the current field.
 9:     '   Since the Enter key also removes focus, have to make sure that the
10:     '   answer is not checked twice in a row.
11:     If m_bAnswerHasChanged Then
12:         If UCase(txtAnswer.Text) = UCase(m_ExpectedAnswer) Then
13:             lblFeedback.Caption = "Correct!"
14:
15:         ElseIf UCase(txtAnswer.Text) = "STATS" Then
16:             ' User is asking how close they are to question limit
17:
18:             svPercent = Int((m_IncorrectAnswerCount / Me.MaxGuesses) * 100)
19:             MsgBox "You have used up " & svPercent & " percent of your " _
20:                     " allowed responses. " & vbCrLf & vbCrLf & _
21:                     "    Responses: " & m_IncorrectAnswerCount & vbCrLf & _
22:                     "    Allowed: " & Me.MaxGuesses, _
23:                     vbOKOnly, "Answer Statistics"
24:         Else
25:             ' Store the incorrect reponse in the array
26:             m_IncorrectAnswerCount = m_IncorrectAnswerCount + 1
27:             ReDim Preserve m_IncorrectAnswers(m_IncorrectAnswerCount)
28:             m_IncorrectAnswers(m_IncorrectAnswerCount) = txtAnswer.Text
29:
30:             ' See if a max number of guesses is in effect
31:             If Me.MaxGuesses > 0 Then
32:                 ' Check to see if maximum allowed guesses has been exceeded
33:                 If m_IncorrectAnswerCount = Me.MaxGuesses Then
34:
35:                     RaiseEvent MaxGuessesExceeded
36:                 End If
37:             End If
38:
39:             If m_DisplayOnIncorrectResponse = ucAnswer Then
40:                 lblFeedback.Caption ="Expected Answer: " & m_ExpectedAnswer
41:             ElseIf m_DisplayOnIncorrectResponse = ucHint Then
42:                 lblFeedback.Caption = "Hint: " & m_Hint
43:                 ' Highlight answer area so user can retry after seeing hint
44:                 txtAnswer.SelStart = 0
45:                 txtAnswer.SelLength = Len(txtAnswer.Text)
46:             End If
47:         End If
48:
49:         ' Set flag so we won't check again until answer has been altered
50:         m_bAnswerHasChanged = False
51:
```

continues

Listing 15.1. continued

```
52:            ' Now send tabkey so focus goes to next question if that
53:            '     property option is set
54:            If EnterCausesTab Then
55:                Call SendTab
56:            End If
57:        End If
58: End Sub
```

ANALYSIS This routine evaluates the user's answer and provides feedback on whether it is correct or incorrect. The number of incorrect responses is also logged. When the incorrect response total reaches the MaxGuesses property, the corresponding event is raised for the host application.

The percentage calculation is a new feature added to this control today. It tells the user what percentage of his guesses have been used, based on a percentage calculation. If the keyword stats has been entered in the question area, the calculation is carried out that determines the percentage of incorrect responses used up. This calculation is based on the formula m_IncorrectAnswerCount divided by MaxGuesses. The resulting percentage is then displayed to the user. To test this for yourself, run the test program and type two consecutive incorrect responses into the *first* question control. Then enter stats into the response area. You will see the response feedback shown in Figure 15.1.

Figure 15.1.

Feedback to the user on percentage of guesses used.

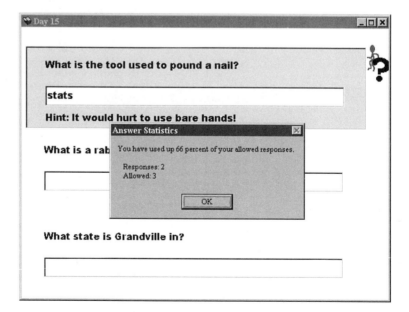

All is not well with this calculation, however. It can cause an error under some conditions. Did you spot it? The error only occurs with certain property states. According to the property convention discussed earlier, the MaxGuesses property does not have to be set with a maximum limit. This property can be set to 0 when no limit is desired. The code never raises the MaxGuessesExceeded event when that is the case. The new percentage calculation does not account for a MaxGuesses property of 0, however. The calculation will attempt to carry out a division with MaxGuesses as the divisor. Because you cannot divide by 0, a runtime error will occur.

This is easy to test. The second and third question controls in the test application have the MaxGuesses property set to 0 so that no maximum response limit is in effect for those questions. Now enter two consecutive incorrect answers in the second question area of the test application. Then enter Stats. You will see the result shown in Figure 15.2.

Figure 15.2.

A runtime error has occurred in the control and is caught by the design environment.

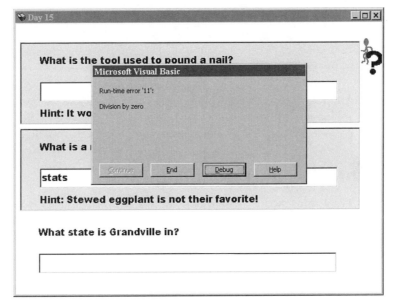

A runtime error occurred when the division by zero was attempted. The Visual Basic design environment caught this error and presented it to you. The ramifications are not so bad in the design-time environment. After all, it's normally only the control or host application developer that uses the control in this mode. You have the option to end the program or debug the problem area. After Visual Basic detects the error, you can debug the control code on-the-fly and resume the application if you want to.

What if this occurred in a host application outside the design environment? After all, that is the environment your users will face. The result is shown in Figure 15.3.

Figure 15.3.

A runtime error has occurred in the control and brings down the host application executable.

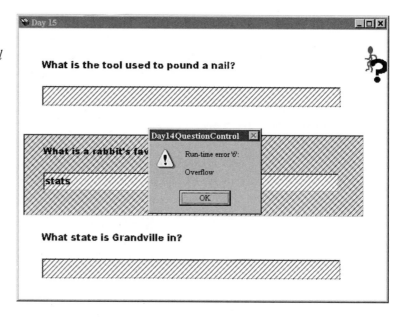

A message box is displayed indicating that a runtime error 6 overflow has occurred. The application is left in a frozen state, and your only choice is to click on the Close box to shut it down. You can imagine what kind of impression that would make on an end user!

Catching and Handling Errors

The way to gracefully handle this type of an error is through the Visual Basic error-handling mechanism. An error handler lets your code catch an unexpected error and process it itself. Once the error is processed, the code can continue on its original course without shutting down. An error can be handled using the Visual Basic On Error statement. On Error Resume Next just tells the code to ignore the current error and continue on with the next statement whenever an error is encountered. This statement typically is placed at the top of a procedure and then is in effect for the entire procedure. Insert this statement at the top of the ProcessAnswer routine, right after the Dim statement:

```
On Error Resume Next
```

Now enter the Stats response in the second question area again. Now, when the divide-by-zero error occurs, the procedure itself catches the error. The On Error Resume Next directive is carried out at the procedure level, and the code continues on its way. The line that calculates the percentage is ignored once the error is caught. The user will never see the error message you saw in Figure 15.3 because the error doesn't ripple up. The message box that

15

displays the percentage is still displayed, but with no percentage visible because that string value was never calculated. You can see the resulting message box in Figure 15.4.

Figure 15.4.

The percent calcula-tion message box after the divide-by-zero error has been caught and ignored.

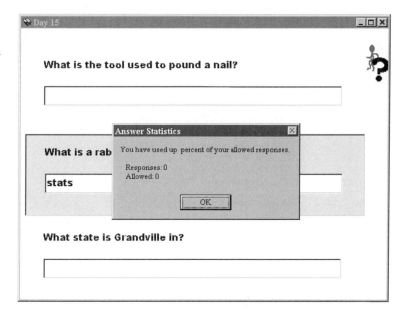

This is an improvement for the user. Although the information in the message box with the missing percentage may be a bit confusing, at least the program hasn't crashed. Providing an error handler that keeps execution chugging along when an unexpected error occurs is better from the user's standpoint than leaving him stranded. There is an even better option, however.

You can catch the error at the procedure level, give the user a message that an error has occurred, and still continue on. This allows the user to realize that something has gone awry. He can notify his support person if he wants to; more importantly, he has a heads-up warning that will help him understand if he sees additional results that look questionable. And the program will still keep running, so he will not face the aggravation of a program crash. The technique for this level of error catching is to use an On Error Goto Label statement. Modify the On Error Resume Next statement you inserted at the top of the ProcessAnswer routine. Make it look like the following statement:

```
On Error Goto ProcessAnswerError
```

This statement will send the flow of code to an area designated by the ProcessAnswerError label when an error occurs anywhere within the routine. Add the ProcessAnswerError label and the associated code in Listing 15.2 to the end of the ProcessAnswer procedure. This code should go immediately prior to the End Sub statement of the procedure. Note that you must precede the ProcessAnswerError label with an Exit Sub statement to keep code from reaching this label under normal, non-error circumstances.

Listing 15.2. The error handler for the ProcessAnswer procedure.

```
 1: Exit Sub
 2:
 3: ProcessAnswerError:
 4:
 5:     ' Handle any errors here so the host application won't crash
 6:     MsgBox "Sorry, a non-fatal program anomaly was detected. " _
 7:         & vbCrLf & vbCrLf & _
 8:         "Error description is (" & Err.Number & ") " & _
 9:         Err.Description & "." & vbCrLf & vbCrLf & _
10:          "Please report this to technical support if " & _
11:          " you experience further problems.", _
12:             vbOKOnly + vbInformation, "User Notice from " & _
13:             " the DoubleBlaze Question Control"
14:
15:     Resume Next
16: End Sub
```

ANALYSIS This error handler will be called whenever an error occurs. It will print out a descriptive message to the user, including information about this specific error that is extracted from the Visual Basic Err object. Then a Resume Next statement is carried out, which will pick up program execution immediately after the statement that caused the error.

Now restart the program and enter stats in the second question area to cause the error again. This time the error is captured and processed by your new error handler. The user first sees the more reassuring, descriptive error message shown in Figure 15.5.

Then the error handler resumes program execution at the statement after the error. This results in the display of the same message box you saw in Figure 15.4 with the blank percentage, but at least this time the user has more context for what has transpired and will not be as puzzled by the missing percentage.

The type of error message shown here is a very appropriate one to use in controls. It accomplishes several important goals. It identifies that the error occurred in your control rather than in the host application through the information in the message box title. It describes the error in language that is important to the end user, including words like "Sorry" and "non-fatal." It describes the error in language that will be helpful to you, the control integrator, if it is reported to you. The error number and description are included in the message text for that purpose. Finally, it tells the user what course of action to take in the message text: The user knows that it is appropriate to report the error if he sees continued problems. The most important aspect of all in dealing with this error, however, is that the error handler carries out a `Resume Next` to continue processing. You never want to risk crashing an application with an error from your control. Nothing could make a worse impression on the integrator or end user of your control!

Figure 15.5.

The error message box generated by the new error handler.

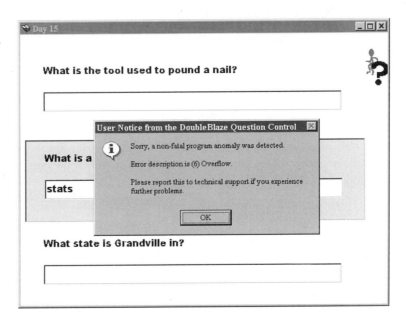

Error Handling and the Call Stack

The error you have seen in this example occurred within the procedure that the error handler was added to. But the error could also have occurred at a lower-level procedure called by this procedure. If that had happened, the error handler still would have caught and processed the error. A procedure can catch an error that occurs in it or in any procedure that it calls. Remember the Call Stack window you saw on Day 14, "More Control Debugging Techniques"? This window showed the sequence of procedure calls that had led up to the current code statement. The concept of a stack of procedure calls also applies to error handling. When an unexpected error occurs, it will bubble up to the top of this stack of procedures and terminate the program unless some routine in the call stack processes the error first.

With that background, you can understand how host application error handling relates to control-generated errors. Consider the cases of the three control interface approaches—properties, methods, and events. A property procedure in your control is only called when host application code references that property. Therefore, the host application itself could include an error handler. If your property procedure generates an unexpected event and you have no error handler in the property procedure, the event will be raised all the way up to the host application. The host application procedure that referenced the property, or some higher-level host application procedure that called that procedure, could capture the error with an error handler. In other words, the host application can protect itself from unexpected errors if it so chooses when it uses the properties of your control.

The same applies when a method in your control is called. A method procedure in your control is called in response to a statement in a host application procedure. If your method procedure causes an unexpected error, the host application procedure can trap that error if an error handler is in place. Unexpected errors that are not caught by an error handler will result in termination of the application. But once again, the host application can protect itself from errors your control raises. The host application just has to include an error handler in the routine that references your control method or in some host application routine that is higher in the call stack.

This situation does *not* exist in the internal event routines in your control, however. An event routine in your control is not called in response to a statement in the host application. Instead, an event routine such as a textbox `KeyPress` event or a `UserControl ExitFocus` occurrence is called in response to some user interaction. If an unexpected error occurs and you don't address it in your control, there is no clear trail of routines back to the host application. No host application error handlers will be able to catch the error. Instead, the error will crash the application.

The Golden Rule of Control Error Handling

The preceding description of error handling in property, method, and event procedures provides the background to the golden rule of robust control coding: You should always have an error handler in any of the control's internal nontrivial event routines. If an unexpected error occurs in any of those routines and you do not have an error handler, you will surely crash the host application because the host application is not capable of catching these errors itself. It is still a good idea to provide error handling in method and property procedures, but it is less critical in those cases because the host application can conceivably protect itself from errors as well.

Raising Errors from Your Control

What if you detect an error condition in your control and you want to notify the host application? You can use the `Raise` statement and raise errors from your control. You would only do this on the assumption that the host application carries out its own error catching and handling. The `Raise` statement takes the form

```
Raise vbObjectError + YourNumber, YourSourceId, YourDescription
```

You supply an error number of your own definition, your source ID, and your own description that the catching application can use for informational purposes. For example, to raise an error to tell the host application that no expected answer had been supplied, you could use this `Raise` statement:

```
Raise vbObjectError + 1, "Day15QuestionControl.Day15Question", _
    "No answer was supplied."
```

While this is a handy interface approach, keep in mind that if the host application does not catch this error, the host application will crash when you raise the error. Therefore, you might want to only raise your own errors up to the host application from your control if you believe the error is critical enough to warrant aborting the application if it is not handled at higher levels.

Generating the Control OCX File

Now you know how to set up all the code for a robust control. The next step is to generate it into an OCX file. You received very brief instructions on how to generate an OCX file early on in Day 2, "Creating a Simple Control." These steps are expanded on in more detail here. Turn your attention to the question control project again. This project will serve as the sample for OCX generation.

The ActiveX OCX file is the means by which you will distribute your control. Other host applications will integrate your ActiveX OCX file in order to have access to your control. This file is a binary format generated according to ActiveX guidelines. It does not include any of your source code statements; it is generated in machine language.

System Registry Information

When an ActiveX OCX file is generated, certain types of information such as Class IDs are generated along with it. These serve as identifiers to the Windows system for that file. In fact, host applications really integrate your control by referring to this identifier. Then Windows itself does the work of matching up the identifier with the location of the OCX file. It does this based on information in the System Registry. You can think of the Registry as a system-configuration database for Windows. You can see that the Class ID portion of your control is quite important.

Part of the process of installing a control involves not only placing the control on a given system, but also registering that control on the new system so that the System Registry has the appropriate entries for the new control. The System Registry–related information is automatically generated along with the OCX file. You'll learn more about System Registry information issues soon when setup issues are addressed. But first, you should have a clear understanding of the fundamentals. For now, the focus will be on simply generating the OCX file.

Making the Project OCX File

It's time to look at the specific steps to generate an OCX file. The process is really very easy. First, go to the project window and click on the control entry to make it the active object. Then select File|Make Day15QuestionControl.ocx from the Visual Basic menu. You will then see the dialog that is shown in Figure 15.6.

Figure 15.6.

The Make Project dialog that is used to specify the location for the new OCX file.

This dialog is somewhat misleadingly named the Make Project dialog. It actually is used to specify the desired location and attributes for the new OCX file. Use the directory navigation tools, if needed, to select the directory in which you want to store the new control. This location may differ depending on where you have placed your sample programs and where you desire to keep your controls. The standard location used during development of these samples was in the directory Samples\OCXFiles. You might want to use the same location on your local drive.

Make Options

After you have specified the target location for the OCX file, click on the Options command button. You will then see the Question Control - Project Properties dialog. The Make tab is initially displayed. You can see this view in Figure 15.7.

Figure 15.7.

The Project Properties Make tab.

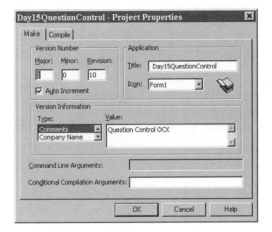

Make sure that the Auto Increment checkbox is checked. This will increment the control's version number each time you generate it. Type in a meaningful name for the Application Title. The Application Icon field can be left blank.

NOTE

> If you want to specify an application icon, you must first make icons available in your project. One way you can do this is to go back to the Project Explorer window and highlight the control project line. Then click the right mouse button and specify Add. Add a form to the control project itself. The form should now be grouped under the control project. Bring up this form and specify an icon for the form's icon property.
>
> Now when you return to the OCX options and click on the Application Icon drop-down list, you will see that your new form name appears in the list. Select it to make the form's icon carry over to be the icon for the control. Note that this icon will not be directly seen by the user of the control or the integrator of the control. The control's separate UserControl ToolbarBitmap property supplies the graphical representation of the control that the integrator sees at design time.

Specify version information for each of the items in the Type drop-down list. Highlight the type and specify a corresponding description. It is important to include version information with your control. This provides a great deal of information to integrators and users of your control. They can tell who it's from, when it was made, and what it is intended for.

Compile Options

Once you have specified all these fields, click on the Compile tab of the Project Properties dialog. You can see the Compile tab view in Figure 15.8.

Figure 15.8.

The Project Properties Compile tab.

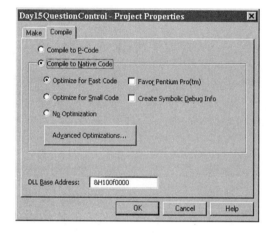

The Compile tab presents many options relating to compilation of the control. For fastest performance, select the Compile to Native Code option. The Compile to P-Code option would generate your control in an interpreted format. It would require more Visual Basic runtime support files to run, but the resulting file itself would be smaller because it relies on support files for much of its function. Unless you have some special need for this approach, use the Compile to Native Code option.

You have many choices when it comes to how the native code can be generated. The compiler is going to generate machine code for your control, but it can do this in many different ways and styles. Each potential style should work on any system. Some have advantages over others, depending on the future you envision for the control. You can optimize the control for fast code if you want it to perform quickly on the standard PC ahead of all else. On the other hand, if you are mainly concerned about the size of the resulting OCX file, you can select the Compile for Small Code. Your OCX file will be smaller, but the code in it may not be as efficient. It is harder for the compiler to generate optimally fast code with the sophisticated decisions that requires while at the same time trying to cut down on the number of instructions used. You can also select No Optimization, which simply means that your control will not be overly slanted toward the fast or the small optimizations.

You could also check the Favor Pentium Pro indicator, in addition to whichever of the preceding options you have chosen. If you choose this, your code will be optimally fast for systems that use the Pentium Pro processor. On other systems, the code will still work, but it won't be fully optimized because the most efficient instructions on the Pentium Pro don't necessarily have the same effect on other processors. Another selection you can make is Create Symbolic Debug Info. This information is mainly of use if you will be using other tools to carry out particular types of advanced debugging.

Base Address

Your choice of the compile Base Address option can make a key difference to the performance of your code. You can think of the Base Address as a specification of where your control will live when it is placed in memory. The frontier that is open for homesteading by your control is located between two borders. Figure 15.9 shows the situation you face as you decide where to stake your claim. The plots within these borders are sequentially numbered in units ranging from &H1000000 and &H80000000. Furthermore, each plot takes up a virtual acreage of &H10000.

Figure 15.9.

Finding a base address to stake claim to.

Now you can build or locate anywhere you want, but you must initially situate yourself at the start of a plot. In other words, you could settle at &H10000000, which is the start of the first plot. You could not set your first stake at &H10000003, which is partially inside the first plot. You could stake claim to &H1010000 because that is the start of the second plot. You can tell this is the start of the second plot because it is located one plot width away from the start of the first plot at &H10000000 + &H10000.

Suppose you locate on exactly the same plot as someone else. That's allowed, but you're going to have to share. Expect the sheriff to come by every now and then to tell you to vacate the premises while the other settlers have their turn at the plot. The more sharing you do, the less work you'll get done, of course. So when you start walking across the plains looking for a place to set roots, you don't want to park yourself at the first plot you find. Odds are, lots of other homesteaders will soon join you there. You probably want to venture way out across the frontier. If you've come with lots of relatives who are also homesteading, spread yourselves out. You might as well all find different plots to settle in on so you don't have to share space yourselves.

Now view this abstraction in more practical Windows terms. The base address is where your control will be located when your code is loaded into memory. Numbers referenced here that begin with an &H are in hexadecimal format. You must locate your code on even, 64KB (&H10000) boundaries due to underlying Windows and processor design. Furthermore, this design dictates that a control must be located between the addresses of 16MB (&H1000000) and 2GB (&H80000000). You can share an address with other code modules. If you do, however, the Windows operating system will make sure that everybody gets a turn. It will swap your module out to disk to give other modules a turn, and then move you back into memory. This is a slow process in computer terms. Consequently, the more Windows has to share your address, the slower your code will be.

Unfortunately, no matter what space you pick, you can't prevent other components made by other developers from selecting exactly the same space. You can end up paying the sharing price no matter where you locate your code. There are a few things you can do to improve your odds, however. For one thing, don't settle on the default address that is presented to you in the Compile tab. Hundreds of thousands of other Visual Basic programmers will see this same default. Many of them, unfortunately, may not be readers of this book and will not understand what the base address is all about. They will blindly settle on the default choice. Their controls will still work fine. But they'll be using the most common base address in the world, and will pay the highest memory-sharing price possible if their components are used on systems that have many other components installed.

Pick a location far away from the commonly used default setting by adding your favorite multiple of 64KB increments to the starting boundary. What if you have 30 different controls that your organization is developing? Then you should give them 30 different base addresses. Code written by other developers might still conflict with these addresses, but at least you're doing everything you can to ensure that your software components don't conflict with one another. For the sake of the current example, supply a base address of &H10F0000 and make sure the Native Code and Fast Code options are selected.

Advanced Optimizations

Next click on the Advanced Optimizations command button. You will see the Advanced Optimizations dialog shown in Figure 15.10.

This dialog presents various compile options that can result in specialized code speedups. At first glance, these may look rather scary and intimidating. At second and third glance, they may still look that way, and for good reason! These options are for the brave of heart. They carry with them a potential element of risk. Essentially, when you select these options you are trading some of the robustness that could be gained through additional machine instructions in your OCX file for the speed that comes from the elimination of those instructions. Notice that even this dialog itself warns you that choosing these options "may prevent correct execution of your program." Not exactly an encouraging thought!

Figure 15.10.
The Advanced Optimizations dialog.

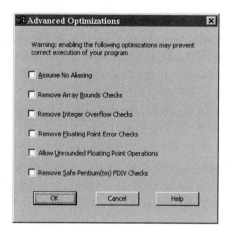

15

You might use these optimizations if you are an advanced developer who knows Windows quite well and has a high knowledge of your own code. They also may be of particular interest to you if you write numerically intensive code. If you fall into these categories, you can get helpful details of each optimization by clicking on the Help command button on this dialog. For most beginning control developers, however, these optimizations don't provide any payoff big enough to warrant the initial risk-associated use. You can create perfectly fine controls even without these optimizations.

Producing the Control

Once you have all the control options set, click OK until you are back at the original Project Make dialog, and then click OK to produce the OCX file. Look in the directory where you specified the control file should be placed. Notice that files with .exp and .lib file extensions exist in addition to the file with the .ocx extension. These are supporting files that are generated at the same time as the OCX file. They are of use to various advanced tools you can use. You don't have to worry about distributing these additional files. As you will soon see, the setup wizard will take care of your OCX file-distribution needs.

Specifying a Compatible Control

There is one more very important consideration when generating a control. You need to make sure that each time you generate a new version of an existing control, the class ID information that is stored in the System Registry information stays the same. If this class ID changed each time you generated a new version of the control, widespread pain and suffering would result! Host applications integrate a control based on this ID. If it changes, all the host applications that once worked with your control would suddenly not be able to reference the control at all.

This problem is easily remedied. You can follow along and observe the solution with the sample question control. Select Project | Day15QuestionControl Properties from the Visual Basic menu. You will see the Project Properties dialog again, but it has some different tab options than when you saw it at the time you created the OCX file. This time there is a Component tab. Select the Component tab and you will see the tab form shown in Figure 15.11.

Figure 15.11.

The Project Properties Component tab.

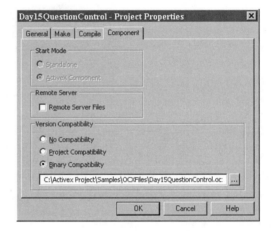

Notice that there are several compatibility options under the Version Compatibility area. The first, No Compatibility, would provide you with no compatibility at all. New class IDs would be generated every time an OCX was built. The second option, Project Compatibility, keeps some information consistent to support project-level integration, but does not guarantee to keep all interfaces the same. The Binary Compatibility option is the one to select. Binary compatibility indicates that you want to keep the Registry-related information consistent from one build of the control to another.

Visual Basic needs to know where to find the previous version of the OCX file in order to enforce this consistency. Therefore, a file-specification box is under the Binary Compatibility option. The location of the OCX file you just generated should be specified here. This specification process is a one-time step. Once you tell Visual Basic where to find your OCX, the file in that location will be considered to be the master location that is used to force consistency in subsequent builds. Therefore, each time you generate a new OCX file, you should place it in this location. Then your latest version will always be used for the consistency checks as you build subsequent versions.

Registration of Controls on Development Systems

When you generate an ActiveX OCX control file, it must be registered on any system before it can be used there. Tomorrow, you will see how a control is registered on other systems. However, the process is slightly different for the development system itself. When you went through the steps to generate the OCX file today, you succeeded in registering the control on your development system. Visual Basic carries this out automatically whenever it generates a new control file. The appropriate entries have been made in the System Registry for your new control. The control is ready to integrate into any ActiveX-compatible development environment on your system.

You can rather easily prove this. Select File | New Project from the Visual Basic menu to start a new project. Select Standard Exe from the resulting dialog. You are presented with a new project. Now select Project | Components from the menu to see the Components dialog. This dialog lists all the controls registered in your system directory. One of the entries in the components list is Day15QuestionControl. Click on this entry to select it. The file location of the OCX file appears in the bottom of the dialog, as you can see in Figure 15.12. You have proof that the System Registry is aware of your new file. You now have the ability to create an OCX file. Tomorrow, you will learn how to rigorously test it before final distribution.

Figure 15.12.

Your new ActiveX OCX file showing up in the components list.

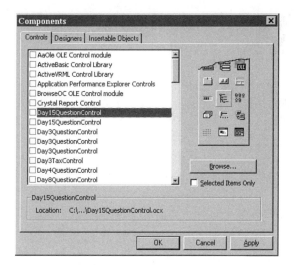

Summary

The focus of today's lesson is on the first steps in preparing controls for subsequent test and distribution. The need to make use of error handling in controls is illustrated today. Control events are not handled by a host application's call stack; therefore, a host application cannot catch errors there. A host application can, on the other hand, catch errors in control property and method procedures. If an unexpected error occurs in a control's event-handling routine, the error will cause the host application to crash. This can be avoided by inserting error handling into the control's event routine. Controls can also raise their own errors for the host application to catch.

Once a control code is complete and is appropriately robust, it can be turned into an ActiveX OCX control. Several steps are required. The location for the new file must be specified, along with version information and optimizing compiler options. Some of the advanced compiler-optimization options are best left untouched unless you have a high knowledge of those areas. You can ensure that your OCX files retain the same System Registry information by setting a Component Binary Compatibility reference to a previous version of the control file. Now that you can produce an OCX file, you're ready to move on to Day 16.

Q&A

Q Is it more important to catch control errors in the method, property, or internal event routines of your control?

A Internal event routines, because there is no higher-level routine in the call stack to handle the errors. If the event routine does not handle the error, the error will rise beyond the host application, and the application will crash.

Q How can you check whether your newly created OCX was registered on your development system?

A One way is to just bring up the Project | Components dialog available from the menu. This lists all components available on your system. You should see your new OCX file listed among these. If you highlight it, the location of the file will be listed at the bottom of the dialog.

Q Why is binary compatibility important when you build multiple versions of a control?

A Binary compatibility is needed to ensure that each new version of the control will still work with preexisting applications that incorporate it.

15

Workshop

Inspect all the internal event routines in the question control. Are there other routines where it would be wise to add error handling? Is there a potential for errors anywhere?

Quiz

NOTE

See Appendix D, "Answers to Quiz Questions," for the answer to this question.

Assume that you want to raise an error from your question control for the host application to catch when no question has been provided. You will provide an error number of 17 for your error code. What is the statement that would be needed to raise the error?

Day **16**

Testing Your Control

The day is drawing near when your control will be ready to be shared with the world. You've learned how to construct a control, carry out preliminary debugging, add robust error handling, and package the control in an OCX file. Now it's time to carry out a systematic test of the control. This test phase is aimed at proving that your control is ready for the real world. You need to bend, shake, poke, and prod the control until you are certain there are no more frailties lurking within it.

You must carry out this level of testing in a methodical, organized manner. It does you no good to perform this final test on your control too early in its development phase because the control is still evolving. You should wait until all your development is wrapped up and the changes have tapered off. Otherwise you are testing a moving target. After the dust of development has settled, it's time to focus on the final control test.

You don't want to test within the safe confines of the development environment only. The end users of host applications that integrate your control won't have this advantage, and it's important to simulate what they are going to encounter when they use your control. Therefore, one of the steps in this test phase involves wrapping up your control in a setup program and trying it on various systems.

Today's lesson includes a detailed first look at control setup. In some cases you might find it helpful to add a special level of logging to your control to support the test phase. Today's lesson also outlines the variety of areas testing can focus on. By the end of this lesson, you still won't have a magic answer to writing bug-free code. None of us do. But you will know how to carry out thorough testing so you can release your controls with confidence in their soundness.

Debugging Versus System Testing

There is often confusion about the process of developing software and the roles of debugging versus systematic testing. You should start out with a clear understanding of the relationship of these activities. Debugging is the act of honing in on a problem to find its cause. It takes place constantly throughout the development process—from the early stages of code entry, through the informal interactive test that occurs during development, and then all the way through final testing of the control. Likewise, informal testing typically takes place in one form or another throughout the Visual Basic development process. This level of testing and debugging aids you in development before you have a final control. System testing, however, occurs when the control is finished. This is very systematic and involves carrying out a test plan made up of specific steps. Its purpose is to prove that your control is ready for release. You might still find problems during this phase that require debugging and modification of your control. If you do, you'll need to repeat the system test again, until you're confident your control works in every context of your system test.

As soon as you start to create the first lines of your software in Visual Basic, you're likely to engage in debugging and informal testing. Visual Basic and the control creation model make it easy to run your control with a test application. Therefore, it is a simple matter to examine the control during development with a quick test. The insights you get from such minitests give you the feedback needed to refine the development even as your control is shaping up. The more frequently you run minitests on your control during development, testing a feature or block of code at a time, the easier it is to catch errors and debug them. After all, if you have a problem that you know was introduced by your last 4 statements of code, it will be quicker to pinpoint than if it was introduced somewhere in your last 200 lines of code. This is the reason it's often efficient to carry out a constant stream of minitests as you add features to your control. You can run your control code over and over with a test application, verifying how a statement works here, chasing down a bug there, and refining aspects of the code's behavior. Then you type in some more code and run the control again, repeating the process again and again. This type of incremental development, debugging, and informal testing often takes place throughout the entire development cycle.

Visual Basic lends itself well to such a test-and-debug-as-you-go approach, and it's really as much development support as testing. It helps you develop your control code quickly, but it generally doesn't go far enough to fully test all aspects of your control. At the end of your development, you have tested a lot of aspects of your code in piecemeal fashion. But the code has continued to change after each informal test. You can't be sure you haven't broken some features as you've added other features. And if your testing has tended to focus on one feature at a time, you can't be sure you've tested the interplay of the features. Likewise, in the thrill of development, you probably haven't taken the time to test each nuance of the control exhaustively. It's more likely that you've done the minimum verification needed to satisfy yourself that a feature is in place and then proceeded to add more code.

System testing is necessary. You must test the control top to bottom in a organized way to ensure that no stone is left unturned. You need to do this on the completed control so you know you're testing the final form of features and implementation. Your system test might still involve plenty of debugging. However, the debugging is now in support of a somewhat different context. Your goal is to prove to yourself that the control is ready for release or to make any changes you find necessary to get it in a releasable form. The most important tool for this systematic test phase is a clear plan of action.

Steps for Testing Your Control

How do you test a control? The key is to have a plan of action. There are several distinct steps to control testing that you should make sure to carry out when control development is complete. The first set of steps can be carried out in the Visual Basic design environment using control source code to aid in the verification process. The following is a list of suggested steps:

1. Verify implementation of properties, methods, and events.
2. Verify design-time behavior.
3. Verify runtime behavior of each property.
4. Verify runtime behavior of each method.
5. Verify runtime behavior of each raised event.

After you have completed phase 1 of the system test plan, you can conclude that the source code version of your control performs correctly under the carefully controlled circumstances of your design environment. Then it is time to produce an OCX file and move on to test under real-world circumstances. Now you need to test your control under the widest variety of circumstances possible to flush out any bugs that your carefully structured testing did not. You want to simulate the real-world environment of your users. Therefore, this round of testing should ideally occur on a system other than the development system you used to create the control. Testing at this point should not be based on control source code in the design environment. Instead, it should be based on the final OCX version of your control installed on an integrator's system with the setup utility. The following list summarizes these steps:

1. Generate the setup for control verification and for use in subsequent steps.
2. Verify that the control can be correctly installed on a nondevelopment system.
3. Verify that the OCX file control can be referenced in an integrator's design environment.
4. Verify integration of the control into the host application.
5. Repeat verification of every property, method, and event from the host application.
6. Test with a variety of host applications using the control in a variety of ways.
7. Incorporate independent integrator beta testing with external logging.

Test Phase 1: Using Control Source Code

The system test process should begin after the coding is complete but before the OCX file is generated. Early system testing should take place using the control's source code in the design environment. The reason for this is perhaps simpler than you might expect—you'll likely be finding lots of bugs, and it's easier to find them and quicker to get rid of them when you already have the source code up. The test phase typically brings many bugs to light as it goes through a methodical wringing. You will want to apply many of the debugging techniques described on Day 13, "Debugging Controls," and Day 14, "More Control Debugging Techniques," as you close in on the bugs. You need to work at the source code level to debug and fix code after you have identified a problem. You might as well start out there. Open up the project group for the question control project. You can step through the test steps for this control as described in the following sections.

NOTE **SAMPLE** If you wish to follow along with the test techniques in this lesson, you can do so using the question control. Keep in mind that this control has already largely been debugged. You won't find as many bugs as you might during a regular system test for a newly created control. You can find the source code for the question control in the Day16QuestionControl.vbg group project file under the Samples\Day16\Your Start directory on the book's CD-ROM. Later today you'll learn about some modifications to support beta testing. This project contains the code intended to be your sample test project as well as the starting point for the modifications described later in today's lesson. Copy the directory to your hard drive so you can make subsequent modifications. The material is presented in a before-and-after format. If you want to see today's changes already implemented,

16

you can view the `Day16QuestionControl.vbg` group project available one
directory level up in the `Samples\Day16` directory.

Verifying Interface Implementation

The system test should start with a look at the interfaces in the control. Your test goal is to
verify that every desired property, method, and event has been implemented. If you have
planned your control well, you should have a list of interface requirements. These requirements should list the properties, methods, and events your control needs to support. Table
16.1 shows the list of property, method, and event interface requirements for the question
control. These interfaces are documented in more detail, including functional descriptions,
in Appendix A, "Question Control Interfaces."

Table 16.1. Question control properties, methods, and events.

Properties

AnswerColor

BackStyle

BorderStyle

DisplayFont

DisplayOnIncorrectResponse

Enabled

EnterCausesTab

ExpectedAnswer

FocusIndicator

Hint

IncorrectAnswer

IncorrectAnswerCount

IncorrectAnswerIndex

MaxGuesses

Question

TabooWords

continues

Table 16.1. continued

Methods

Clear

ForceAnswer

ShowHint

Events

MaxGuessesExceeded

QuestionClick

TabooWordDetected

UserQuestionDetected

Select View|Object Browser from the Visual Basic design environment to start the Object Browser. You can use the browser to inspect the control for the presence of each of the interfaces. Your requirements serve as your guide to this portion of the test plan. You should compare the list of interfaces to those visible in the browser. If all has gone well, everything will be implemented. In many cases, however, even this simple act of comparison can uncover discrepancies between your intentions and reality. This is a good way to catch such discrepancies. It is much easier to find a problem during a simple visual inspection than to uncover it by working backward from a bug or runtime error.

When the Object Browser starts up, go to the Project/Library combobox, which is at the top of the window. Select Day16QuestionControl from the list of available objects. Now you will see only classes related to your control displayed in the browser. One of the classes you see displayed in the Classes listbox is ucDay16Question. Click once on this entry to highlight it. Now, in the Members area to the right, you will see only the members of the ucDay16Question UserControl object displayed.

The Members list shows properties, methods, and events, as well as module-level variables and constituent controls. All these members are intermixed, so the inspection process could be a bit confusing. Right-click to remedy this problem. Select the Group Members option from the resulting submenu. Now all members are sorted by member type. Inspection becomes significantly easier because you can view an alphabetical list of the properties, methods, and events in turn. A hand icon appears before property entries, a green rectangle icon appears before member entries, and a lightning bolt appears before event entries. You can see the Object Browser with the properties displayed in the Members area in Figure 16.1.

Figure 16.1.

Using the Object Browser to inspect properties.

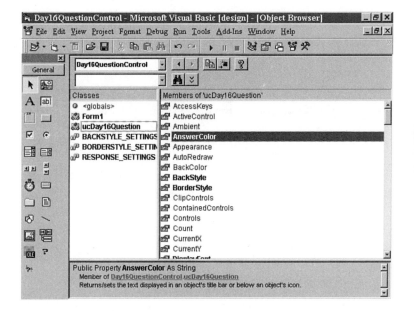

Notice that some of the members are displayed in bold type and others are not. The Object Browser displays all members of an object, but it distinguishes public properties with bold type from private properties with nonbold type. You can then compare your requirements list with the bold entries and make sure there are no discrepancies. At the same time, you can verify the data type and description of your exposed properties. When you click on a member, the full description, including this information, appears at the bottom of the Object Browser window.

Use the information in Table 16.1 to complete the inspection now. If you come across any discrepancies at this stage, you can make the necessary source code changes to bring the control members in sync with your requirements. In some cases, you might decide to change your requirements to match your implementation and revise your documentation accordingly. In either case, the interfaces or documentation presented to the integrator will be improved. After you have completed the comparison, you'll have accomplished an initial requirements verification. You are now done with a significant portion of your testing, and you've barely begun to test!

Verifying Design-Time Behavior

The verification of design-time behavior also consists largely of simple observation. Bring up the test form from the Project Explorer. Then select Project | Components from the menu. You'll see a list of all the components available on the system. Those in use by this test form project will be checked. Make sure that the question control is checked. In addition, click on the question control entry and observe the file location information displayed at the bottom of the window. This tells you the location of the control itself. Since you are testing the control source code, this location should read `Day16QuestionControl.vbp`. Make sure this is your current setting.

If an OCX was given in the file location rather than the `.vbp` file, this means you are not currently testing the source code for the control. There is nothing more frustrating and confusing than testing code that does not correspond to what you believe you are testing. Imagine taking your Ford Escort in for a service check and having the mechanic tell you he can't find the source of the engine thumping you complained about. Picture your reaction as you follow him into the garage to a Mercedes with the hood up and hear him say, "I've been trying to find the problem all afternoon!" It seems superfluous to remind you to be sure you're testing what you think you're testing, but it's very important to be sure during all phases of control testing. Control development often involves several trials of generating OCX files and various test forms. A project group can include many different projects, and each can reference a separate control, with no enforced consistency between them. As a result, it is quite easy to get a test form project in a state where it references a control location other than what you were expecting during extensive development campaigns. Therefore, this simple check should always be a prerequisite to any further testing.

When you're sure you're testing the right control, there are a few more simple checks to carry out in your test form project. First look at the toolbox. Verify that your control icon appears in it. Move the cursor across it. The correct name for your `UserControl` name property should appear in a pop-up display when the cursor is on the control. Then click on the control and add another instance of it to the form. Inspect it visually and make sure it's what you were expecting. If you make it this far with no problems, at least you can know that your control is structured in a correct control framework. Don't rest on your laurels yet, though. Many potential obstacles remain before you're ready to ship your control.

Next return your attention to the control project. Activate it by clicking on the control that appears on the form. Then select View | Properties Window to display the corresponding properties view for the control.

Now the testing, if done correctly, is about to get tedious. You should supply a distinctive value for each and every property you have exposed in the control. Then exit Visual Basic, saving the changes to the project. Start Visual Basic again and reload your project. Return to the test form and corresponding properties view. Inspect each property again, and ensure that the distinctive values are still there.

What has this accomplished? You have exercised and verified the `ReadProperties` and `WriteProperties` routines and confirmed correct usage of the property bag. These routines are involved in saving and loading property values at design time. You've also verified, to a large extent, the property procedures themselves. The property procedures were called to carry out the property assignments and retrievals. It's important that you do this test for each and every property. Many potential problems could affect property code. One frequent problem is the absence of a `PropertyChanged` statement in a `Let` `Property` procedure. In Day 5, "User-Defined Control Properties," you learned that whenever a property is updated in the property procedure, the following statement should be carried out:

```
PropertyChanged "NameOfProperty"
```

This triggers the `WriteProperties` procedure. However, this is an easy statement to omit if you have created your `Property` procedures manually rather than with the wizard or if you have done copy-and-paste operations to create them. This is just one of the potential complications that can occur with any individual property. Some of these complications, such as those resulting from the use of `PropertyChanged`, might only be apparent at design time and not at runtime. A full properties test in design mode is essential. After you have interacted with the control at design time, you can proceed to the runtime tests with confidence that you have implemented the control basics correctly.

Verifying Properties at Runtime

Your runtime tests should make heavy use of all interfaces: properties, methods, and events. Properties are a good place to start. You should construct a test application that makes assignments and retrievals to every single property. In other words, you should use statements like the following two:

```
MyProperty.PropertyName = MyVariable

MyVariable = Property.PropertyName
```

Carrying out the assignments in both directions ensures that both the `Property` `Get` and `Property` `Let` procedures are called.

This type of testing involves exercising the same `Property` procedure areas of your control code that you exercised during your design-time tests. However, you are approaching the testing from a different perspective here. The host application is making the assignments, as opposed to you typing them in design mode. The code paths are slightly different. For example, the design environment property bag will not be updated at runtime. In addition, you can take a more expansive test approach with the runtime assignments. You can hit a breakpoint and then make your property assignments from the Immediate window, as discussed on Day 14. Carrying out these tests from your test host application is a more complete approach, however. You can execute the host application code over and over to make these assignments repeatedly. For example, this is useful in flushing out memory or array-bounds dimensioning issues.

One convenient way to package your tests in the test form is to create a command button to initiate the tests. If there are any special property dependencies with other properties, you might implement a carefully crafted sequence of property assignments and checks based on an underlying knowledge of property interrelationships. Suppose you have BeforeConvert and AfterConvert properties that show the before and after state of a conversion, and then you have BeforeUnits and AfterUnits properties to which you can assign units such as inches and feet. In this case you should have a very specific test procedure that provides sample data and checks for sample results. You can associate such tests with a command button so they are easy to carry out repeatedly.

In most cases, however, you will not have such clear-cut goals for your property tests because of the nature of the properties. Keep in mind that you are not testing methods or events yet. Eventually you'll test the interplay of properties with methods. Right now, however, the goal is just to verify the Property Get, Property Let, and Property Set procedures that are called when property assignments are made.

Another type of test that facilitates property verification is to designate a command button to carry out many property assignments. The command button routine code consists of nothing but a gigantic sequence of property assignments. Then you can click the button repeatedly to carry out the sequence of tests as many times as you desire. Better yet, you can have a loop inside of the routine that cycles through the assignments repeatedly. One small example of such a test routine is shown in Listing 16.1.

Listing 16.1. Testing property handling.

```
 1: Private Sub cmdTest1_Click()
 2: ' This routine tests the control interfaces
 3:
 4:     Dim i
 5:     Dim tmpStr
 6:
 7:     For i = 1 To 1000
 8:         ' Exercise control properties repeatedly
 9:         ucQuestion1.MaxGuesses = i
10:         ucQuestion1.ExpectedAnswer = Time
11:         ucQuestion1.IncorrectAnswerIndex = i
12:         ucQuestion1.Question = ucQuestion1.IncorrectAnswer
13:         MsgBox "Test complete", vbOKOnly, "Testing"
14:     Next
15:
16: End Sub
17:
```

16

ANALYSIS These property assignments are carried out whenever you click on the test button. If there were internal dimensioning or allocation errors in the control property procedures, this type of test could help identify them.

Such tests that seem to assign nonmeaningful values to properties might seem haphazard, but they can bring real problems to the surface. For example, the preceding test will cause an error in the question control when the ucQuestion1.IncorrectAnswer property is assigned. It turns out that the control Get Property procedure for the IncorrectAnswer property causes a runtime subscript error when no corresponding incorrect answers have been entered by the user. This error is caused by an unintended use of the control. You wouldn't expect an integrator's code to look at incorrect answers unless it had checked whether any were present. On the other hand, if you can create this error, so too can the integrator. If the integrator accidentally uses the control in this manner, you might want to give him a more gentle correction than a subscript-out-of-range error. Testing your control in ways not intended by the original implementation can give you important insight into areas you might need to address.

You should do even more than just make a simple assignment to each property if you want to be diligent in your testing. Some problems only occur on boundary conditions. If you have a property you believe you've implemented to correctly handle a range of input from 1 to 100, try assigning values of 0, 1, 50, 100, and 101 to it. Verify that your data value handling is correctly in place. The integrator of your control can potentially provide goofy data values to your properties. You might as well beat him to the task and find out what he'll experience if he does so. You might not be satisfied with the result.

Another way to test is to add statements that assign invalid data to your properties. Assign strings to your integer properties. Assign decimal numbers to your user-defined types. Add a command button and the corresponding test code in Listing 16.2 to the test form.

Listing 16.2. Testing property handling.

```
1: Private Sub cmdTest2_Click()
2:     ' Carry out tests of control interfaces
3:     ucQuestion1.MaxGuesses = "foolproof?"
4:     ucQuestion1.BorderStyle = 17.3
5: End Sub
```

Run the test form and click on the cmdTest2 button. You'll see the result shown in Figure 16.2.

Figure 16.2.

The result of the runtime properties test intended to force errors.

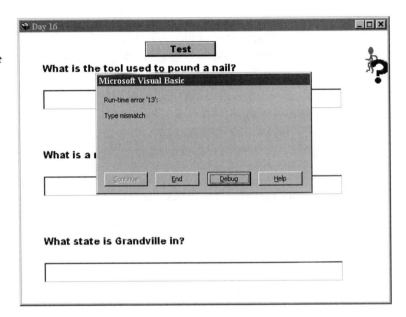

A runtime error results from the mismatched data types. You must make a decision on how to deal with this problem. This is a good example of an issue you'll face frequently in testing. Not every bug has one clear-cut solution—especially when you're dealing with controls and the interface you provide to your user. You can add error handling in the control property procedures that can trap these errors and prevent a misuse of your properties in the host application from causing a visible runtime error. You saw the techniques for error handling on Day 14. On the other hand, if a host application is assigning data of the wrong type to a property, you might not want to hide the problem from the integrator. Maybe the host application has even implemented its own error handlers to catch any such errors that arise from your control. This finding might not be viewed as a bug that must be fixed, depending on your perspective as a control developer.

Properties that affect the user interface of your control sometimes require a special testing approach. You should try to cover all the main combinations of property settings that affect the user interface. For example, you can set the BorderStyle and BackStyle properties of the question control. Even though you probably assume that these standard settings are mutually compatible, it can't hurt to double-check. You don't want the user of your control to be the first one to ever experience some unique combination of user interface settings that render your control in an aesthetically unpleasant way. In other words, make sure you stamp out the uglies before you ship your control! The Immediate window is tailor-made for this type of user interface experimentation. Start your test program and then press the Ctrl+Break key combination to temporarily suspend program execution. Select View|Immediate window from the menu to display the Immediate window. Now it's time to test key combinations of

16

user interface–related properties. You might find it helpful to write down a matrix of all combinations and circle the combinations you wish to hit in your test plan. Then you can adjust settings one at a time from the Immediate window and observe the results immediately. For example, to change the background style of the third question control, just reference the test form, control, and property with a statement in the Immediate window as follows:

```
frmTester.ucQuestion3.BackStyle = Opaque
```

Then press F5 to resume execution of the program, and you can observe the change immediately. If you use this technique, you can cover a wide variety of user interface configurations fairly quickly.

The most important consideration during property testing is to at least identify all problem areas. Then you can make a decision on what to fix based on this assessment. You should test a range of values and test every property. Do this repeatedly, perhaps within a loop triggered by a command button, and try to intentionally introduce errors. You should examine a wide cross-section of user interface settings. Then you can complete this phase of testing knowing that your control properties are ready for the use and abuse that real-world integrators will inflict on them.

Verifying Methods at Runtime

Testing control methods is very similar to testing properties. Set up code-based tests in your host application to test every possible use of your methods. You can enter the statements to trigger the methods from the Immediate window. The are several advantages to supplying test routines associated with command buttons. In a sense, you document your tests so you have a clear view of what you've tested. You can easily repeat the tests. If you make fixes or upgrade the control, repeating all the tests is simple and quick and it ensures that nothing broke.

Test cases for methods might be more detailed. You should try to test each method several ways. Each one should be tested intelligently, comprehensively, and in a random manner. You should carry out intelligent testing to verify that the function of the method is in place. This type of testing is set up in anticipation of the intended use of the control. You might need to make several property assignments if a method has properties that are associated with it. The purpose of some methods is to update property values. You might need to check the results of properties in code to determine whether a test worked.

You should also test methods comprehensively. If they depend on property values to dictate their behavior, add test code that'll test them with a variety of property settings, including boundary conditions. You should also add test code for random testing. *Random testing* is testing that, like testing for properties, uses methods in ways you might not have originally foreseen. This type of testing includes calling property-dependent methods with a wide range of property values or seemingly nonsensical values. For example, imagine a Convert method that must be called to update an After property based on a Before property. Assume also that BeforeUnits and AfterUnits properties determine the units of conversion. You should test what happens when inches are converted to feet. Depending on the units provided by the properties, you might also try an impossible conversion such as converting inches to gallons. Your goal at this phase is to flush out as many errors as possible.

Another important area of testing for methods is testing the sequence in which they are called. Sometimes the order in which you call related methods can make a difference in their behavior. Test the logical relation of methods. Also test random sequences of methods. One test routine that pushes the random sequence testing of methods to an extreme is shown in Listing 16.3.

Listing 16.3. Testing a random selection of methods to look for sequence problems.

```
 1: Private Sub cmdTest3_Click()
 2:
 3: Dim i As Integer
 4: Dim intLoop As Integer
 5: Dim svLog As String
 6:
 7: Randomize
 8:
 9: ' Use random numbers to randomly test different
10: '    sequences of method calls
11:
12:     For intLoop = 1 To 100
13:
14:         i = Int(3 * Rnd())
15:
16:         'Store the test case used in case error occurs and
17:         '  you need to revisit the sequence of method calls
18:         svLog = svLog & "-" & i
19:
20:         'Carry out the randomly selected method
21:         Select Case i
22:             Case 0: ucQuestion1.Clear
23:             Case 1: ucQuestion1.ShowHint
24:             Case 2: ucQuestion1.ForceAnswer
25:         End Select
26:
27:     Next
28:
29: End Sub
30:
```

16

ANALYSIS This routine generates a random number between 0 and 2 on line 14. Then it makes a selection based on the random number. Each selection path is associated with a different control method. A string is used to store the control method selected on each path through the loop. Then if there's a fatal error, you can examine the string to see which sequence caused the problem.

This approach doesn't have much payback for some types of controls, but does for others. The potential for flushing out problems depends on the number and purpose of the control's properties.

A common mistake when testing control methods is to call a method once and then pronounce it tested. If you make sure to approach your method testing from the three perspectives we've discussed, you will avoid this pitfall. The intelligent test cases will verify that your control method functions correctly with a variety of data. The comprehensive test cases will verify that your control method works correctly even when called repeatedly and is robust enough to handle erroneous or unintended property settings. Finally, the sequence test will verify that your method is not unduly affected by the order in which it is called in ways you didn't expect. After your control receives the green flag on all these tests, you can start to feel pretty comfortable with your implementation. You won't be out of the woods yet, however. You still have one more place to search for bugs—the events your control raises.

Verifying Events at Runtime

Testing events has a slightly different flavor than testing the properties and methods of your control. You can force the property and method code of your control to be called by using appropriate statements in the host application. Events your control raises, however, must be caused by the actions internal to your control in reaction to internal events or states detected by the control. The steps needed to cause the control code that raises an event to be executed must be specially considered for each event.

There are no magic answers to streamline this process. Since the path to the `RaiseEvent` statements is not inherently clear, like calling a method is, it is all the more important to verify it. You should locate each `RaiseEvent` statement in your code and identify a test case to trigger each one. Typically you can trigger a `RaiseEvent` statement through a combination of property settings and user actions. You should print out a message box from the corresponding event handler in your test application to verify that the event has occurred as the end result of your test case.

Your control also has procedures that respond to events it catches. Your test plan should include coverage of each of these internal events. You can get a list of the events your control responds to quite easily by looking at the code window. Objects are listed in the drop-down combobox on the top left of the code window. After you select an active code object in the leftmost combobox, the drop-down combobox to the right will display all the corresponding events. Events you've defined as internal event handlers will show up in bold text. Select an event and you'll be taken right to that event routine in your control.

Try out the following steps to see how to navigate among the event routines. Make the control project active through the Project Explorer. Then display the code window for the question control UserControl. Select the txtAnswer textbox object in the left combobox. View the right combobox and you'll see the Change event listed. The txtAnswer_Change event routine appears in the code window. You should test every event routine you've defined. The easiest way is to insert a breakpoint in each. Then determine the circumstances that cause that event to occur and re-create those circumstances.

Logging the Tests

The effectiveness of your testing will increase many times over if you carry out some simple logging steps. This applies throughout all phases of testing and is of particular importance during phase 1. Design environment-level testing is likely to be where you eliminate the greatest number of bugs. By the time you hit OCX file-level testing, the majority of bugs should be gone. So what can you do to pave the way for a smooth phase 1 test? First of all, define all the property, method, and event tests you'll carry out in advance of your test. Then check off each test as you complete it. Log any notes or observations along the way. Many developers shy away from test documentation as an unnecessary burden. This might be the case if testing were a straight point-A-to-point-Z process. But in reality, testing is nearly always a zigzag trail of tests, bug fixes, revised tests, experimentation, more bug fixes, and more tests. Your odds of staying on track are slim without a well-organized plan and a trail of where you've been. Consider it a necessity for professional-caliber testing.

Test Phase 2: Using the OCX File

You have completed design-environment testing. Now it's time to loosen your grip around the control code. You must start to think like the integrator of your control. The integrator won't have the benefit of working with your source code. He will be at the mercy of one main file: the ActiveX OCX file that embodies your control when it is distributed. Likewise, he will be using the control on a PC that's different from your development system. You want to experience what he will experience. You must put your control in a final format so you can proceed with this phase of testing. You need a means to install it on other systems in OCX format so you can test at the integrator level.

Using Setup

On Day 15, "Preparing Your Control for the Real World," you learned the details behind generating an OCX file. You saw that some of the options for generating the OCX file can affect its speed and stability. Now it's time to consider the next step in packaging because it'll be critical to this phase of testing. You need to generate a setup installation program. This will let you move the control to other systems. It'll also let you install it in the same manner as your integrator and will put the same end product in your hands that'll be in his. It'll also allow you to carry out verification of the OCX generation and setup program itself. This packaging is very important to the success of your end product, so the setup process is a key test item in its own right, as well as a tool that lays the groundwork for more tests to follow.

NOTE

> Distribution and licensing issues are considered in more detail on Day 21, "Licensing, Distribution, and Security." The focus today is on the basics of setup distribution to provide the backdrop for phase 2 of system testing.

Setup generation is very easy, thanks to the services of a comforting Setup Wizard. The Setup Wizard is not available directly within the Visual Basic environment, however. Instead, you must start it as a separate program. Click on the Windows Start|Programs|Visual Basic 5.0|Application Setup Wizard selection from the startup menu. The setup program will start and you'll see the initial screen, which is displayed in Figure 16.3.

Figure 16.3.

The Setup Wizard introductory dialog.

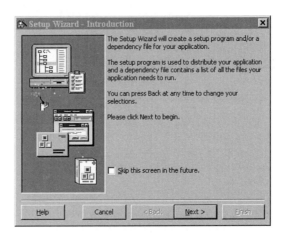

Click the Next command button to proceed to the next wizard page. (This is the way to advance between all wizard pages, so when I refer to "go to the next page" in the rest of this discussion, assume I'm referring to this technique.) The next page is for specifying the project file of the Visual Basic component you wish to distribute. You can see this window in Figure 16.4.

Figure 16.4.

Specifying the project file.

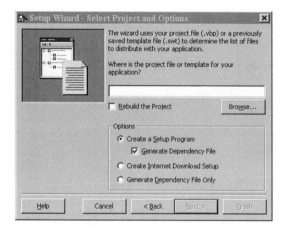

You should specify the location of the control's .vbp file here. You used a project group to combine a control project with an application project and test the control. However, if you just want to distribute your control and not the test software, you should refer to the control project by itself. You can follow along with the steps here to generate a setup program for the question control. The project name to supply is Day16QuestionControl.vbp. You should also check the Rebuild the Project checkbox. This ensures that the project you'll distribute has been built after your latest changes and is up-to-date. You should routinely check this checkbox. It will result in regeneration of the OCX file. Then select the Create a Setup Program option with the Generate Dependency File checkbox on. The dependency file that's generated can be used with some other tools, although today's lesson won't make use of it.

When you proceed to the next page, the project will be rebuilt, so you might notice a slight delay. Then you'll see the distribution page. Specify Disk Directories as the target distribution method. This gives you the most flexibility because then the software can be installed directly from the network or easily moved to floppies later on if need be. You can see the distribution page in Figure 16.5.

Next you'll see a page that lets you specify the directory to which the setup should be generated. Figure 16.6 shows this directory.

16

Figure 16.5.

Specifying the distribution method.

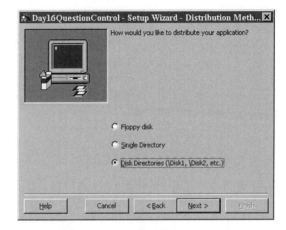

Figure 16.6.

Specifying the directories.

Advance to the next page, which is shown in Figure 16.7. This page is for specifying ActiveX server components, which the question control does not include. This is not likely to apply to a control unless you have produced a fairly sophisticated one that requires advanced knowledge of ActiveX.

When you move to the next page you'll be reminded to include the Property Page DLL if your project provides property pages as the question control does. This DLL is for design-time support on non–Visual Basic development environments. If you know for sure that all users of your control will forever be using Visual Basic, you can elect not to distribute this file. You can see the dialog that is presented when you add the Property Page DLL in Figure 16.8.

Figure 16.7.

ActiveX server
components.

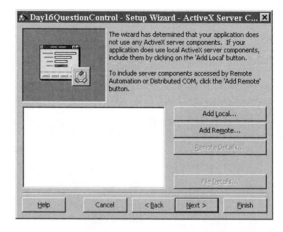

Figure 16.8.

Including the Property
Page DLL.

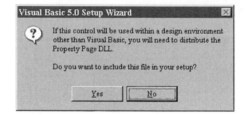

When you proceed to the next page, you see a helpful file summary. Now it's time to step
back into test mode again. The Setup Wizard provides some interesting information about
the distribution. In Figure 16.9 you can see a list of every file that will go into the setup and
why it is being included. You should consider the purpose of each file on the list and verify
that this list of files is the one that you want to put in the hands of your end users.

Figure 16.9.

Viewing the file
summary.

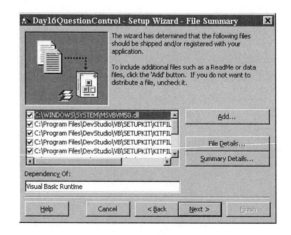

You can get even more information on individual files. Click on the File Details command button. This provides a wealth of information about the currently highlighted file. Figure 16.10 shows the information available.

Figure 16.10.

Viewing the file details for the OCX file.

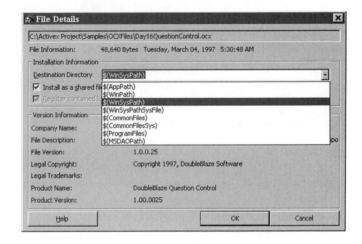

You can see the size, date created, and description for each file. If you are puzzled by the purpose of a file that has been added to your setup distribution, this is the place to get your answers. You can also specify a destination directory of where the control should be installed on the integrator's system.

Now close this page and select the Summary Details command button. You will see the page shown in Figure 16.11. This page shows the grand total size for distributing your control. You need more than 2.4MB of data to install the question control you have been building. Much of this space requirement is due to support files that must be shipped with the control. Additional space on the disk is required by the setup program itself.

You can proceed through the final setup pages to conclude the setup. The whole process has been very quick, but you've made enormous strides toward distributing your control. The specific files distributed with the control are very important. They determine whether the control will have the support it needs to run correctly on another system. You need a thorough understanding of these files to understand, troubleshoot, and solve some of the problems that might confront you during the remainder of phase 2.

Figure 16.11.

Viewing the summary details.

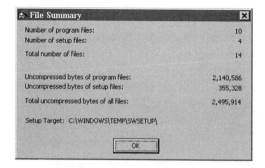

Verifying Installation

It's time to verify your setup. These verification steps should be carried out on a system that doesn't have Visual Basic installed. This ensures that there are no dependencies on Visual Basic files. Start the setup program directly from the directory in which you saved it. Go to the directory and click on the Setup.exe icon, and the setup process will begin. After the setup is complete, verify that the control was installed.

Verifying OCX File Reference

The control's OCX file should now be in the directory you specified when you built the setup program. This directory is the Windows system directory by default. The setup program also registers the control when it installs it. If you had never had the Day16QuestionControl on your system before, it would now exist in your system directory and be registered in the System Registry.

You can verify the registration status with tools such as the Object Browser or the system RegEdit utility if you are an experienced Windows 95 technician. An even easier way is with the Visual Basic component utility. Start Visual Basic, create a new project, and select Project|Components from the menu. You saw how to examine a file location from this window on Day 15. Once again, select the control and verify the filename that appears at the bottom of this window. This should indicate the Day16QuestionControl.ocx file in your system directory. If the control appears in the Components window and is associated with the correct file, you can check off the initial installation test step on your test plan list.

Verifying Control Integration

Now it's time to verify that you can integrate the control. This is a quick and easy check to make sure everything is on course. Go to Visual Basic and create a new project. Use the Components window again for this project. Click to turn on the check mark for the Day16QuestionControl.ocx file in the list. Now it will be available to your project.

Go back to the Visual Basic design environment and go to a form window. You should see the icon for the question control displayed in the toolbox. Click on it and create an instance of the control on your form. Verify that the control looks normal as far as the initial control user interface you see. View the property window for the control. Once again repeat the steps of phase 1. This is to ensure that you did not regress in functionality when you moved from your control source code on your home system to an OCX file on a different system. Change some properties, exit Visual Basic, and return. The property settings should still be in the state in which you last left them.

Repeating Verification of Properties, Methods, and Events

Now it's time to repeat the tests of phase 1. The purpose is twofold. First, you want to make sure that the control hasn't regressed. After all, it's been through a drastic evolution. Think of it as a graceful butterfly emerging from an encompassing cocoon and making its first debut into the sunlight of the real world. (Okay, that imagery might be a little dramatic, but you should be proud of the controls you make!) Your control has grown from source code directly interpreted by Visual Basic to a collection of binary instructions in an OCX file. It has relocated from a safe environment where Visual Basic and its plethora of comforting support files were installed to a completely different system. It had to bring all the files it needs to run along for the ride in order to work. The trip has been fraught with opportunities for error to be introduced. You need to prove that your control still works as well as it did when you carried out your initial testing.

The second thrust of the repeat testing is to see whether the control performs the same on a different system. Many PC-specific factors might influence how your control looks, feels, behaves, or performs. These can range from the existence of other support files that cause conflicts, to a different directory structure where the program is installed, to the amount of available RAM, disk speed, display capabilities and resolution, and processor speed. Many variables might affect your control in subtle ways you couldn't predict in the safety and comfort of your own system.

Fortunately, it should be a simple matter to repeat most of your tests. After all, the majority exist in code in your test application. Just move your test application project over to this system. Move the application project Day16Tester.vbp but not the project group. The project group includes the control source file, and you don't want to test that at this point. Load the test project and go to the Project Explorer window. Click on the project and then right-click the mouse. Select Remove Form to remove the Day16Tester test application form.

The panicky reader might ask at this point, "What? Are you crazy? That's where all the test code is!" Fortunately *you* have more faith in me than that; and it's well founded. The form must be temporarily removed from the project. Open the Project Components window. Remove the reference to the `Day16QuestionControl.vbp` file. Then check the reference to the `Day16QuestionControl` OCX file. You couldn't make this swap if the test form were still part of the project because you can't remove a component reference that's part of a current form. Now return to the Project Explorer window. Right-click on Add. Specify an existing project. Look at the program directory and you'll see the `Day16Tester` form safe and sound. Just add it back to the project, run the test program, and presto! Now your test application is running again; but this time it's exercising the OCX file. Carry out all your original property, method, and event tests, and verify that the results are the same in this test round.

Testing a Variety of Host Applications

You're approaching the final stages of testing. If you've made it this far, you can feel pretty good about your control. The next step requires some creativity. You need to create a variety of test applications that use your control. This time you want to come up with a variety of valid approaches to integrating your control. Often when you attempt to implement real-world solutions, you'll come up with usage patterns or considerations you wouldn't have thought of otherwise. The goal now is to ensure that the control stands up in a variety of these situations. There's no overriding guideline here, except to exercise, exercise, exercise—your control, that is. Try to come up with test applications that cover every aspect of the control features.

One note worth mentioning applies throughout this process. When you find a bug you decide to fix, you must go back to square 1! Or, in keeping with today's lesson, phase 1. Whenever you change your code, you should repeat your testing in the design environment before regenerating a setup and continuing with phase 2. When you make one code change, you could introduce a code change that could break any other aspect of your control.

Beta Testing

Now it's time for the final stage of testing. Find an integrator who was not involved in the control development and has a real-world need for the control. Have him integrate it into his application and provide feedback. This gives you yet another perspective on your control. Very often beta-level testing turns up serious errors after development-level testing would lead you to conclude that a component was as solid as a rock. A different perspective leads to different integration patterns. In this respect, the more beta testers you can comfortably support, the more robust your control will probably end up. Beware of involving beta testers too early, however. Nothing can discourage them more than bug-saturated software. And if your control is still in its early stages, you can probably effectively deal with the early issues yourself. It's in the late stages when you think your control is solid that beta testing has the most payback.

External Logging

What if a beta tester has a problem you can't re-create on your system? How do you debug on his system? In some cases, he might be across the country and Visual Basic design environment debugging might not be feasible. Alternatively, he might not have the space or inclination to accommodate installation of Visual Basic and allow for further debugging. One technique you can use in such cases is to rebuild your control with file I/O trace capability. Supply a routine that takes a parameter of information and writes that information out to a log file. Then sprinkle calls to that routine throughout the control. These routines can indicate their position in code through the parameter. You can even dump data values through the parameter. Regenerate that debug version of your control and ship it to the beta tester. Have him re-create the problem. Then have him ship the trace file back to you. It might not be as helpful as a full-fledged debugging session, but it's much better than nothing!

You won't want these statements in the final version of your control code because they would slow down performance. There is a technique you can use to make it easy to remove such statements in the final version of your code. Add conditional debugging statements around all the trace statements. Refer to the code in Listing 16.4.

Listing 16.4. Conditionally compiling trace code.

```
1: #If FieldDebug Then
2:     Call MyDebugRoutine("At start of program")
3: #End If
```

 This code calls a trace routine. However, it is only included by Visual Basic when the compiler directive FieldDebug is defined.

The statements inside the #If-#End If aren't included in the control code or OCX under normal circumstances, even though they are present in the source code. If you want these statements to be included, you must select Project | Properties. Then go to the Make tab and specify a conditional compilation argument such as the following:

FieldDebug = -1

Now when you run the control code, the statements in the #If are carried out. Likewise, they are generated in the machine code in the OCX when you build your OCX file.

After you go back to the project properties and remove the `FieldDebug` entry, it is as if the statements inside the `#If` do not even exist. They are ignored and will not take up space in the OCX file or be carried out in the design environment.

So you have a painless way to switch between a debugging version of your control and a nondebugging version. One note of caution: It is very easy to forget which is which! If you use this technique, take special care to stay clear on the setting of the conditional compile arguments whenever you generate your OCX file.

The End Result of Testing

You should have a very sturdy control after you have applied these techniques. If you use the approach described in today's lesson, you'll also end up with a very useful test plan and set of automated test code that can be used again and again on future upgrade cycles for your control. Testing should take less time with successive releases. Controls will be prone to more problems than a normal application. A control is typically used on a more widespread basis and in ways not always foreseeable during initial development. The test steps you have examined today are your best means to provide a control that stands the test in the field.

Summary

The consequences of poor testing are even greater with controls than regular applications because a control might be integrated with many different applications in ways that are not easily foreseen. For this reason, comprehensive, well-planned testing is a necessity. Some level of debugging and testing naturally occurs throughout the entire development cycle. When control code is complete, it is time to carry out formal structured testing using a well-defined system test plan. The test plan can be pictured in two phases. Phase 1 consists of tests that are carried out on the control source code to allow easy verification of the basic control behavior. Phase 2 involves testing the control OCX file at the level of the integrator and the end user.

Phase 1 testing starts with a simple Object Browser inspection to ensure that every intended property, method, and event is available in the control. You then verify design-time behavior of the control. After that, each individual property, method, and raised event of the control should be carried out. You can conclude that the control is carrying out its intended job after successful completion of these tests, and you can proceed to phase 2.

Phase 2 testing requires a setup program for the control OCX file. The act of generating the setup program is itself the first form of verification in this test phase. After the setup program is complete, you can verify installation of the control on an integrator's system. Correct references to the control should then be in place on the system and can be verified through various tools. Next, you should again carry out the same verification of properties, methods, and events that you did in phase 1. This time, however, the verification is based on a host application that uses the OCX file rather than control source code. Then the control should be tested with as wide a range of host applications as possible. Finally, the control should undergo beta testing by users of the control with an actual need and desire to integrate it. You can implement a special level of logging in the control to help you understand what occurs when beta users experience problems with the control. Once you've made it past the beta stage, your control is ready to be shared with the world.

16

Q&A

Q How can I tell which files need to be distributed with a control?

A The Setup Wizard will generate a full list of all the required files.

Q Can I control which directory a file is placed in on a user's system when I generate a setup installation?

A Yes, there is an option under File|Details that lets you specify this.

Q Why should I bother to write code to test my control when I can use the Immediate window?

A If you write code, you can use it again and again when you make future changes to the control. The code test routines also provide a level of documentation of what you have covered in your testing and they can help you approach control testing in an organized fashion.

Q Every now and then my control crashes. I suspect it has to do with the order in which methods are called. Is there a way I can verify this?

A Refer to the test code in Listing 16.3 earlier in this chapter that provides a random method exerciser. This host application code calls control methods in random sequences but logs those sequences for subsequent debugging.

Workshop

Think back to all the commercial controls you've integrated. Have you ever discovered a bug in any of them? If so, did it seem like the bug should have been caught prior to release of the control? Would the test process presented in today's lesson have led the developers to catch it?

Quiz

 NOTE   See Appendix D, "Answers to Quiz Questions," for the answer to this question.

Suppose you want to test the user interface of the question control. You want to verify that no problems occur when the BorderStyle and FocusIndicator properties are all set off and BackStyle is Opaque for the third question control. Assume that the test form is currently running. What keystrokes are needed to carry out this test?

Day 17

Data-Bound Controls

If you're a Visual Basic programmer, and even if you're not, you may have heard that most programs written with Visual Basic are client/server–based applications. That is, they access a database, storing data in the database and pulling data out of it for the user. The user's computer, called the *client,* uses the database, which is stored on a computer called the *server.* In many cases, the client computer and the server computer are one and the same. In other cases, the server might be on a network, say at a large corporation. Within the corporation may exist a multitude of client computers, all of which access the database on the server. The Visual Basic program installed on the client computers connects to the database on the server and allows the users on the client computers to access or modify the data.

Visual Basic is a popular tool for building database applications, in part because Microsoft has made it so easy to manipulate data using Visual Basic. One of the easiest ways to connect to a database is to use what's called a *data control.* A data control provides a link between a database and a Visual Basic application. Other controls on a form, such as textboxes, for instance, can then connect to the data control. The data control links the database to the text control so that data from the database automatically appears in the text control. Even better, if the user changes the text in the text control, the controls can be set up so that the changes the user makes in the textbox affect and change the data within the database linked to it. A control that can be connected to a data control this way is called a *data-bound control.*

In today's lesson, you're going to learn how to make an ActiveX control a data-bound control. That is, the program into which a developer places your control will use your control as an interface to a database connected to the program with a data control. Your ActiveX control essentially becomes a window through which the user can see data, and a "control panel" that allows the user to change the data within that database. We'll begin with the fundamentals, exploring in more detail exactly what a bound control is and how it works.

This lesson assumes that you have some familiarity with databases and data controls, but a short primer will be presented to give you an overview of these important concepts. Then you'll dig into the meat of the lesson, learning how to create bindable properties at design time as well as how to use them at runtime. By the end of today's lesson, you will have extended the question control so that the host application can create a database full of questions that can be linked directly into the question control. Furthermore, you'll be able to store the answers the user provides in the database as well, again through the wonderful power of the bound property. So prepare yourself for an exciting adventure with data-bound ActiveX controls!

A Brief Primer on Databases and Data Controls

Before you delve into the subject of bindable properties, you need to understand the basics. The subject of databases and Visual Basic database application programming is indeed very extensive. While we wish we could spend a lot of time explaining every detail about database programming to you, we unfortunately cannot. We'd probably have to write at least one entire book on the topic alone! So our recommendation is this: If you're already very familiar with database programming, specifically within Visual Basic, you can probably skim over this section; you don't need to read it in detail.

If, however, you're somewhat new to database programming and aren't sure how the pieces fit, this section is particularly for you. If you've never heard of database programming and don't know the first thing about a database or how to use one, you may need to get up to speed by reading over the Visual Basic documentation, trying out various sample programs, and reading other books on database programming in Visual Basic. We're going to assume that by the time you read what follows in this lesson, you'll have at least some exposure to database programming. So this primer will serve as a review and a simple overview of database programming, particularly in Visual Basic. Because Visual Basic is very friendly with the

Microsoft Access database application, any databases used in today's lesson will be Microsoft Access databases.

NOTE

Because Visual Basic is able to work directly with Access databases, all the capability to work with an Access database is built into Visual Basic or is available using an add-on that ships with Visual Basic. That means you don't have to go out and buy Access to work with Access databases. It certainly is beneficial, however, to have a copy of Access, because that way you can work with databases in their native programming environment with a full set of features should you need them.

A *database* is essentially a collection of tables with related data. The collection may be small and simple, or it may be very large and complex. You can store a record of the books you have on your bookshelf, your favorite recipes, or a complex collection of employee time-management data all within a database. The beauty of a database is that it gives you the ability to sort, organize, and recall the data in many different ways. Want to find all the books of a certain subject? Want to bring up all your dessert recipes that have less than 100 calories per serving? Or do you want to see how many hours your sales department spent discussing a particular product line with potential clients? All these capabilities and much, much more are available with databases.

So how does a database hold information? The databases most commonly used with Visual Basic store data in entities called *tables*. A table is much like a grid in that it holds data in a series of rows and columns. If you've ever used a spreadsheet program, you've worked with a grid. Each row in a table is called a *record*, and each cell within a particular row, or record, is called a *field*. Figure 17.1 shows a database table graphically, indicating all the entities just mentioned.

Figure 17.1.

A graphical representation of a database table.

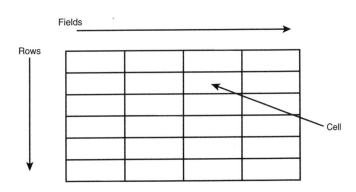

The table is the primary mechanism with which to store data. A single database can contain more than one table. If your database stores employee data, for example, one database may hold the list of employees. Another may hold the departments to which those employees belong. Yet another may hold the projects to which those employees log their time. Finally, you may have another table that brings all this data together and actually stores the time the employee has spent performing a certain task.

Databases can certainly get complex, but I'm going to keep this discussion rather simple. One of the easiest ways to get a database into a Visual Basic application is to use the Microsoft data control. The data control connects to a database, and in particular, a table within that database. It has two properties: DatabaseName stores the name of the database, and RecordSource contains the name of the table that connects to the data control.

Assume for the moment that your recipe table is stored in a database. You could create a Visual Basic application that contains a textbox and a data control. If you connect the data control to the database using the DatabaseName property and you connect the table using the RecordSource property, you have brought the table into the application. Let's suppose you have a database named Recipes.mdb and a table called tblRecipes. Your table consists of the fields Name, Type, Ingredients, and Calories, just to name a few. Figure 17.2 shows the table graphically.

Figure 17.2.

A recipe-storage table.

tblRecipes

Name	Type	Ingredients	Calories
Spaghetti	Meal	Noodles, etc.	120
Pea Soup	Meal	Pea, salt . . .	130
Egg Rolls	Meal	Lettuce . . .	180
Shakes	Dsrt	Ice Cream . . .	210

If you place data in the table and create a Visual Basic application, you can place a data control on the form and connect the database and table to the data control. The data control allows you to access and manipulate the data. As you will see, it also allows you to connect other controls on your form to the database.

What Is a Bound Control?

So now you have a database that contains a table and some data within that table. You also have a data control on your form to connect the database table to the form. The next step is to place controls on your form that show the data to the user. Controls that let you connect directly to the database via the data control are called *bound controls*. The textbox control, for example, is a commonly used bound control.

To bind a textbox control to a database, you need to set two very important properties. The first property, DataSource, is where you specify the data control to which you want to bind the control. But it's not enough just to connect the data control to the textbox control. You also need to specify which field in particular you want to assign to the text control. To do that, you need to set the DataField property. You must set DataSource first, and then when it comes time to set DataField, Visual Basic will automatically show a list of all the fields in the table connected to the data control. The series of connections from the database to the data control and through the data control to the textbox control is shown in Figure 17.3.

Figure 17.3.

The recipe storage table bound to a Visual Basic form using a bound textbox control.

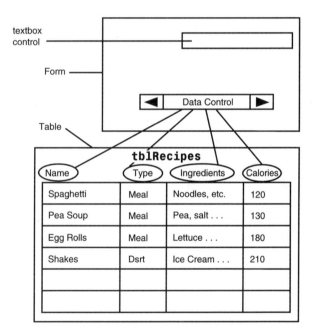

Data controls allow you to bring data into a form one row at a time. So when the data control is set to a specific row, whatever value is in the Name field appears in the text control because the text control is bound to the data control, specifically to the Name field of the data control's set of records. The final result is the series of connections shown in Figure 17.4.

As you can see, a bound control is connected to a database through a data control. It is not possible to bind a control directly to a database; you must work through a data control to make this happen.

Figure 17.4.

*The series of connec-
tions from the textbox
control to the data
control to the
database.*

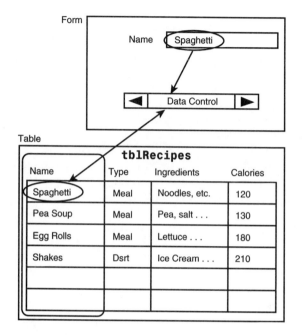

Making Properties Bindable at Design Time

Now let's turn our attention to ActiveX controls. Standard controls like the text control are bound controls because that's the way Microsoft implemented them. Many other controls in the toolbox are not bound controls, however. The grid control, for example, is not a bound control. It does not have a DataSource property, which is the easiest way to tell whether a control is a bound control.

 NOTE

> Just because a control is referred to as a *bound control* does not mean it has to be bound to a data control. You can use a bound control without binding it at all. Perhaps a better term would be a *bindable control* because it is something optional to the developer using the control in his application.

When you work with a control like a text control, it does have the DataSource and DataField properties, so you know very clearly that it's a bound control. When a control is bindable, Visual Basic binds data to a specific property within the control. The text control is an easy one to figure out. When you bind a text control to a data control, the data appears by way of the Text property. A label control, which can also be bound to a data control, funnels the data through to the Caption property. In the case of simple controls like this, there is typically one property that is actually bound to the data control. But there are also more complex controls, such as the data-bound listbox control. That particular control has a DataSource property, but it also has a number of other properties such as ListField, BoundColumn, DataBindings, and RowSource. These properties all work together to present information within a listbox control. In this case, a number of properties can be bound to a data control. So you see that your control can consist of one or more bindable properties. You'll learn how to set up controls using both single and multiple bindable properties next.

Making a Specific Property Bindable

The first, and simplest, case is to make a single property within your ActiveX control a bindable property. All it takes is one bindable property within a control to enable you to call a control a bound control. Again, think of a bound control as a bindable control because the decision to bind the control is really up to the developer.

Let's take a look at the question control at this point. Knowing what you know now about bound controls, you've likely thought of several possible ways of binding the question control to a database. The question is What property should be bindable? There is more than one answer, but in this section, let's consider a simple and very useful property to make bindable: the Question property.

By making the Question property bindable, you'll empower the developer with the ability to connect the ActiveX control to a database and funnel the information into the Question property. This means that the user can set up a database table full of questions and pump those questions through a data control into the question control directly without writing any code. You'll learn how to do this in this section.

Get started by running Visual Basic 5.0 and opening the question control project group in the Your Start directory for Day 17. This will bring up the test application and the control project itself. Bring up the UserControl object and display it in the project window. You can make one of the properties in your control bindable. To choose and set that property, select Tools | Procedure Attributes from the Visual Basic menu. When the dialog appears, click on the Advanced button to expand the dialog.

In this dialog, you can choose a procedure and select various attributes that control the behavior of that procedure. The implication here is that you can only set properties via property procedures. In other words, you cannot set the Caption property of lblQuestion directly. Instead, you have to work through the Question property procedure. Select the Question procedure in the drop-down listbox labeled Name. Then look down at the bottom of the dialog where you see the phrase Property is data bound. Check that checkbox. Three additional checkboxes will then become enabled beneath it. The only one you need to think about right now is the first one, labeled This property binds to DataField. Check that checkbox. The dialog should now look like the one shown in Figure 17.5.

Figure 17.5.

Making a property bindable through the DataField *property with the Procedure Attributes dialog.*

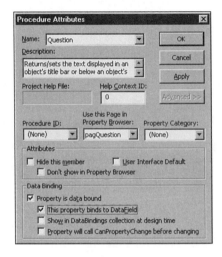

By checking the first checkbox, you expose this property procedure through the DataField property of the ActiveX control. You can only expose one property using the DataField property because DataField can only be tied to a single property. Go ahead and click the OK button. Congratulations! That's all there is to it from the question control development side.

Now that you've made the Question property bindable through the ActiveX control's DataField property, it's time to see how the control operates in the test application. Included in the Your Start directory is a simple database called Question.mdb. This database consists of one table named tblQuestions1 that has only one field within it. The name of the field is Questions. It's a simple text field that can contain up to 20 characters of text. Your task is to connect that database to the ActiveX control.

NOTE

We didn't bother teaching you how to create the database because we assume you're already familiar with that by the time you read this paragraph. If you don't know how to create databases yet, you can read on, but it would be a good idea to learn about them now. Don't worry, though—we've given you a sample database that you can use with this example.

The first step is to bring up the test application form. You should see one question control at the top of the form, as shown in Figure 17.6.

Figure 17.6.

The initial test application form.

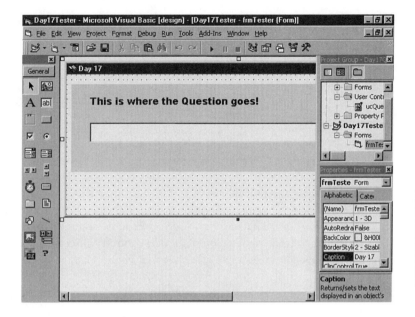

Now, in order to work with the database that exists in this directory, you need to place a data control on the form. Go ahead and select a data control from the toolbox and place it on the test application form. Change the name of the data control to dtcFirst and the caption of the data control to Questions. Go ahead and set the DatabaseName of the data control to Question.mdb. Next, set the RecordSource property of dtcQuestions1 to tblQuestions1. You've now connected the data control to a database using DatabaseName and, using RecordSource, you've connected the data control to a specific table, in this case tblQuestions1. That takes care of the data control.

Go ahead and click on the question control. You'll notice the addition of two properties: DataSource and DataField. These two properties are new on the property sheet because you've made one of the properties of the control bindable to a data control. Go ahead and set the DataSource property to dtcFirst. This connects the question control to the data control. Because you set the data control to point to the table tblQuestions1, when you click on DataField, Visual Basic knows enough to look into the table tblQuestions1 and present you with a list of fields within that table. Because the only field present in the table is Questions, that field name will be the only one that appears in the listbox. Go ahead and select it.

Congratulations again! You've now set all the properties necessary to connect the question control to the database. Go ahead and run the program. The form should look like the one shown in Figure 17.7 when it first comes up.

Figure 17.7.

The test application with a data-bound question control.

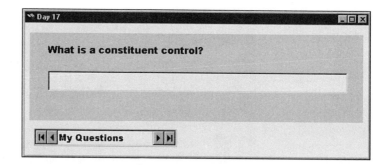

How did that question appear? Was it magic? Not really. The question appears as a result of Visual Basic's going out to the database you connected to the control and retrieving the first entry in the table. That entry is what you see in the question on the control. Go ahead and click on the left and right arrows of the data control. Notice that new questions appear within the ActiveX control as a result, as shown in Figure 17.8.

Figure 17.8.

New questions appear as you click the forward button on the data control.

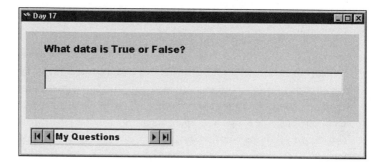

The program is actually moving through the database table and picking up the questions it finds there. Awesome!

Let's review the steps needed to make this happen. The first thing you needed to do was to place a data control on the form. You told Visual Basic what database to connect to using the DatabaseName property of the data control. Then, using the RecordSource property of the data control, you specified a specific table within the database to connect to. Next, you went to the question control and used the DataSource property to connect to the data control. Because the data control was told to connect to a specific table within a database, you can use the DataField property of the question control to indicate a specific field to which you want to connect the question control. This completes the link and connects the question control to a specific field within an Access database.

On the control side, you set up the control so that the DataField property is directly tied to the Question property. The Question property is what changes the label within the question control whenever the Question property is changed. You can still set the Question property manually, but you can now change it via the DataField property of the question control as well.

This is happening because you created a DataField within the question control that connects to a specific field in a table represented through the data control. You did this using the DataSource property of the question control. The data control connects to the table specified by RecordSource in the data control, using the database specified by DatabaseName within the data control. You connected the Question property to the DataField property of the question control, and you connected the DataField property to the field of the table represented by the data control.

By the way, how much code did you have to write in the host application to make all this happen? That's right—el zippo! This is one of the many advantages of using Visual Basic!

Keep in mind that this technique works for one property only. You can set the DataField property of an ActiveX control, but that property is mapped to a property of the ActiveX control exposed through property procedures. Also, you need to remember that some development tools or containers of ActiveX controls do not support data binding. In other words, these properties may not always be available, depending on the environment in which the control is being used. This support is provided by Visual Basic, so you're always guaranteed this functionality when writing programs within Visual Basic.

Making Several Properties Bindable

The DataField technique works fine when all you have is one property that you want to make bindable. But what about a control that may have several properties that you want to bind to a database? What do you do then? In that case, the approach becomes a bit more complicated. In order to make more than one property bindable, you need to use what's called the DataBindings collection.

The DataBindings collection is actually a part of the Extender object. Through the DataBindings collection, the developer using your control gains access to a collection of properties you want to make bindable to a data control. The first thing you need to do is to decide which properties you want to make available within the DataBindings collection. In the case of our question control, it might be useful to make the Question, Hint, and ExpectedAnswer properties bindable. That way, you can create a table that contains three fields—call them Questions, Hints, and ExpectedAnswers. When the data control advances from one row of the table to another, all three fields change. If each of these fields is bound to a respective property in the question control, the program can provide the control with all three pieces of data simultaneously. This allows the program to advance through a series of questions, automatically setting the questions, hints, and expected answers as it goes. What a powerful and useful capability!

To place these three properties within the DataBindings collection, you have to go back to the Procedure Attributes dialog. To do that, bring up the UserControl object and select Tools | Procedure Attributes from the Visual Basic menu. Once you've done that, the familiar dialog will appear as you saw in Figure 17.5. Make sure you click the Advanced button to reveal the attributes you must select. Then select the Name listbox and select the Question property. When you select the Question property procedure, you'll notice that the property is already data bound and that it is bound to the DataField property. You did this in the last section. When the Property is data bound checkbox is selected, that property is automatically a part of the DataBindings collection as well. In this case, the Question property also happens to be bound to the DataField property. You can only assign one property to DataField, but any property with Property is data bound checked will appear in the DataBindings collection.

The checkbox that says Show in DataBindings collection at design time simply makes sure the property appears when you use the DataBindings collection at design time, as you will do in a moment. Go ahead and check the Show in DataBindings collection at design time checkbox. Your dialog should now look like the one shown in Figure 17.9.

Figure 17.9.

Making a property bindable through the DataBindings *collection with the Procedure Attributes dialog.*

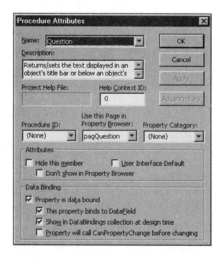

The next step is to select the Hint property procedure and apply the same attribute settings to it. That is, click the Property is data bound item first. That makes the property a part of the DataBindings collection. Then, click the Show in DataBindings collection at design time checkbox. This makes the property appear in the Data Bindings dialog at design time. Note that if you try to set the item This property binds to DataField, you'll see a message box telling you that you can only make one property bindable to the DataField. Because you've already made the Question property the choice, you can't choose another here. Go ahead and set the Hint property, and then set the ExpectedAnswer property the same way.

17

You now have a collection of three properties that will be available when the developer is building an application with your control. To try these newly bound properties, switch back over to the test application. To see these properties at work, you need to bring another data control onto the form. This second data control will connect to a table that contains three fields, one for each property, rather than just the Questions field that you saw before. Name the data control dtcSecond and give the control the caption Questions & Answers. Your figure should now look the one shown in Figure 17.10.

Figure 17.10.

Creating a second data control on the test application form.

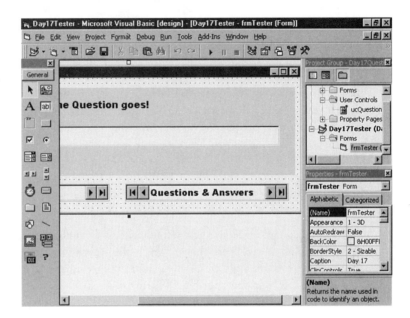

This data control should be bound to the same database as before. Set the DatabaseName property to Question.mdb. The difference is, in the case of the second data control, that you need to set the RecordSource property to tblData rather than tblQuestions2. This connects you to the second table contained in the database.

Now that you've set the data control properly, it's time to connect the bindable properties to the data control's table using the DataBindings property. Click on the question control and look at the property sheet. In order to use the DataBindings collection with the new table, you have to switch over to the new data control. Change the DataSource property of the question control from dtcFirst to dtcSecond. Because both tables contain the field Questions, you don't need to change the DataField property. Now that you've changed the control to connect to the second data control, click on the property named DataBindings. The dialog that appears is shown in Figure 17.11.

Figure 17.11.

The Data Bindings dialog that appears when you select the DataBindings *property of the ActiveX control.*

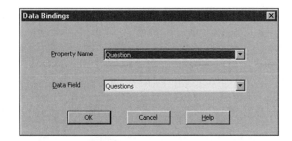

The first drop-down listbox in the dialog, Property Name, shows a list of the properties in the DataBindings collection. Click on the drop-down listbox and you will see three properties. These are the ones you exposed using the Procedure Attributes dialog earlier. The second drop-down list shows the available fields within the table mapped through the data control you've selected for the control. Notice also that you can select None if you don't want to bind a specific property. You'll notice the three table fields are there: Questions, ExpectedAnswers, and Hints. Your job is to connect each of the three question control properties to the corresponding field names of the table supplied through the data control: The Question property should be mapped to the Questions field, the ExpectedAnswer property to the ExpectedAnswers field, and so on. Go ahead and map the properties to the fields at this time. When you're finished, click OK.

Now run the program. Notice first of all that clicking on the data control to the left does no good. That data control is no longer linked to the question control. If, however, you click on the data control to the right, you'll notice that the questions change as you click through the rows in the table. But here's the big difference: You now have three bound properties rather than the single property, Question, that you had earlier. What does this mean?

Table 17.1 shows the contents of the table tblQuestions2. Review the various fields for each row.

Table 17.1. The contents of the table tblQuestions2.

Row	Question	ExpectedAnswer	Hint
1	What is a constituent control?	A control inside an ActiveX control	They're placed in the UserControl object.
2	What data is True or False?	Boolean	This type of data is set to 1 or 0.
3	How many more lessons are left?	4	This is Lesson 17.
4	Are these lessons enjoyable?	Yes	Building ActiveX Controls is fun!

Each of the three fields of these four rows is now directly bound to the question control. Bring up the third question and type in something other than 4. What happens? The hint appears just as you'd expect from looking at the table. Figure 17.12 shows you the result.

Figure 17.12.

Entering an incorrect response based on question (row) 3, as shown in Table 17.1.

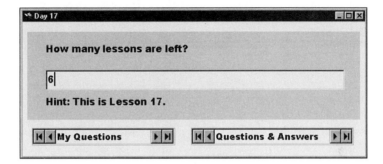

Now type in the correct answer. Hurrah! Everything is working just like you'd expect. The same will be true of all the other questions as well. So in this case, you're able to set three properties at once by scrolling down one row in the data control. Data-bound properties are very powerful, and you can do a great deal when you can make more than one property bindable.

NOTE

You must remember that the DataBindings property and the dialog that appears are designed to work within the Visual Basic programming environment. Other non-Microsoft programming environments may not give you this capability. Although I'd like to give you a list of them, they're subject to change. It's best to try for yourself.

Changing Data Through Bound Properties

So far in this discussion, the bound properties you have used are read-only. The Question and Hint properties appear in labels, so the user has no way to change them. The ExpectedAnswer property is compared with what the user enters into the textbox. The user is not, however, able to change it directly. The only constituent control within the question control that the user can directly modify the contents of is the text control. This control is used to type in the answer, which is then compared with ExpectedAnswer. But there is no way to grab whatever the user enters into the textbox control and bind it to a data control field. At least not yet.

In order to show you how the user can change the contents of a database field through a bound property, you first need to create a new property. This property will be called Answer and will always contain whatever is currently displayed in the textbox within the control. By binding the Answer property to the data control through the DataBindings collection, you'll be able to store the answer in the data control, present it back in the control, and enable the user to change it.

First, you'll create the new Answer property. Switch over to the UserControl object and bring up the ActiveX Control Interface Wizard. Go ahead and add a new property to the control. Map the Answer property to the Text property of the constituent control txtAnswer.

TIP

You should know how to add properties to the control as a result of working through the lessons on Days 4, "Predefined Control Properties" and 5, "User-Defined Control Properties." Refer to those lessons for help in creating this new property.

Once you've created the Answer property, you need to add the Answer property procedure to the DataBindings collection. To do that, bring up the Procedure Attributes dialog and make the Answer property procedure's data bindable. The Procedure Attributes dialog should look like the one in Figure 17.13.

Figure 17.13.

Making the Answer *property bindable in the Procedure Attributes dialog through the* DataBindings *collection.*

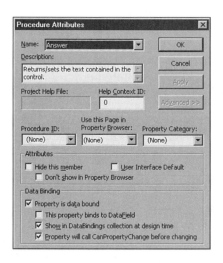

Now that the property is bindable, switch back over to the Test application. You now need to use a table that contains the additional field needed to store the answer. This additional table is available within the Question.mdb database you've been using so far in this lesson. Change the RecordSource property of the second data control, dtcSecond, to the table tblQuestions3. This third table contains the extra field needed to store the answer.

Amazingly enough, that extra field is named Answers. Now click on the question control and bring up the DataBindings collection. Now you will map each bound property of the question control to the appropriate field in the tblQuestions3 table. As before, Question maps to Questions, ExpectedAnswer maps to ExpectedAnswers, and so forth. Map each property to the appropriate field.

Go ahead and run the application. When the first question comes up, type in an answer. Change to a different question and back again to the question you were just on. Is the answer saved in the database? No! Nothing appears in the textbox. Why?

The reason nothing appears is that nobody ever told Visual Basic that the Answer property had changed. When should it change? Whenever the data within the textbox changes. Because the property is data bound, the Property Get procedure is called, but nothing in UserControl ever tells Visual Basic to set the property when the user types in an answer. Let's fix this simple problem. Bring up the UserControl object's code window and bring up the txtAnswer control's Change event. Add the following statement within the Change event:

```
PropertyChanged "Answer"
```

This simple statement makes sure the Answer property is set every time the user makes a change to the textbox control. Now run the application again. This time the answer is saved and stored within the database. Any answer you provide will reappear as you scroll back through the data control.

Using CanPropertyChange

Oftentimes, the user may bind a property to a control for reading purposes only. In other words, it's entirely possible that the user just wants to grab data out of the database and display it in the control. Just because the user can change the data in the control doesn't mean the programmer wants that data to be saved back in the database. Bound properties are great in one respect, because they automatically load data and save changed data based on what the user does with it when it appears, but that isn't always what the programmer wants to happen.

Visual Basic includes a special method called CanPropertyChange that you should always use in your property procedures for bound controls. If the property procedure calls CanPropertyChange before modifying the property, and CanPropertyChange returns False, the property should not be modified at all. Why would CanPropertyChange return False? This would occur if the table opened through the data control is a read-only table. If you forged onward and attempted to change the property anyway, Visual Basic may attempt to write to the table, resulting in an error. Depending on the container your ActiveX control resides in, writing to a read-only table may cause an error. The Property Let procedure for the question control at present is shown in Listing 17.1.

Listing 17.1. The Answer property's Property Let procedure without CanPropertyChange.

```
1: Public Property Let Answer(ByVal New_Answer As String)
2:     txtAnswer.Text() = New_Answer
3:     PropertyChanged "Answer"
4: End Property
```

To make the procedure safe for property changes, all you need to do is change the code so that it reads as shown in Listing 17.2.

Listing 17.2. The correct version of the Answer property's Property Let procedure.

```
1: Public Property Let Answer(ByVal New_Answer As String)
2:     If CanPropertyChange("Answer") Then
3:         txtAnswer.Text() = New_Answer
4:         PropertyChanged "Answer"
5:     End If
6: End Property
```

This will ensure that the property can only be changed when it is permissible to change the data in the table.

NOTE

When this book went to print, Visual Basic documentation stated that CanPropertyChange always returns True, even if the bound field in the data source is read-only. The documentation states that this won't cause an error in Visual Basic because Visual Basic won't return an error if a write is attempted on a read-only field. This may not be true of other environments, however, so we assume this is a bug that will likely be fixed by the time this book gets into your hands.

If you use the CanPropertyChange method, you should select the item Property will call CanPropertyChange before changing in the Advanced section of the Procedure Attributes dialog for that particular property. This notifies the control container that your ActiveX control will always call CanPropertyChange before making any kind of property assignment.

17

NOTE

> At the time this book went to print, this setting was not directly exposed to the host container. It is likely that the definition of this setting will be expanded on in the official documentation for Microsoft Visual Basic 5.0.

Manipulating Bindable Properties at Runtime

You've seen how to create bindable properties at design time for use at runtime. In fact, you haven't even written any code in the Test application yet. This is one of the wonderful aspects of Visual Basic that can make programming so much easier. It's time, however, to learn how to do the same things you've done so far using code at runtime rather than setting all the properties at design time.

At runtime you can set the DataSource and DataField properties of an ActiveX control the same way you set them in the property sheet at design time. No mystery there! What I want to focus on here, though, it how you set the properties in the DataBindings collection at runtime. At design time, a dialog was always presented that let you do the mappings using two listboxes. At runtime, however, all this has to be done in code. How do you do it?

First, you can determine the names of each of the bindable properties by accessing the PropertyName property of the DataBindings collection. The code in Listing 17.3 shows you how to do this.

Listing 17.3. Determining at runtime the properties that are bindable through the DataBindings collection.

```
1: Dim dtb As DataBinding
2: For Each dtb in ucQuestion1.DataBindings
3:     Debug.Print dtb.PropertyName
4: Next
```

Go ahead and put a command button on the test application and enter this code listing into the Click event. When you click the command button, four properties—Question, ExpectedAnswer, Hint, and Answer—appear in the debug window. To assign these properties to database fields at runtime, you could place the four lines of code shown in Listing 17.4 into the form's Load event.

Listing 17.4. Setting the DataBindings collection at runtime.

```
1: ucQuestion1.DataBindings("Question") = "Questions"
2: ucQuestion1.DataBindings("ExpectedAnswer") = "ExpectedAnswers"
3: ucQuestion1.DataBindings("Hint") - "Hints"
4: ucQuestion1.DataBindings("Answer") = "Answers"
```

Here you need to know the field names for each field you want to map to the appropriate property. The strings are automatically matched up with the table fields that the control is made aware of through the DataSource property. Remember that DataSource specifies the data control, which in turn specifies the database and the table within that database.

How would setting these properties at runtime be useful? If you need to make changes to the bindable properties, essentially binding them to different fields depending on what happens in the program, the ability to change them on-the-fly through code is invaluable.

Accessing Data Inside an ActiveX Control

There's one more important concept you should be familiar with before the end of today's lesson. So far, you've been learning how to set up existing properties within an ActiveX control so that the host application can bind those properties to a database. The control never accesses the database directly; all it does is enable the host to bind some of its properties to a database. The action of saving and retrieving the data is handled automatically by Visual Basic when the controls are marked as bound.

It is possible, however, for you to access a database directly inside your ActiveX control. In other words, you can place a data control directly within the UserControl object as a constituent control and access data directly. An obvious benefit is that if you have a large amount of data you need to access within the control, the database makes it possible. Another advantage is that it provides you with a convenient way to store information while the control is being used.

In addition to these useful benefits, however, there are a number of significant drawbacks. For one thing, if your control needs to use a database, you must ship the database with the OCX. Now the user needs two files instead of one. Is this a problem? Probably not, provided that the user has the disk space. But where are you going to put the database? Probably where the control is saved. Most OCX files are saved in the Windows system directory unless otherwise specified. Do you really want to store your database there, cluttering up the user's system directory with additional files? Probably not, and this technique is usually frowned upon among us more sensitive souls.

17

Another big drawback is that, in order for the control to use the database, it also needs to bring with it all the support DLLs and extra baggage to handle the database. In this case, the database support would be Microsoft Access. If someone tried to use your control who didn't have Visual Basic or Microsoft Access, he'd have to copy all the supporting files over to his system. The total number of support files often totals over 2MB to 3MB of storage space! That may be more than what the user bargained for.

The bottom line is, if you want to make your ActiveX control as lightweight and easy to integrate as possible, you should avoid databases. For example, if you plan on users using your control on the Internet, you can forget about databases. There's no way you would want to download all the support files over the Internet. If, on the other hand, you have a corporate intranet, your users may already have all the support files, and the issues wouldn't be as significant. In fact, you may even be able to share the same database among all the users who use the control. You need to weigh these issues carefully. In most cases, databases are not used within controls because controls are never really designed to do so. Once a control starts manipulating a database, it's likely crossed over the line from being a simple control to being a complex control that is more error prone and possibly in greater need of support once released to the user.

Summary

It's a documented fact that more than 80% of all applications written with Visual Basic are database applications. Because the percentage is so high, it's very likely that at some point in your control-creation journey, you'll want to give users the ability to connect databases to your ActiveX controls. Today's lesson has shown you how.

To enable programmers to connect your controls to databases, you must supply bindable properties. Bindable properties are special properties you can assign to the fields of a table connected into an application through a data control. There are two general approaches to making properties of your ActiveX control bindable. You can take one of your control's properties and make it bindable through the `DataField` property. In this way, the user can connect a database field to the `DataField` property and it will automatically create the link between the field in the table and the property you've made bindable.

Or, if you want to make more than one property bindable, you can set up an entire collection of properties and make them all bindable through the `DataBindings` collection. This requires the host program to access a special property called `DataBindings` that allows the program to map each bindable property of the control to a specific field in a database table. This capability is not guaranteed to exist in every environment into which the control is placed, however. If a particular container doesn't support `DataBindings`, you're out of luck because `DataBindings` is an `Extender` property. If, however, the programming environment does support the property, you can make as many properties bindable as you'd like. You've seen several examples of how to make properties bindable and then how to bind and use them at design time and runtime. This capability is very powerful, and we've only begun to scratch the surface in this chapter. An entire book could probably be written on this single topic. But you can round out this week's lessons having the knowledge and experience of a very powerful capability of ActiveX controls created using Visual Basic.

Q&A

Q **Could you tell me one more time what a bound control is?**

A A bound control is a control that has properties that the programmer can connect to specific fields of a database table. When a data control is placed on a form that provides access to the table containing the fields, you can set each bound property to a specific field. Then, when the data control is set and data comes into the data control, that data is automatically passed to the bound property. Likewise, if the user changes the property, the data is automatically saved back to the database. If the property happens to place the data in a text control and the user changes the text in that control, the property can be set to change, which can then change the data inside the database.

Q **Why do I have to use the `DataBindings` collection if I want to bind more than one property?**

A The `DataField` property only allows you to bind one property of your choosing. The nice thing about `DataField` is that it's a property of the `UserControl` object, not a collection that requires more effort to manage. If you have only one property you want to bind, this is ideal. If, however, you have more than one, you should use the `DataBindings` collection. Keep in mind that you can still use `DataField` along with the `DataBindings` collection.

Q **What do you mean by "not all environments support the `DataBindings` collection"?**

A The `DataBindings` collection is a special property that is not necessarily supported anywhere an ActiveX control is used. The reason for this is that `DataBindings` is actually a part of the container, in this case the form, not part of the `UserControl` object itself. If you bring up the `UserControl` object at design time and look in the property sheet, you won't find the `DataBindings` property there. It does appear in the form of the `Test` application, however, because it's a part of the form. If you place the control in a container that doesn't support the `DataBindings` collection, you can't use this capability in that environment.

Workshop

The best way to learn about data-bound controls is to experiment with them and see how they work. In experimenting, you can best determine how to use bindable properties in your own projects. Open a new Visual Basic project and bring in as many data-bound controls as you can find. Experiment with them, checking to see what properties are bindable, why they are bindable, and how they work individually and together. This experience should give you a great deal of additional insight into data-bound control design and use.

Quiz

NOTE

See Appendix D, "Answers to Quiz Questions," for the answers to these questions.

17

1. Suppose you have an ActiveX control named Dictionary1. Write the code necessary to map two bindable properties named Term and Definition of the ActiveX control to two database fields named Word and Meaning.

2. Change the data bindings in the question control so that the Answer property is no longer bound to the table.

3. Modify the table tblQuestion3 to include an additional field named Picture. Place a unique picture in each row for the question. Then make the Picture property of the question control bindable through the DataBindings collection. Set up the application so that each time the user changes a question, the corresponding background picture of the question control changes as well.

Day 18

Multiple Controls, Control Communication, and Advanced Features

You have mastered the basics of creating a simple control. The question control you have progressively developed over the past days can present a question to the user, evaluate the answer, and present feedback. It allows an integrator to build question-based applications and Web pages more quickly than he could from scratch, but the solution still lacks a certain punch. Wouldn't it be nice if you could give the integrator some easy way to consolidate results from all the question controls? Better yet, imagine how wonderful it would be if he could just plop down a results control onto his page and have it magically collect results from his question controls. And how about if you want to add a multiple-choice question into the fleet of controls you provide to integrators? Do you have to do it all from scratch?

Today's lesson shows you how to put these solutions in place. You will implement a results control that communicates with other controls in the same host container. You will see how to package multiple controls in the same OCX and you will learn how to derive a new control from an existing control. There will be plenty of other complementary advanced features introduced as well, ranging from creation of transparent control images to the proper approach for file I/O from a control. You will see that you can go much further than providing controls that just get the job done. Visual Basic control creation allows you to implement features as sophisticated as those on commercial controls you might have used.

The Results Control

The question control developed so far can provide feedback on the question it presents. However, if an integrator adds 50 questions to a Web page, there's no easy way for him to consolidate all the results. It's time to remedy this. Let's add a results control to the question control project to provide this capability. You can see a sample application with two question controls and a results control in Figure 18.1.

Figure 18.1.

An application that uses the results control to score question responses.

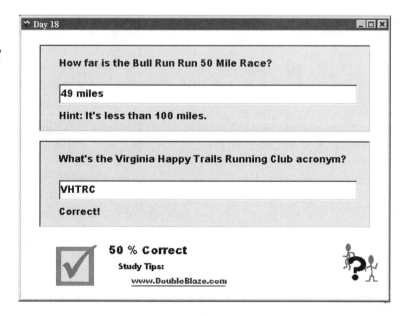

The results control initially appears just as the checkbox icon that you can see at the bottom of Figure 18.1. The control springs into action when the user clicks on this checkbox to indicate completion of a test. Then the results control checks the response entered in each individual question control and compares it to the expected answer. The total percentage correct is displayed on the results control at that point.

A Study Tips URL is also displayed on the results control after the test has been scored. This is a link the user can click on to find further study tips after taking the test. The desired link is specified as a property by the control integrator. Additional changes go on behind the scenes when the results control executes. If the integrator has set the appropriate property to lock out subsequent answers, all question controls are disabled when the answers are checked by the results control. This prevents the user from changing his answers after the test is scored. Another option can be specified by the integrator to save the test results to a log file. There is even a timed test file that enforces a time limit on the overall test and automatically triggers test scoring when that time limit is exceeded.

The properties and methods this new results control will support are summarized in Table 18.1.

Table 18.1. Properties and methods of the results control.

Interface	Description
AutoResultsTime property	Minutes allowed for test before scoring
LockAnswers property	Lock answers after scoring if true
PercentCorrect property	Percentage of all questions correct
ProcessResults method	Scores the test
ResultsFile property	Optional results file
StudyTipsURL property	Location user can link to for tips

The following paragraphs discuss each of these features in turn. The initial step is to create the UserControl object that will host this control. This control is created as part of an OCX containing multiple controls.

Multiple Controls

The first question to consider is how this control will be packaged. Should the results control be in a separate OCX file? Yes, if you intend to sell it or distribute it as a separate product. In that case, you could just create an entirely new project group to develop the results control. Or you could even use the same project group you have been working with and just add a new control project to that group. In either case, when it came time to build the OCX for the project, you'd simply generate a unique OCX file for that control, just as you've done in previous days' lessons for the question control.

Assume that your needs are different, however. You will not be selling the results control as a separate product. You want to provide a bundled control solution to your integrators. Let them install one OCX and have access to everything they need to construct tests and quizzes quickly. That one OCX can include both the familiar question control and the new results control. The integrator will only need to reference this one registered control file to have access to both controls. When this reference is made, both the question control and the results control will show up as available tool icons in the Visual Basic toolbox.

NOTE

> **SAMPLE** Follow along with the examples in this chapter by modify-
> ing the Day18QuestionControl.vbg group project file under
> the Samples\Day18\Your Start\ directory on the book's CD-ROM.
> This project contains the code that is intended to be your starting point
> for the modifications that are described today. Copy the directory to
> your hard drive so you can make subsequent modifications. The
> material is presented in a before-and-after format. If you want to see
> today's changes already implemented, you can view the
> Day18QuestionControl.vbg group project, available one directory level
> up, in the Samples\Day18 directory.

This multiple-controls-in-one-OCX approach is the one to take now to create the results control. Open the same question control project group you've been working with and bring up the Project Explorer window. Click on the Day18QuestionControl.vbp project to select it as the active project. Then select Project|Add User Control from the Visual Basic menu to add a new user control to this existing project. The Add User Control dialog you see pictured in Figure 18.2 will be displayed.

Figure 18.2.

*Using the Add User
Control dialog to add
a second user control
to an existing user
control project.*

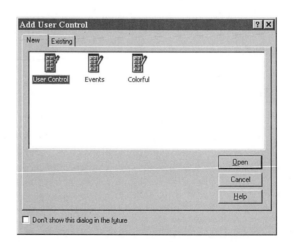

Select the standard user control object from this dialog. The UserControl object will be added to your project. You need to set some properties of this UserControl object, starting with the name. Select the new UserControl object and bring up the corresponding properties window by selecting View | Properties Window from the Visual Basic menu. Set the name property for this UserControl object to ucDay18Results. Then select File | Save As from the Visual Basic menu and save the corresponding control file as ucDay18Results.ctl. The uc prefix used in these names is simply a naming convention that helps you remember that this is a user-defined control.

There are a couple more initial properties to set before you proceed with the exciting new stuff. Set the control's ToolboxBitmap property to the name of the file that should be displayed in the Visual Basic toolbox to control integrators. There is a file in the Samples\Day18 directory named ToolBoxResults.bmp that you should use for this purpose. Click in the ToolBoxBitmap bitmap area to activate this property; then click on the resulting file locator command button to locate and select the file. From now on this bitmap will appear in the toolbox to indicate your results control. Next, change the BackStyle property to set the control's background to Transparent. Now your control has its initial definition in place and you are ready to proceed with the implementation.

Rendering a Control As a Transparent Image

Take another look at the visual representation of the results control in Figure 18.2. The control itself has several distinct visible components. Table 18.2 summarizes these components.

Table 18.2. The visible components of the results control.

Area	Visible Component
The checkbox image	UserControl picture property
Blinking focus indicator on checkbox	Line1 line control caption
The percentage score	lblPercent label control caption property
Study Tips heading	lblStudyCaption label control caption property
The Study Tips link	lblStudyTips label control caption property
The link underline	Line2 line control

You can see from Table 18.2 that the results control incorporates many constituent controls. An interesting thing happens when the application first displays the results control, however. Only the checkbox itself is initially visible on this control. Furthermore, you can click anywhere on the image despite its irregular shape. Notice that the top of the checkmark extends outside the checkbox icon. The top of the checkmark detects a click just as does the area inside the checkbox. Clicking anywhere on this image starts the scoring process. Clicking anywhere else on the entire control has no effect. The rest of the control is transparent in function as well as appearance.

It's easy to create this type of transparent control in Visual Basic 5.0. It's not as easy as you might guess, however. You have already set the BackStyle property of this control to Transparent. The background of the control, under normal circumstances, will not show up, and you will be able to see the underlying form. One small problem remains, though. You need to incorporate a checkmark graphic on your control to give it the look you want. After you load a picture on the control, the control picture shows up instead of the transparent background. The control background itself is still transparent, but it is now obscured by the picture in front of it.

There is a way to get transparency when you use an image for your control. Create the picture that contains the visual image of your control. A sample bitmap is present for this purpose in the Samples\Day18 directory. Click on the file Results.bmp to activate the Windows 95 Paint program with this file loaded. You will see the bitmap displayed in Figure 18.3.

Figure 18.3.

The bitmap that serves as the results control picture image.

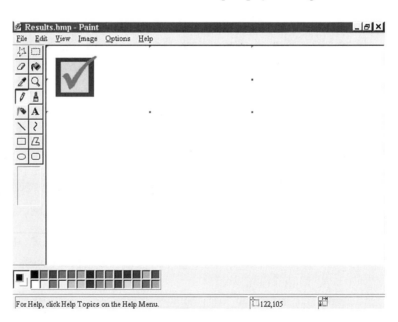

This is the bitmap that you want to appear as the image for your control. You'll want to ensure that everything outside the checkbox is treated as transparent. Don't worry about this for the moment. First make the assignment to associate the entire bitmap with the control, including both the checkbox and surrounding area. Return to the UserControl properties window to

18

make this assignment. Select UserControl's Picture property by clicking in the picture bitmap area. A file finder command button will appear. Click on the button to bring up the file locator dialog, and use that dialog to select the Results.bmp bitmap as the image for the Picture property.

The bitmap is displayed as the current picture image of the control. Resize the borders of UserControl so that they align with the image. Now to help illustrate the response of the control, add a line of code that responds to user clicks on the control. You should add this line of code to the control's MouseUp event because the UserControl object doesn't expose a separate Mouse_Click event. Add the code shown in Listing 18.1.

Listing 18.1. Responding to control clicks.

```
1: Private Sub UserControl_MouseUp(Button As Integer, Shift As Integer, _
2:     X As Single, Y As Single)
3:     Msgbox "Click occurred!"
4: End Sub
```

Close your results control windows and bring up your test form. Make sure that two question controls are present on the test form to support later sections of this example. Reposition the controls as needed so there is space for another control at the bottom of the test form. Try to duplicate the appearance of Figure 18.1. Select the new results control from the toolbox and add it to the bottom of the test form. Then change the BackColor property of the test form itself to be gray so that you can more easily observe the effects of some of the transparency tests to come. Now it's time for your first test!

Run the test application. The new results control is present at the bottom of the test form window. Click on the results control checkbox. As you expect, a message greets you. Now click to the right of the checkbox on the blank white area. The same message greets you! Right now the application is treating the control as one large, rectangular control that encompasses the checkbox and lots of blank space.

There is a way to tell the control to consider itself as the area covered by the checkbox graphic only. You must tell Visual Basic to mask out or ignore the other areas of the UserControl picture image. The MaskPicture property is intended for exactly this purpose. You can specify a secondary picture to designate the areas on the first picture that should be ignored. You can find the bitmap you will use for this masking in the file ResultsMask.bmp. Double-click on this file to bring it up in the Paint program. You'll see the image shown in Figure 18.4.

The area that overlaps the checkbox on the original image has been filled in with black. This specifies the area that is to be displayed and respond to user events. The area outside the filled black region will not be displayed when the control is rendered. Furthermore, this area will not respond to user events such as clicks.

18

Figure 18.4.

The masking bitmap specifies which part of the other image should be ignored.

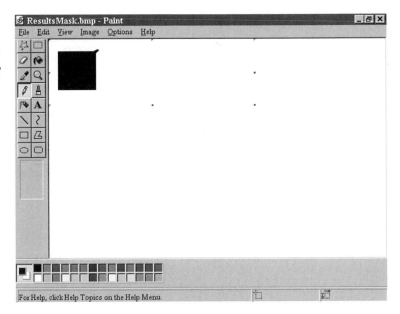

A couple property assignments are necessary to make all this magic work. Set UserControl's MaskPicture property to the ResultsMask.bmp file. This specifies the image that will divide the original image into zones to be ignored or not ignored. Why is it that the masking centers around the region filled with black? This is another characteristic you must specify. Set UserControl's MaskColor property to black to indicate that this is the masking color. Now you are ready to see the results.

Run the test application again. Notice that this time even the image area around the checkbox is transparent. Click on the checkbox. Once again you see the message box appear. Then click just to the right of the checkbox. No response! You have succeeded in placing an image on your control that responds only to clicks on its masked region. This is nice for the question control.

This technique might be useful for other types of controls you wish to tackle. For example, if you wanted to create a circular command button or a clover-shaped listbox, you could use this type of control image display to help craft the user interface.

WARNING

Just because you can drive a car at 150 miles an hour doesn't mean you always should. In the same vein, exercise some restraint on your control creation. You've just learned an easy-to-use secret to create all sorts of wild controls. Use irregular-shaped controls where they are called for, but don't use this feature so much that your programs no longer

18

conform to a standard Windows look and feel. Users are more likely to be confused by the heart-shaped command buttons you've crafted than admire your ingenuity if such innovations are not warranted by the control's function.

There are just a few more steps to carry out to complete the control user interface. Add to UserControl the constituent controls described in Table 18.2. This includes the lblPercent, lblStudyCaption, and lblStudyTips label controls. Consult Figure 18.1 for positioning of the new controls. The lblPercent caption should be set to the text string Score, the lblStudyCaption caption should be set to the text string Study Tips, and the lblStudyTips caption should be set to the text string www.DoubleBlaze.com. Add a line control named Line1 and place the line immediately under the check mark on UserControl. Later you will change this line to a blinking focus indicator. Add another line control named Line2 and place it under the lblStudyTips label. Set its BorderColor property to green so that it resembles a browser text link. Set the Visible property of all the label and line controls to False.

Implementing the Results Control

When you have a control user interface in place, you have much of the work out of the way. Now you can implement the code that's under the hood. First, add the properties and methods described in Table 18.1.

Properties

Start the ActiveX Control Interface Wizard and proceed to the Select a Control dialog. Notice that now there are multiple controls listed for this project because you have defined both the question control and results control within it. Select the ucDay18Results control from the list of available controls. Proceed to the Create Custom Interface Members dialog. Click on the New button and create each of the properties and methods described in Table 18.1. You will soon get a chance to see how each of these properties is implemented. But first define the interfaces so they are available for the code you will enter.

Proceed to the Set Mapping dialog. Only one property is mapped directly to a constituent control. That is the StudyTipsURL property. The linked uniform resource locator specified as a results control property is displayed directly in the label. Associate the StudyTipsURL property with the Caption member of the lblStudyTips label control to complete this mapping.

Now advance to the Set Attributes dialog. Use this dialog to set the attributes for the remaining unmapped properties and methods. The AutoResultsTime property should be an integer and have a default value of 0. The LockAnswers property is a boolean and has a default value of False. The PercentCorrect property is an integer with a default value of 0. The ProcessResults method has no return value or arguments. The ResultsFile property is a string data type with an empty default value. All these properties should have design-time and runtime permissions of read/write, except for PercentCorrect, which is read-only at design time and runtime. You can see descriptions for these properties in Table 18.1.

Triggering the ProcessResults Method

The primary purpose of the results control is to consolidate results and score the test. The end product is a percentage correct that is displayed to the user. This scoring activity should take place when the user initiates it by clicking on the results control or pressing the Enter key when the results control has focus. A routine called ProcessResults will carry out this scoring. Therefore, add the code in Listing 18.2 to UserControl's KeyUp event:

Listing 18.2. Scoring the test in response to a mouse click.

```
1: Private Sub UserControl_MouseUp(Button As Integer, Shift As Integer, _
2:     X As Single, Y As Single)
3:     ' Process the results when user clicks on control
4:     Call ProcessResults
5: End Sub
```

Use this event to trigger the scoring because the UserControl object does not expose a mouse-click event. You could use UserControl's MouseDown event for this purpose as well.

If the control has focus, scoring should likewise begin when the user presses the Enter key. (He could have given the control focus through tabbing.) This gives the user a means to interact with your control through the keyboard as well as with the mouse. It is very important that you provide keyboard support on your controls if you want users to view them as professional efforts. Often new Windows programmers balk at this. I've been asked more than once by Windows programmers in training, "Who in their right mind would use the keyboard instead of a mouse?" The answer is a multitude of people—for a variety of reasons. Many feel they can interact with Windows more quickly through the keyboard. Others use the keyboard because of repetitive stress injuries or disabilities. Others just plain like it better.

It's important for you to include appropriate keyboard support in a control because a control is a building block that can be used in many more ways than you can anticipate when you create it. The bottom line is that if your control doesn't support keyboard interaction, you have earmarked it as a relatively amateurish effort and limited the potential audience of integrators. Add the code shown in Listing 18.3 to UserControl's KeyUp event to add this support.

Listing 18.3. Scoring the test in response to the Enter keypress.

```
1: Private Sub UserControl_KeyUp(KeyCode As Integer, Shift As Integer)
2:     ' Process the results if user types Enter key
3:     If KeyCode = vbKeyReturn Then
4:         Call ProcessResults
5:     End If
6: End Sub
```

Now you've provided the means for the user to trigger the scoring. It's time to face one more law of control design. Always give the integrator of your control the ability to use code to do anything the user can do manually with your control. The user can cause scoring of a test to occur. There is a good chance that sooner or later some developer who integrates this control into his application will want to cause the scoring to occur through code in the host program. The good news is that this is very easily accomplished. The ProcessResults routine that is called to do the scoring just has to be defined as a public method. You already carried out this definition when you defined the ProcessResults method earlier.

You must make the same kind of interface assessment for results that you do for actions. If a user can see a result, there is a good chance that the integrator of a control will want to work with that result as well. Just displaying PercentCorrect in a label does not allow the host application code to retrieve that value. It must be declared as a property. Once again, this property definition has already been carried out. Now you can see the reasoning behind this decision. If you let the user cause an action or see a result directly from your control, you generally should provide the same access to the host container through corresponding interfaces.

The Friend Property Keyword

You should make one more change to the PercentCorrect property. This property was defined as read-only. You don't want the users of your control to update this percentage. It is updated directly from your control based on the number of correct question responses. That means that there's no publicly defined assignment procedure. You do need to be able to update this value from within your control, though. It would be nice to still define it as a property that can only be used within your control and is not visible outside it. You can do this with the Friend declaration, as shown in Listing 18.4. Modify your code so it contains this declaration.

18

Listing 18.4. Allowing updates to a read-only public property only within this module.

```
1: Friend Property Let PercentCorrect(ByVal New_PercentCorrect As Integer)
2:     m_PercentCorrect = New_PercentCorrect
3:     PropertyChanged "PercentCorrect"
4: End Property
```

The Friend keyword makes this property assignment procedure available within the control project but unavailable to host applications that incorporate the control.

The rest of the properties that you need to make use of in the ProcessResults method are already fully defined. The LockAnswers property indicates whether your control code should lock out the answers after a test is scored. Users will not be able to change the values of their question responses after a test has been scored when this property is set to True. You'll provide code that changes the enabled state of the question controls to enforce this restriction.

The StudyTipsURL property provides an Internet address or uniform resource locator. The user will see this address only after a test has been scored. He can click on the label that displays this address for more help on the topic of the questions he's completed. A line appears underneath this address to make it appear similar to a browser link. If no address is supplied in the StudyTipsURL property, then the display of this information is suppressed. You'll add code that carries out the link from the host container to this Internet location later in this lesson.

The ResultsFile property specifies a file that will be used to store the questions and responses to every question evaluated during the scoring session. This is also an optional property. You'll write code that takes no action if this property is left blank, but generates the results file when a filename is specified.

The ProcessResults Method

Now that you have a clear view of the properties that relate to scoring a test, you can tackle the code that does the scoring. The ProcessResults method subroutine is shown in Listing 18.5. Enter this routine into your sample (or copy and paste from the solution in Samples\Day18).

Listing 18.5. The ProcessResults method that carries out scoring of the questions.

```
1: Public Sub ProcessResults()
2: ' Process results of all question controls on page
3:
4:     ' Directory that results file is written to.
5:     '    Results are only stored to this dir to prevent security problems.
```

```
 6:    '       For example, if control is in a web page on the Internet you don't
 7:    '       want to let host app specify that results go to C:\autoexec.bat.
 8:    '       By restricting results file to a given dir, you remove
 9:    '       potential for malicious behavior.
10:    Const RESULTS_DIR = "C:\Questions\"
11:
12:    ' Counter to loop through control collection
13:    Dim intLoop As Integer
14:
15:    ' Temp string used to extract control type
16:    Dim vsCtlType As String
17:
18:    ' Counter variables used to tally correct and total questions
19:    Dim intCorrect As Integer
20:    Dim intTotal As Integer
21:
22:    ' Contains file id for results file
23:    Dim intFileID As Integer
24:    ' Generate results file if specified in property setting
25:    If Me.ResultsFile <> "" Then
26:        If (Dir(RESULTS_DIR) = "") Then
27:            MkDir RESULTS_DIR
28:        End If
29:        intFileID = FreeFile
30:        Open RESULTS_DIR & Me.ResultsFile _
31:            For Output Lock Read Write As intFileID
32:        Print #intFileID, "Test Results for " & _
33:            UserControl.Parent.Name & " generated on " & Date; " " & Time
34:        Print #intFileID, " "
35:    End If
36:    ' Examine every control in the host container
37:    For intLoop = 0 To UserControl.ParentControls.Count - 1
38:        ' See if this is a question control based on type.
39:        '  Look for any type matching "uc*Question", since different
40:        '  versions have different Day descriptors to distinguish lessons
41:        vsCtlType = TypeName(UserControl.ParentControls.Item(intLoop))
42:        If vsCtlType Like "uc*Question" Then
43:
44:            With UserControl.ParentControls.Item(intLoop)
45:
46:                ' Tally the total questions reviewed and number correct
47:                intTotal = intTotal + 1
48:                If .Correct Then
49:                    intCorrect = intCorrect + 1
50:                End If
51:
52:                ' Lock questions from interaction if option
53:                If Me.LockAnswers = True Then
54:                    .Enabled = False
55:                End If
56:
57:                ' Generate results file if specified in property setting
58:                If Me.ResultsFile <> "" Then
59:                    Print #intFileID, String(40, "-")
60:                    Print #intFileID, "Question #" & intTotal & _
61:                        " (Question Control id=" & .Name & ")"
```

continues

Listing 18.5. continued

```
62:                    Print #intFileID, " Question: "; .Question
63:                    Print #intFileID, " User Answer: "; .UserAnswer
64:                    Print #intFileID, " Expected Answer: "; .ExpectedAnswer
65:                    If .Correct Then
66:                        Print #intFileID, " Correct! ";
67:                    Else
68:                        Print #intFileID, " Incorrect. ";
69:                    End If
70:                    Print #intFileID, "Cumulative Score = " & _
71:                        Int((intCorrect / intTotal) * 100) & " Percent"
72:                End If
73:            End With ' Score this question control
74:        End If ' Check if control is a question control
75:    Next ' Process each control on host container
76:
77:    ' Close results file if needed
78:    If Me.ResultsFile <> "" Then
79:        Close #intFileID
80:    End If
81:
82:    ' Update final score in the control property, show results
83:    Me.PercentCorrect = Int((intCorrect / intTotal) * 100)
84:    lblPercent.Caption = Me.PercentCorrect & " % Correct"
85:    lblPercent.Visible = True
86:    ' Show user link to more help if provided
87:    If lblStudyTips.Caption <> "" Then
88:        lblStudyTips.Visible = True
89:        Line2.Width = lblStudyTips.Width
90:        Line2.Visible = True
91:        lblStudyCaption.Visible = True
92:    End If
93:
94: End Sub
```

ANALYSIS This code collects results from each question control on the host container and calculates a total percentage correct. The user will see this score.

File Security

Locate the first line of nondeclaration code, which starts with the following statement:

```
If Me.ResultsFile <> "" Then
```

This statements checks whether the control's ResultsFile property calls for the generation of a results file. If so, a check is made to see whether the results directory already exists. The directory is created if it does not exist. Then the file is opened within that directory. The file is forced to the specific directory predefined by our control in the following declaration:

```
Const RESULTS_DIR = "C:\Questions\"
```

Why is the file forced to this directory? In a normal application, this would likely be the result of a bad, restrictive decision on the part of the application designer. But keep in mind that you are living in the wild frontier of controls now. You don't know how this control will be used by others after you unleash it.

Suppose you did give your users the flexibility to save the results file anywhere. Maybe you picture your coworkers, friends, and neighbors using the control to develop cool Visual Basic and C++ applications. They happily save the results file to a variety of locations. But then your mischievous nephew gets hold of the control and integrates it into a Web page. He specifies the location of the results file to be c:\autoexec.bat. Then he shares his Web page with the whole world. Everyone who visits his Web page and takes a test will have the results file overwrite their system configuration autoexec.bat file—all thanks to *your* question control! When disgruntled users track down the problem, view the page, and inspect the control, it's *your* name that's listed as the control creator. You'll have been the proliferator of an unsafe control. A far more Web-friendly technique is to force the results file into a standard location. Then no malicious overwriting can be carried out by users of your control. The topic of safety and security is a broad one and is addressed in more detail on Day 21, "Licensing, Distribution, and Security."

NOTE

If you are a reader with an inquiring mind, you might have noticed some coding techniques that could use some additional refinement. The file-handling code shown here should ideally have error handling in place to catch any unforeseen errors. There are also many places in the examples in this book where code could be optimized for faster performance with additional code refinements. The code in the samples has been intentionally kept relatively simple for the sake of providing clear, concise examples. If you are going to use the question or results control for your own solutions, you should assess them for areas where you can make them more robust or optimize them for additional performance.

Communicating Between Controls with ParentControls

The next block of code illustrates one of the more powerful features of control construction. Locate the following line:

```
For intLoop = 0 To UserControl.ParentControls.Count - 1
```

This line is the start of a loop that analyzes every control in the host container application. ParentControls is a property of UserControl. The ParentControls property consists of a collection of controls. This collection includes all the controls that belong to the parent of your control. In other words, this collection gives you access to all the controls that the host application integrates.

One of the properties of the collection is `Count`, which tells you how many controls belong to the host application. Five controls are listed in the `ParentControls` collection for the test form host application shown in Figure 18.1. They include the following:

The form itself, `frmTester`

The results control, `ucDay18Results1`

The help control, `ucKeithTimHelp1`

The first question control, `ucDay18Question1`

The second question control, `ucDay18Question2`

The code loop in `ProcessResults` examines each control to see whether it is a question control. This can be deduced by examining the type of the control. This statement extracts the following control type name:

```
vsCtlType = TypeName(UserControl.ParentControls.Item(intLoop))
```

`Item` is another property of the `ParentControls` collection that represents the specific control indicated by the corresponding index. The control collection is essentially an array of controls, and you can reference an individual control by referring to the item element. The Visual Basic `TypeName` function extracts the control type. Then this statement is used to see whether the control is a question control. If it is, it will have a type of `ucDayXXQuestion`, where *XX* is one of the days a question control was produced, as shown in the following code:

```
If vsCtlType Like "uc*Question" Then
```

When a question control is detected, a `With` reference is made so that subsequent references to that control don't require the entire object name:

```
With UserControl.ParentControls.Item(intLoop)
```

After this declaration, you can refer to a property of the control such as its enabled state by a statement like this:

```
.Enabled = False
```

There are a couple advantages to this shorthand form of reference. It makes the code much easier to read. It also improves the speed with which the code will execute in many circumstances.

Within the `With`-`End` `With` statement block, several checks occur, as you can see in Listing 18.6.

18

Listing 18.6. The `With` block provides shorthand references to the current host control.

```
 1:          With UserControl.ParentControls.Item(intLoop)
 2:
 3:              ' Tally the total questions reviewed and number correct
 4:              intTotal = intTotal + 1
 5:              If .Correct Then
 6:                  intCorrect = intCorrect + 1
 7:              End If
 8:
 9:              ' Lock questions from interaction if specified as option
10:              If Me.LockAnswers = True Then
11:                  .Enabled = False
12:              End If
13:
14:              ' Generate results file if specified in property setting
15:              If Me.ResultsFile <> "" Then
16:                  Print #intFileID, String(40, "-")
17:                  Print #intFileID, "Question #" & intTotal & _
18:                      " (Question Control id=" & .Name & ")"
19:                  Print #intFileID, " Question: "; .Question
20:                  Print #intFileID, " User Answer: "; .UserAnswer
21:                  Print #intFileID, " Expected Answer: "; .ExpectedAnswer
22:                  If .Correct Then
23:                      Print #intFileID, " Correct! ";
24:                  Else
25:                      Print #intFileID, " Incorrect. ";
26:                  End If
27:                  Print #intFileID, "Cumulative Score = " & _
28:                      Int((intCorrect / intTotal) * 100) & " Percent"
29:              End If
30:
31:          End With ' Score this question control
```

ANALYSIS   This code analyzes the answer for the referenced host question control. It uses the shorthand `With` notation to refer to the host control.

Several things happen for each control checked within the `With` block. The number of questions is incremented to indicate that this question control has been processed. Then a check is made on the current question control's `Correct` property. This boolean property was added to the question control to indicate whether a correct answer was detected when the user entered the last response to the question. The workshop at the end of this chapter discusses this code. If the current question receives a correct response, the tally of correct answers is incremented.

Next a check is made on the `LockAnswers` property. If this property is set to `True`, the current question control's `Enabled` property is set to `False`. This will prevent users from having any further interaction with the control. They will not be able to go back and change their answers during the current program session.

Then a check is made to see whether a results file has been specified. If it has, the full information for the current question control is generated to that file. The file I/O print lines reference many additional properties of the current question control, including `Name`, `Question`, `ExpectedAnswer`, and `UserAnswer`. The `UserAnswer` property was added for today's lesson and is mapped to directly expose the response the user types in the question control textbox. You have access to all these properties because of `UserControl`'s `ParentControls` collection property. Then when you reference an individual array item in `ParentControl`'s collection through its `Item` property, you can interact with any property of the control as does the code in Listing 18.6. The file output generated by this code for two question controls is shown in Listing 18.7.

Listing 18.7. The results file generated by the results control.

```
 1: Test Results for frmTester generated on 3/16/97 6:46:23 PM
 2:
 3: ----------------------------------------
 4: Question #1 (Question Control id=ucQuestion1)
 5:    Question: How far is the Bull Run Run 50 Mile Race?
 6:    User Answer: 49 miles
 7:    Expected Answer: 50 Miles
 8:    Incorrect. Cumulative Score = 0 Percent
 9: ----------------------------------------
10: Question #2 (Question Control id=ucQuestion2)
11:    Question: What's the Virginia Happy Trails Running Club acronym?
12:    User Answer: VHTRC
13:    Expected Answer: VHTRC
14:    Correct! Cumulative Score = 50 Percent
```

After every host control has been processed, the final percentage can be calculated. Then this percentage and the study tips link are made visible so that the user can get immediate feedback.

Adding a Focus Indicator

The results control has one shortcoming in its user interface. There is no indication of when it has focus. You fixed this problem for the question control on Day 8, "Predefined Events," by adding a `SetFocus` property. When this property is set to `True`, the question control background changes whenever it gains focus. This was rather special handling for the question control, however. It was targeted to the unique situation of stepping the user through a series of sequential questions where the focus is intended as a highly visible indication of the current question.

A more standard, subtle focus indicator might be better for the results control. When you're trying to determine behavior for a control you create, think about what other standard controls do and see whether you can modify the new behavior after those. The textbox control, for example, displays a blinking cursor when it has focus. A command button shows a dotted line as a focus indicator. Which approach is correct for you? There is no one right or wrong answer. Your decision should rest on the type of visual feedback that will be most meaningful to the user of your control.

The following example provides steps to add a blinking underscore to the results control to indicate focus. You can judge whether you like this means of focus feedback or whether you would implement an alternative. But first put it in place so you can observe it for yourself. Add the code in Listing 18.8 to the results control's `EnterFocus` and `ExitFocus` routines.

Listing 18.8. Providing a focus indicator.

```
1: Private Sub UserControl_EnterFocus()
2:      ' Start the focus indicator blinking
3:      tmrLineBlink.Enabled = True
4: End Sub
5: Private Sub UserControl_ExitFocus()
6:      ' Stop the focus indicator from blinking and hide it
7:      tmrLineBlink.Enabled = False
8:      Line1.Visible = False
9: End Sub
```

ANALYSIS This code starts a timer that will periodically blink a line as soon as the results control or any constituent control within it gains focus. Likewise, when the results control and all its constituent controls no longer have focus, the timer will be turned off and the formerly blinking line will be hidden.

Add a timer control to your form to provide support for the focus indicator blink code. Name the timer control `tmrLineBlink` and set its `Visible` property to be `False` initially. Set the `Interval` property to `300` to establish a blink rate of 300 milliseconds. Then the code shown in Listing 18.8 will start the line blinking whenever the control gains focus. Supply the code shown in Listing 18.9 to carry out the periodic blinking action.

Listing 18.9. Timer code for the control focus indicator.

```
1: Private Sub tmrLineBlink_Timer()
2:      ' This timer is turned on and off in the controls
3:      '    EnterFocus and ExitFocus routines.
4:      '    When timer is on, routine displays blinking line focus indicator.
5:
```

continues

Listing 18.9. continued

```
 6: ' Blink the line each time the timer expires
 7:    If Line1.Visible Then
 8:       ' Hide the line to make it blink
 9:       Line1.Visible = False
10:    Else
11:       ' Show the line to complete the blink
12:       Line1.Visible = True
13:    End If
14:
15: End Sub
```

ANALYSIS This timer event is only called after the timer has been started. Then it will be called periodically to toggle the line between a visible and an invisible state. This creates the appearance of a blinking focus indicator.

Adding Timed Behavior to Your Control

As you've just seen, the focus indicator is one example of how you can use a timer to enhance your control. You can also build timed functions directly into the exposed interfaces of your control. The AutoResultsTime property you added earlier fulfills this purpose. When this property is set, it designates a time limit in minutes that the user has to complete the test. After that time period has expired, the control will automatically invoke its ProcessResults method to score the test.

You need to add another timer control to support this feature. Add a second timer control to UserControl and name it tmrAutoResults. Set the Interval property for this timer to 60000 to cause it to have a period of 60,000 milliseconds, or 60 seconds. Set the Enabled state to False. This timer should only be turned on when the host application has set the AutoResultsTime property of the results control to a value greater than 0. Otherwise, the assumption is that no forced time limit is desired. Where is the best place to make this check? Visual Basic already provides you with a properties initialization event subroutine for just such a purpose: the ReadProperties event. Add the code shown in Listing 18.10 to this event routine for your results UserControl.

Listing 18.10. Turning on the timer for runtime use only.

```
1: 'Load property values from storage
2: Private Sub UserControl_ReadProperties(PropBag As PropertyBag)
3:    ' Show designer what control will look like at designer time
4:    If Ambient.UserMode = False Then
5:       ' Display control boundaries for easier layout
6:       UserControl.BorderStyle = 1
7:       ' Display hidden score fields at design time for easier layout
8:       lblPercent.Visible = True
9:       lblStudyCaption.Visible = True
```

```
10:         lblStudyTips.Visible = True
11:         Line2.Width = lblStudyTips.Width
12:         Line2.Visible = True
13:     End If
14:     m_AutoResultsTime = PropBag.ReadProperty _
15:         ("AutoResultsTime", m_def_AutoResultsTime)
16:     ' Start the results timer if requested by host app at runtime
17:     If (m_AutoResultsTime > 0) And (Ambient.UserMode = True) Then
18:         tmrAutoResults.Enabled = True
19:     End If
20:     ' (  More code pertaining to other properties is also contained in
21:     '     this event routine - not shown here in the interest of space  )
```

ANALYSIS This code sets display parameters for the results control when it is in the design environment. It also activates the AutoResults timer when the property is set accordingly at runtime only.

The statement that turns on the timer is

```
If (m_AutoResultsTime > 0) And (Ambient.UserMode = True) Then
        tmrAutoResults.Enabled = True
    End If
```

This code will only be carried out when the user has specified a property greater than 0 in the AutoResultsTime property. When this is the case, the same value will be reflected in the m_AutoResultsTime module-level variable, which is used in the conditional check. In addition, the timer is only started when the control is being used in runtime mode. This state is indicated by the Ambient.UserMode property. If you didn't have this check, the timer would be started even in design mode. Then as the poor integrator worked in design mode, laying out the application, the timer event would occur and chide him about taking too long with his test. This is not a fatal error, but it won't inspire confidence in the integrators of your control either! You have to keep such design-time versus runtime considerations in mind whenever you deal with timer-based code.

Now add the code to the timer event itself (see Listing 18.11). This event will occur every 60 seconds when a timed test has been requested. The number of passing minutes is stored. The user will receive a message when the number of minutes that has gone by reaches the time limit for the test. Then the ProcessResults method will be called to score the test.

Listing 18.11. Timer code for the automatic results generation.

```
1: Private Sub tmrAutoResults_Timer()
2: ' Keep track of seconds expired and score test when time is up
3:     Static lngMinutesExpired As Long
4:
5:     lngMinutesExpired = lngMinutesExpired + 1
6:
```

continues

Listing 18.11. continued

```
 7:      ' Once time is up, tell the user and process results
 8:      If lngMinutesExpired >= Me.AutoResultsTime Then
 9:          MsgBox "The maximum response time allowed by the " & _
10:              "designer of this test has expired. The test will be " & _
11:              "scored now.", vbOKOnly, "Time's Up!"
12:          tmrAutoResults.Enabled = False
13:          Me.ProcessResults
14:      End If
15: End Sub
```

Making Your Control Impressive in Design Time

The block of code at the start of Listing 18.10 reflects another design-time consideration. When the integrator views your results control on a form at design time, it might be hard for him to position it if there are no visible boundaries. In addition, it might be hard for him to understand the purpose of the control because the score-related labels are hidden. You can remedy these shortcomings with a few lines of code. You can use this statement to check whether the application is in design mode:

```
If Ambient.UserMode = False Then
```

If this condition is met, a series of assignments takes place to show borders on the results control and display the labels. Without these additions, the designer would see the control represented as shown in Figure 18.5.

Figure 18.5.

The results control in design mode if special display steps are not taken.

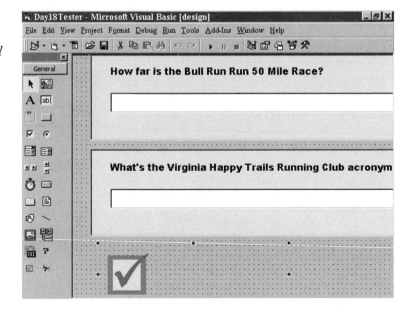

With the check and special design-time display, the control will appear as shown in Figure 18.6. This kind of code will not help the end user who views your control within the application he interacts with. But the second approach is much easier for the integrator—and the integrator is, after all, the customer of your control.

Figure 18.6.

The results control in design mode if special display steps are taken.

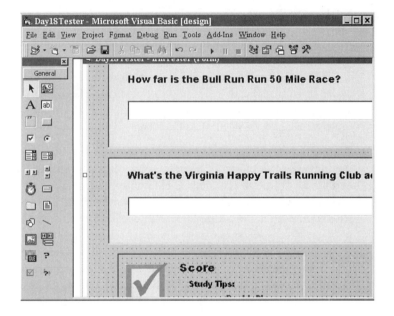

18

The Hyperlink **Object**

You'll learn more about the Hyperlink object used in today's sample on Day 20, "Designing Controls for the Internet." The code is provided in Listing 18.12 so you can completely define all aspects of the results control for today's lesson. Add the code to the lblStudyTips Click event.

Listing 18.12. The code to carry out a hyperlink in response to a click on the StudyTips link.

```
1: Private Sub lblStudyTips_Click()
2:
3:      ' Link to the specified URL
4:      UserControl.Hyperlink.NavigateTo lblStudyTips.Caption
5:
6: End Sub
```

UserControl's Hyperlink object is used to carry out a browser link to a source of additional help on the test material. The link is stored in the lblStudyTips caption, which is mapped to the StudyTipsURL property set by the host application.

Summary

The focus of today's lesson is on multiple controls, communication between controls, and other advanced control features. You have learned about the results control and the steps to create it. This control can total the results from all the question controls incorporated into a given page or application. The results control is packaged in the same control project as the question control. Therefore, they are both included in the same OCX file. A host application can have access to both controls by referencing one OCX file.

The results control renders itself as an irregularly shaped, transparent image. You can set masking properties so that the control only responds to clicks on the irregular image itself, and not on the rest of the control. The control displays borders when it shows up at design time, but it is borderless at runtime. Design-time borders are provided to assist the integrator with control layout. A Let property is declared with the keyword Friend so that it can have public read-only access but full write access within the control itself. A file-logging feature is implemented with a restrictive directory structure so that this control can be considered safe. Communication between controls is carried out with the UserControl's ParentCollection property. A timer is associated with the control, but special precautions should be used to ensure that the timer does not execute at design time. Knowledge of these techniques and others like them will move you from the realm of control apprentice to control craftsman.

Q&A

Q Does it ever make sense to have a control look different at design time than at runtime?

A Yes. For example, consider a control that will have to be positioned or sized in the design environment. If it is a transparent control with no clear indicators of its boundary regions, it might be very hard to see where the control is placed at design time. You can check the Ambient object UserMode property to display a border on the control at design time. Then it will be much easier for the user to position.

Q If a property is declared with the Friend keyword, will it be visible from the host application that integrates my control?

A No. It will only be visible within the control project.

Q How can I write control code to tell how many controls are contained in the host application?

A Use UserControl's ParentControls collection property. The collection object itself has a Count property you can reference. Therefore, a reference to UserControl.ParentControls.Count will provide the total number of controls in the project.

Q Is there a way I can make a control shaped like a star?

A Yes. Associate an image containing a star with the UserControl Picture property. Then use the masking techniques discussed today to mask only the star region as the recognized area of the control. The rest of the control will appear transparent and will not respond to user events such as mouse clicks. As far as the user of the application that contains your control can perceive, it is a star-shaped control.

Workshop

We added two properties to the question control today. One property was the Correct property. This is set by the question control to indicate whether a user response is correct or incorrect. We added this property to the question control to make it easier for the results control to retrieve the answer status from all the questions. The other property we added was the UserAnswer property. This property is simply the exposed caption from the textbox that the user enters his response into. We added this property so that the results control could retrieve the user's answer and place it in the results log file.

Examine the question control code. Search for all occurrences of Correct and UserAnswer. How many lines of code had to be added to define these properties? Consider workarounds to implementing these properties that could have been used to achieve the same goals in the results control. The results control could compare the user answer to the expected answer of each question itself, but then it would be repeating logic already contained in the question control. There is no easy way to extract the answer the user provides in the response textbox without directly exposing the textbox's Text property or adding an additional property to mirror the current response.

Quiz

NOTE   See Appendix D, "Answers to Quiz Questions," for the answer to this question.

Suppose you've included a constituent command button in your control. Supply the code that would display a message box with the number of label controls in the host container in response to a click on that command button.

Day 19

Self-Painting and Invisible Controls

If you've ever needed to create a control that's invisible at runtime and that sits in the background performing a task, this lesson is for you. Or perhaps you've wanted to use some specialized graphics in your control that existing Visual Basic controls just can't provide. Today's lesson discusses both of these cases. You can create ActiveX controls using three different approaches. The first involves using a collection of existing controls. This is the approach you've been taking so far through the lessons in this book. A second approach involves taking an existing control and adding more controls or source code to it. You learned how to do that in yesterday's lesson. In today's lesson, you'll learn about the third approach: creating a user-drawn control. User-drawn controls are different from the others in that you determine your control's appearance, and you interface with it more than with the others. Basically, you place code in the UserControl object's Paint event to do the graphics yourself.

Of course not all controls fall neatly into these three categories. In fact, most controls are hybrids of all three. The controls you'll examine in this lesson are based on what you've learned so far, with some specialized painting added for a few extra effects. Along with the painting technique, you'll also learn how to make a control invisible at runtime and how to represent that control at design time.

Controls That Are Invisible at Runtime

The first case to examine is a control intended to be invisible at runtime. The control is visible at design time, but only for the purpose of providing an interface for the developer so he has access to the property sheet. As soon as the application is run, however, the control doesn't appear on the form. Many standard Visual Basic controls already behave this way. The timer, for example, appears at design time, allowing the programmer to set Interval and various other properties. But when the program that contains the timer runs, the timer is nowhere in sight. It's still there on the form, but it has no visual representation.

Why would you want to create a control like this for yourself? There are many possible reasons. Let's explore one possible use for an invisible control. You've got quite a powerful question control at this point. Perhaps you're an eager entrepreneur ready to sell your control to the huge community of programmers using ActiveX controls. You decide to allow your users to use the control, but you want them to register at some point, pay a registration fee, and receive a registration code. The best way to do this is to remind the user that he needs to register. This is commonly called a "nag screen," and yes, it does a very good job of nagging the user. But when you're on the other side of the fence—a developer who's put a great many hours into designing a control—you want to receive some sort of payback for all your efforts.

The next time you design a control or an application, you might run into the same issue. You want the user to register the control or application before using it further. Perhaps the best way to implement this registration feature is to create an ActiveX control to do the job for you. This has many benefits. For one, you have a consistent, standard interface for all your program registrations. In addition, you don't have to rewrite a lot of code for registration each time you create a new control or application. If you create a control that's invisible, it can sit like a watchdog on the form, ready to be called whenever the host program wants to remind the user of registration.

In this lesson you'll create the simple skeleton of a registration control. For now, the control will provide the host with a method that invokes a message box reminding the user to register the product. You could add a very impressive user interface that steps the user through the entire registration process. We'll help you in that direction by providing you with a starting point. Our purpose here is primarily to show you how to create a control that's invisible at runtime, yet can be manipulated at design time. You'll learn all the concepts you need to know as you go along.

So let's get started. Bring up the question control project in the Your Start directory of Day 19, which is on your CD-ROM or on your hard disk, if you've installed the code to your hard drive. Bring up the Day19QuestionControl project in the design environment. When you get there, add a new UserControl to the existing question control. Click Project | Add User Control on the Visual Basic menu. Verify that you want the UserControl object when the Add User Control dialog appears. A blank UserControl object will then appear, as shown in Figure 19.1.

Figure 19.1.

A brand new
UserControl
object in the design
environment.

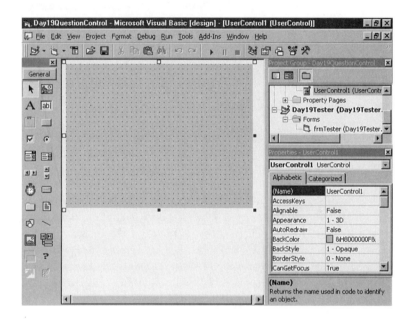

The first step in making a control invisible at runtime is to set the InvisibleAtRuntime property to True. The default setting for this property is, of course, False. Setting the property to True ensures that the control will not appear at runtime. That was easy! While you're in the property sheet, go ahead and set the ToolboxBitmap property, assigning the control with the picture named register.bmp, which is in the Your Start directory. The next step is to give the programmer something to look at while the control sits on the form in design mode. The best way to do this is to put an image control on the UserControl object. Give the image the name imgLogo. Why not use the same register.bmp file to show on the form? Go ahead and place an image control on the UserControl object and set the Picture property of the image to register.bmp. Your control should now look like the one in Figure 19.2.

19

Figure 19.2.

The registration control in the design environment.

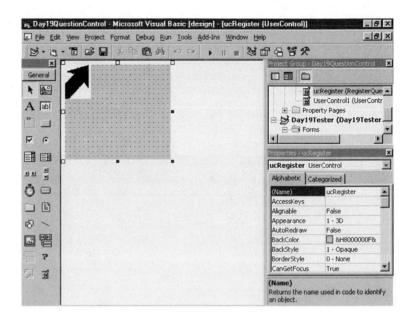

Move the control to the upper-left corner, as shown in Figure 19.2. Notice all the extra space that surrounds the control. When the developer places the control on a form, you want the control to resize itself to show nothing but the image you've placed on the control. In addition, you don't want to allow the user to resize the control when it's on the form. If the developer attempts to do so, you want the control to snap back to its original size when it first displayed. It's very easy to do this. Click on the control, bring up the `Resize` event, and place the following statement in the `Resize` event:

```
Size imgLogo.Width, imgLogo.Height
```

To be safe, go ahead and add this line of code to the `Initialize` event:

```
imgLogo.Move 0,0
```

The first statement resizes the control to the exact dimensions of the image control you placed on the control. The second line of code ensures that the image appears in the upper left of the control when the control is first initialized. This ensures that the entire image is displayed on the control surface. Now, close the registration control and switch over to the test application. You'll notice the registration control on the toolbox to the left. Select it and place a single control on the form. Notice that no matter what size you give the control initially, it snaps back to a fixed size, showing the image you specified when you designed the control. The test application should look like Figure 19.3 at this point.

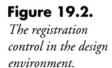

Figure 19.3.

The test application with the new registration control.

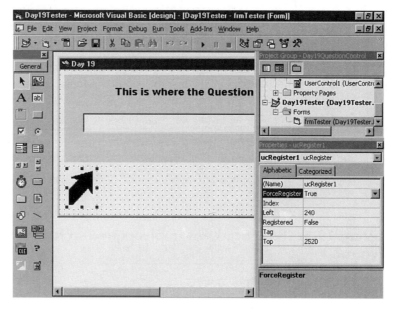

Experiment with resizing the control. You'll notice that no matter what you try, the control always snaps back to its original size. Go ahead and save the project. Run the test application and notice that the registration control doesn't appear on the form at runtime, although it is prominently displayed there at design time, as shown in Figure 19.4.

Figure 19.4.

The registration control does not appear at runtime, even though technically it's still on the form.

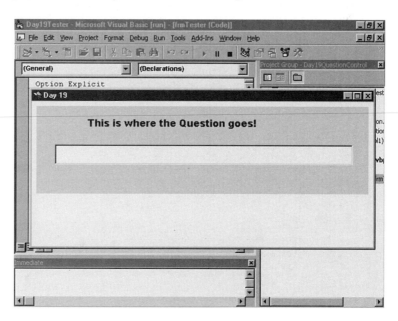

If you follow these steps every time you want to make a control that's invisible at runtime, you'll have in place all the cosmetic ingredients you need. The next step is to add actual functionality to the control. You'll add a property called ForceRegister, which will be a boolean value. When it's set to True, when the registration screen comes up, the user will be forced to register the program to which the control belongs. If it's set to False, the registration screen will come up, but the user will be able to dismiss it. You also need a method called DisplayRegister that brings up the registration form itself.

Use the ActiveX Control Interface Wizard to define the property and the method. The property should be a boolean property, and the method should return a boolean value indicating whether the registration process was a success. When you're finished, the procedures for your registration control should look as shown in Listing 19.1.

Listing 19.1. The procedures implemented so far in the registration control.

```
 1: 'Default Property Values:
 2: Const m_def_Registered = 0
 3: Const m_def_ForceRegister = 0
 4: 'Property Variables:
 5: Dim m_Registered As Boolean
 6: Dim m_ForceRegister As Boolean
 7:
 8: Private Sub UserControl_Initialize()
 9:     imgLogo.Move 0, 0
10: End Sub
11:
12: Private Sub UserControl_Resize()
13:     Size imgLogo.Width, imgLogo.Height
14: End Sub
15:
16: Public Property Get ForceRegister() As Boolean
17:     ForceRegister = m_ForceRegister
18: End Property
19:
20: Public Property Let ForceRegister(ByVal New_
21: ➥ForceRegister As Boolean)
22:     m_ForceRegister = New_ForceRegister
23:     PropertyChanged "ForceRegister"
24: End Property
25:
26: Public Function DisplayRegister() As Boolean
27:
28: End Function
29: 'Initialize Properties for UserControl
30: Private Sub UserControl_InitProperties()
31:     m_ForceRegister = m_def_ForceRegister
32:     m_Registered = m_def_Registered
33: End Sub
34:
```

```
35: 'Load property values from storage
36: Private Sub UserControl_ReadProperties( _
37:                         PropBag As PropertyBag)
38:     m_ForceRegister = PropBag.ReadProperty("ForceRegister", _
39:         m_def_ForceRegister)
40:     m_Registered = PropBag.ReadProperty("Registered", _
41:         m_def_Registered)
42: End Sub
43:
44: 'Write property values to storage
45: Private Sub UserControl_WriteProperties( _
46:                         PropBag As PropertyBag)
47:     Call PropBag.WriteProperty("ForceRegister", _
48:         m_ForceRegister, m_def_ForceRegister)
49:     Call PropBag.WriteProperty("Registered", _
50:         m_Registered, m_def_Registered)
51: End Sub
52:
53: Public Property Get Registered() As Boolean
54:     Registered = m_Registered
55: End Property
56:
57: Public Property Let Registered( _
58:                         ByVal New_Registered As Boolean)
59:     m_Registered = New_Registered
60:     PropertyChanged "Registered"
61: End Property
```

The next step is to add a skeleton form that contains the registration information. Select Project | Add Form and select a standard Visual Basic form. Set the properties for the form as shown in Table 19.1.

Table 19.1. Properties for the registration form.

Property	Setting
Name	frmRegister
BorderStyle	Fixed dialog
Caption	Registration
StartUpPosition	CenterOwner

Then place the controls on the form, as shown in Figure 19.5. The two buttons at the bottom of the form can set a variable indicating whether the user has registered. Create a public variable in the form named bRegister and set the value to True in the Click event of the button that registers the user. Save the form as Register.frm.

Switch back to the register UserControl object and add the statements shown in Listing 19.2 to the DisplayRegister method.

19

Figure 19.5.

The registration form in design mode.

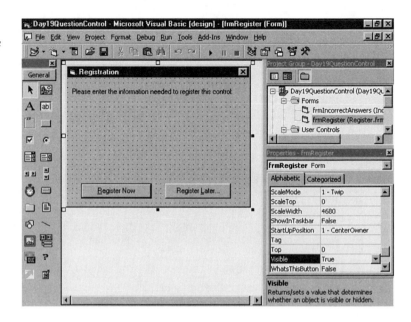

Listing 19.2. The new `DisplayRegister` method.

```
1: Public Function DisplayRegister() As Boolean
2:
3:     frmRegister.Show vbModal
4:
5:     m_Registered = frmRegister.bRegistered
6:
7:     If m_Registered = False And m_ForceRegister = True Then
8:         MsgBox "You must register this control before you can use it."
9:     End If
10:
11: End Function
```

This will bring up the registration form. When the user has clicked on a button to register or wait to register later, the result is analyzed. If the user is forced to register, a message box appears, telling the user that the application is about to exit. If the user has registered successfully, the application continues. All that remains to do now is to call the registration control's `DisplayRegister` method in the test application. Switch to the test application and add a button with the caption Register the Control. In the `Click` event of that control, enter the following code statement:

```
ucRegister1.DisplayRegister
```

Make sure that the ForceRegister property is set to True on the registration control. Now go ahead and run the test application. Click the Register Now button. This will bring up the registration form. Now click Register Later. Because you've specified a forced registration, the message shown in Figure 19.6 appears.

Figure 19.6.

The registration message alerting the user that he must register before moving onward.

If you wanted to take some action after this message, you could modify the Click event of the command button as follows:

```
ucRegister1.DisplayRegister
If ucRegister1.ForceRegister = True And _
    ucRegister1.Registered = False Then
    End
End If
```

This would end the application if the user hasn't registered but is required to. You can then add a registration form and the necessary code to display that form on the screen and handle the registration process for the user.

To summarize, you need to work through several key steps to make a control invisible at runtime. First, you need to set InvisibleAtRuntime to True. Then you should provide some sort of design-time display for the user. The easiest way to do this is to provide an image on the object. Then, in the Resize event, you can make sure the control always resizes itself to the height and width of the image you've placed on the form. The last step is simply to add the code you wish to the control to implement it.

Creating User-Drawn Controls

The next important point in today's lesson is how to create a user-drawn control. What is a user-drawn control? It's a control that requires you to paint its graphics into the UserControl object. Not all controls fall into this category. Many ActiveX controls use constituent controls that produce all the graphics themselves and automatically paint to the screen when necessary. In some cases, however, you might need to provide special graphics to handle certain cases in your control. The entire control might be user drawn, or only certain parts of the control might be.

19

Implementing a user-drawn control is both easy and challenging. It's easy in the sense that all the code you use to draw graphics on the control surface should reside in the Paint event of the UserControl object. The challenging part is coming up with good graphics and the code in the Paint event to make the graphics come together. Oftentimes the various states in which the control is placed can require that the graphics be drawn in different ways. That's no problem, as long as all the logic to decide what to paint is in the Paint event itself. You'll see some examples of this a little later in today's lesson.

If you also have constituent controls on your control, those controls might do their own drawing. In such a case, you don't need to worry about them. Remember, part or all of a control is user drawn when you place code in the Paint event to display graphics on the control that would be difficult, inconvenient, or impossible to do otherwise.

You have many tools at your disposal for drawing. Visual Basic offers a suite of graphics methods that allow you to draw lines, boxes, circles, arcs, and ellipses. You can even set individual pixels. If you need more advanced tools, you can tap into the Windows Application Programming Interface (API). The Windows API is a huge collection of low-level functions that give you advanced capabilities. Visual Basic normally shelters you from these more advanced functions, but they are available if you need them. In today's lesson, we'll focus on graphics you can render in Visual Basic without the need of the API. If you want to learn more about the Windows API, there are some excellent resources that can help you, such as Daniel Appleman's *Visual Basic Programmer's Guide to the Win32 API* by Ziff-Davis Press.

Often you need to cause your control to repaint. To get your control's Paint event to execute, simply call the UserControl object's Refresh event. This will force a Paint event to take place in your application. You'll see this event in action as well.

Let's take a look at an example of a user-drawn control. Actually, we're going to take the existing question control and add some special graphics to it that need to be user drawn. So technically this control will be a mixture of user-drawn graphics and Windows-drawn graphics, based on all the constituent controls already in the control.

The example you'll implement is a set of properties for drawing the question number to the left of the question. You can assign a number of different style attributes for the question number, such as a circular border, a triangular border, or a rectangular border.

To begin, use the ActiveX Control Interface Wizard to add the three properties shown in Table 19.2.

Table 19.2. Three new properties of the question control.

Property	Description
QuestionNumber	Indicates the number to draw next to the question.
DisplayQuestionNumber	Indicates whether you want the question number displayed.
QuestionNumberStyle	Indicates the style of the question. The style can be SQUARE, CIRCLE, or RECTANGLE.

When you've added each of the properties, create the following enumerated type:

```
Public Enum QNUMSTYLE
    styNone
    styCircle
    stySquare
    styTriangle
End Enum
```

NOTE

Enumerated types are new to Visual Basic 5.0. They enable you to create variables that can be set to the values inside the enumerated type declaration. In this example, any variable declared with the enumerated type, say Dim Style as QNUMSTYLE, can be set to styNone, styCircle, stySquare, or styTriangle. Rather than having to set these variables to integer values or strings, you can use the enumerated type to make life easier for the programmers using your control.

Set the property parameters for each Property procedure to this enumerated type. Then set the data type of the default property variable, located in the declarations section of the UserControl module, to the same enumerated type. The next step is to add the code necessary in the Paint event to draw the graphics on the screen. The code you need to enter into the Paint event is shown in Listing 19.3.

Listing 19.3. The Paint event of the question control.

```
1: Private Sub UserControl_Paint()
2:     If m_DisplayQuestionNumber = True Then
3:
4:         ' Draw the question number
5:         Font = lblQuestion.Font
6:         FontSize = lblQuestion.FontSize
7:         CurrentX = 700
8:         CurrentY = 240
```

continues

19

Listing 19.3. continued

```
 9:           Print Str(m_QuestionNumber)
10:
11:           ' Draw the question border
12:           Select Case m_QuestionNumberStyle
13:
14:               Case styCircle
15:                   Circle (875, 400), 300
16:
17:               Case stySquare
18:                   Line (650, 200)-Step(500, 500), , B
19:
20:               Case styTriangle
21:                   Line (850, 100)-(600, 600)
22:                   Line (850, 100)-(1100, 600)
23:                   Line (600, 600)-(1100, 600)
24:
25:           End Select
26:
27:       End If
28: End Sub
```

The first thing the Paint event does is check the state of the question control, specifically whether the DisplayQuestionNumber property is set to True. If the property is set to False, the Paint event paints nothing. If, however, the user has specified that the question numbers are to appear, the first thing the Paint event does is paint the number on the control. Then the event checks the DisplayQuestionStyle property to see what the style of the border should be. It draws a circle, a square, or a triangle based on the style setting. If none of these are specified, nothing is drawn around the question number itself.

Go ahead and switch over to the test application. Set the DisplayQuestionNumber property to True. At this point, you'd expect the question number to be displayed. If you look at the QuestionNumber property, you'll see that it's indeed set to 1. Why, then, doesn't the control paint itself? Go ahead and change the style property and the question number property. Note that they have no effect. Where's the problem here?

The problem is that the control only painted once, immediately after the Initialize event. At that point the DisplayQuestionNumber property was set to its default value of False. When you changed the property, the variable within the control was changed, but the display wasn't updated.

The problem here is that you need to add the Refresh statement to every Property procedure where any of these three properties is changed. Go ahead and change each of the Property Let statements to those shown in Listing 19.4.

19

Listing 19.4. The revised `Property` procedures that allow for proper painting.

```
1: Public Property Let QuestionNumber(ByVal New__
2:                            QuestionNumber As Integer)
3:     m_QuestionNumber = New_QuestionNumber
4:     UserControl.Refresh
5:     PropertyChanged "QuestionNumber"
6: End Property
7: Public Property Let QuestionNumberStyle(ByVal New__
8:                            QuestionNumberStyle As QNUMSTYLE)
9:     m_QuestionNumberStyle = New_QuestionNumberStyle
10:    UserControl.Refresh
11:    PropertyChanged "QuestionNumberStyle"
12: End Property
13: Public Property Let DisplayQuestionNumber(ByVal New__
14:                            DisplayQuestionNumber As Boolean)
15:    m_DisplayQuestionNumber = New_DisplayQuestionNumber
16:    UserControl.Refresh
17:    PropertyChanged "DisplayQuestionNumber"
18: End Property
```

As you can see, each `Property` procedure that changes the user-drawn portion of the control must have a `Refresh` statement. This forces the `Paint` event to take place, which then triggers the code shown in Listing 19.3.

Now go ahead and try the different configurations in the design environment. Observe the result shown in Figure 19.7 when the question number is set to 1 and the style is set to the triangle.

Figure 19.7.

The corrected question control in the design environment of the test application.

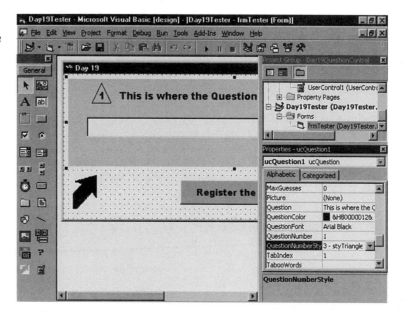

As you can see, the control now paints properly because Paint is called after each relevant property setting. The moral of the story here is that you should make sure you execute Refresh every time you paint the control. If you neglect to trigger the Paint event at some point in your code, the user won't see the result when he changes a property setting.

This simple example shows how you can implement your own user-drawn effects on controls. You might be wondering why you can't just use a label and a shape control to achieve these effects. You can for the circle and square, but the triangle requires three line shapes. It's much easier to write code to handle this display issue. Another important consideration is when the question climbs to the number 10 or higher. You need to write code that makes sure the border is drawn around the number in the correct way. Right now, everything looks fine until the question count gets higher than 9. Then the border needs to be expanded. In the case of a shape control, it would be much more inconvenient to have to resize a graphics control versus the easier approach of changing the drawing using graphics methods.

Important Do's and Don'ts of User-Drawn Controls

You need to consider a few more things when doing your own control painting. First of all, never set the BackStyle property of your UserControl object to False. If you do so, Visual Basic will never send any Paint events to your control. Why is this? The graphics sent to your UserControl object are sent to three layers of the form. Each layer sits on the one beneath it. So graphics on the highest layer overlap graphics created in the lower layers. The topmost layer holds things like command buttons, textboxes, and most other constituent controls. The middle layer is reserved for graphics created using graphics controls such as the shape control. The lowest layer is where all the graphics you create in the Paint event using graphics methods appear. They have the lowest priority in the layers. This layer is often referred to as the *background layer*.

All the graphics you create using graphics methods are sent to the background layer of your UserControl object. Setting BackStyle so it is transparent effectively cancels out the entire background layer. So make sure this property is always set to True. Then the Paint event will be fired whenever it's needed, and your code in the Paint event will be executed as it should.

It's also important that you avoid using the DoEvents statement in the Paint event. DoEvents can cause errors in this event because it causes Windows to process messages in the operating system. This message processing can cause Windows to get confused when code is executing in the Paint event.

Generating Graphics to Indicate Control Focus

At times, you might need to use graphics methods to indicate that your control has focus. This is typically done by drawing a small, dotted rectangle around the border of UserControl. You might wish to create a variable that keeps track of whether the control has the focus. In the GotFocus event of UserControl, you can set the state variable to True, and then to False in the LostFocus event. In both events, you should call the Refresh event of UserControl to add or remove the rectangular border. If the control has focus, the border should appear. Otherwise, it should not. The easiest way to implement the border is to use the Windows API function DrawFocusRect. Refer to the Windows documentation for information on how to use this function.

Generating Graphics to Show a Disabled Control

You might also want to show your control in a disabled state as well as in an enabled state. Again, it's best to use a state variable. You can create your own user-defined property named Enabled. When Enabled is set to False, set your state variable to False and call the Refresh event. That will cause the control to redraw in the disabled state. You can simply place an If-Then statement in the Paint event to handle this case. When the control is disabled, you simply need to paint the control differently. How you do this is up to you.

Generating Graphics to Treat Controls As Default Buttons

One final drawing effect you might wish to implement in a user-drawn control can be useful when the control behaves like a default button. Suppose, for example, your control behaves like a normal button, but you've added some special effects. The button might change size or color, or perhaps it is animated in some way. If you select the button to be a default button, you need to place a special shadow around it. You must implement this functionality yourself in the Paint event. Remember to set the DefaultCancel property of the UserControl object to True in order for the Cancel and Default properties to appear on the property sheet of your control in the design environment of the host.

Draw the border around the control only if Extender's DisplayAsDefault property is set to True. This cues your Paint event in on the fact that this particular control is set as the default and therefore the shadow must be drawn. DisplayAsDefault will only be set to True when your control has its Default property set to True and no other button has the focus at the time.

Summary

Today's lesson gives you experience working with some special features you can apply to ActiveX controls. Often it is necessary to write controls that you want to appear at design time only and not at runtime. In such cases, you can set the InvisibleAtRuntime property to False to ensure that the control doesn't appear at runtime. But you need to do some other things to make the control behave properly. You should also make sure the control looks correct in the design environment. One way to do this is to add an image control and put some code in the resize event.

User-drawn controls are necessary when you need your control to do some specialized drawing that you can't do with constituent controls. The simple example in this lesson is only one possible way you can use a user-drawn control. Often you might not have any constituent controls in the control and must rely completely on code within the Paint event to draw the graphics for you on the control. The techniques you've learned in today's lesson will help enable you to write the code necessary to make sure your controls paint properly on their own.

Q&A

Q Why would I want to create a user-drawn control in the first place?

A User-drawn controls are useful because they allow you to place special graphic effects within a normal ActiveX control. It is often impossible to achieve the graphic effects you want using the standard graphics controls that you can place on the control at design time. In such a case, you have to resort to graphics methods or the Windows API to get the effects you want. Other times, you don't even use any constituent controls and render all the graphics in the Paint event. This can happen when you're producing a control with very customized graphics. When that time comes, you need to know how to design your control to paint on its own.

Q Why is it important for an invisible control to appear at design time?

A A control should never be invisible at design time. Controls can be placed on a form at design time so that the developer can set properties and write code easily for the control. Then at runtime the control doesn't appear.

Q How do I learn how to do advanced drawing using Visual Basic?

A The best place to start is to consult the Visual Basic online help or documentation that ships with the product. Focus on graphics methods; if they don't give you the power and flexibility you need, you might need to use the Windows API instead.

Workshop

Enhance the registration control by adding a form that enables you to completely register the control. Take the user's name, address, and other information and store it in a database or the System Registry. Can you think of other ways to make the registration control more useful? Go ahead and build up the registration control as far as you can. You will find it useful if you decide to market your controls to the public!

Quiz

NOTE   See Appendix D, "Answers to Quiz Questions," for the answers to these questions.

1. Add code to the question control to dynamically redraw the borders for the question number when the question count reaches two digits. Restrict the question count so that it can never exceed 99.

2. Modify the question control so that the default question number is equal to the number at the end of the question control name upon initialization. For instance, if you create the control from scratch, you might name it ucQuestion4. In this case, the default question number should be four.

   Hint: The easiest way to do this is to parse the question name in the proper UserControl event. Take the digits to the right of the text ucQuestion and use them in the question number property.

3. Use the Windows API to set the focus around the question control when the control has focus in the container in which it is placed.

Day 20

Designing Controls for the Internet

Up to this point, the controls you've been building have all been targeted for a regular Visual Basic application. But ActiveX controls can operate in a wide variety of environments, including environments for the Internet such as Web browsers. You've probably heard a great deal about ActiveX controls for the Internet. In fact, ActiveX control technology was created, in part, for the Internet. ActiveX controls are typically small and easy to download, making them very suitable for the Internet. Before the advent of ActiveX controls, it was realistically impossible to download and use the typically larger OLE controls that came before ActiveX technology. ActiveX controls add new dimensions to the Internet, particularly to the World Wide Web. ActiveX controls make Web pages much more powerful and functional than the traditional, static Web pages of the past.

In today's lesson you're going to learn how to create ActiveX controls targeted for use on the Internet. You'll learn what it takes to write an ActiveX control for the Internet, and you'll see what special considerations you have to take into account when your control is used on the Internet. You'll also learn about some of the special features you can use specifically for controls that are on the Internet or can connect to it. Today's lesson primarily focuses on using ActiveX controls within Web browsers such as Microsoft's Internet Explorer. If you haven't already done so, make sure you've installed Internet Explorer on your system for the controls in this lesson.

Using ActiveX Controls on the Internet

So how do you go about using an ActiveX control on the Internet, anyway? Actually, it's easier than you might think. At this point, you have two primary ways of doing this. The first way is to place an ActiveX control into an HTML document using the <OBJECT> tags that are a part of HTML. The second way is to create what's called an *ActiveX document*, which essentially is a full-fledged application that runs within a Web browser. It has limitations, of course, because it's running in a browser. But you can place ActiveX controls in an ActiveX document just like you do on a form, and they will appear that way when you load them into a browser. Let's consider both approaches, determining how to get your control to work in these environments.

Placing an ActiveX Control in an HTML Document

Begin by starting Visual Basic 5.0 and bringing up the project group named Day20QuestionControl in the Your Start directory for Day 20. The result will be the project as you left it in yesterday's lesson. If you look in the Your Start directory, you'll see the OCX for this lesson. Select Project|Day20QuestionControl Properties from the Visual Basic menu, which will bring up the property sheet for the project. Click the Component tab and make sure Project Compatibility is checked in the Version Compatibility area. Then make sure the name of the control is specified in the textbox below the radio button. The dialog should now look like the one in Figure 20.1.

Then select File|Make Day20QuestionControl.ocx from the Visual Basic menu. This will compile the OCX. Overwrite the existing OCX when prompted. You'll need to do this several times throughout the lesson today because you need to create the OCX each time you want to put the control into a Web page or an ActiveX document.

The next step is to bring up an HTML document and place the ActiveX control within that document. I've already done the work of providing you the HTML document; it's called BegPage.htm. The Web page that appears should look like the one shown in Figure 20.2.

Open Internet Explorer and load the HTML document into the browser. When the page is loaded, choose View|Source from the Explorer menu. The source code for this document should look as shown in Listing 20.1.

Figure 20.1.

Making sure the project is set to compile properly.

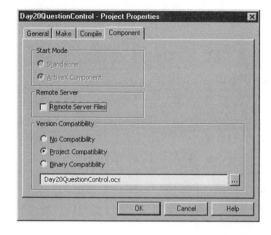

Figure 20.2.

The initial Web page for the question control.

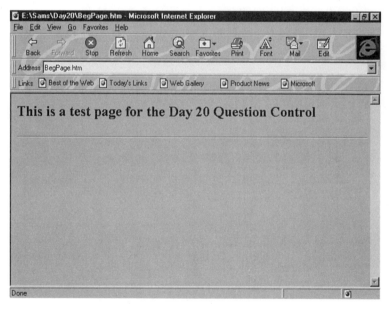

Listing 20.1. The initial HTML source code for the question control Web page.

```
1: <HTML>
2: <HEAD>
3: <TITLE>Question Control Test Page</TITLE>
4: </HEAD>
5: <BODY>
```

continues

Listing 20.1. continued

```
6: <H1>This is a test page for the Day 20 Question Control</H1>
7: <HR>
8: </BODY>
9: </HTML>
```

In order to display the ActiveX control within the Web page, you need to specify the ActiveX control using a special HTML tag called the <OBJECT> tag. The <OBJECT> tag is similar to the standard HTML <BODY> tag format in many respects. It has both a start tag (<OBJECT>) and an end tag (</OBJECT>). Within the start tag, you can define additional attributes that further describe characteristics common to all objects. Listing 20.2 shows the same HTML document with the question control included in the Web page.

Listing 20.2. The HTML source code for the question control Web page with the ActiveX control included.

```
 1: <HTML>
 2: <HEAD>
 3: <TITLE>Question Control Test Page</TITLE>
 4: </HEAD>
 5: <BODY>
 6: <H1>This is a test page for the Day 20 Question Control</H1>
 7: <HR>
 8: <OBJECT
 9:    CLASSID="CLSID:C020C87D-9D8C-11D0-ABCE-444553540000"
10:    ID="ucQuestion1"
11: >
12: </OBJECT>
13: </BODY>
14: </HTML>
```

Figure 20.3 shows the question control in its initial configuration.

All the statements shown in Listing 20.2 following the <OBJECT portion of the tag but preceding the > are attributes. These attributes, which are specifically defined by the HTML draft standard for objects, describe standard object characteristics to the browser.

NOTE

At this point, I'm assuming you have a working knowledge of HTML and, to some extent, of the use of the <OBJECT> tag. This book focuses more on how to create ActiveX controls for the Internet, not necessarily how to add existing ActiveX controls to HTML pages. So this discussion is primarily intended for your review. If you need to learn HTML and/or how to integrate ActiveX controls into Web pages, you can consult many useful books such as Laura Lemay's *Teach Yourself Web Publishing with HTML 3.2 in a Week* (Sams.net Publishing), among others.

Figure 20.3.

The question control as it appears in the Web browser.

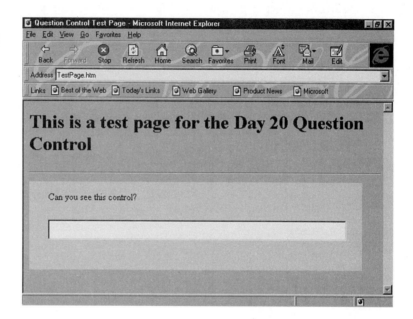

At a minimum, you must include the CLASSID attribute in your object declaration. CLASSID is an essential part of any ActiveX object declaration. It identifies the implementation of an object to the browser; in other words, it provides the browser with a path to the code behind an object. It describes what kind of class an object belongs to and thereby identifies the code that defines its behavior. The information supplied for CLASSID is a tag that enables the browser to look up information for the control in the class system registration database. The browser then uses the information it finds in the Registry to locate the OCX file and properly bring up the control within the HTML document.

So how do you go about finding the CLASSID for your ActiveX control? There are at least two ways to do this. One way is to obtain a utility such as Microsoft's ActiveX Control Pad or FrontPage 97. These tools allow you to select the ActiveX control from a list, much like you do in Visual Basic. The utilities then automatically insert the control into the HTML document for you, complete with the <OBJECT> tag and all the necessary attributes. You can even set the initial properties using a handy interface.

NOTE

You can obtain the Microsoft ActiveX Control Pad by downloading it from the Microsoft site at http://www.microsoft.com.

Another way to get at the CLASSID is to place the control within a Visual Basic form. Switch over to Visual Basic and open up the test application. Make sure the question control is on the form. Then go to the Windows Explorer, find the file Day20Tester.frm, and load it into a text editor such as Notepad. You should see a listing that looks something like the one shown in Listing 20.3.

Listing 20.3. The Visual Basic test form in its ASCII representation.

```
 1: VERSION 5.00
 2: Object = "{C020C875-9D8C-11D0-ABCE-444553540000}#2.0#0";
 3:           ➥ "Day20QuestionControl.ocx"
 4: Begin VB.Form frmTester
 5:     BackColor       =    &H00FFFFFF&
 6:     Caption         =    "Day 20"
 7:     ClientHeight    =    3345
 8:     ClientLeft      =    165
 9:     ClientTop       =    450
10:     ClientWidth     =    8835
11:     BeginProperty Font
12:         Name        =    "Arial Black"
13:         Size        =    11.25
14:         Charset     =    0
15:         Weight      =    400
16:         Underline   =    0    'False
17:         Italic      =    0    'False
18:         Strikethrough =  0    'False
19:     EndProperty
20:     Icon            =    "Day20Tester.frx":0000
21:     LinkTopic       =    "Form1"
22:     ScaleHeight     =    3345
23:     ScaleWidth      =    8835
24:     StartUpPosition =    2    'CenterScreen
25:     Begin Day20QuestionControl.ucQuestion ucQuestion1
26:         Height      =    2160
27:         Left        =    120
28:         TabIndex    =    0
29:         Top         =    120
30:         Width       =    8580
31:         _ExtentX    =    15134
32:         _ExtentY    =    3810
33:         BackStyle   =    1
34:         BeginProperty QuestionFont {0BE35203-8F91-11CE-9DE3-00AA004BB851}
35:             Name    =    "Arial Black"
36:             Size    =    12
```

```
37:          Charset        =    0
38:          Weight         =    400
39:          Underline      =    0     'False
40:          Italic         =    0     'False
41:          Strikethrough  =    0     'False
42:       EndProperty
43:       BeginProperty AnswerFont {0BE35203-8F91-11CE-9DE3-00AA004BB851}
44:          Name           =    "Arial Black"
45:          Size           =    12
46:          Charset        =    0
47:          Weight         =    400
48:          Underline      =    0     'False
49:          Italic         =    0     'False
50:          Strikethrough  =    0     'False
51:       EndProperty
52:       BeginProperty HintFont {0BE35203-8F91-11CE-9DE3-00AA004BB851}
53:          Name           =    "Arial Black"
54:          Size           =    12
55:          Charset        =    0
56:          Weight         =    400
57:          Underline      =    0     'False
58:          Italic         =    0     'False
59:          Strikethrough  =    0     'False
60:       EndProperty
61:    End
62: End
63: Attribute VB_Name = "frmTester"
64: Attribute VB_GlobalNameSpace = False
65: Attribute VB_Creatable = False
66: Attribute VB_PredeclaredId = True
67: Attribute VB_Exposed = False
68: Option Explicit
```

In line 2 of the listing, you'll see the statement

```
Object = "{C020C875-9D8C-11D0-ABCE-444553540000}#2.0#0";
    ➥ "Day20QuestionControl.ocx"
```

This statement specifies that the ActiveX control named Day20QuestionControl.ocx is included in the form. You'll also notice the CLASSID listed in quotes. This is the value used in the CLASSID attribute within the HTML document. You can copy the relevant information from the form into the HTML document to bring the control onto a Web page.

To set properties for the ActiveX control, you need to use <PARAM> tags. These tags take the syntax

```
<PARAM NAME="propertyname" VALUE="propertyvalue">
```

where propertyname is the name of a property, and propertyvalue is the value you want to assign the property. The code in Listing 20.4 shows the ActiveX control, complete with property assignments.

20

Listing 20.4. The object specification for the question control, complete with property settings.

```
1: <OBJECT
2:  ID="ucQuestion1"
3:  CLASSID="CLSID:C020C87D-9D8C-11D0-ABCE-444553540000" >
4:  <param name="BackStyle" value="1">
5:  <param name="question" value="Can you see this control?">
6:  <param name="expectedanswer" value="Yes">
7:  <param name="hint" value="You must be using Internet Explorer">
8: </OBJECT>
```

The properties will then be applied to the question control when the HTML page is loaded into the browser.

Using an ActiveX Control in an ActiveX Document

Another way to bring ActiveX controls into a Web browser is by creating an ActiveX document. ActiveX documents are actually executable files that the browser references through a special file with the extension .vbd. ActiveX documents are easier to work with because they can be constructed just like a form within the Visual Basic environment.

To create an ActiveX document, bring up a new project in Visual Basic. When asked to specify the project type, choose the ActiveX Document EXE option. A blank project comes up with a special object called a UserDocument object. This object is very similar to the UserControl object you've worked with throughout the book, except that UserDocument is used to build a document, whereas the UserControl object is used to build a control.

Bring up the default UserDocument object and rename it AXDQuestion. Save it as AXDTest.dob. The .dob extension is used to store a UserDocument file. Then select Project | Components and include the Day20QuestionControl and KeithTimHelp controls in the toolbox by selecting them from the list of components. When the question, results, and KeithTimHelp controls appear in the toolbox, select them and place them on the UserDocument object. Go ahead and include a label on the document as well. Make sure you set the LockControls property of the results control to False so you can continue to interact with the document. The document should look like the one shown in Figure 20.4.

To bring up the document in the browser, you should first save the project. Give the project the name AXDTest, for ActiveX Document Test, and save the project file as AXDTest.vbp. Now choose File | Make AXDTest.exe from the Visual Basic menu and create the executable file for the project. This will create two new files: AXDTest.exe and AXDQuestion.vbd. The .vbd document file is the one you can load into your browser. Bring up Internet Explorer and specify the AXDQuestion.vbd file. Your browser will load the ActiveX document into the browser; it should look like Figure 20.5.

Figure 20.4.

The question and help controls, as they appear in the UserDocument *object.*

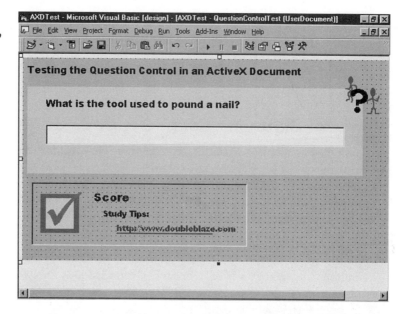

Figure 20.5.

The question control ActiveX document, as it appears in Internet Explorer 3.0.

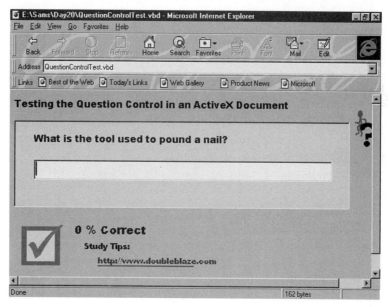

You can build an entire application, placing controls on the document and bringing them into the browser. As you can see, ActiveX documents give you a very powerful means of using ActiveX controls within the browser. Rather than make you deal with the rather restrictive HTML approach, this gives you a great deal of flexibility and additional capability.

Throughout the rest of this lesson, we'll be showing you how to implement ActiveX controls for the Internet using the ActiveX document approach. This approach is on the cutting edge of technology and is likely to become the standard way of bringing ActiveX controls onto the Internet.

Control Behavior Often Depends on the Container

As you've seen in these examples, controls can behave quite differently, depending on the container in which they are placed. This is a good time to remind you that when you place an ActiveX control in an HTML document, you must remember that HTML document containers do not behave the same way Visual Basic forms do. ActiveX documents, another type of container, also act differently from VB forms or HTML documents, even though both HTML documents and ActiveX documents can be loaded into a Web browser.

In the case of HTML documents, you must remember that they do not save design-time information. When an HTML document is loaded into a browser, it always comes up as though it's being created for the very first time. The control receives the `Initialize` event, then the `InitProperties` event, and finally the `Resize` and `Paint` events. Any of the attributes you assign to the control using `<PARAM>` tags are not assigned to the control until after it is running. After the `Resize` and `Paint` events take place, the `ReadProperties` event executes and the properties are assigned using `PropertyBag`, which essentially consists of any properties passed in through the `<PARAM>` attributes of the HTML document container. The properties can also be changed if any scripts, such as VBScript, exist in the document.

NOTE

For more information on scripting and how it applies to ActiveX documents, an excellent reference is *Teach Yourself VBScript in 21 Days* by Keith Brophy and Tim Koets, from Sams.net Publishing.

Another important issue to be aware of is that even different Web browsers may behave differently. Because each is a different container, you cannot rely on consistent operations between them. In some cases, for example, if you don't use any attributes in the `<PARAM>` tags other than those that set `Extender` properties (such as `Left` and `Top`), the control may set those properties using `InitProperties` rather than `ReadProperties`. The point is, you cannot count on the order one way or the other. What does this mean to you, the control developer? Test, test, test! Make sure the control behaves the way you want it to in all the containers you're targeting it for!

Navigating the World Wide Web with the Hyperlink **Object**

Now that you've seen how to present ActiveX controls on the Internet, let's take a look at some of the features you can take advantage of within an ActiveX control to use the Internet effectively. You will now learn about a series of useful objects that enable you to add extra features to your controls to make them take advantage of access the user has to the Internet. The first of these objects is the Hyperlink object.

The Hyperlink object provides you with the means of accessing the Internet from within your control. When the right properties and methods of the Hyperlink object are used, the control's container can jump to a particular address on the World Wide Web. If, for example, the container happens to be a Web browser such as Internet Explorer, the container is automatically able to access the address. If the container is a standard Visual Basic form, it cannot access the Web by itself. In some cases, however, Windows is smart enough to bring up the user's default browser and access the site anyway. The Hyperlink object is actually a property of the UserControl object, so it's very easy to access. Let's explore the Hyperlink object properties and methods to see what it can do.

The NavigateTo **Method**

The NavigateTo method enables the ActiveX control to initiate a hyperlink on its container. It's just one of several methods you can use to navigate the World Wide Web. NavigateTo uses the syntax

```
Hyperlink.NavigateTo Target [, Location [, FrameName]]
```

where *Target* is the address, or URL, of the hyperlink, *Location* is an optional parameter specifying the location within the target URL, and *FrameName* is an optional parameter specifying the frame within the target URL. When this method is called, the ActiveX control takes a look at the container on which the control exists. If that container supports hyperlinking, such as Internet Explorer does, the hyperlink is attempted. If the container doesn't support hyperlinking (say it's a Visual Basic form, for example), Windows tries to find a registered application that does support hyperlinking and starts that application to handle the request.

Keep in mind, however, that depending on the container you've placed your control into, the container might not be smart enough to make this call to another application and may simply do nothing. Therefore, it's important to thoroughly test the control within its intended container to make sure the hyperlink takes place properly.

20

To see how the `NavigateTo` method works, reexamine the code you wrote on Day 18, "Multiple Controls, Control Communication, and Advanced Features," which activates the link in the results control. Bring up the Day20QuestionControl project within Visual Basic. Switch to the `ucDay209Results` UserControl in the project and bring up the `UserControl` object on the display. Your screen should now look like the one shown in Figure 20.6.

Figure 20.6.

The results control in the design environment.

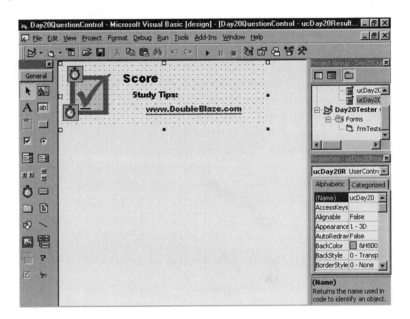

Bring up the `Click` event code for the label `lblStudyTips`, in which the statement

```
UserControl.Hyperlink.NavigateTo lblStudyTips.Caption
```

exists. This statement takes the string in the label's caption and hyperlinks to that location. If you run the test application from within Visual Basic, you can see the `Hyperlink` object in action. Running the test application brings up a standard Visual Basic application. If you enter an answer and click on the results control, the number of correct responses comes up. Then, if you select the link that appears in the results control, you will automatically link to the Internet. Even though you're working with a Visual Basic form, Windows 95 will call up your browser and make the connection for you. Likewise, if you're running the application as an ActiveX document already within Internet Explorer, the connection to the DoubleBlaze site will be made. Figure 20.7 shows the test application at runtime.

Now, when the user clicks on the DoubleBlaze link, Internet Explorer is brought up and the Web site shown in Figure 20.8 appears.

Figure 20.7.

The test application at runtime.

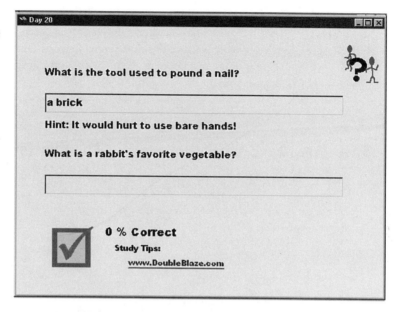

Figure 20.8.

The DoubleBlaze Web site that appears as a result of the NavigateTo *method.*

NOTE
If the DoubleBlaze site looks different from what you see in the figure, it's probably because I've made some updates to the site. The point here is that you can get to the best site on the Internet right from within your ActiveX control!

The `GoForward` and `GoBackward` Methods

The next two useful methods are the `GoForward` and `GoBackward` methods. They can be called the same way the `NavigateTo` method is called, except that in this case, they don't require any parameters. These two methods simply navigate the history stack of the browser. The syntax for the `GoForward` method is

```
UserControl.Hyperlink.GoForward
```

and for the `GoBackward` method is

```
UserControl.Hyperlink.GoBackward
```

If the user is at the end of the history stack, the `GoForward` method will fail and return an error. The same will happen when using `GoBackward` if you're at the beginning of the history stack. Suppose, for example, that you have loaded pages A, B, C, and D into the browser. You're currently viewing page D. All four pages are in the history stack for this browser session. If you execute the `GoForward` method at the end of the history stack, the browser will raise an error and stay at page D. If you use `GoBackward`, however, the browser will move to pages C, B, and A. Then `GoBackward` will raise an error if you try to keep moving backward. Page A will remain in the browser. You should make sure to use error handling in the procedure where you call these methods so that your program can gracefully recover from such an error. For example, you might enter the code as

```
On Error Resume Next
UserControl.Hyperlink.GoForward
```

so that if an error occurs, the program will continue forward without raising an ugly error on the user.

Downloading Files with the `UserControl` Object

Another useful capability you get with the `UserControl` object is the ability to download files from the Internet while the control is running. This capability is referred to as asynchronous downloading. First, I'll discuss a bit about what this term means to you. Then, I'll show you how to take advantage of this useful capability in your ActiveX controls.

What Is Asynchronous Downloading?

The term *asynchronous downloading* simply means that you can download a file from the Internet and you don't have to stop and wait for the file to come in. In other words, you can start the download and then go merrily on your way, executing other code and letting the information come in. When it's arrived, Visual Basic triggers an event that lets you do something with the data that has come in.

The advantage of this capability is quite apparent if you try to download a bitmap that takes 10 minutes to get. If the control was locked up while that bitmap was being downloaded, your user would probably think the application locked up and would most likely shut off the computer in frustration. With asynchronous downloading, however, the user can continue to use the application and the control. When the file arrives, the control will take the appropriate action. Also keep in mind that the term *download* does not necessarily mean you have to get the data from the Internet. You could just as easily specify a file on the local hard drive and load it without even going out to the Internet. How do you put asynchronous downloading in your control? The following sections outline the steps you need to take to carry this out.

Step 1: Calling the AsyncRead Method

The first step is to place a call to the AsyncRead method within your code. The AsyncRead method is part of the UserControl object, so you can call it from anywhere within your control code. The purpose of this method is to initiate the download of a file. The syntax for AsyncRead is

```
UserControl.AsyncRead Target, AsyncType [, PropertyName]
```

where *Target* is the URL or file that you want to download and *AsyncType* is an integer value that tells Visual Basic how the file being downloaded is to be represented. *AsyncType* can be set to the values shown in Table 20.1.

Table 20.1. Possible values for AsyncType.

Setting	Description
vbAsyncTypeFile	The incoming data is placed into a file that Visual Basic creates.
vbAsyncTypeByteArray	The data to be retrieved is provided as a byte array. It is assumed that the control author will know how to handle the data.
vbAsyncTypePicture	The data to be retrieved is a picture file of some sort.

20

If you want to download a file such as a picture from the Internet, use the vbAsyncTypePicture value. If you are downloading a file such as an executable or a compressed file, use the vbAsyncTypeFile constant. For any other data that you're downloading, you can use the vbAsyncTypeByteArray, which simply means "pass a big chunk of data to the control." If you use this constant, you must know how to handle the data. Perhaps you are storing the data in an array or some other structure. This constant is therefore used when you don't have a simple picture or file to download.

The third parameter, PropertyName, is optional. This parameter can be set to tag the download with a name so that when the data arrives, you can determine where to send it. Because any incoming data triggers an event called AsyncReadComplete, you must be able to keep track of where the data is coming from. You'll see how this is used in a moment. Remember that PropertyName has nothing to do with any of the properties of the UserControl object. Think of this value as a tag, or label, you can use to keep track of a number of simultaneous downloads.

To see how this is carried out, let's create a new method in the question control called GetPictureFromURL. This method will allow the user to specify a URL that loads a picture into the background of the picture control. To bring this method into existence, add the procedure shown in Listing 20.5 to the UserControl object.

Listing 20.5. Adding the GetPictureFromURL method to the question control.

```
1: Public Sub GetPictureFromURL(URL As String)
2:     On Error Resume Next
3:     ' Only perform the download if the URL is not empty.
4:     If URL <> "" Then
5:         UserControl.AsyncRead URL, vbAsyncTypePicture, GetPictureFromURL
6:     End IF
7: End Sub
```

Now when the test application calls the GetPictureFromURL method, passing in a valid filename or Internet reference to a picture file, the download will begin. Notice that the method checks to make sure that a valid string has been passed in for the URL address.

Step 2: Responding to the AsyncReadComplete Event

When the download request completes, the AsyncReadComplete event is called. Therefore, the next step is to write code within the AsyncReadComplete event that does something with the data that arrives. This is where the PropertyName comes in handy. Add the code shown in Listing 20.6 to the AsyncReadComplete event as shown.

Listing 20.6. Adding the `GetPictureFromURL` method to the question control.

```
 1: Private Sub UserControl_AsyncReadComplete(AsyncProp As AsyncProperty)
 2:
 3:     On Error Resume Next
 4:
 5:     Select Case AsyncProp.PropertyName
 6:
 7:         Case "GetPictureFromURL"
 8:             Set Picture = AsyncProp.Value
 9:             Debug.Print "Picture has arrived!"
10:
11:     End Select
12:
13: End Sub
```

This event passes in a special object called `AsyncProp`. This object contains three values: `AsyncType`, `PropertyName`, and `Value`. `AsyncType` indicates the type of data coming in. `PropertyName` is the tag you used to indicate the download in the statement

`UserControl.AsyncRead URL, vbAsyncTypePicture, GetPictureFromURL`

that initiated the download, in this case `GetPictureFromURL`. `Value` is the actual data itself. That's why this event checks the *PropertyName* value of the `AsyncProp` object and, if it is equal to `GetPictureFromURL`, it takes the `Value` property, which contains the actual data, and passes it along to the `Picture` property of `UserControl`. The `Select Case` statement is used so that if more than one download takes place, you can continue to add `Case` statements into the procedure to handle all the different types of data that come down the pike.

It's very important to place error-handling code in this event because the download process may have been stopped by some error. When the download is stopped, `AsyncReadComplete` is still called, but when you try to access the `Value` property, the error rears its ugly head. To avoid this problem, you can place error-handling code in the procedure to either respond to errors or just pass them by. The procedure shown in Listing 20.6 simply fails to process the download if some sort of error occurs.

Now close the question control and switch over to the test application. Add a button to the form with the caption Get Picture. Name the command button `cmdDownload`. Add the following code to the `Click` event of `cmdDownload`:

`ucDay20Question1.GetPictureFromURL App.Path & "\leafbg.jpg"`

This statement loads a picture found in the subdirectory on the CD-ROM for this lesson. You can actually use any picture you want to here. Go ahead and run the application. When the form appears, click on the Get Picture button and wait for the picture to load. When you

20

see the text Picture has arrived! in the debug window, click back on the first control and observe the bitmap that now appears in the control.

You can also specify a file from the Internet if you know its location. For instance, you can specify the URL of a Web site that contains a picture and include that picture in the URL address.

Canceling an Asynchronous Download

If, for some reason, you want to cancel an asynchronous download while it's in progress, there's an easy way to do so. You simply call the UserControl object method CancelAsyncRead and pass along with it the property name of the download to only stop the one you want. CancelAsyncRead uses the following syntax:

```
UserControl.CancelAsyncRead [PropertyName]
```

If you leave off the property name, the last download invoked without a property name will be canceled. As a rule, it's a good idea to always assign a property name to each of your downloads, even if there's only one. That way, when you complete the download or cancel it, you can easily see what's being canceled or received in your code. When you cancel a particular download, all the other download requests will continue as normal unless an error occurs, the user terminates the application, or the requests are canceled one by one.

Summary

ActiveX controls are useful in a variety of environments, not the least of which is the Internet. You can use ActiveX controls within a Web browser in many ways. The two most common ways are to use ActiveX controls in a traditional HTML document or to create an ActiveX document and use the controls in that document. In both cases, the control appears in a Web page. In the case of the HTML document, however, the user must specify the initial property values using <PARAM> tags in the object definition. With an ActiveX document, on the other hand, the developer has as much flexibility in coding techniques as he does when creating a standard Visual Basic form.

ActiveX controls created with Visual Basic can take advantage of the Internet in many ways. You can use the NavigateTo, MoveForward, and MoveBackward methods of the Hyperlink object to bring up various Web pages in a browser. This is a useful technique whenever you want to provide an application that uses your control access to the Internet. It gives you the ability to provide links within your controls that hook up to addresses on the Internet. In the case of the question control discussed throughout this book, it's a great way to provide more information on particular questions the user must answer.

20

Another useful feature you can implement in your controls is the ability to do asynchronous downloads of data using the `UserControl` object's `AsyncRead` method and `AsyncReadComplete` event. Asynchronous downloading enables you to load data files such as pictures into a control while the computer is doing other things. When the appropriate file is downloaded, you can then tell the control what to do with the file. This technique is very useful for cases when you want to download information for the user without halting the program within which the control is being run.

Above all, you must remember that ActiveX controls can behave differently, depending on the container in which they are placed. In today's lesson, the question, results, and TimKeithHelp controls were all used within ActiveX documents as well as in HTML documents. You need to make sure you include lots of error handling in all your code to handle the unexpected, and you should certainly test as much as possible in all the environments you are targeting your control to be used within.

Q&A

Q Why do ActiveX controls behave so much differently in different containers?

A The reason controls react differently in different containers is that the designers of each container handle ActiveX controls differently. Some containers aren't even able to recognize ActiveX controls, while others recognize and support them extensively. Netscape Navigator 3.0, for instance, is incapable of recognizing ActiveX controls, while Internet Explorer most certainly recognizes them. Visual Basic is perhaps one of the best containers for an ActiveX control, but Borland Delphi will also work with ActiveX controls. The simple reality is that the technology is very new and belongs to Microsoft. Some companies haven't decided to support ActiveX controls, and even the various Microsoft containers handle them differently. It is hoped that, as this technology matures, results will be more consistent across containers.

Q What's the advantage of using an ActiveX document to host my control versus regular old HTML?

A Well, there are advantages and disadvantages. One of the biggest advantages is that you can develop an application using all the design-time editing tools you've come to expect when creating forms. Then, when you're ready to put it on the Internet, you don't have to mess around with static HTML. The downside is that not all browsers support ActiveX documents, so you're restricting the usability of your application. Then again, Netscape 3.0 doesn't support ActiveX controls at all yet, so you face that limitation either way.

20

Q **Controls that work just great on a form are riddled with errors and problems when I bring them over to Web pages. What's the problem?**

A You're one of many who have stumbled into this roadblock. You'll find a great many differences between forms and Internet containers such as Internet Explorer. To keep your head straight, use the testing and debugging techniques outlined for you on Days 13 through 16. And remember that no two containers are guaranteed to behave the same way every time. Only testing and experimentation can weed out the difficulties.

Workshop

You've learned quite a bit about various features you can add to controls to make them work on the Internet. Go through the current list of properties, methods, and events of the question control. Would it be possible to design a Web site that could supply an endless list of questions and answers as the control requests them? How would you go about designing a control for such a Web site, and how would you lay out the Web site? Give some thought to these issues because you might find yourself building controls that can tie into Web sites quite heavily. This capability makes ActiveX controls very powerful; they can leverage the power and capabilities of the entire Internet!

Quiz

 NOTE
See Appendix D, "Answers to Quiz Questions," for the answer to this question.

Bring up the UserDocument object used to test the controls in this chapter. Add a command button labeled Load Picture and invoke the question control's GetPictureFromURL method in the Click event of the command button. Place a text control on the ActiveX document that lets the user enter his own file path or address for the picture.

20

Day **21**

Licensing, Distribution, and Security

Some of the most important issues to a control author do not even involve the technical implementation of the control. They involve the support issues of licensing, distribution, and security. If you do not have an adequate means of licensing a control, your entire motivation for creating it in the first place may be undermined. If you can't effectively distribute it to the users who need it, it does little good. Suppose you surmount these issues. You're still not out of the woods. A distributed control with improper security may be worse than never having distributed the control in the first place.

Problems of how to safely distribute and manage controls continue to be addressed by the industry. By now your head may be spinning as you contemplate how to proceed. Don't worry, though. You'll find guidance on these issues in today's lesson. These issues have been saved for the final lesson in this book so that you can approach them with a well-versed control-creation background. Some initial solutions are largely in place today, ranging from the Microsoft licensing scheme to the handy Setup Wizard to code signing. You will learn about these today. However, more developments are likely to occur as the pace of control development in general and Internet control distribution in particular quicken. Look at the material today as a good starting point.

Licensing

Licensing is a way you can protect design-time rights to your control. Once you create the control, you may wish to restrict access to who can develop applications with it. The primary reason for this is commercial motivations, of course. It is hard to sell something to someone if he can get it for free. You would have a hard time selling a control to a developer who could just lift the OCX file off a page on the World Wide Web for free and dive into development with it.

Licensing really addresses this problem on two levels. First of all, a license is required to use the control in design time, so the logistics of an integrator incorporating an unauthorized version of your control become more complicated. Second, the mere fact that you provide the control as a licensed control in effect stakes your claims to it. This is a clear sign to integrators that you do not intend for the control to be freely distributed for design purposes. Much of the control kidnapping that goes on is not malevolent in nature. Integrators simply stumble across controls and don't know any better than to share them willy-nilly. But when an integrator receives a clear signal like a license requirement, he knows he is crossing ethical boundaries if he helps others use your control without a license. He is less likely to share your control with his Great Aunt Edna for the pages she is designing. Instead, he will send Aunt Edna to you to purchase the control directly from you.

There is often confusion about a couple aspects of control licensing. The first is whether you have to do it at all. If you are not worried about others freely designing applications around your control, you don't need licensing. Licensing is intended, in the words of Microsoft, to "protect your investment" in your control. Many developers are control philanthropists and gladly share their controls with no restrictions. If you are in this noble category, accept thanks on behalf of control users everywhere. *Don't* skip over the rest of this section, though. Even if you won't license controls yourself, you are likely to run into licensed controls and may find the information that follows helpful.

Another point of confusion is over whether licensing controls affects the end user of applications or Web pages that use the controls. The answer is no. End users typically do not need to purchase licenses to use an application that uses a control. And the licensing technology does not require that they do. The industry model is that end users have free access to controls that support an application or a Web page. Developers who build those applications or Web pages must obtain a legal copy of the control to enable their development. Keep in mind that this is based on human convention. Could you demand every end user to purchase your control if they use an application that incorporates it? I don't recommend it, and will provide the standard jack-of-all-trades disclaimer. This section only talks about the technical realities and conventions of licensing. Consult with your lawyer (or your Great Aunt Edna) for an official interpretation of any legalities relating to control distribution.

Okay, now let's talk specifics. When you build an application in Visual Basic, you can specify that a license is required. Select Project | Properties from the Visual Basic menu to make this specification. The Project Properties dialog will appear, as shown in Figure 21.1. In the bottom-left corner is a Require License Key checkbox. Check the box and click OK to close the dialog. The ease of Visual Basic control development pays off again. Now you are ready to produce a licensed control. Generate the OCX for the control. Inspect the directory where the OCX was generated, and you'll notice a new file. A .vbl file has been generated. This contains license information.

Figure 21.1.

Specifying that a control project requires a license.

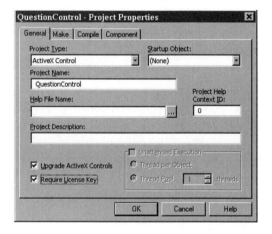

Now the next time you run the Setup Wizard, this information will be automatically used in generating the setup for your control. When an integrator obtains your control setup program and installs your control, the setup program will install the license key for him as well. The license key is stored as an entry in the integrator's Windows 95 System Registry. This allows the integrator to work with your control in the development environment. If an integrator tried to reference your OCX file in Visual Basic without the license key entry, he would get an error message and be unable to use the OCX.

When an integrator adds your control to an application, the license key is copied from the Registry and built directly into the application that uses it. The setup program for the application will not register the license key for the controls it incorporates. However, it will install the application and the required OCX files.

21

Consider what happens when that application is installed on the end user's system. The application and the OCX it requires are placed on the user's system. The end user can run that application directly. The control still requires license validation, but that license information is now available directly in the application itself. There is no need to extract the information from the System Registry since the key is right in the .EXE of the application. However, if the end user brings up Visual Basic and tries to reference the OCX file to design a new application around it, he will fail. Visual Basic will check the System Registry and find that there is not a license key entry for design-time use of the OCX.

Some special rules apply for non–Visual Basic applications. What if your aggregate control uses a licensed constituent control that someone else made? Then your setup program for the control will need to pass on the license information for both controls to integrators that install it. Both keys will be registered on the integrator's system when your control is installed. This means that you are redistributing licensed work of another developer. You will have to gain his permission (and likely pay him a royalty for each control so distributed). Another means to ensure that you have respected the license of his control is to require that every installer of your control also have purchased and installed the developer's separate control product. The best approach is to check with that control developer directly on the requirements for distribution to use.

The Microsoft controls are an exception to this policy. Most have special licensing that allows you to redistribute them as constituent controls of your aggregate controls. You can do this as long as you have enhanced the function of the Microsoft controls for your own purposes and don't just try to repackage the Microsoft work. In other words, Microsoft might not look very kindly on it if a Keith and Tim's Label Control product suddenly hit the market and consisted only of a direct repackaging of the Visual Basic label control. But a Keith and Tim's Question Control product that included the label control would be fine. These restrictions are spelled out in the licensing agreement that comes with Visual Basic. (Check with your lawyer or Great Aunt Edna if you need help interpreting it.) The one exception to this is the DBGrid control. That control does require a license to redistribute.

The license model is a little different for Microsoft Office and browser applications. Microsoft Office requires that you have a design-time license for each control added to a document. When you compose an Internet Web page, you must also have the license available. You provide a license reference in the page itself when you declare the object.

The license reference refers to a license package file. You must create this license package file before you distribute the control. You can use LPK_TOOL.EXE, which comes in the Visual Basic Tools\LPK_TOOL directory. Once you have created this file, any Web page that wants to incorporate your control can simply reference it. For example, Listing 21.1 shows the HTML object references to the question and results control that refer to the license pack.

Listing 21.1. HTML object declarations that reference the control license pack.

```
 1:<HTML>
 2.<OBJECT ID="ucQuestion" WIDTH=572 HEIGHT=146
 3: CLASSID="CLSID:B7D6D241-9F30-11D0-B9C1-0080C82BD9D5"
 4: CODEBASE="Question.CAB#version=1,0,0,28">
 5: <PARAM NAME="LPKPath" VALUE="LPKfilename.LPK">
 6: </OBJECT>
 7: <OBJECT ID="ucResults" WIDTH=349 HEIGHT=104
 8: CLASSID="CLSID:B7D6D247-9F30-11D0-B9C1-0080C82BD9D5"
 9: CODEBASE="Question.CAB#version=1,0,0,28">
10: <PARAM NAME="LPKPath" VALUE="LPKfilename.LPK">
11: </OBJECT>
12. <!… more HTML lines … ->
13: </HTML>
```

Security

Several aspects of security must be considered when you design and distribute a control. The Internet imposes many of these considerations. Controls are shared over the Web on a more widespread basis than ever. Web page viewers encounter new pages every time they browse the Web. These pages can contain new controls that will execute on their PCs when the page is loaded in the browser. Several security precautions are provided to help users browse the Web without undue risk from controls. You need to understand these user-level precautions in order to understand the issues that affect your control distribution.

Browser Safety Levels

First and foremost as a user-level security option is the browser safety-level option of the Microsoft Internet Explorer. You can select the View|Options menu choice, go to the Security tab, and select the Safety Level button to bring up a dialog of available security levels. You can see this dialog in Figure 21.2.

If you select the high level of content, you will get a warning whenever you try to view a page that contains an unsigned ActiveX control and you will not be able to view it. In the words of the browser dialog, "You are protected from all security problems. Potentially unsafe content is avoided, and you are notified [of unsafe content]."

Potentially unsafe content is any control that is not signed. Control signing is the process of embedding digital identification in a control so that it can be tracked back to you, the developer. This does not guarantee that your control will not cause damage, intentionally or inadvertently, to someone's system. It does imply a higher level of accountability to the end

21

user than a control that has no such signing, however. Consider the analogy of purchasing a new computer to put this into perspective. Who would you rather buy a new computer from? the company down the street that has a clear sign on its business and an address where you can contact it if problems occur? or the shady anonymous character lurking in a dark alley who says "Pssst...I can give you a Pentium 200 real cheap...but don't ask my name"? Identification and traceability implies a certain level of trust with controls just as it does with computer purchases. Control signing is considered in the next section.

Figure 21.2.

Browser security levels.

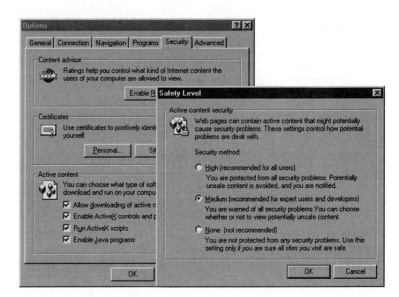

When your security options are on the high setting and the browser encounters a page with an unsigned control, you will not be able to view it at all, even after you get the warning message telling you the control is present. To view it, you would have to downshift to medium security and revisit the page.

With the medium level of security, you will get a warning about unsafe controls that you can override to view the controls, if desired. Once you see the warning that an unsigned control exists on the page, you can still view the page if you so choose. If you're really impatient with error messages, you could downshift your security even lower, to the none threshold.

The none level of security will let you view anything on any page you come across, with no restrictions. You will not even get warnings before unsigned controls are displayed. You could stumble across a page that contains an unsigned control written by the College Hackers, Virus Spreaders, and Evildoers of America. This page and its control would be loaded with no warning to you, and the control could proceed to reformat your hard drive as you stand helplessly by.

You can see now why control signing is significant to the end user. If you attempt to distribute unsigned controls, you may lock yourself out of a significant integrator and end user market.

Marking Your Control As Safe

Before moving on to the steps necessary to obtain a digital signature, first consider the more easily implemented aspect of control identification—safety markings. When you distribute a control on the Internet, you can mark it as safe for scripting and safe for initialization. These are judgments that you make as the developer of the control. This might sound a little bit like asking a used car salesman if his car runs smoothly. To a certain extent, it is true that this may be a biased judgment since it comes from developers. However, Microsoft offers some fairly clear suggestions to guide developers in marking their controls. A *script* is a program the Web page developer can write to run in a host environment and interact with various objects, including controls. A control is considered unsafe for scripting if it exposes any properties or methods that can be used from a script to alter the system state. The following are specific no-nos:

Allowing the script to specify the name for a file to read or write
Allowing the script to specify the key to read or write Registry information
Allowing a Windows API to be carried out based on script settings
Controlling other objects such as a Word document with class IDs supplied by the script

The results control created on Day 18, "Multiple Controls, Control Communication, and Advanced Features," violates the first guideline because the integrator can specify a property where the results file is written. Consider the code in Listing 21.2.

Listing 21.2. Code that writes to a file from a control.

```
 1: Public Sub ProcessResults()
 2: ' Process results of all question controls on page
 3:
 4:     ' Directory that results file is written to.
 5:     '     Results are only stored to this
 6:     '     directory to prevent security problems.
 7:     '     For example, if this control is included in a
 8:     '     web page on the Internet you don't want to
 9:     '     let the host app specify that the results can
10:     '     go to C:\autoexec.bat.  By restricting the
11:     '     results file to a given directory, you remove
12:     '     potential for malicious behavior.
13:     Const RESULTS_DIR = "C:\Questions\"
14:
15:     ' Counter to loop through control collection
16:     Dim intLoop As Integer
17:
```

continues

Listing 21.2. continued

```
18:    ' Temp string used to extract control type
19:    Dim vsCtlType As String
20:
21:    ' Counter variables used to tally correct and total questions
22:    Dim intCorrect As Integer
23:    Dim intTotal As Integer
24:
25:    ' Contains file id for results file
26:    Dim intFileID As Integer
27:
28:    ' Generate results file if specified in property setting
29:    If Me.ResultsFile <> "" Then
30:        If (Dir(RESULTS_DIR) = "") Then
31:            MkDir RESULTS_DIR
32:        End If
33:        intFileID = FreeFile
34:        Open RESULTS_DIR & Me.ResultsFile For Output Lock Read Write _
35:            As intFileID
36:        Print #intFileID, "Test Results for " & UserControl.Parent.Name & _
37:            " generated on " & Date; " " & Time
38:        Print #intFileID, " "
39:    End If
40:
41:    ' Examine every control in the host container
42:    For intLoop = 0 To UserControl.ParentControls.Count - 1
43:
44:        ' See if this is a question control based on type.
45:        '  Look for any type matching "uc*Question", since different
46:        '  versions have different Day descriptors to distinguish lessons
47:        vsCtlType = TypeName(UserControl.ParentControls.Item(intLoop))
48:        If vsCtlType Like "uc*Question" Then
49:
50:            With UserControl.ParentControls.Item(intLoop)
51:
52:                ' Tally the total questions reviewed and number correct
53:                intTotal = intTotal + 1
54:                If .Correct Then
55:                    intCorrect = intCorrect + 1
56:                End If
57:
58:                ' Lock the questions from further interaction if specified
59:                '   as an option
60:                If Me.LockAnswers = True Then
61:                    .Enabled = False
62:                End If
63:
64:                ' Generate results file if specified in property setting
65:                If Me.ResultsFile <> "" Then
66:                    Print #intFileID, String(40, "-")
67:                    Print #intFileID, "Question #" & intTotal & " _
68:                        (Question Control id=" & .Name & ")"
69:                    Print #intFileID, "  Question: "; .Question
70:                    Print #intFileID, "  User Answer: "; .UserAnswer
```

```
 71:                         Print #intFileID, "  Expected Answer: "_
 72:                         ;.ExpectedAnswer
 73:                         If .Correct Then
 74:                             Print #intFileID, "  Correct! ";
 75:                         Else
 76:                             Print #intFileID, "  Incorrect. ";
 77:                         End If
 78:                         Print #intFileID, "Cumulative Score = " & _
 79:                             Int((intCorrect / intTotal) * 100) & " Percent"
 80:                     End If
 81:
 82:             End With ' Score this question control
 83:
 84:         End If ' Check if control is a question control
 85:
 86:     Next ' Process each control on host container
 87:
 88:     ' Close results file if needed
 89:     If Me.ResultsFile <> "" Then
 90:         Close #intFileID
 91:     End If
 92:
 93:     ' Update final score in the control property, show results
 94:     Me.PercentCorrect = Int((intCorrect / intTotal) * 100)
 95:     lblPercent.Caption = Me.PercentCorrect & " % Correct"
 96:     lblPercent.Visible = True
 97:     ' Show user link to more help if provided
 98:     If lblStudyTips.Caption <> "" Then
 99:         lblStudyTips.Visible = True
100:         Line2.X2 = Line2.X1 + lblStudyTips.Width
101:         Line2.Visible = True
102:         lblStudyCaption.Visible = True
103:     End If
104:
105: End Sub
```

The actual implementation used is probably perfectly safe. The file can only be written to the C:\Questions directory, so it would seem that it would have little potential for damage. However, it does fall out of the criteria presented earlier and is probably in a gray area between safe and unsafe for this reason. You, as the control developer, could decide how to mark this control when you distribute it. A good solution might be to modify the code so that the results file always starts with the string results. This would prevent the user from generating an Autoexec.bat file, which is not a good capability to have even if this file is just generated to the Questions directory. The question control can safely be considered safe for scripting since it does not read or write any files or Registry information.

Marking a control as safe for initialization implies that no property setting can be made that will interfere with any system setting, data, file, or Registry entry. The results and question controls that you developed can be considered to fall under this category.

21

Running Internet Setup and Marking the Control

The hard part of control marking is understanding what the criteria are and making a decision based on this. The easy part is actually marking the controls. The Setup Wizard makes this a snap. Start up the Setup Wizard by selecting Programs | Visual Basic 5 | Application Setup Wizard. Specify the question control project file Question.vbp as the name of the project to build on the Select Project and Options dialog. Also specify that this is to be an Internet download setup.

NOTE

SAMPLE Follow along with the examples in this chapter by modifying the QuestionControl.vbg group project file under the Samples\Day21 directory on the book's CD-ROM. This is the final version of the question control and therefore does not have a specific day associated with it.

Proceed to the Internet Package dialog shown in Figure 21.3. This dialog has an option to indicate whether required runtime components should be downloaded from Microsoft or a different location. The advantage of downloading from Microsoft is that you can generally count on the support components to be there. Otherwise, you have to supply them yourself in another server location.

Figure 21.3.

Specifying safety.

The other action to carry out here is to click the Safety command button. Then you will see the Safety dialog shown in Figure 21.4. The Components listbox shows all the controls in a project. Two controls are listed for the question control project—the results control and the question control. Mark the results control as safe for initialization but not for scripting since it can write to a local file. Mark the question control as safe for both initialization and scripting.

Figure 21.4.

The Safety dialog.

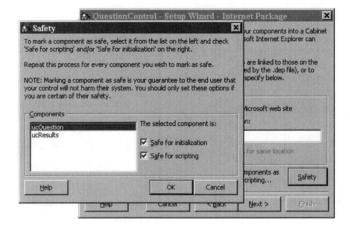

Other Aspects of Internet Setup

When you proceed to the Setup Wizard | Working dialog, activity will take place to process the working files. You will also get a reminder that if you created any property pages, you don't have the property pages DLL in your setup configuration. Since a property page is declared for the question control, respond yes to this prompt.

NOTE

> The Setup Wizard was covered in detail on Day 15, "Preparing Your Control for the Real World," which includes a discussion of inspecting the details behind various files that are included by Visual Basic. You can reach this file information from the File Summary dialog.

When you generate the setup for the question control, you will also see a dialog prompt that asks if you want to install licensing on the end user's system. This dialog can be seen in Figure 21.5. Respond yes to generate a setup that enforces licensing.

The Setup Wizard determines the dependency files that must be shipped with your control. Table 21.1 lists the files that must be included with the question control. This information can be obtained from the Setup Wizard's File Summary dialog.

Table 21.1. Control dependency information.

File	Purpose
MSVBVM50.DLL	VB runtime—Virtual Machine
AsycFilt.DLL	VB runtime—OLE

continues

Table 21.1. continued

File	Purpose
Question.OCX	Your question control OCX file
Question.LIC	The license file needed for Web pages
MSStkPrp.DLL	Question.OCX dependency—properties

Figure 21.5.

The licensing install dialog.

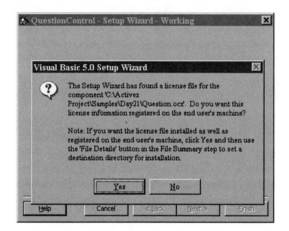

The grand total size of the distribution for the question control is 2MB. 1.3MB of this is from the MSVBVM50.DLL file. This file provides Visual Basic runtime support and is needed even though the question control was generated in native code format. If you knew that all your end users already had the runtime installed on their systems, you could save yourself 1.3MB of space in the distribution. However, unless you are making your control available for a very well-known and limited set of users, this is not a safe assumption to make. You should include all the recommended files with the setup.

The last dialog you see from the Setup Wizard is shown in Figure 21.6. It reminds you to check for viruses before distributing your control more widely. Once your setup is done, a .CAB file is generated in the target directory you specified at the start of the setup session. This is a cabinet file that contains information about the files to be installed. This serves as the starting point for the Internet distribution. Now your control is ready to distribute.

Code Signing

So far the distribution steps you have seen could be carried out within the Visual Basic environment. Code signing, however, is not something you can do within Visual Basic. You must obtain a certificate from a certification authority in order to proceed with code signing.

21

Perhaps the best known Certificate Authority is VeriSign. The VeriSign Web site is at `http://digitalid.verisign.com/codesign.htm`; you can go there to make arrangements with them to certify one of your controls.

Figure 21.6.

The virus reminder dialog.

You can seek one of two kinds of certificates. A Class 2 certificate is intended for individuals and costs only $20 per year. The following is the information you must supply to get a Class 2 license:

Name
Address
E-mail address
Birthdate
SSN

A Class 3 certificate, on the other hand, is intended for commercial software producers. The following is the information you need to provide to get this level of certificate:

Company name
Company location
Company contacts

What happens after you get your certificate? Then you are ready to embed the digital ID you get with it into your control. There are tools in the ActiveX SDK that you can use for this purpose. You will receive two important pieces of information: a private key and a public key. These keys are your digital identification. Run a utility program that embeds the private key in the control. Then this can be used in conjunction with the public key to form a unique identification for the control. Once you have embedded the information, you can run the Setup Wizard to create a setup for your signed control.

Now whenever the control is downloaded, the browser will cause a check to occur. This check will ensure that the content is exactly the same as when it was first produced. This action is carried out transparently by the browser. What does this check buy you as a user of controls? You know the control hasn't been tampered with. You also know that you are using the

21

certified control from whichever company provided it. Traceability back to the control owner will be available. A signed control is the professional way to go when you distribute controls. Then you are doing all you can to assure the user of your control that it is safe and backed by someone who can be held accountable.

Summary

The way you distribute your control and approach safety, security, and licensing concerns can ultimately be as important to its success or failure as the code behind it. Security issues for controls take on a special concern because of the Internet distribution that's possible. Someone browsing the World Wide Web might link to a page that contains an unknown control. The browser provides various forms of protection against such controls. One level of protection is digital signing. You can obtain a certificate for your control from a certified certificate authority. This certificate provides you with a digital identification that can be embedded in your control. Then the Internet Explorer browser can automatically identify your control and verify that it has not changed since you released it.

The browser also has various security levels the user can choose that block out controls altogether or allow only controls that are explicitly approved. When you distribute your control, you can mark it as safe for scripting or safe for initialization. The browser can also screen controls based on this criteria. Your control could still provide the means for a malicious script creator to harm an end user's system no matter how carefully the code is signed and marked if you do not carefully consider its feature set. For example, features like methods to save data to a file should be implemented in a way that prevents the user from overwriting other data on the system. If it is not practical to implement your controls in a safety-first manner, you should include documentation that clearly outlines any risk areas.

Another issue of concern to many control developers is how to avoid having controls freely distributed and lifted into other development projects. Visual Basic provides a licensing scheme that addresses this problem. You can specify that a development-time license is required when you create a control. The setup program for your control will register the license on the systems of those that install your program. This allows them to use it in Visual Basic and design applications around it. Then they can freely distribute your control with their applications, but only a runtime license is included. Their end users will not be able to design applications around the control. Even Web pages can include a license reference. The license enforcement is somewhat less secure, but still reinforces the message to the development community that a control should not be freely integrated into other development projects.

Distribution of controls is made easy by the Visual Basic Setup Wizard. This application steps you through the generation of setup programs. It automatically carries out the most challenging aspects of generating a setup in response to your direction. It even pulls together the list of all the dependency files that must be distributed with your application. And you will have dependency files. Even a control compiled with the Visual Basic Native Code option still requires runtime support files. You will have an installation program that installs all needed files and registers your control on the end user's system once you have generated the setup program. Then your control will be ready for the world.

Q&A

Q **Can users on the World Wide Web view pages that incorporate my control even if it has not been digitally signed?**

A Yes, if they set their browser security options to the No Security level. Then they can use their controls through the browsers. They will be at increased risk of security breaches as long as they use their browsers in this mode.

Q **If I license my control, does it prevent someone from shipping an application that uses the control without my permission?**

A No. Licensing encourages integrators of host applications to have licensed versions of your control on their systems at design time. Once they build host applications around your control, they can freely distribute those applications and your control. This is the industry-standard model. Typically you would retain rights to a control used to design applications. Then free distribution of that control will be allowed when it is distributed with the applications that use it.

Q **In the preceding answer the phrase "Licensing encourages..." was used. Doesn't licensing completely enforce integrators to have a licensed version of the control rather than just encourage it?**

A The licensing scheme is a good one, but there are ways that it can be circumvented. It should meet the needs of most developers since it clearly sends the message to integrators that you do not intend your control to be freely distributed for design purposes. However, you should realize that it is not completely tamper proof if this is an area of special concern to you.

Q **I don't plan to make any money from my control or restrict usage in any way. Is there any reason I should worry about licensing?**

A There are easy answers to some questions. No! Licensing doesn't buy you anything if you have no desire to restrict the free flow of your control for design purposes.

Q **I never plan for my control to be used outside of Visual Basic applications. Do I need to worry about any of this stuff?**

A For the short term, perhaps not, but for the long term, definitely. You never know where a control might end up. Perhaps some other user of it will decide to try to integrate it into his Web page. Furthermore, the line between traditional Visual

21

Basic applications and the Internet is already becoming blurred. A Visual Basic application can be easily converted to a Visual Basic ActiveX document that can be distributed over the Web. Upcoming releases of Windows 95 will further blur the distinction between the user's desktop and the Internet. Given these factors, you should assume that any control you make could end up as a World Wide Web citizen if you want to be a responsible developer.

Q Yikes! I have no clue which Visual Basic support files are needed by my control. Bill Gates isn't returning my calls. What do I do?

A Never fear, the handy-dandy Setup Wizard stands ready to assist you. The wizard will automatically identify your dependency files and even summarizes this information for you on a wizard dialog. The only dependencies the wizard can't help with are if you are redistributing a third-party control that did not include an appropriately structured dependency list. But the wizard will automatically figure out everything it needs to know as far as appropriately structured controls and the Visual Basic support files themselves.

Workshop

Fire up the Microsoft Internet Explorer browser. You can obtain it from the www.microsoft.com site if you do not already have it. Select View|Options from the menu. Then select the Security tab and the Safety Level command button on this tab. You will reach the dialog that lets you specify High, Medium, or None for security. Alternate between each of these options in turn, and browse safe sites on the Web with each option in effect. *Be aware that you do this at your own risk.* You are vulnerable to malicious behavior of software you may encounter on the Web when you have lower security options in effect. Be careful not to explore any unknown sites with lowered security options. Check out various known safe sites such as www.DoubleBlaze.com, www.microsoft.com, and www.tmn.com/~asad. Observe what kind of security notices or restrictions you run into with each level of security. Can you fully appreciate a site with high security in effect? Be sure to change your security options back to their original settings when you're done.

21

Quiz

NOTE

See Appendix D, "Answers to Quiz Questions," for the answer to this question.

Examine the following code:

```
' This code called in response to a user SaveGraphData method
    intFileID = FreeFile
    ' Use the control's DataPath property to save the file
    Open me.DataPath For Output Lock Read Write As intFileID
    Print #intFileID, "Data saved on " & Date; " " & Time
    For intLoop = 0 To MAXPOINTS - 1
        ' Write the data points
        Print #intFileID, DataArray(intLoop)
    Next
    Close #intFileID
```

Assume that it is part of a graph control. Assess whether it poses any security risk if provided as a component for World Wide Web pages.

21

In Review

This week has introduced a wide range of advanced issues. These issues include not only advanced features you can add to your controls, but ways of targeting controls for various environments, such as the Internet and client/server applications. But you not only learned about new techniques; you also learned many important concepts that apply to the entire process of designing a control. After all, learning how to debug, test, and support an ActiveX control in a multitude of environments is just as important as learning how to implement a property, a method, or an event. This week, therefore, helped to round out what you need to know in order to design controls that are easy to use and easy to install, and that work exactly the way you intend them to. Congratulations! You have now gained a state-of-the-art, fundamental knowledge of what ActiveX controls are and how to create them.

Where You Have Been

You learned quite a few of the more advanced features of ActiveX controls this week. Day 17 introduced you to controls that can be bound to databases. Then on Day 18 you learned how to create controls that are invisible at runtime or must be painted on the screen in a special way. You also learned how to create aggregate and subclassed controls on Day 19. Day 20 gave you a great deal of helpful advice and new techniques for building controls for the Internet. You wrapped up the week with an informative discussion on control security, distribution, and licensing. You are now ready to create your own ActiveX controls! With all the techniques and strategies you've learned about throughout this book, you can fully and effectively use this new capability Visual Basic provides. Before Visual Basic made it so easy to create ActiveX controls, it was up to the C++ gurus to build them. This long, tedious process made it almost impossible to create the controls you can now create with just a few hours of work. ActiveX controls will likely become more and more powerful as new capabilities are added. Now that you've read this book, you'll be able to keep up with these ever-changing technologies and stay ahead of the pack. Whatever you do, don't stop learning. And remember that experience is definitely the best teacher.

Question Control Interfaces

The question control is used as a sample throughout this book. Its capabilities are incrementally expanded from day to day as new concepts are introduced. A comprehensive summary of all the properties, methods, and event interfaces that the question control supports is presented here.

This control is provided with this book for educational purposes only. You are welcome to include it in your own host applications if you keep this in mind and are willing to use it at your own risk. If you integrate it into a host application you will distribute, please indicate "Question Control from DoubleBlaze Software" in your program about box, splash screen, or other viewable area. Since capabilities of the control are progressively expanded throughout the book, be sure to use the Day 21 version of the question control, Day21QuestionControl.ocx, if you are going to integrate it into a host application.

You can verify that you have the latest version of this control by checking the www.DoubleBlaze.com Web site, where any updates to this book and its samples will be posted.

Properties

Table A.1 provides a list of the properties available in the final version of the question control, Day21QuestionControl. It also lists the specific day that each property was introduced.

Table A.1. Question control properties.

Property	Lesson	Description
AnswerColor	Day 5	The color to display the answer text in.
BackStyle	Day 4	Indicates whether the background is transparent or opaque.
BorderStyle	Day 4	Indicates whether the border should be displayed as None or FixedSingle for control.
DisplayFont	Day 4	The characteristics of the display font.
DisplayOnIncorrectResponse	Day 2	Indicates whether the action to take on incorrect response is ucNone, ucHint, or ucAnswer display.
Enabled	Day 4	The boolean indicator if the control is enabled.
EnterCausesTab	Day 2	The boolean indicator if the Enter key should cause focus to shift from this control to the next.
ExpectedAnswer	Day 2	The string that is to be regarded as correct when evaluating an answer.
FocusIndicator	Day 8	The boolean indicator if the control border and background should change to indicate when the control has the focus.
Hint	Day 2	The hint string to display to the user when the DisplayOnIncorrectResponse property is set to ucHint.
IncorrectAnswer	Day 5	An array that stores the incorrect responses of the user.
IncorrectAnswerCount	Day 5	The number of incorrect responses entered so far by the user.

Property	Lesson	Description
IncorrectAnswerIndex	Day 5	The index number of the current incorrect response in the IncorrectAnswer array property.
MaxGuesses	Day 9	The maximum number of responses the user is permitted to supply before the MaxGuessesExceeded event is raised. If this property is set to 0, no limit is in effect and the event is never raised.
Question	Day 2	The question to display to the user.
TabooWords	Day 9	A string specifying all the words that are considered taboo, with a semicolon used to separate words. If this string is not empty, the TabooWordDetected event is raised when a taboo word is found.

Methods

Table A.2 provides a list of the methods available in the final version of the question control, Day21QuestionControl. It also lists the specific day that each method was introduced.

Table A.2. Question control methods.

Method	Lesson	Description
Clear	Day 7	Clears out all the user's incorrect answers stored in the IncorrectAnswer() array property and resets the Incorrect AnswerCount property to 0.
ForceAnswer	Day 7	Displays the answer to the question immediately, overwriting the current response entry.
ShowHint	Day 7	Displays the hint in the hint area.

Events

Table A.3 provides a list of the events available in the final version of the question control, Day21QuestionControl. It also lists the specific day that each event was introduced.

Table A.3. Question control events.

Event	Lesson	Description
MaxGuessesExceeded	Day 9	Raised when the number of incorrect user guesses exceeds the limit specified in the MaxGuesses property.
QuestionClick	Day 8	Raised when the user clicks on the question area.
TabooWordDetected	Day 9	Raised when one of the words specified in the TabooWords property has been detected in the user's question response.
UserQuestionDetected	Day 9	Raised when the user enters a question mark as part of his reply.

APPENDIX

B

Syntax Summary

Visual Basic controls are created using a class module and are built on the same syntax you use for regular Visual Basic programs. Control interfaces are based on properties, methods, and events raised by the control. The general structure for each of these interface types is summarized in this appendix through sample code.

Properties

Properties are introduced on Day 4, "Predefined Control Properties," and Day 5, "User-Defined Control Properties." A Property Let procedure in the control is called when the host application assigns a value to a control property. A sample Property procedure for a property named BackStyle is shown in Listing B.1.

Listing B.1. Property Let **procedure example.**

```
1: Public Property Let BackStyle(ByVal New_BackStyle As BACKSTYLE_SETTINGS)
2:     UserControl.BackStyle() = New_BackStyle
3:     PropertyChanged "BackStyle"
4: End Property
```

The generic form of the syntax is summarized in Listing B.2.

Listing B.2. Property Let **procedure generic syntax.**

```
1: Public Property Let PropertyName(ParameterList)
2:     ' Your code here
3:     PropertyChanged "PropertyName"
4: End Property
```

ANALYSIS Declare your control property as a public property, as shown on line 1. Use Let to specify that it is the procedure called when a value is assigned to that property. Use the PropertyChanged call of line 3 to notify Visual Basic that a property has changed. This enables subsequent property saves at design time.

A Property Set procedure in the control is called when the host application assigns an object reference to a control property. A sample property procedure for a property named DisplayFont is shown in Listing B.3.

Listing B.3. Property Set **procedure example.**

```
 1: Public Property Set DisplayFont(ByVal NewFont As Font)
 2:
 3:     Dim objCtl As Object
 4:
 5:     UserControl.Font = NewFont
 6:
 7:     For Each objCtl In Controls
 8:         objCtl.Font = NewFont
 9:     Next
10:
11:     PropertyChanged "DisplayFont"
12:
13: End Property
```

The generic form of the syntax is summarized in Listing B.4.

Listing B.4. Property Set **procedure generic syntax.**

```
1: Public Property Set PropertyName(ParameterList)
2:     ' Your code here
3:     PropertyChanged "PropertyName"
4: End Property
```

 Declare your control property as a public property, as shown on line 1. Use Set to specify that it is the procedure called when an object reference is assigned to that property. Use the PropertyChanged call of line 3 to notify Visual Basic that a property has changed. This enables subsequent property saves at design time.

A Property Get procedure in the control is called when the host application retrieves a value from a control property. A sample property procedure for a property named BackStyle is shown in Listing B.5.

Listing B.5. Property Get **procedure example.**

```
1: Public Property Get BackStyle() As BACKSTYLE_SETTINGS
2:     BackStyle = UserControl.BackStyle
3: End Property
```

The generic form of the syntax is summarized in Listing B.6.

Listing B.6. Property Get **procedure generic syntax.**

```
1: Public Property Get PropertyName(ParameterList) As type
2:     ' Your code here
3: End Property
```

ANALYSIS Declare your control property as a public property, as shown on line 1. Use Get to specify that it is the procedure called when a value is retrieved from that property.

Methods

Methods are introduced on Day 6, "Predefined Control Methods," and Day 7, "User-Defined Control Methods." A method procedure in the control is called when the host application makes the corresponding call. A sample method procedure for a method named ForceAnswer is shown in Listing B.7.

Listing B.7. A method procedure sample.

```
1: Public Sub ForceAnswer()
2:     txtAnswer.Text = "Answer = " & m_ExpectedAnswer
3: End Sub
```

The generic form of the syntax is summarized in Listing B.8.

Listing B.8. A method procedure generic syntax.

```
1: Public Sub MethodName(ParameterList)
2:     ' Your code here
3: End Sub
```

 Declare your method property as a public property, as shown on line 1.

Events Raised by the Control

Events raised by the control are introduced on Day 8, "Predefined Events," and Day 9, "User-Defined Events." An event routine in a host application is called after the control code raises the corresponding event. A sample event declaration statement for an event named TabooWordDetected is shown in Listing B.9.

Listing B.9. The TabooWordDetected event declaration example.

```
Event TabooWordDetected(svTabooWord As String)
```

The generic form of the syntax is summarized in Listing B.10.

Listing B.10. The TabooWordDetected event declaration generic syntax.

```
Event EventName(ParameterList)
```

 You must declare an event in your control with the event declaration statement before you can raise that event.

A sample statement that raises the event TabooWordDetected is shown in Listing B.11.

Listing B.11. The `TabooWordDetected` `RaiseEvent` **statement example.**

```
RaiseEvent TabooWordDetected(svReplacement)
```

The generic form of the syntax is summarized in Listing B.12.

Listing B.12. The `RaiseEvent` **event declaration generic syntax.**

```
RaiseEvent EventName(ParameterList)
```

 This statement can appear anywhere in your control code. It will raise for the host application the event name you specify in the `RaiseEvent` statement.

APPENDIX

C

Sources of Additional Information

What if you want to dig a little deeper into some of the topics addressed in this book? Here's your starting point! Several sources of additional information on the Web are provided here. Of course, the location of areas on the Web can change with time, so if in doubt, just carry out your own Internet search on the control topic of interest to you. Odds are, you'll find a wealth of information out there.

Book Update Information

Check the Web site with information about this book to see if there are any pertinent changes or updates to the material in this book. You can check `www.DoubleBlaze.com` to see information from the authors themselves. Refer to `www.mcp.com` for the Sams.net Publishing site.

Microsoft Site

Many locations on the Microsoft Web site contain information relevant to control development in Visual Basic. A good place to start is `www.Microsoft.com/vbasic`, the Visual Basic site. From there you can specify a search on `ActiveX`. Another source of information is `www.Microsoft.com/workshop`. View the Programming area for a list of articles related to ActiveX.

VeriSign Site

The `www.Verisign.com` site has information pertaining to digital security.

Full Syntax Rules

Full syntax information on the Visual Basic syntax, including the control-related property, method, and event interfaces, is contained right within your Visual Basic help file. You can highlight any keyword—such as `Event`—in the code window and then select F1 to automatically bring up the syntax description for that keyword.

APPENDIX

D

Answers to Quiz Questions

Day 1

1. `UserControl`
2. methods, events
3. aggregate control

Day 2

1. requirements, user interface
2. `BackColor`, `UserControl`
3. description, default

Day 3

You could take various approaches to implementing this control. For example, you might have named your constituent controls differently. Nevertheless, the overall construction of any solution should be similar. One solution is shown here:

```
 1: Option Explicit
 2: 'Default Property Values:
 3: Const m_def_TaxRate = 0.04
 4: 'Property Variables:
 5: Dim m_TaxRate As Single
 6:
 7: Public Property Get TaxRate() As Single
 8:     TaxRate = m_TaxRate
 9: End Property
10:
11: Public Property Let TaxRate(ByVal New_TaxRate As Single)
12:     m_TaxRate = New_TaxRate
13:     PropertyChanged "TaxRate"
14: End Property
15:
16: ' Apply tax rate after enter is pressed
17: Private Sub txtPrice_KeyPress(KeyAscii As Integer)
18:
19:    If KeyAscii = vbKeyReturn Then
20:         lblTax.Caption = Format(txtPrice.Text * Me.TaxRate, "Currency")
21:         ' Use CSng to treat values as single precision during calculation
22:         lblTotal.Caption = Format(CSng(txtPrice.Text) + _
23:             CSng(lblTax.Caption), "Currency")
24:    End If
25:
26: End Sub
27:
28: 'Initialize Properties for User Control
29: Private Sub UserControl_InitProperties()
30:     m_TaxRate = m_def_TaxRate
31: End Sub
32:
33: 'Load property values from storage
34: Private Sub UserControl_ReadProperties(PropBag As PropertyBag)
35:
36:     m_TaxRate = PropBag.ReadProperty("TaxRate", m_def_TaxRate)
37: End Sub
38:
39: 'Write property values to storage
40: Private Sub UserControl_WriteProperties(PropBag As PropertyBag)
41:
42:     Call PropBag.WriteProperty("TaxRate", m_TaxRate, m_def_TaxRate)
43: End Sub
```

The test form for this solution is shown in Figure D.1.

Figure D.1.

The sales tax control test form.

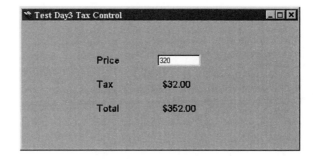

NOTE

SAMPLE The sales tax control solution is included on the CD-ROM under the Samples\Day3\SalesTax directory. You can load the Day3Tax.vbg project into Visual Basic to see the control definition and the test form used.

ANALYSIS The control uses one property, TaxRate. The standard InitProperties, ReadProperties, and WriteProperties property events are included to support this property. The Property Let and Get routines are also present. These handle the storage and retrieval of the property value when the host application uses it. All those routines, and the corresponding variable declarations, were supplied by the ActiveX Control Interface Wizard. The only real custom code needed was for the txtPrice_KeyPress event. This routine is called whenever the end user types a key in the price textbox control. A check is made to see if the end user pressed the Enter key. If so, the assumption is that a price has been supplied. The tax amount is calculated based on the user-supplied price and the current TaxRate property setting. This tax amount is displayed in a label on the control and then added to the original price to derive the grand total. The total is then displayed on a label on the control as well.

Day 4

1. No, you cannot use the name Visible because Visible is a property of the Extender object. If you expose the property with the same name, the user will never get access to it because the Extender object will take precedence.

2. The following is the code:

```
Public Property Get BackColor() As OLE_COLOR
    BackColor = UserControl.BackColor
End Property

Public Property Let BackColor(ByVal vNewColor As OLE_COLOR)
    UserControl.BackColor = vNewColor
    PropertyChanged "BackColor"
End Property
```

3. The following is the code:

```
Public Property Get Feedback() As String
    Feedback = lblFeedback.Caption
End Property

Public Property Let Feedback(ByVal vNewCaption As String)
    lblFeedback.Caption = vNewCaption
    PropertyChanged "Feedback"
End Property
```

Day 5

1. The following is the code:

```
Private Sub UserControl_ReadProperties(PropBag As PropertyBag)

    UserControl.Enabled = PropBag.ReadProperty("Enabled", True)

    UserControl.BackStyle = PropBag.ReadProperty("BackStyle", 0)

    UserControl.BorderStyle = PropBag.ReadProperty("BorderStyle", 0)

    Question = PropBag.ReadProperty("Question", _
                              m_def_Question)

    AnswerColor = PropBag.ReadProperty("AnswerColor", _
                              vbWindowText)

    DisplayOnIncorrectResponse = PropBag.ReadProperty( _
                              "DisplayOnIncorrectResponse", _
                              m_def_DisplayOnIncorrectResponse)

    ExpectedAnswer = PropBag.ReadProperty("ExpectedAnswer", _
                              m_def_ExpectedAnswer)

    Hint = PropBag.ReadProperty("Hint", m_def_Hint)

    m_EnterCausesTab = PropBag.ReadProperty("EnterCausesTab", _
                              m_def_EnterCausesTab)

    Set DisplayFont = PropBag.ReadProperty("DisplayFont", _
                              Ambient.Font)

End Sub

Private Sub UserControl_WriteProperties(PropBag As PropertyBag)
```

```
    Call PropBag.WriteProperty("BackStyle", _
                            UserControl.BackStyle, 0)
    Call PropBag.WriteProperty("BorderStyle", _
                            UserControl.BorderStyle, 0)
    Call PropBag.WriteProperty("Question", _
                            lblQuestion.Caption, _
                            m_def_Question)
    Call PropBag.WriteProperty("DisplayOnIncorrectResponse", _
                            m_DisplayOnIncorrectResponse, _
                            m_def_DisplayOnIncorrectResponse)
    Call PropBag.WriteProperty("ExpectedAnswer", _
                            m_ExpectedAnswer, _
                            m_def_ExpectedAnswer)
    Call PropBag.WriteProperty("Hint", _
                            m_Hint, _
                            m_def_Hint)
    Call PropBag.WriteProperty("EnterCausesTab", _
                            m_EnterCausesTab, _
                            m_def_EnterCausesTab)
    Call PropBag.WriteProperty("AnswerColor", _
                            txtAnswer.ForeColor, _
                            vbWindowText)
    Call PropBag.WriteProperty("AnswerFont", _
                            txtAnswer.Font, _
                            UserControl.Font)
    Call PropBag.WriteProperty("Enabled", _
                            Enabled, True)
    Call PropBag.WriteProperty("DisplayFont", _
                            DisplayFont, Ambient.Font)

End Sub
```

Notice that you must use the Set statement to set the DisplayFont properly because you're actually passing an object to the property rather than a variable declared using a standard data type.

2. The following is the code:

```
Private Sub UserControl_InitProperties()

    lblQuestion.Caption = m_def_Question
    m_DisplayOnIncorrectResponse = m_def_DisplayOnIncorrectResponse
    m_ExpectedAnswer = m_def_ExpectedAnswer
    m_Hint = m_def_Hint
    m_EnterCausesTab = m_def_EnterCausesTab
    lblQuestion.Font = Ambient.Font
    txtAnswer.Font = Ambient.Font
    lblFeedback.Font = Ambient.Font

End Sub
```

3. The reason `DisplayFont` was used rather than `Font` is because of all the possible collisions and naming conflicts you'd run into with the `Ambient` object, the `UserControl` object, and the `Extender` object. To avoid all these difficulties, a unique property name is always desirable.

Day 6

1. The `Size` method requires two arguments—`Width`, expressed as a decimal number, and `Height`, also a decimal number.

2. The following is the code:

```
Public Sub Size(Width As Single, Height As Single)
    UserControl.Size Width, Height
End Sub
```

3. The ActiveX Control Interface Wizard generates the following method procedure:

```
Public Sub Size(Width As Single, Height As Single)
    UserControl.Size Width, Height
End Sub
```

If you got question 2 right, the procedures should be identical except for the comments at the top. Also, you might have named your arguments differently.

4. The following is the code:

```
Public Sub Refresh()
    UserControl.Refresh
End Sub
```

Day 7

1. To implement this solution, all you have to do is add an additional timer to the form, name it tmrHint, and set its `Interval` property to `30000`. Then simply enter the following statement within the `Timer` event:

```
Private Sub tmrHint_Timer()
    ucQuestion1.ShowHint
End Sub
```

While this procedure shows the hint after 30 seconds, there is no way to start or stop the timer. The best solution would be to have the control notify the host application when the user has provided the correct answer. This solution would require an `Event`, which you'll learn about in the next two days' lessons. Then you can shut the timer off. The timer can be turned on again when the host sets the `Question` property, indicating that the user has a fresh question with a new duration of time to answer.

2. Here is the code needed for the `Countdown` method:

```
Public Function Countdown(Interval as Integer) as Boolean
    If Interval > 0 Then
        tmrCountdown.Interval = Interval
        tmrCountdown.Enabled = True
        Countdown = True
    Else
        Countdown = False
    End If
End Function
```

This method checks to make sure the timer is greater than `0` because the timer interval must start with a value of `1` or higher. The upper limit is not checked, however, because the Visual Basic `Integer` data type does not allow the user to pass a value in higher than what the Timer's `Interval` property allows.

3. Here's the code:

```
Public Sub PasteAnswer()
    Clipboard.SetText txtInformation.Text
End Sub
```

Note the use of the term `CopyAnswer` in the method. If you were to name the method `Copy`, it would conflict with an existing method and would be unclear. This makes it very clear what the method will do.

Day 8

You could take various routes in implementing this control. For example, you could have named your label controls differently. Nevertheless, the overall construction of any solution should be similar. The following is the code for one solution:

```
Private Sub ucQuestion1_DragDrop(Source As Control, X As Single, Y As Single)
    ' Make sure the Question Control has focus
    ucQuestion1.SetFocus
    ' Send over the caption of the label that was dragged here.
    ' Follow it up with a simulated Enter key to cause the answer
    '    to be evaluated
    SendKeys Source.Caption & "{Enter}"
End Sub
```

NOTE

SAMPLE The `DragDrop` modification is included on the CD-ROM under the `Samples\Day08\DragDrop` directory. You can load the `Day8Drag.vbg` project into Visual Basic to see the modified test application.

ANALYSIS Four label controls are used to contain the multiple-choice answers. These label controls have their DragMode property set to Automatic so that Windows allows them to be dragged. Once they are dropped on the question control, the DragDrop event occurs. First, a statement is carried out to ensure that the question control has focus, so that any subsequent text that is typed will go to that control. Then the Visual Basic SendKeys statement is used to send the keystrokes of the label caption over to the control.

If the question control exposed a UserAnswer property, you could have modified that directly instead of using the SendKey statement. However, the question control does not support that statement in its current form.

Day 9

The following is the modified keypress routine that raises the UserQuestionDetected event:

```
' This event is raised when the user enters a question mark as part
'    of their reply. The users entire reply string is passed with the event.
Event UserQuestionDetected(svUserText As String)

' Process answer in response to enter key
Private Sub txtAnswer_KeyPress(KeyAscii As Integer)

    ' Declare a constant for the question mark since VB doesn't define one
    Const vbKeyQuestion As Integer = 63 'ASCII63 code represents question mark

    ' Censure any taboo words that have been entered in the textbox so far
    Call TabooWordCensor

    ' Check if enter key was pressed
    If KeyAscii = vbKeyReturn Then
        KeyAscii = 0
        Call ProcessAnswer
    ElseIf KeyAscii = vbKeyQuestion Then
        ' Raise event to signify that user entered a question.
        '     Pass the entire text response entered by user with the event.
        RaiseEvent UserQuestionDetected(txtAnswer.Text & vbKeyQuestion)
    End If
End Sub
```

The original txtAnswer_KeyPress routine carried out a check to see if the Enter key had been pressed. The modified version carries out an additional check to see if a question mark was pressed if an Enter keypress is not detected. If the question mark is present, the RaiseEvent routine is used to raise the UserQuestionDetected event up to the host application level. The user's answer in the txtAnswer textbox, along with the question mark character still being processed, is passed as an argument with the event so that the host application will have a complete copy of the question that was found.

This code would raise the `UserQuestionDetected` event. Then the host application could supply code to respond to it through the appropriate event-handling routine, such as `ucQuestion1_UserQuestionDetected`. The completed version of today's test control includes a sample of this event-handling routine.

NOTE

SAMPLE You can find this sample solution in the `Day9QuestionControl.vbg` group project file under the `Samples\Day09` directory on the book's CD-ROM. This project contains the final solution code for today's lesson. The code that was intended to be your starting point without these modifications can be found in the `Samples\Day09\Your Start` directory.

Day 10

1. None! If you've already saved to disk the form that contains the control, then you've already created the control. `InitProperties` is only called when you first place a control onto a form in Visual Basic. Therefore, you should only place code in the `InitProperties` event that sets default properties of the event.

2. For cases where you need to initialize the variables of a control, you must place that code in the `Initialize` event. For instance, to get the application path that the control belongs to, you would enter this code:

```
Private Sub UserControl_Initialize()
    m_svPath = App.Path
End Sub
```

where `m_svPath` is a module-level variable used to store the path of the application and `App.Path` is the command referencing the `Application` object to read in the appropriate value.

3. With the addition of the following simple statements you can ensure that your control will behave correctly with no errors:

```
Private Sub UserControl_WriteProperties(PropBag As PropertyBag)

    On Error Goto WriteProperties_Error
```

D

```
    Call PropBag.WriteProperty("Caption", m_Caption, m_def_Caption)
    Call PropBag.WriteProperty("Language", m_Language, m_def_Language)
    Call PropBag.WriteProperty("Answer", m_Answer, m_def_Answer)

    Exit Sub

WriteProperties_Error:

    MsgBox "An error has occurred writing the properties!", _

            vbExclamation, "Property Write Error"

    Resume Next

End Sub
```

Make sure every procedure you have in your control ultimately has some form of error-handling support.

Day 11

1. Using the ActiveX Control Interface Wizard, you should see the following property procedures for the Picture property:

```
Public Property Get Picture() As Picture
    Set Picture = UserControl.Picture
End Property

Public Property Set Picture(ByVal New_Picture As Picture)
    Set UserControl.Picture = New_Picture
    PropertyChanged "Picture"
End Property
```

In addition to these two property procedures, the wizard also adds the following statement to the ReadProperties event:

```
Set Picture = PropBag.ReadProperty("Picture", Nothing)
```

and this statement to the WriteProperties event:

```
Call PropBag.WriteProperty("Picture", Picture, Nothing)
```

Both of these set the UserControl object's Picture property, as you want them to. When you add the StandardColor property page to the PropertyPages property of the UserControl object, it will appear in the Test application at design time. Notice in Figure D.2 what the property page should look like.

Figure D.2.

The `StandardPicture` *property page in the test application with a picture being previewed.*

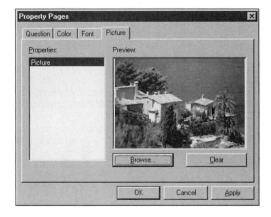

Notice that the picture actually appears in the preview window, and that if you accept the picture, it is placed in the background on the `UserControl` object itself, as shown in Figure D.3!

Figure D.3.

A great picture placed on the question control through the use of the `Picture` *property. Cool!*

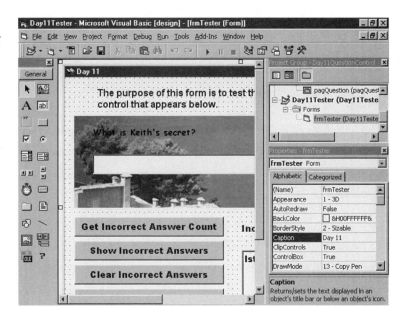

2. The property `QuestionColor` maps directly to the `ForeColor` property of the label control `lblQuestion`, which displays the question. After you use the ActiveX Control Interface Wizard, the two property procedures for the new property appear as follows:

```
Public Property Get QuestionColor() As OLE_COLOR
    QuestionColor = lblQuestion.ForeColor
End Property

Public Property Let QuestionColor(ByVal New_QuestionColor As OLE_COLOR)
    lblQuestion.ForeColor() = New_QuestionColor
    PropertyChanged "QuestionColor"
End Property
```

In addition, the following statement is added to the `ReadProperties` event:

```
lblQuestion.ForeColor = PropBag.ReadProperty("QuestionColor", &H80000012)
```

and this statement is added to the `WriteProperties` event:

```
Call PropBag.WriteProperty("QuestionColor", lblQuestion.ForeColor, _
    &H80000012)
```

These two statements round out the code required for the property. Now, when the `Test` application's property pages are brought up and the user clicks on the Color tab, the additional property appears. This allows the programmer to change the color of the question.

Day 12

1. The easiest way to add these properties to the Question property page is to do so using the ActiveX Control Wizard. Doing so gives you the following procedures in the Question property page:

```
Private Sub txtExpectedAnswer_Change()
    Changed = True
End Sub

Private Sub txtMaxGuesses_Change()
    Changed = True
End Sub

Private Sub PropertyPage_ApplyChanges()
    SelectedControls(0).MaxGuesses = txtMaxGuesses.Text

    On Error Resume Next

    SelectedControls(0).Question = txtQuestion.Text

    If Err.Number <> 0 Then
        MsgBox "Error: " & Err.Description & _
```

```
                "(" & Err.Number & ") has occurred in setting the Question
              ➡property. Please enter the value correctly.",
              ➡vbExclamation, "Question Property Error"
        txtQuestion.SetFocus
        Changed = True
        Exit Sub
    End If

    SelectedControls(0).Hint = txtHint

    If Err.Number <> 0 Then
        MsgBox "Error: " & Err.Description & _
              "(" & Err.Number & ") has occurred in setting the Hint
              ➡property. Please enter the value correctly.",
              ➡vbExclamation, "Hint Property Error"
        txtQuestion.SetFocus
        Changed = True
        Exit Sub
    End If

    SelectedControls(0).DisplayOnIncorrectResponse = _
        cboDisplayOnIncorrectResponse.ListIndex

End Sub

Private Sub PropertyPage_SelectionChanged()

    txtExpectedAnswer.Text = SelectedControls(0).ExpectedAnswer
    txtMaxGuesses.Text = SelectedControls(0).MaxGuesses

    txtQuestion = SelectedControls(0).Question
    txtHint = SelectedControls(0).Hint

    cboDisplayOnIncorrectResponse.Clear
    cboDisplayOnIncorrectResponse.AddItem "0 - ucNone"
    cboDisplayOnIncorrectResponse.AddItem "1 - ucHint"
    cboDisplayOnIncorrectResponse.AddItem "2 - ucAnswer"

    cboDisplayOnIncorrectResponse.ListIndex = _
        SelectedControls(0).DisplayOnIncorrectResponse

End Sub

Private Sub txtHint_Change()
    Changed = True
End Sub

Private Sub txtQuestion_Change()
    Changed = True
End Sub
```

The new Question property page appears, as shown in Figure D.4.

Figure D.4.

The new Question page.

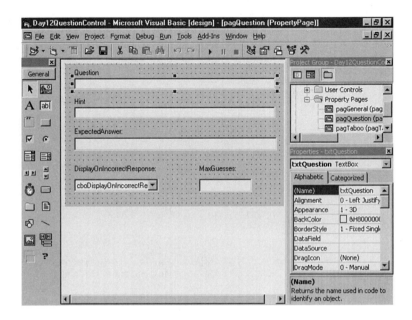

2. Again, the best approach here is to use the wizard. The procedure is as follows:

```
Private Sub chkEnabled_Click()
    Changed = True
End Sub

Private Sub chkFocusIndicator_Click()
    Changed = True
End Sub

Private Sub chkEnterCausesTab_Click()
    Changed = True
End Sub

Private Sub PropertyPage_ApplyChanges()
    SelectedControls(0).Enabled = (chkEnabled.Value = vbChecked)
    SelectedControls(0).FocusIndicator = _
            (chkFocusIndicator.Value = vbChecked)
    SelectedControls(0).EnterCausesTab = _
            (chkEnterCausesTab.Value = vbChecked)
End Sub

Private Sub PropertyPage_SelectionChanged()
    chkEnabled.Value = (SelectedControls(0).Enabled And vbChecked)
    chkFocusIndicator.Value = _
            (SelectedControls(0).FocusIndicator And vbChecked)
    chkEnterCausesTab.Value = _
            (SelectedControls(0).EnterCausesTab And vbChecked)
End Sub
```

The new General property page appears, as shown in Figure D.5.

Figure D.5.

The new General page.

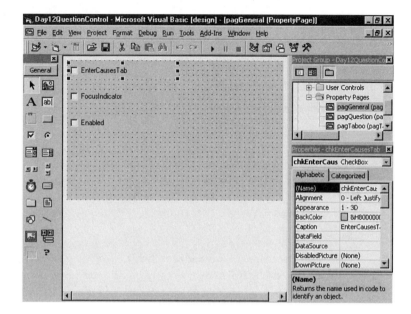

Day 13

You should place the breakpoint on the following line:

```
txtAnswer.SelStart = Len(txtAnswer.Text)
```

You cannot place a breakpoint on a comment line in Visual Basic, so only two of the four lines in the listing are candidates for breakpoints. A breakpoint halts the program when it is reached, *without* carrying out the current statement. If you placed the breakpoint on the line of the string assignment, the program would halt but the assignment would not yet have been carried out and you couldn't yet verify its correctness. If you place the breakpoint on the subsequent line, the string assignment will already have been completed, and you can inspect the resulting string value to see if it is correct.

If you did place the breakpoint on the string assignment line, however, you could inspect the string values before and after the assignment. You could inspect the values first, then single step with the F8 key to the next statement, and then inspect the values after the assignment. Either approach will work, so this is a quiz question where you're right either way!

Day 14

The following is the modified property procedure:

```
Public Property Let Question(ByVal New_Question As String)

    ' A breakpoint will occur when a string of 50+ characters is assigned.
    '   Then the problem condition exists and further probing can take place.
    Debug.Assert Len(New_Question) < 50

    If Len(New_Question) >= 60 Then
        MsgBox "The Question must be no more than 30 characters in length!", _
               vbExclamation, "Error"
    Else
        lblQuestion.Caption() = New_Question
        PropertyChanged "Question"
    End If
End Property
```

A Debug.Assert statement was added to help isolate the problem. This is just one way you can isolate the problem. Many other steps are also appropriate, such as a traditional breakpoint or a Debug.Print statement to provide information.

 The Debug.Assert statement will cause a breakpoint to occur whenever a string of more than 50 characters is assigned to the Question property. Further debugging can proceed from there.

Day 15

Here's the code:

```
Raise vbObjectError + 17, "Day15QuestionControl.Day15Question", _
    "No question was supplied."
```

This statement raises your own error code by providing it as an offset from the vbObjectError constant and associating the corresponding source description and problem description in the next two parameters.

Day 16

First press Ctrl+Break to suspend the program. Then select View | Immediate Window to bring up the Immediate window so you can enter debug statements. Type the following three statements in the Immediate window:

```
frmTester.ucQuestion3.BorderStyle = None
frmTester.ucQuestion3.FocusIndicator = False
frmTester.ucQuestion3.BackStyle = Opaque
```

Then press F5 to resume execution of the program (or select Run | Start from the menu, or click the Continue icon on the toolbar). You will see the results of your test displayed immediately on the form.

Day 17

1. The following is the code:

```
Dictionary1.DataBindings("Term") = "Word"
Dictionary1.DataBindings("Definition") = "Meaning"
```

2. To do this, you can bring up the Data Bindings dialog in the design environment of the host application. Select the Answer property and set the Data Field to (none). That will detach the Answer property from the field in the table so that the user's answers are not stored each time they are entered.

3. You're on your own for this one!

Day 18

The following is the code:

```
Private Sub Command1_Click()

    Dim intCount As Integer
    Dim intLabelCount As Integer

    For intCount = 0 To UserControl.ParentControls.Count - 1
        If TypeName(UserControl.ParentControls.Item(intCount)) = "Label" Then
            intLabelCount = intLabelCount + 1
        End If
    Next
    MsgBox "There are " & intLabelCount & " labels on the host application " & _
        UserControl.Parent.Name, vbOKOnly, "Host Analysis"
End Sub
```

The labels in the host application are inspected through UserControl's ParentControls collection.

ANALYSIS   Each control in UserControl's ParentControls collection is examined. The Visual Basic TypeName function is called to see whether the control's type is that of the label. If so, the label count is incremented. After the loop, the grand total is displayed in a message box. The Parent property is used to provide the name of the host container itself in the message.

D

NOTE

You can find more information about the `Parent` and `ParentControls` properties in the Visual Basic help file. Select Help | Microsoft Visual Basic Help Topics from the Visual Basic menu. Then enter `parent` in the Index tab.

Day 19

1. To properly handle the question numbers, you need to modify the `Paint` event as follows:

```
Private Sub UserControl_Paint()
    If m_DisplayQuestionNumber = True Then

        ' Draw the question number
        Font = lblQuestion.Font
        FontSize = lblQuestion.FontSize
        CurrentX = 700
        CurrentY = 240
        Print Str(m_QuestionNumber)

        ' Draw the question border
        Select Case m_QuestionNumberStyle

            Case styCircle
                Circle (875, 400), 300

            Case stySquare
                Line (650, 200)-Step(500, 500), , B

            Case styTriangle

                Line (850, 100)-(600, 600)
                Line (850, 100)-(1100, 600)
                Line (600, 600)-(1100, 600)

        End Select

    End If
End Sub
```

This will ensure that the border properly paints around the question numbers as long as they range from 0 to 99.

2. The way to implement this feature is to write code in the `InitProperties` event. The event should look as follows:

```
Private Sub UserControl_Initialize()
Dim svNumber as String
Dim iPos as Integer
iPos = InStr(UserControl.Name, "1")
```

```
svNumber = Right$(UserControl.Name, iPos+1)
m_QuestionNumber = Cint(svNumber)
End Sub
```

This procedure works correctly because there is only one character in the string ucQuestionControlxx, where *xx* is the number appended to the end of the control. You can rest assured that the control will always be named this way in the Initialize event because that event is only called once—when the control is first created.

3. Refer to Microsoft Visual Basic documentation for steps on making this possible.

Day 20

The first step is to bring up the AXDTest project. Add the text control, label, and command button to the UserDocument as shown in Figure D.6.

Figure D.6.

The revised
UserDocument *with*
the hyperlink com-
mand button and edit
control.

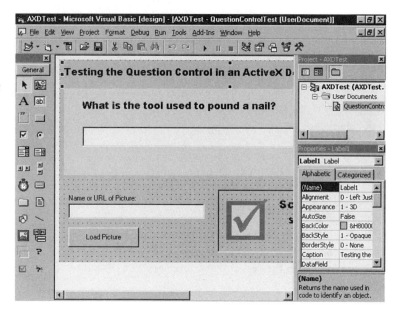

Now add the following code to the command button's Click event:

```
ucQuestion1.GetPictureFromURL txtPicture.Text
```

When the user enters an Internet address such as http://www.doubleblaze.com/general/ leafbg.jpg, the bitmap automatically loads into the picture control background, as shown in Figure D.7.

Figure D.7.

*The new ActiveX
document in use
within the Web
browser.*

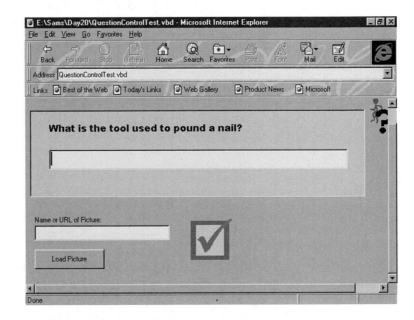

Because the method already exists in the control, all you need to do is call it here with one
line of code. The control does all the rest!

Day 21

The code writes data to a file. The file location used is based on a control property that is
specified by the host application. This presents a potential security problem. If the file
location were set to specify the same location as a key system file, this code would wipe out
the critical file. The file location should be restricted through code to a known safe area on
the computer if file I/O must be used. In the case of this sample, this could have already been
done through the me.DataPath property Let procedure.

INDEX

W-Z

Watch window, 375
Web pages
    integrating controls into,
    4-13
    OCX file, 510
    referencing, 532
    results control, 466
    results file, 479
Web sites
    DoubleBlaze, 550, 559
    Microsoft, 560
    Sams Publishing, 560
    VeriSign, 560
Width property, 253
**Window menu commands,
 Tile Vertically, 78**
Windows
    API (Application Program-
    ming Interface), 500
    module swapping, 406

    programmers, 474
    System Registry, 401
windows (IDE)
    code window, 65-67
        event coding, 70-73
        property settings, 67-70
    dockable, 37, 58
    project window, 34, 56
        opening projects, 57-58
        viewing objects, 60-65
    resizing, 36-37
    undockable, 59
    viewing, 34, 58-60
With reference, 480
**wizard-generated question
 control source code
 (Listing 3.1), 65-67**
wizards
    ActiveX Control Interface
    Wizard
        exposing methods,
        156-163

    locating object descrip-
    tions, 214
    properties, setting for
    controls, 44-52
    user-defined events,
    224
    defined, 24
    errors, 295
    installing as add-ins, 43-44
    Setup, 429, 538
**World Wide Web (WWW),
519**
WriteProperties event, 259
    Listing 5.3, 136-137
    Listing 8.6, 210-211
    UserControl object,
    136-137, 205, 209
**WriteProperty method
(PropertyBag object), 135**

**ZOrder method (Extender
object), 164**

Teach Yourself Visual Basic 5 in 21 Days, Fourth Edition

Nathan Gurewich & Ori Gurewich

Using a logical, easy-to-follow approach, this international bestseller teaches readers the fundamentals of developing programs. It starts with the basics of writing a program and then moves on to adding voice, music, sound, and graphics.

Price: $29.99 USA/$42.95 CDN   *New—Casual*
ISBN: 0-672-30978-5   *1,000 pages*

Teach Yourself Database Programming with Visual Basic 5 in 21 Days, Second Edition

Michael Amundsen & Curtis Smith

Visual Basic, the 32-bit programming language from Microsoft, is used by programmers to create Windows and Windows 95 applications. It can also be used to program applications for the Web. This book shows those programmers how to design, develop, and deploy Visual Basic applications for the World Wide Web.

Price: $45.00 USA/$63.95 CAN   *New—Casual—Accomplished*
ISBN: 0-672-31018-X   *1,000 pp*

ActiveX Programming Unleashed

Weiying Chen et al.

ActiveX is Microsoft's core Internet communication technology. This book describes and details that technology, giving programmers the knowledge they need to create powerful ActiveX programs for the Web and beyond.

Price: $39.99 USA/$56.95 CDN   *Accomplished—Expert*
ISBN: 1-57521-154-8   *700 pages*

Laura Lemay's Web Workshop: ActiveX and VBScript

Paul Lomax & Rogers Cadenhead

ActiveX is an umbrella term for a series of Microsoft products and technologies that add activity to Web pages. VBScript is an essential element of the ActiveX family. With it, animation, multimedia, sound, graphics, and interactivity can be added to a Web site. This book is a compilation of individual workshops that show the reader how to use VBScript and other ActiveX technologies within their Web site.

Price: $39.99 USA/$56.95 CDN   *Casual—Accomplished*
ISBN: 1-57521-207-2   *450 pages*

VBScript Unleashed

Brian Johnson

In *VBScript Unleashed*, Web programming techniques are presented in a logical and easy-to-follow sequence that helps readers understand the principles involved in developing programs. The reader begins with learning the basics to writing a first program and then builds on that to add interactivity, multimedia, and more to Web page designs.

Price: $39.99 USA/$56.95 CDN   *Casual—Accomplished—Expert*
ISBN: 1-57521-124-6   *650 pages*

Teach Yourself Visual Basic for Applications in 21 Days, Third Edition

Matthew Harris

This book covers all fundamental aspects of this programming language and teaches novice programmers how to design, create, and debug macro programs written in the VBA programming language.

Price: $39.99 USA/$56.95 CAN   *New —Casual*
ISBN: 0-672-31016-3   *1,000 pages*

Visual Basic for Applications Unleashed

Paul McFedries

Combining both power and ease of use, Visual Basic for Applications (VBA) is the common language for developing macros and applications across all Microsoft Office components. Using the format of the best-selling *Unleashed* series, users will master the intricacies of this popular language and exploit the full power of VBA. Covers user interface design, database programming, networking programming, Internet programming, and stand-alone application creation.

Price: $49.99 USA/$70.95 CDN   *Accomplished—Expert*
ISBN: 0-672-31046-5   *800 pages*

Teach Yourself Microsoft Visual InterDev in 21 Days

Michael Van Hoozer

Using the familiar, day-by-day format of the best-selling *Teach Yourself* series, this easy-to-follow tutorial will provide users with a solid understanding of Visual InterDev, Microsoft's new Web application development environment. In no time, they will learn how to perform a variety of tasks, including front-end scripting, database and query design, content creation, server-side scripting, and more.

Price: $39.99 USA/$56.95 CDN   *New—Casual—Accomplished*
ISBN: 1-57521-093-2   *800 pages*

Add to Your Sams.net Library Today
with the Best Books for Internet Technologies

ISBN	Quantity	Description of Item	Unit Cost	Total Cost
0-672-30978-5		Teach Yourself Visual Basic 5 in 21 Days, Fourth Edition	$29.99	
0-672-31018-X		Teach Yourself Database Programming with Visual Basic 5 in 21 Days, Second Edition (book/CD-ROM)	$45.00	
1-57521-154-8		ActiveX Programming Unleashed (book/CD-ROM)	$39.99	
1-57521-207-2		Laura Lemay's Web Workshop: ActiveX and VBScript (book/CD-ROM)	$39.99	
1-57521-124-6		VBScript Unleashed (book/CD-ROM)	$39.99	
0-672-31016-3		Teach Yourself Visual Basic for Applications in 21 Days, Third Edition	$39.99	
0-672-31046-5		Visual Basic for Applications Unleashed (book/CD-ROM)	$49.99	
1-57521-093-2		Teach Yourself Visual InterDev in 21 Days (book/CD-ROM)	$39.99	
		Shipping and Handling: See information below.		
		TOTAL		

Shipping and Handling: $4.00 for the first book, and $1.75 for each additional book. If you need to have it NOW, we can ship product to you in 24 hours for an additional charge of approximately $18.00, and you will receive your item overnight or in two days. Overseas shipping and handling adds $2.00. Prices subject to change. Call between 9:00 a.m. and 5:00 p.m. EST for availability and pricing information on latest editions.

201 W. 103rd Street, Indianapolis, Indiana 46290

1-800-428-5331 — Orders   1-800-835-3202 — FAX   1-800-858-7674 — Customer Service

Book ISBN 1-57521-245-5

MACMILLAN COMPUTER PUBLISHING USA
A VIACOM COMPANY

Technical Support:

If you need assistance with the information in this book or with a CD/Disk accompanying the book, please access the Knowledge Base on our Web site at **http://www.superlibrary.com/general/support**. Our most Frequently Asked Questions are answered there. If you do not find the answer to your questions on our Web site, you may contact Macmillan Technical Support **(317) 581-3833** or e-mail us at **support@mcp.com**.

MISCELLANEOUS

If you acquired this product in the United States, this EULA is governed by the laws of the State of Washington.

If you acquired this product in Canada, this EULA is governed by the laws of the Province of Ontario, Canada. Each of the parties hereto irrevocably attorns to the jurisdiction of the courts of the Province of Ontario and further agrees to commence any litigation which may arise hereunder in the courts located in the Judicial District of York, Province of Ontario.

If this product was acquired outside the United States, then local law may apply.

Should you have any questions concerning this EULA, or if you desire to contact Microsoft for any reason, please contact the Microsoft subsidiary serving your country, or write: Microsoft Sales Information Center, One Microsoft Way, Redmond, WA 98052-6399.

LIMITED WARRANTY

NO WARRANTIES. Microsoft expressly disclaims any warranty for the SOFTWARE PRODUCT. The SOFTWARE PRODUCT and any related documentation is provided "as is" without warranty of any kind, either express or implied, including, without limitation, the implied warranties or merchantability, fitness for a particular purpose, or noninfringement. The entire risk arising out of use or performance of the SOFTWARE PRODUCT remains with you.

NO LIABILITY FOR DAMAGES. In no event shall Microsoft or its suppliers be liable for any damages whatsoever (including, without limitation, damages for loss of business profits, business interruption, loss of business information, or any other pecuniary loss) arising out of the use of or inability to use this Microsoft product, even if Microsoft has been advised of the possibility of such damages. Because some states/jurisdictions do not allow the exclusion or limitation of liability for consequential or incidental damages, the above limitation may not apply to you.

use the resulting upgraded product only in accordance with the terms of this EULA. If the SOFTWARE PRODUCT is an upgrade of a component of a package of software programs that you licensed as a single product, the SOFTWARE PRODUCT may be used and transferred only as part of that single product package and may not be separated for use on more than one computer.

4. **COPYRIGHT.** All title and copyrights in and to the SOFTWARE PRODUCT (including but not limited to any images, photographs, animations, video, audio, music, text, and "applets" incorporated into the SOFTWARE PRODUCT), the accompanying printed materials, and any copies of the SOFTWARE PRODUCT are owned by Microsoft or its suppliers. The SOFTWARE PRODUCT is protected by copyright laws and international treaty provisions. Therefore, you must treat the SOFTWARE PRODUCT like any other copyrighted material except that you may install the SOFTWARE PRODUCT on a single computer provided you keep the original solely for backup or archival purposes. You may not copy the printed materials accompanying the SOFTWARE PRODUCT.

5. **DUAL-MEDIA SOFTWARE.** You may receive the SOFTWARE PRODUCT in more than one medium. Regardless of the type or size of medium you receive, you may use only one medium that is appropriate for your single computer. You may not use or install the other medium on another computer. You may not loan, rent, lease, or otherwise transfer the other medium to another user, except as part of the permanent transfer (as provided above) of the SOFTWARE PRODUCT.

6. **U.S. GOVERNMENT RESTRICTED RIGHTS.** The SOFTWARE PRODUCT and documentation are provided with RESTRICTED RIGHTS. Use, duplication, or disclosure by the Government is subject to restrictions as set forth in subparagraph (c)(1)(ii) of the Rights in Technical Data and Computer Software clause at DFARS 252.227-7013 or subparagraphs (c)(1) and (2) of the Commercial Computer Software—Restricted Rights at 48 CFR 52.227-19, as applicable. Manufacturer is Microsoft Corporation, One Microsoft Way, Redmond, WA 98052-6399.

7. **EXPORT RESTRICTIONS.** You agree that neither you nor your customers intend to or will, directly or indirectly, export or transmit (i) the SOFTWARE or related documentation and technical data or (ii) your software product as described in Section 1(b) of this License (or any part thereof), or process, or service that is the direct product of the SOFTWARE, to any country to which such export or transmission is restricted by any applicable U.S. regulation or statute, without the prior written consent, if required, of the Bureau of Export Administration of the U.S. Department of Commerce, or such other governmental entity as may have jurisdiction over such export or transmission.

2. DESCRIPTION OF OTHER RIGHTS AND LIMITATIONS.

a. Not for Resale Software. If the SOFTWARE PRODUCT is labeled "Not for Resale" or "NFR," then, notwithstanding other sections of this EULA, you may not resell, or otherwise transfer for value, the SOFTWARE PRODUCT.

b. Limitations on Reverse Engineering, Decompilation, and Disassembly. You may not reverse engineer, decompile, or disassemble the SOFTWARE PRODUCT, except and only to the extent that such activity is expressly permitted by applicable law notwithstanding this limitation.

c. Separation of Components. The SOFTWARE PRODUCT is licensed as a single product. Its component parts may not be separated for use by more than one user.

d. Rental. You may not rent, lease, or lend the SOFTWARE PRODUCT.

e. Support Services. Microsoft may provide you with support services related to the SOFTWARE PRODUCT ("Support Services"). Use of Support Services is governed by the Microsoft policies and programs described in the user manual, in "online" documentation, and/or in other Microsoft-provided materials. Any supplemental software code provided to you as part of the Support Services shall be considered part of the SOFTWARE PRODUCT and subject to the terms and conditions of this EULA. With respect to technical information you provide to Microsoft as part of the Support Services, Microsoft may use such information for its business purposes, including for product support and development. Microsoft will not utilize such technical information in a form that personally identifies you.

f. Software Transfer. You may permanently transfer all of your rights under this EULA, provided you retain no copies, you transfer all of the SOFTWARE PRODUCT (including all component parts, the media and printed materials, any upgrades, this EULA, and, if applicable, the Certificate of Authenticity), **and** the recipient agrees to the terms of this EULA. If the SOFTWARE PRODUCT is an upgrade, any transfer must include all prior versions of the SOFTWARE PRODUCT.

g. Termination. Without prejudice to any other rights, Microsoft may terminate this EULA if you fail to comply with the terms and conditions of this EULA. In such event, you must destroy all copies of the SOFTWARE PRODUCT and all of its component parts.

3. UPGRADES. If the SOFTWARE PRODUCT is labeled as an upgrade, you must be properly licensed to use a product identified by Microsoft as being eligible for the upgrade in order to use the SOFTWARE PRODUCT. A SOFTWARE PRODUCT labeled as an upgrade replaces and/or supplements the product that formed the basis for your eligibility for the upgrade. You may

b. Electronic Documents. Solely with respect to electronic documents included with the SOFTWARE, you may make an unlimited number of copies (either in hardcopy or electronic form), provided that such copies shall be used only for internal purposes and are not republished or distributed to any third party.

c. Redistributable Components.

(i) Sample Code. In addition to the rights granted in Section 1, Microsoft grants you the right to use and modify the source code version of those portions of the SOFTWARE designated as "Sample Code" ("SAMPLE CODE") for the sole purposes of designing, developing, and testing your software product(s), and to reproduce and distribute the SAMPLE CODE, along with any modifications thereof, only in object code form provided that you comply with Section c(iii), below.

(ii) Redistributable Components. In addition to the rights granted in Section 1, Microsoft grants you a nonexclusive royalty-free right to reproduce and distribute the object code version of any portion of the SOFTWARE listed in the SOFTWARE file REDIST.TXT ("REDISTRIBUTABLE SOFTWARE"), provided you comply with Section c(iii), below.

(iii) Redistribution Requirements. If you redistribute the SAMPLE CODE or REDISTRIBUTABLE SOFTWARE (collectively, "REDISTRIBUTABLES"), you agree to: (A) distribute the REDISTRIBUTABLES in object code only in conjunction with and as a part of a software application product developed by you that adds significant and primary functionality to the SOFTWARE and that is developed to operate on the Windows or Windows NT environment ("Application"); (B) not use Microsoft's name, logo, or trademarks to market your software application product; (C) include a valid copyright notice on your software product; (D) indemnify, hold harmless, and defend Microsoft from and against any claims or lawsuits, including attorney's fees, that arise or result from the use or distribution of your software application product; (E) not permit further distribution of the REDISTRIBUTABLES by your end user. The following **exceptions** apply to subsection (iii)(E), above: (1) you may permit further redistribution of the REDISTRIBUTABLES by your distributors to your end-user customers if your distributors only distribute the REDISTRIBUTABLES in conjunction with, and as part of, your Application and you and your distributors comply with all other terms of this EULA; and (2) you may permit your end users to reproduce and distribute the object code version of the files designated by ".ocx" file extensions ("Controls") only in conjunction with and as a part of an Application and/or Web page that adds significant and primary functionality to the Controls, and such end user complies with all other terms of this EULA.

END-USER LICENSE AGREEMENT FOR MICROSOFT SOFTWARE

Microsoft Visual Basic, Control Creation Edition

IMPORTANT—READ CAREFULLY: This Microsoft End-User License Agreement ("EULA") is a legal agreement between you (either an individual or a single entity) and Microsoft Corporation for the Microsoft software product identified above, which includes computer software and may include associated media, printed materials, and "online" or electronic documentation ("SOFTWARE PRODUCT"). By installing, copying, or otherwise using the SOFTWARE PRODUCT, you agree to be bound by the terms of this EULA. If you do not agree to the terms of this EULA, do not install or use the SOFTWARE PRODUCT; you may, however, return it to your place of purchase for a full refund.

Software PRODUCT LICENSE

The SOFTWARE PRODUCT is protected by copyright laws and international copyright treaties, as well as other intellectual property laws and treaties. The SOFTWARE PRODUCT is licensed, not sold.

1. **GRANT OF LICENSE.** This EULA grants you the following rights:

    a. Software Product. Microsoft grants to you as an individual, a personal, nonexclusive license to make and use copies of the SOFTWARE for the sole purposes of designing, developing, and testing your software product(s) that is designed to operate in conjunction with any Microsoft operating system product. You may install copies of the SOFTWARE on an unlimited number of computers provided that you are the only individual using the SOFTWARE. If you are an entity, Microsoft grants you the right to designate one individual within your organization to have the right to use the SOFTWARE in the manner provided above.